Yale Language Series

أهلا وسهلا

العربية الوظيفية للمبتدئين

مهدي العش

دار جامعة ييل للنشر
نيوهيڤن ولندن

Ahlan wa Sahlan

Functional Modern Standard Arabic for Beginners

Mahdi Alosh

Yale University Press
New Haven and London

Printed in the United States of America.

Library of Congress Cataloging-in-Publication Data

Alosh, Mahdi.
Ahlan wa-sahlan : li-ta' alum al-'Arabīyah waẓīfīyan lil-mubtadi 'īn / Mahdī al-'Ush = Ahlan wa sahlan : functional modern standard Arabic for beginners / Mahdi Alosh.
p. cm. — (Yale language series)
English and Arabic.
Includes bibliographical references (p. –) and index.
ISBN 0-300-05854-3 (alk. paper)
1. Arabic language Textbooks for foreign speakers—English. I. Title. II. Series
PJ6307.A39 2000
492.7'82421—dc21 99-36606
CIP

A catalogue record for this book is available from the British Library.

The paper in this book meets the guidelines for permanence and durability of the Committee on Production Guidelines for Book Longevity of the Council on Library Resources.

10 9 8 7 6 5 4 3 2 1

To

my wife, Ibtissam
my mother, Falak
the memory of my father

Acknowledgments

I am indebted to so many people whose direct and indirect contribution made this work better, including students of Arabic at my institution and elsewhere as well as colleagues who used an earlier version and took some of their valuable time to provide me with feedback. Professor Frederic Cadora, former chair of the Department of Near Eastern Languages and Cultures, provided much sound advice and paved the way for the conception, development, and implementation of an earlier version of this volume. I am especially indebted to my wife, Ibtissam, for putting up with the endless hours I spent on developing the materials and for designing and programming the computer-assisted program that accompanies this textbook. I would like to acknowledge the expert assistance of Fayez Al-Ghalayini whose meticulous editing of the Arabic portion of this textbook and assiduous input and profuse comments on the linguistic aspect improved the quality of this work and made it more accurate. My thanks also go to Kimberly Schreiber, who edited part of this volume and the *Teacher's Handbook* with much care and insight, to Stafford Noble for proofreading and editing the greater part of this textbook, and to Charles Grench, Judith Calvert, Richard Miller, Paul Royster, Lawrence Kenney (all of Yale University Press) for providing very useful editorial comments on parts of this volume. Credit is also due to Marjorie Healey for editing part of the *Teacher's Handbook*. Their editorial remarks have been invaluable. I thank Nonie Williams and Lana Khodary for the many hours they devoted to the recording of the audio material, and Lauren Aland for her unlimited technical support. I thank Lalainya Goldsberry, Hibah Abdalla, and Nevine Demian for providing factual and cultural information about Egypt. I thank Professors Ernest MacCarus and Raji Rammuny for granting permission to use some diagrams from their book *A Programmed Course in Modern Literary Arabic Phonology and Script*. My thanks also go to Rami Kamhawi, Fadi Abu-Humaidan, and Lana Khodary for their permission to use their likenesses in the textbooks.

Last, but not least, I would like to acknowledge the support I have received from the College of Humanities at the Ohio State University and the Department of Near Eastern Languages and Cultures, which made the completion of this work possible.

محتويات الكتاب

Introduction

Purpose and Approach

Ahlan wa Sahlan introduces learners of Arabic to the sound and writing systems of this language and provides them with basic structural and lexical knowledge to enable them to say things in Arabic, such as greeting others, thanking someone, introducing oneself, describing one's background, seeking and providing information, and so forth. The ability to perform these langugage functions in real-life or lifelike situations is developed by engaging the learner in structured functional activities and grammatical exercises. In every lesson, a variety of such activities are designed to build up overall proficiency gradually. In this fashion, learners can take part in communication with classmates and instructor in Arabic, keeping in mind that communication is not only oral. The focus, therefore, is on performing language functions using the language forms learned, not on analyzing them grammatically. This does not mean, however, that grammar is not important. On the contrary, it enables learners to use the language forms appropriately and correctly. By "enabling" I mean putting grammatical structures and explanations in the service of language *use*. For example, presenting, explaining, and practicing the subjunctive mood in Arabic should always be related to a language function or functions accomplished through its use. In this textbook, it is dealt with in the contexts of expressing obligation, intention, and reason. As the learner tries to acquire the ability to express these functions, he or she will at the same time internalize accurate usage of the subjunctive, not for its own sake, but in order to express a given language function.

In addition, presenting and practicing the Arabic language from functional and structural perspectives attempts to accommodate the needs and learning styles of most learners. Learners learn differently; some benefit primarily from a functional presentation and practice, others find structural information useful. A functional presentation normally activates inductive cognitive processes and structural presentations deductive processes. Research tells us that the human mind, regardless of how it acquires knowledge, assimilates, modifies, and reconstructs this knowledge and then uses it in ways appropriate for it specifically. The aim, in both modes of presentation, is developing overall proficiency in using Arabic.

Audience

This textbook is designed to take learners from the absolute beginner stage to the intermediate range. At the university level, this can be translated into a first-year program, providing approximately 150 contact hours, the equivalent of three academic quarters or two semesters.

Lesson Format

Lessons have similar formats. They start with a listing of learning objectives (both functional and structural) to familiarize the user with the content, topics, and grammatical points discussed. At the bottom of the list, there is a reminder concerning the tape-recorded material and parts of the Arabic software program *Ahlan wa Sahlan* where drills, exercises, vocabulary, and reading passages relevant to a particular lesson can be found.

Learning Objectives: The objectives listed at the beginning of each lesson are of two types: (1) functional objectives which describe what learners will be able to do in Arabic at the end of a given lesson and (2) structural objectives which specify exactly which language forms need to be practiced and used in order to perform the functional objectives correctly.

Activities: Each lesson contains activities associated with each type of objective. There are two major types of activities: (1) classroom activities (not described in the student's textbook) designed to develop oral communicative competence and (2) out-of-class activities. The latter involve reading passages of varying lengths, listening to tapes, and doing computer-assisted and written exercises. Written exercises follow the reading passages and are subdivided into five types: vocabulary, reading comprehension, writing, listening comprehension, and grammar exercises. There are also integrative exercises that combine two types, such as reading comprehension and writing. Each exercise is made up of one or more sections. For example, a vocabulary exercise may contain several sections, such as matching, categorization, odd-man-out, and multiple choice. Vocabulary, reading comprehension, and writing exercises immediately follow each reading passage to encourage immediate review and recall of the reading material. Grammar exercises have one or two sections each, since each grammar exercise deals with a specific point. They are structured and proceed from simple to complex.

Listening exercises (marked by an audiocassette icon in the right margin) provide practice in pronunciation, word recognition, and dictation. They also try to develop the ability to communicate orally by guiding learners step by step through exchanges which together constitute dialogues. Each dialogue or set of communicative phrases is presented at the beginning of each segment followed by oral practice of its component parts.

Listening comprehension exercises usually comprise three types: content questions, multiple choice, and true-false. Content questions should be read before listening to the passage in order to guide learners to what they should listen for. Learners are expected to deal with true-false exercises at a level higher than mere recognition and labeling items true or false. They should either elaborate on each item, amplify it, or correct it in order to reflect their understanding of the text.

It is recommended that the exercises be done after the vocabulary has been covered, since the purpose of written vocabulary exercises is to reinforce the learning of the new words. The same thing applies to reading comprehension exercises, which must be done during or immediately after reading. Most of the written activities are expected to be done out of the classroom. The instructor may provide feedback, though, in class or on paper.

Reading Passages: The reading material can either be simple communicative phrases, dialogues, expository prose, or personal journals written by the two main characters, Michael Brown and Adnān Mārtīnī. The reading passages are usually accompanied by illustrations, graphics, or maps. They are designed to provide the necessary contexts for language functions represented by the objectives. They also constitute a source for the vocabulary and language forms needed to realize these functions. The reading passages, in addition, provide cultural glimpses of both the target culture and the local one. The content of these passages is expected to promote general knowledge *through* Arabic. At an intermediate level, such as the one served by part of this textbook and by its sequel, the amount of knowledge imparted to the learner through Arabic makes it partially content-based. In most foreign-language courses, content-based materials represent the first step toward discipline-based materials, where the learner is prepared to embark on dealing with original texts within a particular field of study.

Most of the passages here are developed specifically for this textbook. Thus, the language is rather controlled, i.e., it is not "authentic" in the traditional sense of the term, although it is written by a native speaker. Authenticity is interpreted here, however, in a functional sense, where the language used by teacher and learner is considered authentic if it serves some genuine functional or communicative purpose regardless of whether or not native speakers use the same forms orally to accomplish this purpose (see the section on the language situation in the Arab world below). The written passages, on the other hand, can be considered both authentic in function and sociolinguistically appropriate, since the majority of them are either expository passages, written communication (messages, postcards, letters), or personal diaries, which places them in the realm of Standard Arabic.

Arabic Script: The Arabic writing system is presented gradually over the first six lessons along with communicative phrases and new vocabulary. During this initial phase (at least the first five lessons), learners are of course unable to read. Instead, they should depend on tapes and classroom communicative activities to learn the language content. Although Arabic script might seem exotic and undecipherable at first encounter, it is in fact quite consistent and, to the pleasant surprise of most learners, can be acquired quickly and easily. Unlike the English system, the Arabic has a high degree of correspondence between sound and symbol (each symbol represents one sound). The explanations are immediately followed by a writing practice exercise that is based on visual information only, which is followed by two or more exercises that combine visual and aural cues for word recognition. Practice of the script culminates in a dictation exercise on tape.

Arab Culture: The content of the reading passages offers cultural insights into the target and local (American) cultures. Since the two main characters have roles as university-level students (one studying Arabic in Cairo, Egypt and the other computer science in Columbus, Ohio), Arabic students using this textbook might be able to identify with their activities and interests. Arabic students must realize that there is no single Arab culture, but rather a multiplicity of cultures. In fact, diversity rather than homogeneity characterizes the cultures of the Arab world. No one textbook can provide a comprehensive look at the culture. Instead, the reading passages and the storyline maintained through the lessons in this textbook attempt to show selected aspects of Arab culture. These include food and drink, clothing, customs, family, entertainment, sports, homes, schools, geography of the Arab world, significant Arab personalities, and festivities. The presentation of the cultural and language items proceeds from the immediate to the wider environment.

Grammatical Explanations and Exercises: The grammatical notes in this textbook are by no means comprehensive, nor do they constitute a reference grammar for the student. However, they are adequate for the tasks at hand, providing the necessary knowledge about structures that occur in the reading passages and the practice needed to internalize this knowledge. Grammar acquisition is not the goal of instruction, but rather a facilitating element to achieve the goal, which is developing the ability to *use* the Arabic language (Standard Arabic) as native speakers would use it in formal and semiformal situations. Therefore, the importance of the grammar section lies in its facilitating function. The ultimate test of its success is the students' ability to perform functional tasks specified in functional exercises following the reading passages where they are expected, for example, to provide a biographical sketch of themselves or of people they know, describe possessions and activities, express preferences and opinions, and be able to read and understand simple passages.

It is suggested that grammatical explanations and exercises be read and done out of the classroom, thus preserving valuable class time for conducting lifelike interactive activities which cannot be done outside the classroom for lack of interaction with classmates and an instructor. Students can read the grammar section even before reading the lesson, because this is information *about* the language and does not require special language skills. Grammatical explanations are basically information, or knowledge, that can be learned without external help, whereas language abilities are skills which must be developed physically as well as cognitively with the assistance of an instructor and interaction with classmates. Instructors can, of course, provide brief feedback on their students' work on grammar exercises in class.

Glossaries: Each lesson ends with an Arabic-English glossary of the new words. After the thirtieth lesson, there is a cumulative glossary, or dictionary, of all the words used in the textbook marked with the lesson number where each word first appears.

Appendices: Appendix A contains the Arabic alphabet with the different forms of the letters according to their positions in the word and the Roman symbol representing each letter. Appendix B contains a key to the sound system of Arabic and the transliteration system used in this textbook (i.e., the Roman symbols used to represent Arabic letters). Appendix C has a representative sample of thirteen verb conjugation paradigms, showing tense, mood, imperative, verbal nouns, and active and passive participles. Appendix D contains an answer key to all the exercises in the book, including listening comprehension exercises.

Modern Standard Arabic

The Arabic variety used in this textbook is known in the West as Modern Standard Arabic (MSA) and *al-fuṣḥā* (meaning "most beautiful," "most eloquent," "purest") in the Arab world. It is more or less invariable throughout the Arab world and is used for specialized functions, including classroom instruction, the electronic and print media, and formal situations. It is used neither at home nor on the street for interpersonal communication. These features differentiate it from the various spoken regional and local dialects which vary considerably from place to place. They are exclusively oral. Variation among the dialects takes place at all linguistic levels: phonological, morphological, syntactic, and lexical. The dialects are numerous, but for convenience they may be grouped roughly into five categories: (1) Levantine (Syria, Lebanon, Palestine, and Jordan), (2) Iraqi, (3) Arabian (the Arabian peninsula), (4) Egyptian (Egypt and the Sudan), and (5) North African (Libya, Tunis, Algeria, and Morocco). Somalia and Djibouti are not included

although they are members of the Arab League. The reason is that Arabic is used there mostly as a liturgical language and in some areas as a second language learned formally, thus making this variety classifiable with MSA, or even classical Arabic, rather than with the dialects.

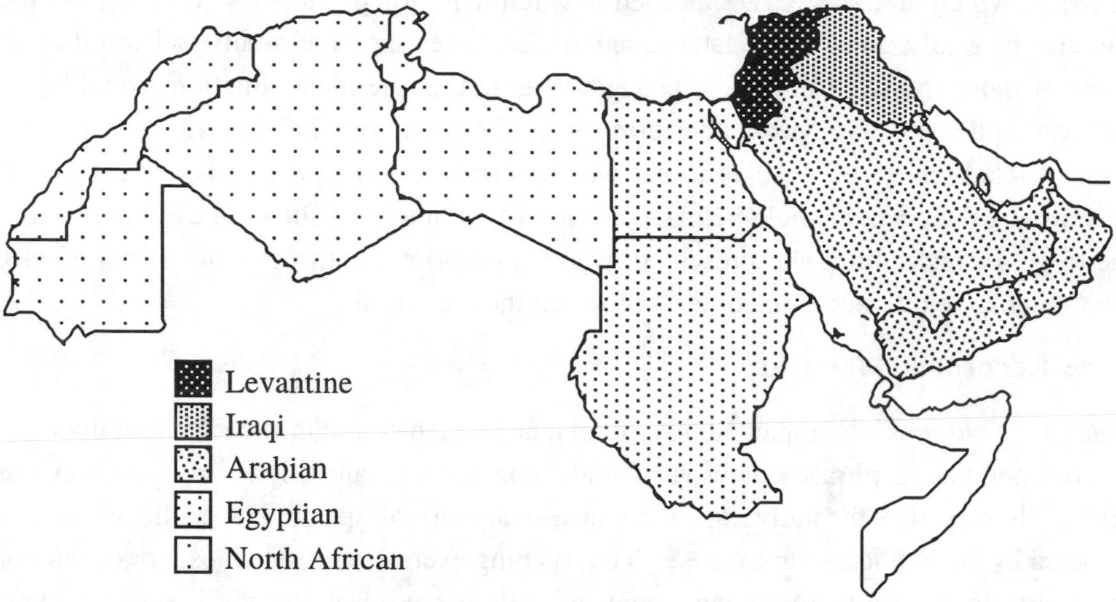

Figure 1. Dialectal Regions of the Arab World

The dialects are known collectively as colloquial Arabic (CA), which is distinct from MSA at all linguistic levels. Learning MSA before any colloquial variety provides learners with two advantages. First, a good foundation in MSA facilitates the acquisition of any dialect a learner might wish to learn later, for generally dialects are structurally less complex than MSA. Therefore, it may be easier for learners to learn a colloquial variety after they have learned MSA, because learning colloquial utterances involves applying deletion rather than augmentation rules.[1] Second, and unlike local dialects, MSA is readily understood anywhere in the Arab world. In addition, by learning MSA, learners will be literate and have access to a vast heritage of ancient and modern literature, scholarly work, and the media.

Given this situation, some Arabists might object to using MSA as a vehicle for oral communication in situations normally reserved for colloquial Arabic. I am aware of this sociolinguistic discrepancy and finds that the response to that view may rest on educational and pedagogical grounds. First of all, for most Arabic programs, reading is the primary goal, especially at institutions where there is a graduate program. Second, in order to

[1] Cadora, Frederic. 1967. The Teaching of Spoken and Written Arabic. *Language Learning*, Vol. 15, Nos. 3&4; and personal communication.

avoid confusing learners with two varieties at the beginning stage, MSA may be used to fulfill both its own linguistic function (reading and writing primarily) as well as that of CA (speaking). In addition to the expected reading skills, learners will develop oral skills in MSA, which are, at any rate, needed as a requisite for proficiency in MSA, but they can also be easily transferable later to any dialect when the opportunity to learn it arises. Most of those involved in Arabic pedagogy agree that the ideal situation would be one that can replicate native-speaker performance in the classroom, but they also acknowledge the restricted nature of the classroom, which cannot accommodate this ambitious goal. Nevertheless, students should be made aware of this linguistic situation even if CA is not the target of instruction and presented, when appropriate, with CA equivalents of MSA communicative utterances in contexts in which they are used.

Tape-Recorded Material

Ahlan wa Sahlan is accompanied by a set of tapes which contains a rendition of dialogues or communicative phrases, new vocabulary, reading passages, listening passages, and oral drills recorded by native speakers at a near-normal speed. The audio material is signaled by an audiocassette icon. The listening exercises include those for developing the ability to discriminate among sounds as well as exercises for word recognition and listening comprehension. All the audio material of a given lesson is recorded in the sequence in which it appears in the textbook. That is to say, new vocabulary, dialogues, and reading passages are followed by listening exercises and finally by a listening comprehension passage. In the first few lessons, learners are guided word by word and phrase by phrase on how to communicate orally and to recognize and produce the language forms correctly.

Computer-Assisted Materials

Available with this textbook is a computer-assisted language learning (CALL) program. It provides drill and practice in the sound and writing systems of Arabic and contains a large number of vocabulary, grammar, and reading comprehension exercises. The language material contained in the CALL program is generally based on objectives similar to those in this textbook. However, the vocabulary and structures vary a little, and the stories in the reading passages have a different content from those in the textbook, which provides variety. And since the program is also self-contained, it may be used independently of the text.

The CALL program contains drills and exercises designed to help in learning the sound

and writing systems of Arabic quickly and easily. It combines the printed word, digitized voice, and picture for efficient learning. The exercises include matching, multiple choice, word construction, categorization, and scrambled sentences and paragraphs. Each exercise format is supposed to activate a different cognitive subskill. Multiple-choice items make learners view a word in a linguistic context, matching lets them look at lexical items as pairs which share at least one semantic trait, and categorization makes them view words as collocations which have some common function in the language. Such cognitive exercises improve learning by reorganizing lexical items in the learners' cognitive structures. Listed next to an icon of a computer diskette is the section or sections of the software where relevant material can be found.

The computer program incorporates a testing component that comprises fifteen Stage Tests. Each one of these tests covers material equivalent to one credit hour in the quarter system (or ten contact hours); thus the fifteen tests cover first-year Arabic at the university level. The computer generates a record for each test taker in which answers and scores are recorded. Students can have access to their responses in order to discuss them with their instructor. The program allows students to take a test more than once to enhance their grade. However, each time a test is requested, all the items and the alternatives within each item are automatically scrambled to preserve a measure of test validity.

This textbook, along with the peripheral material that is available with it, attempts to provide a learning environment conducive to effective acquisition of specific language abilities. These abilities, in their totality, create a measure of proficiency in Arabic. Upon completing this course, the average learner may achieve a proficiency level within the Intermediate Mid range by the American Council on the Teaching of Foreign Languages (ACTFL). Naturally, some learners may achieve a higher or a lower level.

Lesson One الدَرْسُ الأوَّل

Objectives

- Two common greetings.
- Introducing oneself.
- Leave-taking.
- Arabic alphabet: one-way connectors ا و د ذ ر ز.
- Arabic numbers.
- Listen to the recorded material for this lesson.
- Do relevant Stage 1 computer drills and exercises (see Introduction for details).

1. Common Greetings

There are several common greetings you may use in Arabic. The first greeting represented above is equivalent to the English greeting *hello*. Its response is a different word, though it has the same function. This greeting can be said to anyone at any time of the day.

The second greeting below is one of the most common in the Arab and Islamic worlds. Literally it means "*peace be upon you*," but functions as "hello." It can be addressed to a single person or a group of people in any situation, formal or informal. One of its functions is to announce one's presence when entering a home or a room. It is the obligation of one or more of the people present to respond audibly. Further, you may use it even if its use would interrupt some activity that is going on, such as a conversation. Many people, when greeting or upon responding to a greeting, place the right hand on the chest, as the man on the left is doing. You will notice, when listening to the greeting and its response, that the response has the reverse word order of the greeting.

2 1

2. Introducing Oneself

When meeting someone for the first time, you may introduce yourself by saying *anā* "أنا" (*I am*...) plus your name, or you can say *ismī* "اسْمي" (*my name is*...) plus your name. The other person responds by saying *tašarrafnā* "تَشَرَّفْنا", which is the equivalent of *how do you do* (literally: *we've been honored*). The exchange is repeated with the other person saying his or her name.

3. **Leave-Taking**

Just like other greetings, leave-taking involves two different phrases. The phrase *ila lliqā'* إلى اللقاء is roughly equivalent to "*I'll see you later.*" The response phrase *ma'a s-salāma* مَعَ السَلامَة literally means "[*go*] *with safety.*" Normally, the phrase *ma'a s-salāma* (مَعَ السَلامَة) is said by the person(s) staying behind, but it can also be used by the one leaving, as is the case in many regions, including the Gulf.

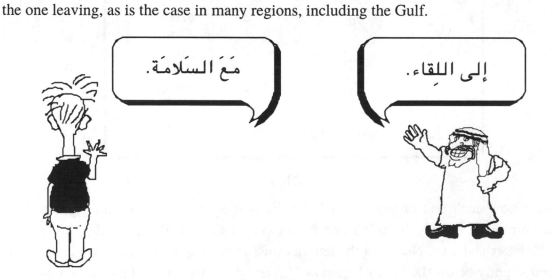

4. **Arabic Alphabet: One-Way Connectors** ا، و، د، ذ، ر، ز

The Arabic writing system is easy to learn and master because the Arabic alphabet has a high correspondence between sound and symbol. This means that a letter is pronounced almost the same in every word position.

The Arabic alphabet contains twenty-eight letters in addition to the *hamza* and two variants of existing letters (see the alphabet chart in Appendix A). A number of diacritical marks complement the alphabet. These are signs written above or below the letters. Words are written from right to left.

Arabic is written cursively, with the letters connected to one another. However, some letters connect only to preceding letters, or from the right side. These are known as one-way connectors. Table 1 lists them along with their pronunciations (see the transliteration system used in this textbook in Appendix B).

One-Way Connectors

Letter	Name	Symbol	Example
ا	*alif* ألِف	*ā*	*dad, far*
و	*wāw* واو	*ū, w*	*boot, wet*
د	*dāl* دال	*d*	*dim*
ذ	*ḏāl* ذال	*ḏ*	*then*
ر	*rā'* راء	*r*	*trilled **r***
ز	*zāy* زاي	*z*	*busy*

Table 1

Examine how each one of the letters below is written, proceeding from right to left. Strokes are made from right to left and from top to bottom. If there is a dot, it is placed after the letter is drawn. Note that the letters *wāw* (و), *rā'* (ر), and *zāy* (ز) are curved and descend slightly below the line, whereas *dāl* (د) and *ḏāl* (ذ) are angled and do not descend below the line.

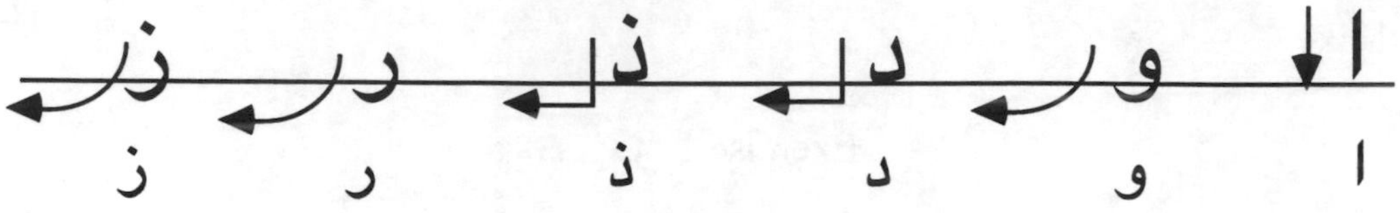

a. **The Letter** ***alif*** (ا): This letter is written from top to bottom in the independent position. But if it is connected to a preceding letter, it is drawn from bottom up. Remember that it never connects to a following letter. The long vowel *ā* represented by this letter has two variations, as in the vowels in *far* and *dad*.

b. **The Letter** ***wāw*** (و): The letter *wāw* (و) functions as both a vowel (e.g. *boot*) and a semivowel which has a consonantal value (e.g. *wet*). It is easy to distinguish between the two because an Arabic syllable does not start with a vowel, nor does it allow two vowels consecutively. Thus, any و followed or preceded by a vowel is certainly a semivowel. Consider the following examples of *wāw*:

1 واد: consonant (followed by a vowel)

2 دود: vowel (preceded and followed by consonants)

3 داوود: consonant (preceded and followed by vowels)

Example 3 above contains two syllables دا and وود. The first one is made up of a consonant and a vowel (CV) and the second contains a consonant, a vowel, and another consonant (CVC). Join the two syllables and you will get a typical Arabic word structure (CVCVC), where consonants and vowels alternate. Two general rules follow:

Rule 1 An Arabic syllable always starts with a consonant, never with a vowel.
Rule 2 Two vowels do not occur consecutively in a syllable.

c. **The Arabic** ***r*** (ر): The Arabic *r* sound is very different from the American *r*. The Arabic *r* resembles the *r* sound in the Spanish word *pero*, where the tip of the tongue flaps against the alveolar ridge behind the upper front teeth (see Figure 1 in Lesson 3). It

sounds more or less like the *t* sound in *auto* and *writer*. By contrast, American *r* is vowel-like.

Exercise 1 تمرين

Trace over the light-toned letters and copy them several times on a ruled sheet of paper. Remember to write from right to left. Your strokes should go from top to bottom.

ا و د ذ ر ز

ا و د ذ ر ز

ا و د ذ ر ز

d. **Combining Sounds/Letters into Syllables and Words:** The combination of د and ا is pronounced *dā:* دا = ا + د. Add another د to the syllable and you get a word: داد. Try to sound it out.

Likewise, the letters ز and ا make the syllable زا. What is the syllable made by the letters ر and و? Write it down in this box [ ], moving from right to left. Now combine the first and second syllables into one word and write it down in this box [ ].

e. **Distinguishing Among Similar Letters:** The letter *ḏāl* ذ (*ḏ*) differs from *dāl* د (*d*) only by a dot placed above it (ذ). The letter *rā'* ر (*r*) differs from *dāl* د in the way it is drawn. Instead of the angled shape of د, it has a slanting, curved shape (ر).

The letter *zāy* ز (*z*) is written like ر but with a dot above it. Therefore, it is important to attend to the placement and number of dots of particular letters. Remember that one-way connectors do not connect to each other.

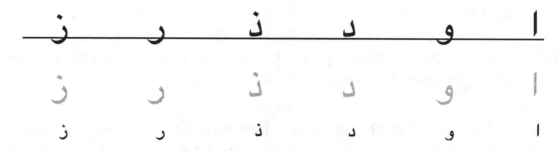

Exercise 2 تمرين

Listen to each word and repeat during the pause. Then trace over the light-toned words and copy them several times on a ruled sheet of paper. Pronounce each word as you copy it. Note that the letters ر ز و descend slightly below the line, whereas د ذ and ا do not.

دود راد واز زار ذاد زود

دود راد واز زار ذاد زود

5. **Numbers**: Until the Arabic numerals are covered, the following numeral conversion chart will help you recognize the numbers in exercise items.

Numerals Chart										
	1	2	3	4	5	6	7	8	9	0
	١	٢	٣	٤	٥	٦	٧	٨	٩	٠

Exercise 3 تمرين

Listen to each word and repeat during the pause. Remember to read from right to left. There are two items on each line:

١- زاد ٢- زور

٣- ذود ٤- دارو

٥- زادو ٦- دوراد

٧- داوود ٨- ذاد

٩- واد ١٠- رادود

١١- زورو ١٢- وازو

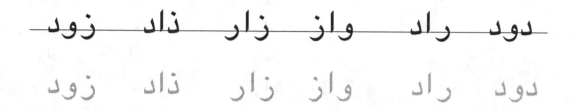

تمرين Exercise 4 🔘

Listen to a word read to you for each item and check the box next to the appropriate word. Remember to read from right to left.

رادو ❑		دارو ❑	١ـ
راز ❑		زار ❑	٢ـ
راوا ❑		وار ❑	٣ـ
ذاد ❑		زاد ❑	٤ـ
رود ❑		زود ❑	٥ـ
زارو ❑		رازو ❑	٦ـ
داوو ❑		وادو ❑	٧ـ
داذ ❑		ذاد ❑	٨ـ

تمرين Exercise 5

Join the letters in each set to form words, as in the example. Then indicate whether the letter *wāw* (و) represents a consonant or a vowel and explain why. Note that one-way connectors do not connect to each other.

Vowel	Consonant		
☑	❑	داذود ⬅	د + ا + ذ + و + د =

Explanation: Preceded and followed by consonants

❑	❑	....	١ـ ز + ا + ر + و =
❑	❑	....	٢ـ د + و + ذ + ا =
❑	❑	....	٣ـ ر + ا + و + ا + د =
❑	❑	....	٤ـ و + ا + د + ا + د =
❑	❑	....	٥ـ ز + ا + د + و + ر =

Exercise 6 تمرين

Listen to the words and syllables dictated to you on tape and write them down in the blank spaces next to item numbers.

١- .... ٢- ....

٣- .... ٤- ....

٥- .... ٦- ....

Exercise 7 تمرين

Listen to each phrase, determine whether it is a greeting or a response to a greeting, and mark the appropriate boxes:

	Greeting	Response
1.	❑	❑
2.	❑	❑
3.	❑	❑
4.	❑	❑
5.	❑	❑
6.	❑	❑

Exercise 8 تمرين

Examine this excerpt from Arabic print media and identify the letters ا و د ذ ر ز by circling them. Check the answer key to confirm your choice.

درجات الحرارة العظمى والصغرى المتوقعة
اليوم ٣٢/١٨. زخات من المطر بعد الظهر.

Vocabulary المُفْرَدات

Vocabulary items are listed in alphabetical order. Nouns are followed by their plurals after the letter ج for جَمْع *"plural,"* and verbs are listed in the past tense third person masculine singular form, followed by the present tense form in parentheses and the verbal noun after the parentheses. Nouns starting with the definite article are listed according to the first letter of the word.

name.......... (n., m.) اِسْم ج أسْماء
good-bye.......... إلى اللقاء
name of the letter *alif* .... (n., f.) ألف
I.......... (pro.) أنا
hello, welcome (response to a greeting).......... أهْلاً
nice to meet you .... تَشَرَّفْنا
name of the letter *dāl* .... (n., f.) دال
name of the letter *ḏāl* .... (n., f.) ذال
name of the letter *rā'* .... (n., f.) راء
name of the letter *zāy* .... (n., f.) زاي
peace be upon you (greeting) .... السلامُ عَلَيْكُمْ
hello (greeting).......... مَرحَباً
good-bye.......... مَعَ السلامَة
name of the letter *wāw* .... (n., f.)واو
response to السلامُ عَلَيْكُمْ.......... وَعَلَيْكُمُ السلام

بِسمِ اللهِ الرحمنِ الرَحيم
An ornate calligraphic representation of the Arabic phrase
"In the Name of God the Compassionate the Merciful"

Lesson Two — الدَرْسُ الثاني

Objectives

- Identifying yourself and others.
- Arabic alphabet: two-way connectors ب، ت، ث، ن، ي.
- Long and short vowels.
- Separate personal pronouns.
- Listen to the recorded material for this lesson.
- Do relevant computer drills and exercises, Stage 1.

1. Identifying Yourself and Others

You have learned how to introduce yourself by saying *anā* أنا *"I"* plus your name, which may also be used to identify yourself. You can introduce or identify a third person by using *huwa* هُوَ "*he*" and *hiya* هِيَ "*she*" plus that person's name.

Similarly, you may identify the addressee by using *anti* أَنْتِ "*you*" (feminine) and *anta* أَنْتَ "*you*" (masculine) plus the person's name. The exchanges in the drawings above and below proceed from right to left.

2. **Arabic Alphabet: Two-Way Connectors** ب، ت، ث، ن، ي

In Lesson One, we covered the letters of the alphabet which connect to preceding letters only, known as one-way connectors. The remaining letters of the alphabet are two-way connectors; that is, they connect both to preceding and following letters. Because of this feature, each one of them may have up to four different forms, depending on its position in the word. The five letters selected for this section are grouped because in the initial and medial positions they look the same and differ only in the number and placement of dots, as you can see in Table 1 below. Note that in the independent and final positions, the first three letters, *bā'* (ب), *tā'* (ت), and *ṯā'* (ث), have the same basic form. The other two, *yā'* (ي) and *nūn* (ن), are different.

Examine the manner of writing these five letters and their shapes in different word positions (Table 1).

Note that the initial form is also used in the middle of words following a one-way connector, as in (دابو), where (ب) assumes an initial form after *alif* (ا), which is a one-way connector.

Forms of Some Two-Way Connectors

Initial	Medial	Final connected	Final unconnected	Name	Symbol
بـ	ـبـ	ـب	ب	*bā'*	*b*
تـ	ـتـ	ـت	ت	*tā'*	*t*
ثـ	ـثـ	ـث	ث	*ṯā'*	*ṯ*
نـ	ـنـ	ـن	ن	*nūn*	*n*
يـ	ـيـ	ـي	ي	*yā'*	*ī/y*

Table 1

The independent forms of the letters in question differ also in their basic shapes. The letters ب, ت, and ث share the same basic shape differentiated by the number and placement of dots. The letters ي and ن have different shapes in an independent position and they descend below the line, as in the illustration below.

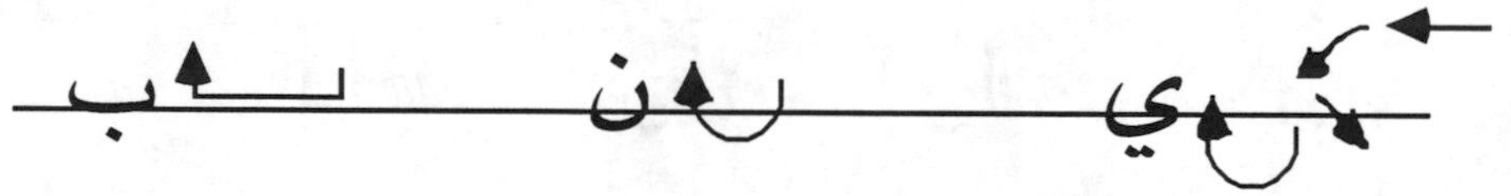

a. **The Letter *yā'* (ي) as a Vowel and a Semivowel:** As you recall, the letter *wāw* (و) has two values: a long vowel (*ū*) and a semivowel (*w*). The same thing is true of the letter *yā'* (ي): it functions as a long vowel (*ī*) and as a semivowel (*y*). As a semivowel, it has a consonantal value, which allows a short vowel to follow it. Thus, the letter *yā'* (ي) followed by any long or short vowels should automatically be interpreted as a semivowel with a consonantal value.

3. **Long and Short Vowels**

The Arabic alphabet has three long vowels. We covered two of them in Lesson One (ا and و). The third one is the vowel *yā'* ي, which is equivalent to the vowel sound in *deed.*

For the three long vowels, there are three short counterparts, which are roughly half as long. Short vowels, however, are not represented by letters like long vowels. Rather, they are represented by diacritics, or signs, placed above or below the consonants they follow.

a. **Vowel Length**: Just as in English, vowel length in Arabic is distinctive. That is, sometimes the only difference in the pronunciation of two words is vowel length. An example in English is *deed* and *did.*

In Arabic, the same process applies. The verbs for "he wrote" كَتَبَ *kataba* and "he corresponded" كاتَبَ *kātaba* are distinguished by the length of the first vowel:

kataba كَتَبَ *kātaba* كاتَبَ

b. **The Short Vowel *fatḥa*** (ـَ): The first short vowel is called *fatḥa.* It is represented by a short slanting stroke placed above the letter it follows (e.g. دَ). The difference between a *fatḥa* and an *alif* (ا) is that *alif* is twice as long. Here are three consonants with long and short vowels:

zā زا *za* زَ *rā* را *ra* رَ *dā* دا *da* دَ

c. **The Short Vowel *ḍamma*** (ـُ): The second short vowel is called *ḍamma*. It is the short counterpart of the long vowel *wāw* (و) [*ū*] and is written above the consonant it follows. It looks like a raised tiny *wāw* (e.g. دُ). The difference between *ḍamma* and *wāw* is roughly similar to the difference between *foot* and *food* or *sun* and *soon.*

zū زو *zu* زُ *rū* رو *ru* رُ *dū* دو *du* دُ

d. **The Short Vowel *kasra*** (ـِ): The third short vowel is called *kasra.* It is represented by a short slanting stroke placed below the letter it follows (e.g. دِ). Its long counterpart is the vowel *yā'* (ي). The difference between the two is similar to that

between the vowels in *deep* and *dip*. Examine and pronounce the three pairs of syllables.

دِ *di* دي *dī* رِ *ri* ري *rī* ذِ *di* ذي *dī*

تمرين ١

Listen to the following words as you read them and repeat each one during the pause. Then trace over the light-toned words and copy them several times on a ruled sheet of paper. Remember that the letters و, ز, ر descend slightly below the line, whereas د and ذ do not. Proceed from right to left.

رَذاذ دُوار رِداد ذُرور

رَذاذ دُوار رِداد ذُرور

رَذاذ دُوار رِداد ذُرور

e. **Different Handwriting Styles**: The letters you have been imitating and copying are used for printing. There is a special style called *ruq'a*, used for writing notes and letters. Although handwriting varies widely in any language, Arabic script, whether handwritten or printed, follows certain conventions shared by both varieties. Note, however, that in handwriting the two dots above the *tā'* and below the *yā'* are usually replaced with a short horizontal stroke, and the three dots above the (ث) are replaced with a caret, which is a small angle facing downwards (^). Other than that, only slight variations exist. Examine these handwritten words:

بيت ثيابي

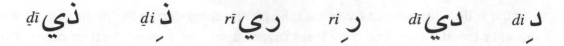

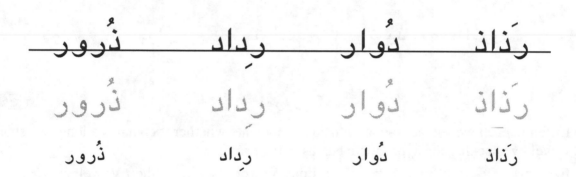

تمرين ٢

Listen to the following words as you read them and repeat during the pause. Then trace over the light-toned words and copy them several times on a ruled sheet of paper. Pay attention to the letters that descend below the line and those that do not. Four words contain the letter *yā'*. Indicate which ones are vowels and which ones are consonants and explain why (see Answer Key).

تين بَيان ثِياب نَبيذ بارود

تين بَيان ثِياب نَبيذ بارود

تين بَيان ثِياب نَبيذ بارود

تمرين ٣

Listen to each word read to you on tape and indicate whether it contains a long or a short vowel by checking the appropriate box as in the example.

	Long Vowel	Short Vowel	
Example:	☑	☐	
	☐	☐	١-
	☐	☐	٢-
	☐	☐	٣-
	☐	☐	٤-
	☐	☐	٥-
	☐	☐	٦-
	☐	☐	٧-
	☐	☐	٨-

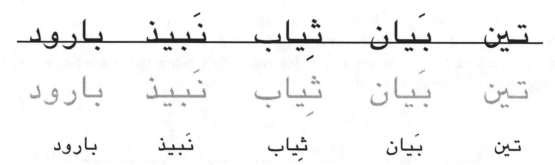

تمرين ٤

Read the following words as you listen to them on tape. Move from right to left. There are two items on each line:

١- رَتيب	٢- نُذور
٣- ثابِت	٤- ثَرو
٥- زِرياب	٦- ثِياب
٧- يَدان	٨- بَنان

تمرين ٥

Listen to the words on tape and check the appropriate box next to the word you hear:

١- دَني	❑	داني	❑
٢- بَرود	❑	بارود	❑
٣- روبى	❑	رُبى	❑
٤- داري	❑	دَري	❑
٥- ثُبور	❑	ثوبور	❑
٦- نَدير	❑	نادِر	❑
٧- بارِد	❑	بَريد	❑
٨- رَباب	❑	رابَب	❑

تمرين ٦

Listen carefully to the words read to you and write them down in the blank spaces below. Each word will be read twice.

١- .... ٢- ....

٣- .... ٤- ....

٥- .... ٦- ....

تمرين ٧

Combine the letters in each set to form words, as in the example. Do not forget to copy the short vowels. Remember that one-way connectors connect to two-way connectors only from the right side.

ثَ + ر + ي + د = ⇦ ثَريد

١- نُ + ر + ي + د =

٢- زُ + بَ + ي + د + ي =

٣- رَ + ت + ي + ب =

٤- ي + ا + ب + ا + ن =

٥- بُ + د + و + ر =

4. Separate Personal Pronouns

The words which you have used to introduce and identify yourself and others are called personal pronouns. So far, we have covered five singular pronouns (Table 2). You will notice that Arabic distinguishes between masculine (m.) and feminine (f.) in second person pronouns (you).

Separate Singular Personal Pronouns

Pronoun	Meaning	Pronunciation
أنا	I	*anā*
أنتَ	you (m.)	*anta*
أنتِ	you (f.)	*anti*
هُوَ	he	*huwa*
هِيَ	she	*hiya*

Table 2

تمرين ٨

Listen to the utterances on tape and determine whom the speaker is identifying. Mark your choice by checking the appropriate box, as in the example.

	Self	Addressee (f.)	Addressee (m.)	Third person (f.)	Third person (m.)	
Example:	☐	☑	☐	☐	☐	أنتِ
1.	☐	☐	☐	☐	☐	
2.	☐	☐	☐	☐	☐	
3.	☐	☐	☐	☐	☐	
4.	☐	☐	☐	☐	☐	
5.	☐	☐	☐	☐	☐	
6.	☐	☐	☐	☐	☐	

SUMMARY

1. There are twenty-eight letters in the Arabic alphabet in addition to the *hamza* and two variants of existing letters. Six of the letters connect only to preceding letters. They are called one-way connectors. The rest connect both to preceding and following letters. The latter group has different shapes depending on the position of the letter in a word.

2. In the Arabic sound system, there are three long vowels represented by the letters و, ا, and ي and three short vowels, which are counterparts of the long vowels, represented by diacritical marks placed above and below the letters they follow: ـَ ـُ ـِ.

3. Common greetings and leave-taking are exchanges made up of a phrase and an appropriate response.

4. Arabic personal pronouns distinguish between masculine and feminine in the second person (you).

تمرين ٩

Examine these excerpts from Arabic print media and try to identify the letters ب, ت, ث, ن, ي in all word positions.

عملية السلام تتعثر في واشنطن لكن
الأمريكيين متفائلون بالنتائج.

قام وزير الدولة الإيراني بزيارة ثانية إلى
تونس في هذا الشهر.

Vocabulary المُفْرَدات

proper noun (man's name).................... (n., m.) أديب
you (singular, masculine) .... (pro., m.) أنْتَ
you (singular, feminine).................... (pro., f.) أنْتِ
name of the letter *bā'* .... (n., f.) باء
name of the letter *tā'* .... (n., f.) تاء
name of the letter *ṯā'* .... (n., f.) ثاء
no .... (negative particle) لا
proper noun (man's name) .... (n., m.) نزار
yes.................... (particle) نَعَم
name of the letter *nūn*.................... (n., f.) نون
he.................... (pro., m.) هُوَ
she .... (pro., f.) هِيَ
name of the letter *yā'*.................... (n., f.) ياء

Calligraphic representation of the phrase
اللهُ وَحدَهُ "Allah is the sole God."

Lesson Three الدَرْسُ الثالِث

Objectives

- The morning greeting.
- Asking about well-being.
- Arabic alphabet: two-way connectors س ش ج ح خ ف ق ة.
- Listen to the recorded material for this lesson.
- Do relevant computer drills and exercises, Stages 1 and 2.

1. The Morning Greeting

The morning greeting has the same function as its English counterpart. You may respond to this greeting, using the same phrase or another one which differs only in the second word, as the man does in the drawing. Listen to the taped material for oral practice.

2. **Asking about Well-Being**

الحَمْدُ للّهِ بِخَيْر.
كَيفَ الحال؟

Usually, when two people greet each other, they also ask about each other's well-being. More often than not, Arabs also ask about the well-being of the family and even the extended family. The culturally appropriate response is a positive one. That is, one is not expected to complain even if one is not faring well. The initial response (الحَمْدُ للّه بِخَيْر) literally means "Thank God, I'm well." Later in the conversation, it is all right to express dejection or complain about an ailment, for example. Many people, however, hedge their complaints by the phrase الشَكوى للّه "*aš-šakwā li-llāh*" which means "I complain to God." The young man in the picture does not seem to be very happy, yet he uses the appropriate response.

3. **Arabic Alphabet: Two-Way Connectors** س ش ج ح خ ف ق ة

a. **The Letters *sīn* (س) and *šīn* (ش) and Their Sounds**: As you may have noticed, there are groups of letters in the alphabet. Each group shares a basic form. For example, the letters *sīn* س (s) and *šīn* ش (š) have one basic form. They are differentiated by the three dots placed above the *šīn* ش. The curved part descends below the line.

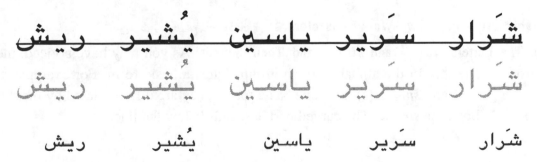

These letters pose no pronunciation problems; س is pronounced *s*, as in *Sam*, and ش is pronounced *š*, as in *shine*. Examine their different forms in Table 1.

Forms of Two-Way Connectors (س and ش)

Initial	Medial	Final connected	Final unconnected	Name	Symbol
سـ	ـسـ	ـس	س	*sīn*	*s*
شـ	ـشـ	ـش	ش	*šīn*	*š*

Table 1

Usually, in handwriting the three dots above ش may be written as a caret ˆ placed above the basic form after writing it. Also, the three "teeth" of these letters may disappear, leaving an elongated horizontal stroke, as in this sample: ســ شــ .

تمرين ١

Listen to the following words as you read them and repeat each one during the pause. Then trace over the light-toned words and copy them several times on a ruled sheet of paper. Remember to proceed from right to left.

شَرار سَرير ياسين يُشير ريش

شَرار سَرير ياسين يُشير ريش

شَرار سَرير ياسين يُشير ريش

تمرين ٢

Check the box next to the word read to you on tape, as in the example.

Example: نَسيب ☑ يُثيب ☐

١ـ تَشريد ☐ تَسديد ☐
٢ـ شَراب ☐ سَراب ☐
٣ـ روسي ☐ سوري ☐
٤ـ راس ☐ راش ☐
٥ـ شَنَب ☐ سَبَب ☐
٦ـ نَشاز ☐ ناشِز ☐
٧ـ ساري ☐ يَسار ☐
٨ـ سودان ☐ ياسين ☐

تمرين ٣

Combine the letters in each set, including short vowels, to form words, as in the example:

نِ + ب + ر + ا + س = نِبراس
١ـ تَ + ش + ر + ي + ن = ...
٢ـ شَ + ر + ي + د = ...
٣ـ سَ + ي + ا + ر + ي + ن = ...
٤ـ شَ + ر + ا + ش + ي + ب = ...
٥ـ تَ + شْ + و + ي + ش = ...
٦ـ ي + ا + ب + و + س = ...

تمرين ٤

Listen to each word dictated to you and write it down below or on a ruled sheet of paper. Each word will be read twice.

١- .... ٢- ....

٣- .... ٤- ....

٥- .... ٦- ....

b. **The Letters *jīm* (ج), *ḥā'* (ح), *ḫā'* (خ) and Their Sounds**: As you can see, these letters share one basic form and are differentiated by the dot and its placement.

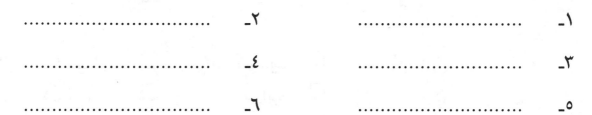

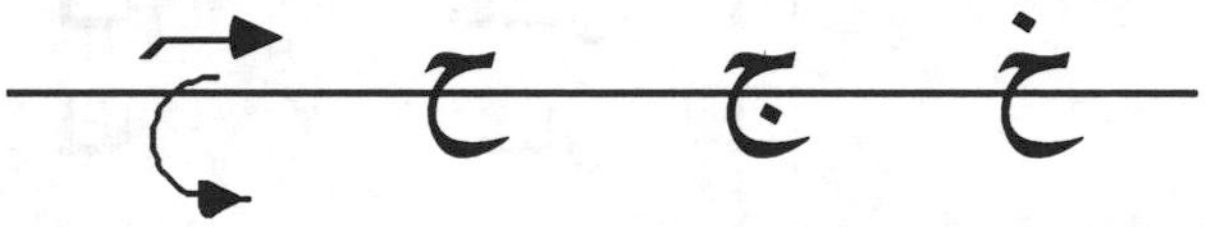

i. **A Brief Phonetic Background**: Several factors contribute to how a consonant is sounded. The first is place of articulation. This refers to how the speech organs come into contact with one another to obstruct the flow of air in some way in order to produce a sound. Figure 1 illustrates the speech organs and places of articulation.

Second, manner of articulation refers to the ways in which the articulation of a sound is performed. For example, a consonant may be oral (the air escapes through the mouth, as in *s*) or nasal (the air escapes through the nose, as in *m*). It may be a stop, where speech organs stop the flow of the air completely and then release it explosively (e.g. *b*). A consonant may also be produced with an amount of friction when two organs come very close to each other, not stopping the air flow completely but rather allowing it to escape with friction (e.g. *s*). Fricative sounds are produced in this manner.

The third important factor is the state of the vocal cords. A consonant is said to be voiced if the vocal cords vibrate during its production. To experience this, place your fingers on your throat while saying *ssssss* and then change to *zzzzzz*. Alternate them until you feel the difference. The first sound (*s*) is voiceless, where no vibrations in the throat can be felt, whereas the latter (*z*) is voiced, and you will feel the vibrations.

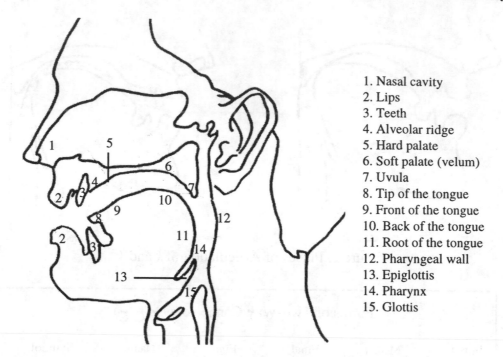

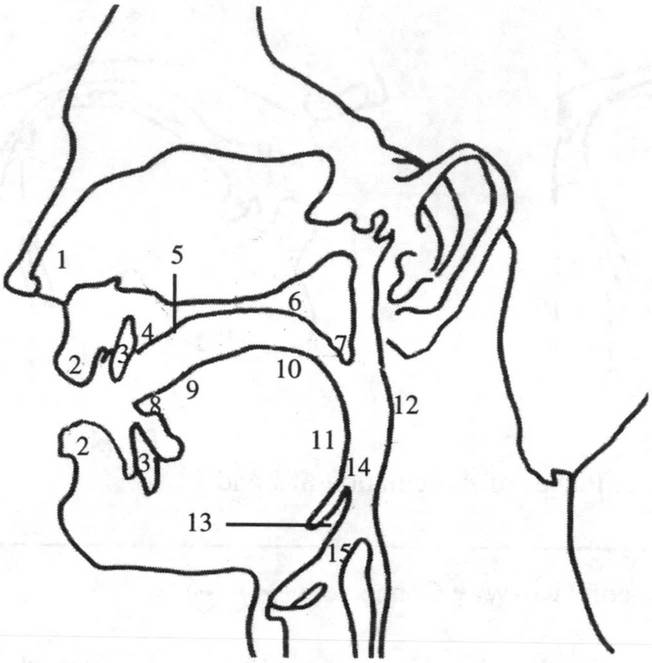

Figure 1. Organs of Speech

ii. **The Sound of the Letter** (ح): The sound represented by the letter *ḥā'* ح is called by some learners of Arabic "hard *h*", meaning that it is produced like an *h*, but with accompanying friction in the throat. There is a great deal of truth in this description. The mechanisms involved in producing the sound ح are the same used in producing the *h* sound, but with the epiglottis brought so close to the pharyngeal wall that the air escapes with friction. This consonant is voiceless; that is, no vibrations of the vocal cords occur.

iii. **The Sound of the Letter** (خ): The sound represented by the letter *ḳā'* خ is similar to the final consonants in German *Bach* and Scottish *loch*. The back of the tongue lightly touches the soft palate (velum) and the air escapes with friction. It is produced in the same place where the sharp *k* sound is produced as you can see in Figure 2. The sound *ḳ* is voiceless.

iv. **The Sound of the Letter** (ج): This letter is usually pronounced just like the *s* in *pleasure*. Note, however, that in formal recitations (e.g. recitation of the Holy *Qur'ān*), it may be pronounced like the *j* in *judge*. In parts of Egypt and Yemen it is pronounced *g* as in *gap*. In colloquial speech in the Gulf area, it is pronounced *y* as in *yet*. Despite these variations, the spelling remains unchanged. Table 2 shows the four forms of these letters in dfferent word positions.

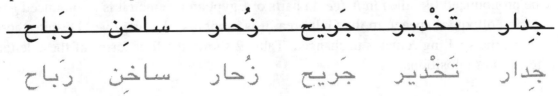

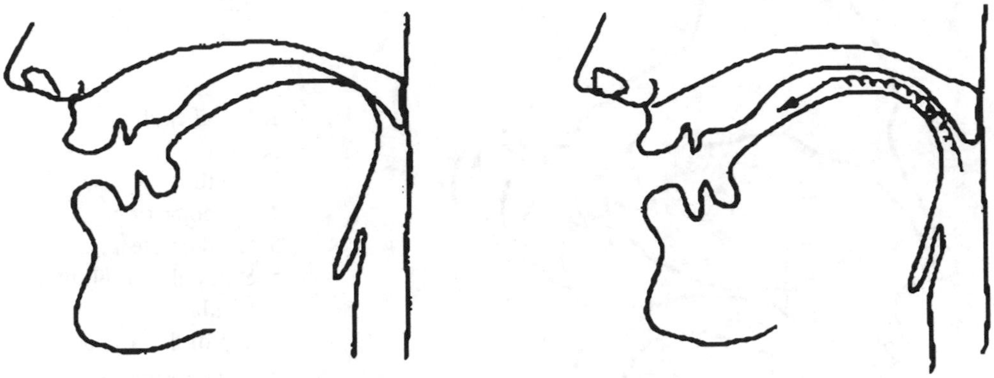

ك *k* خ *ḳ*

Figure 2. Places of Articulation of *k* and *ḳ*

Forms of Two-Way Connectors (ج ح خ)					
Initial	Medial	Final connected	Final unconnected	Name	Symbol
جـ	ـجـ	ـج	ج	*jīm*	*j*
حـ	ـحـ	ـح	ح	*ḥā'*	*ḥ*
خـ	ـخـ	ـخ	خ	*ḳā'*	*ḳ*

Table 2

تمرين ٥

Listen to the following words as you read them and repeat each one during the pause. Then trace over the light-toned words and copy them several times on a ruled sheet of paper. Remember to proceed from right to left.

جِدار تَخْدير جَريح زُحار ساخِن رَباح

جِدار تَخْدير جَريح زُحار ساخِن رَباح

تمرين ٦

Check the box next to the word read to you on tape, as in the example.

جاري	☑	جَري	☐
١- خَراب	☐	حَرب	☐
٢- جَرير	☐	حَرير	☐
٣- حَديث	☐	حُدوث	☐
٤- جَرَش	☐	حَرَس	☐
٥- جَديد	☐	خَرير	☐
٦- تَحْذير	☐	تَخْزين	☐

تمرين ٧

Combine the letters in each set, including short vowels, to form words, as in the example:

ج + ا + ر + و + ر = جارور

١- رِ + ح + ا + ب = ...

٢- سِ + ن + ج + ا + ب = ...

٣- شَ + خ + ي + ر = ...

٤- خَ + س + ي + س = ...

٥- رَ + ب + ي + ح = ...

٦- ج + و + ر + ي = ...

٧- س + ا + خِ + ر + و + ن = ...

٨- سَ + ح + ا + ب = ...

تمرين ٨

Listen to the words and write them down in the blank spaces or on a ruled sheet of paper. Each word will be read twice.

١- .... ٢- ....

٣- .... ٤- ....

٥- .... ٦- ....

c. **The Letters** ***fā'*** **(ف) and** ***qāf*** **(ق) and Their Sounds**: Although the independent shapes of these two letters are different, the shapes in the initial and medial positions resemble each other. The letter *fā'* ف (*f*) is written flush on the line, whereas the letter *qāf* ق (*q*) has a bowl-like shape and descends below the line.

The sound represented by the letter *fā'* ف is the same as the English *f.* The sound represented by the letter *qāf* ق is slightly similar to the *k* sound in *cot*, but with the back of the tongue touching the uvula (Figure 3). This means that its place of articulation is further back than that of *k.* You may feel the difference between the two places of

articulation if you alternate pronouncing *cot* and *cat*. But remember that the place of articulation of *qāf* is even further back. Also, the vowels (*a* and *ā*) that follow *qāf* differ in quality from the same ones when they follow *kāf*. After *q*, the vowel *ā* is pronounced like the vowel in *far*, whereas following *k*, it is pronounced like the vowel in *dad*.

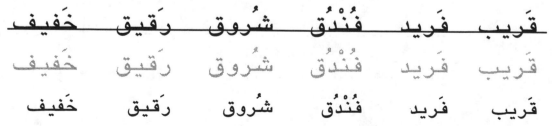

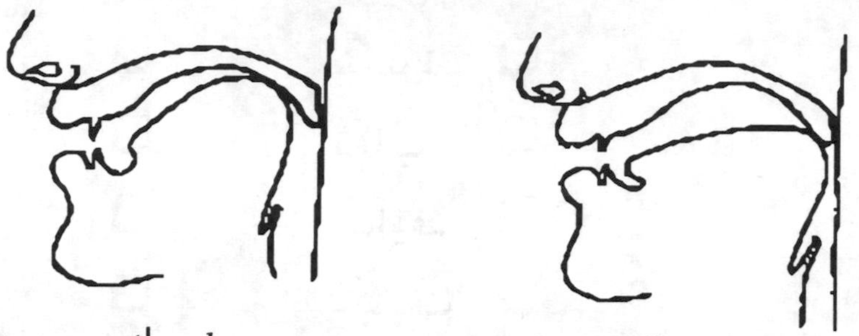

ك *k* ق *q*

Figure 3. Places of Articulation of *qāf* and *kāf*

Forms of Two-Way Connectors (ف and ق)

Initial	Medial	Final connected	Final unconnected	Name	Symbol
ﻓ	ﻔ	ﻒ	ف	*fā'*	*f*
ﻗ	ﻘ	ﻖ	ق	*qāf*	*q*

Table 3

تمرين ٩

Listen to the following words as you read them and repeat each one during the pause. Then trace over the light-toned words and copy them several times on a ruled sheet of paper. Remember to proceed from right to left.

قَريب فَريد فُنْدُق شُروق رَقيق خَفيف

قَريب فَريد فُنْدُق شُروق رَقيق خَفيف

قَريب فَريد فُنْدُق شُروق رَقيق خَفيف

تمرين ١٠

Check the box next to the word read to you on tape, as in the example.

Example:	رَفيق	☑	فَريق	☐
١-	سَخيف	☐	خُسوف	☐
٢-	ثُقْب	☐	ثِقاب	☐
٣-	فَنادِق	☐	قَذايِف	☐
٤-	فِراخ	☐	خَفيف	☐
٥-	رافِق	☐	رِفاق	☐
٦-	فُسْتُق	☐	فاسِق	☐
٧-	فِردَوْس	☐	فَراديس	☐

تمرين ١١

Combine the letters in each set, including short vowels, to form words.

١- رَ + ق + ي + ب = ...

٢- تَ + ق + ا + ر + ي + ر = ...

٣- فُ + نْ + و + ن = ...

٤- ث + ا + قِ + ب = ...

٥- فُ + ر + ا + ت = ...

٦- نُ + ق + و + د = ...

d. **The Letter *tā' marbūṭa* and Its Sound**: The letter *tā' marbūṭa* (ة) is a variant of the regular *tā'* (ت). It serves only as a suffix. The function for which it is best known is the feminine marker. When this letter is attached to most masculine nouns and adjectives, it makes them feminine.

The *tā' marbūṭa* may or may not be pronounced, depending on the grammatical function of the word to which it is suffixed and on its structure. If the word is said by itself or is followed by an adjective, then the *tā' marbūṭa* may not be pronounced. But if a personal pronoun or some other suffix is attached to the word, or if the word forms a special relationship of belonging with the following noun (*iḍāfa*), then it must be pronounced just like a regular *t*.

The position of a *tā' marbūṭa* is at the end of a word. There are only two forms: one connected to a preceding two-way connector and one after a one-way connector. The way to draw the two forms of this letter is illustrated below and in Table 4.

ة 

Unconnected

ـة 

Connected

Forms of the Letter *tā' marbūṭa*	
Following a one-way connector	Following a two-way connector
ة (جَريدَة)	ـة (قَرْيَة)

Table 4

i. **Attaching a Suffix to a Word Ending in ة**: If a suffix is attached to a word ending in a *tā' marbūṭa,* this letter assumes the medial shape of a regular *tā'*, as in: قَرْيَتي (قَرْيَة+ي) and جَريدَتي (جَريدَة+ي), where the possessive pronoun ي "*my*" is attached to the examples in Table 4 above.

تمرين ١٢

Combine the letters in each set, including short vowels, to form words. Remember to change ة into a regular ت if a suffix follows, e.g.

خَ + شَ + بَ + ة = خَشَبَة

١- خِ + شْ + يَ + ة = ...

٢- جَ + ر + ي + دَ + ة + ي = ...

٣- دَ + ف + ي + نَ + ة = ...

٤- شَ + ر + ي + فَ + ة = ...

٥- ح + ا + رِ + سَ + ة = ...

٦- ق + ا + ر + و + رَ + ة + ي = ...

تمرين ١٣

Listen to the following words as you read them and repeat each one during the pause. Then trace over the light-toned words and copy them several times on a ruled sheet of paper. Remember to proceed from right to left.

سارَة نُسَيْبَة سورية قِيادَة فَرْحَة رَبْوَة

سارَة نُسَيْبَة سورية قِيادَة فَرْحَة رَبْوَة

سارَة نُسَيْبَة سورية قِيادَة فَرْحَة رَبْوَة

تمرين ١٤

Write down the six words dictated to you on a ruled sheet of paper. Each word will be read twice. Note that words ending in *tā' marbūṭa* not followed by a suffix or another noun are pronounced simply with a final short *a* (*fatḥa*) with the *t* sound suppressed. The word خَبيرَة, for example, is pronounced *ḳabīra* with no *t* on its end.

تمرين ١٥

Identify the letters س, ش, ج, ح, خ, ف, ق, ة in these excerpts from Arabic newspapers.

آخِرُ خَبَر

سَتَبْدأُ غداً الأحَدَ أعْمالُ الدورَةِ التدريبيَّةِ للإعلامِ الزراعيِّ والَّتي تُقامُ برِعايَةِ السَيِّدِ خَليل عَرنوق وَزيرِ الزِراعَة.

حَرَكَةُ القِطارات

مِن دمَشقَ مُباشَرَةً دونَ تَوَقُّفٍ إلى حَلَبَ ١٦,١٠. من دمَشقَ إلى حِمْصَ، حَماة، حَلب الرَقَّةَ دَيرِ الزَوْر الحَسَكَة القامِشلي ١٧,٢٥ إلى طَرطوس واللاذِقِيَّة ٣١,٠.

المُفْرَدات

fine, well .... بِخَيْر
name of the letter *jīm* .... (n., m.) جيم
name of the letter *ḥā'* .... (n., m.) حاء
condition, circumstance .... (n., f.) (أحْوال) حال
Thank God, praise be to God .... الحَمدُ لِلّه
name of the letter *ḳā'* .... (n., m.) خاء
name of the letter *sīn* .... (n., m.) سين
name of the letter *šīn* .... (n., m.) شين
good morning .... صَباحُ الخَيْر
good morning (response) .... صَباحُ النور
name of the letter *fā'* .... (n., m.) فاء
name of the letter *qāf* .... (n., m.) قاف
how .... كَيفَ
How are you? .... كَيفَ الحال؟

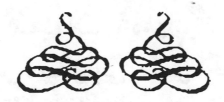

Lesson Four الدَرْسُ الرابِع

Objectives

- Inquiring about and identifying place of origin.
- Subject and predicate.
- Colloquial Arabic.
- Separate pronouns.
- Arabic Alphabet: Two-way connectors ص ض ط ظ ع غ.
- Identifying and inquiring about Arab countries, capitals, and cities.
- Arab states, political systems, and capitals.
- Listen to the recorded material for this lesson.
- Do relevant computer drills and exercises, Stage 3.

1. **Inquiring about and Identifying Place of Origin**

You may inquire about and identify place of origin by using simple structures. The question is equivalent in meaning to *"Where are you from?"* The Arabic question, however, is made up of the preposition *min* مِنْ (*from*), the question word *ayna* أَيْنَ (*where*), and a personal pronoun, referring to the person or persons about whom you are

however, is made up of the preposition *min* مِـنْ (*from*), the question word *ayna* أيْـنَ (*where*), and a personal pronoun, referring to the person or persons about whom you are inquiring. Thus, asking a woman about her place of origin requires the insertion of the second person singular feminine pronoun *anti* أنتِ, as in the example:

١ مِن أيـنَ أنتِ؟

But if you are asking about where a certain man comes from, you must use the third person singular masculine pronoun *huwa* هُوَ (*he*). Use هِيَ to refer to a woman.

٢ مِن أيـنَ هُوَ/هِيَ؟

The response to such questions involves the use of a personal pronoun, the preposition مِن "*from*," and the place of origin, which may be a town, a region, or a country, as in the example in the drawing below.

You may inquire about the location of a town with a question that contains the question word أيـنَ "where" plus the name of that town. The answer to this question involves the use of the name of that town, the preposition *fi* فـي "in," and the name of the country or state in which it is located, as in the example above.

2. Subject and Predicate

You may have noticed from the exchanges above that there is no verb *to be* (e.g. is, are) in these structures. Let's examine the sentences more closely. For example, to inquire about a woman's place of origin, you may say:

١ مِنْ أَيْنَ أنتِ؟ *min ayna anti?*

from where you (f.)? (Where are you from?)

In order to identify your place of origin, you might say:

٢ أنا مِنْ فاس. *anā min fās*

I from Fez (I'm from Fez).

And to inquire about the location of a town, you may ask:

٣ أَيْنَ فاس؟ *ayna fās?*

where Fez? (Where's Fez?)

The answer to such a question is made up of the name of that town, the preposition for *in*, and the name of the wider region:

٤ فاسُ في المَغْرِب. *fās fī al-maġrib*

Fez in Morocco (Fez is in Morocco).

Clearly, there is no verb *to be* in the above sentences. In most instances, this verb does not materialize in the present tense in Arabic. Sentences that lack the verb *to be,* or do not start with a verb, are known as nominal sentences—the term *nominal* refers to the word *noun.* A nominal sentence does not start with a verb. The subject (or topic of the sentence) may be a noun or a pronoun. The predicate (or the information or comment about the subject) can be a noun or a prepositional phrase, as in these examples:

٥ أَنْتِ | ريما | You are Reema.

٦ أنا | مِن فاس | I am from Fez.

All examples above are made up of two parts: *subject* and *predicate*. The *subject* is the focus, or topic, of the sentence, such as أنا *"I"* in *2* and فاس "Fez" in *4*. The *predicate* is the information, or comment, about the subject, such as مِنْ فاس "from Fez" in *2* and في المَغْرِب *"in Morocco"* in *4*. Table 1 illustrates this point.

Examples *1* and *3*, on the other hand, are questions and, therefore, the order of the subject and predicate is reversed. Thus, أنتِ "*you*" (f.) in *7* and فاس "*Fez*" in *8* are subjects, and مِن أينَ "from where" and أينَ "*where*" are predicates.

٧ أنتِ مِن فاس. ← مِن أينَ أنتِ؟

٨ فاسُ في المَغْرِب. ← أينَ فاس؟

Subject and Predicate	
Predicate	Subject
من فاس	أنا
فى المغرب	فاسُ

Table 1

3. Colloquial Arabic

The type of Arabic presented in this textbook is the standard language used in education, the media, and formal situations. The difference between Standard Arabic and any local colloquial Arabic may be limited to variations in pronunciation or could be marked by major syntactic changes. For example, the word أينَ in this lesson is وين (*wēn*) or فين (*fēn*) in colloquial speech. Thus, one would ask وين/فين دمَشق؟ instead of أينَ دمشق؟. In Syrian Arabic, for example, the question مِن أينَ أنتِ؟ is formed as follows: مْنين إنتِ؟. Note that مِن أين (*min ayna*) changes into مْنين (*mnēn*), where the two words are collapsed into one. Note that the first word loses the short vowel *i* and the diphthong *ay* in the second changes to the long vowel *ē*.

4. Separate Pronouns

There are other separate pronouns which have not been covered yet. The pronouns we have covered include pronouns that refer to one person (*s.* singular). Those we have not covered include pronouns that refer to two persons (dual, *d.*) and to more than two (plural, *p.*). Plural separate pronouns in Arabic distinguish between masculine (*m.*) and

feminine (*f.*) entities. That is, you use one pronoun if you are referring to a group of women and another one when referring to a group of men. Table 2 lists all separate pronouns arranged according to person.

Separate Pronouns

Person	Pronoun	Meaning
First Person	أنا	I
	نَحنُ	we
Second Person	أنتَ	you (m.s.)
	أنتِ	you (f.s.)
	أنتُما	you (f./m., dual)
	أنتُم	you (m. p.)
	أنتُنَّ	you (f. p.)
Third Person	هُوَ	he
	هِيَ	she
	هُما	they (f./m., d.)
	هُم	they (m. p.)
	هُنَّ	they (f. p.)

Table 2

5. **Arabic Alphabet:** Two-Way Connectors ص ض ط ظ ع غ

a. **The Letters** ***ṣād*** ص **and** ***ḍād*** ض **and Their Sounds:** These two letters share one basic shape. They are differentiated only by a dot placed above ض. Examine these letters

below. They are written *in one stroke*, moving clockwise. The dot is placed above the letter ض after its stem is written.

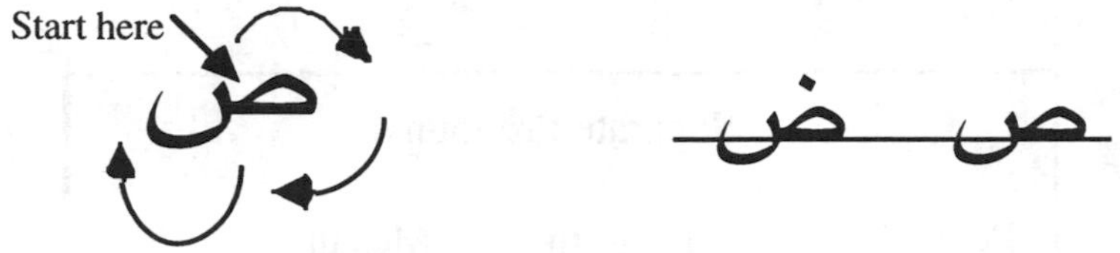

i. **Pronunciation of** (ص): To your ear, at least at this stage, the sound represented by the letter *ṣād* ص (*ṣ*) might at first resemble very closely the sound of *sīn* س (*s*), but in fact they are produced differently. The ص sound is said to be pharyngealized. This means that the back of the tongue is raised toward the soft palate during articulation and the front of the tongue (not tip) is lowered or hollowed, causing a change in sound quality (see Figure 4 below). The Arabic sound ص is similar to the *s* in *sod*, whereas the sound represented by the letter *sīn* س is more like the *s* in *seen.* Again, to your ear, the difference might be in the following vowel rather than in the consonant itself. In essence, then, Arabic has two versions of the sound *s*, one plain, or regular, and the other pharyngealized.

ii. **Pronunciation of** (ض): The sound represented by the letter *ḍād* ض (*ḍ*) is the pharyngealized counterpart of *dāl* د (*d*), and is produced with the back of the tongue raised toward the soft palate. It sounds like the *d* in *dark*, whereas د sounds like the *d* in *dad*. Figure 4 illustrates the difference between a pharyngealized sound and its counterpart.

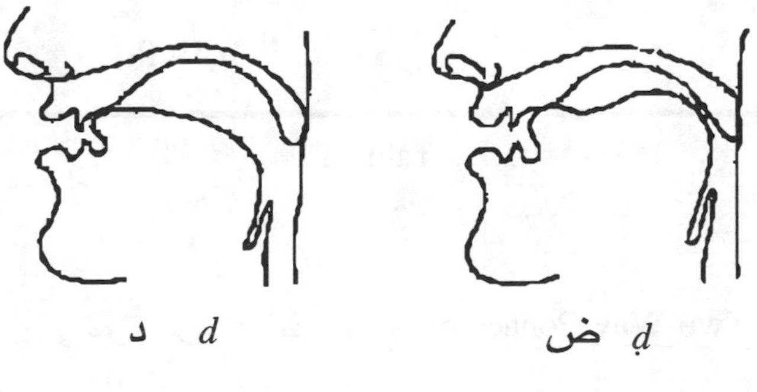

Figure 4. Plain *(d)* versus Pharyngealized *(ḍ)* articulation

Initial	Medial	Final connected	Final unconnected	Name	Symbol
صـ	ـصـ	ـص	ص	*ṣād*	*ṣ*
ضـ	ـضـ	ـض	ض	*ḍād*	*ḍ*

Table 3. Forms of the letters ص and ض in different word positions

تمرين ١

Listen to the following words as you read them and repeat during the pause. Then trace over the light-toned words and copy them several times on a ruled sheet of paper.

صَبور بَصير فُرْصَة بَيْض ضَرير نُضوب

صَبور بَصير فُرْصَة بَيْض ضَرير نُضوب

صَبور بَصير فُرْصَة بَيْض ضَرير نُضوب

تمرين ٢

Check the box next to the word read to you on tape, as in the example.

Example: صورة ☑ سيرة ❑

١- فَصيحة ❑ فَضيحة ❑

٢- رَصين ❑ نَصير ❑

٣- ضَجيج ❑ صَفيح ❑

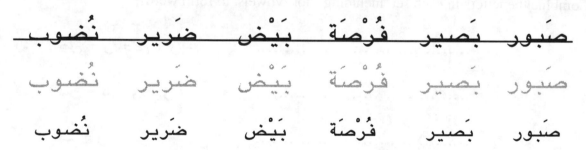

٤- رُضوض	❑	صوص	❑
٥- فَريضَة	❑	فُرْصَة	❑
٦- صاد	❑	ضاد	❑
٧- رَصيف	❑	ضَريبَة	❑
٨- ضاري	❑	داري	❑
٩- ساري	❑	صاري	❑
١٠- يَصْرِفُ	❑	يُسْرِفُ	❑

تمرين ٣

Combine the letters in each set, including short vowels, to form words.

١- ضَ + ر + ي + ر = ...

٢- صُ + د + و + ر = ...

٣- فُ + رَ + ص = ...

٤- ضَ + ف + ي + رَ + ة = ...

٥- يَ + صْ + فِ + رُ = ...

٦- قَ + و + ا + رِ + ض = ...

٧- رَ + ص + ي + ن = ...

٨- قَ + و + ا + نِ + ص = ...

تمرين ٤

Listen to each word dictated to you and write it down below or on a ruled sheet of paper. Each word will be read twice.

١-	٢- ....
٣-	٤- ....
٥-	٦- ....

b. **The Letters** ***ṭā'*** **ط and** ***ẓā'*** **ظ and Their Sounds**: These two letters also share one basic form. They are distinguished by a dot placed above the loop in *ẓā'* ظ. Note that they are written flush on the line.

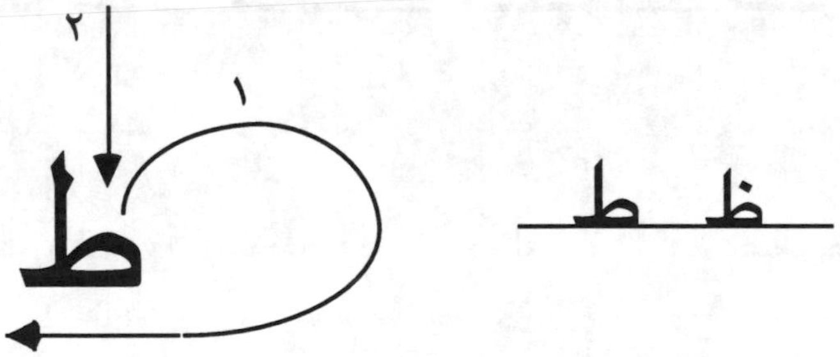

Two-Way Connectors ط and ظ			
Initial	Medial	Final connected	Final unconnected
ط	ـطـ	ـط	ط
ظ	ـظـ	ـظ	ظ

Table 4

i. **Pronunciation of ط and ظ**: Like ص and ض the sounds represented by these two letters are pharyngealized. That is, the back of the tongue is raised toward the soft palate. The difference between *tā'* ت (plain *t*) and *ṭā'* ط (pharyngealized *ṭ*) is almost similar to

the difference between the *t* sounds in *Tim* and *Todd*. While this difference is not distinctive in English, it is in Arabic. For example, the word for "*mud*" is طين (*ṭīn*) and the word for "*figs*" is تين (*tīn*). The same explanation applies to *ẓā'* ظ. It is pharyngealized, while its counterpart *ḏāl* ذ is not. The difference between the two is similar to that between the *th* sounds in *thine* and *this*, respectively. Table 4 shows the forms of the letters ط and ظ in different positions.

تمرين ٥

Listen to the following words as you read them and repeat each one during the pause. Then trace over the light-toned words and copy them several times on a ruled sheet of paper. Remember to proceed from right to left.

طَروب ظَريف خَطير حَظيرة خُطوط قَيْظ

طَروب ظَريف خَطير حَظيرة خُطوط قَيْظ

طَروب ظَريف خَطير حَظيرة خُطوط قَيْظ

تمرين ٦

Check the box next to the word read to you on tape, as in the example.

	طَباشير	☑	تَباشير	☐
١-	رَتيب	☐	رَطيب	☐
٢-	ظَريف	☐	طَريف	☐
٣-	ذاخِر	☐	ظافِر	☐
٤-	بِطريق	☐	طارِق	☐
٥-	بَسيط	☐	بَساط	☐
٦-	قَيْظ	☐	فَيْض	☐

تمرين ٧

Combine the letters in each set, including short vowels, to form words.

١- طَ + ر + ب + و + ش = ...

٢- قِ + ط + ا + ر = ...

٣- فَ + ظ + ا + ظ + ة = ...

٤- رُ + طَ + ب = ...

٥- ب + و + ص = ...

٦- ظَ + بْ + يٌ = ...

تمرين ٨

Listen to each word dictated to you and write it down below or on a ruled sheet of paper. Each word will be read twice.

١- .... ٢- ....

٣- .... ٤- ....

٥- .... ٦- ....

c. **The Letters *'ayn* ع and *ġayn* غ and Their Sounds**: These two letters share the same basic shape although they are two different sounds. As you can see below, the basic shape in the independent position is made up of two semicircles on top of each other facing right. They are written in one uninterrupted stroke. The lower, larger segment descends below the line. The medial shape is written as a loop flush on the line.

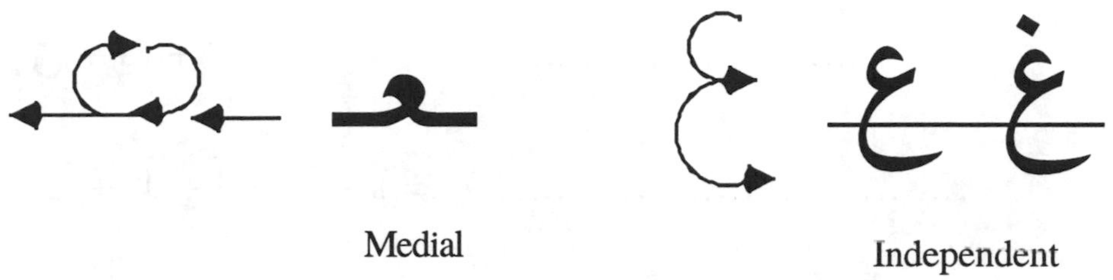

i. **The Sound of** ع: The sound represented by the letter *'ayn* ع has the same place of articulation as that of ح (i.e., in the throat), but it is voiced; that is, the vocal cords vibrate.

Two-Way Connectors ع and غ			
Initial	Medial	Final connected	Final unconnected
عـ	ـعـ	ـع	ع
غـ	ـغـ	ـغ	غ

Table 5

ii. **The Sound of** غ: The sound represented by the letter *ġayn* غ is the voiced counterpart of the sound represented by خ. It roughly resembles the Parisian *r*. The place of articulation is between the back of the tongue and the soft palate. The stream of air passing through the stricture creates a sound similar to that of gargling. The vocal cords should be vibrating; otherwise you produce the sound خ.

تمرين ٩

Listen to the following words as you read them and repeat each one during the pause. Then trace over the light-toned words and copy them several times on a ruled sheet of paper. Remember to proceed from right to left.

عَزيز غَدير شُغور بَعير سَريع فَراغ

عَزيز غَدير شُغور بَعير سَريع فَراغ

تمرين ١٠

Check the box next to the word read to you on tape, as in the example.

Example:	تَغريب	☑	تَخريب	☐
١-	غَدير	☐	عَديد	☐
٢-	يَعرِف	☐	يَغرِف	☐
٣-	يُذيع	☐	يُزيغ	☐
٤-	صِباغ	☐	طِباع	☐
٥-	عَريف	☐	غَريق	☐
٦-	يَغار	☐	بَعيد	☐

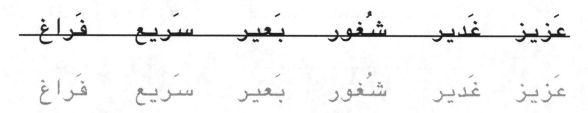

تمرين ١١

Combine the letters in each set, including short vowels, to form words.

١ـ عِ + ف + ر + ي + ت = ...

٢ـ فَ + ر + ا + غ = ...

٣ـ شُ + غ + و + ر = ...

٤ـ دَ + غْ + د = ...

٥ـ بَ + د + ي + ع = ...

٦ـ تُ + ب + و + غ = ...

6. Inquiring about and Identifying Arab Cities

The map below displays the names and locations of some Arab cities. For practice, ask someone or yourself where a certain town is located and answer the question, using the name of that city and the country. Here is an example:

أينَ بَغْداد ؟ (Where is Baghdad?) ⇦ بَغْداد في العِراق. (Baghdad is in Iraq).

Although you are able to read some of these names at this point, you might wish to postpone this activity until you have covered the whole alphabet if you want to combine reading and speaking at the same time. For oral practice only, refer to "Identifying Arab Cities" in Lesson Four.

تمرين ١٢

Listed in this exercise are ten names of Arab and American towns and states. Decode each one and write their English equivalents next to them.

١ـ بَيْروت	....	٦ـ سورية	....
٢ـ يوتا	....	٧ـ بويزي	....
٣ـ أريزونا	....	٨ـ تونِس	....
٤ـ باتن روج	....	٩ـ دِمَشق	....
٥ـ إندِيانا	....	١٠ـ ويتشِتا	....

Figure 5. Map of the Arab World

7. Arab States, Political Systems, and Capitals

There are currently twenty-one Arab states which are members of the Arab League. Their combined population is about 240 million. Arab states vary in their political systems. There are republics, monarchies, and emirates. Republics are ruled by presidents, some of whom are democratically elected. Monarchies are ruled by kings, who come from families

that have ruled the country for centuries (e.g. Morocco) or that came to power relatively recently (e.g. Jordan). An emirate (e.g. Kuwait) is ruled by an *emir* "leader, prince." An *emir* is usually a leader of a powerful tribe or clan. He assumes the regular responsibilities of a head of state.

Arab states are developing countries. Some of them, however, have become fairly wealthy and have modernized their economies and their lifestyles. A few countries are still rather poor and underdeveloped (e.g. Somalia, Mauritania). The chart in Table 6 lists countries which are members of the Arab League along with their capitals.

Arab Countries and their Capital Cities

Capital	Country	Capital	Country
مَسْقَط	١٢ـ عُمان	عَمّان	١ـ الأردُن
القُدس	١٣ـ فِلَسطين	أبو ظَبي	٢ـ الإمارات
الدَوحة	١٤ـ قَطَر	المَنامة	٣ـ البَحرَين
الكُوَيْت	١٥ـ الكُوَيْت	تونِس	٤ـ تونِس
بَيْروت	١٦ـ لُبْنان	الجَزائِر	٥ـ الجَزائِر
طَرابُلْسَ الغَرْب	١٧ـ ليبيا	جيبوتي	٦ـ جيبوتي
القاهِرة	١٨ـ مِصْر	الرياض	٧ـ السُعوديّة
الرَباط	١٩ـ المَغرِب	الخُرطوم	٨ـ السودان
نواكشوط	٢٠ـ موريتانيا	دِمَشْق	٩ـ سورية
صَنْعاء	٢١ـ اليَمَن	موقاديشو	١٠ـ الصومال
		بَغْداد	١١ـ العِراق

Table 6

تمرين ١٣

A. Examine these headings from Arabic print media and try to identify the letters ص, ض, ط, ظ, ع, غ printed in different fonts by circling them.

١- **طريق الحرير: ٩ دول اسلامية تسعى الى إحيائه**

٢- **الهواتف الضرورية**

٣- الصيدليات المناوبة

٤- **حظك اليوم**

٥- أسعار العملات

٦- **على رغم الحب لا تزال زوجته غريمته**

تمرين ١٤

For each item, one word will be read to you on tape. Check the box next to the word read on tape.

١-	سَليل ❑	صَليل ❑
٢-	ظَربان ❑	طَربان ❑
٣-	رَديد ❑	غَدير ❑
٤-	ذَرْف ❑	ظَرْف ❑
٥-	رُطَب ❑	رُتَب ❑
٦-	ضاري ❑	داري ❑
٧-	ثَعلَب ❑	ثالَب ❑
٨-	عُلَب ❑	لُعَب ❑

المُفْرَدات

Abu Dhabi (*abū ẓabī*)........(n., m.) أبو ظَبي
Jordan (*al-urdun*)........(n., m.) الأُردُن
Arizona........(n., f.) أريزونا
United Arab Emirates (*al-imārāt*)........(n., f.) الإمارات
Indiana........(n., f.) إنديانا
where (question particle)........أَيْنَ
Baton Rouge........(n., f.) باتِن روج
Bahrain (*al-baḥrayn*)........(n., f.) البَحرَين
Baghdad (*baġdād*) (capital of Iraq)........(n., f.) بَغْداد
Boise........(n., f.) بويزي
Beirut (capital of Lebanon)........(n., f.) بَيْروت
Tunis, Tunisia........(n., f.) تونس
Algiers (*al-jazā'ir*), Algeria (*al-jazā'ir*)........(n., f.) الجَزائِر
Djibouti (*jībūti*)........(n., f.) جيبوتي
Khartoum (*al-ḵurṭūm*) (capital of the Sudan)........(n., f.) الخُرطوم
Damascus (*dimašq*) (capital of Syria)........(n., f.) دِمَشْق
Doha (*ad-dawḥa*) (capital of Qatar)........(n., f.) الدَوحة
Rabat (*ar-rabāṭ*) (capital of Morocco)........(n., f.) الرَباط
Riyadh (*ar-riyāḍ*) (capital of Saudi Arabia)........(n., f.) الرِياض
Saudi Arabia (*as-su'ūdiyya*)........(n., f.) السُعودية
the Sudan (*as-sūdān*)........(n., m.) السودان
Syria (*sūrya*)........(n., f.) سورِيَة
San'a (*ṣan'ā'*) (capital of Yemen)........(n., f.) صَنْعاء
Somalia (*aṣ-ṣōmāl*)........(n., m.) الصومال
Tripoli (*ṭarāblus al-ġarb*) (capital of Libya)........(n., f.) طَرابُلُس الغرب
Iraq (*al-'irāq*)........(n., m.) العراق
Arab........(n., m.) عَرَبيّ ج عَرَب

Amman (*çammān*) (capital of Jordan)........ (n., f.) عَمّان
Oman (*çumān*)........ (n., f.) عُمان
Fez (*fās*) (town in Morocco)........ (n., f.) فاس
Palestine (*filasṭīn*)........ (n., f.) فِلَسطين
in........ (prep.) في
Cairo (*al-qāhira*) (capital of Egypt)........ (n., f.) القاهِرة
Jerusalem (*al-quds*) (capital of Palestine)........ (n., f.) القُدْس
Qatar (*qaṭar*)........ (n., f.) قَطَر
Kuwait (*al-kuwayt*)........ (n., f.) الكُوَيت
Lebanon (*lubnān*)........ (n., m.) لُبنان
Libya (*lībyā*)........ (n., f.) ليبيا
Muscat (*masqaṭ*) (capital of Oman)........ (n., f.) مَسْقَط
Egypt (*miṣr*)........ (n., f.) مِصْر
Morocco (*al-maġrib*)........ (n., m.) المَغرِب
from, of........ (prep.) مِن
Manama (*al-manāma*) (capital of Bahrain)........ (n., f.) المَنامة
Mauritania (*mōritānyā*)........ (n., f.) موريتانيا
Mogadishu (*muqadīšō*) (capital of Somalia)........ (n., f.) موقاديشو
Nwakshot (*nwakšot*) (capital of Mauritania)........ (n., f.) نواكشوط
homeland........ (n., m.) وَطَن ج أوطان
Wichita........ (n., f.) ويتشتا
Yemen (*al-yaman*)........ (n., m.) اليَمَن
Utah........ (n., f.) يوتا

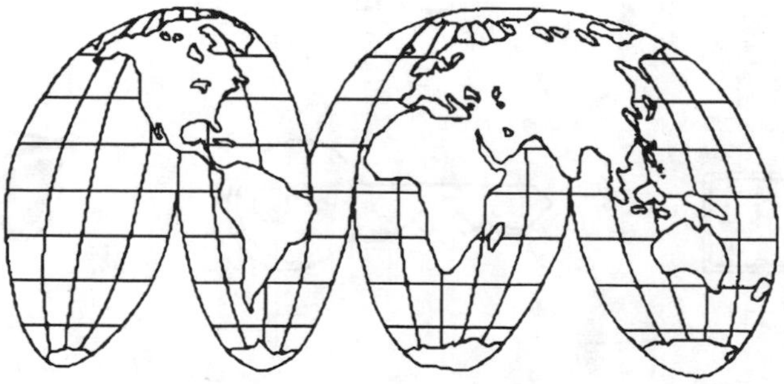

أينَ الوطن العربي؟

Lesson Five الدَرْسُ الخامِس

Objectives

- Identifying objects from the immediate environment.
- Expressing possession.
- Attached pronouns.
- Colloquial Arabic.
- Arabic alphabet: two-way connectors ل ،ك ،م ،هـ.
- Describing national and regional affiliation.
- The relative "noun" (*nisba*) اِسْمُ النِسبة.
- Gender in Arabic nouns.
- Listen to the recorded material for this lesson.
- Do relevant computer drills and exercises, Stages 1, 2, and 3.

1. Objects from the Immediate Environment

دَفتَر

كِتاب

جَريدَة

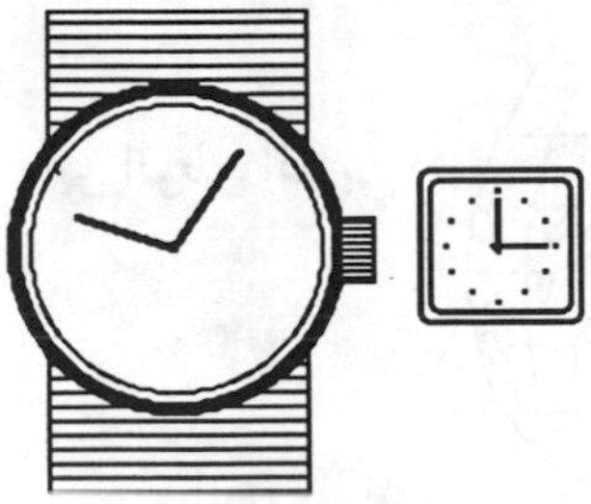

ساعَة

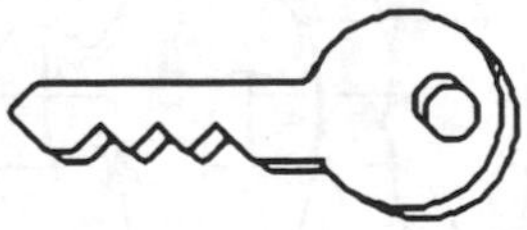

مِفْتاح

نَظّارة

حاسوب

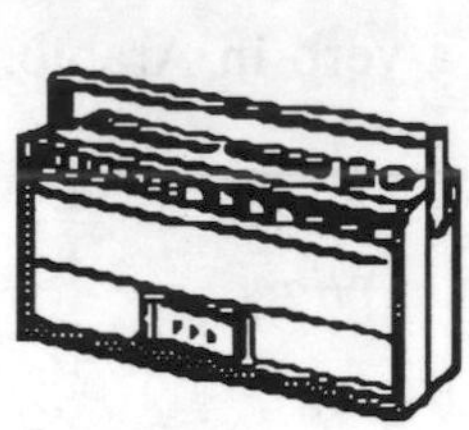

مُسَجِّلَة

دَرّاجَة

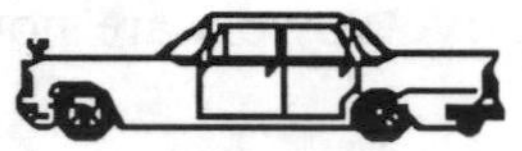

سيارة

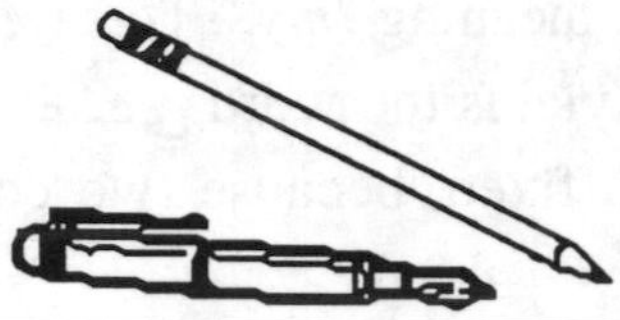

قَلَم

تلْفاز

هاتِف

2. Expressing Possession

One way of expressing possession is by using a phrase made up of the adverb عِنْدَ (literally, *"at"*) and an attached pronoun. Together they form one word. Thus, in order to say to a man, "*You have a notebook*," you begin with the word عِنْدَ and the attached

pronoun كَ "*you*" suffixed to it, referring to the second person masculine singular. Then you add the object in question, دَفْتَر, in this case. Note that although the word عِنْدَكَ translates as "*you have,*" it is not a verb in Arabic. The process may be represented as follows:

١	عِنْدَ + كَ = عِنْدَكَ	*You* (m. s.) *have*
٢	عِنْدَكَ + دَفْتَر = عِنْدَكَ دَفْتَر .	*You have a notebook.*

You are already familiar with another possessive suffix which you have used when introducing yourself, using "*my name is...*" *ismī* (... اسمي). The final long vowel *yā'* (*ī* = ي) of this word is an attached pronoun, meaning "*my.*" To say, "*I have,*" use عِنْدَ plus the attached pronoun ي. The combination yields the word عِنْدي. Note that the *fatḥa* on the end of عِنْدَ is dropped when ي is suffixed, because two consecutive vowels are not permissible.

You can also express possession by attaching possessive pronouns to nouns (e.g. كتابي "*my book*"). It is the same process described above, but with a possessive pronoun attached to a noun instead of to the adverb عِنْدَ.

3. Colloquial Arabic

Variation between Standard Arabic and the different colloquial varieties can be at the phonological, lexical, morphological, syntactic, and lexical levels. In this lesson, we are concerned with lexical variation, where Standard Arabic and colloquial versions have different words to express the same ideas. In this lesson, the word for computer is حاسوب in the standard language, but many people also use كُمبيوتَر, which is a close representation of the English word. In areas such as Syria, Iraq, and Saudi Arabia the word حاسوب is used fairly frequently. The same thing applies to هاتف where the Arabized version تَلفون (*talifōn*) is often used in speech. The word تَلفاز is an Arabized form of the French word *télévision* (pronounced تِلْفِزيون-- *tilfiziōn*).

4. Attached Pronouns

Every separate pronoun (e.g. أنا، أنتَ "*I, you*") has an attached counterpart that is suffixed to the end of nouns, prepositions, and verbs. When suffixed to nouns, they serve as possessive pronouns (e.g. ي، كَ "*my, your*"). When suffixed to verbs, they serve as direct objects (with a verb, ي requires a ن before it: ني). Table 1 lists separate pronouns

and their attached counterparts with examples of attached pronouns suffixed to nouns. Note that the third person singular pronoun هُ (*-hu=his*) is pronounced ـهِ (*-hi*) when preceded by either a *kasra* or the letter ي (e.g. فيهِ).

Separate and Attached Personal Pronouns

Person	Separate	Attached	Example	Meaning
First Person	أنا	ي	دَفتَري	my (notebook)
	نَحْنُ	نا	دَفْتَرُنا	our
Second Person	أنْتَ	كَ	دَفْتَرُكَ	your (m.s.)
	أنْتِ	كِ	دَفْتَرُكِ	your (f.s.)
	أنْتُما	كُما	دَفْتَرُكُما	your (m./f. dual)
	أنْتُمْ	كُمْ	دَفْتَرُكُمْ	your (m.p.)
	أنْتُنَّ	كُنَّ	دَفْتَرُكُنَّ	your (f.p.)
Third Person	هُوَ	هُ	دَفْتَرُهُ	his
	هِيَ	ها	دَفْتَرُها	her
	هُما	هُما	دَفْتَرُهُما	their (m./f. dual)
	هُمْ	هُمْ	دَفْتَرُهُمْ	their (m.p.)
	هُنَّ	هُنَّ	دَفْتَرُهُنَّ	their (f.p.)

Table 1

5. **Arabic Alphabet:** Two-Way Connectors ل ك م هـ

a. **The Letter *lām* (*l*) ل and Its Sound**: The sound of the letter *l* in Arabic is mostly *light*. That is to say, it is pronounced with the back of the tongue lowered and the tip touching the alveolar ridge just behind the upper teeth. By contrast, in American English, the *l* sound is usually dark, with the back of the tongue raised toward the soft palate. The

word *little* has two occurrences of *l*, the first one light and the second one dark. If you can perceive the difference, it would be easy for you to pronounce the Arabic *l*, which is a light one in most cases. There are, however, instances of dark *l* in Arabic. The best-known one occurs in the word *allah* الله *"God."* Also, dark *l* occurs when it precedes or follows pharyngealized sounds (e.g. ص ض ط ظ).

This letter has a distinct shape in final and independent positions. Make sure not to confuse it with an *alif* in the initial and medial positions. The difference is that an *alif* does not connect to a following letter, whereas a *lām* does. Note the direction of writing the different shapes of *lām*.

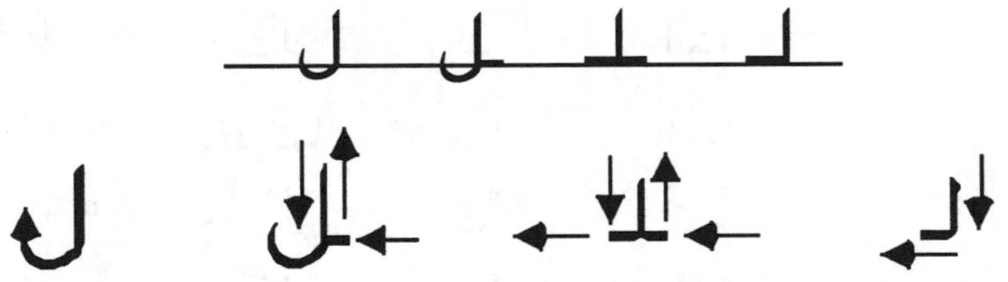

Independent Final connected Medial Initial

Figure 6. Shapes of the Letter ل in Different Word Positions

When an *alif* follows a *lām*, the *alif* is written embedded inside *lām*, slanting to the right. In print, it looks like this لا when the *lām* is not connected to a preceding letter and like this ـلا when it is connected to a preceding letter. In handwriting, however, the *lām-alif* combination resembles the latter shape, as illustrated below.

Figure 7. Shaping the letters *lām* and *alif*

تمرين ١

Listen to the following words as you read them and repeat each one during the pause. Then trace over the light-toned words and copy them several times on a ruled sheet of paper. Remember to write from right to left.

لَبيب بَليد نيل نِبال شَلَبي

لَبيب بَليد نيل نِبال شَلَبي

تمرين ٢

Check the box next to the word read to you on tape, as in the example.

	سَبيل	☑	شِبل	☐
١-	بِلال	☐	نَبيل	☐
٢-	والي	☐	وَيلي	☐
٣-	بُلبُل	☐	بِلال	☐
٤-	لادِن	☐	لَدِن	☐
٥-	لَبيب	☐	لَباب	☐
٦-	بِلادي	☐	بَلَدي	☐
٧-	والِدي	☐	وَلَدي	☐
٨-	روني	☐	روبي	☐

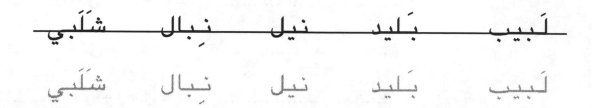

تمرين ٣

Combine the letters in each set, including short vowels, to form words.

١- لَ + ي + ل = ...

٢- بُ + ل + بُ + ل = ...

٣- عَ + سَ + ل = ...

٤- جَ + ل + ا + ل = ...

٥- صَ + ل + ي + ب = ...

٦- نَ + و + ا + ل = ...

تمرين ٤

Listen to each word dictated to you and write it down below or on a ruled sheet of paper. Each word will be read twice.

١- .... ٢- ....

٣- .... ٤- ....

٥- .... ٦- ....

b. **The Letter *kāf* ك and Its Sound**: The sound represented by this letter is pronounced just like the *k* in *kit*. In the independent position, it is written much like the letter *lām*, but with a flat base rather than a bowl-shaped one. Compare the letters *lām* ل and *kāf* ك.

The arrows below show the direction you should follow in drawing ك. The diacritical mark embedded within the letter *kāf* is used to distinguish *kāf* from *lām* in the final and independent positions. Table 2 illustrates the shapes of the letter *kāf* in the other two word positions.

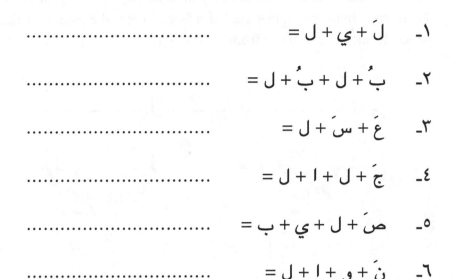

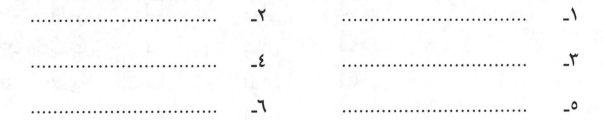

Figure 8. The Independent Shape of the Letter *kāf*

Shapes of the Letter *kāf*

Initial	Medial	Final Connected	Final Unconnected
كـ	ـكـ	ـك	ك

Table 2

تمرين ٥

Listen to the following words as you read them and repeat each one during the pause. Then trace over the light-toned words and copy them several times on a ruled sheet of paper.

كِبريت باكِر تَكبير فَلَك سُلوك

كِبريت باكِر تَكبير فَلَك سُلوك

كِبريت باكِر تكبير فَلَك سُلوك

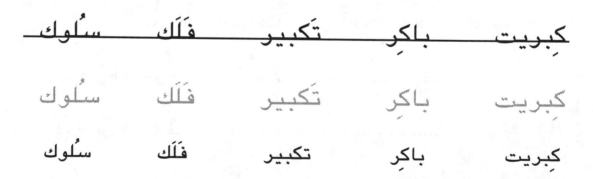

تمرين ٦

Check the box next to the word read to you on tape, as in the example.

	كَبير	☑	أكبَر	☐
١ـ	كوت	☐	كُوَيت	☐
٢ـ	شاكِر	☐	شَكَر	☐
٣ـ	فُكوك	☐	كُفوف	☐
٤ـ	كاسي	☐	قاسي	☐
٥ـ	كَسَب	☐	كاسِب	☐
٦ـ	تَدليك	☐	رَكيك	☐

تمرين ٧

Combine the letters in each set, including short vowels, to form words.

١ـ كُ + رْ + د + و + س = ...

٢ـ كُ + س + و + ف = ...

٣ـ شُ + ك + و + ك = ...

٤ـ بُ + ر + ك + ا + ن = ...

تمرين ٨

Listen to each word and write it down below. Each word will be read twice.

١- .... ٢- ....

٣- .... ٤- ....

٥- .... ٦- ....

c. **The Letter *mīm* م and Its Sound**: The sound represented by the letter *mīm* resembles the English *m*. Its independent and initial forms are written as follows:

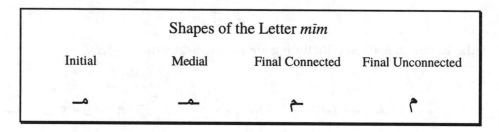

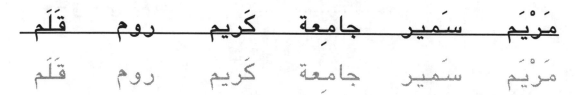

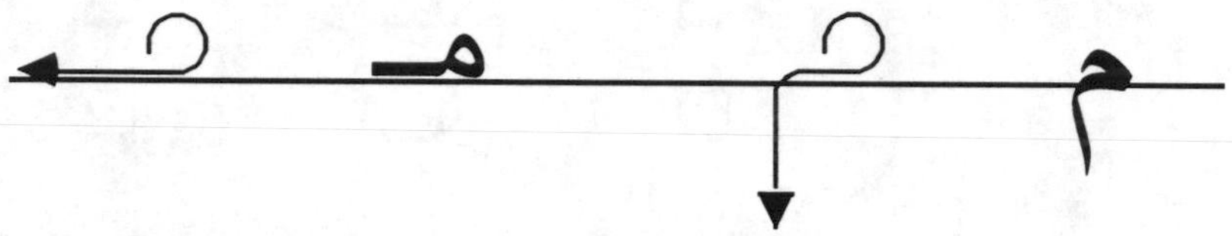

Figure 9. Writing the Letter *mīm* in the Independent and Initial Positions

Shapes of the Letter *mīm*

Initial	Medial	Final Connected	Final Unconnected
مـ	ـمـ	ـم	م

Table 3

تمرين ٩

Listen to the following words as you read them and repeat each one during the pause. Then trace over the light-toned ones and copy them several times.

مَرْيَم سَمير جامِعة كَريم روم قَلَم

مَرْيَم سَمير جامِعة كَريم روم قَلَم

تمرين ١٠

Check the box next to the word read to you on tape, as in the example.

Example:		مُدير	☑	مُريد	☐
	١-	مَيْسان	☐	مَسار	☐
	٢-	ديماس	☐	دَمَس	☐
	٣-	صَميم	☐	صَمَم	☐
	٤-	مُراد	☐	مارِد	☐
	٥-	لَميس	☐	سَليم	☐
	٦-	مُسْلِم	☐	سَلام	☐

تمرين ١١

Combine the letters in each set, including short vowels, to form words.

١- بَ + ل + سَ + م = ...

٢- مُ + س + لِ + م + و + ن = ...

٣- كِ + ر + ا + م = ...

٤- مُ + ق + ي + م = ...

تمرين ١٢

Listen to each word dictated to you and write it down below. Each word will be read twice.

١- .... ٢- ....

٣- .... ٤- ....

٥- .... ٦- ....

d. **The Letter *hā'* هـ and Its Sound**: The sound represented by this letter is pronounced like the *h* in the word *house*. The difference between the English and Arabic *h* is that in English it is found mainly at the beginning of a syllable, whereas in Arabic it can be at the beginning or the end (e.g. English *hen*; Arabic هابَ and تاهَ).

Examine how the different forms are written. The initial form is written as two loops, one within the other and with one stroke. The handwritten medial shape is somewhat different from the printed shape ـهـ. The two final shapes are similar to the *tā' marbūṭa* minus the dots.

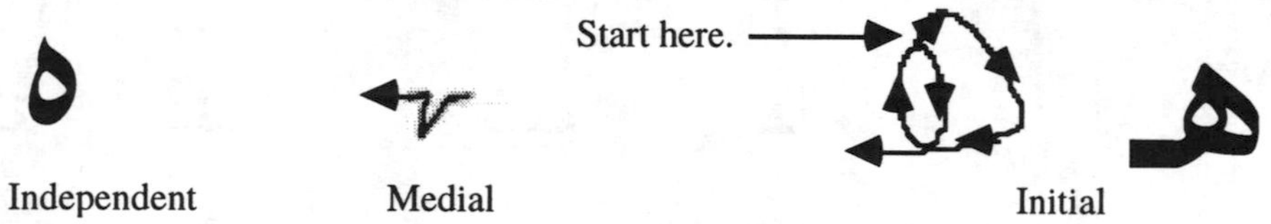

Shapes of the Letter *hā'*			
Initial	Medial	Final Connected	Final Unconnected
هـ	ـهـ	ـه	ه

Table 4

تمرين ١٣

Listen to the following words as you read them and repeat each one during the pause. Then trace over the light-toned ones and copy them several times.

هادي مَهْدي شاه تيه تَهافُت

هادي مَهْدي شاه تيه تَهافُت

تمرين ١٤

Check the box next to the word read to you on tape, as in the example.

Example:	رَفاه	☑	وَفاة	☐
١-	هِشام	☐	حُسام	☐
٢-	نَبِيّة	☐	نَبيه	☐
٣-	مَحروم	☐	مَهروم	☐
٤-	دَواليهِ	☐	دالِيَة	☐
٥-	زَهْرَة	☐	زَهْرَه	☐
٦-	هاتِها	☐	حافِلة	☐

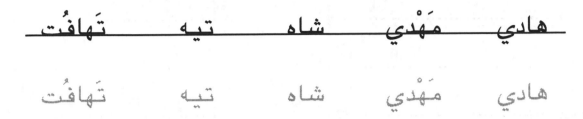

تمرين ١٥

Combine the letters in each set, including short vowels, to form words.

١ـ بَ + ه + ل + و + ل = ...

٢ـ مُ + ه + ا + تَ + ر + ا + ت = ...

٣ـ ا + ل + مَ + ل + ا + ه + ي = ...

٤ـ سَ + ف + ي + ه = ...

٥ـ فِ + د + ا + هُ = ...

تمرين ١٦

Listen to each word dictated to you and write it down below. Each word is read twice.

١ـ ....   ٢ـ ....

٣ـ ....   ٤ـ ....

٥ـ ....   ٦ـ ....

6. Describing National and Regional Affiliation

Describing one's national or regional affiliation involves providing information about one's place of origin or residence. This function requires the use of a noun called "noun of *nisba*." Examine the passages below.

هو مِصْريّ.

هو مِن مَدينـةِ القاهِرة.

مارتِن لوثَر كِنغ أمِريكيّ.

هُوَ مِن مَدينَـةِ أتلانتا في

وِلايَةِ جورجَة.

7. The Relative Noun *nisba* (اِسْمُ النِسبة)

The noun used to indicate affiliation is called a *relative "noun."* The Arabic word for it is *nisba* (lit. "relation"). It is derived from a noun that refers to a city, country, region, ethnic group, etc. This process is fairly simple in Arabic. It involves adding one suffix to nouns. This suffix is made up of a doubled consonantal *yā'* يّ (*-iy*). Here is how to make relative nouns:

a. If a noun from which we wish to derive a *nisba* noun ends with a consonant, simply add to it a doubled (i.e. with a *šadda*) consonantal *yā'* يّ (-iy):

تونِس ⇦ تونِس + يّ = تونِسيّ (Tunisian)

b. If a noun ends with a *tā' marbūṭa* (ة) or *alif* (ا), drop them and add يّ:

بَرْزَة ⇦ بَرْز + يّ = بَرْزِيّ (of Barza)

فَرَنْسا ⇦ فَرَنْس + يّ = فَرَنْسِيّ (French)

c. If a noun ends with *yā'* and *tā' marbūṭa* (ـية) or *yā'* and *alif* (ـيا), simply drop the *tā' marbūṭa* (ة) or *alif* (ا) and attach *yā'* ي, which will make a doubled *yā'* with the original one:

١ سورية ⇦ سوريّ (Syrian)

٢ ليبيا ⇦ ليبيّ (Libyan)

d. If a noun has the definite article الـ "*the*" prefixed to it, drop it and attach the suffix يّ:

٣ السودان ⇦ سودان + يّ = سودانيّ (Sudanese)

e. Forming *nisba* nouns from some nouns having a long vowel requires dropping this long vowel (e.g. مدينة "*city*"):

٤ مَدينة ⇦ مَدَن + يّ = مَدَنيّ (*civilian*)

f. A small class of nouns, where an original letter (و) is deleted, requires the restoration of this letter before adding the suffix يّ:

٥ أب ⇦ أَبَ + و + يّ = أبَويّ (*paternal*)

g. Some nouns end with alif and hamza, such as سَماء "sky." A relative noun may be formed by replacing the *hamza* with wāw (سَماويّ) or by keeping it (سَمائِيّ).

8. Gender in Arabic Nouns

All Arabic nouns, even those denoting abstract notions, are either masculine or feminine. Many, but not all, feminine nouns are marked by a *tā' marbūṭa* (ة). Most masculine nouns and adjectives can be made feminine by attaching this ending to them. Note, however, that not all nouns without a *tā' marbūṭa* are masculine (e.g. أرْض "floor, ground" is feminine).

٦ تونِسيّ (Tunisian, m.) + ة = تونِسيّة (Tunisian, f.)

Note that names of all cities and towns are feminine. Country names may be masculine or feminine.

تمرين ١٧

Derive relative nouns (*nisba*) from the following nouns and then make each one feminine, as in the example.

لُبْنان ⇦ لُبْنانيّ ⇦ لُبْنانيّة

١- الهِند (India)	....	٥ - لُغة	....
٢- قَطَر	....	٦- فَرَنسا	....
٣- السُعوديّة	....	٧- العِراق	....
٤- أَخ	....	٨- دِمَشق	....

SUMMARY

1. Possession may be expressed by using the preposition عِنْد plus one of the attached pronouns, e.g. عِنْدي كِتاب.
2. A relative noun (*nisba*) is derived by adding the suffix يّ to a noun, e.g. تونِس ⇦ تونِسيّ.
3. Arabic nouns are either feminine or masculine. Many, but not all, feminine nouns have *tā' marbūṭa* (ة) as a suffix. A few masculine nouns end with *tā' marbūṭa* as well.

تمرين ١٨

Match words or phrases from the right-hand column with words or phrases in the left-hand column. Copy the matching word from the left-hand column and write it down in the blank space provided next to its match.

١ـ كَيفَ الحال؟	....	نَعَم
٢ـ اسمي خالِد	....	المَغرِب
٣ـ مَرحَباً	....	الحَمدُ لِلّه
٤ـ أنتَ	....	مِن
٥ـ لا	....	إلى اللِقاء
٦ـ مِصْر	....	أهْلاً
٧ـ مَعَ السلامَة	....	هِيَ
		تَشَرَّفنا

تمرين ١٩

Underline the word that does not belong in each set of words and explain your choice in English.

١ـ كِتاب ـ دَفتَر ـ مُسَجِّلَة ـ جَريدَة

٢ـ نَظّارَة ـ دَرّاجَة ـ سَيّارَة

٣ـ تِلفاز ـ مُسَجِّلَة ـ مِفتاح ـ حاسوب

٤ـ مَدينَة ـ دَرّاجَة ـ وِلايَة – وَطَن

تمرين ٢٠

Identify the letters ه، م، ك، ل in different word positions in these excerpts from Arabic-language newspapers.

حَظُّكَ اليَوم

الحَمَل: الحياةُ مَليئةٌ بِمثلِ هذهِ المَواقِف فتَقبَّلْ ذلِكَ بِصَدرٍ رَحب.	الأَسَد: لا تَأبَهْ بوشايةِ إنْسانٍ مُغرِض يَقْصِدُ بها الإساءَةَ إلَيْك.

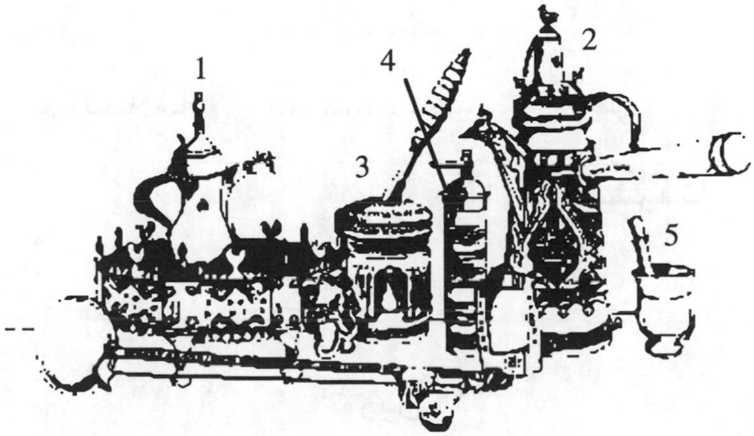

A Traditional Coffee Set

1. Brass coffee serving pot resting on hot embers.
2. Large brass serving pot.
3. This wooden mortar-like utensil is called *mihbāj*. It is used to crush roasted coffee beans. In the process of pulverizing the beans with the pestle, the user makes rhythmic, musical sounds, informing neighbors that there is a guest in his or her house.
4. Manual brass coffee grinder.
5. A brass mortar used to crush the seeds of cardamom, an aromatic spice.

المُفْرَدات

you (m. pl.) .... (pro., m., pl.) أنتُمْ
you (f./m. dual) .... (pro., m/f., dual) أنْتُما
you (f. pl.) .... (pro., f., pl.) أنتُنَّ
television .... (n., m.) تلفاز ج تِلفازات
newspaper .... (n., f.) جَريدَة ج جَرائد
computer .... حاسوب ج حَواسيب
bicycle .... (n., f.) دَرّاجَة ج دَرّاجات
notebook .... (n., m.) دَفتَر ج دفاتر
watch, clock .... (n., f.) ساعَة ج ساعات
car .... (n., f.) سَيّارة ج سيّارات
at (expresses possession with possessive pronouns) .... (prep.) عندَ
pen, pencil .... (n., m.) قَلَم ج أقلام
book .... (n., m.) كتاب ج كُتُب
town, city .... (n., f.) مَدينَة ج مُدُن
tape recorder .... (n., f.) مُسَجِّلة ج مُسَجِّلات
key .... (n., m.) مِفْتاح ج مَفاتيح
we .... (pro., pl.) نَحْنُ
relative adjective .... (n., f.) نِسْبَة
eyeglasses .... (n., f.) نَظّارة ج نَظّارات
telephone .... (n., m.) هاتف ج هَواتف
they (m. pl.) .... (pro., m., pl.) هُمْ
they (m./f. dual) .... (pro., m/f., dual) هُما
they (f. pl.) .... هُنَّ
state .... (n., f.) وِلايَة ج وِلايات

Lesson Six — الدَرْسُ السادِس

Objectives

- Identifying objects in the school environment.
- The letters *alif maqṣūra* and *hamza* (ء ى).
- Diacritical marks (*šadda, madda, tanwīn, sukūn, short alif*).
- Representation of foreign sounds.
- Colloquial Arabic.
- Listen to the recorded material for this lesson.
- Do relevant computer drills and exercises, Stages 1, 2, and 3.

1. Familiar Objects at School

لَوْح

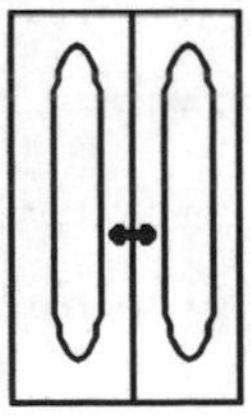

باب

نافِذَة

حَقيبَة

مِسْطَرَة

كُرْسِيّ طاوِلَة

صورَة

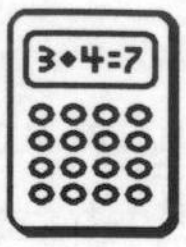

حاسِبَة

مِمْحاة

مِبْراة

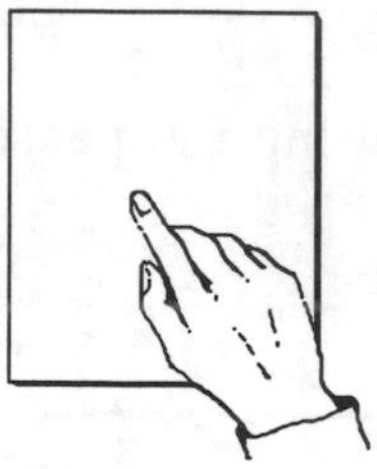

هذه ورَقَة

هذا قلَم.

2. **The Letters *Alif Maqṣūra (ā)* ى and *Hamza* ء**

a. **The Letter *Alif Maqṣūra (ā)* ى and Its Sound**: This letter is a variant of the regular *alif*. It is pronounced the same as *alif* (ā), but it is restricted to a final word position. It is written with one uninterrupted stroke, just like a *yā'* minus the two dots below it. Sometimes a tiny regular *alif* is written above it to distinguish it from *yā'* in regions where the two dots are not used below the final form of *yā'* (e.g. Egypt). If a suffix is attached to a word that ends in *alif maqṣūra*, it automatically changes to either a regular alif or to a medial yā':

فَتى + كِ = فَتاكِ

عَلى + كَ = عَلَيْكَ

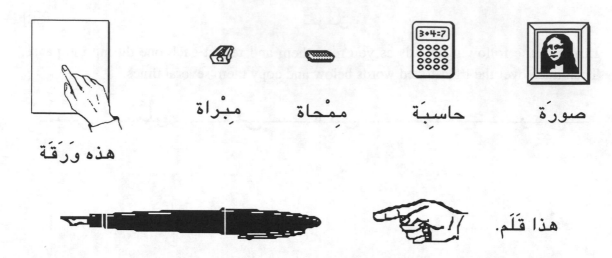

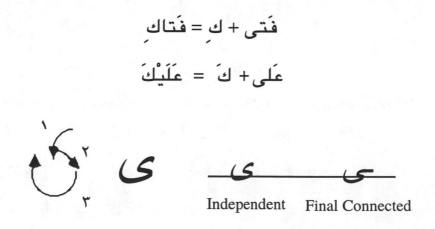

Figure 10. The Letter *alif maqṣūra*

تمرين ١

Listen to the following words as you read them and repeat each one during the pause. Then trace over the light-toned words below and copy them several times.

لَيْلى سَلْوى عَلى هُدى موسى رَمى

لَيْلى سَلْوى عَلى هُدى موسى رَمى

تمرين ٢

Check the box next to the word read to you on tape, as in the example.

Example:	عَلى	☑	عَليّ	☐
١-	لَمى	☐	لاما	☐
٢-	سودي	☐	سُدى	☐
٣-	رَمى	☐	رَمي	☐
٤-	لَبَنيّ	☐	لُبْنى	☐
٥-	دَوى	☐	دَوي	☐

تمرين ٣

Combine the letters in each set, including short vowels, to form words, as in the example:

نِ + ب + ر + ا + س = نِبراس

١- رَ + ع + ى = ...

٢- يُ + شْ + تَ + ر + ى = ...

٣- وَ + ف + ى = ...

٤- فَ + دْ + و + ى = ...

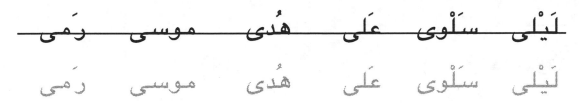

تمرين ٤

Listen to each word dictated to you and write it down. Each word will be read twice.

١- .... ٢- ....

٣- .... ٤- ....

b. **The Letter *Hamza* ء and Its Sound**: The sound represented by the letter *hamza* is a consonant produced by stopping the breath momentarily in the glottis and then releasing it explosively as when you lift something heavy. It is part of the English sound system, but it is not represented by a letter. For example, the words *above*, *in,* and *air* start with a glottal stop (i.e., *hamza*) which signals the release of the initial vowel in these words. In Arabic, this sound can appear in any word position and it is represented by a letter.

The letter *hamza* can be written independently only in the final word position. It can also be placed above any one of the three long vowels, which serve only as seats for the *hamza* and have no phonetic value.

The basic form of *hamza* is illustrated below. It is disproportionately enlarged for you to see how it is written. Write it in one uninterrupted stroke. It is written flush on the line in an independent position. Examine its size in the word باء.

Figure 11. The Letter *hamza*

In the initial position, if followed by a *fatḥa* or *ḍamma*, the *hamza* is written above an *alif*. If it is followed by a *kasra*, it is usually written below an *alif*. Remember that the *alif* has no phonetic value at all: it only serves as a seat for the *hamza*. When the *hamza* is followed by a *kasra*, it is usually placed below an *alif*, and there is no need to indicate the *kasra*.

إِ　　أُ　　أَ

Figure 12. The Letter *hamza* in the Initial Position

Writing the *hamza* above long vowels in medial and final positions follows a set of rules which will be covered gradually. The *hamza* in the final position is written flush on the line if it is preceded by a long vowel (e.g. سـوء، باء) or if it is preceded by a consonant with a *sukūn*, e.g. شَيْء، بَدْء (the detailed rules for writing the *hamza* are in Lesson 30).

تمرين ٥

Listen to the following words as you read them and repeat each one during the pause. Then trace over the light-toned words below and copy them several times.

رِفاء　　إذا　　راء　　إزار　　أنْتِ　　أُذَيْنَة

رِفاء　　إذا　　راء　　إزار　　أنْتِ　　أُذَيْنَة

تمرين ٦

Check the box next to the word read to you on tape, as in the example.

Example:		بَلاء	☑	بَلى ☐
	١-	أديب	☐	أُريد ☐
	٢-	نَقاء	☐	بَقاء ☐
	٣-	ثَناء	☐	نَشاء ☐
	٤-	أُذُن	☐	إذْن ☐
	٥-	أبي	☐	أُبَيّ ☐
	٦-	أيْنَ	☐	إناء ☐

تمرين ٧

Combine the letters in each set, including short vowels, to form words.

١- أُ + سْ + ت + ا + ذ = ...

٢- إِ + ز + ا + ءَ = ...

٣- أ + بَ + و + ك = ...

٤- رِ + ي + ا + ء = ...

3. Diacritical Marks

a. **The *šadda*** (ـّ): This mark indicates a doubled consonant. It is called *šadda* (شَـدّة) in Arabic. Doubling a consonant involves pronouncing it twice, such as the *k* in "bookkeeping" and the *n* in "non-native." A *shadda* is placed above the doubled consonant. Examine the enlarged illustration.

Figure 13. The Diacritical Mark *shadda* above د and in isolation

The short vowel following a doubled consonant marked by a *šadda* is indicated above or below the *šadda*. The short vowels *fatḥa* and *ḍamma* are placed above the *šadda* and the *kasra* below it, as in these examples:

الصَفَّ الصَفُّ الصَفِّ

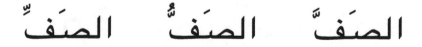

تمرين ٨

Listen to the following words as you read them and repeat each one during the pause. Then trace over the light-toned words below and copy them several times.

دَرّاجَة بَسّام سَيّارَة بَرّاد نَظّارَة مُسَجِّلَة

دَرّاجَة بَسّام سَيّارَة بَرّاد نَظّارَة مُسَجِّلَة

دَرّاجَة بَسّام سَيّارَة بَرّاد نَظّارَة مُسَجِّلَة

تمرين ٩

Check the box under "Doubled" if the word read to you on tape contains a doubled consonant (i.e. with a *šadda*) and check the box under "Not doubled" if the consonant is not doubled, as in the example.

	Doubled		Not doubled	
Example:	بَرّاد	☑	بَراد	☐
١-		☐		☐
٢-		☐		☐
٣-		☐		☐
٤-		☐		☐
٥-		☐		☐
٦-		☐		☐

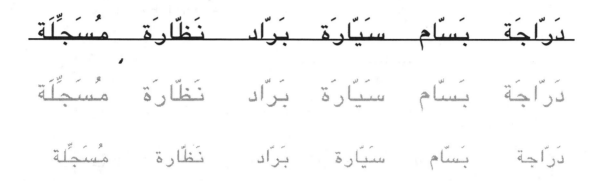

تمرين ١٠

Combine the letters in each set, including short vowels and other diacritical marks, to form words.

١ـ بَ + شْ + ش + ا + ر = ...

٢ـ حَ + دْ + د + ا + د = ...

٣ـ خَ + بْ + ب + ا + ز = ...

٤ـ رَ + سْ + س + ا + م = ...

b. **The** ***madda*** (آ): This mark is written above the letter *alif* to indicate a *hamza* followed by the long vowel *alif*. The mark *madda* (مَـدّة) resembles a short, wavy line. The combination of sounds which result in a *madda* are illustrated below.

ء + ا = آ

Figure 14. The Combination of Letters which Constitute the *madda*

تمرين ١١

Listen to the following words as you read them and repeat each one during the pause. Then trace over the light-toned words below and copy them several times.

آداب   آلات   قَرَآ   مَآثِر   شَآم

آداب   آلات   قَرَآ   مَآثِر   شَآم

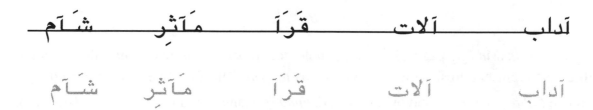

تمرين ١٢

Check the box under "*Madda*" if the word read to you on tape contains a *hamza* plus a long *alif* and check the box under "No *madda*" if a long *alif* only or a *hamza* only are pronounced, as in the example.

		No *madda*		*Madda*	
Example:		❑	مادِر	☑	مَآبِر
		❑		❑	١-
		❑		❑	٢-
		❑		❑	٣-
		❑		❑	٤-
		❑		❑	٥-

تمرين ١٣

Combine the letters in each set, including diacritics, to form words.

١- ء + ا + ر + ا + ء = ...

٢- م + رْ + ء + ا + ة = ...

٣- ء + ا + ل + ا + ف = ...

٤- ء + ا + فَ + ة = ...

٥- قُ + رْ + ء + ا + ن = ...

c. **The *tanwīn*** (تَنْوين): This is a phonological process that gives a *nūn*-like sound to three different endings, which are known as *tanwīn.* The first one is represented by a double *fatḥa* (ً), the second by a double *ḍamma* (ٌ), and the third by a double *kasra* (ٍ). They are pronounced *-an, -un, -in*, respectively.

Grammatically, *tanwīn* indicates case and an indefinite status. It appears in the final word position only, and, like short vowels, it is written above and below the letters it follows. A double *fatḥa* most often requires a silent *alif* as a seat (e.g. كتاباً). But if a word ends in a *hamza* preceded by a long *alif,* an *alif maqṣūra,* or a *tā' marbūṭa*, the double *fatḥa* may be placed above these three letters directly:

عَصاً　　مَساءً　　مَلْهًى　　جريدةً

Note that words ending in a *hamza* but preceded by a consonant require an *alif* as a seat for *tanwīn* (e.g. بَدْءاً). A double *ḍamma* and a double *kasra* require no added seat. They are placed above and below the final letters, respectively:

جُزْءاً　　شَيْئاً　　كِتابٌ　　كِتابٍ

Note: In case *alif* is required for *tanwīn* after a *hamza*, the *hamza* is written on the line and the *alif* stands independent if the letter preceding it (ز) is a one-way connector (جُزْءاً). It is placed on a *yā'* if the preceding letter (ي) is a connector (شَيْئاً).

A double *ḍamma* may be written as two *ḍammas* one above the other or as a diacritical mark that resembles a *ḍamma* with a little hook attached to it, as illustrated below.

لٌ

تمرين ١٤

Listen to the following words as you read them and repeat each one during the pause. Then trace over the light-toned words below and copy them several times.

أَهْلاً　　سيّارَةً　　مَساءً　　حاسوبٍ　　غُرْفَةٌ

أَهْلاً　　سيّارَةً　　مَساءً　　حاسوبٍ　　غُرْفَةٌ

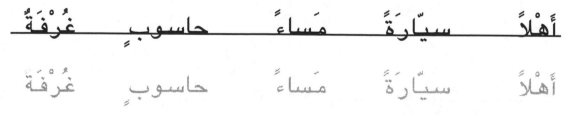

تمرين ١٥

Listen to each word and mark the box under the appropriate *tanwīn*:

ً	ُ	ٍ	
☐	☐	☐	١-
☐	☐	☐	٢-
☐	☐	☐	٣-
☐	☐	☐	٤-
☐	☐	☐	٥-
☐	☐	☐	٦-

d. **The *sukūn*** (ْ) سُكون: This diacritical mark is represented by a tiny circle placed above a letter to indicate the absence of a vowel after that sound. The following words contain a sequence of two consonants, the first of which has a *sukūn* to indicate that there is no vowel to break the sequence of consonants.

مَكْتَب   غُرْفة   اِسْمي

تمرين ١٦

Write down the words dictated to you and indicate all the short vowels and other diacritical marks, including the *sukūn*.

....	٢-	....	١-
....	٤-	....	٣-
....	٦-	....	٥-

e. **The short *alif***: There are a few words in Arabic that contain a regular long *alif*, but are spelled without one. You may have wondered why the word هذا, for example, is pronounced هاذا, but spelled هذا, and why لكنْ is thus spelled, but pronounced لاكنْ. In fact, the long *alif* may be indicated by a special marker which resembles a tiny *alif* placed above the consonant it follows. This is referred to as the *dagger alif*. In practice, however, it is usually not written. Only in certain publications, such as the *Qur'ān* (the holy book of Muslims), can you find this diacritical mark. Since only a limited number of words that contain a long *alif* and are spelled without one exist, you will be able to recognize them even without the marker. Some of these words include the following:

هذا　　هذِهِ　　هؤُلاءِ　　ذلِكَ　　لكِن　　الله

Most of these words are already familiar to you. The third one (هؤلاء) is a demonstrative like the first two, but it has plural reference. The fourth one (ذَلك) is also a demonstrative, but it refers to a distant masculine object. The short *alif* follows the first letter in all these words except in الله where it follows the second *lām*.

4. **Representation of Foreign Sounds**

A few sounds that exist in other languages are not in the Arabic sound system. Of these, the following three are most commonly used because they are part of the sound systems of most European languages with which Arabic has close contact. Certain conventions in Arabic spelling address this deficiency.

Foreign Sound	Representation in Arabic
p	پ
v	ڤ
g	غ

The sound *g*, however, is represented by ج in Egypt because the letter ج is pronounced *g* in most parts of Egypt, Yemen, and Oman. It is represented by غ in the eastern part of the Arab world (the Levant) and in other regions where the ج is pronounced *j*. Some publications in the eastern part also use ج to represent *g*.

تمرين ١٧

Test your ability to identify and spell in Arabic at least ten American cities of those marked on the map of the United States. Write in complete sentences as in the example. This will allow you to apply the skills you have developed in using the Arabic script. Provide short vowels and other diacritical marks and use special conventions to represent non-Arabic sounds where necessary. Note that not all cities marked are state capitals.

Example: مَدينَةُ شيكاغو في وِلايَةِ إلينوي.

5. Colloquial Arabic

Phonological Variation: One aspect of variation of colloquial speech at the phonological level involves sound variation. For example, the word قَلَم "*pen*" is pronounced *alam* in most of Syria and urban areas in Egypt, ظَريف "*nice*" *zarīf*, نَظّارَة "*eyeglasses*" *naḍḍāra*, ذَهَب "*gold*" *dahab*, لَذيذ "*tasty*" *lazīz*, ثوم "*garlic*" *tūm*, ثانَوِيّ "*secondary*" *sānawī*. As you can see, one sound may have up to two variants in colloquial speech in the Levantine area (i.e. Greater Syria). Note that these variants are not interchangeable. Below is a list of some sounds and their cognates in the colloquial Arabic spoken in the Levant.

Sound	Example	Standard	Colloquial
ق	قَلَم	*qalam*	*alam* (urban)
	قَلَم	*qalam*	*galam* (rural)
ظ	نَظّارَة	*naẓẓāra*	*naḍḍāra*
	ظَريف	*ẓarīf*	*ẓarīf*
ث	ثوم	*ṯūm*	*tūm*
	ثانَويّ	*ṯānawiy*	*sānawī*
ذ	ذَهَب	*ḏahab*	*dahab*
	لَذيذ	*laḏīḏ*	*lazīz*

تمرين ١٨

Match words from the right-hand column with words in the left-hand column. Copy the matching word from the left-hand column and write it down in the blank space provided next to its match.

مِمْحاة	....	نافِذَة
باب	....	أمريكيّ
كُرْسيّ	....	حَقيبَة
حاسوب	....	مِبْراة
عَرَبيّ	....	حاسِبَة
		طاوِلَة

تمرين ١٩

A. Identify the letter *hamza* (ء) in different word positions and the letter *alif maqṣūra* (ى) in these excerpts from the Arabic print media (airport activities).

حركة المطار

الطائرة السُعوديّة من الرياض ٥,٣٠
السُعَوديّة إلى الرياَض ٦,٣٠
الإيطاليّة إلى روما ٧,٣٠
السوريّة إلى إستنبول وموسكو ٧,٣٥
الألمانيّة إلى فرانكفورت ٧,٤٠
الطائرة السوريّة إلى دَير الزور والكُوَيْت ٨,٠٠
السوريّة إلى حلَب وبرلين وكوبنهاغن ٨,٠٠
الطائرة اللبنانيّة من بَيْروت ٨,٢٠
السوريّة إلى حلَب وباريس ٩,٠٠
السوريّة إلى حلَب وفرانكفورت ٩,١٠
اللبنانيّة إلى بَيْروت ٩,٢٠
الخليجيّة من أبو ظبي ١٠,١٠
الإمارات العربيّة من دُبَيّ ١٠,٣٠
الخليجيّة إلى أبو ظَبي ١٠,٤٥
الإمارات العربيّة إلى أبو ظَبي ١١,٢٠

B. Read and copy these samples of handwritten words:

محاريب ثعالب نيروز جيوش سلوى بيئة

مباراة نزيه فلك كريم لواء تنظير

A Traditional Family Room in a Small Arab Town or Village.

Notice the kerosene lamp on the wall along with the electric lightbulb. A diesel oil space heater is used to heat and boil water in a kettle for tea. The cushions are placed against the walls where there is a wood floor. The floor is covered with wool rugs and carpets. People usually take their shoes off before stepping into the sitting area.

Courtesy of the Arab Culture Notebook

المُفْرَدات

door .... (n., m.) باب ج أبْواب

tanwīn (diacritical mark, grammatical marker) .... تَنْوين

calculator .... (n., f.) حاسِبة ج حاسِبات

bag .... (n., f.) حَقيبة ج حَقائِب

sukūn .... (n., m.) سُكون

šadda (diacritical mark that signifies a doubled consonant) .... (n., f.) شَدَّة

picture .... (n., f.) صورة ج صُوَر

table .... (n., f.) طاوِلة ج طاوِلات

chair .... (n., m.) كُرسِيّ ج كَراسٍ

blackboard .... (n., m.) لَوْح ج ألواح

pencil sharpener .... (n., f.) مِبراة ج مَبارٍ/مِبرايات

madda (a diacritical mark that signifies a *hamza* followed by *alif*) .... (n., f.) مَدّة ج مَدّات

city, town .... (n., f.) مَدينة ج مُدُن

ruler .... (n., f.) مِسطَرة ج مَساطِر

eraser .... (n., f.) مِمحاة ج مَماحٍ/مِمحايات

window .... (n., f.) نافِذة ج نَوافِذ

this .... (n., m.) هذا

this .... (n., f.) هذه

sheet of paper .... (n., f.) وَرَقة ج وَرَقات

state .... (n., f.) وِلاية ج وِلايات

Decorative calligraphy of a Quranic phrase that reads
وما بِكُم مِن نِعمةٍ فَمِنَ الله "Whatever blessings you have come from God"

Lesson Seven الدَرْسُ السابِع

Objectives

- Identifying objects from school surroundings.
- The prepositions عَلى and في and the noun phrase بِجانِب.
- Enumerating, using the coordinating particle وَ.
- Demonstratives هذا هذه هُنا هُناك.
- Contrasting with لكنْ and لَكِنَّ.
- Negating with لَيْسَ.
- The nominal sentence and cases of its nouns.
- The definite article الـ, assimilating, and nonassimilating sounds.
- Definite and indefinite nouns.
- Listen to the recorded material for this lesson.
- Do relevant computer drills and exercises, Stage 4.

1. **School Surroundings**

غُرْفَةُ الصَفِّ

اِسْمي هالَة بُسْتاني. أنا طالِبَةٌ هُنا في جامِعَةِ حَلَب. لكِنَّني مِن مَدينةِ دِمَشْق. هذهِ غُرفةُ صَفّي. وَهذا أُستاذي. اِسْمُهُ اِلياس زِيادَة. هُوَ أسْتاذُ رِياضِيّات.

هالة بُستاني

هُناكَ طاوِلةٌ وَكُرْسيٌّ في غُرْفَةِ الصَفّ. على الجِدارِ لَوْحٌ وَصورَةٌ وَساعَةٌ. في الغُرفَةِ أيْضاً بابٌ وَنافِذَة. هُناكَ صورةٌ على الجِدارِ بِجانِبِ الباب.

2. The Prepositions في عَلى, and the Phrase بِجانِب

Prepositions usually acquire specific meanings from the context in which they are used. In the passage above, the preposition على means *on* and في *in*. The prepositional phrase بِجانب (*beside, next to*) is made up of the preposition بِـ added to the noun جانِب *side*.

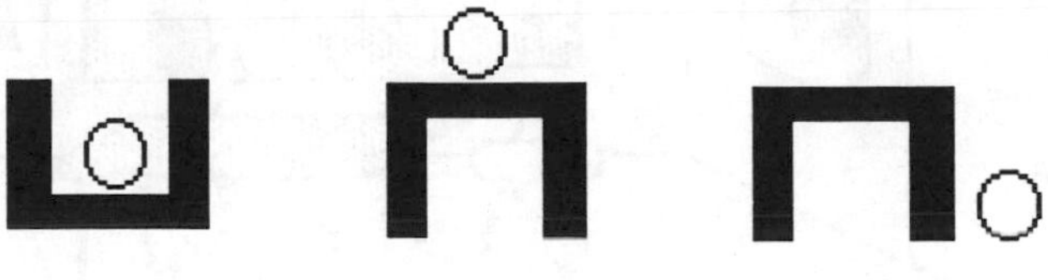

في عَلى بِجانِب

تمرين ١

Fill in the blanks in the following sentences with information from the reading passage:

١- هالَة مِنْ مَدينةِ ....

٢- هِيَ طالِبةٌ في .... حَلَب.

٣- في الصورَة لَوْحٌ وَ........................ وَ................ عَلى الجِدار.

٤- هُناكَ طاوِلَةٌ وَ........................ عَلى الأرْض.

٥- هُناكَ .... بِجانِبِ الباب.

٦- الياس زِيادَة أُسْتاذُ ....

3. Enumerating: The Coordinating Particle وَ

Listing and enumerating things is a common language function used almost daily. It involves stringing a number of words together (e.g. *She speaks Italian, French, German, and Russian*). Unlike English, where the conjunction *and* is used only before the last enumerated item, Arabic requires the use of the conjunction وَ before *every* enumerated item, as in the example:

١ في غُرْفَتي طاوِلَةٌ وَكُرسِيٌّ وَحاسوبٌ وَمُسَجِّلَة.

Important: The coordinating particle in Arabic is a prefix rather than an independent word. It should never be separated from the word it modifies (i.e., the word it precedes).

تمرين ٢

Using the conjunction وَ as in the examples below, list several objects that you own, which have been covered in this and the previous lesson. Also, enumerate objects that may be found in your room or classroom.

عِنْدي سَيّارةٌ وَ.... وَ.....

في غُرْفَتي طاوِلةٌ وَ.... وَ......

4. Demonstratives: Gender Agreement

Demonstratives are used to identify entities by making reference to them. In English a demonstrative (e.g. *this, that*) is called a determiner, which is part of a noun phrase (e.g. *this* room). In Arabic it is considered a noun. For example, the sentence هذا أسْتاذي is made up of a subject (هذا) and a predicate (أسْتاذي). This, as noted in Lesson 4, is a nominal sentence because it starts with a noun.

In English, demonstratives agree with the nouns they modify in number, but not in gender (e.g. *this man/woman, those men/women*). In Arabic, on the other hand, they agree with the following noun in number and gender. At this point, we shall consider the two forms used with singular masculine and feminine nouns. In the first example below, the word كتاب "*book*", which is masculine, is the noun modified by the demonstrative هذا. The second example contains the noun صورة "*picture,*" which is feminine. It is modified by the demonstrative هذه.

١ هذا كِتاب. This is a book.

٢ هذِهِ صورَة. This is a picture.

Two other demonstratives are used in the text above: هُنا "*here*" and هُناكَ "*there.*" The demonstrative هُناكَ, however, is also used in the sense of *there is/are* to indicate the existence of an entity. It is used with singular (3), dual (4), and plural (5) nouns.

٣ هُناكَ كِتابٌ عَلى الطاوِلة. *There is a book on the table*

٤ هُناكَ كِتابانِ عَلى الطاوِلة. *There are two books on the table*

٥ هُناكَ كُتُبٌ عَلى الطاوِلة. *There are books on the table*

تمرين ٣

Indicate the existence of five items, using في and هُناكَ, as in the following examples. Select five words that have been covered in this and previous lessons.

Examples:

هَناكَ كتابٌ عَلى الطاوِلَة.

في الصَفِّ طالِبَة.

تمرين ٤

Indicate objects by using هذا or هذه, as in the example. You may need to check the gender of each noun.

كِتاب ⇦ هذا كِتاب

صورَة ⇦ هذِهِ صورَة

١ هاتِف ⇦ ....

٢ وَرَقَة ⇦ ....

٣ قَلَم ⇦ ....

٤ تِلفاز ⇦ ....

٥ـ لَوْح ⇦ ....

٦ طالِبَة ⇦ ....

5. Contrasting: The Particles لكِنْ and لكِنَّ

Showing contrasts between objects, people, states of affairs, and so forth may be achieved by using the word لكِنْ. There are two versions of this particle: (1) the weak version لكِنْ (pronounced *lākin*) and (2) the strong version لكِنَّ (pronounced *lākinna*).

a. **The Strong Version** (لكنَّ): The strong version, as used in the text above, must have either an attached pronoun suffixed to it or a noun following it and subordinated by it, where the noun or pronoun functions as the subject of لكنَّ. In the reading passage, there is the sentence:

٦ أنا طالِبَةٌ في جامِعَةِ حَلَب لكنَّني مِن دِمَشق.

The word لكنَّني is a combination of لكنَّ and the suffix ني, which is the attached counterpart of the separate pronoun أنا, serving as the subject. لكنَّ may be followed by a noun which is also the subject of the nominal sentence following لكنَّ.

رَنا عَرَبيةٌ لكنَّ
ساندي أمريكيةٌ.
ساندي
رَنا

b. **The Weak Version** (لكِنْ): You may also use the weak version لكِنْ in order to make contrasts, as in the examples below. The contrasted part after لكِنْ is a nominal sentence (e.g. عندي درّاجة) whose preposed predicate is a phrase made up of the adverb عند and the attached pronoun ي. A sentence beginning with such a phrase may be contrasted with another, using the weak version لكِنْ. No changes occur in the forms of the constituents of the contrasted sentences as a consequence of the use of لكِنْ:

٧ عِندي سيّارَة لكِنْ لَيْسَ عِندي دَرّاجَةٌ.

However, a more acceptable and simpler style is to begin with the negative part:

٨ لَيسَ عِندي دَرّاجَةٌ لكِنْ سيّارَة.

6. **Nominal Sentences**: Arabic sentences that do not start with a verb are called nominal sentences. The first noun is the subject, or topic, and the second is the predicate, or comment. Both nouns are in the nominative case. Nouns in the nominative case are marked by a *ḍamma* on the end. If the noun is indefinite, the marker is double *ḍamma*, as in 9 (عَرَبِيَّةٌ).

٩ الطالبَةُ عَرَبِيَّةٌ.

When the particle لكنَّ is used with a nominal sentence, it causes the subject to change its grammatical case from nominative to the accusative. Nouns in the accusative case are marked by a *fatḥa* for definite nouns and double *fatḥa* for indefinite nouns:

١٠ الطالِبَةُ تونِسيَّةٌ لكنَّ الطالِبَ مَغرِبِيٌّ.

7. **Negating with** لَيْسَ: The statement in the example below is negated by لَيْسَ, which is used to negate nominal sentences. In a nominal sentence, such as the one in the example, the predicate acquires the accusative case with the use of لَيْسَ (see also 11-13).

١١ نادِيَةُ طالِبَةٌ. ⇦ لَيْسَتْ نادِيَةُ طالِبَةً.

١٢ الأُسْتاذُ لُبْنانيٌّ. ⇦ لَيْسَ الأُسْتاذُ لُبْنانِيّاً.

Notice that لَيْسَ agrees with the noun it is negating in gender. Thus, if the noun at the beginning of the sentence is feminine, لَيْسَ must agree with it in gender and should have the form لَيْسَتْ.

Note also that the use of لَيْسَ makes the predicate accusative, as in لُبْنانيّاً، طالِبَةً in 11 and 12. Accusative nouns are marked by *fatḥa* or double *fatḥa*. Regular plurals with ونَ take the ending ينَ. When لَيْسَ *follows* the noun or pronoun, which is permitted, it should agree with it in number and in gender:

١٣ هُمْ كَنَديّون. ⇦ هُمْ لَيْسوا كَنَديّين.

Forms of لَيْسَ

Conjugation	Pronoun	Conjugation	Pronoun
لَيْسا	هُما	لَسْتُ	أنا
لَيْسَتا	هُما	لَسْتَ	أنتَ
لَسْنا	نَحْنُ	لَسْتِ	أنتِ
لَسْتُم	أنتُم	لَيْسَ	هُوَ
لَسْتُنَّ	أنتُنَّ	لَيْسَت	هِيَ
لَيْسوا	هُم	لَسْتُما	أنتُما
لَسْنَ	هُنَّ	لَسْتُما	أنتُما

Table 1. Conjugations of لَيْسَ

In the above example, لَيْسَ agrees with the pronoun هُم in gender and number (m., pl.). Note that the predicate in 10, a plural noun, takes the plural accusative marker ينَ instead of ونَ as a result of the use of لَيْسَ. If the predicate, however, is a prepositional phrase (مِن فِلَسطين in 13), no change takes place in the form of words:

١١ مَحمود مِن فِلَسطين. ⇦ مَحمود لَيْسَ مِن فِلَسطين.

تمرين ٥

Underline the predicate in each sentence, which may be a word or a phrase. Then negate these sentences and phrases, using appropriate forms of لَيْس. Make changes to the predicate if necessary.

١- أُسْتاذُنا مِصْرِيٌّ.
٢- سوزانُ أوستراليّةٌ.
٣- نَحنُ سوريّون.
٤- هؤُلاءِ الطُلّابُ مِن جامِعَتِنا.
٥- هُما طالِبَتانِ أمريكيّتانِ.

تمرين ٦

Use لكِنَّ to contrast these sentences. Remember that the noun that follows this particle must be in the accusative case and it must be marked as such. Example:

سَيّارَتَكَ يابانيّةٌ. سَيّارَتُها أمريكيّةٌ. ⇦
سَيّارَتُكَ يابانيّةٌ لكِنَّ سَيّارَتَها أمريكيّةٌ.

١- صورَةُ هالَة عَلى الجِدار. صورَتُك عَلى الباب.
٢- دِمَشقُ في سورية. عَمّانُ في الأردُنّ.
٣- أنتِ مِصريّةٌ. أنا سودانيٌّ.
٤- حاسوبُ الأستاذِ أمريكيٌّ. حاسوبُ الطالِبِ يابانيٌّ.

تمرين ٧

Express contrasts in Arabic, using لكنْ and لكِنَّ. Remember that لكنْ has no effect on the structure of the sentence, but with لكِنَّ, the subject is in the accusative case:

I don't have a computer but I have a calculator. لَيسَ عِنْدي حاسوب لكِنْ حاسِبَة.

Your teacher is from Cairo but her teacher is from Tunis (note the two endings on أستاذ).

أُسْتاذُكَ مِنَ القاهِرة لكِنَّ أُسْتاذَها مِن تونِس.

Use the following sentences as guides to form your Arabic sentences. Remember to provide the appropriate endings.

1. Your school is in Damascus but his school is in Cairo.
2. She doesn't have a bicycle but she has a car.
3. There's no newspaper in my bag but there is a book on my table. (هُناكَ)
4. This is a tape recorder but this is a television.
5. There's no calculator on the table but there's an eraser and a ruler.
6. His car is American, but his computer is Japanese.

تمرين ٨

Match words from the right-hand column with words in the left-hand column. Copy the matching word from the left-hand column and write it down in the blank space provided next to its match.

١ـ لَوْح	....	صورَة
٢ـ غُرفَة	....	لكِنْ
٣ـ أُسْتاذ	....	صَفّ
٤ـ جِدار	....	في
٥ـ هُنا	....	باب
٦ـ عَلى	....	هُناكَ
		طالِب

8. The Definite Article ال: Assimilating and Nonassimilating Sounds

The definite article in Arabic (the prefix equivalent to *the*) is made up of the letters *alif* and *lām* (ال) and is prefixed to nouns and adjectives. It is pronounced *al* when prefixed to

words beginning with a sound that belongs to a group of sounds known as "moon" letters. They are so called because long ago Arab grammarians used the word *qamar* قَمَر "moon" to exemplify this group of sounds. If you prefix the definite article to this word, you have القَمَر, which is pronounced *al-qamar*. The sound represented by the letter ق and those in its class do **not** assimilate the ل of the definite article. In other words, the *lām* is pronounced as an *l* sound when prefixed to a word starting with one of these sounds. The sounds of this group are known as أحرُف قَمَرية "moon letters."

Moon Letters (Nonassimilating)													
ء	ب	ج	ح	خ	ع	غ	ف	ق	ك	مَ	هـ	و	ي

Table 2

In contrast, there are words which start with sounds that do assimilate the *lām* of the article; that is, a sound of this group causes the *lām* to be pronounced just like it. These are the "sun" letters, so named for the same reason cited above: Arab grammarians have used the word *šams* شَمس "sun" to exemplify this class of sounds. If you prefix the article to this word, you have الشَمس, which is pronounced *aš-šams* (*š*= *sh* as in *shoe*). As you can see, the *l* sound changes to *š*, thus resulting in two *š* sounds: one is the result of assimilating the *lām* of the article and the other is the original initial sound of the word. The sounds of this group are known as أحْرُف شَمسيّة "sun letters." They are listed in Table 3.

Sun Letters (Assimilating)													
ت	ث	د	ذ	ر	ز	س	ش	ص	ض	ط	ظ	ل	ن

Table 3

You have been using the process of assimilation unconsciously. The morning greeting صَباحُ الخَيْر, for example, contains the article in the second word followed by a "moon" letter خ, which allows the *lām* of the article to be pronounced as *l*. Its response صَباحُ

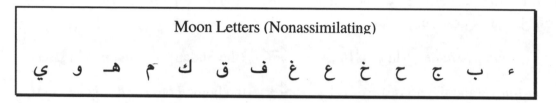

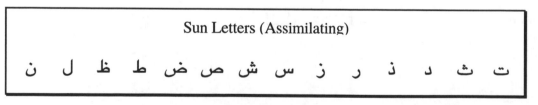

النور, on the other hand, contains the word النور, which starts with a "sun" letter ن that causes the *lām* of the article to assimilate to ن, thus resulting in *an-nūr*.

The article, whether or not it has an assimilated *l*, starts with an initial *a-* sound, which is basically a *hamza*. Thus, the word الســودان "the Sudan" is pronounced *as-sūdān* and البَيْت "the house" is pronounced *al-bayt* . This is only when these words are pronounced independently, that is, when they are not preceded by a word or a prefix. The definite article, however, loses the *hamza*, or the initial *a-* sound, if a word precedes it, such as the coordinating particle *wa* وَ "and" or a preposition. This type of *hamza* is call *hamzatul waṣl* هَمزَةُ الوَصْل. , e.g.

١٢ السودان *as-sūdān* (the Sudan) ⇦ مِنَ السودان *mina s-sūdān*

١٣ الْبَيْت *al-bayt* (the home/house) ⇦ وَالْبَيْت (and the house) *wa-l-bayt*

Important: Note that these processes affect the pronunciation of the article only, not its spelling.

تمرين ٩

Listen to each word and mark the appropriate box. If the *l* of the article is pronounced *l*, then mark the box under the phrase حَرْفٌ قَمَري "moon letter." If the *l* is not pronounced as an *l* and you hear a doubled consonant, then mark the box under حَرْفٌ شَمْسِيّ "sun letter." If you wish, you may write down the words.

	حَرْفٌ شَمْسِيّ		حَرْفٌ قَمَريّ		
Example:	❑	الطَريق	☑	القَلْب	
	❑		❑		١-
	❑		❑		٢-
	❑		❑		٣-
	❑		❑		٤-
	❑		❑		٥-

❑	❑	٦-
❑	❑	٧-
❑	❑	٨-

9. **Definite and Indefinite Nouns**

Obviously, nouns marked with the definite article are definite and those which are not marked are indefinite. For example, the word كِتاب is indefinite and الكِتاب is definite. There are other ways of making a noun definite, such as a suffixed possessive pronoun, e.g. كِتابي "my book." Unlike English, which has indefinite articles (*a* and *an*), Arabic has no indefinite article, though, as you have seen, the three *tanwīn* markers (double *fatḥa*, double *ḍamma*, and double *kasra*) on the end of a noun indicate indefinite status.

تمرين ١٠

Listen to the words pronounced and mark the appropriate box to indicate your ability to distinguish between definite and indefinite nouns. A definite word either contains the definite article ال whether or not it is assimilated to the following sound or has a possessive pronoun suffixed to it (e.g. كِتابي). Indefinite nouns end with a *tanwīn*.

Indefinite	Definite	
❑	❑	١-
❑	❑	٢-
❑	❑	٣-
❑	❑	٤-
❑	❑	٥-
❑	❑	٦-
❑	❑	٧-
❑	❑	٨-
❑	❑	٩-
❑	❑	١٠-

المُفْرَدات

professor, teacher .... أُسْتاذ ج أساتِذَة (n., m.)
too, also .... أَيْضاً (adv.)
on, in, by, with, for .... بِـ (preposition)
university .... جامِعَة ج جامِعات (f.)
side .... جانِب (n., m.)
wall .... جِدار ج جُدْران (n., m.)
Aleppo .... حَلَب (n., f.)
mathematics, calculus .... رياضِيّات (n., f.)
of the sun .... شَمْسِيّ (adj.)
class .... صَفّ ج صُفوف (n., m.)
male student .... طالِب ج طُلّاب (n., m.)
female student .... طالِبة ج طالِبات (n., f.)
on .... عَلى (prep.)
room .... غُرْفَة (غُرَف) (n., f.)
of the moon .... قَمَرِيّ (adj.)
but .... لكِنْ (particle, weak version)
but .... لكِنَّ (particle, strong version)
not .... لَيْسَ (particle)
there, there is/are .... هُناكَ (demonstrative)
and .... وَ (conjunction)

Lesson Eight الدَرْسُ الثامِن

Objectives

- Describing school surroundings and facilities.
- *Nisba* revisited.
- The *iḍāfa* structure.
- Identifying objects: demonstratives.
- Colloquial Arabic.
- Listen to the recorded material for this lesson.
- Do relevant computer drills and exercises, Stages 4 and 5.

1. School Surroundings and Facilities

جامِعَتي

اِسْمي هَيْثَم نَجّار. أنا طالِبٌ في كُلِّيَّةِ العُلومِ في جامِعَةِ دِمَشْق. في جامِعَتي عِدّةُ كُلِّيّات. هُناكَ كُلِّيَّةُ الهَنْدَسَةِ وَكُلِّيَّةُ الآدابِ وَكُلِّيَّةُ العُلومِ وَكُلِّيَّةُ الطِبِّ وَكُلِّيَّةُ التِجارَةِ وَكُلِّيَّةُ الحُقوق.

هُناكَ مَلعَبٌ رِياضِيٌّ وَمَسْبَحٌ بِجانِبِ كُلِّيَّتي. في كُلِّيَّتي مَخبَرٌ عِلْمِيٌّ، وَهُناكَ مَخبَرٌ لُغَوِيٌّ في كليةِ الآداب. المَكتَبةُ بِجانِبِ كُلِّيَّةِ الحُقوق.

غُرفَةُ مَكتَبي

اِسْمي راغِب طَبّاع. أنا أستاذُ رِياضِيّات في الجامِعةِ الأُرْدُنِيَّة. في غُرفَةِ مَكتَبي طاوِلةٌ وَكُرْسِيٌّ وَلَوْحٌ وَمَكْتَبَة. عِندي هاتِفٌ في مَكتَبي. هاتِفي على الطاوِلَةِ، لكِنْ لَيْسَ عِندي حاسوبٌ في المَكتَب. هذه حَقيبَتي عَلى الأرضِ بِجانِبِ الطاوِلَة. مَكتَبي في كُلِّيَّةِ العُلومِ في الجامِعَةِ الأُردُنيَّة.

تمريـن ١

Fill out these identification cards for the persons described in the above passages. Indicate in the box (by writing down the appropriate word) whether this person is a student or a faculty member. Then complete the sentences with information from the texts.

الاسْم: ____________

الكُليّة: ____________

الجامعَة: ____________

الاسم: ____________

الكُليّة: ____________

الجامعَة: ____________

١ـ هُناكَ .... كُلِّيّات في جامِعَةِ دِمَشْق.

٢ـ هُناكَ .... وَ............... بِجانِبِ كُلِّيَّةِ العُلوم.

٣ـ هُناكَ .... في كُلِّيَّةِ الآداب.

٤ـ راغِب طَبّاع .... في الجامِعَةِ الأردُنِيَّة.

٥ـ هوَ أُسْتاذُ ....

٦ـ مَكْتَبُ الأُسْتاذِ راغِب في ....

٧- هُناكَ .... على طاوِلةِ الأُسْتاذِ راغِب.

٨- حَقيبَةُ الأُسْتاذ راغِب عَلى ....

تمرين ٢

Study the first passage in this lesson about هَيْثَم نَجّار and replicate it, providing information about yourself and your school. You may provide actual names of buildings, colleges, and streets as applicable to your own situation.

تمرين ٣

Study the second passage in this lesson about راغِب طَبّاع and compose another passage similar to it, but in the third person, describing a professor you know. Make necessary changes in content and form to fit the new situation.

تمرين ٤

Underline the word that does not belong to each set of words and explain your choice in English.

١-	جانِب	جامِعَة	كُلِّيَّة	طِبّ
٢-	مَلعَب	مَسْبَح	هَندَسَة	مَخبَر
٣-	مَكتَب	غُرْفَة	صَفّ	عِدَّة
٤-	هذا	ذلِكَ	رِياضِيّ	تِلكَ

تمرين ٥

Match words from the right-hand column with words in the left-hand column. Copy the matching word from the left-hand column and write it down in the blank space provided next to its match.

١- رِياضَة	....	طِبّ
٢- مَخْبَر	....	عُنوان
٣- ذلِكَ	....	مَلعَب
٤- كُلِّيَّة	....	سَكَن
٥- كِتاب	....	لُغَوِيّ
		تِلْكَ
		مَكتَبَة

2. ***Nisba* Revisited**

In Lesson Five, we derived relative nouns called *nisba* (اِسْمُ نِسْبَة) (which function more like adjectives) from names of countries. The process involves adding a doubled يّ to a noun. This process, in fact, applies to the majority of nouns. In the passage above, three *nisba* nouns are derived from the words رِياضَة "sports", عِلْم "science", and لُغَة "language." If you recall, deriving a *nisba* from some nouns requires the addition of the letter و before suffixing يّ, as in لُغَوِيّ. In addition to the rules of derivation specified in Lesson Five, note that if a noun is plural, it is generally changed to the singular before a *nisba* is derived. For example, the plural noun عُلوم "sciences" must be changed to the singular عِلْم "science" before deriving the word عِلمي.

a. **Word order and gender agreement:** Adjectives in Arabic *follow* nouns and they agree with them in gender, number, and case. For example, the noun مَخْبَر may be modified by the adjective-like *nisba* عِلميّ (مَخْبَرٌ عِلمِيّ) which follows the noun and agrees with it in number (both being singular) and gender (both being masculine). If the noun is feminine, such as كُلِّيَّة, the adjective must also be feminine, e.g. كُلِّيَّةٌ عِلمِيَّة, where the *tā' marbūṭa* on the end of عِلمِيَّة marks the *nisba* as feminine.

تمرين ٦

Construct noun phrases made up of nouns and *nisba* nouns (adjectives) from the pairs of words below. Derive a *nisba* from the second noun of each pair, which must agree with the first noun in number and gender as in the examples. You may need to review the derivation rules explained in Lesson Five.

Examples:

مَخبَرٌ / لُغَةٌ ⇦ مَخبَرٌ لُغَوِيٌّ

كُلِّيَّةٌ / عِلْمٌ ⇦ كُلِّيَّةٌ عِلْمِيَّةٌ

١- جَريدَةٌ / رِياضَةٌ ⇦

٢- كِتابٌ / طِبٌّ ⇦

٣- غُرْفَةٌ / تِجارَةٌ ⇦

٤- صَفٌّ / صَباحٌ ⇦

٥- طالِبَةٌ / جامِعَةٌ ⇦

٦- سَيّارَةٌ / اليابانُ ⇦

3. The *Iḍāfa Structure* (الإضافة)

The phrases مَدينَةُ دمَشق "city of Damascus" and جامِعَةُ حَلَب "University of Aleppo" may be familiar to you by now. They represent a structure in Arabic called *iḍāfa*. The term إضافَة literally means "addition." It denotes "adding" one noun to another to form a relationship of possession or belonging. The *iḍāfa* structure binds the two (or more) nouns together, forming one entity. The main referent of this entity is represented by the *first* word of the structure. This structure is parallel to three English structures: (1) the of-structure (e.g. top of the hill); (2) the apostrophe-*s* used on the end of nouns (e.g. Tom's hat); and (3) compound nouns (e.g. stock market). The Arabic structure which is equivalent to the three English structures is the *iḍāfa*. Examples:

City of New York ١ مَدينَةُ نيويورك

Sandy's room (literally, room of Sandy) ٢ غُرفَةُ ساندي

a car key (literally, a key of a car) ٣ مِفتاحُ سَيّارَةٍ

So far, you have used a number of *iḍāfa* phrases, including the following:

the classroom (literally, the room of the class) ٤ غُرفَةُ الصَفِّ

University of Aleppo ٥ جامِعَةُ حَلَب

City of Damascus ٦ مَدينَةُ دِمَشق

As you can see in the six examples above, the first noun is the focus of the phrase. When reference is made to Sandy's room, for example, the reference is to the room (غُرفَةُ) rather than to Sandy. The second noun in an *iḍāfa* structure serves as added information to define the referent.

a. **Cases of the Constituents of the *iḍāfa* Structure**: An *iḍāfa* structure is made up of two or more nouns. The first noun in an *iḍāfa* structure can be in any grammatical case, depending on the position of the *iḍāfa* phrase in the sentence (cases of the noun will be dealt with at later points). The second noun of the *iḍāfa* structure (and others, if any), however, is always in the genitive case. The genitive case (known as حالَةُ الجَرّ) is one of three grammatical cases of the Arabic noun. Nouns in the genitive are marked in a variety of ways. One of them is appending the short vowel *kasra* to the end of a definite noun. Examine the end of the second word in the examples below. You will notice that a *kasra* is written on the end of each one of them.

the professor's car (the car of the professor) ٧ سَيّارَةُ الأستاذِ

the classroom (the room of the class) ٨ غُرفَةُ الصَفِّ

b. **Definiteness of an *iḍāfa* Structure**: The above phrases are definite by virtue of the definite article prefixed to the last noun. An *iḍāfa* structure is definite if the definite article الـ is prefixed to the *last* noun of the structure, an attached possessive pronoun is suffixed to it, or if it is a proper noun. The first noun *never* receives the definite article or an attached pronoun. It is, however, considered definite if the last noun of the structure is definite. Examine the following indefinite *iḍāfa* phrase:

a car key (a key of a car) ٩ مِفتاحُ سَيّارَةٍ

Notice that the last noun is marked with a double *kasra (tanwīn)*. This marker denotes both a genitive case and an indefinite state (double *fatḥa* and double *ḍamma* also denote an indefinite state). Thus, if the last constituent of an *iḍāfa* structure is indefinite, the whole structure is indefinite. And if the last noun is definite, the whole structure is definite.

Recognizing an *iḍāfa* phrase is relatively easy. First, it is made up of nouns that constitute the phrase. Second, the first noun is always indefinite and the second noun may be definite or indefinite.

Important: Note that in an *iḍāfa* structure the *tā' marbūṭa* must be pronounced as a regular *t* in all nouns that contain it except in the last one where its pronunciation is optional (e.g.غُرفةُ الصَفِّ pronounced *ġurfat**u** ṣ-ṣaffi*).

SUMMARY

- An *iḍāfa* structure is made up of two or more nouns.
- The first noun is the main noun of the phrase.
- The second noun is always in the genitive case (marked by a single or double *kasra*).
- The first noun is always indefinite; the second noun may be definite or indefinite.
- An *iḍāfa* phrase is indefinite if the last noun is indefinite.
- An *iḍāfa* phrase is definite if the last noun in the phrase has the definite article, an attached pronoun is suffixed to it, or if it is a name.
- Indefinite nouns take *tanwīn* (-ً -ٌ -ٍ) on their ends.

تمرين ٧

Identify the *iḍāfa* phrases in the two passages above entitled جامِعَتي and غُرفةُ مكتَبي and copy them down. There are sixteen phrases altogether, including repeated phrases.

تمرين ٨

Form *iḍāfa* phrases to express the following meanings, as in the example. Pay attention to the noun that is the focus of the phrase and the one that should receive the definite article.

Example: the door of the room بابُ الغُرفَةِ

1. The college of medicine
2. The window of my room
3. The car key
4. Eyeglasses of a female student
5. Sandy's professor
6. A bicycle of a male student

4. Identifying Objects: Demonstratives

The **demonstrative** "nouns" هذا and هذه refer to objects that are **near**. In order to refer to objects or people located **far** from the speaker, other forms are used. For the masculine singular, ذلِكَ is used and for the feminine singular, تِلكَ is used.

The woman in the drawing is identifying her car (سيارة), which is feminine, by using the demonstrative تِلكَ and her house (بَيت), which is masculine, by the demonstrative ذلِكَ. Both are far from her.

Dual and Plural Demonstratives

هذانِ (m., dual, nominative, close)	هذَينِ (m., dual, genitive/accusative, close)
هاتانِ (f., dual, nominative, close)	هاتَينِ (f., genitive/accusative, close)
ذانِكَ (m., dual, nominative)	ذَيْنِكَ (m., genitive/accusative, far)
تانِكَ (f., dual, nominative)	تَيْنِكَ (m., genitive/accusative, far)
هؤلاءِ (pl., m., f., close)	أولائِكَ (pl., m., f., far)

SUMMARY

- Demonstratives in Arabic are considered nouns.
- The Arabic demonstrative system distinguishes among referents in terms of gender, number, and proximity.
- The demonstratives هذا and هذه (masculine and feminine, respectively) are used to refer to something close.
- The demonstratives ذلكَ and تلكَ (masculine and feminine, respectively) are used to refer to something far.

تمرين ٩

Identify the people and objects in the following pictures, using appropriate demonstratives (هذا, هذه, ذلك, تلك). Those that are closer to the pointing hand are therefore close and those that are farther from it are considered to be far. Write on the blank lines.

Examples:  هذا حاسوب.   تِلكَ طالِبَة.

 ١ ____________________ 

 ٢ ____________________ 

 ٣ ____________________ 

 ٤ ____________________ 

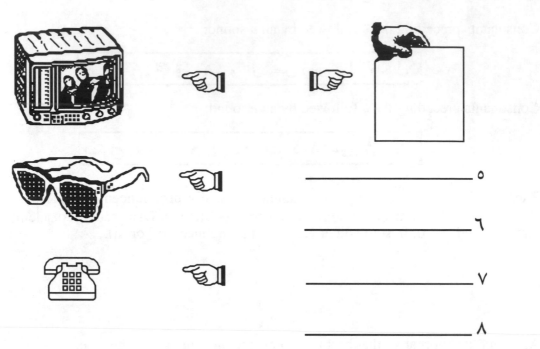

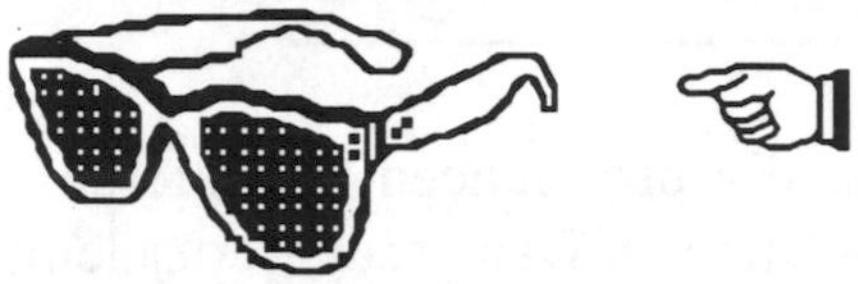

٥ ________________

٦ ________________

٧ ________________

٨ ________________

5. **Colloquial Arabic**

a. **Suppression of Short Vowels:** A distinct aspect of phonological variation in colloquial Arabic is the suppression of one or more internal short vowels. For example, the word كـتـاب is pronounced *kitāb* in Standard Arabic, but in urban areas in the Levant it is pronounced *ktāb*, where the *i* sound is dropped. The same process applies to جـامـِعـة (*jāmi'a*), which is pronounced *jām'a* in colloquial speech, where the short vowel *i* is deleted.

b. **Quality of the Vowel Preceding ة:** The word (مُـسَـجِّـلَة) exemplifies another phonological process in Levantine colloquial Arabic: the change of the *a* sound preceding the *tā' marbūṭa* into an *e* sound (as in *net*) after certain consonants in feminine nouns. For example, no change in the final vowel occurs in صـورة, but the word طاولة (*ṭāwila*) is pronounced *ṭāwle* in Syrian colloquial speech, where the *a* sound changes into an *e* sound. Below is a classification of consonants in final word positions that are followed by the sound *a* in feminine nouns and adjectives in Syrian colloquial speech as well as those followed by the *e* sound. Please note that this is a general rule and that variations do exist.

Consonants preceding the ة followed by an *a* sound:

ح خ ع غ ق هـ و ر ص ض ط ظ ل.

Consonants preceding the ة followed by an *e* sound:

ب ج ف ك م ي ت ث د ذ س ش ن.

Pronunciation of the Letter ق: This sound is usually pronounced as a glottal stop (i.e. *hamza*) in Arabic dialects in some urban centers, such as Damascus, Jerusalem, Beirut, Amman, and Cairo. In some other areas, it is pronounced [g] or [q].

تمرين ١٠

A. Select the alternative that best represents the information on the tape.

١- اِسمُ الأسْتاذِ نَديم ......

☐ ساحوري ☐ ساهوري ☐ سَمْهوري

٢- الأستاذُ نَديم مِن جامِعَةِ ......

☐ القُدْس ☐ الآداب ☐ بير زَيْت

٣- مكتَبُ الأستاذ نَديم في كُلِيَّة ......

☐ الآداب ☐ العُلوم ☐ الطِبّ

٤- في مكتبِ الأستاذِ نَديم صورَةُ مَدينةِ ......

☐ بير زَيْت ☐ القُدْس ☐ فِلَسطين

B. Mark the following statement صَحْ or خَطَأ based on the information in the passage and correct any false statements.

٥- لَيْسَ عندَ الأستاذِ نَديم حاسوب.

٦- هُناكَ هاتِفٌ عَلى طاولَةِ الأستاذ نَديم.

٧- صورَةُ مَدينَةِ القُدْسِ عَلى جِدارِ المَكْتَب.

المُفْرَدات

literature .... (n., m.) أدَب ج آداب
ground .... أرْض ج أراضٍ
those .... (pl., demonstrative) أولائِكَ
house, home .... (n., m.) بَيْت ج بُيوت
those .... (dual, nom.) تانِكَ
trade, business, commerce .... (n., f.) تِجارة
that .... (n., f., s.) تِلكَ
those .... (dual, acc., g.) تَيْنِكَ
right, law .... (n., m.) حَقّ ج حُقوق
that .... (n., m., s.) ذلِكَ
sport .... (n., f.) رِياضَة ج رِياضات
of sports .... (adj.) رياضِيّ
medicine .... (m.) طِبّ
a number of, several .... (n., f.) عِدَّة
science, discipline .... (n., m.) عِلْم ج عُلوم
of science, scientific .... (adj.) علميّ
college .... (n., f.) كُلِّيَّة ج كُلّيات
language .... (n., f.) لُغَة ج لُغات
of language, linguitic .... (adj.) لُغَويّ
laboratory .... (n., m.) مَخْبَر ج مَخابِر
swimming pool .... (n., m.) مَسْبَح ج مَسابِح
office .... (n., m.) مَكْتَب ج مَكاتِب
library, bookstore, bookcase .... (n., f.) مَكْتَبة ج مَكْتَبات
playground, sports field .... (n., m.) مَلْعَب ج مَلاعِب
these .... (dual, f., nominative) هاتانِ
these .... (dual, f., acc., g.) هاتَيْنِ

these.. (dual, m., nom.) هذانِ
these... (dual, m., accusative, genitive) هذَيْنِ
engineering.. (n., f.) هَنْدَسَة
these... (pl., m.) هؤُلاءِ

مِئذَنةُ مَسجِدٍ
A Minaret of a Mosque

Lesson Nine الدَرْسُ التاسِع

Objectives

- Seeking and providing information.
- Question words.
- The Arabic verb.
- Expressing knowledge and the inability to do so.
- Eliciting information.
- The particle يا.
- Expressing admiration.
- The question particle كَم.
- Cardinal numbers 1-10.
- Listen to the recorded material for this lesson.
- Do relevant computer drills and exercises, Stage 4.

1. **Seeking and Providing Information**

أنا مِنْ جَبْلة

الإمْرَأة: مَرحباً.

الرَجُل: أهلاً.

الإمْرَأة: ما اسْمُك؟

الرَجُل: اِسْمي نِزار حَدّاد.

الإمْرَأة: مِنْ أينَ أَنْت؟

الرَجُل: أنا مِنْ جَبْلة.

الإمْرَأة: أينَ جَبْلة؟

الرَجُل: هذِهِ بَلْدَة في سوريَة.

الإمْرَأة: ما عُنوانُك؟

الرَجُل: ٥ شارِعُ ابنِ خَلدون.

الإمْرَأة: أتَسكُنُ في شَقَّةٍ أَمْ في بَيْت؟

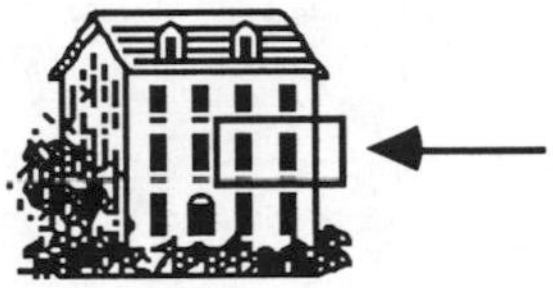

شَقّة

الرَجُل: أسكُنُ في شَقَّة.

الإمْرَأة: عِنْدَكَ سَيّارَة؟

الرَجُل: نَعَم.

الإمْرَأة: هَل عِندَكَ هاتِف في شَقَّتِك؟

الرَجُل: نَعَم عِنْدي هاتِف.

الإمْرَأة: ما رَقْمُ هاتِفِك؟

الرَجُل: سِتّة صِفْر واحِد خَمْسَة سَبْعَة تِسْعَة أرْبَعَة.

الإمْرَأة: هَل عِندَكَ حاسوب؟

الرَجُل: لا. لَيْسَ عِندي حاسوب.

الإمْرَأة: شُكْراً.

الرَجُل: عَفْواً.

تمرين ١

A. Select the best alternative according to the dialogue above:

١ـ اِسْمُ الرَجُلِ ......

☐ نزار ☐ جَبْلَة ☐ ابنُ خَلدون

٢ـ يَسكُنُ الرَجُلُ في ......

☐ بَيْت ☐ شَقَّة ☐ الجامِعَة

٣ـ عِنْدَ الرَجُلِ ......

☐ سَيّارَة ☐ حاسوب ☐ دَرّاجَة

٤ـ رَقْمُ هاتِفِ الرَجُلِ ......

☐ ٦٠١٥٧٩٤ ☐ ٤٩٧٥١٠٦ ☐ ١٠٦٤٩٧٥

B. Respond in Arabic or English to these questions with reference to the dialogue:

5. What does the word جَبْلَة refer to?

6. What is the woman's name?

7. Copy the man's address.

تمرين ٢

Listen to and study the dialogue above then provide written answers to the following questions in full sentences about yourself. You may wish to read Section 3 before doing this exercise.

١ـ ما اسْمُك؟

٢ـ ما عُنْوانُك؟

٣ـ مِنْ أيْنَ أنْت؟

٤- ما اسْمُ جامِعَتِك؟

٥- هَل عِنْدَكَ/عِنْدَكِ دَرّاجَة (سَيّارَة، حاسوب، هاتِف)؟

٦- هَلْ تَسكُن/تَسكُنينَ في شَقَّة أَمْ في بَيْت؟

تمرين ٣

Form questions to ask your interlocutor about the following:

1. location of the library
2. whether he/she has a car
3. number of rooms in his/her apartment/house
4. his/her telephone number
5. identity of the professor of Arabic (who he/she is)

تمرين ٤

Interview a classmate or an imaginary character, using the questions listed in Exercise 2 or those in the dialogue above. Then write a short paragraph, providing information about that person in terms of name, address, origin, school, possessions, and place of residence. Imitate the model below, which gives information about هالَة بُسْتاني, the student who was described in Lesson Seven.

هالَة بُسْتاني طالِبَةٌ مِن مَدينَةِ دِمَشق. عُنْوانُها ٨ شارِع الكَواكِبيّ في مَدينَةِ حَلَب. هِيَ طالِبَةٌ في جامِعَةِ حَلَب. لَيْسَ عِندَ هالَة دَرّاجَة، لكِنْ حاسوب. تسكُنُ هالَة في شَقَّة. هِيَ لا تَسْكُنُ في سَكَنِ الطالِبات.

2. **Question Words**

a. **Yes/No Questions:** Yes/no questions may be asked either by using a rising intonation only or the question particles هَلْ and أ. As you can see from the exchanges between the woman and the man above, these particles are inserted at the beginning of a sentence to render it a question without causing any changes either in word order or in the forms of the words.

Note: The particle أَمْ "or" is used in questions (e.g. عِندَكَ سَيّارة أم دَرّاجة؟), its counterpart أَوْ "or" in statements.

b. **Content Questions:** Questions that seek information concerning, for example, time, place, manner, or reason use other question particles, or words. In the above interview the question particles أينَ "where" and ما "what" are used. The first one inquires about the location of someone or something, and the latter inquires about the identity of something. The particle ما is followed by a noun or a pronoun (e.g. ما اسْمُكَ؟ "What's your name?" ما هُوَ؟ "What is it?). On the other hand, أينَ "where" and مَنْ "who" may be followed by either a noun, a pronoun, or a verb:

١ أينَ جَبْلَة؟ مَنْ هُناك؟

٢ مَن هُوَ؟ أينَ هِيَ؟

٣ أينَ تَسْكُن؟

٤ مَنْ يَسْكُنُ في الشَقَّة؟

The particle ماذا "what" is usually used before verbs, e.g. ماذا يَدْرُسُ زِياد؟.

The question word كَيْفَ "how"is used to inquire about a state of affair, that is, the process or manner of doing something:

٥ كَيْفَ الحال؟

Note that these question words cause no change either in the form or order of the words in a sentence.

SUMMARY

1. The particle هَلْ is used for forming yes/no questions. It is inserted at the beginning of a sentence, causing no structural change.

2. Question particles cause no change either in word form or order. The following are some of these words:

هَلْ – أ – أيْنَ – ما – ماذا – مَنْ – ث

3. The Arabic Verb

a. **Verb Stem and Root**: The above dialogue introduces the first verb in this textbook. There are two instances of the verb "*to live*": the first one for second person masculine singular (تَسْكُنْ) "*you live*" and the second for first person singular (أسْكُنْ) "*I live.*" In English, both instances have the same form: *live*. In Arabic, however, verbs vary in form because person is indicated in verbs as a prefix, suffix, or both. In addition, the form of a verb is affected by tense, number, and gender. At this point, we will consider the present tense, or imperfect, which indicates uncompleted, or unfinished, action. Table 1 shows five forms which correspond to five personal pronouns. In Arabic, there are fourteen pronouns.

If you look closely, you will find that the verb forms change on the basis of the initial letter, which is a prefix added to the stem of the verb (سْكُنْ). In the second person feminine, the verb form takes a suffix in addition. Thus, present tense conjugations contain prefixes *and* suffixes, as exemplified by the second person singular feminine form ("*you*" when addressing a female). The prefix and suffix are boxed in the enlarged word to make the stem (سْكُنْ) stand out.

٦ أنْتِ تَسْكُنينَ

[تَ] سْكُنـ [ينَ]

Verb Form	Separate Pronoun	English Verb Form
أَسْكُنُ	أنا	live
تَسْكُنُ	أنتَ	live
تَسْكُنينَ	أنتِ	live
يَسْكُنُ	هُوَ	lives
تَسْكُنُ	هِيَ	lives

Present Tense Conjugations of the Verb (سَكَنَ)

Table 1

Arabic verbs (and almost all derivatives) are generally cited in the dictionary according to their root, which is the minimal form of a word. The root of the above verb is the three letters (س ك ن). Unlike English, Arabic cites verbs in the third person masculine singular past tense (e.g. سَكَنَ "*he lived*"), as you can see in the header of Table 1.

b. **Negating the Present Tense Verb**: Negating the present is done simply by using the negative particle لا (which also doubles as "no") before the verb. The use of لا does not affect the form of the verb in any way:

٧ أَسْكُنُ في بَيْت. *I live in a house.*

٨ لا أَسْكُنُ في بَيْت. *I don't live in a house.*

تمرين ٥

Seek and provide the information by asking questions in Arabic. Remember that the question mark faces to the right.

1. Ask a woman where she lives.
2. Say that you do not live on Lincoln Street.
3. Ask a man whether he lives in an apartment.
4. Say that your teacher lives in (name of a town).

4. Expressing Knowledge or the Inability to Do So

عادِل: كَمْ لُغةً تَعرفينَ يا سَناء؟

سَناء: أعْرِفُ أربَعَ لُغات.

عادِل: ما هِيَ؟

سَناء: العَرَبيّةُ والإنكليزيّةُ والفَرَنسيّةُ واليابانيّة.

عادِل: ما شاءَ اللّه!! ما مَعْنى كَلِمةِ "لُغَة" بِاليابانِيّة؟

سناء: آسِفَة. لا أعْرِف.

The verb عَرَفَ "to know" in the dialogue above expresses knowledge about something. The phrase لا أعرف "I don't know" expresses lack of knowledge of something. It is made up of the negative particle لا and the verb أعرف. It has a high functional value, especially when you do not know the answer to a question in class.

5. Eliciting Information

In order to inquire about the meaning of a word you do not know in Arabic, you may use the phrase ما مَعْنى كَلِمَة ...؟ "*What is the meaning of the word...*" followed by the English word you wish to know. For example, to find out the word for "police," you may ask:

٩ ما مَعْنى كَلِمةِ "police" بِالعَرَبِيّة؟

Note that the words معنى and كلمة are both nouns and together they form an *iḍāfa* structure. Notice also the preposition بـ prefixed to the noun العَرَبيَّة (بالعَرَبيَّة) It is one of a few prepositions that are prefixed to nouns. In this context, it means "in."

تمرين ٦

Ask an imaginary native-speaker informant about the meanings of at least six words in Arabic you would like to know, but don't know, as in the example above.

6. Expressing Admiration

One way of expressing admiration is by using the phrase ما شاءَ اللّه (literally "what God willed"). If someone informs you, for example, that he or she has nine children or has won a million dollars, this would be the appropriate response. It connotes joy for someone else's good fortunes devoid of any envy.

7. The Particle يا

This particle is called "vocative" because it is used to call the attention of someone (e.g. يا سَناء! ، يا أُسْتاذ!). It is used before names, terms of address, and titles, but never by itself. It has no equivalent in modern English usage although the particles "Hey" and "O" are close in meaning. Examine this sentence:

١٠ كَيْفَ الحالُ يا أَحْمَد؟ *How are you, Ahmed?*

8. The Question Particle كَم

In the dialogue above, inquiring about the number of languages the woman knows is accomplished by the question particle كَم "how many." Note that this particle should be followed by a singular, indefinite noun which is in a case called accusative (نَصْب). By contrast, in English the noun after *how many* is plural. Thus, to inquire about the number of books someone has, use a singular indefinite noun (marked by a double *fatḥa* on its end). Example:

١١ كَمْ كِتاباً عِنْدَك؟

Remember that the *alif* above which the double *fatḥa* is written in كتاباً serves only as a seat for this marker. It has no phonetic value. Remember that a silent *alif* must be provided except in words ending in ء preceded by a long vowel, ة, and ى.

SUMMARY

- The particle كَمْ is followed by a singular, indefinite noun in the accusative case.
- The noun following كَمْ thus has a double *fatḥa* (ً) on its end (كِتاباً).

تمرين ٧

Complete the following questions with the appropriate form of the noun in parentheses, as in the example. Remember that كَمْ must be followed by an accusative, singular, indefinite noun, and that the ة, ى, and ء do not require an *alif* to seat a double *fatḥa*.

Example: كَمْ (كِتاب) ......كِتاباً...... عِندَك ؟

١- كَمْ (دَرّاجَة) .... عِندَك ؟

٢- كَمْ (مِفْتاح) .... على الطاوِلة ؟

٣- كَمْ (قَلَم) .... في حَقيبَتِك ؟

٤- كَمْ (مُسَجِّلَة) .... عِندَك ؟

٥- كَمْ (هاتِف) .... في بَيتِك ؟

٦- كَمْ (جامِعة) .... في هذِهِ المدينة ؟

٧- كَمْ (كَلِمَة) .... في هذا التمرين ؟

٨- كَمْ (أُسْتاذ) .... في هذِهِ الجامعة ؟

9. Cardinal Numbers 1-10

Cardinal numbers may be used for counting and labeling things. Let's consider counting first. The numbers in the exercise below represent the printed form, which is very similar to the manuscript form, except for number *two* which is written as follows: ٢. It starts from the top righthand side, moves to the left and then down.

تمرين ٨

Listen and repeat after the tape. Read the numbers (and words) below from right to left. Copy them several times, paying attention to the manuscript form of the number *two*.

٠ صِفْر　　١ واحِد　　٢ اِثْنان　　٣ ثَلاثَة

٤ أرْبَعَة　　٥ خَمْسَة　　٦ سِتّة　　٧ سَبْعَة

٨ ثَمانِيَة　　٩ تِسْعَة　　١٠ عَشَرَة

٠　١　٢　٣　٤　٥　٦　٧　٨　٩　١٠

The above numbers are known as **cardinal numbers**, which are also used for numbering things (telephone numbers, car numbers, house numbers, etc.).

At this point, you may say telephone numbers one digit at a time from left to right, as in English. Thus, the man on the telephone in the drawing might say his telephone number in the following manner:

أرْبَعَة - سِتَّة - ثَمانِيَة - اِثْنان - ثَلاثَة - سَبْعَة - خَمْسَة

How do you think the man below might say his ID number?

بطاقة هَوِيّة

تمرين ٩

Do the following calculations:

١- ٣ + ٥ = ...
٢- ١ + ٧ = ...
٣- ٩ − ٤ = ...
٤- ١٢ − ٥ = ...
٥- ٢ + ٨ = ...
٦- ٦ + ٤ = ...
٧- ٨ − ١ = ...
٨- ٧ − ٣ = ...

Note that the word for the plus sign is زائِد, for the minus sign is ناقِص, and for the word "equal" is يُساوي.

تمرين ١٠

Examine the following identification card. List these data about this person in English, including the institution that issued the card, to whom it was issued, the permanent address of this person, her telephone number, and card number.

جامِعَةُ حَلَب

بِطاقَة هَوِيّة

الاسم: هالَة بُستاني

اِسمُ الأب: وَحيد

العُنوان: ٥٢ شارِع المَنصور-دِمَشق

رَقْم الهاتِف: ٨٥٦٩-٢٨٤

رَقْم الهَوِيَّة: ٩٧١٤٥٢

تمرين ١١

Underline the word that does not belong to each set of words. Explain your choice in English.

١- سَكَن - شَقَّة - تِسْعة - بَيْت

٢- هَلْ - لَيْسَ - ماذا - كَمْ

٣- عِلْمِيّ - يابانِيّ - عَرَبِيّ - إنْكليزِيّ

٤- هاتِف - رَقْم - عُنْوان - طاوِلَة

تمرين ١٢

Provide the information requested in the following items in numbers. If it is not available, indicate the reason in Arabic:

١- رَقْمُ غُرْفَةِ صَفِّ اللُّغَةِ العَرَبِيّة: ....

٢- رَقْمُ هاتِفِكِ: ....

٣- رَقْمُ سيّارَتِك: ....

٤- رَقْمُ شَقَّتِك: ....

٥- رَقْمُ هَوِيّتِك: ....

٦- رَقْمُ بَيْتِك: ....

تمرين ١٣

A. Select the appropriate alternative according to the information in the taped passage:

١- وَفاءُ مِن ......

☐ مَدينَةِ دِمَشق   ☐ بَلْدَةِ الباب   ☐ مَدينَةِ حَلَب

٢- تَدْرُسُ وَفاءُ ......

☐ اللغةَ العَرَبِيَّةَ   ☐ اللغةَ الإنكليزِيَّةَ   ☐ التِجارَةَ

٣- عِندَ وَفاءَ ......

☐ هاتِف   ☐ حاسوب   ☐ حاسِبَة

B. Mark these statements خَطَأ or صَــواب according to the taped passage. Correct any false statements.

٤- تَسكُنَ وَفاءُ في شَقَّة.

٥- وَفاءُ طالِبَةٌ في جامِعَةِ دِمَشق.

٦- تَعرِفُ وَفاءُ ثَلاثَ لُغات.

تمرين ١٤

Match words from the right-hand column with words in the left-hand column. Copy the matching word from the left-hand column and write it down in the blank space provided next to its match. Explain your choice if necessary.

١- بَلْدَة	....	تِجارة
٢- عُنوان	....	ثَلاثَة
٣- العَرَبيّة	....	عَفْواً
٤- رَقْم	....	مَدينَة
٥- بِطاقة	....	شارِع
٦- شُكْراً	....	لُغة
		هَوِيّة

جَمَل

المُفْرَدات

a question particle to form yes/no questions .... أ

God .... (n., m.) الله

14th-century Arab historian and sociologist .... (proper noun) ابْنُ خَلْدون

two .... (n., m.) اثنان

four .... (n., f.) أَرْبَعة

sorry .... (n., f.) آسِفة /(n., m.) آسِف

or (particle used in questions) .... (conjunction) أَمْ

woman .... (n., f.) امرأة ج نِساء

now .... (n.) الآنَ

English (language) .... (adj.) الإنكليزية

or (used with statements) .... (conjunction) أو

in, with, by .... (preposition) بِـ

card .... (n., f.) بِطاقة ج بِطاقات

small town .... (n., f.) بَلْدة ج بَلْدات

nine .... (n., f.) تِسْعة

three .... (n., f.) ثَلاثة

eight .... (n., f.) ثَمانية

name of a town in Syria .... (n., f.) جَبْلة

five .... (n., f.) خَمْسة

man .... (n., m.) رَجُل ج رِجال

number .... (n., m.) رَقْم ج أَرْقام

plus .... (n., m.) زائِد

to equal .... (v.) ساوى (يُساوي)

seven .... (n., f.) سَبْعة

six .... (n., f.) سِتّة

to live	سَكَنَ (يَسْكُنُ) (v.)
(student) living, residence, dormitory	سَكَنُ (الطُلاّب) (verbal noun, m.)
street	شارِع ج شَوارِع (n., m.)
want, will	شاءَ (يَشاءُ) (v.)
apartment	شَقّة ج شُقَق (n, f.)
thank you	شُكْراً
zero	صِفْر ج أصْفار (n., m.)
Arabic (language)	العَرَبيّة (n., f.)
to know	عَرَفَ (يَعرِفُ) (v.)
ten	عَشَرَة (n., f.)
you're welcome (response to "thank you")	عَفْواً
address	عُنوان ج عَناوين (n., m.)
French (language)	الفَرَنْسيّة (n., f.)
word	كَلِمَة ج كَلِمات (n., f.)
how many/much	كَمْ (interrogative particle)
what (question particle used in front of nouns)	ما
what (used with verbs)	ماذا
meaning	مَعْنى ج مَعانٍ (المعاني) (n., m.)
minus	ناقِص (n., m.)
question particle for yes-no questions	هَلْ
identity	هَوِيّة ج هَوِيّات (n., f.)
one	واحِد (n., m.)
vocative particle used to call the attention of the addressee	يا
Japanese (language)	اليابانِيّة (n., f.)

Lesson Ten الدَرْسُ العاشِر

Objectives

- Describing situations.
- Forming dual nouns.
- Number-noun agreement.
- Plurals of nonrational nouns.
- Listen to the recorded material for this lesson.
- Do relevant computer drills and exercises, Stages 4 and 5.

1. **Describing Background**

طالِبَتانِ في جامِعَةِ حَلَب

هالة بُستاني

سَحَر حلاّق

هالَة بُسْتاني وسَحَر حَلاّق طالِبَتانِ في جامِعَةِ حَلَب. هالَة مِن دِمَشْق وَسَحَر مِن دِمَشْق أيْضاً. تَسكُنُ هالَة في شَقَّةٍ مَعَ سَحَر حَلاّق، والشَقَّةُ في البِنايَةِ رَقْمِ خَمسَة في شارِعِ الحَمَداني. رَقْمُ شَقتِهِما ٩. في شَقَّةِ هالَة وسَحَر غُرفَتانِ وسَريرانِ وطاوِلَتانِ وكُرسيّان. هالَة وسَحَر لا تَدرُسانِ في مَكتَبَةِ الجامِعَةِ بَلْ في شَقَّتِهِما.

تَدرُسُ هالَة الطِبَّ وعِندَها الآن ثَلاثُ مَوادَّ وهِيَ الأحْياءُ والكيمْياءُ واللُغةُ الإنكليزيَّة. تَدرُسُ سَحَر التِجارة، وهِيَ تَعرِفُ ثَلاثَ لُغاتٍ هِيَ العَرَبِيَّةُ والفَرَنسِيَّةُ والإنكليزيَّة.

تمرين ١

Select the best alternative according to the information in the passage above.

١- هالَة بُستاني طالِبَةٌ في ......

☐ جامِعَة دِمَشق ☐ مَدينَة حَلَب ☐ كُلِّيَّة الطِبِّ

٢- تسكُنُ هالَة في ......

☐ بَيت ☐ شَقَّةٍ ☐ غُرفَةٍ

٣- تَسكُنُ سَحَر حلاّق ...... هالَة بستاني.

☐ مَعَ ☐ مِن ☐ عَلَى

٤- هالَة وَسَحَر ...... دِمَشق.

☐ مِن ☐ في ☐ مَعَ

٥- رَقْمُ شَقَّة هالَة وَسَحَر ......

☐ خَمْسَة ☐ سَبْعَة ☐ تِسْعَة

٦- تَدرُسُ سَحَر ......

☐ التِجارَة ☐ الأحْياء ☐ اللُغة الفَرَنسِيَّة

تمرين ٢

Read the following statements and check the box next to each if the statement is correct according to the reading passage. Put an ✗ if it is wrong and correct it in the blank space.

١- سَحَر أُختُ هالَة. ☐ ....

٢- تَدرُسُ سَحَر حلاّق ثَلاثَ مَوادّ. ☐ ....

٣- تَسكُنُ هالَة مَعَ طالِبةٍ مِن دِمَشق. ☐ ....

٤- تَدرُسُ هالَةُ الطِبَّ في جامِعَة دِمَشق. ☐ ....

٥- في غُرفَةِ هالَة سَريران. ☐ ....

تمرين ٣

Match words from the right-hand column with words in the left-hand column. Copy the matching word from the left-hand column and write it down in the blank space provided next to its match.

١- مادّة	....	سَرير
٢- لُغَة	....	أيْضاً
٣- كُرسيّ	....	تَسكُنُ
٤- بِناية	....	مَعَ
٥- تَعرِف	....	الإنكليزيّة
٦- في	....	أحْياء
		شَقّة

تمرين ٤

Underline the word that does not belong to each set and explain your choice in English.

١- الرياضيّات - الفَرَنْسيّة - الأحْياء - الكيمياء

٢- شَقّة - بِنايَة - بَيْت - كُلِيّة

٣- دَرّاجَة - طاوِلَة - كُرْسيّ - سَرير

2. Forming Dual Nouns

As you may have noticed, nouns (and adjectives) in Arabic have three states with regard to number: singular, dual (two), and plural (more than two). The dual is predictable and is easy to form. You can use one of two endings, depending on the case of the noun (or adjective).

1. If the noun is in the nominative case, the ending *-āni* (انِ) is suffixed to it:

١	هذا كِتابٌ	⇦	هذانِ كِتابانِ
	singular		dual

Note that the demonstrative هذا is a noun which serves as the subject in the above example. The word كِتابٌ is a noun that functions as a predicate. In the dual, both acquire the suffix *-āni* (انِ). This suffix is used for both definite and indefinite nouns. Normally the *kasra* on the end of the suffix is not pronounced in casual speech (e.g. the word كِتابانِ is pronounced *kitābān*).

2. If the noun is the direct object of a verb (e.g.أدرُسُ مادّةً) or a preposition (e.g.في جامعةٍ), the suffix *-ayni* (ـيْنِ) is attached to it. These are called the *accusative* (نَصْب) and the *genitive* (جَرّ) cases, respectively:

٢	أدرسُ مادّةً	⇦	أدرسُ مادّتَيْنِ
٣	في جامِعةٍ	⇦	في جامِعَتَيْنِ

Notice the change of the ة to a regular *tā'* (ت) when the suffix ـَيْنِ is attached to it. Just like انِ, the suffix *-ayni* ـَيْنِ is used with definite and indefinite nouns.

3. Number-Noun Agreement

In order to express quantity, a number is combined with a noun. In the dialogue in Section 4, the woman specifies the number of languages she knows by saying: أعرفُ أربعَ لُغاتٍ. You may wonder why the number is without the feminine marker ة although the word for *language* (لُغة) is feminine. Using numbers requires the knowledge of a few rules.

Rule 1. **The numbers *one* and *two* *follow*** the noun, because they serve as adjectives describing the nouns, thus agreeing with them in gender, number, and case. They are usually used for emphasis, since the suffixes ان and ـَيْنِ denote dual number (see Section 2 above on dual formation):

	Dual	Singular
Masculine	كتابانِ اثنانِ	كِتابٌ واحدٌ.
Feminine	سيّارتانِ اثنَتانِ	سيّارةٌ واحدةٌ.

Rule 2. **The numbers *three* through *ten* (3-10):**

(a) These numbers *precede* the noun they modify.

(b) They have a *reverse gender agreement* with the singular counted noun; that is, if the counted noun is masculine, the number is feminine (by suffixing ـة to it) and vice versa:

٤ أربَعُ سَيّاراتٍ أربَعَةُ كُتُبٍ.

Since the plural noun سيارات "*cars*" is feminine, the number modifying it (أربَع) should be masculine. Similarly, the singular of كُتُب "*books*" كتاب is masculine, therefore, the number modifying it should be feminine (with a *tā' marbūṭa*).

(c) The specified noun being counted must be indefinite (no ال), hence the *tanwīn* on the end of the words.

(d) The numbers 3-10 form with the following noun an *iḍāfa* structure, because these numbers are nouns. The plural counted nouns are thus marked with a double *kasra*, being genitive (جرّ) and indefinite.

Note that the feminine form of the number *10* is pronounced عَشَرَة (e.g. عَشَرَةُ كُتُبٍ) and the masculine form is pronounced عَشْر (e.g. عَشْرُ سَيّاراتٍ).

SUMMARY

The Numbers *1, 2*

They *follow* the noun they modify. These numbers function as adjectives and, therefore, they agree with the preceding noun in gender, number, and case.

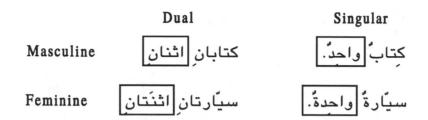

The Numbers *3-10*

These numbers *precede* the noun they modify and have a reverse gender agreement with it. They form with the noun an *iḍāfa* structure. The noun following them is indefinite, genitive, and plural.

Numbers 1-10 with Nouns

(fem.) سَيّارة ج سيّارات	(mas.) كِتاب ج كُتُب
سيّارةٌ واحِدةٌ	كِتابٌ واحِدٌ
سيارتانِ اثنَتان	كِتابانِ اثنان
ثلاثُ سيّاراتٍ	ثلاثةُ كُتُب
أربَعُ سياراتٍ	أربَعَةُ كتبٍ
خَمسُ سياراتٍ	خَمسَةُ كتبٍ
سِتُّ سياراتٍ	سِتَّةُ كتبٍ
سَبعُ سياراتٍ	سَبعَةُ كتبٍ
ثَماني سياراتٍ	ثَمانِيَةُ كتبٍ
تِسعُ سياراتٍ	تِسعَةُ كتبٍ
عَشْرُ سياراتٍ	عَشَرَةُ كتبٍ

Table 1

تمرين ٥

Use the appropriate form of the number and put it in the right word order with respect to the singular noun provided, as in the example. Refer to Section 6 and check plurals of nouns in previous glossaries.

٤ (كِتاب)	⇦	أربَعةُ كُتُبٍ	Example:
٦ (سَيّارَة)		سِتُّ سيّاراتٍ	
١- (٣ طاوِلة)	⇦		
٢- ١ (سَيّارة)	⇦		
٣- ٧ (دَفْتَر)	⇦		
٤- ٢ (هاتِف)	⇦		
٥- ٢ (حَقيبَة)	⇦		
٦- ١ (حاسوب)	⇦		
٧- ٨ (مِسْطَرَة)	⇦		
٨- ٦ (قَلَم)	⇦		

تمرين ٦

Express whether or not you own the items listed below.

Example: two cars — عِندي سَيّارتان./ لَيْسَ عِندي سَيّارتان.

١- 1. A watch

٢- 2. Four books

٣- 3. Three bicycles

٤- 4. Two computers

٥- 5. Two pairs of eyeglasses

٦- 6. Five notebooks

تمرين ٧

Inquire from an imaginary person about the following, addressing him or her in the second person.

Example: Number of pens she has/he has — كَم قَلَماً عِندَكِ/عِندَكَ؟

١- 1. Number of languages she knows

٢- 2. Number of houses on his street

٣- 3. Number of Arab cities he knows
٤- 4. Number of students in the Arabic class
٥- 5. Number of students she knows in this class
٦- 6. Number of Arab students he knows

4. Plurals of Nonrational Nouns

In the dialogue in Section 4, the man refers to the four languages the woman knows, using the separate pronoun هيَ "*she*," which is singular feminine. He asks, ما هيَ؟. The reason for using هيَ is that all nonrational (or non-human) nouns are usually referred to in the singular feminine regardless of gender. That is, the plural noun كُتُب, which is masculine, is referred to by هي, هذه and تلكَ, which are used to refer to singular feminine entities. The same pronouns (هيَ، هذه، تلكَ) are also used to refer to both the singular feminine noun ساعة and the feminine plural noun ساعات. Thus, the man's question ما هيَ؟ may be translated in this context "what are *they?*" rather than "what is *it*?" or "what is *she*?" Examples:

٥ هذهِ الكُتُبُ *these books* هذهِ السَيّاراتُ *these cars*

٦ تِلْكَ الشَوارِعُ *those streets* تِلكَ الصُفوفُ *those classrooms*

By contrast, rational plurals (those referring to people) are referred to by pronouns and demonstratives that agree with them in gender and number, e.g.

٧ هؤلاء الأساتذة. *these (male) teachers*

٨ هُم طُلاّب. *They are (male) students.*

٩ هؤلاءِ النِساءِ. *these women*

١٠ هُنَّ طالِبات. *They are (female) students*

SUMMARY

Nonrational plurals are referred to by feminine *singular* pronouns and demonstratives regardless of their gender, e.g.

هيَ سَيّارات (feminine)، هيَ كُتُب (masculine)

هذهِ سَيّارات (feminine)، هذه كُتُب (masculine)

تمرين ٨

Use the appropriate pronoun and demonstrative to refer to each of the following nouns. Note that the nouns listed may be singular, plural, masculine, or feminine. Also, use the proper demonstrative based on its proximity to the pointing hand.

هذا، هذِهِ، هؤلاءِ، تِلكَ، هُوَ، هِيَ، هُم، هُنَّ

قَلَم  ⇦ هُوَ قَلَم / هذا قَلَم

١- حَقيبة  ⇦

٢- كَراسٍ  ⇦

٣- ساعَة  ⇦

٤- بُيوت  ⇦

٥- طُلّاب  ⇦

٦- تِلفاز  ⇦

٧- مَفاتيح  ⇦

٨- طالِبة  ⇦

٩- نَظّارَة  ⇦

١٠- سَيّارات  ⇦

تمرين ٩

A. Select the appropriate alternative according to the information in the taped passage:

١- اسمُ الطالِبِ المَغرِبيِّ ......

☐ عَبدُ الرحمن ☐ عَبدُ الرَحيم ☐ عَبدُ الله

٢- يَدرُسُ عَبدُ اللهِ ......

☐ الأدَبَ العَرَبيَّ ☐ اللُغَةَ الإنكليزية ☐ الطِبَّ

٣- الطالِبُ المَغرِبيّ مِن مَدينةِ ......

☐ القاهِرة ☐ وُجْدة ☐ عَيْن شَمْس

٤- في شَقَّةِ هذا الطالِبِ ......

☐ حاسوبان ☐ تِلفازان ☐ سَريران

B. Mark these statements خَطَأ or صَواب according to the taped passage. Correct any false statements.

٥- يَدرُسُ عَبْدُ الرحمنِ الأدَبَ العَرَبيّ.

٦- يَسكُنُ عَبدُ الرحمنِ في شَقَّة.

٧- يَسكنُ مَعَ عبدِ الرحمن طالِبٌ مَغرِبيّ.

٨- يَعرِفُ عَبدُ الرحمن اللُغةَ الفَرَنسيّة.

المُفْرَدات

biology .... أحْياء (n., pl.)

rather, but .... بَلْ (particle)

building .... بِناية ج بِنايات (n., f.)

study (v.) .... دَرَسَ (يَدرُسُ) دِراسة / دَرْس

bed .... سَرير ج أسِرّة (n., m.)

school subject, course .... مادّة ج مَوادّ (n., f.)

with .... مَعَ (prep.)

Decorative Calligraphy

Lesson Eleven الدَرْسُ الحادي عَشَر

Objectives

- Family.
- School subjects.
- Arabic last names.
- Objects of verbs.
- Objects of prepositions.
- Ordinal numbers I.
- Pronouns of separation.
- Listen to the recorded material for this lesson.
- Do relevant computer drills and exercises, Stages 4 and 5.

عائِلَةُ مازِن نَجّار

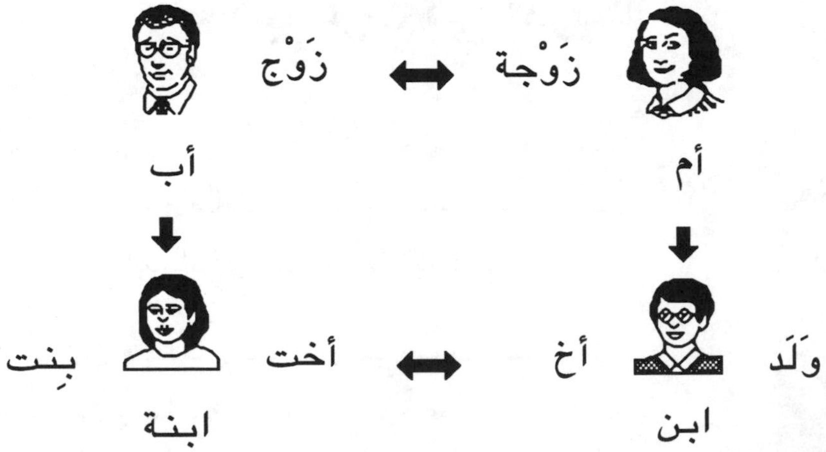

هذِهِ عائِلَةُ مازِن نَجّار. اِسمُ زَوجَتِهِ ناديا الخولي. عِندَهُ ابنٌ واحِدٌ اسمُهُ أحْمَد وَابنتانِ: واحِدَةٌ اسْمُها رانِيَة وَواحِدَةٌ اسمُها رِحاب.

أحْمَد في المدرسَةِ في الصَفِّ الثالثِ الإبْتِدائيِّ وَأختُهُ رانيَة في الصَفِّ الرابعِ وَرِحابُ في الصَفِّ السادِس. أحمَدُ الوَلَدُ الوَحيد في عائلَةِ مازنِ وَناديا.

Culture Note: Women in most Arab countries (e.g., Syria, Egypt) retain their maiden names after marriage.

1. School Subjects

طُلاّبٌ عَرَبٌ في أمريكا

هذا عَدْنانُ مارتيني. يَدْرُسُ عَدْنانُ عِلْمَ الحاسوبِ في جامِعَةِ وِلايَةِ أوهايو. هُوَ طالِبٌ عَرَبِيٌّ مِن سورية. يَدْرُسُ عَدنانُ الآنَ مادَّةَ الرِياضِيّاتِ وَ مادَّةَ اللُغَةِ الإنكليزيَّة.

أبو عَدْنانَ وأمُّ عَدْنانَ يَسْكُنانِ في مَدينَةِ حَلَبَ في سورية ويَسْكُنُ مَعَهُما في البَيتِ إخوَةُ عَدْنانَ الثَلاثَةُ وأختاهُ. لكِنَّ عَدْنانَ يَسْكُنُ في شَقَّةٍ في مَدينةِ كَلَمبَس مَعَ طالِبَيْنِ عَرَبِيَّيْن، واحدٌ مِن فِلَسطين اسمُهُ زِياد نابلُسي وَواحِدٌ مِن لُبنان اسمُهُ وَليد صايِغ. يَدرُسُ زِيادُ الهَندَسَة ويَدرُسُ وَليدُ الكيمياء.

الهَنْدَسَة

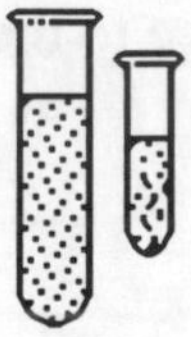

الكيمْياء

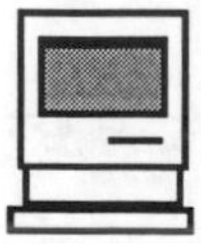

عِلمُ الحاسوب

في هذا الفَصْلِ الدِراسيِّ يَدرُسُ زِياد هذِهِ المَوادَّ: اللُغَةَ الإنكليزيةَ والفيزياءَ والتَفاضُل. ويَدرُسُ وَليدُ في هذا الفَصلِ مادَّتَيْنِ فَقَط هُما اللُغَةَ الإنكليزيَّةَ والأحياء.

تمرين ١

A. Check the alternative in each item that corresponds with the information in the above passages.

١- عائِلةُ النَجّارِ فيها ......

❑ ابنٌ واحِد ❑ ابنانِ ❑ ثلاثَةُ أبناء

٢- رانِية في الصَفِّ ...... الابْتِدائيّ.

الثالِث الرابِع السادِس

٣- وَليد صايِغ طالِبٌ ......

❑ سوريّ ❑ لُبنانيّ ❑ فِلَسطينيّ

٤- يَدْرُسُ عَدْنان مارتيني ......

❑ عِلمَ الحاسوب ❑ الهَندَسَةَ ❑ الكيمْياءَ

٥- يَدْرُسُ زياد في هذا الفَصلِ ......

❑ مادّةً واحِدة ❑ مادَّتَين ❑ ثلاثَ مَواد

٦- يَسْكُنُ عَدْنان مارتيني في ......

❑ سكَنِ الطلاّبِ ❑ بَيتٍ ❑ شَقَّةٍ

٧- يَدْرُسُ وَليدُ في جامِعَةِ وِلايَةِ ......

❑ كاليفورنيا ❑ أوهايو ❑ تِكساس

B. Answer these questions with reference to the passages.

٨- ما اسْمُ أبي رانِيَة؟

٩- مَنْ يَدرُسُ مادّةَ التَفاضُل؟

١٠- مَعَ مَنْ يَسْكُنُ عَدْنان مارتيني؟

١١- كَم مادّةً يَدرُسُ عَدْنان في هذا الفَصل؟

١٢- ماذا يَدْرُسُ زياد نابُلسي في جامِعَةِ ولايةِ أوهايو؟

تمرين ٢

Read the following statements and then mark the box next to each statement with a check mark if the statement is correct according to the reading passage on the Najjār family. If the statement is wrong, mark it with an ✗ and then correct it in the blank space.

١- رانِيَة أختُ رِحاب. ❑ ....

٢- مازِن ابنُ ناديا. ❑ ....

٣- أحْمَد أخو رانِيَة. ❑ ....

٤- رِحابُ ابنةُ أحْمَد. ❑ ....

٥- ناديا زَوجةُ مازِن. ❑ ....

٦- أحْمَد أبو مازِن. ❑ ....

٧- أحْمَد زَوجُ ناديا. ❑ ....

تمرين ٣

Check the appropriate box to indicate the family role of the people specified below. Each one may have more than one role.

	أب	أم	زَوْج	زَوْجَة	اِبْن	اِبْنَة	أخ	أُخْت
١- أنا	☐	☐	☐	☐	☐	☐	☐	☐
٢- أبي	☐	☐	☐	☐	☐	☐	☐	☐
٣- أمّي	☐	☐	☐	☐	☐	☐	☐	☐
٤- أخي	☐	☐	☐	☐	☐	☐	☐	☐
٥- أُختي	☐	☐	☐	☐	☐	☐	☐	☐

تمرين ٤

Underline the word that does not belong in each set of words and explain your choice in English.

١-	تَفاضُل	أحْياء	أُخْت	كيمياء
٢-	وَحيد	فَصْل	مادَّة	فيزياء
٣-	زَوْج	اِبْن	وَلَد	أوَّل
٤-	اِبنَة	عَلى	مَنْ	في

تمرين ٥

Match words from the right-hand column with words in the left-hand column. Copy the matching word from the left-hand column and write it down in the blank space provided next to its match.

١-	فِلَسطين	....	وَلَد
٢-	فَصْل	....	عائلة
٣-	بِنْت	....	لُبنان
٤-	سِتَّة	....	دِراسيّ
			سادِس

تمرين ٦

Select words from the list below that best complete the following sentences.

(الثاني – زَوْجَة – مادَّةً – الابْتِدائِيّ – تَدْرُسُ)

١- .... هالَة مادّةَ الرياضيّات في هذا الفَصْل.

٢- كَم ....عِندَكَ يا سالِم؟

٣- هَل أنتَ الابنَ ....في عائِلَتِك؟

٤- أخي في الصَفِّ الرابِع ....

تمرين ٧

Answer these questions about yourself:

١- ماذا تَدْرُسُ في هذا الفَصْل؟

٢- أينَ تَسْكُن؟

٣- ما اسْمُ جامِعَتِك؟

٤- كَم طالِباً في صَفِّك؟

٥- كَم أخاً وأُختاً لَك؟

تمرين ٨

Compose a paragraph about yourself modeled after the passage on the three Arab students. Describe who you are, where you come from, what you are majoring in, what courses you are currently taking, where you live, where your parents live, and whether you live with others. If you live with others, give a brief biographical sketch of at least one of your roommates.

2. **Arabic Last Names**
Arabic last names refer generally either to place of origin, profession, an attribute acquired by one of the forebears of the family, or they are the person's father's and/or grandfather's names. Other variations also exist. For example, the surname مــارتيـنـي in the passage above is derived from the name of a small town in northern Syria near the city of إدْلِب called مــارتـين. As you can see, the name is a relative noun, or adjective, derived from مــارتـين. The surname نـابُلسي refers to نـابُلُس, a town on the west bank of the river Jordan, Palestine; and the surname صـايغ is the word for a profession (goldsmith). There are names composed of two or more proper names. The second name is usually the father's first name and the third one is the grandfather's first name (e.g. نـزار أحْــمَــد صـالِح). In regions like the Arabian peninsula and North Africa, some names may have the word بِـن (for ابْـن) "son of" inserted after the first name, which explicitly shows the relationship (e.g. عَبّاس بِـن مَـسعود *'abbas bin mas'ūd*).

تمرين ٩

A. The following is an advertisement for a book. What is the author's last or family name? Explain your answer in terms of the explanations above.

كلمات
لها إيقاع
بقلم: هشام علي حافظ

B. This is a heading from an Arabic magazine. Identify the two last names of the persons mentioned. A font called *Kūfī* is used in this headline.

أحمد الشيباني كاتب العام
وفهمي هويدي يفوز بجائزة الأقليات الإسلامية

3. Objects of Verbs

An object of a verb is a noun or a pronoun that is modified by the verb. In English, nouns that are direct objects are not marked for case (i.e., being subject or object), though pronouns are. Notice that the word *apples* remains unchanged in both positions in examples 1 and 2 below. However, if a pronoun is used instead of *apples* in sentence 1, the pronoun *them* would be used (not *they*).

	Subject	Verb	Direct Object
1	I	like	apples (them).
2	Apples (they)	are	good food.

In Arabic, on the other hand, nouns that are direct objects are marked for case. The case of an object of a verb is called accusative in Western grammars and نَصْب in Arabic. There are different markers or endings that indicate this case:

a. A *fatḥa* (فَتحة) on the end of the object if it is definite:

	verb	subject	direct object
٣	يَدْرُسُ	وَليدُ	الأحْياءَ.

where يَدْرُسُ is the verb, وَليدُ the subject who performs the action, and الأحْياءَ the definite direct object (traditionally Arabic sentences start with the verb, but they may also start with the subject).

b. A double *fatḥa* (*tanwīn*) (تَنوين) on the end of an object if it is indefinite:

٤ يَدْرُسُ وَليدُ مادّةً واحِدةً.

where مادّةً is the direct object, which is indefinite (hence the use of *tanwīn*).

c. The suffix *-ayni* (َيْنِ) is attached to dual nouns and *-īn* (ين) to some plural nouns. These suffixes are used with both definite and indefinite nouns. e.g.

٥ يَدْرُسُ وَليدُ مادّتَيْنِ. أعرِفُ ثلاثةَ أمريكيين.

4. Objects of Prepositions: A noun preceded by a preposition is in a case called جَرّ in Arabic and genitive in Western grammars. An Arabic noun is marked in this case in four ways, three of which will be discussed at this point:

a. A *kasra* (كَسْرة) on the end of an object if it is definite:

٦ يَدْرُسُ عَدْنانُ في الجامعَةِ.

b. A *double kasra* (تَنوين) on the end of an indefinite noun:

٧ يَدْرُسُ عَدْنانُ في جامِعَةٍ أمريكيَّةٍ.

c. The suffix *-ayni* (ـَيْنِ) is attached to dual nouns and *-in* (ـين) to some plural nouns:

٨ في جامِعَتَيْنِ أعرِفُ مِصْريين

Note that these suffixes are used with both definite and indefinite nouns (e.g. في الجامعتَين). Remember that adjectives agree with preceding nouns in number, gender, and case.

SUMMARY

The direct object of a verb is marked by a *fatḥa* on its end if it is definite, a double *fatḥa* if it is indefinite, and by suffixing (ـَيْن) to both definite and indefinite dual nouns and (ـين) to some plural nouns.

The object of a preposition is marked on its end by a *kasra* if it is a definite noun, a double *kasra* if it is indefinite, and by suffixing (ـَيْن) to both definite and indefinite dual nouns and (ـين) to some plural nouns.

تمرين ١٠

Identify the objects of verbs by using an underline and the objects of prepositions by drawing a rectangle around them and provide the endings if necessary. There may be more than one object in each sentence.

١- يَسْكُنُ أحمد شَقّة في شارِع الاستِقْلال.

٢- أدرسُ مادّتَين في هذا الفَصْلْ.

٣- لا تَعْرِفُ سامية عُنْوان أمين.

٤- تدرس هالة مادّة الأحياء في جامعة القاهِرة.

تمرين ١١

Convey the following information to someone in Arabic. Provide the appropriate endings to nouns and adjectives.

Say that you ......
1. are taking (studying) two courses in this term.
2. live in an apartment with two students.
3. study computer science.
4. know three French students.
5. live in the City of (name of your town).

5. Ordinal Numbers I

Ordinal numbers are used to order items (e.g. first, second, etc.). Arabic ordinal numbers are derived from cardinal numbers (e.g. one, two, etc.). While cardinal numbers 3-10 *precede* the noun they modify and form an *iḍāfa* structure with it, an ordinal number *follows* the noun and functions as an adjective. Examine the examples below:

Cardinal number	"five lessons"	خَمْسَةُ دُروسٍ	٩
Ordinal number	"the fifth lesson"	الدَّرْسُ الخامِسُ	١٠

Ordinal numbers may be feminine or masculine. As adjectives, they agree with a preceding noun in gender, number, case, and definiteness:

"this is the tenth lesson" هذا هُوَ الدَّرْسُ العاشِرُ ١١

"a third book" كِتابٌ ثالِثٌ ١٢

"in the first two lessons" في الدَّرْسَيْنِ الأَوَّلَيْنِ ١٣

Note that the cardinal number واحِد and its ordinal counterpart أوَّل have different forms. Ordinal numbers 11 and 12 are invariable (i.e., they do not vary in case and exhibit a *fatḥa* only on their ends).

Cardinal and Ordinal Numbers

Ordinal (f.)	Ordinal (m.)	Cardinal	Digit
الأولى	الأوّل	واحد	١
الثانِية	الثاني	اثنان	٢
الثالثة	الثالث	ثَلاثة	٣
الرابعة	الرابع	أربَعة	٤
الخامسة	الخامس	خَمْسة	٥
السادسة	السادس	ستّة	٦
السابعة	السابع	سَبْعة	٧
الثامنة	الثامن	ثَمانية	٨
التاسعة	التاسع	تسْعة	٩
العاشرة	العاشر	عَشَرة	١٠
الحادِيةَ عَشْرةَ	الحاديَ عَشَرَ	أحَدَ عَشَرَ	١١
الثانِيةَ عَشْرةَ	الثانيَ عَشَرَ	اثنا عَشَرَ	١٢

Table 1. Cardinal and Ordinal Numbers

6. Pronouns of Separation ضَمائِر الفَصل

Separate personal pronouns (e.g. هُوَ، هِيَ) may be used to separate subjects and predicates and also in order to distinguish sentences from phrases. In this usage, personal pronouns are analogous with the verb *be* in English, as you can see in these examples from the passage:

١٤ هذِهِ هِيَ عائلةُ مازِن. — This *is* Mazen's family.

١٥ أحمَدُ هُوَ الوَلَدُ الوَحيد. — Aḥmed *is* the only child.

The subjects in 14 and 15 above are هذه and أحمَد, respectively. The predicates represent the information about the subjects. The first predicate happens to be an *iḍāfa* structure عائلةُ مازن (lit., family of Mazen) and the second one is a noun phrase الوَلَدُ الوَحيد (the only child) made up of a noun and an adjective. Note that both predicates are definite. Note also that these pronouns agree with the subjects in gender and number. Pronouns of separation are not used with indefinite predicates.

The use of pronouns of separation is especially called for when the predicate is a single noun defined by the article, as in:

١٦ هذا الكِتابُ.	This book.

The use of هُوَ in this context spells the difference between a noun phrase (16) and a sentence (17).

١٧ هذا هُوَ الكِتابُ.	This *is* the book.

SUMMARY

1. Pronouns of separation are separate personal pronouns.
2. They are used to separate subjects and predicates
3. They distinguish a noun phrase from a sentence.
4. The predicate must be definite.
5. Pronouns of separation agree in number and gender with subjects.

تمرين ١٢

Change the following phrases into sentences by using the appropriate pronoun in the right place.

١- هذهِ المِبراة.

٢- الأستاذُ راغِب طَبّاع.

٣- أخي نِزار.

٤- هذا دفْتَرُ العائلة.

٥- هذانِ الطالبان.

٦- هؤُلاءِ إخوَتي.

تمرين ١٣

In some Arab countries there is what is called "a family identification card." In Arabic, it is called دَفْتَرُ العائلة. Fill out the first page of this document as per the information about the Najjār family in the reading passage.

دَفْتَر العائلة

اِسْم الأب:

اِسْم الأم:

الوَلَدُ الأوَّل:

الوَلَدُ الثاني:

البِنتُ الأولى:

البِنتُ الثانية:

تمرين ١٤

Answer these questions about yourself.

١- هَل عِندَك أخ؟ ماسمُه؟

٢- هَل عِندَك أُخت؟ ماسمُها؟

٣- هَل أنتَ الابنُ الوَحيدُ / الابنَةُ الوَحيدَةُ في العائِلَة؟

تمرين ١٥

A. Select the appropriate alternative according to the information in the tape-recorded passage:

١- نَدى هِيَ أستاذَةُ اللُغةِ ......

☐ الإنكليزيَّة ☐ الفَرَنسيَّة ☐ العَرَبيَّة

٢- نَدى لَها ......

☐ ابْنٌ واحِد ☐ ابنانِ ☐ ثَلاثةُ أبناء

٣- اسمُ زَوْجِ نَدى ......

☐ سامِر ☐ رامِز ☐ سَميح

٤- سامِر في الصَفِّ ......

☐ الثالِث ☐ الخامِس ☐ السابِع

B. Mark these statements خَطَأ or صَواب according to the meaning of the taped passage and correct the false ones.

٥- تَسكُنُ أمُّ سَميح في دارِها.

٦- سَميح بارودي هو زَوْجُ نَدى حَفّار.

٧- يَسْكُنُ سَميحُ وعائِلَتُهُ في مَدرَسةِ بَنات.

٨- لِهذهِ العائِلَةِ ابنانِ وابْنَة.

المُفْرَدات

father	أب ج آباء (n., m.)
elementary	ابْتِدائيّ (adj.)
son	ابْنٌ ج أبْناء (n., m.)
daughter	ابْنَة ج بَنات (n., f.)
brother	أخ ج إخوة (n., m.)
sister	أُخْت ج أَخَوات (n., f.)
mother	أُمّ ج أُمَّهات (n., f.)
English	إنْكليزيّ (n.)
first	أوّل ج أوائِل (n., m.)
girl	بِنْت ج بَنات (n., f.)
ninth	تاسِع (adj.)
differential equations	تَفاضُل (n., m.)
second	ثانٍ (الثاني) (n., m.)
third	ثالِث (adj.)
eighth	ثامِن (adj.)
fifth	خامِس (adj.)
of school, academic	دِراسِيّ (adj.)
fourth	رابِع (adj.)
husband	زَوْج ج أزْواج (n., m.)
wife	زَوْجَة ج زَوْجات (n., f.)
seventh	سابِع (adj.)
sixth	سادِس (adj.)
tenth	عاشِر (adj.)
family	عائِلَة ج عائِلات (n., f.)
(academic) term, season	فَصْل ج فُصول (n., m.)

only, no more .... (particle) فَقَطْ
physics .... (n., f.) فيزياء
chemistry .... (n., f.) كيمياء
who .... (question particle and relative noun) مَنْ
sole, only .... (n., m.) وَحيد ج وَحيدون
boy .... (n., m.) وَلَد ج أَوْلاد

Calligraphic representation of the Qur'anic phrase
وَوَسِعَت رَحْمَتي كُلَّ شَيْءٍ
"And my mercy has encompassed every thing."

Lesson Twelve الدَرْسُ الثاني عَشَر

Objectives

- Terms of address I.
- Expressing regret or apology.
- Expressing lack of knowledge.
- Expressing degree.
- Present tense: negation and conjugation.
- Cardinal numbers 11-100.
- Listen to the recorded material for this lesson.
- Do relevant computer drills and exercises, Stages 4 and 5.

يا آنِسَة!

1. Terms of Address

As in many languages, when people address each other in Arabic, they use terms of address. Some Arabic terms of address also serve as titles. For example, the term آنسة is equivalent to the English "Miss," سَيِّدة is similar to "Mrs." and the word سَيِّد is like "Mr." However, people may also use the words أخ "brother" and أخت "sister" to address strangers. The use of these terms is perceived to make the addressee feel safe, respected, and close. In direct oral interaction, these terms may be preceded by the vocative يا, which is a particle used to call attention, as you can see in the exchanges above and below. However, in indirect speech (e.g. when referring to someone) or in writing, the definite article الـ may be prefixed to the different terms of address (e.g. الأستاذ أحمد).

يا أخ! أينَ مَكتَبُ أستاذِ الرياضيّات؟
هُناك. في الغُرفة رَقم ٣٧.

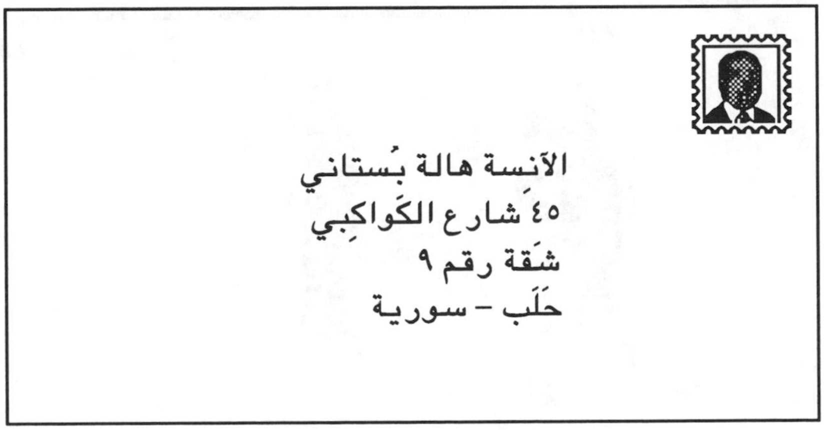
الآنسة هالة بُستاني
٤٥ شارع الكَواكِبي
شَقة رقم ٩
حَلَب - سورية

السيدة نِداء خَيّاط

- مَنْ أمينةُ المكتَبَة ؟
- اِسْمُها السَيِّدة نِداء خَيّاط.
- شُكراً.
- عَفواً.

- أينَ كِتابُكَ يا صَلاح ؟
- آسِف يا أسْتاذ. كِتابي لَيْسَ مَعي.

In speech you may use the article يا with either the first or the last names (e.g. an educated person named خَليل حدّاد may be addressed as أسْتاذ خَليل or أسْتاذ حَدّاد).

The plural forms of سَيِّد (سادة) and سَيِّدة (سيِّدات) may be used to address groups of people, as in public gatherings. Consider the following example where the MC is introducing a man named حُسَيْن زاهِر:

سَيِّداتي وَسادَتي...
الأسْتاذ حُسَين زاهر.

Use of Terms of Address

	Written (formal)	Oral (informal)
١	السَيِّد أحْمَد ناجي	يا سَيِّد أحْمَد!
٢	السَيِّدة رَنا غَلاييني	يا سَيِّدة رَنا![1]
٣	الآنِسَة هَنادي زَيْتونة	يا آنِسَة هَنادي!
٤	الأسْتاذ خَليل حَدّاد	يا أسْتاذ خَليل!
٥	الأخ مُنذِرْ الدَجاني	يا أخ مُنذِرْ!
٦	الأخْت مُزْنة القائِد	يا أخت مُزْنة!

تمرين ١

Review the dialogues once more and check the alternative in each item that corresponds with the information in these dialogues.

١- مَكْتَبُ أسْتاذِ الرياضِيّات في ......

❑ الجامِعَة ❑ لا نَعْرِفَ أيْنَ هُوَ ❑ الغُرفة رَقْم ٣٧

٢- تَسْكُنُ هالة بُسْتاني في ......

❑ شَقَّة رَقْم ٩ ❑ غُرْفَة رَقْم ٩ ❑ شارِع رَقْم ٩

٣- اِسْمُ أمينَة المَكْتَبة ......

❑ هالَة بُسْتاني ❑ سامِية ❑ نِداء خَيّاط

٤- صَلاح ......

❑ لَيْسَ مَعَهُ كِتاب ❑ لَيْسَ مَعَهُ مِحفَظة ❑ لَيْسَ في الصَفِّ

٥- سامِية ...... اسْمَ أستاذِ الأحياء.

❑ تَعْرِفُ ❑ لا تَعْرِفُ ❑ لا تَتَكَلَّمُ

٦- صَلاح ......

❑ طالِبٌ ❑ أُسْتاذٌ ❑ أمينُ مَكتَبة

---

[1] In informal, colloquial speech, the word سيّدة is usually replaced with ست.

تمرين ٢

Address these persons appropriately according to the contexts described below:

1. Writing to a man on official business. His name is وَليد طَرَزي and he has a university degree.
2. Addressing a lower-level employee in your office named مَحمود سالِم.
3. Addressing orally a young, single female secretary named ريم مَعلوف.
4. Writing to a lady named رَباب كَحّال.
5. Writing to an older, little-educated man named عبد الرحيم حُسَين.
6. Addressing orally your professor فَريد قَدّورة.
7. Writing to a female student named أمان عَطِيّة.

2. Expressing Regret or Apology

One way of expressing regret or apology is by using the word آسِف "I'm sorry" by a man or with reference to a man. The word آسِفة is used by a woman or with reference to a female. These words are considered nouns in Arabic. Therefore, they are amenable to manipulation in terms of number in the same way as regular nouns. The dual form is formed by suffixing ان to the masculine and the feminine forms (آسِفان، آسِفَتان) and plural by suffixing ون to the masculine form (آسِفون) and ات to the feminine form (آسِفات).

Note that when the dual suffix ان is appended to the feminine form, the feminine suffix (*tā' marbūṭa*) is retained, but it changes into a regular *tā'*. However, when the plural feminine ending ات is suffixed to the word آسِفة, the feminine marker (ة) is dropped.

تمرين ٣

In the first exchange in this lesson, the form for expressing regret or apology is used. Determine the context in which it is used. Write down your explanation in English.

تمرين ٤

Write down one word in each bubble to describe what the person or persons should say in order to express regret or apology. Proceed from right to left.

3. Expressing Lack of Knowledge

You already know that the phrase لا أعْـرِف "I don't know" expresses lack of knowledge. It has occurred in the first exchange above. There are, however, other ways of expressing lack of knowledge. One of them involves the use of the phrase اللّهُ أعلَم (pronounced *allāhu a'lam*) which literally means "God is the most knowledgeable." It is one of many phrases with various functions that involve the use of the word اللّه, which will be covered gradually. This phrase occurs in the exchange below, signifying lack of knowledge on the woman's part.

4. Expressing Degree

Expressing degree refers to how well one does something. In the exchange below the woman tries to find out whether Marwān speaks English well. His response shows that he does not.

The adverbs جَيِّداً "well" and قَليلاً "a little" are derived from the adjectives جَيِّد "good" and قَليل "little," respectively, by suffixing a *tanwīn* (seated on an *alif*). These adverbs are generally placed in the final sentence position.

تمرين ٥

Match words from the right-hand column with words in the left-hand column. Copy the matching word from the left-hand column and write it down in the blank space provided next to its match.

١- جَيِّداً	....	لُغَة
٢- آنِسَة	....	أعْلَم
٣- يتَكلَّم	....	مِئَة
٤- أمينَةُ	....	قَليلاً
٥- اللّهُ	....	سَيِّدَة
		مَكْتَبَة

تمرين ٦

Complete the following sentences with words from the list.

(اللهُ أعْلَم، الأخ، قليلاً، الآنِسة، سَيِّداتي، آسِفة)

١- .... هالة لا تَسْكُنُ هُنا بَلْ في سَكَنِ الطالِبات.

٢- أنا .... قَلَمي لَيسَ مَعي.

٣- .... وَسادَتي، أهلاً بِكُم.

٤- أينَ مِفتاحُ السَيّارَة؟ ....

٥- أتَكلَّمُ اللُغةَ الإنكليزيَّةَ جَيِّداً والفَرَنْسِيَّةَ ....

تمرين ٧

Respond to the following questions in Arabic with reference to the dialogues contained in this lesson.

1. Does the woman know where the School of Law is? How do you know that?
2. What is Hala Boustani's address? Copy it in Arabic.
3. How would you introduce your favorite celebrity to an audience in Arabic?
4. How do you say in Arabic that you speak a little Arabic?
5. Someone asks you about your professor's address, but you have no idea. How do you express that?
6. How would a woman express regret or apology? How would a man do that?

تمرين ٨

اخترِ الكلمةَ المُناسِبَة:

١- أدْرُسُ في الإسكَندريَّة ...... يسكنُ أخي.

❑ حَيْثُ ❑ أيْنَ ❑ في

٢- هذا كِتابٌ ......

❑ عَليم ❑ جَيِّد ❑ أمين

٣- ريم علاّف ...... مَكتَبةٍ في جامِعَةِ تِشرين.

❑ صَيْدَلَة ❑ مِئَة ❑ أمينَة

٤- ...... لا أعرِفُ أينَ كُليَّةُ الصَيْدَلَة.

❑ شُكراً ❑ آسِف ❑ مِن

٥- ...... هالة الإنْكليزيّةَ جَيِّداً.

❑ تَتَكلَّمُ ❑ تَأكُلُ ❑ تَسْكُنُ

5. The Present Tense: Negation and Conjugation

Negation: You have already used the present tense of the verb سَكَنَ "to live" in order to describe where one lives. For example, to indicate that you live in an apartment, you say: أَسْكُنُ في شَقّة. However, if you do not live in an apartment, you can express that by inserting the negative particle لا in front of the verb:

١ لا أَسْكُنُ في شَقّة.

Negating present tense verbs with the negative particle لا entails no change either in the structure of the verb or in word order.

Conjugation: So far, only five conjugations have been used to refer to yourself, to an addressee (singular masculine and feminine), and to a third person (singular masculine and feminine). The table below lists all verb conjugations in the present tense classified according to number.

As noted earlier, remember that لا is generally used to negate present tense (مُضارِع) verbs. Its use in this manner does not change either the form of the verb or the order of the words in any way. Table 1 shows the thirteen conjugations of the verb تَكَلَّمَ "speak" in the present tense (imperfect).

SUMMARY The particle لا negates present tense verbs, causing no change either in the verb form or word order.

تمرين ٩

Describe how well you speak the following languages. If you do not speak one of them at all, indicate that as well. If there are other languages that you know but are not listed, list them and indicate your proficiency.

١ـ الإنْكليزيّة
٢ـ العَرَبيّة
٣ـ الإسْبانيّة
٤ـ الفَرَنسيّة
٥ـ اللاتينيّة

Present Tense Conjugations of تَكَلَّمَ

	الضَمير (pronoun)	الفعل (verb)
Singular	أنا	أتَكَلَّمُ
	أنتَ	تَتَكَلَّمُ
	أنتِ	تَتَكَلَّمِينَ
	هُوَ	يَتَكَلَّمُ
	هِيَ	تَتَكَلَّمُ
Dual	أنتُما	تَتَكَلَّمان
	هُما	يَتَكَلَّمان
	هُما	تَتَكَلَّمان
Plural	نَحنُ	نَتَكَلَّمُ
	أنتُم	تَتَكَلَّمونَ
	أنتُنَّ	تَتَكَلَّمنَ
	هُم	يَتَكَلَّمونَ
	هُنَّ	يَتَكَلَّمنَ

Table 1

6. **Cardinal Numbers 11-100**

a. **Cardinal Numbers 11 and 12:** These compound numbers *precede* the noun which they modify and they agree with the specified noun in gender, e.g. (using كِتاب m. and سَيّارة f. as examples),

٢ أحَدَ عَشَرَ كِتاباً		إحْدى عَشْرَةَ سيارةً

٣ اِثنا (اِثني) عَشَرَ كِتاباً		اثنَتا (اثنَتَي) عَشْرَةَ سيّارةً

Note that the number *11* is invariable; that is, it does not change according to case. However, the number *12* changes its form according to case, where the forms اثنَي (m.) and اثنَتَي (f.) are used when the noun is the object of a verb or a preposition (in the accusative or genitive cases--more on cases later).

b. **Cardinal Numbers 13-19**: Like the numbers 3-10, these numbers have reverse agreement in gender with the following noun. However, the reverse agreement is limited to the ones, not the tens, as you can see in the following example:

٤ ثلاثةَ عشَرَ كِتاباً　　　ثلاثَ عَشْرَةَ سيّارةً

Cardinal Numbers 11-19

سيّارة	كتاب
١١ إحْدى عَشْرَةَ سيّارةً	١١ أحَدَ عَشَرَ كتاباً
١٢ اثنتا (اثْنَتَي) عَشْرَةَ سيّارةً	١٢ اثنا (اثْنَي) عَشَرَ كتاباً
١٣ ثلاثَ عَشْرَةَ سيّارةً	١٣ ثلاثةَ عَشَرَ كتاباً
١٤ أربَعَةَ عَشْرَةَ سيّارةً	١٤ أربَعَةَ عَشَرَ كتاباً
١٥ خَمسَ عَشْرَةَ سيّارةً	١٥ خَمسَةَ عَشَرَ كتاباً
١٦ ستَّ عَشْرَةَ سيّارةً	١٦ ستّةَ عَشَرَ كتاباً
١٧ سَبعَ عَشْرَةَ سيّارةً	١٧ سَبعَةَ عَشَرَ كتاباً
١٨ ثَماني عَشْرَةَ سيّارةً	١٨ ثَمانِيَةَ عَشَرَ كتاباً
١٩ تِسْعَ عَشْرَةَ سيّارةً	١٩ تِسْعَةَ عَشَرَ كتاباً

The reverse agreement is between the first word of the number (the ones) and the noun. Notice that ثلاثة and كتاباً exhibit a reverse gender agreement, while عَشَرَ and كتاباً agree in gender. Thus, the ones have a reverse agreement in gender with nouns, not the tens. Tens have gender agreement with the modified nouns.

All numbers *11* through *19* (except for the number *12*, which shows a case marker) are invariable with a *fatḥa* on their ends in all cases. Remember that the counted nouns are indefinite singular accusative (e.g. سيّارةً ,كِتاباً).

c. **Cardinal Numbers *20-90***: These numbers (i.e., the tens) are nouns and therefore they change in form with case. The ending ون is used for the nominative case (subject) (e.g. عشرون) and ين for the accusative and genitive cases (e.g. عِشرين). Like the numbers 11-19, the noun following them is singular, indefinite, and accusative with a *tanwīn* (ً) on its end. They are invariable with regard to gender; that is, they do not vary in form with the gender of the counted noun. In the examples below the number *30* changes according to case, but not gender.

٥ عِندي ثَلاثونَ كِتاباً — في ثَلاثينَ كِتاباً

٦ هُناكَ ثَلاثونَ جامِعةً — في ثَلاثينَ جامِعةً

Tens (العُقود) (20-90) with masculine and feminine nouns:

٢٠. عِشرونَ كِتاباً / سيّارةً — ٣٠. ثَلاثونَ كِتاباً / سيّارةً

٤٠. أربَعونَ كِتاباً / سيّارةً — ٥٠. خَمسونَ كِتاباً / سيّارةً

٦٠. سِتّونَ كِتاباً / سيّارةً — ٧٠. سَبعونَ كِتاباً / سيّارةً

٨٠. ثَمانونَ كِتاباً / سيّارةً — ٩٠. تِسعونَ كِتاباً / سيّارةً

SUMMARY

The Numbers 11 and 12

Both words in the number agree in gender with the noun. The number *11* is invariable (i.e. does not change with case), exhibiting a *fatḥa* on the ends of both words, whereas the words اثنا and اثنَتا in the number *12* change to اثنَي and اثنَتَي in the accusative and genitive cases.

The Numbers 13-19

The first word of the number has a reverse gender agreement with the noun, while the second word (ten) agrees with the noun in gender. They do not vary with case; they always have a *fatḥa* on their ends.

The numbers *20-90*

These numbers have two forms: (1) nominative (e.g. عِشْرون) and (2) accusative and genitive (e.g. عِشْرين). The noun following these numbers is singular, indefinite, accusative (e.g. سِتّون/ستّين سيّارةً).

d. **The Number *100*** (مِئة): This is also a noun, which means that its case varies according to its position in the sentence. The counted noun following it is singular indefinite. It forms with the following noun an *iḍāfa* structure. The noun following it is, therefore, genitive and indefinite, displaying a double *kasra*:

٧ مِئَةُ كِتابٍ   مِئَةُ سيّارةٍ

Here is a list of multiples of *100* used with nouns:

٢٠٠ مِئتا / مِئَتَي كِتابٍ / سَيّارَةٍ

٣٠٠ ثلاثُمئة كِتابٍ / سيّارَةٍ

٤٠٠ أربَعُمِئة كِتابٍ / سَيّارَةٍ

٥٠٠ خمسُمِئة كِتابٍ / سيّارَةٍ

٦٠٠ ستُمِئة كِتابٍ / سَيّارَةٍ

٧٠٠ سَبعُمِئة كِتابٍ / سيّارَةٍ

٨٠٠ ثَمانمِئة كِتابٍ / سَيّارَةٍ

٩٠٠ تِسعُمِئة كِتابٍ / سيّارَةٍ

Note that the number *200* with a following noun loses its final ن because it is the first word of an *iḍāfa* structure (المُضاف).

Since the word مـئـة is a noun, it is subject to being made dual and plural. The dual is formed by suffixing ان or يْن to it, depending on case. The plural is formed by suffixing ات because it is a feminine noun, thus resulting in مِئات "hundreds." However, the plural form مِئات is never used with the numbers *100-999*, but it is used in phrases such as:

٨ مِئاتُ الكُتبِ "hundreds of books"

Notice that in this usage, the counted noun is plural, definite, and genitive.

تمرين ١٠

Write out in words the numbers listed below and provide the correct form of the nouns with the appropriate short vowels.

١- ٨ (نظّارة)

٢- ٤ (مَختبَر)

٣- ١١ (دَفتَر)

٤- ١٤ (دَرّاجة)

٥- ٥٠ (طالِب)

٦- ٨٠ (بِنت)

٧- ١٠٠ (قَلَم)

٨- ٢٠٠ (جامِعة)

٩- ٧٠٠ (رَجُل)

تمرين ١١

A. Listen to the tape-recorded passage and check the best alternative according to the passage.

١- يَسْكُنُ عادِل مَحْمود في ......

❑ الإسْكَندَرية ❑ طَنطا ❑ القاهِرة

٢- عادِل مَحْمود هُوَ ...... سامية.

❑ أخو ❑ أبو ❑ أخت

٣- تدرسُ سامية في جامِعةِ ......

❑ طَنطا ❑ القاهِرة ❑ الإسكندرية

٤- لِعَبدِ الحَليم ......

❑ أخت واحِدة ❑ أختان ❑ ثَلاث أخَوات

٥- تسكُنُ سامية محمود الآن في ......

❑ سكَنِ الطالِبات ❑ بيتِ أبيها ❑ كُليّةِ التِجارة

B. Answer these questions with reference to the listening passage.

٦- كَم أخاً لِسامية؟

٧- مَن زَينَب؟ أهِيَ في المَدْرَسَةِ أم في الجامعة؟

٨- مَن تَهاني وماذا تَدْرُسُ؟

9. Describe Samia's room in Arabic.

10. Compose a biographical sketch about yourself modeled after the listening passage.

المُفْرَدات

sorry	آسِف (m.) / آسِفة (n.) (f.)
most knowledgeable	أعلَم (n. superlative)
librarian	أمين/ أمينةُ مَكتَبةٍ (n., m./f.)
to speak	تَكَلَّمَ (يَتَكَلَّمُ) (v.)
good	جَيِّد (adj.)
well	جَيِّداً (adv.)
where, when	حَيْثُ (adv.)
pharmacology	صَيْدَلَة (n., f.)
knowledgeable	عَليم (adj.)
group of ten	عَقْد ج عُقود (n., m.)
little	قَليل (adj.)
a little	قَليلاً (adv.)
to, for, by	لِـ (prep.)
hundred	مِئة ج مِئات (n., f.)

دمَشقُ القَديمة

Lesson Thirteen — الدَرْسُ الثالِثَ عَشَر

Objectives

- Arabic print media.
- Inquiring about and describing activities.
- Requesting and offering something politely.
  - a. The imperative.
  - b. Doubly transitive verbs.
  - c. The pronunciation of the pronoun ه (*h*).
- Cases of the noun.
- Expressing possession with مَع.
- Attached pronouns suffixed to verbs.
- More on Arabic names.
- Listen to the recorded material for this lesson.
- Do relevant computer drills and exercises, Stage 4, Text 2.

جَرائِدُ ومَجَلاّتٌ عَرَبيّة

هُناكَ جَرائدُ ومَجَلاّتٌ عربيّةٌ في مكتبةِ الجامعةِ.

جَريدةُ الأهرامِ مِصريّةٌ.

جَريدةُ تِشرين سوريّةٌ.

جَريدةُ الشَرقِ الأوسَطِ سُعوديّةٌ.

جريدةُ العَلَم عِراقية.

مَجَلّةُ الفِكْر تونسيّة.

مَجلّةُ الإكليل يَمَنيّة.

مجلّة الفُنون مَغربية.

مَجَلّةُ العَرَبيِّ كُوَيتيّة.

جَريدة

مَن يَقرأ هذه الجرائدَ والـمَجلاّت؟

يَقْرأُ الـمَجلاّتِ والجرائدَ العربيّةَ طُلاّبٌ عَرَبٌ في الجامِعَةِ وطُلاّبٌ أمريكيّونَ يَدرُسونَ اللُّغةَ العربِيَّةَ.

ماذا يَقرَأون؟

يَقْـرَأُ الطُلابُ العَـرَبُ في أمـريكا الجَـرائِدَ والمَجَـلاّتِ العَـرَبِيَّـةَ في مَكتَبَةِ الجامِعَةِ عادَةً. يَقْرَأ عَدنان مارتيني جَريدَةَ «تِشرينَ» ومَجَـلَّةَ «المَعرفـة» السـوريّتَين عـادةً، ويَقْرَأ أحياناً مَجَلّةَ «روز اليـوسِف» المِصريَّة.

وَليد صايِغ

يَقْـرَأُ وَليـد صـايِغ عـادةً جَـريدةَ «النَهـارِ» اللُبنـانيَّـة ومَـجَلّةَ «المَجلّةِ» السُعودية، ويَقْرَأ أحياناً جَريدَةَ «الأهرامِ» المصرية.

زِياد نابلسي

يَقْرَأ زِياد نابلسي عادَةً جَريدةَ «الثَورةِ» العِراقيّة، لكِنَّهُ يقرأ جريدة «الشرقِ الأوسَط» السُعودية و«الأخبارَ» المِصرية. يَقرَأ زِياد أحيانـاً مَجَلَّةَ «الإكليل» اليَمَنيّة ومَجَلّةَ «مَواقِف أدَبِيّة» السورية.

أيّةَ مَجلّةٍ تقرأ يا عَبدَ اللَطيف؟

أقرأ جَريدةَ النَهار.

- أيّةَ جَريدَة تقرأ يا عَبدَ اللَطيف؟
- أقرأ جَريدةَ النَهار عادَةً
  وأقرأ جَريدةَ المُجاهِد أحياناً.
- هَل جَريدةُ النهار سورَية؟
- لا. هي لُبنانيّة، والمُجاهِد جَزائريّة.
- هَل تَكتُبُ في جَريدة؟
- لا. أنا لا أكتُبُ في أيّةِ جَريدة. أنا أقرأ الجَرائِد.

1. Inquiring about and Describing an Activitiy or Object

Inquiring about or describing an activitiy involves describing an action, which is expressed by a verb of action. However, in the first exchange above, the focus is on the object being read rather than on the action, hence the use of أيّة "*which*" (أيّ for masculine nouns) for inquiring about something. Alternatively, asking about the process of doing something requires the use of the question word ماذا followed by a verb. If the nature of the activity is known, the verb denoting it may be used. But if the activity is not known, then the verb فَعَلَ "*to do*" should be used, as in the exchange below.

In summary, the interrogative (question) word used to inquire about objects is أيّ "*which*" and the question word used to inquire about actions is ماذا "*what.*"

The Question Words أيُّ and أيَّةُ

The question words أيُّ/أيَّةُ are nouns (masculine and feminine). They can, therefore, form with a following noun an *iḍāfa* structure and function as subject or object.

In the dialogue, the woman uses the verb تَفْعَل "*do*" which is replaced in the answer with the verb describing the action being inquired about (e.g. أقرأ).

If the request cannot be fulfilled, the words (m.) آسِف / (f.) آسِفَة "*sorry*" may be used, as in the exchange above.

2. Requesting and Offering Something Politely

In the exchange below, the use of the prepositional phrase مِن فَضْل and one of the second person attached pronouns (كَ، كِ، كُما، كُم، كُنَّ) denotes a polite request. A positive response to a request usually involves the use of a particular imperative verb (تَفَضَّل/تَفَضَّلي), which also signifies politeness. This verb carries many meanings which

are made specific only by context. For example, if you are requesting a pen, the use of تَفَضَّل in the response is more like "*there you are*." However, if someone knocks on the door and you answer to let him in, the meaning would be "*come in*."

a. **The Imperative**: Requesting and offering something might involve the use of the imperative form of the verb you are using. Two imperative verbs أَعْطِ and تَفَضَّلْ are used in the dialogue below. The verb أَعْطِ "*give!*" is the second person masculine singular conjugation, as it is addressed to a man. The form تَفَضَّلي is second person feminine singular, because it is addressed to a woman. There are basically five imperative forms of the verb, corresponding to the five second person pronouns (refer to the verb conjugation table below). The verb تَفَضَّلْ has several meanings as noted above, depending on the context in which it is used. Literally, it means "*if you please*," but in particular contexts, it may mean "*go ahead, after you, please sit down, here you are*," and so forth.

b. **Forming the Imperative**: It is derived from the present tense conjugation as follows:

1. Drop the prefix of the present tense verb. If the letter following the prefix has a short vowel on it, do nothing (e.g. يَتَفَضَّلُ becomes تَفَضَّلْ; the *tā'* is followed by a *fatḥa*). Note that the final *ḍamma* is also dropped.
2. If the letter following the prefix is not followed by a vowel (that is, it has *sukūn*), replace the prefix with a *hamza* (e.g. يَكْتُبُ ⇨ أُكْتُبْ).
3. The short vowel on the initial *hamza* is *fatḥa* if the past tense verb has four letters (e.g. أَعْطى ⇨ أَعْطِ), *ḍamma* if the middle letter of the present tense verb has a *ḍamma* (e.g. يَكْتُبُ ⇨ أُكْتُبْ), and *kasra* if the middle letter has a *kasra* (e.g. يَجْلِسُ ⇨ اِجْلِسْ).

Conjugation of أعْطى (يُعْطي)

Imperative	Present	Past	Pronoun
	أُعْطي	أعْطَيْتُ	أنا
	نُعْطي	أعْطَيْنا	نَحنُ
أعْطِ	تُعْطي	أعْطَيْتَ	أنتَ
أعْطي	تُعْطينَ	أعْطَيْتِ	أنتِ
أعْطِيا	تُعْطِيانِ	أعْطَيْتُما	أنتُما
أعْطوا	تُعْطونَ	أعْطَيْتُم	أنتُم
أعْطينَ	تَعْطينَ	أعْطَيْتُنَّ	أنتُنَّ
	يُعْطي	أعْطى	هُوَ
	تُعْطي	أعْطَتْ	هِيَ
	يُعْطِيانِ	أعْطَيا	هُما
	تُعْطِيانِ	أعْطَيَتا	هُما
	يُعْطونَ	أعْطَوا	هُم
	يُعْطينَ	أعْطَيْنَ	هُنَّ

Table 1

Imperative Forms of the Verb تَفَضَّل

أنتَ	أنت	أنتُما	أنتُم	أنتُنَّ
تَفَضَّلْ	تَفَضَّلي	تَفَضَّلا	تَفَضَّلوا	تَفَضَّلْنَ

Table 2

c. **Doubly Transitive Verbs:** Verbs that take an object are called transitive verbs. For example, in the sentence *I wrote a letter*, the verb *wrote* is transitive because the word *letter* is the direct object of the verb *wrote*. A limited number of verbs are transitive to two objects, not only one. One of them is the verb أَعْطى "*to give*." In the sentence أَعْطِني جَريدةً "*give me a newspaper*" in the dialogue below, the two objects are the pronoun ني "*me*" suffixed to the verb and the noun جَريدةً "*newspaper*." Note that this noun has a double *fatḥa* on its end, marking it indefinite and accusative (being the direct object of the verb أعطِ).

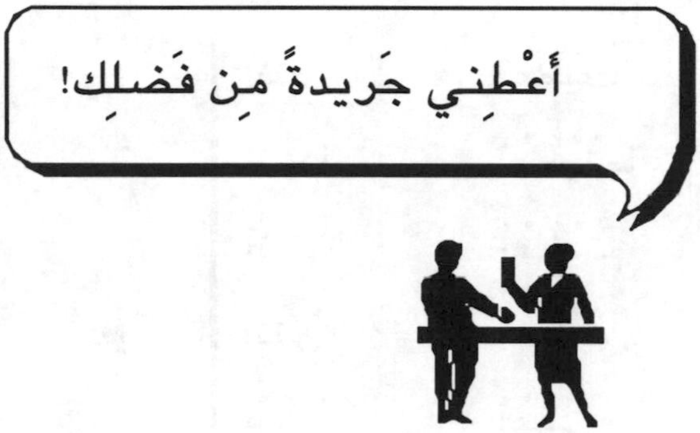

- أعطِني جَريدةً مِن فَضلِك!
- أيّةَ جَريدة؟
- جَريدَةَ «الدُسْتور» مِن فَضلِك.
- تَفَضَّلي!
- شُكراً.
- عَفواً.

d. **Pronunciation of the Attached Pronoun** هُ: As you know, this pronoun can function only as a suffix and is pronounced *hu*. However, if the preceding vowel is a *kasra* (i.e. the short vowel *i*) or the long vowel ي (*ī*), this pronoun is pronounced *hi*, as in these examples:

فيهِ - إلَيْهِ - بِهِ - في بيتِهِ - أعطِهِ

تمرين ١

أ- اِخْتَرِ الكلِمةَ المُناسِبةَ حَسَبَ النص:

١- «العَلَم» ...... عِراقيّة.

❑ مَكتَبَةٌ ❑ مَجَلّةٌ ❑ جَريدَةٌ

٢- هُناكَ ...... عَرَبيّةٌ في مَكتبةِ الجامِعةِ.

❑ طالِباتٌ ❑ طُلّابٌ وَطالِباتٌ ❑ مَجَلّاتٌ وَجَرائِدُ

٣- الفُنونُ ...... مَغربيّة.

❑ جَريدةٌ ❑ مَجَلّةٌ ❑ طالِبةٌ

٤ـ يَقْرَأُ الجَرائِدَ العربيةَ في المكتبة طلابٌ ......

❑ أمريكيونَ ❑ مِصريّونَ ❑ يعرفونَ العربية

٥ـ يَقْرَأُ عَبدُ اللَطيفِ ......

❑ جَريدةً لُبنانيَّةً ❑ جَريدةً سوريَّةً ❑ مَجلّةً جَزائِريَّةً

٦ـ أعْطى الرجُلُ الامرأةَ جَريدةَ ......

❑ النَهارِ ❑ المُجاهِدِ ❑ الدُسْتورِ

٧ـ يَقرأُ عَدنان مارتيني عادةً مَجلَّةَ ......

❑ روز اليوسف ❑ المجلّة ❑ المَعرِفَة

٨ـ يَقْرَأُ وَليد صايغ جَريدةَ ...... أحياناً.

❑ الأهرامِ ❑ النَهارِ ❑ تِشرينَ

٩ـ يَقْرَأُ زِياد نابُلسي جَريدةَ ...... عادةً.

❑ الأهرامِ ❑ الأخبارِ ❑ تِشرينَ

تمرين ٢

أكمِلِ الجُملَ التاليةَ بِكَلِماتٍ مِن بين القَوسَين:

(تَفَضَّلي، آسِفَة، عادَةً، جَيِّداً، أيّةَ، مِن فَضلِك، تَشَرَّفنا)

١ـ ...... مَجلّةٍ تقرأينَ يا هُدى؟

٢ـ أقرأُ مَجَلَّةَ العَرَبيّ ......

٣ـ أينَ مَكتَبُ الأسْتاذِ طَبّاع ....؟

٤ـ ...... لَيسَ مَعي قَلَم.

تمرين ٣

وافِقْ بَيْنَ الكَلِماتِ في العَمودَين (match words in the two columns):

١- جَريدة	....	تَفَضَّلْ
٢- عادَةً	....	مَعَهُ
٣- اعطِني	....	مَجَلَّة
٤- يَقْرَأ	....	أحْياناً
		يَكتُبُ

تمرين ٤

Respond to the following in Arabic.

How do you ......

1. Request a pen from a woman politely?
2. Hand *Time* magazine to a woman politely?
3. Ask the newstand attendant whether he has got الرأي newspaper?
4. Apologize for not having an eraser with you?

3. **Cases of the Noun**

There are three cases of the noun in Arabic:

a. **The Nominative Case** (الرَفْع): A noun is nominative (مَرْفوع) if it is:

(i) the doer of the action (agent, subject) of a verb in a sentence, where the word الطالِبُ "*student*" below stands for the doer of the action (فاعِل):

١ يَقْرَأُ الطالِبُ جَريدَةً. *The student reads/ is reading a newspaper*.

(ii) the subject (مُبْتَدَأ) of a nominal sentence (الطالِبُ) (see example 2 below).

(iii) the predicate (خَبَر) of a nominal sentence (أمريكيٌّ), as in 2 below.

٢ الطالِبُ أمريكيٌّ. *The student is American.*

Note that both nouns above are nominative, being the subject and predicate (topic and comment) of the sentence, yet الطالِبُ is marked with a *ḍamma* because it is definite,

and أمـريكيٌّ is marked with a double *ḍamma* because it is indefinite. A nominative noun is then marked with a *ḍamma* on its end if it is definite, double *ḍamma* if it is indefinite. The ending ان is suffixed to dual nouns, and ون to some masculine plural nouns. The dual and plural forms of the above example are as follows:

٣ الطالبـانِ أمريكيّـانِ. *The two students are American.*

٤ الطُلاّبُ أمريكيّـونَ. *The students are American.*

b. **The Genitive Case** (الجَـرّ): A noun is in the genitive case (مَـجْرور) if:

(i) it is the object of a preposition (مَجْرور بِحَرْفِ الجَرّ):

٥ في الصَفِّ *in the classroom*

(ii) it is the second part of an *iḍāfa* structure (مُضاف إلَيْه):

٦ مَخْبَرُ الكيمياءِ. *lab of chemistry*

The genitive markers include the *kasra,* the double *kasra,* ـيْنِ (*-ayni*) on the end of dual nouns, and ـين (*-īna*) on the end of some plural nouns.

c. **The Accusative Case** (النَـصْب): Nouns in all grammatical positions other than the nominative and genitive are accusative (مَنْصوب). You already know two of them:

(1) the object of a verb (المَفْعول بِـه):

٧ تَعرفُ سَلوى اللُغةَ الفرَنْسيَّةَ. *Salwa knows (is familiar with) French.*

(2) specification of quantity (التَمْييز):

٨ كَم كتاباً عِندَك ؟ *How many books do you have?*

٩ خَمْسونَ كتاباً. *50 books*

The accusative markers include the *fatḥa*, double *fatḥa*, ـيْنِ (*-ayni*) on the end of dual nouns and ـين (*-īna*) on the end of some plural nouns.

تمرين ٥

Describe the case of the underlined word(s) in each sentence, indicate their markings, and explain your description, using Arabic terminology:

١- أسْتاذُ الصَفِّ مِن مَدينةِ سوسَة في تونِس.

٢- السَيّارة في الشارِعِ.

٣- كَمْ طالبٍ في الصَفِّ؟

٤- يَعْرِفُ أحْمَدُ عُنوانَ هالَة.

4. Expressing Possession with the Prepositions لِـ and مَعَ

Possession has been expressed so far with the adverb of place عِنْدَ plus a noun or an attached pronoun:

١٤ عِنْدَ سامي سَيّارةٌ. *Sami has a car.* عِنْدي سَيّارةٌ. *I have a car.*

Possession may also be expressed with the preposition (لِـ) in the same manner by prefixing لِـ [2] to an attached pronoun or a noun:

١٥ لي أخْتان. *I have two sisters.* لِعادِلٍ أخْتان. *Adil has two sisters.*

This prepositional phrase may also translate into "*I have*" although there is no verb involved in Arabic.

Note that the two phrases may not be used interchangeably. With reference to people, both the preposition لِـ and the adverb عِنْدَ may be used to express possession of something whether acquired or inherent (e.g. *I have a car*; *I have two hands*), but when it is used with reference to inanimate objects, only لِـ may be used (e.g. لِغُرفَتي شُبّاكان, "*my room has two windows*").

Notice that when the preposition لِـ (*li-*) is prefixed to a noun, it is pronounced *li*, but when prefixed to a pronoun, it is pronounced *la-* (e.g. لَكَ، لَنا، لَهُ).

The use of the preposition مَعَ with a possessive pronoun (e.g. مَعي) denotes a form of possession. The phrase مَعي قَلَم, for example, means "*I have a pen*" or "*I have a pen with me.*" It may not be necessarily *my* pen. In this context, this preposition means "*with*" or "*along with.*"

---

[2] Note that this preposition can only be a prefix.

تمرين ٦

Express possession, using عِنْدَ, لِـ, and مَعَ:

1. Reema (feminine name) has two bicycles.
2. Our house has three doors.
3. Ahmed has got a car with him now.
4. I have a brother and a sister.
5. Do you have your eyeglasses (with you)?
6. Mrs. Boustani has a son and a daughter.

5. Attached Pronouns Suffixed to Verbs

Up to this lesson, you have seen attached pronouns suffixed to nouns where they function as possessive pronouns (e.g. كتابي "*my book*", قَلَمُها "*her pen*"). However, when these pronouns are suffixed to verbs and prepositions they serve as object pronouns, such as the English *him, them*, etc. The word أتَكَلَّمُها in Section 4 has the third person, feminine, singular attached pronoun, meaning "*I speak it*" where the ـها suffix refers back to لُغة "*language.*"

Remember that nonrational (i.e. inanimate) plurals have singular feminine reference, as indicated in the use of the third person feminine singular suffix, e.g.

١٦ أعْرِفُ ثَلاثَ لُغاتٍ وأتَكلّمُها جَيِّداً.

where the suffix ها (third person, singular, feminine) in أتَكلّمُها means "*them*" (not "*it*" or "*she*") because this attached pronoun refers back to لُغات, which is a nonrational plural. Reference to all such plurals is made in the third person, singular, feminine regardless of the gender of the noun.

The attached pronouns suffixed to nouns and prepositions are basically the same as those suffixed to verbs. The only difference is in the first person singular pronoun ي, which becomes ني when suffixed to verbs:

١٧ تَعرِفُني نادية مِنَ الجامعة. *Nadia knows* me *from college*

تمرين ٧

With reference to Table 1 of attached pronouns in Lesson 5 and to the verb conjugation tables, rewrite in Arabic the meaning of the sentences below, providing the appropriate forms of the verbs with the correct attached pronouns.

1. I know her.
2. He gave us a newspaper.
3. They (m.) know Arabic and speak it at home.
4. Give me that magazine, please.
5. They (f.) know me.
6. Do you (f.) know them (m.)?
7. Give him your phone number.

6. More on Arabic Names

Most Arabic first names have meanings. For example, the name وَليد (m.) means "*boy*" or "*newborn*," and the name تَهاني (f.) means "*congratulations*." There are also compound names (e.g. عَبْدُ الله). Such compound names containing عَبْد are only for males. The first word عَبْد means "*servant, slave.*" The second word is either الله "*God*" or any one of the ninety-nine other names of *Allah*, such as عَبْدُ اللّطيف and عَبْدُ الهادي (pronounced *'abdu-l-latīf* and *'abdu-l-hādī*). Thus, the popular belief that the word *Abdul* is an Arabic name is partially mistaken, since this word represents only the first part of the name (عَبْد) plus the definite article (ال) of the second part.

تمرين ٨

Examine these excerpts from an Arabic magazine and try to identify some foreign names. There are five in the first excerpt (on the right) and three in the second.

يقول جون كلارك غيبل "لقد قررت
أن أجرب حظي في التمثيل عندما
أحضر كلايد وير نص الفيلم (جيم
السيئ) لأنني أحببته كثيراً. سأمثل
هذا الفيلم مع ممثلين مجربين هما
جيمس برولين وريتشارد راوندتري.

ساهم الكاتبان غراهام غرين وجون
لو كاريه في ظهور نوع جديد من
أدب الرواية الجاسوسية يتحدث عن
جرائم فظيعة ترتكب على كلا
الجانبين من جدار برلين أيام الحرب
الباردة.

تمرين ٩

A. Listen to the tape-recorded passage and check ✔ the best alternative according to the passage.

١ـ أحمَد زَوج ......

❑ فاطِمة ❑ رانِيَة ❑ سَميرَة

٢ـ يَقرأ أحْمَدُ جَريدةَ ...... أحْياناً.

❑ الدُسْتورِ ❑ الشَرْقِ الأوسَطِ ❑ الأهرامِ

٣ـ فَريد ...... فاطِمَة.

❑ اِبنُ ❑ زَوْجُ ❑ أبو

B. Complete these sentences according to the information in the passage:

٤ـ فاطِمَة لَها ابنَتان هُما ...... و......

٥ـ تَقرَأ فاطِمَةُ جَريدةَ ......

٦ـ يَقرأ أحمَدُ عادَةً جَريدَةَ ......

C. On the basis of the information in the recorded passage, mark these statements خَطَأ or صَواب and correct the false ones.

٧ـ يَقْرَأُ أحْمَدُ مَجلَّةَ الهِلال.

٨ـ سَميرَة أختُ بَشير.

٩ـ تَسكُنُ عائِلَةُ أحْمَد في عُمان.

المُفْرَدات

أحياناً (adv.)	sometimes
أعطى (يُعطي) أعْطِ (v.) (imperative) إعْطاء (verbal noun)	to give
أيٌّ (n., m.)/أيّةٌ (n., f.)	which
تَفَضَّلْ/تَفَضَّلي (imperative verb)	if you please
عادَةً (adv.)	usually
فَعَلَ (يَفعَلُ) (v.)	to do
قَرَأَ (يَقرَأُ) (v.)	to read
كَتَبَ (يَكْتُبُ)	to write
مَجَلَّة ج مَجَلاّت (n., f.)	magazine
مِنْ فَضْلِك (polite phrase)	please

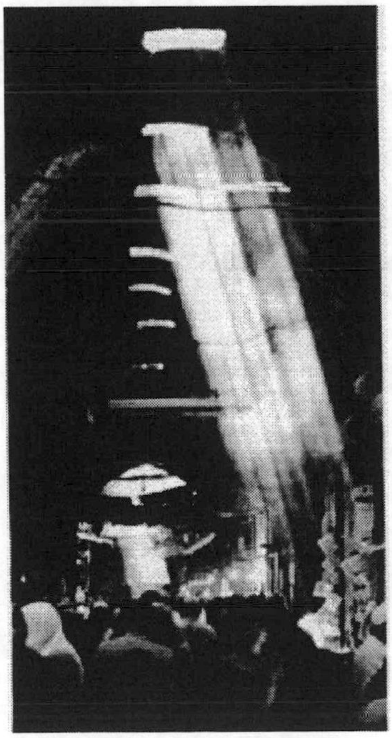

سوق قديمة في حَلَب

Lesson Fourteen الدَرْسُ الرابِعَ عَشَر

Objectives

- Requesting and declining things politely.
- Food and drink.
- Describing daily activities.
- The imperative.
- Prepositions and attached pronouns.
- Expressing likes and dislikes.
- Plurals of nouns.
- Adverbials.
- *Iḍāfa* structure revisited (multiple *iḍāfa*).
- Listen to the recorded material for this lesson.
- Do relevant computer exercises, Stage 5 (Texts 1 and 2) and Stage 7.

شاي مِن فَضْلِك!

- تُريدينَ قَهْوَةً يا آنِسَة؟
- لا. شُكراً. شاياً مِن فَضلِك.
- مَعَ السكَّر؟
- نَعَم.
- حاضِر.

- قَهْوة يا سَيِّد؟
- لا شُكراً. عَصير بُرتُقال مِن فَضلِك.

1. Requesting and Declining Things Politely

In the dialogues above, the woman and the man decline politely what the waiter is offering by using the expression لا شُكراً. They request their preferences also politely by stating directly what they want, using the phrase مِن فَضلِك "if you please."

Note the appropriate use of terms of address by the two waiters (آنسة and سَيِّد).

Also, the waiter responds to a request politely by the word حاضِر "*ready, all set,*" meaning that the order will be done instantly.

2. Food and Drink

Types of foods and drinks consumed in different cultures and the manner in which different people consume them vary tremendously. Below are descriptions of what some people in the Arab and American cultures in different situations drink and eat for breakfast.

ماذا يشربون ويأكُلون صباحاً؟

هذا مايكل بْراون. يَشْرَبُ مايكل صَباحاً فِنجانَ قَهوَةٍ مَعَ الحَليبِ والسُكَّرِ. ويأكُلُ مايكل في الصَباحِ الحُبوبَ مَعَ الحَليبِ عادَةً. لكِنَّ مايكل الآنَ في القاهِرةِ ويَأكُلُ هُناكَ صَباحاً الخُبْزَ والجُبْنَ والبَيْضَ ويَشرَبُ الشاي. يُحِبُّ مايكل القَهْوَةَ العَرَبِيَّةَ أَيْضاً.

هذه هالَة بُستاني. تَشْرَبُ هالَة كأسَ ماءٍ صَباحاً وتأكُلُ الخُبْزَ والجُبْنَ والزَيتونَ مَعَ فِنجانِ شاي. تَشْرَبُ هالَة الشاي مَعَ السُكَّرِ عادَةً في الصَباحِ لكِنَّها تَشْرَبُ القَهْوَةَ دونَ سُكَّرٍ أحياناً.

هذه كاثي وايت. هي تَدرُسُ اللُغَةَ العَرَبِيَّةَ في جامِعَةِ آركانسو. تَشْرَبُ كاثي فِنجانَ قَهْوَةٍ صَباحاً دونَ سُكَّرٍ أوْ تَشْرَبُ كَأسَ عَصيرِ بُرتُقال، لكِنَّها لا تَشْرَبُ الشاي. تأكُلُ قِطْعَةَ خُبزٍ مَعَ الزُبدَةِ ومُرَبّى البُرتُقالِ أو العَسَلِ.

- يأكُلُ الأمريكيّونَ صباحاً الحُبوبَ مَعَ الحَليبِ عادةً أو البَيْضَ ولَحْمَ الخِنْزيرِ ويَشْرَبونَ عَصيرَ البُرتُقالِ أوِ القَهْوَةَ أو الحَليب.
- يأكُلُ الفَرَنسِيّونَ عادَةً الخُبزَ والمُرَبّى في الصَباحِ ويَشْرَبونَ القَهْوَةَ.

- يأكُلُ العَرَبُ عادَةً الخُبْزَ والجُبْنَ والزَيْتونَ صَباحاً ويَشْرَبونَ الشاي.

وأنتَ يا طالِبَ اللُغَةِ العَرَبِيَّةِ ماذا تَشْرَبُ صَباحاً وماذا تأكُل؟

تمرين ١

Respond to this question: ماذا تَشْرَبُ صَباحاً وماذا تأكُل؟. Describe what you normally eat and drink in the morning for breakfast, or you may use the pictures below.

جُبْن

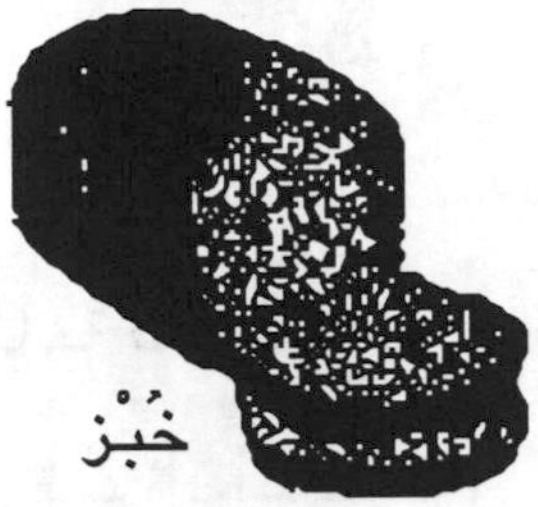
خُبْز

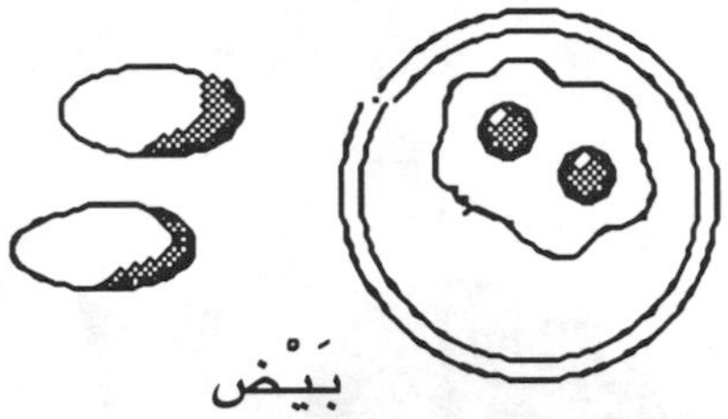
بَيْض

بُرتُقالة

تُفّاحة

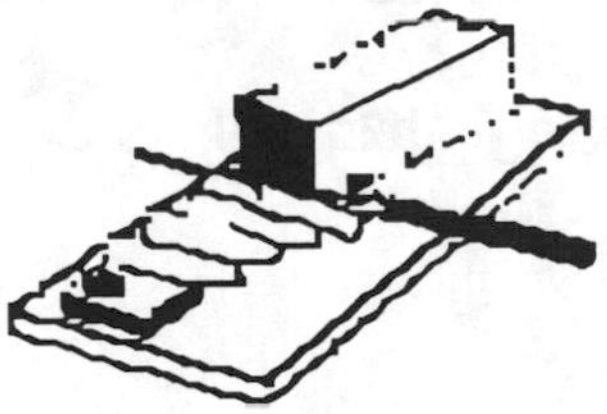
زُبْدة

فِنجان قَهْوة

3. **Describing Daily Activities**

Describing activities involves the use of verbs. Some activities are performed habitually (e.g. *eat*), others are in progress (e.g. *am eating*). The former type of activity is described by the simple present in English and the latter by the present continuous, or progressive. In Arabic, the simple present is called the indicative, or المضارع المرفوع, which is used for both the habitual and progressive aspects (e.g. أقرأ *I read/am reading*).

ماذا يَفْعَلُ مايكل براون؟

أنا مايكل بْراون. أدْرُسُ اللُّغَةَ العَرَبِيَّةَ في الجامِعَةِ الأمريكيَّةِ في القاهِرة في هذا الفَصْلِ الدِراسيّ. أسْكُنُ في

شَقَّةٍ في شارِعِ المازِنيّ. آكُلُ عادَةً في شَقَّتي صَباحاً الخُبزَ والبَيْضَ وأشرب الشايَ. عِندَ الظُّهْرِ آكُلُ أحْياناً في مَطعَمٍ اِسْمُهُ «نِعْمة». آكُلُ هُناكَ الفولَ أو الطَعْمِيَّةَ (الفلافِل). أُحِبُّ الفولَ والطَعْميّةَ كَثيراً، لكِنَّني لا أُحِبُّ اللَحْمَ. أحْياناً آكُلُ سَلَطةً في مَقْصَفِ الجامِعَة. مَساءً آكُلُ في مَقْصَفِ الجامِعةِ أو في مَطعَمٍ أو في شَقَّتي.

زِيادُ يَقْرَأُ الجَريدَةَ

- مَرْحَباً زِياد. ماذا تَفْعَلُ هُنا؟
- أقْرَأُ الجَريدَةَ وأشرَبُ قَهوَةَ. تَفَضَّلي اجْلِسي، يا هادية.
- لا شُكراً. أيّةَ جَريدَةٍ تَقْرَأ؟
- جَريدَةَ «النَهار». هُناكَ قَهوَةٌ في المَطْبَخ.
- لا أريدُ قَهوَةَ. شُكراً. أشْرَبُ الشاي.

تمرين ٢

A. Place a check mark (✔) next to the alternative in each item that matches the information in the passages and dialogues for this lesson.

١- الآنِسةُ في ......

❑ غُرفَةِ الصَفِّ ❑ المَطعَمِ ❑ البَيْتِ

٢- يُريدُ الرجلُ ......

❑ كأسَ ماءٍ ❑ فِنجانَ قَهوةٍ ❑ عَصيرَ بُرتُقالٍ

٣- مايكل براون في مِصرَ الآن. يَأكُلُ صَباحاً ......

❑ البَيْضَ ❑ الفولَ ❑ الحُبوبَ

٤- يُحِبُّ مايكل ...... كَثيراً.

❑ القَهوةَ الأمريكيةَ ❑ القَهوةَ العَرَبيَّةَ ❑ الشايَ

٥- تَشرَبُ هالَة بُستاني القَهوَةَ ......

❑ مَعَ السُكَّر ❑ دونَ سُكَّر ❑ مَعَ العَسَل

٦- تأكلُ كاثي وايْت صَباحاً الخُبزَ وَ......

❑ لَحْمَ الخِنزيرِ ❑ البَيْضَ ❑ العَسَلَ

٧- يأكلُ مايكل الطَعميّةَ في ......

❑ مَقْصَفِ الجامِعَةِ ❑ مَطعَمِ نِعمَةَ ❑ شَقَّتِه

٨- لا يُحِبُّ مايكل ......

❑ السَلَطةَ ❑ الفَلافِلَ ❑ اللَحْمَ

٩- يَقرأُ زِيادُ ......

❑ كِتاباً ❑ مَجَلَّةً ❑ جَريدةً

١٠- يَجلِسُ زِيادُ في ......

❑ البَيْتِ ❑ الشارِعِ ❑ المَطبَخِ

B. Mark these sentences either خَطَأ or صَـــواب according to the information in the reading passages and correct the false ones.

١١- تُريدُ هادية فِنجانَ قَهوة.

١٢- يَشْرَبُ مايكل القَهوَةَ مَعَ الحَليبِ والسُكَّر.

١٣- تَشرَبُ كاثي كأسَ عَصيرِ بُرتُقالٍ صَباحاً.

١٤- تأكلُ هالَة قِطعةَ خُبزٍ مَعَ الزُبدةِ والعَسَلِ صَباحاً.

C. Answer the following questions on the basis of the information in the reading passages.

١٥- مَتى يَشرَبُ مايكل الشايَ في القاهِرة؟

١٦- أينَ يأكلُ مايكل ظُهراً؟

١٧- مَتى تَشرَبُ هالَة الشاي؟

١٨- ماذا تأكُلُ كاثي صَباحاً؟

تمرين ٣

وافِق بَينَ الكَلِماتِ في العَمودَين:

١- شاي	....	مساءً
٢- مُرَبّى	....	حاضِر
٣- لَحْم	....	قَهوَة
٤- صَباحاً	....	بُرتُقال
٥- مَعَ	....	عَسَل
٦- مَطْعَم	....	كَأس
٧- يَشرَب	....	خِنزير
٨- عَصير	....	دونَ
		مَقصَف
		يَأكُل

تمرين ٤

Underline the word that does not belong in each set and explain your choice in English.

١- فول	طَعمِيَّة	مُرَبّى	فَلافِل
٢- دونَ	ظُهر	صَباح	مَساء
٣- عَصير	شاي	قَهوة	بُرتُقال
٤- ماء	حَليب	خُبز	شاي

تمرين ٥

اِختَرِ الكَلِمةَ المُناسِبة:

١- أشرَبُ صَباحاً ......

❑ قِطعَةَ خُبزٍ ❑ عَصيرَ بُرتُقال ❑ لَحْمَ خِنزير

٢- يَأكلُ سامي في ...... عِندَ الظُهر.

❑ مَطعَم ❑ مكتَب ❑ كُلِّيَّة

٣- يَأكلُ أبي صَباحاً الزُبدَةَ مَعَ ......

❑ الزَيتونِ ❑ الجُبنِ ❑ العَسَل

٤- تَشرَبُ أختي صَباحاً ...... فقَط.

❑ الماءَ ❑ المَقصَفَ ❑ المُرَبّى

٥- يَأكلُ الأمريكيّونَ في الصَباحِ عادةً ...... مَعَ الحَليب.

❑ القَهوَةَ ❑ السكَّرَ ❑ الحُبوبَ

تمرين ٦

Rearrange the words in each item to make meaningful sentences.

١- مِن، كَأس، أريدُ، فَضلِك، ماءٍ
٢- صَباحاً، سَمير، وَالجُبنَ، الشايَ، ويَشرَبُ، الخُبزَ، يَأكُلُ
٣- اللَحْمَ، الفَلافِلَ، يُحِبُّ، يُحِبُّ، لكِنَّهُ، مايكل، لا

4. The Imperative

The imperative form of the verb جَلَسَ "*sit*" is اجلِسْ for the second person masculine and اجْلِسي for the second person feminine. The latter form is used in the dialogue above. It immediately follows another imperative verb (تفضَّلي) "*if you please*," which is also imperative. The imperative is one of three forms of the Arabic verb: past, present, and imperative. It is normally used with the second person, as you can see in Table 1.

Notice the changes which the verb undergoes in order to assume the imperative form for the five persons. The stem of the present tense is used without the indicative prefix (يجلس ➡ جلِس) then a *hamza* with a *kasra* is prefixed (اجلِسْ). This is the form for the second person masculine singular. The dual takes an *alif* for a suffix (e.g. اجلِسا), the masculine plural takes the long vowel و and a final silent *alif* (اجلِسوا), and the feminine plural takes نَ as a suffix.

تمرين ٧

Ask the following people politely to sit down, as in the example.

Two men or women   اجلِسا مِن فَضْلِكُما.

1. A woman
2. A mixed group of five
3. A man
4. Four women
5. Three boys

Conjugation of جَلَسَ (يَجلِسُ)

	Imperative	Present	Pronoun	
		أجلِسُ	أنا	Singular
	اِجلِسْ	تَجلِسُ	أنتَ	
	اِجلِسي	تَجلِسينَ	أنتِ	
		يَجلِسُ	هو	
		تَجلِسُ	هي	
	اِجلِسا	تَجلِسانِ	أنتُما	Dual
		يَجلِسانِ	هُما (m.)	
		تَجلِسانِ	هُما (f.)	
		نَجلِسُ	نَحنُ	Plural
	اِجلِسوا	تَجلِسونَ	أنتُم	
	اِجلِسْنَ	تَجلِسْنَ	أنتُنَّ	
		يَجلِسونَ	هُم	
		يَجلِسْنَ	هُنَّ	

Table 1

5. **Expressing Likes and Dislikes**

The verb أَحَبَّ/يُحِبُّ "*to like*" is used to express likes. In order to express dislike, the same verb may be used with the negative particle **لا**. Examples:

١ أُحِبُّ عَصيرَ البُرتُقالِ. *I like orange juice*.

٢ لا أُحِبُّ الحَليبَ. *I don't like milk*.

Remember that the noun (e.g. عَصيرَ البُرتُقالِ، الحليبَ) following أُحِبُّ "*I like*" is the object of this verb and it must, therefore, be in the accusative case marked by a *fatḥa* for singular nouns or يـنَ for dual and some plural nouns.

6. **Prepositions and Attached Pronouns**

Attached pronouns may be suffixed to prepositions. In the exchange below, the first person singular attached pronoun ي "*me*" is suffixed to the preposition مِـن "*from*", resulting in مِنّـي "*from me.*"

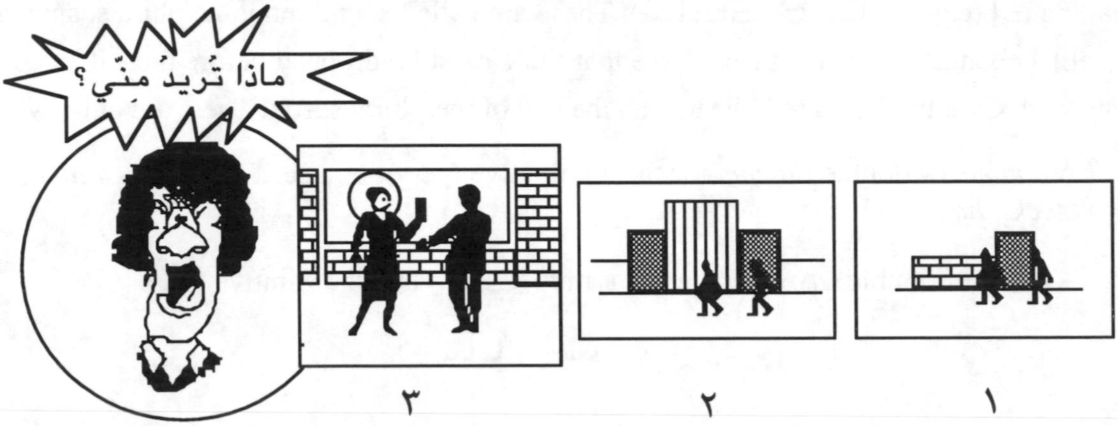

تمرين ٨

List three things you like and three things you do not like, as in the reading passages in this lesson. Provide inflectional markers on the ends of words.

١-	٤-
٢-	٥-
٣-	٦-

7. **Plurals of Nouns**

a. **Sound Masculine Plurals** (جَمْع مُذَكَّر سالِم): Some masculine nouns do not undergo any changes internally when transformed into a plural form. Such a noun usually refers to humans and is made plural by suffixing the ending ون to it if it is the subject of a sentence (nominative رَفْع) and by ين if it is the object of a verb (accusative نَصْب) or a preposition (genitive جَرّ). Such nouns are called sound masculine plurals:

٣ أمريكيّ ⇦ أمريكيّون/أمريكيّين *Americans*

Such nouns are called *sound* because no internal changes in the word occur and the same sequence of letters is retained intact in the plural form.

b. **Sound Feminine Plurals** (جَمع مُؤنَّث سالِم): Some feminine plurals display the ending ات (e.g. ساعة ⇦ ساعات). These are called sound feminine plurals, since no internal changes ever take place. Note that the ة must be dropped before the suffix ات is attached. Case markers are indicated on the end of the plural suffix. There are only two:

1. A *ḍamma* or double *ḍamma* for the nominative (رَفع): ساعاتُ، ساعاتٌ *watches, clocks, hours.*
2. A *kasra* or double *kasra* for the accusative (نَصب) and the genitive (جَرّ):

ساعاتِ ساعاتٍ

c. **Broken Plurals** (جَمْع تَكسير): Other nouns, feminine and masculine, are made plural through internal changes whereby addition and/or deletion of long and short vowels occur. These are called broken plurals, e.g.

٤	جَريدة	⇦	جَرائِد
٥	كِتاب	⇦	كُتُب.

Note that the consonants remain unchanged in the plural form. Only short and long vowels are dropped, added, or changed from one position to another. Case markers appear on the end of the plural form just as they would on the end of a singular form:

كُتُبٌ - كُتُباً - كُتُبٍ

You are advised to learn the plural form of a noun along with the singular.

SUMMARY

1. Sound masculine plural nouns are formed by suffixing ون to subjects and ين to objects.
2. Sound feminine plural nouns are formed by suffixing ات to the noun.
3. Broken plurals are formed through internal changes in the word.

تمرين ٩

Underline all sound masculine plural nouns and adjectives, place a dotted line under sound feminine plurals, and box broken plurals, as in the examples. There may be more than one plural form in each sentence.

أساتذةٌ أمريكيون – أميناتٌ مكتَبات – طلاّبٌ عرَب.

١ـ السَيّاراتُ اليابانِيّة سَيّاراتٌ جَيِّدة.

٢ـ هؤلاءِ طلاّبٌ ماليزيّون.

٣ـ هُناكَ بَناتٌ وأبناءٌ كَثيرون في عائلاتِ المِصريّين.

٤ـ في كُلِيَّتي حَواسيبُ كَثيرة.

٥ـ يأكُلُ السوريّونَ الجُبنَ والزَيتونَ صَباحاً.

٦ـ مَن مَعَهُ أقلامٌ في حَقيبَتِه؟

تمرين ١٠

Express these meanings in Arabic with reference to the information about Arabic plural nouns and to previous glossaries to verify broken plurals.

1. We have three French (female) students in our class.
2. I have three pencils with me.
3. There are five telephones in this room.
4. Do you know any Korean students?
5. There are three tables and six chairs in the teachers' room.

8. Adverbials

An adverbial modifies a verb, indicating the time, place, or manner in which it occurred. Usually, it is an indefinite noun to which a double *fatḥa* is suffixed, indicating that it is in the accusative case (نَصْب):

٦ صَباح ⇦ صَباحاً مَساء ⇦ مَساءً

The adverbial meaning may also be expressed with a prepositional phrase. For example, the adverbial صَباحاً *"in the morning"* may be expressed as follows: في الصَباحِ (a prepositional phrase). Note that the noun in the prepositional phrase is definite. The same preposition may be used to refer to the evening (في المساء). But with reference to noontime, another preposition is used (عِندَ الظُهْرِ).

Another adverbial used in this lesson is كَثيراً *"a great deal."* It is based on the adjective كَثير *"much."* This adverbial is used in the passage above to modify the verb أُحِبُّ, expressing degree, as in أُحِبُّ العَسَلَ كَثيراً *"I like honey very much."*

تمرين ١١

List three activities which you do at three different times of the day, using adverbials or prepositional phrases to indicate the time of the activity.

9. *Iḍāfa* Structure Revisited

In this lesson, extensive use of the *iḍāfa* structure is made. There are seventeen instances of it altogether throughout the passages and dialogues, including repeated ones. One example is قطعةُ خُبزٍ *"piece of bread."* This phrase is indefinite because the second (or last) part of the phrase is indefinite (خُبزٍ), whereas the phrase عَصير البُرتُقال is definite because of the definite article prefixed to the second part (البُرتُقال).

One of the *iḍāfa* structures is كَأس عَصيرِ بُرتُقال. Literally, it means *"a glass of juice of orange,"* in this order. The phrase contains more than two words. This is known as a multiple *iḍāfa*, where more than two parts constitute the structure. This is also an indefinite *iḍāfa* phrase.

تمرين ١٢

Identify at least six *iḍāfa* structures in the reading passages above and provide their meanings.

تمرين ١٣

A. Listen to the tape-recorded passage and check the best alternative according to the passage.

١ـ تَشرَبُ سُعادُ صَباحاً ......

❑ قَهوةً ❑ ماءً ❑ سُكَّراً

٢ـ تَشرَبُ سُعادُ الشايَ صَباحاً مَعَ ......

❑ السُكَّرِ والحَليبِ ❑ الخُبزِ والجُبنِ ❑ الدَجاجِ واللَحمِ

٣ـ تَأكلُ سُعادُ ظُهراً ......

❑ الدَجاجَ أو اللَحمَ ❑ الجُبنَ أو الزَيْتونَ ❑ العَسَلَ أو المَرَبّى

B. Mark these statements خطأ or صواب according to the recorded passage and correct the false ones:

٤ـ لا تُحِبُّ سُعادُ صيداوي أكلَ اللَحمِ.

٥ـ تأكلُ سُعادُ السَلَطةَ مَساءً.

٦ـ تَشرَبُ سُعادُ القَهوةَ العَرَبيَّةَ.

C. Answer these questions according to the passage:

٧ـ مَتى تَأكُلُ سُعادُ البُرتُقالَ؟

٨ـ ماذا تَأكُلُ سُعادُ مَساءً؟

المُفْرَدات

to like .... أحَبَّ (يُحِبُّ) حُبّ، مَحَبّة (v.)
to want .... أراد (يُريدُ) (v.)
to eat .... أكَلَ (يأكُلُ) (v.)
orange .... بُرتُقال (n., m.)
egg .... بَيْض (n., m.)
apple .... تُفّاح (n., m.)
cheese .... جُبْن ج أجْبان (n., m.)
to sit down [14] .... جَلَسَ (يَجلِسُ) جُلوس (اجلِسْ) (v.) (imperative)
ready, all set (polite expression) .... حاضِر (participle)
grain, cereal .... حَبّ ج حُبوب (n., m.)
milk .... حَليب (n., m.)
bread .... خُبْز (n., m.)
pig, swine .... خِنزير ج خَنازير (n., m.)
without .... دونَ (prep.)
butter .... زُبْدة (n., f.)
olive .... زَيْتون (n., m.)
sugar .... سُكَّر (n., m.)
salad .... سَلَطة ج سَلَطات (n., f.)
tea .... شاي (n., m.)
to drink .... شَرِبَ (يَشْرَبُ) (v.)
morning .... صَباح (n., m.)
patty made from ground beans and spices fried in oil (Egypt) .... طَعْمِيّة (n., f.)
noon .... ظُهْر (n., m.)
honey .... عَسَل (n., m.)

juice .... (n., m.) عَصير

patty made from ground beans and spices fried in oil (Syria) .... (n., m.) فُلفُل ج فَلافِل

cup .... (n., m.) فِنْجان ج فَناجين

fava beans .... (n., m.) فول

piece .... (n., f.) قِطْعة ج قِطَع

coffee .... (n., f.) قَهْوة

glass .... (n., f.) كَأس ج كُؤوس

a great deal .... (adverbial) كَثيراً

meat .... (n., m.) لَحْم ج لُحوم

water .... (n., m.) ماء ج مِياه

when .... (question particle) مَتى

jam, preserve .... (n., m.) مُرَبّى ج مُرَبَّيات

evening .... (n., m.) مَساء

kitchen .... (n., m.) مَطْبَخ ج مَطابِخ

restaurant .... (n., m.) مَطْعَم ج مَطاعِم

cafeteria .... (n., m.) مَقْصَف ج مَقاصِف

Lesson Fifteen الدَّرْسُ الخامِسَ عَشَر

Objectives

- Describing activities and background.
- Daily schedules.
- Telling time formally and informally.
- Breaking consonant clusters.
- The initial sound of the article.
- Mass and count nouns.
- Numbers: reading hundreds and thousands.
- Listen to the recorded material for this lesson.
- Do relevant computer drills and exercises, Stage 5 (Telling Time), Stage 7.

سَحَر في جامِعةِ حَلَب

تَدرُسُ سَحَر حَلاّق التِجارةَ في جامِعةِ حَلَبَ في سورية. هِيَ مِن دِمَشقَ وتَسكُنُ مَعَ طالِبَةٍ مِن دِمَشقَ أيْضاً اِسمُها هالَة بُستاني. عِندَ سَحَر أربَعُ مَوادَّ في هذا الفَصلِ هِيَ الرِياضِيّاتُ واللُغَةُ الإنكليزيَّةُ والمُحاسَبةُ والإحْصاء.

مَوْعِدُ دَرسِ الرياضيّاتِ في الساعَةِ التاسِعَةِ صَباحاً، ومَوْعِدُ دَرْسِ اللُغَةِ الإنكليزيَّةِ في العاشِرة. بَعْدَ دَرْسِ الإنكليزيَّةِ تَقرَأُ سَحَر مَجَلاّتٍ وَجَرائِدَ إنكليزيَّةً في المكتَبَةِ. عِندَ الظُهْرِ تَأكلُ سَلَطةً أو فَلافِلَ أو حِمَّصاً في مَقْصَفِ الجامِعَة. أحْياناً تأكلُ الكَبابَ الحَلَبِيّ. في الساعَةِ الواحِدةِ مَوْعِدُ دَرْسِ المُحاسَبَةِ، وفي الساعَةِ الثالِثةِ تَدرُسُ الإحْصاءَ. بَعدَ ذلِكَ تَدرُسُ سَحَر في المَكتَبَةِ مِنَ الساعَةِ الرابِعَةِ إلى السادِسةِ مَعَ طُلاّبٍ وطالِباتٍ مِن صَفِّها.

مايْكل بْراوْن في القاهِرَة

اسمي مايكِل بْراوْن. أنا مِن وِلايةِ أوهايو في الوِلاياتِ المُتّحِدةِ الأمريكيّةِ. يَسكُنُ أبي وأمّي (جاك ومارثا بْراون) في مَدينَةِ سِنسِناتي وتَسكُنُ أختي لين في توليدو، وهي لا تَدرُسُ الآن. يَدرُسُ أخي ريتشارد في جامِعَةِ وِلايةِ أوهايو في كَلَمبَس. هذِهِ جامِعَتي أيْضاً أدرُسُ فيها العَلاقاتِ الدوْلِيَّة.

أنا الآنَ في الجامِعَةِ الأمريكيَّةِ بِالقاهِرة أدرُسُ اللُغَةَ العَرَبِيَّةَ وأدَبَها. مَوعِدُ دَرسِ اللُغَةِ العَرَبِيَّةِ في الساعَةِ الثامِنةِ صَباحاً وأسْتاذَةُ هذِهِ المادةِ هِيَ زَيْنَب طه.[3] ومَوعِدُ دَرسِ الأدَبِ العَرَبيِّ في الساعَةِ الحادِيةَ عَشْرَةَ واسمُ أُسْتاذِها عَبّاس التونِسي. أحِبُّ دُروسَ العَرَبِيَّةِ كَثيراً.

في مَقصَفِ جامِعَةِ القاهِرَةِ أتَكَلَّمُ عادَةً بِالعَرَبيّةِ مَعَ سَمير عَبدِ الفَتّاح وهُوَ طالِبٌ مِصريّ مِن مَدينةِ طَنْطا في مِصر. هذا هو أوَّلُ حَديثٍ بِاللُغةِ العَرَبيةِ مَعَ سَمير.

سَمير: مَرحباً.

مايْكِل: أهلاً.

سَمير: اسمي سَمير عَبدُ الفَتّاح.

مايْكِل: تَشَرَّفنا. أنا مايْكِل بْراون.

سَمير: تَشَرَّفنا. مِن أيْنَ أنْت؟

مايْكِل: أنا مِن وِلايَةِ أوهايو في أمريكا.

---

3 Pronounced ṭāhā.

سَمير: ماذا تَفعَلُ هُنا في القاهِرة؟

مايْكِل: أدرُسُ اللغةَ العربيـة. وأنت؟

سَمير: أنا أدرُسُ الهَندَسَة. تَتَكلَّمُ العَرَبِيَّةَ جَيِّداً.

مايْكِل: شكراً. لَيْسَ جَيِّداً جِدّاً. وأنتَ، هل تَتَكلَّمُ الإنكليزيَّة؟

سَمير: نَعَم. قَليلاً. أينَ تَسكُنُ الآن؟

مايْكِل: هُنا في القاهِرة.

سَمير: أعرِف.... يَعني هل تَسكُنُ في سَكَنِ الطلاّب؟

مايْكِل: لا. في شَقَّة.

سَمير: مَن يَسكُنُ مَعَك؟

مايْكِل: لا يسكُنُ مَعي أحَد. أسكُنُ وَحْدي.

تمرين ١

A. Check the alternative in each item that best corresponds with the information in the reading passages above.

١- سَحَر حَلاّق مِن مَدينَةِ ......

❑ دِمَشق ❑ حَلَب ❑ القاهِرة

٢- تَسكُنُ سَحَر ......

❑ وَحدَها ❑ مَعَ طالِبَة ❑ مَعَ ثَلاثِ طالِبات

٣- تَدرُسُ سَحَر في هذا الفَصْلِ ......

❑ مَجلاّتٍ وَجَرائِدَ ❑ اللُّغَةَ الإنكليزيَّة ❑ اللُّغَةَ العَرَبيَّة

٤- تأكلُ سَحَر عِندَ الظُهرِ في ...... الجامِعة.

❑ مَكتَبَةِ ❑ مَقصَفِ ❑ مَطعَمِ

٥- مَوعِدُ دَرْسِ المُحاسَبَةِ في الساعَةِ ......

❑ العاشِرَةِ صَباحاً ❑ الواحِدةِ بَعْدَ الظُهرِ ❑ الثالِثةِ بَعْدَ الظُهرِ

٦- اِسْمُ أُختِ مايْكِل بْراون ......

❑ مارثا ❑ لين ❑ كاثي

٧- يَدرُسُ مايْكِل الآنَ في مَدينَةِ ......

❑ سِنسِناتي ❑ كَلَمبَس ❑ القاهِرة

٨- يَتَكلَّمُ مايْكِل العَرَبيَّةَ في مَقصَفِ الجامِعَةِ مَعَ ......

❑ سَمير عَبدِ الفَتّاح ❑ زَينب طه ❑ عبّاسِ التونِسيّ

٩- يَدرُسُ سَمير عَبدُ الفَتّاح ......

❑ العَلاقاتِ الدَوْليّة ❑ الأدَبَ العَرَبيَّ ❑ الهَندَسَةَ

B. Mark the following statements خطأ or صَـواب according to the information in the reading passages and correct the false ones.

١٠- عِندَ سَحَر حَلاّق ثَلاثُ مَوادٍّ في هذا الفَصْل.

١١- تَقرَأُ سَحَر الجَرائِدَ في المَكتَبَةِ بَعدَ دَرسِ المُحاسَبَة.

١٢- تَدرُسُ سَحَر مَعَ طُلاّبٍ وطالِباتٍ مِن صَفِّها بَعدَ دَرسِ الإحْصاء.

١٣- يَدرُسُ مايكل الأدَبَ العَرَبيَّ مَعَ الأستاذِ عبّاس التونِسيّ.

١٤- يَدرُسُ أخو مايكل في جامِعةِ ولايَةِ أوهايو.

تمرين ٢

A. Fill in Saḥar's daily schedule as per the information in the above passage. List the types of activities she is involved in next to the appropriate times.

الساعةَ	ماذا تَفعلُ سَحَر ؟
٨	
٩	
١٠	
١١	
١٢	
١	
٢	
٣	
٤	
٥	

B. Provide your own schedule on a particular day, showing at least three times and the activities involved.

Womens' Islamic Dress: Women's Islamic dress includes a headdress which covers the hair. Islamic attire has become very popular among women in the Arab world.

تمرين ٣

Fill in the names in the Brown family tree (Chart A) with information from the passage above. Fill in the boxes in the other tree (Chart B) with information about your own family or another family you know. Insert additional names as needed. In part C, write

down details about the members of the family in Chart B in a manner similar to Michael Brown's account of his family.

A. عائلَةُ بْراوْن

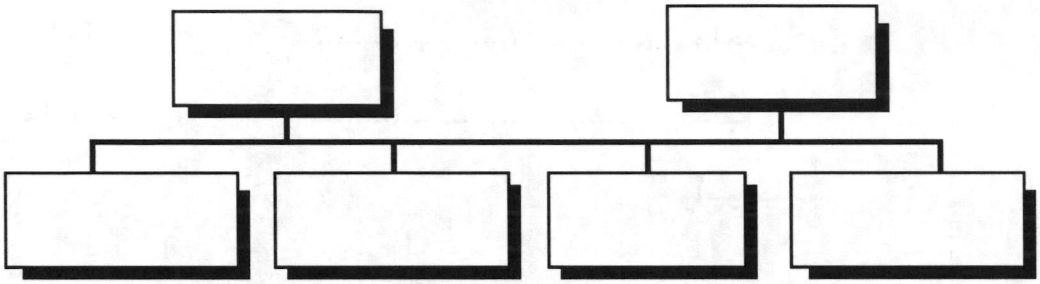

B. عائلَةُ ....

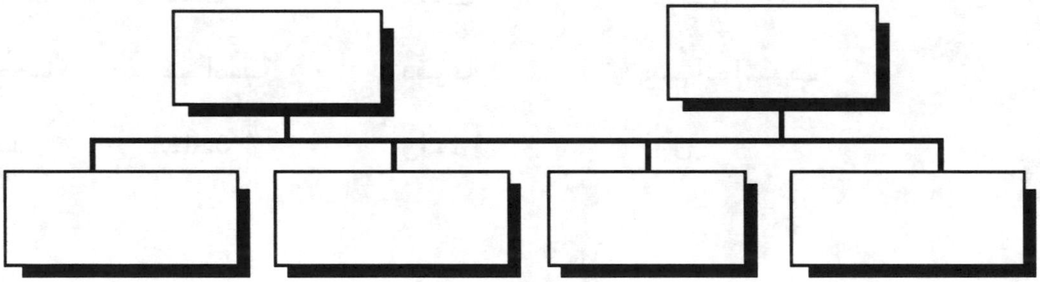

C.

تمرين ٤

وافِق بَينَ الكَلِماتِ في العَمودَين:

١- أوّل	....	دَقيقَة
٢- الوِلاياتُ المُتّحِدةُ	....	العَلاقاتُ الدَوْليّةُ
٣- ساعَة	....	واحِد
٤- مادّة	....	كُليّة
		أمريكا

تمرين ٥

Underline the word that does not belong in each set and explain your choice in English.

١-	رُبْع	نِصْف	ثُلْث	كَثير
٢-	مَوعِد	حِمّص	كَباب	فَلافِل
٣-	إحْصاء	مُحاسَبَة	دَقيقَة	عِلمُ الحاسوب
٤-	أحَد	حاضِر	واحِد	أوّل

تمرين ٦

Rearrange the words in each item to make meaningful sentences.

١- مِن، كَأسَ، أريدُ، فَضلِك، ماءٍ

٢- صَباحاً، سَمير، وَالجُبنَ، الشايَ، وَيَشرَبُ، الخُبزَ، يأكُلُ

٣- الساعةِ، الظُهر، المُحاسَبَةِ، في، مَوعِدُ، الواحِدةِ، بعدَ، دَرْسِ

1. Telling Time

كَمِ الساعَة؟

الساعَةُ الواحِدَة

Telling time formally in Arabic involves the use of ordinal numbers. Formal telling of time is a daily practice on the radio and television throughout the Arab world, and it is the form used in this lesson. However, reference will be made to the manner of telling time in informal situations. You may have noticed from the caption below the clock face that الواحدة is not an ordinal number, yet it is used to tell time. This is, in fact, the only exception. The feminine form of the cardinal number واحد is used with the definite article, forming an adjective that agrees with the noun السَاعَة.

a. **Grammatical Structure**: The phrase used in telling time is a noun phrase; that is, it is made up of a noun and an adjective:

١ الساعَةُ الثانيةُ *two o'clock*

where الساعَةُ is the feminine noun and الثانيةُ is the adjective modifying it. Note that they agree in number, gender, and case. For example, in response to the question مَتى دَرسُ العربية؟ *"At what time is the Arabic class?"* you may say: في الساعةِ الثانيةِ. Notice that both the noun and the adjective acquire a *kasra* on their ends as a marker of the genitive case brought about by the preposition في. This description applies to times from *one o'clock* through *ten o'clock.* For *11* and *12*, compound numbers are used.

Remember that compound numbers *11-19* are invariable; that is, they have one form that does not change regardless of case. Notice how السـاعـةُ changes to السـاعـةِ following the preposition فـي, but not the number:

٢ السـاعَةُ الحادِيـةَ عَشْرَةَ ⇦ في السـاعـةِ الحادِيـةَ عَشْرَةَ

٣ السـاعَةُ الثانِيـةَ عَشْرَةَ ⇦ في السـاعـةِ الثانِيـةَ عَشْرَةَ

b. **Fractions of an Hour**: Telling time with fractions of an hour differs a little from the way it is done in English. The fractions used are the words for *half, third, quarter,* and *minute.* Examine the examples below:

The time on the right is 5:07 and the one on the left is 1:20 p.m. Note that hours and fractions are connected with the conjunction وَ, and that they are all definite with the exception of minutes. Examples:

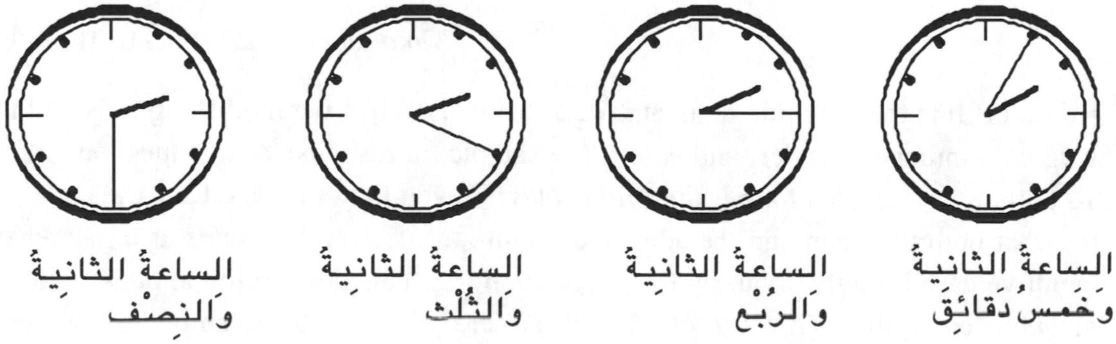

For the times above, the minute hand is on the right-hand side of the clock dial and the particle وَ *"and"* is used. When the minute hand is on the left-hand side, another particle is used with hours and fractions. This particle is إلاّ "*except, minus.*" It is used with all times in the left-hand side except with the first nine minutes after the half-hour mark. The noun following إلاّ is accusative (مَنصوب) and indefinite:

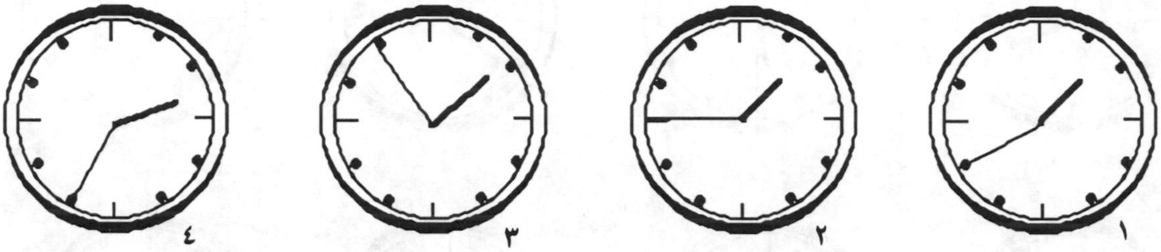

١ الساعةُ الثانيةُ إلاّ ثُلْثاً

٢ الساعةُ الثانيةُ إلاّ رُبْعاً

٣ الساعةُ الثانيةُ إلا خَمْسَ دَقائِق

٤ الساعةُ الثانيةُ وَالنصْفُ وَخَمْسُ دَقائِق

There is a variation to example 4, which is used to tell time up to 39 minutes after the hour. It makes use of hours and minutes only:

الساعَةُ الثانِيةُ وَخَمْسٌ وَثَلاثونَ دَقيقية

The diagram below summarizes the information about the uses of وَ and إلاّ.

SUMMARY

- In telling time, a noun phrase is used where the number indicating the time is an ordinal number: الساعَةُ الثانِيةُ وَالنِصْفُ.
- The numbers *11* and *12* are invariable: الساعةُ الثانيةَ عَشْرَةَ.
- The fractions of an hour used are: نِصْف، ثُلْث، رُبْع، دَقيقة.
- The particle وَ is inserted between the hour and fractions.
- The particle إلاّ is used to indicate times *until* the hour (40-59 minutes).

تمرين ٧

Under each clock face, indicate the time shown. Provide the short vowels on the ends of all words, assuming that السـاعـةُ is nominative (مَرفوع).

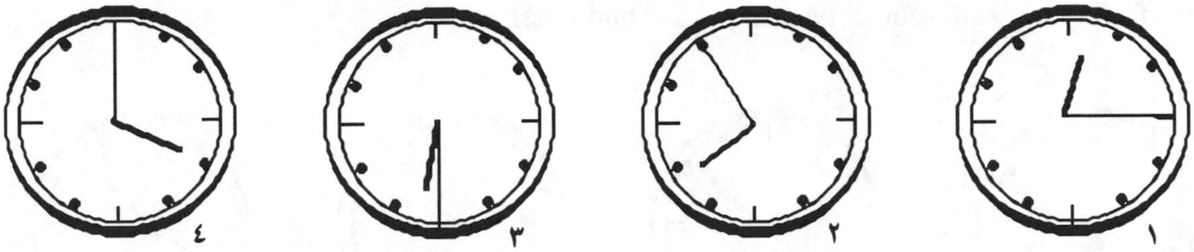

١ ٢ ٣ ٤

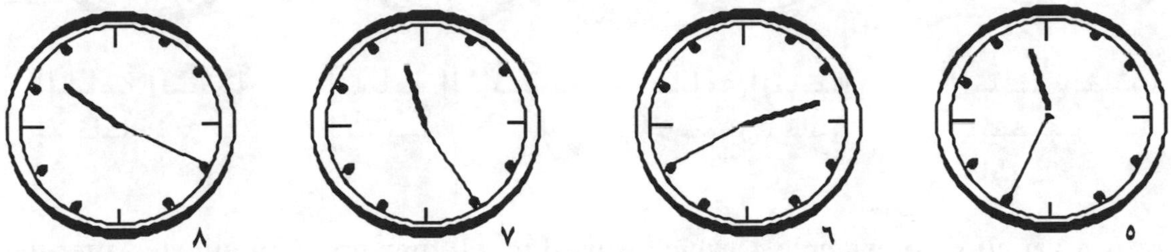

٥ ٦ ٧ ٨

c. **Telling Time Informally**: Telling time informally almost verges on using colloquial forms. In many Arabic colloquial varieties cardinal numbers are used instead of ordinal numbers. Also, the forms are not definite. Thus, to indicate *7:30* and *10:15*, for example, in an informal way, you say:

٤ الساعة سَبعة ونِصف[4]

٥ الساعة عَشَرة ورُبْع

This practice may still be acceptable in a formal setting when used orally so long as the phonology and morphology (pronunciation and structure) of the words comply with the standard norms. Remember, however, that in writing it is recommended that you use the standard forms discussed above.

In order to indicate minutes after or before the hour, you may drop the word for "minutes." Examine these examples:

[4] The word نِصْف "half" is pronounced نِص in several Arabic dialects.

٦ الساعة سَبعة وعَشَرة

٧ الساعة أربعة إلاّ خمسة

Notice also that the conjunction وَ (*wa*) is pronounced *w* without the *fatḥa* (e.g. *sab'a w 'ashara*).

2. Breaking Consonant Clusters

The question particles مَن and كم, which end in consonants, acquire a *kasra* on their ends to prevent two consonants from coming together (the final consonant of the particle and the first consonant of the following word). Thus, to avoid a consonant cluster, which is not tolerated in Arabic, a short vowel (*kasra*) is inserted between the two consonants. Examples:

٨ كَمِ الساعة؟

٩ مَنِ الأستاذ؟

3. Suppressing the Initial Sound of the Article

The initial sound of the definite article (the glottal stop plus *-a*), is normally dropped when a prefix is attached to the word or preceded by another word. For example, the word العربية starts with the definite article *al-*, and is pronounced *al-'arabiyya* when the word stands independently. But with the prefix بِـ the *a-* part is dropped (*bil-'arabiyya*). The same process occurs when the conjunction وَ is prefixed (وَالعربية is pronounced *wa-l-'arabiyya*).

4. Mass and Count Nouns

A noun may refer to the general class of something, *cheese*, for example. This noun is known as a mass noun. In Arabic, one way of creating a count noun from a mass noun is by simply adding a *tā' marbūṭa* to the noun:

١٠ تُفّاح *apple* ⇦ تُفّاحة *an apple*

تمرين ٨

Form count nouns from the following mass nouns that occurred in the previous lesson. Provide the meaning of each count noun you form.

١- بُرتُقال ٢- خُبز

٣- زَيتون ٤- بَيْض

٥- فول ٦- سُكَّر

5. Numbers: Reading Hundreds and Thousands

The Arabic word for *thousand* is ألف (plural آلاف). It is a noun and, therefore, it forms with the counted noun an *iḍāfa* structure, where the noun must be singular, genitive, indefinite:

ألفُ رَجُلٍ

The word رَجُلٍ is genitive marked by a double *kasra* because it is indefinite. Traditionally, Arabic numbers used to be read from *right to left*; that is, ones, tens, hundreds, and then thousands. For example, the number 1246 is read from right to left in this manner:

١١ سِتٌّ وأربَعون ومِئَتانِ وألف ١ ٢ ٤ ٦

Although this style is still practiced by a few radio and television announcers, another style of reading numbers is more prevalent today. When reading a number, you start with the highest category. Thus, in order to read 5246, read from *left to right*, as in English. Start with the thousands, then read the hundreds, skip the tens, read the ones, then finally read the tens, as follows:

١٢ خَمسةُ آلافٍ ومِئتان وسِتٌّ وأربعون ٥ ٢ ٤ ٦

Start here

The conjunction وَ is inserted before every category, as you can see in the examples above.

تمرين ٩

Spell out these numbers in words:

١- ٩٠٧

٢- ٤٧٨٣

٣- ١٣٦٨٥

تمرين ١٠

Make questions in Arabic to inquire about the following and then answer them, as in the example:

What is Michael's sister's name? (Use ما to form this question.)

ما اسمُ أختِ مايكل؟
اِسمُ أختِ مايكل لين.

1. When does Saḥar eat in the cafeteria? (مَتى)
2. At what time does Saḥar have statistics? (في أيّةِ ساعَة)
3. What's the name of Michael Brown's Arabic language professor? (ما)
4. Where do Michael's parents live? (أينَ)

تمرين ١١

A. Listen to the tape-recorded passage and check the best alternative according to the passage.

١- اِسْمُ هذا الطالبِ ......

❑ عَبدُالله ❑ عادِل ❑ أشرَف

٢- يَدرُسُ هذا الطالِبُ الأدَبَ ......

❑ العَرَبيَّ ❑ الإنكليزيَّ ❑ الفَرَنسيَّ

٣- أُستاذُ مادّةِ اللُغَةِ الإنكليزيّةِ هو الدُكتور ......

❑ جَزائِري ❑ ديفيس ❑ عَبدُ السلام

٤- أستاذُ مادّةِ الأدَبِ الإنكليزيِّ مِن ......

❑ الأردن ❑ مِصر ❑ بريطانيا

B. Mark the following statements صَواب or خطأ based on the information in the tape-recorded passage and correct the false ones.

٥- يَدرُسُ عادِل في جامِعَةٍ بريطانيّة.

٦- أشرَفُ طالبٌ في الجامِعةِ الأردُنيّة.

٧- أستاذُ مادةِ اللُغَةِ الإنكليزيّةِ بريطانيٌ.

٨- مَوعِدُ مادّةِ الأدَبِ في الساعةِ الواحِدَة.

C. Do the following:

9. Write out the daily schedule of the person described in the listening passage.

10. What is the title used in the listening passage to refer to a university professor?

المُفْرَدات

أَحَد ج آحاد (n., m.)	one
إِحْصاء (n., m.)	statistics
إلاّ (particle)	except, minus
أَلْف ج آلاف (n., m.)	thousand
بَعْدَ (preposition)	after
ثُلْث ج أَثْلاث (n., m.)	a third
حَديث ج أحاديث (n., m.)	conversation
حمّص[5] (n., m.)	dip prepared from chickpeas, sesame seed paste, lemon juice
دَقيقَة ج دَقائِق (n., f.)	minute
دَوْلِيّ (n., m.)	international
رُبْع ج أَرْباع (n., m.)	quarter
ساعَة ج ساعات (n., f.)	o'clock, hour
عَلاقة ج عَلاقات (n., f.)	relation
عَنى (يَعْني) (v.)	to mean
كَباب (n., m.)	kebob, minced meat on a skewer with parsley and onion
مُتَّحِد (adj., m.)	united
مُحاسَبة (n., f.)	accounting
مَوْعِد ج مَواعيد (n., m.)	time, appointment
نِصْف ج أَنْصاف (n., m.)	half
هُنا (demonstrative)	here
وَحْدَهُ (adv.)	alone, by himself
الوِلاياتُ المُتَّحِدةُ الأمريكيّة (n., f.)	the United States of America

[5] In colloquial speech, this word is pronounced حُمُّص (*ḥommoṣ*)

Lesson Sixteen الدَرْسُ السادِسَ عَشَرَ

Objectives

- Describing people, objects, possessions, and activities.
- Culture notes (family, women, geography, history, headgear).
- The past tense: conjugation and negation الماضي.
- Verbal nouns المصدر.
- Noun-adjective agreement revisited (number, gender, case, definiteness).
- Listen to the recorded material for this lesson.
- Do relevant computer drills and exercises, Stages 5 and 6 (Text 1).

لُؤلُؤَة القَطامي

فَتاةٌ عَرَبيّةٌ مِن قَطَر

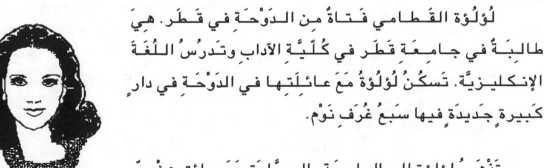

لُؤلُؤة القَطامي فَتاةٌ مِن الدَوْحَةِ في قَطَر. هِيَ طالِبَةٌ في جامِعَةِ قَطَر في كُلّيَّةِ الآدابِ وتَدرُسُ اللُغَةَ الإنكليزيَّة. تَسكُنُ لُؤلُؤةُ مَعَ عائِلَتِها في الدَوْحَةِ في دارٍ كَبيرةٍ جَديدَةٍ فيها سَبعُ غُرَفِ نَوْم.

تَذْهَبُ لؤلؤة إلى الجامِعَةِ بِالسيَّارَةِ مَعَ سائِقٍ هِنْديّ. هُناكَ سائِقٌ ثانٍ مِنَ الباكِسْتان تَذهَبُ مَعَهُ أمُّها إلى السوقِ وإلى بُيوتِ صَديقاتِها. لِعائِلَةِ القَطامي ثَلاثُ سَيّارات. الأولى سَيارةٌ أمريكيّةٌ كَبيرة (كاديلاك) وهِيَ لِلأُم.

والسيّارةُ الثانِيةُ مَرسيدس ألمانيةٌ وهِيَ لِلأب. والسَيّارةُ الثالِثةُ تويوتا يابانِيّةٌ تَذهَبُ بِها لُؤلُؤةُ وإخوَتُها إلى الجامِعةِ والمَدارِس.

لُؤلُؤةُ فَتاةٌ جَميلَة. هِيَ لَيْسَتْ طويلةً ولَيْسَتْ قَصيرة، لكِنَّ أُختَها الصَغيرة عائِشة طَويلَة. تُحِبُّ لُؤلُؤة دِراسَةَ اللُغَةِ الإنكليزيَّة، وهِيَ تَذهَبُ إلى مَكتَبَةِ الجامِعَةِ بَعدَ الظُهرِ وتَقْرَأُ هُناكَ الجَرائِدَ والمجلاّتِ الإنكليزيّة.

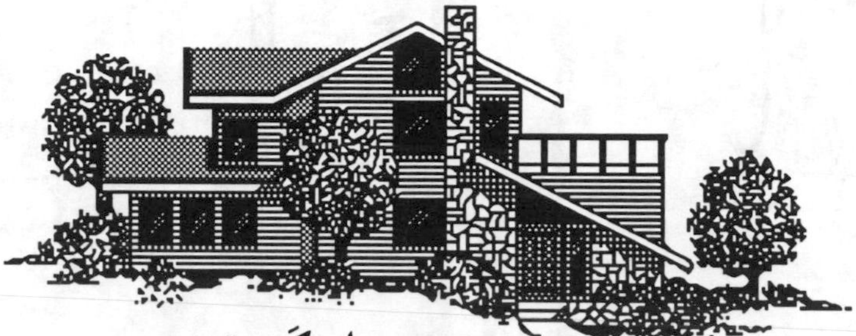

دار كَبيرة

دار صَغيرة

لِلُؤلُؤةُ أُخْتانِ وأخَوان. أُخْتاها دانَة وعائِشة في المدرسةِ الثانَوِيّة. أخوها الصَغيرُ حَسَن في الصَفِّ العاشِرِ الثانَويّ. أخوها الكَبيرُ حُسَيْن في الكُوَيْتِ الآن. وهُوَ يَسكُنُ ويَعْمَلُ هُناك. يَسكُنُ حُسَيْنُ في شَقَّةٍ في شارِعِ حَمَدِ المُبارَك. عِندَ حُسَيْن سَيّارة پورش ألمانيّة وهِيَ سَيّارَةٌ حَديثَةٌ وجَميلَة لَها مُحَرِّكٌ قَويّ. يُحِبُّ حُسَيْنُ السَيّاراتِ الألمانيةَ كَثيراً.

حسين القطامي

سيارة حَديثة

سيّارة قَديمة

دَرَسَ حُسَيْن التِجارةَ في لندن وسكن فيها أربعَ سَنَوات. يحِبُّ حسين العَمَلَ بالحاسوب لكِنَّهُ ما دَرَسَ عِلمَ الحاسوب.حُسَيْن رجل طويل ووَسيم، لكنْ لَيسَ له زَوجة الآن ولا يسكن أحدٌ معه في شقّتِهِ. يَلبَسُ حُسَيْن الكوفيّةَ والعِقال.

فتاةٌ جَميلة

رَجُلٌ وَسيم

قَلَمٌ قَصير

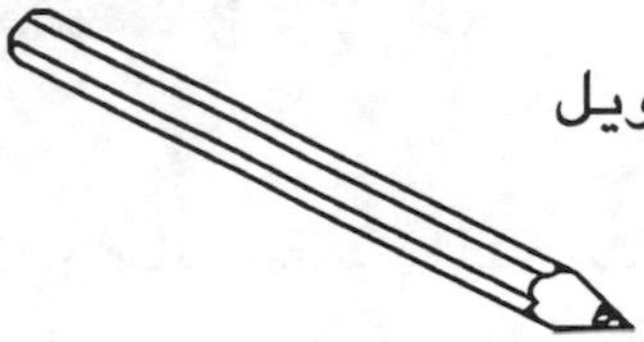

قَلَمٌ طَويل

تمرين ١

Explain these items in Arabic or English according to the reading passage.

١ـ الدَوْحَة ٢ـ سَيّارَةُ حُسَيْن ٣ـ شارِعُ حَمَدِ المُبارَك

تمرين ٢

A. Check the alternative in each item that corresponds with the information in the passage above:

١ـ لُؤلُؤةُ فَتاةٌ مِن ......

❑ الكُويتِ ❑ قَطَرَ ❑ الباكستان

٢ـ تَدرُسُ لُؤلُؤةُ ......

❑ اللُغَةَ الإنكليزيَّة ❑ التِجارةَ ❑ الحُقوقَ

٣- تَقرأُ لُؤلُؤةُ المَجلاّتِ الإنكليزيّةَ في ......

❑ البَيْتِ ❑ الصَفِّ ❑ المَكتَبَةِ

٤- تَسْكُنُ لُؤلُؤةُ في ......

❑ سكَنِ الطالِباتِ ❑ شَقّةٍ ❑ دارِ أُسْرَتِها

٥- عِندَ عائِلةِ القَطامي ......

❑ سَيّارتانِ ❑ ثَلاثُ سَيّاراتٍ ❑ أربَعُ سَيّاراتٍ

٦- دَرَسَ حُسَيْنُ التِجارةَ في ......

❑ الدَوْحَةِ ❑ الكُوَيْتِ ❑ لَنْدَن

٧- يَعمَلُ حُسَيْنُ في ......

❑ الكُوَيْت ❑ الدَوْحَة ❑ لَندَن

٨- لِحُسَين سَيّارَةٌ ......

❑ أمريكيّة ❑ يابانيّة ❑ ألمانيّة

B. Mark the following sentences صَح "true" or خَطأ "false" according to the information in the reading passage and correct the false ones.

٩- في دارِ عائِلةِ القَطامي تِسعُ غُرَف.

١٠- تَذهَبُ أمُّ لُؤلُؤة مَعَ السائِقِ إلى السوق.

١١- تَقرأُ لُؤلُؤةُ المجلاّتِ الإنكليزيةَ في كُلّيّةِ الآداب.

١٢- سَيّارةُ حُسَينِ لَها مُحَرِّكٌ قَوِيٌّ وجَميل.

١٣- يَسكُنُ حُسَيْنُ مَعَ زَوجَتِهِ في بَيتٍ كبير.

C. Describe a person you know (male or female), replicating one of the biographical descriptions in the reading passage.

تمرين ٣

Select the best alternative to complete these sentences.

١- سَيّارَتي لَها ...... قَويّ.

❑ عِقالٌ ❑ شُبّاكٌ ❑ مُحَرِّكٌ

٢- في شَقَّتي ...... نَوْمٍ واحِدة.

❑ غُرفةٌ ❑ كوفيّةٌ ❑ مَجَلّةٌ

٣- يسكنُ أبي في ...... كَبيرة.

❑ مَطعَمٍ ❑ دارٍ ❑ وَسيمٍ

٤- لي ...... مِنَ اليابان.

❑ قَديمٌ ❑ قَصيرٌ ❑ صَديقٌ

٥- يَعمَلُ حامِدُ ...... في القاهِرة.

❑ سائِقاً ❑ طَويلاً ❑ جَميلاً

تمرين ٤

Write down matching pairs of words from the two columns in the blanks provided.

١- سيّارة	....	جَميلة
٢- مَكتَبَة	....	بَيْت
٣- دار	....	قَويّ
٤- طَويل	....	حَديث
٥- وَسيم	....	مَجلّات
٦- قَديم	....	قَصير
		سائِق

تمرين ٥

Underline the word that does not belong to each set and explain your choice in English.

١- حَليب مكتبَة مَجلّات كُتُب جَرائِد

٢- سيّارة مُحَرِّك نِصْف سائِق كاديلاك

٣- اليابان ألمانيا الهِند مُحاسَبة سورية

٤- أخ أُخت أب أَرْض أُم

1. Culture Notes

a. **Family:** Arab families tend to be overly protective of their children, even after they reach the age of eighteen. Their offspring generally remain financially dependent on their parents and continue to live at home until they are married.

b. **Women:** Female children in particular are not allowed to be on their own, especially in the region of the Arabian peninsula. Although young women are legally allowed to drive cars, they normally do not (Saudi Arabia is the only country in that region that prohibits women from driving, hence the need for chauffeurs). Chauffeurs, mostly from India, Pakistan, and Bangladesh, drive the females of a household wherever they wish to go. Hiring foreign chauffeurs on a large scale has become an affordable practice thanks to oil revenues. Women do work, even in Saudi Arabia. Professional opportunities, though, are limited for women in the Arabian peninsula. Most working women are teachers. From the author's observation, these restrictions seem to have had a positive effect on women's motivation and desire to excel and outperform men. Some women have achieved excellence in several fields, including education, literature, and the arts.

In the more secular Arab countries, such as Algeria, Egypt, Syria, Lebanon, Palestine, and Iraq, women have equal opportunities and they can be found in almost all fields. Some of them have cabinet positions.

Men, on the other hand, have much more freedom of movement and work, though young men are not expected to live by themselves until they are married.

c. **The Gulf**: Arab states call it the Arabian Gulf (الخَليج العَرَبي), and Iran calls it the Persian Gulf (الخَليج الفارسي). As you can see on the map below, it is both Arab and Persian. Iran overlooks the eastern part of the Gulf, while the United Arab Emirates, Qatar, Saudi Arabia, and Kuwait are on the western part, and Iraq has a narrow outlet to the Gulf in the north. Bahrain is a small island on the western (Arab) side of the Gulf.

- Which countries listed on the map are not Arab countries?
- What Arab countries appear on the map but are not named? (Check answers in the answer key.)

أينَ قَطَر والكُوَيْت؟

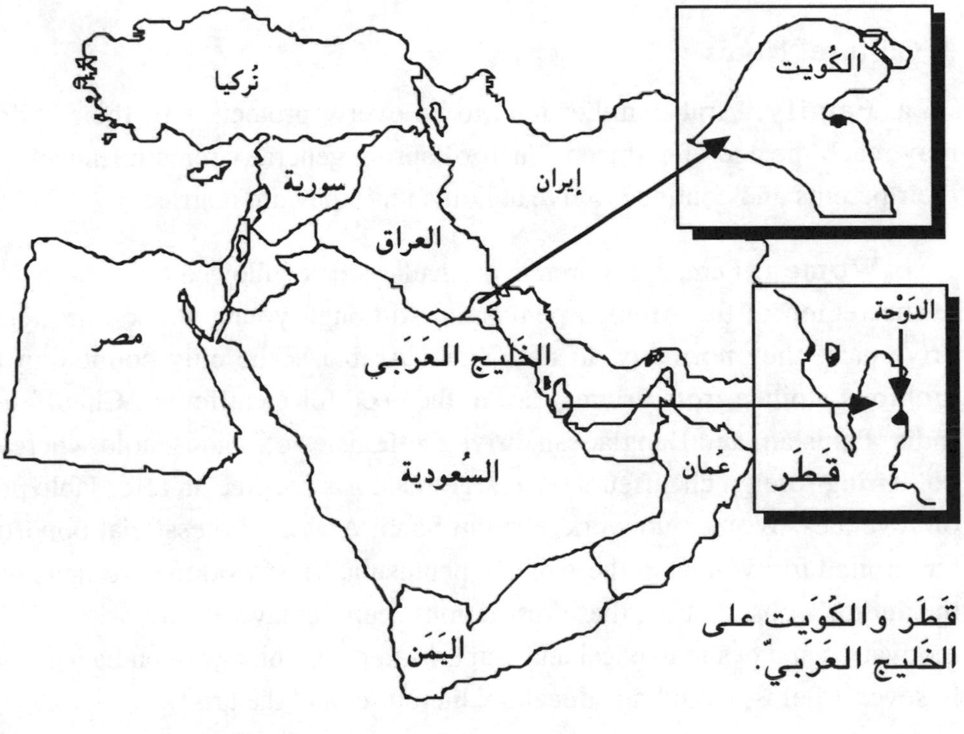

d. **Names and Recent History**: The personal name لُؤلُؤة "pearl" is a common name for females in the Gulf area. It is reminiscent of the times that preceded oil discovery and its revenues when the mainstays of the region were pearl diving and fishing. As in most Arabic dialects, the Gulf dialect changes the *hamza* into either a *wāw* or a *yā'*. Thus, this name is pronounced *lulwa* in that part of the Arab world. Another popular name has occurred in the reading passage which has reference also to the ancient trade of pearl diving. This name is دانة "big pearl."

e. **Men's Headgear:** The male headgear, such as the one shown below, is called غُتْرة in the Gulf area (also known as كوفيّة in the region of Greater Syria --بِلاد الشام-- where it is still in use in rural areas). It is made of fine white cotton held in place with two thick bands made from a thick, black cord called عقال which has tassels that descend along the back of the head. This headdress is worn all year round. It protects against the intense heat of the long, hot season as well as against the cold. In wintertime, the white cotton material is usually replaced with a checkered woolen material (black or red on white), such as the one worn by Palestinian head of state ياسِر عَرَفات (on the right below). The one on the left represents the more formal headdress.

الكوفيّة (الغُترة) والعِقال

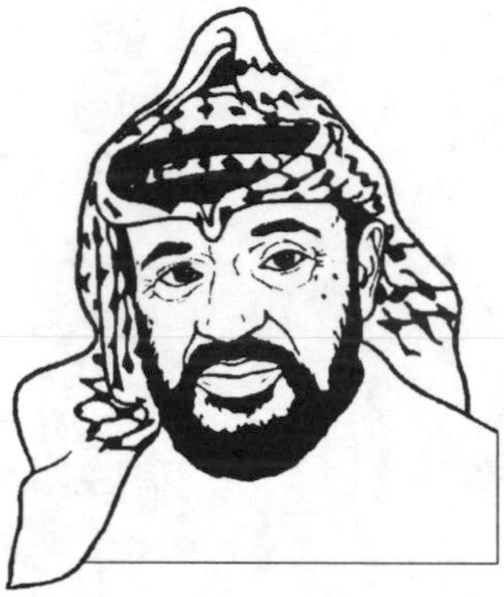

2. **The Past Tense**

Verbs are conventionally cited in the simplest form, that of the past third person masculine singular. All the verbs you have encountered are thus cited although they have not been used in the past tense. In the passage above, there are two occurrences of the past: سَكَنَ "*he lived*" and دَرَسَ "*he studied.*" They are both third person singular masculine. As you can see in the table below, the past tense is formed by adding suffixes to the root. These suffixes range from a single *fatḥa* to three letters in addition to long or short vowels.

a. **Past Tense Conjugation of the Verb** دَرَسَ "*he studied*": The stem of the past tense verb for all conjugations is دَرَسْ to which the various suffixes, which denote person, gender, and number, are attached. For example, for the first person plural (we), the suffix is نا. Here is how it is formed:

١ دَرَسْ + نا = دَرَسْنا

The same process is followed in forming the different conjugations with the other suffixes. Examine the different forms of the past for دَرَسَ in the table below, paying attention to suffixes and how they correspond to pronouns.

Suffix	Past tense form	Pronoun
ـتُ	دَرَسْتُ	*I* أنا
ـتَ	دَرَسْتَ	*you* (s., m.) أنتَ
ـتِ	دَرَسْتِ	*you* (s., f.) أنتِ
ـَ	دَرَسَ	*he* هُوَ
ـَتْ	دَرَسَتْ	*she* هِيَ
ـتُما	دَرَسْتُما	*you* (m. & f., dual) أنتُما
ا	دَرَسا	*they* (m., dual) هُما
ـَتا	دَرَسَتا	*they* (f., dual) هُما
نا	دَرَسْنا	*we* نَحْنُ
تُم	دَرَسْتُم	*you* (*pl*., m.) أنتُم
تُنَّ	دَرَسْتُنَّ	*you* (pl., f.) أنتُنَّ
silent *alif* وا	دَرَسوا	*they* (pl., m.) هُم
نَ	دَرَسْنَ	*they* (pl., f.) هُنَّ

Note that the third person plural masculine form دَرَسوا has a silent *alif* on its end. The verb is pronounced *darasū*. The *alif* has no phonetic value at all.

b. **Negating the Past Tense**: One way of negating a past tense verb is by using the particle ما before the verb. It does not cause any changes either in the word itself or in the order of words within the sentence:

٢ دَرَسْتُ التِجارَةَ. ⇦ ما دَرَسْتُ التِجارَةَ.

3. Verbal Nouns (المَصْدَر)

A verbal noun is a noun derived from a verb. For instance, the noun دِراسة "*study, studying*," which occurred in the reading passage, is derived, as you may have guessed, from the verb دَرَسَ. It is treated exactly like a noun in the sense that it takes the definite article, allows possessive pronouns to be suffixed to it, and changes according to number and case. The pattern of دِراسة (فِعالة) is only one of several verbal noun patterns which you will encounter later. By comparing the pattern of the verb دَرَسَ "*he studied*" and the verbal noun دِراسة "*studying*," you will find that there are three differences indicated by the boxed letters:

Verb	دَ رَ سَ	⇦	دَرَسَ	٣
Verbal Noun	[دِ] ر [ا] س [ـة]	⇦	دِراسة	٤

1. The first consonant is followed by a *kasra* instead of *fatḥa*.
2. The second, or middle, consonant is followed by an added *alif*.
3. A *tā' marbūṭa* is suffixed to the resulting word.

The verbal noun for the verb قَرَأَ has a similar pattern:

he read	قَرَأَ	٥
reading	قِراءة	٦

Notice how the spelling of the *hamza* has changed because of the change in the preceding vowel (see Lesson 30 for detailed rules for writing the *hamza*).

There is another verbal noun pattern that entails no changes in the basic form of the triliteral verb; only short vowels are manipulated. Examine the verb أَكَلَ "*he ate*" and its verbal noun.

eating, food أَكْل	⇦	*eat* أَكَلَ	٧

The consonants remain intact, but some vowels change. The vowel on the middle consonant, for example, is dropped. Note that the short vowel on the last consonant is not indicated. This is done on purpose because this word, being a noun, can have any one of the three short vowels to indicate case, depending on its position in the sentence. In the examples below, another verbal noun pattern of the verb دَرَسَ is used. This verb has two verbal noun patterns, the one listed above (دِراسة) and the one below (دَرْس).

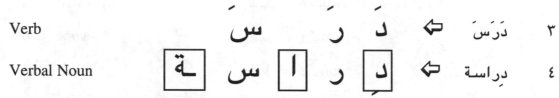

٨ دَرْسُ العَرَبِيَّةِ جَيِّدٌ. *Studying Arabic is good*

٩ أحِبُّ دَرْسَ العَرَبِيَّةِ. *I like the Arabic class*

١٠ في دَرْسِ العَرَبِيَّةِ. *in the Arabic class*

Other verbs that have a verbal noun pattern with no change in consonants include:

١١	شَرِبَ *drink*	⇦	شُرْب *drinking*
١٢	سَكَنَ *live, reside*	⇦	سَكَن *living, residing, residence*
١٣	عَمِلَ *work*	⇦	عَمَل *work (n.)*
١٤	فَعَلَ *do*	⇦	فِعْل *doing, deed*
١٥	دَرَسَ *study*	⇦	دَرْس *studying, lesson*
١٦	لَبِسَ *wear*	⇦	لُبْس *wearing, attire*

Remember that a verbal noun has the same form whether you derive it from a past or a present tense verb.

تمرين ٦

Make use of verbal nouns to express the following meanings, using the verbs يُحِبُّ and يُريد, as in the example. Note that all the verbal nouns in these items should be definite.

تُحِبُّ لُؤْلُؤَةُ دِراسَةَ اللغةِ الإنكليزية.

1. Say that you like reading in the morning.
2. My friend عُمَر wants to study (studying) mathematics.
3. Say that you live in the dorm (residence of students).
4. Say that you and your friends like drinking coffee with no sugar.
5. Your younger sister likes Arab food.
6. Husein likes working in Kuwait.
7. Her brother likes wearing the *kūfiyya.*

4. Noun-Adjective Agreement Revisited

If you recall, adjectives *follow* nouns and they agree with them in number, gender, case, and definiteness. Let's review these points one by one.

a. **Number**: Singular nouns require singular adjectives to follow. Likewise, dual (two) nouns must be followed by dual adjectives and plural nouns by plural adjectives:

١٧ وَلَدٌ طَويلٌ

١٨ وَلَدانِ طَويلانِ

١٩ أولادٌ طِوالٌ

Remember, however, that plural nonrational nouns (those referring to inanimate objects) agree with singular feminine adjectives regardless of their gender:

٢٠ كُتُبٌ قَديمَةٌ

٢١ سيّاراتٌ قَديمَةٌ

where كُتُب is a masculine plural and سَيّارات is a feminine plural and yet both are modified by the same adjectival form, قَديمَة, which is feminine singular.

تمرين ٧

Underline the adjectives in the following sentences and then place a check mark next to those which show correct noun-adjective agreement in number and an ✘ next to those that do not and then correct the incorrect ones.

١- عِندي هاتِف يابانيّان.

٢- تأكلُ سَلمى في مَطعَمٍ صَغير.

٣- عِندَ أخي كُتُبٌ قَديمات.

٤- إِخْوَةُ مَحمود طِوال.

٥- هَل أولادُها الصَغيرُ مَعَها؟

٦- في صَفِّنا كَراسٍ قَديم.

b. **Gender**: Masculine nouns must be followed by masculine adjectives and feminine nouns by feminine adjectives:

٢٢ مَطعَمٌ حَديثٌ

٢٣ مَدرَسةٌ حَديثَةٌ

Note that nonrational plural nouns, regardless of gender, are modified by feminine, singular adjectives (see examples 20 and 21 above).

تمرين ٨

Underline the adjectives in the following sentences and then place a check mark next to the sentences which show correct noun-adjective agreement in *gender* and an **✗** next to those that do not and then *correct* the incorrect ones.

١- باريس مدينةٌ فرنسيٌّ.

٢- عَدنان طالبٌ سوريٌّ.

٣- مينيسوتا ولايةٌ أمريكيةٌ.

٤- جامِعتنا كبيرٌ.

٥- صَفّنا صغيرٌ.

٦- حُسَين رجلٌ قَطَريّةٌ.

c. **Case**: The adjective should have the same case as that of the noun it modifies. Examine these examples:

٢٤ لُغَتي الأولى اللُغَةُ العَرَبيَّةُ.

٢٥ يَعرِفُ مايكل اللُغَةَ العَرَبيَّةَ.

٢٦ أتكلَّمُ مَعَ أستاذي باللُغَةِ العَرَبيَّةِ.

In sentence 24, the noun اللُغةُ is the predicate of the sentence and therefore it is nominative, as is the adjective العَرَبيَّةُ. As you can see, both display the same case marker: the *ḍamma*. In 25, the noun اللُغَةَ is the object of the verb يَعْرِف and is marked by a *fatḥa*, which also shows on the end of the adjective العَرَبيَّةَ. In 26, the noun اللُغةِ is the object of the preposition بِـ and is therefore marked by a *kasra*. The modifying adjective العَرَبِيَّةِ displays a similar marker. Note that there are case markers other than the three short vowels and their doubled forms (*tanwīn*). These include ان, ـَيْن for dual nouns, and ون, ين for sound plural nouns.

تمرين ٩

Underline the adjectives in the following sentences and then place a check mark next to the sentences which show correct noun-adjective agreement in *case* and an ✗ next to those that do not and then *correct* the incorrect ones.

١- عِندي كِتابانِ جَديدَينِ.

٢- يدرسُ سامي لُغَةً جَديدةٌ.

٣- يَدرُسُ عَدنان في الجامِعةِ الأمريكيَّةِ.

٤- أعرِفُ رِجالاً وَسيمون.

٥- هذهِ شَقَّةُ الطالِبَةِ السوريَّةُ.

d. **Definiteness**: Both a noun and its modifying adjective should be either definite or indefinite. A *noun* is definite if:

1. The definite particle ال is prefixed to it (e.g. الكتاب).
2. A possessive pronoun is suffixed to it (e.g. كتابي).
3. It is the first part of an *iḍāfa* structure, where the second or last part is definite (e.g. كتابُ العَرَبيَّة).
4. It is a proper noun; that is, a personal name (e.g. مايكل، عَدنان).

Remember that a string of two words in which both the noun and the adjective are definite or indefinite is considered a noun phrase (not a sentence). But if the noun is definite and the adjective is indefinite, this string is no longer a noun phrase; it is a sentence:

Noun Phrases	*big door* بابٌ كبيرٌ	*the big door* البابُ الكبيرُ	٢٧
Sentence		*the door is big.* البابُ كبيرٌ	٢٨

Thus, agreement in definiteness, where both the noun and the adjective are either definite or indefinite, signifies a noun phrase. Remember, however, that a string of two nouns, where the first one is indefinite and the second definite, is an *iḍāfa* structure, e.g.

An *iḍāfa* phrase	*the door of the classroom* بابُ الصفِّ	٢٩

تمرين ١٠

Based on the information in Section 4.d, label the following items "phrase" or "sentence" with a check mark or an ✗ whether the phrases are acceptable or unacceptable in terms of agreement and then *correct* the anomalous word.

١- أستاذُ العَرَبِيَّةِ.
٢- المَدينةُ القَديمةُ.
٣- الكُرسيُّ صَغيرٌ.
٤- سَيّارةٌ حَديثَةٍ.
٥- صورةُ الجميلةُ.
٦- الفَتاةُ قَطَرِيَّةٌ.
٧- هاتِفُ جَديدٌ.
٨- رَجُلُ الوَسيمُ.
٩- مُدُنُ الخَليجِ.
١٠- سيّارتُك جديدةَ.
١١- مَكتَبُها كبيرٌ.
١٢- حاسوبٌ قديمٌ.

تمرين ١١

Select a suitable adjective to complete each item.

١- تِلكَ هيَ كُلِّيَّةُ الآدابِ ......
❑ جَديدةٌ ❑ جَديدٍ ❑ الجَديدَةُ ❑ الجَديدِ

٢- أين الكُتُبُ ......؟
❑ القَديمُ ❑ القَديمةُ ❑ القُدَماءُ ❑ القديماتُ

٣- تُحِبُّ هالَة مَدينَةَ دِمَشق ......
❑ قَديمٌ ❑ القَديمَ ❑ قَديمَةً ❑ القَديمَةَ

٤- عِندي دَرّاجَتانِ ......
❑ فَرَنسيٌّ ❑ فَرَنسيّانِ ❑ فَرَنسِيَّتانِ ❑ فَرَنسيّاتٍ

٥- اِسمُ الطالِبِ ...... سامي.
❑ الجَديدَ ❑ الجَديدُ ❑ الجَديدِ ❑ جَديدٌ

٦- تَسكُنُ الطالِباتُ ...... في سَكَنِ الطالِبات.
❑ الجَديدُ ❑ الجُدُدُ ❑ الجَديدَةُ ❑ الجديداتُ

تمرين ١٢

Complete these sentences with the correct form of the adjective صَغير, as in the examples. Note that the masculine plural of صَغير is صِغار.

عِندي بَيتٌ صَغيرٌ. أُختي صَغيرَةٌ.

١- عِندَ سالِمٍ سَيّارةٌ ......

٢- أذهَبُ إلى الجامِعَةِ بِالسَيّارَةِ ......

٣- يُحِبُّ أبي الأولادَ ......

٤- ريما وغادَةُ بِنتانِ ......

٥- ثَلاثَةُ مَفاتيحَ ......

٦- هَل دِمَشقُ وبغدادُ مدينتانِ ....؟

٧- هَل أخوكِ .... يا سَميرة؟

٨- يجلِسُ عِماد في المكتبِ ......

تمرين ١٣

A. Select the best alternative as per the information in the listening passage:

١- سَعيدٌ طالِبٌ ......

❑ سوريّ ❑ تونِسيّ ❑ أمريكيّ

٢- يَدرُسُ سَعيدٌ ......

❑ عِلمَ الحاسوبِ ❑ الكيمياءَ ❑ الطِبَّ

٣- يَسكُنُ سَعيدٌ في ......

❑ شَقَّةٍ ❑ بَيْتٍ ❑ سكَنِ الطُلاّبِ

٤- لِسَعيدٍ ......

❑ أختان ❑ ثَلاثُ أخَواتٍ ❑ أربَعُ أخَواتٍ

B. Read these sentences then mark each of them صَواب or خَطأ according to the information in the listening passage and *correct* the false information.

٥- يَدرُسُ سَعيدُ في جامِعَةِ ماساتشوسِتس.

٦- يَدرُسُ بْرايَن الطِبَّ الآن.

٧- فَرَحُ صَديقةُ سَعيد.

٨- تَدرُسُ عَلياءُ في الجامِعةِ.

٩- عِندَ بْرايَن سَيّارةٌ.

١٠- سَعيد لَيْسَ عِندَهُ دَرّاجةٌ.

11. Write a brief summary of the passage in English.

المُفرَدات

Germany	ألمانيا (n., f.)
German	ألمانيّ (adj.)
Pakistan	الباكِسْتان (n., f.)
Porsche (German car)	پورش (n.)
secondary	ثانَوِيّ (adj.)
new	جَديد ج جُدُد (adj., m.)
beautiful, good-looking	جَميل ج (–ون) (adj.)
modern	حَديث (adj.)
house	دار ج دور (n., f.)
study	دراسة ج دراسات (n., f.)
to go	ذَهَبَ (يَذْهَبُ) ذَهاب (إلى) (v.)
driver, chauffeur	سائِق ج سائقون (n., m.)
market	سوق ج أسْواق (n., f.)
friend	صَديق ج أصْدِقاء (n., m.)
small, child, young child	صَغير ج صِغار (n., m.)
tall	طَويل ج طِوال (n., m.)
cord used to hold a male's headdress in place	عقال ج عُقُل (n., m.)
to work	عَمِلَ (يَعْمَلُ) عَمَل (v.)
a male's headdress	غُتْرَة ج غُتَر، غُترات (n., f.)
girl, young woman	فَتاة ج فَتَيات (n., f.)
old, ancient	قَديم ج قُدَماء (adj.)
short	قَصير ج قِصار (n., m.)
powerful, strong	قَويّ ج أقوِياء (adj.)
big, large, old (in age)	كَبير ج كِبار (n., m.)
headdress	كوفيّة ج كوفيّات (n., f.)
to wear	لَبِسَ (يَلبَسُ) لُبْس (v.)

particle used to negate past tense verbs .... (particle) ما

engine, motor .... (n., f.) مُحَرِّك ج مَحَرِّكات

handsome .... (adj., m.) وَسيم ج (–ون)

India .... (n., f.) الهِنْد

Japan .... (n., f.) اليابان

Lesson Seventeen — الدَرْسُ السابِعَ عَشَرَ

Objectives

- Describing activities in the past, present, and future.
- Arab and Muslim calendars.
- Reporting other people's speech (قالَ إنَّ).
- Expressing sequence (قَبلَ - بَعدَ).
- Comparing and contrasting entities (the superlative and comparative degrees).
- Expressing certainty and lack of it (أظُنُّ أنَّ).
- *Iḍāfa* structures (dual and plural).
- The verb كانَ.
- The five nouns.
- The preposition بِـ.
- Listen to the recorded material for this lesson.
- Do relevant computer drills and exercises, Stage 6.

يومِيّاتُ طالبٍ عَرَبِيّ
في أمريكا

هذا عَدنان مارتيني. هو طالِبٌ عَرَبِيٌّ مِن سورِيَة يَدرُسُ عِلمَ الحاسوبِ في جامِعَةِ ولايَةِ أوهايو. كَتَبَ عَدنانُ هذِهِ اليَومِيّاتِ حينَ أتى إلى أمريكا.

الخَميس ١٤ أيْلول ١٩٩٥

وَصَلتُ اليومَ إلى مَطارِ كِنيدي في نيويورك في الساعَةِ السادسةِ مَساءً. ذَهَبتُ إلى فُندُقِ شيراتُن في المطارِ وأكَلتُ في مَطعَمِ الفُندُق. بَعْدَ ذلِكَ ذَهَبتُ إلى

غُرفَتي ونِمْتُ حَتّى الساعةِ السابِعةِ مِن صَباحِ يومِ الجُمْعة. مَوعِدُ طائِرَتي في الساعةِ العاشِرةِ والنِصْفِ صَباحاً.

الجُمْعَة ١٥ أيلول ١٩٩٥

وَصَلتُ إلى مَطارِ كَلَمبَس في الساعةِ الثانيةَ عَشْرةَ ظُهْراً. حينَ وَصَلتُ إلى المطارِ كانَ هِشامُ هُناكَ (هِشامُ هو صَديقُ أخي رامي). نَزَلتُ في شَقَّةِ هِشام. يوجَدُ في شَقّتِه غُرفَتا نَوْمٍ وغُرفةُ جُلوسٍ واحِدة. غُرفَةُ نَومِ هِشام أَكْبَرُ مِن الغُرفَةِ الثانية. أظُنُّ أنّي سَأسكُنُ مَعَهُ في هذا الشَهْر.

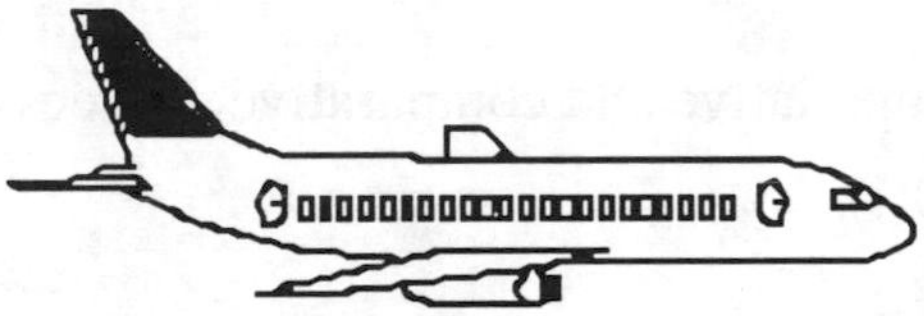
طائِرَة

مَطار

تَقويم

الأربعاء ٢٠ أيلول ١٩٩٥

الثُلاثاء ١٩ أيلول ١٩٩٥

الإثنين ١٨ أيلول ١٩٩٥

الأحَد ١٧ أيلول ١٩٩٥

السبت ١٦ أيلول ١٩٩٥

الجمعة ١٥ أيلول ١٩٩٥

الخميس ١٤ أيلول ١٩٩٥

اللغة الإنكليزية ٩ صباحاً
الرياضيّات ١٢ ظُهراً
الكيمياء ٣ بَعدَ الظهر

تشرين الثاني ١٩٩٥

تشرين الأوّل ١٩٩٥

أيلول ١٩٩٥

السبت	الأحد	الإثنين	الثلاثاء	الأربعاء	الخميس	الجمعة
						١
٢	٣	٤	٥	٦	٧	٨
٩	١٠	١١	١٢	١٣	١٤	١٥
١٦	١٧	١٨	١٩	٢٠	٢١	٢٢
٢٣	٢٤	٢٥	٢٦	٢٧	٢٨	٢٩
٣٠						

السَبْت ١٦ أيلول ١٩٩٥

ذَهَبنا أنا وهِشامُ أمْسِ إلى السوقِ بِالسيّارةِ وهي بَعيدةٌ عَنِ الشَقّةِ. اشْتَرَيْتُ وِسادةً وشَرشَفَين وبَطّانيَّتَينِ لِسَريري، واشْتَرى هشام قَميصاً جَديداً بِخَمسةٍ وعِشرينَ دولاراً. بَعدَ ذلِكَ أكَلنا في مَطعَمٍ مِكسيكيٍّ قَريبٍ مِن شقّتِه. أكَلَ هِشام فاهيتا بِاللَحْمِ وأنا أكلتُ فاهيتا بِالدَجاج. يُحِبُّ هِشامُ الأكلَ المِكسيكيّ. سَآكُلُ غداً في مَطعَمٍ عَرَبِيٍّ إنْ شاءَ الله.

الأرْبعاء ٢٠ أيلول ١٩٩٥

كُنتُ اليَومَ في الجامِعَة. ذَهَبتُ إلى دُروسي ومَشَيْتُ في الجامِعة. أظُنُّ أنَّ جامعةَ ولاية أوهايو كبيرةٌ جداً. يَقولُ هِشام إنَّها أكْبَرُ جامعةٍ في الولايات المُتَّحِدة الأمريكيّة. في الساعةِ الخامِسةِ مَساءً مَشيْتُ إلى الشَقَّة. قَبْلَ ذلكَ مَشَيْتُ إلى مكتبةِ «إس بي إكس» القَريبةِ مِن الجامعة واشتَرَيْتُ كُتبي منها. اشتَريتُ سَبعَةَ كُتُبٍ وثَلاثَةَ دَفاتِرَ بِمِئتَينِ وسِتَّةٍ وسَبعينَ دولاراً. سأقرأُ قَليلاً قَبلَ النَومِ وسَوْفَ أكتُبُ إلى أبي وأمّي.

عُطلةُ نِهايةِ الأسبوعِ في البِلادِ العَرَبيَّة

يَذهَبُ الطُلّابُ إلى المدارسِ سِتّةَ أيّامٍ في الأسبوعِ في البِلادِ العَرَبِيَّةِ ويَعمَلُ الناسُ سِتّةَ أيّامٍ في الأسبوعِ أيضاً. في هذا التَقويمِ العَرَبيِّ يَومُ الجُمْعَةِ هو عُطلةُ نِهايةِ الأسبوعِ. لكن في لُبنانَ عُطلةُ نِهايةِ الأسبوعِ هي يَوما الجُمْعَةِ والأحَد.

تشرين الأول ١٩٩٥ م

السبت	الأحد	الإثنين	الثلاثاء	الأربعاء	الخميس	الجمعة
٧	٨	٩	١٠	١١	١٢	١٣

التَقويمُ الميلاديّ

1. **Calendars in the Arab World**

Generally, two calendars are used: the Islamic lunar calendar and the Western solar calendar. The names of the months of the Western calendar vary within the Arab world. In the eastern part, the names of indigenous Babylonian-semitic months are still in use, whereas in Egypt and North African countries two varieties of the Roman months are used.

The week normally starts with Saturday, the first working day of the week. In most Arab countries, the weekend is on Friday. In Lebanon, for example, where there is a substantial Christian community, Sunday is considered an additional weekend.

a. **The Islamic Calendar**: The Islamic calendar is based on the lunar cycle, and its beginning is marked by the emigration (هِجْرة) of the Prophet Muḥammad from Mecca to Yathrib (*Medīna*) in 622 A.D. Hence the designation هِجْـريّة of the Islamic calendar (abbrivated as هـ). A lunar year is eleven days shorter than the year based on the Gregorian calendar.

شُهورُ السنةِ الهِجريّة

١- مُحَرَّم
٢- صَفَر
٣- رَبيعُ الأوَّل
٤- رَبيعُ الآخِر
٥- جُمادى الأولى
٦- جُمادى الآخِرة
٧- رَجَب
٨- شَعبان
٩- رَمَضان
١٠- شَوّال
١١- ذو القَعْدة
١٢- ذو الحِجّة

رَجَب ١٤١٦ هـ

السبت	الأحد	الإثنين	الثلاثاء	الأربعاء	الخميس	الجمعة
٣	٤	٥	٦	٧	٨	٩

التَقويمُ الهِجريّ (الإسلاميّ)

b. **The Western Calendar**: It is based on the Gregorian calendar and is called التَقويم الغَربي (western calendar) or الميلادي in reference to the birth of Christ. The abbreviation م is used to indicate it. The names of the months used in Egypt are listed in parentheses next to the indigenous names used in Greater Syria and Iraq.

شُهورُ السنةِ الميلاديّة

١	كانون الثاني (يَنايِر)	٧	تَمّوز (يوليو/يولية)
٢	شُباط (فِبرايِر)	٨	آب (أغسطس)
٣	آذار (مارِس)	٩	أيْلول (سبتمبر)
٤	نيسان (أبريل)	١٠	تِشرين الأوَّل (أكتوبر)
٥	أيّار/مايِس (مايو)	١١	تِشرين الثاني (نوفمبر)
٦	حَزيران (يونيو/يونية)	١٢	كانون الأوَّل (ديسمبر)

تمرين ١

A. Select the best alternative according to the reading passages to complete these sentences.

١- وَصَلَ عَدنان إلى مطارِ كِنيدي ......

❑ في الساعَةِ العاشِرة ❑ في الساعَةِ السادِسَة ❑ بِالسَيّارَة

٢- كانَ مَوْعِدُ طائِرَةِ كَلَمبَس في الساعَةِ ......

❑ السادِسَة ❑ العاشَرةِ والنِصْف ❑ الثانيَةِ عَشْرَة

٣- هِشامُ ......

❑ صَديقُ عَدنان ❑ أخو رامي ❑ صَديقُ رامي

٤- حينَ وَصَلَ عَدنانُ إلى مَطارِ كَلَمبَس كانَ هاني في ......

❑ المطار ❑ الجامِعة ❑ الشَقَّة

٥- يوجَدُ في شَقَّةِ هاني ......

❑ غُرفَةُ نَوْمٍ واحِدة ❑ غُرفَتا نَوْم ❑ ثَلاثُ غُرَفِ نَوْم

٦- في هذا الشَهرِ سَوفَ يَسكُنُ عَدنانُ في ......

❑ شَقَّةِ هاني ❑ فُندُق ❑ سكَنِ الطُلاّب

٧- اشترى هاني ......

❑ كُتُباً ❑ قَميصاً ❑ وِسادةً

٨- اشترى عَدنانُ كُتُباً بِـ ...... دولاراً.

❑ ٧٢٦ ❑ ٦٢٧ ❑ ٢٧٦

B. Mark the following sentences صح or خطأ and correct the false ones.

٩- سَيَسكُنُ عَدنانُ في غُرفَةٍ كَبيرة.

١٠- وَصَلَ عَدنانُ إلى كَلَمبَس يَومَ الجُمْعَة.

١١- ذَهَبَ عَدنانُ إلى دُروسِهِ في الجامِعَةِ يَومَ الثُلاثاء.

١٢- يَظُنُّ عَدنانُ أنَّ جامِعَةَ ولايَةِ أوهايو أكبَرُ مِن جامِعَةِ دِمَشق.

تمرين ٢

Underline the word that does not belong in each set and explain your choice, in English if necessary.

١- وَصَلَ شَهر ذَهَبَ نامَ

٢- غُرفَة فُندُق مَطعَم مَقصَف

٣- الجُمْعَة يَوْم الإثنَين أيْلول

٤- كَبير بَعيد حينَ قَريب

٥- وِسادَة ساعَة بَطّانيَّة شَرشَف

تمرين ٣

Write down matching words from the left column in the blanks next to their matches.

١- آب	....	أسبوع
٢- مَساءً	....	سَوفَ
٣- نامَ	....	المِكسيك
٤- شُباط	....	السَبت
٥- وِسادَة	....	فُندُق
٦- فاهيتا	....	سَرير
٧- شَهْر	....	ظُهراً
٨- الأحَد	....	فِبرايِر
٩- كانون الثاني	....	طائِرة
١٠- مَطار	....	يَنايِر
		أغُسطُس

تمرين ٤

Complete the following sentences with appropriate words.

١- يَأتي شَهْرُ تَمّوزَ بَعْدَ شَهرِ ......

٢- يَأتي شَهْرُ آذارَ قَبْلَ شَهرِ ......

٣- شَهرُ ...... هو الشهرُ السادِسُ في التَقويمِ الميلادي.

٤- الشَهرُ الثاني عَشَر هُوَ ......

٥- شَهرُ ...... هُوَ الشهرُ الثامِنُ في التَقويمِ الإسلامي.

٦- في الأُسبوعِ ...... أيّام.

٧- يَأتي يَومُ الخَميسِ قَبلَ يَومِ ......

٨- يَومُ الإثنَينِ بَعدَ يَوم ......

٩- يَومُ عُطلَةِ نِهايَةِ الأسبوعِ في البِلادِ العَرَبِيَّة هُوَ ......

١٠- عُطلَةُ نِهايَةِ الأسبوعِ في أمريكا هِيَ يَومَي ......

2. Describing Activities in the Past, Present, and Future

You are already familiar with the past and present forms of some Arabic verbs. The present describes an action that is not yet complete, and it is formed by adding prefixes and suffixes to the root of the verb. The past denotes an action that has been completed, and it is formed through adding suffixes. The future describes an action that has not yet occurred, but will take place some time in the future. It is formed by prefixing the future particle سَـ to the present tense form of the verb (indicative المُضارع المرفوع) or by inserting the future word سَوْفَ right before the present tense verb:

	Present		Future
١	يَدْرُسُ *he studies*	⇦	سَيَدْرُسُ / سَوْفَ يَدْرُسُ *he will study*

As you can see, no change in the verb form is involved.

تمرين ٥

Describe in Arabic future activities in which you will engage. Starting a sentence with a verb is more acceptable stylistically.

Example: You will drink a cup of coffee in the cafeteria.

سَأشرَبُ فِنْجانَ قَهوَةٍ في المَقصَف. *I'll drink a cup of coffee in the cafeteria*

1. You will read a magazine in the library.
2. Your Arab friend will stay in your apartment this month.
3. You will go to Washington, D.C., on Monday.
4. You will go to bed (sleep) at 10 p.m. on Sunday.
5. You will study chemistry on Monday and Wednesday.
6. Your friend's flight will arrive at 7:30 p.m.
7. You will eat chicken at the restaurant tomorrow.
8. You will buy a magazine, two newspapers, and three books from the market.

3. Expressing Certainty and Lack of It

When you are not absolutely certain of something, you may use the verb ظَنَّ "*think*" to express the degree of certainty you have about something. This verb is immediately followed by the particle أنَّ "*that*," which must be followed by either a pronoun or a noun:

٢ أينَ هالة؟ – أظُنُّ أنَّها في المدرسةِ الآن.

٣ أينَ كتابي؟ – أظُنُّ أنَّ الأستاذَ يقرأه.

a. **The Particle** أنَّ: In example 2, the suffix ـها attached to أنَّ refers back to هالة. In *3*, أنَّ is followed by a noun (الأستاذَ). Note that the noun has a *fatḥa* on its end. This is the effect of أنَّ on the noun it modifies; it makes it مَنصوب (accusative). Remember that other markers of the accusative include a double *fatḥa* and ـين.

Remember that the subject and predicate in a nominal sentence are nominative (مَرفوع) if it is not modified by أنَّ. But when it is modified by أنَّ, only the subject is made accusative (مَنصوب); its predicate remains unchanged (مَرفوع/nominative):

٤ أظُنُّ أنَّ أختَكِ طَويلةٌ.

b. **Verbs with Doubled Consonants**: The verb ظَنَّ, as you can see, has two different consonants, one of them doubled. The conjugation of such verbs is slightly different from those with three different consonants. Note that the doubled consonant (e.g. the doubled نّ in أظُنُّ, تَظُنُّ, and يَظُنُّ) occurs in all conjugations in the present and in the third person in the past (e.g. ظَنَّ), but not in the first and second persons in the past.

Conjugation of the Verb ظَنَّ
in the Present and Past Tense

Present Tense	Past Tense	Separate Pronoun
أظُنُّ	ظَنَنْتُ	أنا
نَظُنُّ	ظَنَنّا	نَحْنُ
تَظُنُّ	ظَنَنْتَ	أَنْتَ
تَظُنّينَ	ظَنَنْتِ	أَنْتِ
تظُنّانِ	ظَنَنْتُما	أَنْتُما (m. and f.)
تَظُنّونَ	ظَنَنْتُم	أَنْتُم
تَظنَنَّ	ظَنَنْتُنَّ	أنتُنَّ

هُوَ	ظَنَّ	يَظُنُّ
هِيَ	ظَنَّتْ	تَظُنُّ
هُما (m.)	ظَنّا	يَظُنّانِ
هُما (f.)	ظَنَّتا	تَظُنّانِ
هُم	ظَنّوا (silent *alif*)	يَظُنّونَ
هُنَّ	ظَنَنَّ	يَظْنُنَّ

4. Reporting Other People's Speech

Reporting someone's speech may be performed through the use of the verb قالَ "say."

a. **The Particle إنَّ**: Like the verb ظَنَّ, the verb قالَ is followed by the particle إنَّ "*that,*" which is very similar to أنَّ, especially in its grammatical function (the difference is in either the *fatḥa* or the *kasra* following the *hamza*). The particle must be followed by either a pronoun or a noun, which must be مَنصوب (accusative). Remember that if a noun is the subject of a nominal sentence and is preceded by أنَّ or إنَّ, the predicate of the sentence remains مَرفوع (nominative):

٥ يَقولُ عَبدُ الرحمنِ إنَّ مَكتَبَهُ كَبيرٌ.

where مَكتَبَ is مَنصوب (accusative indicated by a *fatḥa*) and كَبيرٌ is مَرفوع (nominative indicated by a double *ḍamma*). Note: another marker of the accusative is ين, e.g. كِتابَين. The particle إنَّ follows the verb قال, and أنَّ follows all other verbs that require it.

تمرين ٦

Use either أنَّ or إنَّ before the nouns in parentheses and provide the correct endings for the nouns which follow them.

١- يَظُنُّ سَميحُ ..... (الجامِعَة) بَعيدة.

٢- تَقولُ ريم ..... (سَيّارتَها) قَديمةٌ.

٣- هَل تَظُنّين ..... (الكِتاب × ٢) بِعشرينَ دولاراً؟

٤- أظُنُّ ..... (مَدينَة) سان فرانسيسكو جَميلةٌ.

٥- يَقولُ صَديقي بَشّار ..... (الطلاّب) لَيْسوا في الصَفِّ.

٦- تَقولُ سُعادُ ..... (السَيارة × ٢) (جَديدَة × ٢).

5. **Expressing Sequence** (قَبْلَ، بَعْدَ)

The word for adverb in Arabic is ظَرف, which means "vessel" or "container" in which an action or a state is situated, as in أشربُ الحليبَ صباحاً *"I drink milk in the morning,"* where the action is specified to take place in the morning. The words قَبلَ *"before"* and بَعدَ *"after"* are adverbs of time and place. In the reading passages above, they are used with reference to time.

These two adverbs behave just like prepositions in that the noun that follows them is مَجرور (genitive) marked by a *kasra* or ين.

6. **Comparing and Contrasting Entities** (اسم التَفضيل)

To compare or contrast entities one compares the attributes of two things or more. This should involve the use of adjectives. In English, there are two degrees of comparison: the comparative and the superlative degrees. The former is formed by the suffix *-er* appended to some adjectives or the word *more* used before other adjectives. The word *than* is placed right before the entity to which the first one is being compared. The superlative degree is formed by suffixing *-est* to adjectives or by using the word *most* before them:

6 John is taller than his brother. (comparative)

7 John is the tallest boy. (superlative)

In Arabic, both degrees of comparison are indicated by a single pattern (أفْعَل). This pattern is a noun (اسمُ تَفضيل) derived from a verb and is more like an adjective. It indicates that two entities have a common attribute, but one of them has more of this attribute.

The comparative and superlative degrees in Arabic are distinguished by the manner in which this noun relates to the other words in the sentence. First, here are some selected adjectives and their comparative nouns:

٨	كَبير	أكْبَر
٩	بَعيد	أبْعَد
١٠	جَميل	أجْمَل

a. **The Comparative**: To compare two entities in terms of size, for example, insert the preposition مِن after the comparative noun formed on the pattern أفْعَل:

١١ هالَة أطْوَلُ مِن أُختِها.

When the preposition مِن is followed by a pronoun, this pronoun should be an *attached* pronoun:

١٢ هالَة أطولُ منها (مِن + ها=).

b. **The Superlative**: In order to describe a superlative attribute of something, use a noun derived from the adjective in question formed on the pattern أفْعَل followed immediately by a noun which refers back to the noun that is the subject of comparison (e.g. أطول and طالب in 12 below). Being a noun, the superlative forms an *iḍāfa* structure with the following noun. The following noun may be singular, dual, or plural, and the plural form may be definite or indefinite:

١٣ هِشامُ أطْولُ طالب في الصَفِّ.

١٤ هِشامُ وسامي أطْوَلُ طالبَين في الصَفِّ.

١٥ هِشامُ وسامي وعبدُ الرَحيم أطْوَلُ طلابٍ (أو:الطلاب) في الصَفِّ.

تمرين ٧

Compare the following entities, using comparative nouns formed on the pattern أفْعَل. Remember that comparing two entities requires the use of مِن after the comparative noun, as in examples 10 and 11, while expressing the superlative degree requires the use of a noun after the superlative form, as in examples 12-14.

١- سان فرانسيسكو (جَميل) ديترويت.

٢- جامِعةُ ويسكونسن واحِدةٌ مِن (كبير) الجامِعاتِ في أمريكا.

٣- سَناء (طَويل) طالبةٍ في الصَفِّ.

٤- أريحا[1] (قَديم) مَدينةٍ في العالَم.[2]

[1]Jericho, [2]world

٥- حاسوبُ هُدى (كَبير) حاسوبي.

٦- اشتَرى هاني (حَديث) سَيّارةٍ في السوق.

٧- باريس وروما (جميل) مَدينَتَين في أوروبا.

٨- سَناءُ (طَويل) أنا.

7. *Iḍāfa* Structure: Dual and Plural

If you recall, an *iḍāfa* structure is made up of at least two parts: the first one is a noun called مُضاف "added," and the second part is a noun called مُضاف إلَيْه "noun to which another noun is added." If the first part (مُضاف) is dual, it loses the final *nūn* ن. Similarly, nouns whose plural is formed by the suffix ون also lose the final ن:

١٦ غُرفَتان + نَوم = غُرفَتا نَوم.

١٧ سائِقون + السَيّارات = سائقو السَيّارات.

The ن in غُرفَتان and سائقون is dropped because these nouns function as مُضاف (i.e., the first part of an *iḍāfa* structure), meaning "*rooms of, drivers of.*"

تمرين ٨

Examine these two advertisements (the middle rectangles) and identify all instances of *iḍāfa* structures even if the words are not familiar to you. There are nine *iḍāfa* structures.

للمراجعة الرجاء الاتصال بالهاتف ٤٥٧٩٨٤٤.	مغر. يرجى الاتصال على الهاتف ٦٦٧٤٦٣٢-إياد.
دار في شارع الجلاء مع هاتف وبراد وغسالة وتلفاز. ثلاث غرف نوم وغرفتا جلوس وغرفة طعام مع المفروشات. الإيجار السنوي ٦٠٠ ألف ليرة.	مطلوب سائقو شاحنات للعمل في شركة المطاحن. يتراوح الراتب الشهري من مئتي دينار إلى ثلاثمئة دينار.
محل تجاري في وسط المدينة	قطعة أرض في صحنايا صالحة

١-
٢-
٣-
٤-
٥-
٦-
٧-
٨-
٩-

8. The Verb كانَ

The verb كانَ is the Arabic equivalent of the verb "to be" and it conjugates like any other verb. Although its present tense form may not be needed in most present tense sentences, it is used in past tense sentences and when you want to express future time. There are present tense sentences, however, that require the use of this verb, as in *18*:

١٨ أكونُ في مكتبي في الساعة الثامنة صباحاً. *I am present in my office...*

١٩ سأكونُ في مكتبي في الساعة الثامنة غداً. *I will be in my office...*

٢٠ كُنتُ أمْسِ في مكتبي في الساعة الثامنة. *I was in my office yesterday..*

The adverbs غَداً "*tomorrow*" in *19* and أمْس "*yesterday*" in *20* define the time of the occurrence of an action. The adverb غَداً requires the use of the present tense with the future particle and أمس the use of the past tense. The conjugations of كانَ are classified according to person (first, second, third).

Conjugation of the Verb كانَ
in the Present and Past Tense

Present Tense	Past Tense	Separate Pronoun
أكونُ	كُنْتُ	أنا
نَكونُ	كُنّا	نَحْنُ
تَكونُ	كُنْتَ	أنْتَ
تَكونينَ	كُنْتِ	أنْتِ
تَكونانِ	كُنْتُما	أنْتُما (m. and f.)
تَكونونَ	كُنْتُم	أنْتُم
تَكُنَّ	كُنْتُنَّ	أنتُنَّ
يَكونُ	كانَ	هُوَ
تَكونُ	كانَتْ	هِيَ
يَكونانِ	كانا	هُما (m.)
تَكونانِ	كانَتا	هُما (f.)
يَكونونَ	كانوا (silent *alif*)	هُم
يَكُنَّ	كُنَّ	هُنَّ

The verb كَانَ (and others in its class) differs from other regular verbs in that (1) it provides a time frame for a nominal sentence and (2) it has an effect on the case of the predicate of a nominal sentence. You are already familiar with another member of its group used for negation (لَيْسَ). Note the case of the predicate in examples 21 and 22:

٢١ الفَتاةُ جَميلةٌ *The girl is beautiful*

٢٢ كانَت الفَتاةُ جَميلةً *The girl was beautiful*

The predicate جَميلة in *22* is preceded by كانَ and it is accusative (مَنصوب) marked by a double *fatḥa*.

تمرين ٩

Use the correct from of كَانَ to complete these sentences, where it may assume past or present forms.

١ـ .... عَليٌّ في الدارِ البَيضاء* غَداً.

* Casablanca

٢ـ صَديقي أحمَد وزَوجَتُه .... في المَطعَمِ أمس.

٣ـ مَن .... في المطارِ حينَ وَصَلَتْ طائِرةُ دانة؟

٤ـ أنا وعائِلَتي .... عِندَكُم في الأسبوعِ المُقبِل.

٥ـ الأستاذُ والطُلابُ .... أمامَ بابِ الجامِعَةِ بَعدَ ظُهرِ أمس.

٦ـ هِيَ وأخوها .... في المَطعَمِ يَومَ الأحَدِ الماضي.

٧ـ أينَ .... أمسِ يا هالَة؟

٨ـ مَتى .... في مَكتَبِكَ يا أستاذُ عادَةً؟

Note on عِندَ: In addition to expressing possession, the adverbial phrase عِندَ + a noun or a pronoun signifies being at a particular location. For example, the phrase عِندَ البابِ means "at the door."

9. The Five Nouns (أب and أخ)

There are five nouns in Arabic which behave in a different manner from other nouns. Whereas regular nouns are marked for case by short vowels, these five nouns are marked by long vowels. You already know two of them: أب and أخ. Examine these pairs of examples:

٢٣	هذا كتابُ حازِم.	اشتَريتُ كتابَ حازِم.	لكتابِ حازِم.
٢٤	هذا أبو حازِم.	إنَّ أبا حازِم في الدار.	لأبي حازِم.

The noun أبو in 24 serves as the predicate of the sentence; أبا is modified by the particle إنّ, which makes the subject of a nominal sentence accusative; and أبي is the object of a preposition. The five nouns are marked for the nominative (رَفْع) by a و, for the accusative (نَصْب) by an *alif* (ا), and for the genitive (جَرّ) by a ي.

تمرين ١٠

Provide case markers on the ends of the nouns in parentheses, using short or long vowels as appropriate and making the necessary changes:

١- هَل هذا الكِتابُ لِـ (أخ+هي)؟

٢- أدرُسُ (اللُّغة) العَرَبيَّة.

٣- يَعمَلُ (أب) سامية في الدارِ البَيضاء.

٤- هذا (الكِتاب) لَيْسَ لي.

٥- يَدرُسُ صَديقي في (جامِعَة) دِمَشق.

٦- إنَّ (أب) سَليم صَديقُ أبي.

10. The Preposition بِـ

As is the case with most prepositions, بِـ acquires its meaning from context. So far, three meanings have been used, as exemplified by these sentences:

٢٥ اشترَيتُ كِتاباً **بـعشرينَ** دولاراً. *for the amount of*

٢٦ ما مَعْنى "police" **بـالعَرَبيَّةِ**؟ *in Arabic*

٢٧ أنا أكبَرُ مِن أختي **بـسَنَتَين.** *by two years*

The preposition بـ, as you can see, functions as a prefix only and causes the modified noun to be مَجْرور (genitive), as indicated by the ي in عِشرين and سَنَتَين and the *kasra* on the end of العَرَبيَّةِ.

تمرين ١١

A. Check the alternative in each item that agrees with the information in the tape-recorded listening passage.

١ـ ذَهَبَ حَسّانُ إلى ......
❑ دمَشْقَ ❑ الرِياض ❑ القاهِرة

٢ـ حَسّانُ لَهُ ......
❑ ابنٌ واحدٌ ❑ ابنٌ وبِنتٌ ❑ ثَلاثةُ أبناء

٣ـ نَزَلَ حَسّانُ في ......
❑ فُندُقٍ ❑ شَقَّةِ أخيهِ ❑ دارِ أبيه

٤ـ في بَيتِ أبي حَسّانَ ......
❑ غُرفَتا نَوْم ❑ ثَلاثُ غُرَفِ نَوْم ❑ أربَعُ غُرَفِ نَوْم

B. Mark the following sentences صَح or خَطأ based on the information in the listening passage and correct the false statements.

٥ـ ذَهَبَ حَسّانُ إلى الرياضَ بِالسَيّارةِ مَعَ زَوْجَتِهِ.

٦ـ كانَ أبو حَسّان في المطارِ حينَ وَصَلَ حَسّانُ وعائِلَتُه.

٧ـ حَسّانُ طالبٌ في مَدرَسَةٍ ثانَويةٍ في دمشق.

٨ـ رانِية أصغَرُ من رائِد بِسَنَتَيْن.

المُفْرَدات

August.......... (n., m.) آب

to come.......... (v.) أتى (يَأتي)

Monday.......... (n., m.) الإثْـنَين

Sunday.......... (n., m.) الأحَد

March.......... (n., m.) آذار

Wednesday.......... (n., m.) الأرْبِعاء

week.......... (n., m.) أُسْبوع ج أسابيع

to buy.......... (v.) اشتَرى (يَشتري)

yesterday.......... (adv.) أمْسِ

that (after verbs similar to "think").......... (particle) أنَّ

that (after the verb for "say").......... (particle) إنَّ

hopefully (lit. God willing).......... (set phrase) إنْ شاءَ الله

May.......... (n., m.) أيّار

September.......... (n., m.) أيْلول

Saturday.......... (n., m.) السَبْت

calendar.......... (n., m.) تَقويم ج تَقاويم

July.......... (n., m.) تَمّوز

Tuesday.......... (n., m.) الثُلاثاء

sitting.......... (verbal n.) جُلوس

Islamic month (*Jumādā al-ākira*).......... (n., f.) جُمادى الآخِرة

Islamic month (*Jumādā al-'ūlā*).......... (n., f.) جُمادى الأولى

Friday.......... (n., m.) الجُمْعة

till, until.......... (particle) حَتّى

June.......... (n., m.) حَزيران

when .... (adv.) حينَ
Thursday .... (n., m.) الخَميس
lesson .... (n., m.) دَرْس ج دُروس
Islamic month (*ḏū al-ḥijja*) .... (n., m.) ذو الحِجّة
Islamic month (*ḏū al-Qi'da*) .... (n., m.) ذو القِعدة
Islamic month (*Rabī' al-'āḵir*) .... (n., m.) رَبيع الآخِر
Islamic month (*Rabī' al-'awwal*) .... (n., m.) رَبيع الأوَّل
Islamic month (*Rajab*) .... (n., m.) رَجَب
Islamic month (*Ramaḍān*) .... (n., m.) رَمَضان
shall, will .... (future particle) سَـ
year .... (n., f.) سَنة ج سَنَوات/سِنون
shall, will .... (future particle) سَوْفَ
February .... (n., m.) شُباط
bedsheet .... (n., m.) شَرْشَف ج شَراشِف
Islamic month (*ša'bān*) .... (n., m.) شَعبان
month .... (n., m.) شَهْر ج أشْهُر/شُهور
Islamic month (*šawwāl*) .... (n., m.) شَوّال
Islamic month (*ṣafar*) .... (n., m.) صَفَر
airplane .... (n., f.) طائِرة ج طائِرات
to think, to believe .... (v.) ظَنَّ (يَظُنُّ)
tomorrow .... (adv.) غَداً
hotel .... (n., m.) فُنْدُق ج فَنادِق
to say .... (v.) قالَ (يَقولُ)
before .... (adv.) قَبْلَ
close, near .... (adv.) قَريب
shirt .... (n., m.) قَميص ج قُمْصان
to be (was, were) .... (v.) كانَ (يَكونُ) كَوْن
December .... (n., m.) كانون الأوَّل

January .... (n., m.) كانون الثاني
Islamic month (*muḥarram*) .... (n., m.) مُحَرَّم
walk .... (v.) مَشى (يَمْشي) مَشي
airport .... (n., m.) مَطار ج مَطارات
to sleep .... (v.) نامَ (يَنامُ) نَوم
to stay (in a place) .... (v.) نَزَلَ (يَنْزِلُ) نُزول
sleeping .... (verbal n.) نَوْم
April .... (n., m.) نيسان
pillow .... (n., f.) وسادة ج وَسائد
to arrive, to reach a destination .... (v.) وَصَلَ (يَصِلُ) وُصول
day .... (n., m.) يَوْم ج أيّام
today .... (adv.) اليَوْم
diary, daily journal .... (n.) يَوْمِيّة ج يومِيّات

عمّانُ الحَديثة

Lesson Eighteen الدَرْسُ الثامِنَ عَشَر

Objectives

- Describing the four seasons.
- Describing the weather.
- Converting temperature scales.
- Partitive nouns (بعض، كلّ، مُعظم).
- Listen to recorded material for this lesson.
- Do relevant computer drills and exercises, Stage 6.

الفُصولُ الأَرْبَعَة والطَقْس

أزهار

في السَنَةِ أربَعَةُ فُصول هِيَ الرَبيعُ والصَيْفُ والخَريفُ والشِتاءُ. فَصْلُ الرَبيعِ جَميلٌ. الأشْجارُ خَضْراءُ والأزْهارَ مِن كُلِّ لَوْن. يَسْقُطُ المَطَرُ أحْياناً، لكِنَّ الطَقْسَ مُعْتَدِلٌ دائماً. الشَمسُ ساطِعَةٌ في مُعْظَمِ الأيّام. أشْهُرُ هذا الفَصْلِ هِيَ آذارُ ونيسانُ وأيّار.

الشَمس

يَأتي فَصْلُ الصَيْفِ بَعْدَ فَصْلِ الرَبيع. الطَقْسُ حارٌّ في الصَيْفِ والسَماءُ صافِيَةٌ. يَذهَبُ الناسُ في الصَيفِ عادةً إلى شاطِئِ البَحْرِ أو البُحَيْرةِ ويَسْبَحون هُناك. شُهورُ الصَيْفِ هِيَ حَزيران وتَموز وآب.

غُيوم

أشْهُرُ فَصْلِ الخَريف هِيَ أَيْلولُ وتِشْرينُ الأوّلُ وتِشْرينُ الثّاني ويَأتي هذا الفَصْلُ بَعْدَ فَصْلِ الصَيْف. هُناكَ غُيومٌ في السَماءِ في الخَريف وتَهُبُّ الرياحُ وتَسقُطُ أوراقُ الأشْجار. يَذهَبُ كُلُّ الطُلّاب إلى المَدارِسِ والجامِعاتِ في هذا الفَصْل.

هُناكَ ثَلاثةُ أشْهُرٍ في الشِتاءِ أيْضاً وهي كانونُ الأوّلُ وكانونُ الثاني وشُباط. في هذا الفَصْلِ يَسْقُطُ المَطَرُ أو الثَلْجُ ويَكونُ الطَقْسُ بارِداً عادَةً. يَذهَبُ بَعْضُ الناسِ في أمريكا في الشِتاءِ عادةً إلى وِلايَتَيْ أريزونا وفلوريدا لأنَّهُما دافِئَتانِ في هذا الفَصلِ.

الطَقْسُ

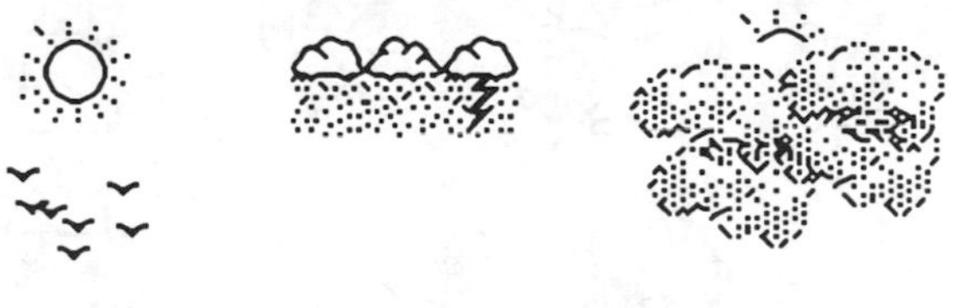

دَرَجةُ الحَرارة

يَوم= نَهار + لَيْل

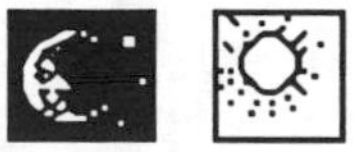

نَهار لَيْل

الجمعة ١٧ آذار ١٩٩٥

الطقس اليوم

ماطِر

مطَر كُلَّ اليوم. تصل
درجة الحرارة إلى ١٢
مِئوية نَهاراً و ٦ درَجات
لَيْلاً. رياح خَفيفة.

الثلاثاء ١٨ تموز ١٩٩٥

الطقس اليوم

حارّ وصَحو

تصل درجة الحرارة إلى
٣٦ مئوية. رياح خَفيفة.
اَلسماء صافية.

الإثنين ٢ تشرين الأول ١٩٩٥

الطقس اليوم

معتدل وغائم

تصل درجة الحرارة إلى
١٨ مئوية نهاراً و١٢
درجة ليلاً. رياح قويّة.
غُيوم في النهار.

الجمعة ٢٦ كانون الثاني ١٩٩٦

الطقس اليوم

بارد

يسقط الثلج من الصباح
حتى المساء. تصل درجة
الحرارة إلى -٢ مئوية.
ليس هناك رياح.

Note that the word يَوْم means "*day*," whereas اليَــوْم, with the definite article, means "*today*."

تمرين ١

A. Complete the following sentences with the most appropriate alternatives according to the information in the reading passages.

١- في السَنَةِ أربَعَةُ ......

❑ شُهور ❑ فُصول ❑ أسابيع ❑ أيّام

٢- شَهْرُ تِشرينَ الأوَّلِ مِن أشهُرِ ......

❑ الخَريف ❑ الشِتاء ❑ الرَبيع ❑ الصَيْف

٣- الطَقسُ في الرَبيعِ ......

❑ حارٌّ ❑ بارِدٌ ❑ مُعتَدِلٌ ❑ كَبيرٌ

٤- يَذهَبُ بَعضُ الناسِ في أيّامِ الصَيْفِ الحارَّةِ إلى ......

❑ البَحْرِ ❑ الغُيومِ ❑ الرِياحِ ❑ الشَمسِ

٥- يَذهَبُ بَعْضُ الأمريكيّين في الشِتاءِ إلى ......

❑ المَدينَة ❑ ألاسكا ❑ الغُيومِ ❑ أريزونا

٦- تَهبُّ الرِياحُ في فَصلِ ......

❑ الرَبيعِ ❑ الصَيفِ ❑ الخَريفِ ❑ الشتاءِ

B. Answer these questions according to the information in the reading passages.

٧- في أيِّ فَصلٍ تَكونُ الأشْجارُ خَضراء؟

٨- مَتى تَكونُ الشَمسُ ساطِعةً في مُعْظَمِ الأيّام؟

٩- هَل توجَدُ بُحَيرَةٌ قَريبَةٌ مِن مَدينَتِك؟ ما اسْمُها؟

١٠- في أيِّ فَصلٍ يَكونُ الطَقسُ حارّاً؟

C. According to your general knowledge and the current situation, label these sentences صَح or خَطَأ and correct the false ones:

١١- يَسقُطُ الثلجُ في الخَريف.

١٢- تَصِلُ دَرَجَةُ الحَرارَةِ في الشِتاءِ إلى -٢ (ناقِص اثنَين) مِئَويَّة.

١٣- الطَقسُ غائِمٌ في الصَيفِ في مُعظمِ الأيّام.

١٤- طَقْسُ اليَومِ ماطِرٌ.

تمرين ٢

Write down matching words from the left column in the blanks next to their matches.

١- رَبيع	....	مَطَر
٢- حارّ	....	مِئويّة
٣- غائِم	....	خَريف
٤- شاطِئ	....	صَحْوٌ
٥- لَيْل	....	سَماء
٦- ثَلج	....	بَحْر
٧- دَرَجَة	....	نَهار
		بارِد

تمرين ٣

Underline the word that does not belong in each set and explain your choice:

١- شَجَرة	زَهْرة	خَضراء	ثَلْج
٢- طَقْس	بُحَيْرة	مُعْتَدِل	دَرَجة حَرارَة
٣- مَطَر	شاطِئ	بَحْر	بُحَيْرة
٤- دافِئ	بارِد	فَصْل	حارّ
٥- ريح	مَطَر	ثَلْج	أسْبوع

تمرين ٤

Describe today's weather, using the models above and making the necessary changes.

تمرين ٥

Rearrange the words in each item to make meaningful sentences.

١- أمريكيَّة - هذهِ - لَيْسَتْ - سَيّارتُها
٢- أُختي - مِفتاحُ - هذا - شَقَّةِ - بابِ
٣- أيّار - حَزيران - شَهْرُ - شَهْرِ - بَعْدَ - يَأتي
٤- غدٍ - الطَقْسُ - بَعْدَ - سَيَكونُ - صَحْواً
٥- الصَيفِ - شاطِئِ - في - إلى - الناسُ - البَحْرِ - يَذهَبُ
٦- لِصَديقاتِها - غداً - قالَت - إلى - إنَّها - زَيْنَب - المَغرِبِ - سَتُسافِر
٧- جَيِّدَةٌ - العَرَبِيَّةَ - إنَّ - لي - لُغَتي - أُسْتاذي - قالَ
٨- مِن - السَبتِ - إلى - في - بِالقِطارِ - حَلَبَ - دِمَشقَ - ذَهَبْتُ - يَوْمِ

تمرين ٦

Convey the following meanings in Arabic, using the verb وَصَلَ. Remember that you may need to use the preposition إلى after this verb when the destination is specified.

1. Hani's flight arrived at 9:30.
2. I arrived in this town in 1990.
3. The temperature in the summer reaches 40 degrees Celsius in my town.
4. We have reached lesson 18.
5. The temperature will reach minus five at night.

1. **Converting Temperature Scales**

You may convert a Fahrenheit scale to a Celsius scale by simply subtracting 32 from the temperature reading, multiplying the result by 5, and then dividing by 9. For example, to convert 78 F to the decimal scale, here is what you do:

78 - 32 = 46	٤٦ = ٣٢ – ٧٨	١
46 x 5 = 230	٢٣٠ = ٥ x ٤٦	٢
230 ÷ 9 = 25.55	٢٥,٥٥ = ٩ ÷ ٢٣٠	٣

In order to convert from Celsius to Fahrenheit, follow the reverse process: multiply by 9, divide by 5, and then add 32.

تمرين ٧

What is the equivalent of each of these temperature readings?

٣٨ مِئَوِيَّة   26C   ٨٤ فَرنهايت   32F

2. **Partitive Nouns**

There are words that denote part of a whole. We have encountered three of them so far: مُعْظَم "*most*," بَعْض "*some*," and كُلّ "*every, all, the whole*." These Arabic words are nouns and they occur with a following noun or nouns, forming with them *iḍāfa* structures.

The meaning of these nouns varies, depending on whether the modified noun is definite, indefinite, singular, or plural, as in these examples:

٤	مُعْظَم	"*most of the*"	مُعْظَمُ اليَوْمِ
٥		"*most of the*"	مُعْظَمُ الأيّامِ
٦		"*most of the*"	مُعْظَمُ أيّامِ الأسبوعِ
٧	بَعْض	"*part/some of the*"	بَعْضُ اليَوْمِ
٨		"*part of a*"	بَعْضُ يَوْمٍ
٩		"*a number of*"	بَعْضُ أيّامٍ
١٠		"*some of the*"	بَعْضُ الأيّامِ
١١		"*some of the*"	بَعْضُ أيّامِ الأسبوعِ
١٢	كُلّ	"*the whole*"	كُلُّ اليَوْمِ
١٣		"*every*"	كُلُّ يَوْمٍ
١٤		"*all of*"	كُلُّ الأيّامِ
١٥		"*all of*"	كُلُّ أيّامِ الأسبوعِ

The second part of an *iḍāfa* is مَجرور "genitive" marked by a *kasra* or a double *kasra*. Note that الأيّامِ and أيّامِ الأسبوعِ are both definite, marked by a *kasra* and that indefinite nouns are marked by a double *kasra*. These structures may be used as adverbs of time (دَرَسْتُ مُعْظَمَ اليَومِ) or according to their position in a sentence (كُلُّ الأيّام بارِدَةٌ).

تمرين ٨

Convey these meanings in Arabic, using مُعْظَمُ ,بَعضُ, and كلُّ, and provide inflectional endings.

1. All the books.
2. Every month.
3. Some of my friends.
4. Most of the day.
5. The whole week.
6. Some of the year.

تمرين ٩

Listen to the recorded passage and select the best alternative.

١- في أوَّلِ يَومٍ كانَ الطَقْسُ في النَهارِ ......

❑ بارِداً ❑ مُعْتَدِلاً ❑ حارّاً

٢- ذَهَبَ الزَوْجُ والزوجةُ إلى صافيتا في فَصْلِ ......

❑ الشِتاءِ ❑ الرَبيعِ ❑ الصَيْفِ

٣- وَصَلَ الزَوْجُ وزَوْجَتُهُ إلى صافيتا يَومَ ......

❑ الخَميسِ ❑ الجُمْعةِ ❑ السَبْتِ

٤- يَعملُ الزَوْجُ في مَدينَةِ ......

❑ صافيتا ❑ دِمَشق ❑ حَلَب

Mark each sentence صَح or خطأ according to the recorded passage and *correct* or comment on the false ones.

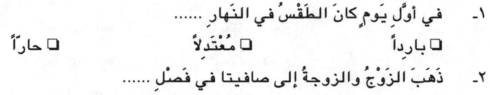

٥- ذَهَبَ الزَوْجُ والزَوْجَةُ إلى صافيتا بِالقِطار.

٦- كانَتِ الأشْجارُ خَضْراءَ في صافيتا.

٧- تُريد الزَوْجَةُ السَكَنَ في حَلَب.

٨- الطَقْسُ بارِدٌ في اللَيْلِ في صافيتا.

9. Write down all that you can understand of the passage in idiomatic English. Do not translate literally.

المُفْرَدات

green	أَخْضَر ج خُضْر (adj., m.)
cold	بارِد (adj., m.)
sea	بَحْر ج بِحار (n., m.)
lake	بُحَيْرة ج بُحَيْرات (n., f.)
some	بَعْض (n.)
snow	ثَلْج ج ثُلوج (n., m.)
hot	حارّ (adj., m.)
heat	حَرارة (n., f.)
autumn	خَريف (n., m.)
green	خَضْراء ج خَضْراوات (adj., f.)
warm	دافِئ (adj., m.)
degree (temperature), step	دَرَجة ج دَرَجات (n., f.) (درجة حرارة)
spring	رَبيع (n., m.)
wind	ريح ج رِياح (n., f.)
flower	زَهْرة ج زَهْرات/أَزْهار (n., f.)
brilliant, shining	ساطِع (adj., m.)
to swim	سَبَحَ (يَسْبَحُ) سِباحة (v.)
to fall	سَقَطَ (يَسْقُطُ) سُقوط (v.)
sky	سَماء ج سَماوات (n., f.)
beach	شاطِئ ج شَواطِئ (n., m.)
winter	شِتاء (n., m.)
tree	شَجَرة ج شَجَرات (n., f.)
sun	شَمْس ج شُموس (n., f.)
pure, clear, not cloudy	صافٍ (adj., m.) صافِية (f.)
clear, fine (of weather)	صَحْوٌ (adj., m.)

طَقْس ج طُقوس (n., m.)	weather
عامِل ج عُمّال (n., m.) (عيد العُمّال)	worker, laborer (Labor Day)
غائِم (adj., m.)	cloudy
غَيْمة ج غُيوم (n., f.)	cloud
كُلّ (n.)	every, all, the whole
لَوْن ج ألْوان (n., m.)	color
لَيْل (n., m.)	night
ماطِر (adj., m.)	rainy
مَطَر ج أمْطار (n., m.)	rain
مُعْتَدِل (adj.)	moderate
مُعْظَم (n.)	most
ناقِص (n., m.)	minus
نَهار ج (n., m.)	daytime

مَسجِدٌ دِمَشقيّ

Lesson Nineteen — الدَّرْسُ التاسِعَ عَشَرَ

Objectives

- Describing daily activities.
- Partitive nouns revisited (كأس حليب – فنجان شاي – قِطعة خُبز).
- Asking someone not to do something (negating imperative verbs).
- Defective and hollow verbs.
- Expressing reason: the particle لأنَّ.
- Verb position in the Arabic sentence.
- The preposition وَ.
- Listen to recorded material for this lesson.
- Do relevant computer drills and exercises, Stage 7.

ماذا تفعلُ هالة بُسْتاني كُلَّ يَوْم؟

هالَةُ بُستاني طالِبةٌ تَدْرُسُ الطِبَّ في جامِعَةِ حَلَب. تَسْكُنُ في شَقّةٍ مَعَ صَديقَتِها سَحَر حلاّق.

تَنهَضُ هالَةُ مِن النَومِ في الساعَةِ السابِعَةِ والرُبْعِ صَباحاً وتَذهَبُ إلى الحَمّام وتَسْتَحِمُّ أو تَغْسِلُ يَدَيْها ووَجهَها بِالماءِ والصابونِ وتُنَظِّفُ أسْنانَها بِفُرشاةِ الأسْنانِ والمَعْجون.

بَعدَ ذلكَ تَذهَبُ إلى المَطْبَخِ وتُحَضِّر طَعامَ الفَطورِ. تأكُلُ هالَةُ عَلى الفَطورِ عادَةً بَيضَتَينِ أو قِطعَةَ خُبْزٍ وقِطعَةً مِنَ الجُبْنِ مَعَ كأسِ حَليب.

في يَوْمِ الجُمْعةِ تُحَضِّرُ هالَةُ وسَحَرُ البَيْضَ أو الفولَ المُدَمَّسَ عَلى الفَطورِ وتَشرَبانِ الشايَ بَعدَ الطَعامِ.

في الساعَةِ الثامِنَةِ تَذهَبُ هالَةُ إلى الجامِعَةِ بِالحافِلةِ. لا تَذهَبُ إلى الجامِعةِ بِالسَيّارَةِ لأنَّها لَيْسَ عِندَها سَيّارة.

في الساعَةِ الثامِنَةِ والنِصْفِ تَصِلُ إلى الجامِعَةِ وتَذهَبُ إلى المَكتَبَةِ وتدرُسُ هُناكَ حَتّى الساعةِ الحاديةَ عَشْرَةَ.

في الساعَةِ الحادِيَةَ عَشْرَةَ تَذهَبُ إلى دَرْسِ الكيمياءِ مَعَ صديقَتِها غادة. وفي الساعةِ الثانيَةَ عَشْرةَ تَذهبانِ مَعاً إلى مَقْصَفِ الجامِعةِ وتأكُلانِ الغَداءَ هُناك. تأكُلُ هالَةُ أحْياناً الكَبابَ الحَلَبيَّ وأحْياناً الفَلافِلَ، لكِنَّ غادَة تأكُلُ لَبَناً أو سَلَطَةً فَقَط، وأحْياناً تأكلُ التَبّولَة.

بَعْدَ ذلكَ تَذهَبُ هالَة إلى المَخْبَرِ من الساعَةِ الواحِدةِ إلى الساعَةِ الثالِثة. بَعْدَ المَخْبَرِ تَذهَبُ إلى دَرسِ الأحْياء.

في الساعَةِ الخامِسَةِ تَرْجِعُ إلى البَيْتِ وتَكونُ في شَقَّتِها في الساعَةِ الخامِسَةِ والرُبْع. في المساءِ تُحَضِّرُ هالَةُ طَعامَ العَشاء، وتأكلُ عادةً الزَيْتونَ والجُبنَ أو الخُضَرَ أو البَيْضَ المَقْليَّ وتَشرَبُ فِنجانَ شايٍ بَعْدَ العَشاء.

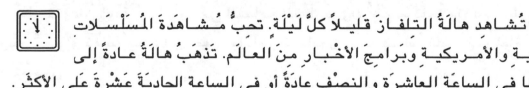

تُشاهِد هالَةُ التِلفازَ قَليلاً كلَّ لَيْلَةٍ. تحِبُّ مُشاهَدَةَ المُسَلْسَلاتِ العَرَبيةِ والأمريكيةِ وبَرامِجَ الأخْبارِ مِنَ العالَم. تَذهَبُ هالَةُ عادةً إلى سَريرِها في الساعَةِ العاشِرَةِ والنِصْفِ عادَةً أو في الساعةِ الحادِيَةَ عَشْرةَ عَلى الأكثَر.

يَوْمِيّات عدنان مارتيني

الثُلاثاء ١٠ تِشرينَ الأوَّل ١٩٩٥

نَهَضْتُ اليَوْمَ مِنَ النَومِ في الساعَةِ السابِعَةِ إلاّ ثُلثاً. استَحْمَمْتُ وحَلَقْتُ ذَقْني بِرُبعِ ساعَةٍ ثُمَّ أكَلْتُ فَطوري (كأس حَليبٍ وقِطعَةَ خُبزٍ مَعَ الجُبْنِ) ومَشَيْتُ إلى الجامِعَةِ.

وَصَلتُ إلى صَفّي في الساعَةِ الثامِنَةِ والنِصْفِ تَماماً. لا أحِبُّ هذه المادَّةَ (لُغات الحاسوب) لأنَّها في وقتٍ مُبَكِّرٍ جداً. وَصَلَ بعضُ الطلابِ مُتَأخِّرينَ إلى الصَفِّ اليَوْمَ. حينَ رَجَعتُ إلى البَيْتِ مَساءً كانَ هُناكَ وَرَقَةٌ مِن زِياد عَلى بابِ غُرفَتي. كَتَبَ فيها: «لا تَنسَ العَشاءَ اليومَ في مَطعَمِ عَلي بابا في الساعَةِ السابِعَةِ مَعَ تِم وَليسا.» نَسيتُ مَوعِدَ هذا العَشاءِ وَالله.

الأربِعاء ١١ تِشرينَ الأوَّل ١٩٩٥.

بَعدَ دَرسِ لُغاتِ الحاسوبِ ذَهَبْتُ إلى المَكتَبَةِ وقَرأتُ ساعَتَينِ ثُمَّ أكَلتُ الغَداءَ في مَقصَفِ الجامِعَةِ وذَهَبتُ إلى عَمَلي في مَخبَرِ الحاسوب. أعْمَلُ هُناكَ خَمسَ عَشْرَةَ ساعةً في الأسبوع. بَعْدَ الظُهرِ ذَهَبتُ إلى دَرسَيْ الرياضيّاتِ واللُغةِ الإنكليزية. رَجَعتُ إلى المَكتَبَةِ مَرةً ثانيَةً وقَرأتُ دُروسي حَتّى الساعَةِ الثامِنَةِ مَساءً. بَعدَ ذلِكَ مَشَيْتُ إلى شَقَّتي وأكَلتُ العَشاءَ مَعَ زِيادَ في الشَقَّة.

ما أكَلْنا أمْسِ في مَطْعَمِ عَلي بابا. تَكلّمَتْ ليسا أمسِ بِالهاتِفِ وقالَتْ إنَّها مَشغولَةٌ جِدّاً. سَنَأكُلُ مَعاً (أنا وزِيادُ وليسا وتِم) مَساءَ يَوْمِ الجُمْعَةِ إنْ شاءَ الله. ذَهَبْتُ إلى النَوْمِ في السّاعَةِ الحاديَةَ عَشْرَةَ بَعدَ مُشاهَدَةِ بَرنامَجِ "سِتّونَ دَقيقَةَ" عَلى التلفاز. أُحِبُّ مُشاهَدَةَ هذا البَرنامَج. لا أحِبُّ كِتابَةَ الرسائِلِ عادةً لكِنَّني سَأكتُبُ رِسالَةً إلى أبي وأُمّي غَداً إنْ شاءَ الله.

تمرين ١

A. Complete the following sentences with the appropriate alternatives according to the information in the reading passages.

١- تَسكُنُ هالَةَ بُستاني الآنَ في ......

❑ حَلَب ❑ القاهِرة ❑ دِمَشْق

٢- تَنهَضُ هالَةُ مِنَ النَوْمِ في الساعَةِ ......

❑ السادِسَةِ ❑ السابِعَةِ ❑ الثامِنَةِ

٣- تَذهَبُ هالَةُ إلى الجامِعَةِ ......

❑ بِالحافِلَةِ ❑ بِالسَيّارَةِ ❑ مَشْياً

٤- تَأكلُ هالَةُ الغَداءَ مَعَ صَديقَتِها ......

❑ سُعاد ❑ غادَة ❑ سَحَر

٥- مَوعِدُ دَرسِ الأحْياءِ في الساعَةِ ......

❑ الواحِدَةِ ❑ الثانِيَةِ ❑ الثالِثَةِ

٦- يَأكلُ عَدنانُ عَلى الفَطورِ ......

❑ الزَيْتونَ ❑ البَيْضَ ❑ الجُبْنَ

٧- وَصَلَ عَدنان إلى دَرْسِ لُغاتِ الحاسوبِ ......

❑ في مَوْعِدِهِ ❑ مُبَكِّراً ❑ مُتَأخِّراً

٨- ما أكَلَ عَدْنانُ العَشاءَ مَعَ أصْدِقائِهِ يَوْمَ الثُلاثاءِ لأنَّ ليسا كانَت ......

❑ مُبَكِّرَةً ❑ مَشغولَةً ❑ مُتَأخِّرَةً

٩- يَعمَلُ عَدنانُ في مَخبَرِ الحاسوبِ ...... في الأُسْبوع.

❑ عَشْرَ ساعاتٍ ❑ خَمسَ عَشْرَةَ ساعَةً ❑ عِشْرونَ ساعَةً

١٠- يُحِبُّ عَدنانُ ......

❑ مُشاهَدَةَ التِلفازِ ❑ كِتابَةَ الرَسائِلِ ❑ بَرنامَجَ سِتّونَ دَقيقَة

B. Complete these sentences with information from the reading passages.

١١- تَسْكُنُ هالَة بُستاني مَعَ ......

١٢- تَرجِعُ هالَةُ إلى شَقَّتِها في الساعَةِ ......

١٣- تَذهَبُ هالَة إلى السَريرِ في الساعَةِ ......

١٤- لا يُحِبُّ عَدنانُ مادّةَ لُغاتِ الحاسوبِ لأنَّها ......

١٥- نَسِيَ عَدنانُ مَوعِدَ ......

١٦- يَقرَأُ عَدنانُ دُروسَهُ عادَةً في ......

C. Mark the following sentences صَـواب or خَطأ and correct the false ones according to the reading passages.

١٧- تأكُلُ هالَة بُستاني الفولَ عَلى الفَطورِ كلَّ يَوم.

١٨- تَذهَبُ هالَةُ إلى النَومِ في الساعَةِ العاشِرةِ مَساءً.

١٩- تُنَظِّفُ غادَةُ وَجهَها بِالفُرشاةِ والمَعْجون.

٢٠- لَيسَ عِندَ هالَة سَيّارَة.

٢١- تُحِبُّ هالَةُ مُشاهَدَةَ بَرنامَجِ سِتّونَ دَقيقَة.

٢٢- يَحلِقُ عَدنانُ ذَقنَهُ قَبلَ النَوم.

٢٣- نَسِيَ عَدنانُ دَرْسَ لُغاتِ الحاسوب.

٢٤- تَكَلَّمَ عَدنانُ بِالهاتِف وَقالَ إنَّهُ مَشغول.

٢٥- سَيأكلُ الأَصْدِقاءُ الأَرْبَعَةُ العَشاءَ مَعاً يَومَ الجُمْعَة.

٢٦- سَيَكتُبُ عَدنانُ رِسالةً يَومَ الأربِعاء.

تمرين ٢

Complete the following sentences with words from the list.

الحَلوى – تَنهَضينَ – عيدُ – المَعجونِ – الشايَ – تَبّولَةً – فَجْرُ – الصابونِ

١- تَشرَبُ هالَةُ .... بَعْدَ الفَطور.

٢- أغسِلِ يَدَيَّ بالماءِ و ....

٣- هَلْ تَأكُلُ .... بَعدَ الطَعام؟

٤- مَتى .... مِنَ النَومِ يا لَيْلى؟

٥- أُنَظِّفُ أسْناني بِالفُرشاةِ و...........

٦- آكُلُ .... فَقَط عَلى الغَداء.

تمرين ٣

Write down matching words from the left column in the blanks next to their matches.

١- اسْتَحَمَّ	....	مَعْجون أسْنان
٢- فُرشاة	....	ذَقْن
٣- نَسِيَ	....	حافِلَة
٤- سَرير	....	غَسَلَ
٥- كَباب	....	مَطعَم
٦- حَلَقَ	....	فَلافِل
٧- مَقْصَف	....	مَوْعِد
		نَوْم

تمرين ٤

Select the word that does not belong in each set and explain your choice.

١ـ	فُرشاة	ماء	قَهوة	شاي
٢ـ	فَطور	غَداء	طِبّ	عَشاء
٣ـ	حافِلَة	سَيّارَة	درّاجَة	حاسِبَة
٤ـ	كَباب	صابون	فَلافِل	فول
٥ـ	سِنّ	وَجْه	لَبَن	يَد
٦ـ	مادَّة	مُسَلسَل	بَرنامَج	تِلفاز
٧ـ	نَهَضَ	اِسْتَحَمَّ	غَسَلَ	مَرَّة
٨ـ	ورَقَة	مُشاهَدَة	كِتابَة	رِسالَة

تمرين ٥

Construct a meaningful paragraph by rearranging the following sentences. Do not change the position of the first sentence.

١ـ اِسْمي رَوضَة قَطّان.

أُحَضِّرُ عادَةً فَطوراً كَبيراً لي ولِزَوجي وأولادي.

نَرجِعُ إلى البَيْتِ في الساعَةِ الثامِنَةِ مَساءً.

في الساعَةِ الرابِعَةِ بَعْدَ الظُهْرِ أذْهَبُ وَأولادي إلى دارِ أبي وأمّي.

أعْمَلُ أمينَةَ مَكتَبَةٍ في الجامِعَةِ الأُردُنِيَّةِ في عَمّان.

لكِنَّني أنهَضُ مُتَأخِّرَةً في يَوْمِ الجُمْعَة (في التاسِعَةِ أو العاشِرَةَ).

وأحْياناً نَأكُلُ الحِمَّصَ إلى جانِبِ الزَيتونِ والجُبْن.

حَيْثُ أتَكَلَّمُ مَعَهُما ومَعَ أُختي وأخي.

بَعدَ الفَطورِ أُنَظِّفُ الدارَ وأغسِلُ القُمْصان.

أُحَضِّرُ أحْياناً الفولَ المُدَمَّسَ والبَيْضَ المَقْليّ.

أذهَبُ إلى عَمَلي في الساعَةِ السابِعَةِ كُلَّ يَوْم.

تمرين ٦

Rearrange the words in each item to make meaningful sentences.

١- عَلى - الفولَ - هالَةُ - الغَداءِ - تَأكُلُ - المُدَمَّسَ

٢- صَباحاً - مُشاهَدَةَ - الأخْبارِ - أحِبُّ - بَرامِجَ

٣- السَبْتِ - السَيّارَةَ - زَوجي - يَوْمَ - يَغسِلُ

تمرين ٧

Construct three sentences, describing in the first one an activity which you do every day, in the second an activity you usually do, and in the third an activity you sometimes do. You may use the adverbials كُلَّ يَوم، عادَةً، أحْياناً, as in the example below.

آكُلُ الكَبابَ الحَلَبِيَّ عَلى الغَداءِ عادَةً.

تمرين ٨

In one paragraph, describe your daily activities either on a typical day of the week or on a weekend. Model your description after the reading passages above.

1. **Partitive Nouns and Phrases**

Just like the noun بَعْضُ, which denotes part of a whole, there are nouns which, when used with other nouns as *iḍāfa* structures, effect a partitive meaning. In this lesson, three such phrases occurred: (1) كَأسُ ماء "*glass of water,*" فِنجانُ شاي "*cup of tea,*" and قِطعَةُ خُبْز "*piece of bread.*" The first word of each phrase signifies a specific amount of the complete whole.

Note also that a partitive meaning can also be achieved through a prepositional phrase, as in قِطعَةٌ مِنَ الخُبز, which literally means "*piece of bread,*" the same meaning conveyed by an *iḍāfa* structure.

تمرين ٩

How do you express these meanings in Arabic? Use both *iḍāfa* and prepositional phrases.
1. A glass of orange juice.
2. A cup of coffee.
3. A piece of cheese.

2. Negating Imperative Verbs

An imperative verb is used for making requests or giving commands, such as أعْطِ، اِجْلِسْ and تَفَضَّلْ (see lesson 13). Negating an imperative verb is done with the negative particle لا. It is used before the verb and it affects its form. With لا, the verb changes its form from the imperative to a form of the present tense called المُضارِع المَجزوم (jussive).

١ أُكْتُبْ ⇦ لا تَكْتُبْ

This form of the present is similar to the regular (indicative) present (المضارع المرفوع), but with two differences: (1) the inflectional marker *ḍamma* on the end of the regular present is replaced with a *sukūn*:

٢ تَكتُبُ ⇦ تكتُبْ

and (2) in some conjugations which end with a نون, this letter is dropped:

٣ تَكتُبون ⇦ تكتُبوا

Note that the final *alif* in the third person masculine plural conjugation of المضارع المجزوم (jussive) (example 3 above) is silent. It is, however, dropped when an attached (object) pronoun is suffixed to the verb:

٤ تَكتُبوا + ها = تَكتُبوها

3. Weak Verbs

A weak verb is called مُعتَلّ in Arabic because it contains حَرف علّة, which is a vowel in the first, second, or third position of the verb (e.g. نَسِيَ، وَصَلَ، قالَ). It is called a hollow verb if it has a long vowel as the middle letter (e.g. قالَ). Notice that in المُضارِع المجزوم, the long vowel is replaced with its short vowel counterpart (e.g. *alif* becomes *fatḥa*) in the second person masculine singular (see also the imperative conjugation of these verbs in Appendix C):

٥ تَقولُ ⇦ تَقُلْ

٦ تَنسى ⇦ تَنسَ

٧ تُعطي ⇦ تُعطِ

This process occurs only with the second person masculine singular (*you* m.). The other difference between المضارع المرفوع and المضارع المجزوم is that the final *nūn* is deleted:

<u>مَرفوع</u> <u>مَجزوم</u>

٨ تَقولينَ ⇦ تَقولي

٩ تَنسَيْنَ ⇦ تَنسَيْ

١٠ تُعطينَ ⇦ تُعطي

Note that the feminine, second person plural form does not undergo any changes, e.g.

١١ تَقُلْنَ ⇦ تَقُلْنَ

١٢ تَنسينَ ⇦ تَنسينَ

١٣ تُعطينَ ⇦ تُعطينَ

تمرين ١٠

Express each of these situations in Arabic in one imperative sentence, using the negative particle لا and the appropriate form of the verb (المُضارع المجزوم).

1. In order to decrease the amount of graffiti, you write a sign asking people not to write on the walls.
2. You remind a male friend not to forget the time of his flight.
3. Ask a woman not to give her phone number to someone (him).
4. Ask a man not to sit on a particular chair.
5. Inform two friends that there is no class today (ask them not to go to class).

4. Expressing Reason

Expressing a reason is accomplished by using the particle لأنَّ "*because*." It is made up of the preposition لِـ "*for*" and the particle أنَّ "*that*". Just like إنَّ and أنَّ, لأنَّ must be followed by a noun or a pronoun. For example, the phrase "because I" is expressed as لأنّي, and "because the teacher" is rendered لأنَّ الأستاذَ. Remember that the following noun must be مَنصوب, as indicated by the *fatḥa* on the end of الأستاذَ (see lesson 17 for a discussion of أنَّ and إنَّ). Questions whose answer requires the use of لأنَّ start with لِماذا (e.g. لماذا تسكن هُنا؟).

تمرين ١١

Express reason in Arabic, using لأنَّ:

1. Sāmi does not have a car because he is a student.
2. This man doesn't know what you're saying because he doesn't speak English.
3. I'll visit some Arab countries next spring because I'm learning Arabic.

5. Verb Position in Arabic Sentences

Conventionally, the Arabic verb occupies an initial sentence position, as in example *14*:

١٤ تَدرُسُ الطالباتُ في المَكتَبَةِ.

In this case, the verb agrees with the following noun, which is the subject (or doer of the action), in gender, but not in number. The verb is singular though the subject is plural. However, a sentence may also start with the subject (الفاعل):

١٥ الطالباتُ يدرسنَ في المَكتَبَةِ.

As you can see, the verb in example 15 agrees with the preceding subject not only in gender, but also in number. If the subject is of a mixed gender, use the gender of the first noun (e.g. يَسكُنُ أخي وأختي في بَيْتي).

Examine this sentence from lesson 19:

١٦ تَحضَرُ هالَةُ وسَحَرُ البَيْضَ على الفَطورِ و تَشرَبانِ الشايَ.

In the first occurrence, the verb is singular while the subject is dual (هالَةُ وسَحَر). In the second occurrence, the verb is dual because it follows the dual subject.

SUMMARY

If the verb *precedes* the subject, it agrees with it only in gender, and it is in the singular. If the verb *follows* the subject, it agrees with it in gender *and* number.

تمرين ١٢

Provide the correct form of the verb in parentheses (tense, gender, and number). The verbs are listed in the past tense third person masculine singular. Look for time clues to determine tense.

Example: أخَواتُ صَديقي (عَمِل) الآنَ في سوقٍ كَبيرَة.

أخَواتُ صَديقي ...يعْمَلنَ... الآن في سوقٍ كَبيرَة.

١- كُلُّ الطُّلاّبِ (دَرَس) ...... اللُغةَ الإنكليزيَّةَ في المَدارِسِ الآنَ.

٢- (وَصَلَ) ...... صَديقاتي مِنَ الرَباطِ أمْسِ.

٣- (عَمِلَ) ...... أبي وأمّي في مَدينَةِ الرياضِ حينَ كُنْتُ صَغيراً.

٤- أخي وزَوجَتُهُ (سَكَن) ...... في مَدينَةِ حَلَبَ في سوريَة حَتّى الآن.

٥- صَديقي وعائِلَتُهُ (انتَقَلَ) ...... إلى دارٍ جَديدَةٍ في الشَهرِ الماضي.

٦- (لَبِس) ...... سامي وأخوه الكوفِيَّةَ والعِقالَ عادَةً.

٧- (دَرَسَ) ...... مُعْظَمُ صَديقاتِ هالَة اللُغَةَ الإنكليزِيَّةَ.

6. The Preposition وَ

This preposition is used either to add emphasis to one's words or to swear solemnly (e.g. وَاللّه). The noun modified by it is مَجرور (genitive) marked either with a *kasra* on the end of singular and broken plural nouns or ي instead of *alif* and *wāw* و in dual and sound plural nouns (see Cases of the Noun in lesson 13).

١٣ تمرين

A. Listen to the taped passage, then check the alternative in each item that agrees with the information in the tape-recorded passage.

١ـ سَيَغْسِلُ هاني قُمْصانَهُ يَوْمَ ......

❑ الجُمْعةِ ❑ السَبْتِ ❑ الأحَدِ

٢ـ سَيَذهَبُ هاني عِنْدَ الظُهرِ إلى ......

❑ مَكتَبةِ الفارابي ❑ مَطعَمِ الصَحّة ❑ دارِ صَديقِهِ

٣ـ يَدرُسُ غسّانُ في جامِعَةِ ......

❑ دِمَشقَ ❑ بِرمِنغهام ❑ حَلَبَ

٤ـ في السَنَةِ المُقبِلَةِ سَيَكونُ غسّانُ في ......

❑ سوريَة ❑ بريطانيا ❑ أمريكا

٥ـ سَيأكُلُ الأصدِقاءُ الثلاثَةُ العَشاءَ في مَطعَمِ ......

❑ الفارابي ❑ الصَحّةِ ❑ الجامِعَةِ

B. Mark the following sentences صَح or خَطأ and correct the false ones.

٦ـ عِندَ هاني سَيّارَة.

٧ـ يَدرُسُ غَسّانُ الأدَبَ الأمريكيّ.

٨ـ سَيأكُلُ الأصْدِقاءُ الثَلاثَةُ العَشاءَ في الساعَةِ السابِعَة.

٩ـ عامِر صَديقُ هاني وغَسّان.

10. Describe in Arabic what the narrator will do on that weekend morning.

11. Compose in Arabic a biographical sketch of the narrator's friend.

المُفْرَدات

to bathe, to take a bath or shower .... اسْتَحَمَّ (يَستَحِمُّ) استِحْمام (v.)

program .... بَرنامَج ج بَرامِج (n., m.)

salad made with finely chopped parsley, cracked wheat, tomatoes, lemon juice, and olive oil .... تَبّولة (n., f.)

then, and again .... ثُمَّ (conjunction)

bus, tram .... حافلة ج حافلات (n., f.)

to prepare, to make .... حَضَّرَ (يُحَضِّرُ) تَحْضير (v.)

to shave .... حَلَقَ (يَحْلِقُ) حَلْق (v.)

bathroom .... حَمّام ج حمّامات (n., f.)

news story .... خَبَر ج أخْبار (n., m.)

vegetables .... خُضرة ج خُضَر (n., f.)

chin (when used with 'shave' it signifies 'beard') .... ذَقْن ج ذُقون (n., f.)

to return, to go back .... رَجَعَ (يَرْجِعُ) رُجوع (v.)

letter, message .... رِسالة ج رَسائِل (n., f.)

tooth .... سِنٌّ ج أسْنان (n., m.)

soap .... صابون (n., m.)

world .... عالَم ج عَوالِم (n., m.)

dinner .... عَشاء ج أعْشِية (n., m.)

lunch .... غَداء ج أغْدية (n., m.)

to wash .... غَسَلَ (يَغْسِلُ) غَسْل (v.)

brush .... فُرْشاة ج فَراشٍ (n., f.)

breakfast .... فَطور (n., m.)

writing .... كِتابة

much, a great deal .... كَثير ج كَثيرون / كِثار (n., m.)

because .... لأنَّ (particle)

yogurt .... لَبَن (n., m.)
why .... لماذا (particle)
one coming early .... مُبَكِّر ج مُبَكِّرون (n., m.)
one coming late .... مُتَأخِّر ج مُتَأخِّرون (n., m.)
stewed .... مُدَمَّس (adj.)
once, one occurrence .... مَرّة ج مَرّات (n., f.)
(television) series .... مُسَلسَل ج مُسَلسَلات (n., m.)
watching .... مُشاهَدة (verbal noun)
busy .... مَشْغول ج مَشْغولون (n., m.)
together .... مَعاً (adv.)
paste .... مَعْجون ج مَعاجين (n., m.)
fried .... مَقليّ (adj.)
to forget .... نَسِيَ (يَنسى) نِسْيان (v.)
to clean .... نَظَّفَ (يُنَظِّفُ) تَنظيف (v.)
to get up .... نَهَضَ (يَنهَضُ) نُهوض (v.)
by God, I swear, really (used to add emphasis) .... وَاللّهِ
face .... وَجْه ج وُجوه (n., m.)
hand .... يَد ج أيْدٍ (n., f.)

دارُ الحِكْمَة في بَغداد.

Lesson Twenty — الدَرْسُ العِشرون

Objectives

- Describing activities in the past, present, and future.
- Expressing contrast with (أمّا ... فَـ).
- Expressing reason with لِذلِكَ.
- Structural notes.
- Listen to recorded material for this lesson.
- Do relevant computer drills and exercises, Stage 8.

يَومِيّاتُ مايْكِل بْراوْن

الأربِعاء ٢٣ أغسطس (آب) ١٩٩٥

بَعْدَ دَرسِ العَرَبيَّةِ بَعْدَ ظُهرِ اليَومِ ذَهَبتُ إلى مَطعَمٍ مَشْهورٍ في حَيِّ المُهَندِسينَ اِسْمُهُ «العُمْدَة» مَعَ أصدِقائي حُسَيْن أحْمَد وَهِبَة عَبد الله وَجِنِفَر كولي. يَدرُسُ حُسَينُ التِجارَةَ وتَدرُسُ هِبَةُ الصَحافَةَ. أمّا جِنِفَر فَهي طالِبةٌ أمريكيَّةٌ مِن جامِعَةِ واشِنطَن في سانت لويس تَدْرُسُ اللُغَةَ العَرَبِيَّةَ في الجامِعَةِ الأمريكيَّةِ في القاهِرَة. أكَلْنا هُناكَ "الكُشَري" وهِيَ أكْلَةٌ مِصْرِيَّةٌ مِنَ الأرُزِّ والعَدَسِ والمَعكَرونَةِ والبَصَل. أحِبُّ الكُشَريَّ كَثيراً، لكِنَّني حينَ آكلُ الكُشَريَّ أشرَبُ كَثيراً من الماءِ بَعدَ الطَعام. لِذلِكَ ما أكَلتُ كَثيراً مِنَ الكُشَريّ. كانَ المَطعَمُ نَظيفاً وكانَ هُناكَ بَعضُ الناسِ البريطانِيّينَ والإيطالِيّين.

الخَميس ٢٤ أغسطس (آب) ١٩٩٥

يَقولُ حُسَيْنُ إنَّ الطَقسَ غداً سَيكونُ حاراً. قُلتُ لَهُ إنّي سَأذهَبُ في عُطلَةِ نِهايَةِ الأسْبوعِ هذهِ إلى مَدينَةِ المِنيا. قالَ لي إنَّ المِنيا حارَّةٌ أيْضاً، وهِيَ أحَرُّ مِنَ القاهِرَة. سأزورُ أُسْرَةَ صَديقي سَمير أحْمَد هُناكَ وسَأنزِلُ عِندَهُم. سَأذهبُ بِالقِطارِ مِن مَحَطَّةِ الجيزَة. ثَلاثُ ساعاتٍ ونِصْفٌ مِن هذه المَحَطَّةِ إلى المِنيا. مَوعِدُ القِطارِ في الساعَةِ السابِعَةِ صَباحاً مِن كُلِّ يَوْم. سَيَكونُ أخو سَمير في مَحَطَّةِ القِطار حينَ أصِلُ إلى هُناك.

يَومِيّات عَدنان مارتيني

الجُمْعَة ١ أيلول ١٩٩٥

بَعْدَ دُروسي اليَومَ ذَهَبْتُ إلى المكتَبةِ وقَرَأتُ أكْثَرَ مِن ساعَتَيْن. كانَ هُناكَ صَديقي تِم نِكَلز وقالَ لي إنَّ الطَقسَ سَيكون حاراً غداً وبَعدَ غدٍ وإنَّ عُطلةَ نِهايَةِ الأسبوعِ هذهِ طَويلةٌ لأنَّ يَومَ الإثنَيْن ٤ أيلول هو عيدُ العُمّال، لِذلكَ سَيَذهَبُ يَومَ السَبتِ مَعَ صَديقَينِ إلى «سيدَر پوينت» وهي مَدينَةُ مَلاهٍ عَلى شاطِئِ بُحَيْرةِ إيري، والطَقسُ هُناكَ أبْرَدُ مِن طَقسِ كَلَمبَس. قال لي تِم "تَفَضَّلْ مَعَنا." سَأذهبُ مَعَهُم إنْ شاءَ الله لأنّي ما زُرتُ «سيدَر پوينت» حَتّى الآن.

الإثنَين ٤ أيلول ١٩٩٥

كانَ الطَقسُ جَميلاً جِداً في "سيدَر پوينت" وكانَت الشَمْسُ ساطِعةً ودَرَجَةُ الحَرارةِ مُعْتَدِلَة. بُحَيرةُ إيري كَبيرَةٌ، وهي أكبَرُ مِن كُلِّ البُحَيراتِ القَريبَةِ مِن كَلَمبَس. كانَ هُناكَ ناسٌ كَثيرونَ عَلى شاطِئِ البُحَيْرة وكانَ بَعْضُ الناسِ يَسبَحونَ في الماء. كانَ يَومُ السَبْتِ هذا مِن أجْمَلِ أيّامِ الصَيف. سَأزورُ "سيدَر پوينت" مَعَ أصدِقائي في الصَيفِ المُقْبِلِ إن شاءَ الله.

تمرين ١

Select the best alternative with reference to the Brown and Martini diaries:

١- «العُمْدة» اِسْمُ ......

❑ صَديقِ مايكل　❑ حَيٍّ في القاهِرة　❑ مَطعَمٍ

٢- الكُشَريُّ أَكْلةٌ ......

❑ مصرية　❑ بريطانية　❑ إيطالية

٣- كانَ المَطعَمُ ......

❑ قَريباً　❑ نَظيفاً　❑ جَميلاً

٤- سَيذهَبُ مايكل إلى المِنْيا مِن ......

❑ مَطارِ القاهِرةِ　❑ مَحَطّةِ الجيزَةِ　❑ حَيّ المُهَندِسينَ

٥- ذَهَبَ عدنانُ بَعدَ دُروسِهِ إلى ......

❑ المَكتَبةِ　❑ الصَفِّ　❑ الشارِعِ

٦- ذَهَبَ عَدنانُ في عُطلَةِ نِهايَةِ الأسْبوعِ إلى مَدينَةِ ......

❑ كلَمبَس　❑ دِمَشقَ　❑ مَلاهٍ

٧- عيدُ العُمّالِ في يَومِ ......

❑ السَبْتِ　❑ الأحَدِ　❑ الإثْنَينِ

٨- اِسْمُ صَديقِ عَدْنان ......

❑ تِم　❑ مايْكِل　❑ جِنِفَر

Mark the following sentences صح or خطأ and correct the false ones.

٩- مِنَ القاهِرَةِ إلى المِنيا خَمسُ ساعاتٍ بِالقِطار.

١٠- مَوعِدُ قِطارِ المِنيا في الساعَةِ التاسِعَةِ.

١١- كانَ الطَقسُ في «سيدَر پوينت» غائِماً.

١٢- سَيَذهَبُ عَدنانُ إلى «سيدَر پوينت» في الصَيفِ المُقبِلِ.

13. Form three questions about the reading passages.

تمرين ٢

A. Complete these sentences with the appropriate word:

١- جِمي كارتَر رَجُلٌ ......

❑ مَشْهور ❑ مُتَوَسِّط ❑ مُهَندِس

٢- ذَهَبَ سالِم إلى تونِس في ...... الصَيف.

❑ بَلْدةٍ ❑ بِطاقَةٍ ❑ عُطْلَةٍ

٣- تَسكُنُ سَناء في ..... «القَنَوات» في مَدينةِ دِمَشق.

❑ حَديث ❑ حَيّ ❑ حَبّ

٤- سَتَدرسُ أختي في جامعةِ الجَزائِر في فَصلِ الخَريفِ ......

❑ الحارّ ❑ الأوَّل ❑ المُقبِل

B. Select the word that does not belong in each set and explain your choice if necessary.

٥-	شَمْس	حارّ	بَصَل	صَيْف
٦-	مَوْعِد	سَرير	قِطار	مَحَطّة
٧-	أرُزّ	عَدَس	بَصَل	طَقْس
٨-	عيد	شاطِئ	بَحْر	بُحَيْرة

تمرين ٣

Rearrange the words in each item to make meaningful sentences.

١- فِلَسطينِيَّةٌ - "المُسَخَّنُ" - مَشهورَةٌ - أكْلَةٌ

٢- الإسْكَندَرِيَّة - بْراون - زارَ - مايْكِل - مَدينَةَ

٣- شاطِئِ - هُناكَ - عَلى - البَحرِ - ناسٌ - كانَ - كَثيرون

٤- مَساءً - القِطارِ - سامية - مَحَطّةِ - وَصَلَتْ - إلى

تمرين ٤

Reshuffle the order of the following sentences to create a meaningful paragraph, leaving the first sentence intact.

١- أحْمَد حِجازي رجُلٌ مِن مدينة حَلَب.

بَعدَ أربعِ ساعاتٍ ونِصْف وَصَلوا إلى طَرْطوس.

لكِنَّ طَرطوسَ لَيْسَتْ قَريبَةً ولَيْسَ عِندَ أحْمَد سَيّارَة.

بَعْدَ خَمسةِ أيّامٍ رَجَعوا إلى حَلَبَ بِالقِطارِ أيْضاً.

أرادَ أحْمَدُ زِيارةَ مَدينَةِ طَرطوسَ مَعَ عائِلَتِه.

نَزَلوا في طَرطوسَ في فُندُقٍ قَريبٍ مِن شاطِئِ البَحْر.

وطَرطوسُ مَدينَـةٌ صَغيرَةٌ على الشاطِئِ السوريّ.

كانوا في مَحَطَّةِ القِطارِ في حَلَبَ في الساعَةِ السابِعَةِ صَباحاً.

لِذلِكَ ذَهَبوا إلى هُناكَ بِالقِطار.

1. **Expressing Contrast with** أمّا ... فَـ

The combination of the particles أمّا ... فَـ serves as a device to express contrasts. They may roughly be translated "however, as for, as to, but, yet." The contrastive clause starts with أمّا signaling the entity or situation being contrasted. It must be followed immediately by the noun or noun phrase in question (the underlined word in the example). The conjunction فَـ introduces the attribute which distinguishes the second entity from the first. It may be followed directly by the attribute (جديدة), as in the example:

١ سَيّارَةُ يوسُفَ قَديمَةٌ [أمّا] سَيّارَةُ أحْمَدَ [فَجَديدَةٌ.]

The particle فَـ is usually followed directly by a verb if the sentence contains one, as in example 2.

٢ أتَكَلَّمُ العَرَبيّةَ [أمّا] مايكل [فَيَتَكَلَّمُ] الإنكليزيَّة.

Note that the grammatical case of the item after أمّـا should be similar to that of the one being contrasted. In example 1 above, both سَيّارَةُ أحْمَد and سَيّارَةُ يوسُف are nominative (مَرفوع), since they function as subjects. Examine the following example:

٣ أتكَلّمُ العَرَبيّةَ جيدًا أمّا الفرَنسيةَ فأتكلّمُها قليلاً.

In example 3, since the word العَرَبيّةَ is the direct object of the verb أتكَلّمُ, therefore, it is accusative (مَنصوب), and so is its contrast الفرَنسيةَ.

تمرين ٥

With reference to the structural discussion in section 2 above, contrast the following entities and situations, using the structure أمّا ... فـ, as in the following example:

مَدينةُ نيويورك كَبيرَةٌ/مَدينَةُ توليدو صَغيرَة

مَدينةُ نيويورك كَبيرَةٌ أمّا مَدينةُ توليدو فَصَغيرَة.

١- نَهرُ النيلِ طويل/نَهرُ بَرَدى قَصير

٢- يَسْكُنُ نادِر في شَقّة/تَسكُنُ ناديا في سَكَنِ الطالِبات

٣- أخي مُهَندِس/أختي أستاذة

٤- اشتَرَيتُ مِحفَظةً/اشتَرَتْ زَوجَتي نَظّارة

٥- مَدينَةُ طَرابُلُسَ الشامِ في لُبنان/مَدينَةُ طَرابُلُسَ الغَربِ في ليبيا

٦- أحِبُّ عَصيرَ البُرتُقالِ/أنتِ تُحبّينَ الحَليب

2. Expressing Reason

One way of expressing reason is by using the prepositional phrase لذلكَ (pronounced *lidālika*). It is made up of the preposition لـ "*for*" and the demonstrative ذلكَ "*that.*" Together, they mean "*for that reason.*" The use of لذلكَ makes your sentences look complex and more sophisticated, and it does not affect the sentence structurally at all. Example:

٤ أحِبُّ الفولَ المُدَمَّسَ لِذلِكَ آكُلُهُ كُلَّ يومٍ.

If you want to ask about reason, you may use the particle لِماذا "*why.*" Example:

لِماذا تَدرُسُ اللغةَ العَرَبِيَّةَ؟

تمرين ٦

A. Join the two parts of these sentences together with لذلكَ.

١- المكتبةُ قريبةٌ / مَشَيْتُ إلَيْها.

٢- يُحِبُّ مَحْمودُ البيتزا كثيراً / يأكُلُها كُلَّ يوم.

٣- سَحَر مِن دِمَشقَ وتَدرُسُ في جامِعَةِ حَلَب / تَسكُنُ في شَقَّةٍ هُناك.

B. Express these meanings in Arabic, using لِذلِكَ.

4. I don't have a car. Therefore, I went by train.
5. We sat in the classroom for a half-hour, but the teacher did not show up. So, we went to the library.
6. Souha likes swimming. For this reason, she lives on a lake.

3. Structural Notes

a. **The Preposition following the verb قال**: The verb قالَ is followed by the preposition لِ when the addressee is specified. This preposition is pronounced *li* when prefixed to nouns (e.g. قال لِعدنان) and *la* when prefixed to pronouns (قال لَهُ).

تمرين ٧

Express the following meanings in Arabic, using the verb قالَ.

1. My professor told me that he would be in his office at nine.
2. Maḥmūd said to his wife that he stayed at the Sheraton Hotel in Damascus.
3. He told her also that he ate at al-Sharq Restaurant every day.
4. Marwān says that his brother will arrive at the train station at 4 p.m.

b. **The Position of Demonstratives in Relation to the Modified Noun**: Demonstratives in Arabic (e.g. هذا) are nouns. Thus, they function just like nouns. They may be objects of verbs (e.g. أَعْطني هذا) or of prepositions (e.g. أَعْطني مِن هذا), or they may be subjects of nominal sentences:

٥ هذا هُوَ أُسْتاذُ العَرَبيّةِ. *This is the Arabic teacher*

٦ هذا أُسْتاذٌ. *This is a teacher*

A demonstrative may be one of the constituents of a noun phrase (not a sentence):

٧ هذا الكِتابُ *this book*

In a noun phrase, however, if the noun modified by a demonstrative has a possessive pronoun suffixed to it (e.g. كتابي) or it is part of an *iḍāfa* structure عُطْلَةُ الأسْبوعِ, the demonstrative should *follow* this noun or noun phrase, as in the examples:

٨ كِتابي هذا *this book of mine*

٩ عُطلَةُ الأسْبوعِ هذِهِ *this weekend*

where هذا (m.) refers to كتاب (m.) and هذه (f.) refers to عُطلَةُ (f.). Otherwise, if the demonstrative precedes a noun or noun phrase of this sort, the combination is a sentence, e.g.

١٠ هذا كِتابي *This is my book.*

١١ هذه عُطلَةُ الأسْبوعِ *This is the weekend.*

تمرين ٨

Express these phrases and sentences in Arabic, using appropriate demonstratives in the right positions:

1. This is our professor.
2. your holiday (f., sing.)
3. my friends
4. This is my car.
5. my mother's eyeglasses

c. **More on the Derivation of Relative Nouns** (نِسْبَة): The relative noun (*nisba*) مِئَوِيّ is derived from مِئَة by dropping the final *tā' marbūṭa* and suffixing a *wāw* (و) and then the relative suffix يّ. When deriving relative nouns, an additional و is required before the relative suffix in some nouns, such as سَماء، مِئَة، سَنَة، أُسرة (see lesson 5, section 6).

Note that relative adjectives are normally derived from singular nouns, but as you will see later they may also be derived from plurals.

تمرين ٩

Derive relative adjectives from these words:

١- أوروبا	٥- ميلاد
٢- سَنَة	٦- مِئَة
٣- سَماء	٧- خَريف
٤- شِتاء	٨- أُسْرَة

تمرين ١٠

Describe a visit you made to a place outside your hometown, imaginary or real. Mention your destination, your reason for going there, when you went and how, where you stayed, and when you returned. Describe the place briefly in terms of size, people, and weather. Also describe what you did there.

تمرين ١١

A. Complete the following sentences with the appropriate alternatives according to the information in the listening passage.

١- رامِز الخولي مِن مَدينَةِ ......

❑ طَرابُلُسَ ❑ حِمْص ❑ دِمَشق

٢- أَكَلَ رامِز وزوجَتُهُ فَطوراً صَغيراً لأنَّهُما ......

❑ لا يَأكلانِ الفَطورَ ❑ في طَرابُلُسَ ❑ سَيَأكلانِ غَداءً كَبيراً

٣- وَصَلَ رامِز وَزَوجَتُهُ إلى طَرابُلُسَ في الساعَةِ ......

❑ التاسِعَةِ ❑ الحادِيَةَ عَشْرَةَ ❑ الواحِدَةِ

٤- أَكَلَ رامِز وَزَوجَتُهُ عَلى الغَداءِ ......

❑ فولاً ❑ كَباباً ❑ أطعِمَةً لُبنانِيَّةً

B. Complete these sentences with information from the listening passage.

٥- يَعمَلُ رامِز ......

٦- يَسكُنُ رامِزُ وَزَوجَتُهُ في مَدينَةِ ......

٧- ذَهَبَ رامِزُ وزَوجَتُهُ إلى طَرابُلُسَ في فَصلِ ......

٨- أَكَلَ رامِزُ وزَوجَتُهُ طَعامَ الغَداءِ في مَطعَمٍ اِسْمُهُ ......

C. Mark the following sentences صَح or خطأ and correct the false ones.

٩- اِسْمُ زَوجَةِ رامِز سِهام.

١٠- مَشى رامِزُ وزوجتُهُ في السوقِ بَعدَ الغَداء.

١١- كانَ الطَقسُ بارِداً وجلَسا في غُرفَةٍ دافِئَة.

١٢- ذَهَبَ رامِزُ وزَوْجَتُهُ إلى طَرابُلُسَ بِالحافِلَة.

المُفْرَدات

rice .... (n., m.) أرُزّ

extended family .... (n., f.) أُسْرة ج أُسَر

onion .... (n., m.) بَصَل

neighborhood, borough .... (n., m.) حَيّ ج أحْياء

to visit .... (v.) زارَ (يَزورُ) زِيارة

journalism .... (n., f.) صَحافة

worker, laborer (Labor Day) .... (n., m.) عامِل ج عُمّال (عيدُ العُمّال)

lentils .... (n., m.) عَدَس

break, vacation .... (n., f.) عُطْلة ج عُطلات

weekend .... (n., f.) عُطْلَةُ نِهايَةِ الأُسْبوعِ

mayor .... (n., m.) عُمْدَة ج عُمَد

celebration, festivity, feast day, holiday .... (n., m.) عيد ج أعْياد

train .... (n., m.) قِطار ج قِطارات

for this reason, therefore .... (demonstrative) لِذلكَ

station .... (n., f.) مَحَطّة ج مَحَطّات

famous, well known .... (participle) مَشْهور ج (ون)، مَشاهير

pasta, macaroni .... (n., f.) مَعْكَرونة

place of entertainment .... (n., m.) مَلْهىً ج مَلاهٍ

engineer .... (n., m.) مُهَنْدِس ج مُهَنْدِسون

clean .... (adj., m.) نَظيف

end .... (n., f.) نِهاية ج نِهايات

Lesson Twenty-One — الدَّرْسُ الحادي والعِشرون

Objectives

- Describing events (national and religious festivities).
- Providing personal data and background.
- Structural notes: the five nouns; uninflected nouns; the passive; the verb صار.
- Listen to recorded material for this lesson.
- Do relevant computer drills and exercises, Stages 5 and 6.

أعيادٌ عَرَبيةٌ وإسلاميةٌ ومسيحيةٌ وأمريكيةٌ

في البِلادِ العَرَبيَّةِ هُناكَ أعيادٌ عَرَبيةٌ وإسلاميةٌ ومسيحيةٌ. يَحْتَفِلُ كلُّ بَلَدٍ عربيٍّ عادةً بعيدِ اسْتِقلالِهِ أو بِعيدِ ثَوْرتِهِ. هذه أعيادُ الاستقلال والثورة في بَعضِ البِلادِ العَرَبيَّةِ.

البَلَد	عيدُ الاستِقلال	عيدُ الثَورة	
تونِس	٢٠ آذار	-----	
الجَزائِر	-----	١ تشرين الثاني	
سورية	١٧ نيسان	٨ آذار	
العِراق	-----	١٧ تَمّوز	

عُمان	١٨ تشرين الثاني	-----	
لُبْنان	٢٢ تشرين الثاني	-----	
مِصْر	-----	٢٤ تمّوز	
المَغْرِب	٣ آذار	-----	
اليَمَن	٢٢ أيّار	-----	

تَحتَفِلُ كُلُّ البِلادِ العَرَبيةِ بالأعيادِ الإسْلاميّة، لكِنَّ بَعضَ البِلادِ العَرَبيَّةِ تَحتَفِلُ بالأعيادِ المَسيحيّة أيْضاً، ويكونُ هذا في سوريةَ ولُبنانَ وفِلَسطينَ والأردُنِّ والعِراقِ ومِصرَ.

عيدان إسلاميّان

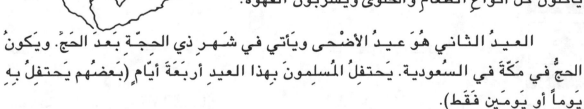

مِن الأعيادِ الإسلاميّة عيدُ الفِطْرِ ويأتي بعدَ شَهرِ رَمَضان. في شَهرِ رَمَضان يَصومُ المُسْلِمون عَنِ الأكْلِ والشُربِ من الفَجْرِ حتّى المَغرب. بَعدَ رَمَضان كُلُّ المُسلِمينَ يحتَفِلونَ بعيدِ الفطر ثلاثةَ أيّام، يأكلون كُلَّ أنواعِ الطَعامِ والحَلْوى ويشربون القَهْوة.

العيدُ الثاني هُوَ عيدُ الأضْحى ويأتي في شَهرِ ذي الحِجّةِ بَعدَ الحَجّ. ويَكونُ الحجُّ في مَكّةَ في السُعودية. يَحتفِلُ المُسلِمونَ بِهذا العيدِ أربَعَةَ أيّامٍ (بَعضُهم يَحتفِلُ بِهِ يَوماً أو يَومَين فَقَط).

بَعضُ البِلادِ الإسلاميَّةِ تَحتَفِلُ بِعيدِ ميلادِ رَسولِ اللهِ مُحَمَّد صلّى اللهُ عَلَيهِ وسَلَّم وبَعضُ البِلادِ لا تَحتَفِلُ بِهِ، ويُسَمّى هذا العيدُ "عيدُ المَوْلِد".

عيدان مَسيحيّان

عيدُ الميلادِ يَعني ميلادُ السيِّدِ المَسيحِ عيسى عَلَيْهِ السلام ويَحتفِلُ بِه المسيحيون في ٢٥ كانون الأوَّل.

عيدُ الفِصْح

شَجَرَةُ عيدِ الميلاد

العيدُ المسيحيُّ الثاني هو عيدُ الفِصْحِ ويُحْتَفَلُ بِهذا العيدِ في يَومِ أحَد بَيْنَ ٢٢ آذار و٢٥ نيسان.

أعْياد أمريكيّة

عيدُ الشُكْر

ديك حَبَش

يَحتَفِلُ الأمريكيّون بِعيدِ الشُكْرِ في رابِعِ يَوْمِ خَميس مِن شهرِ تِشرينَ الثاني. يأكلُ الأمريكيّون في هذا اليومِ ديكَ حَبَش (ديك رومي) وحَلوى تُسمى فَطيرةَ القَرْع.

عيدُ الاستِقلال

تَحتَفِلُ أمريكا بِعيدِ الاستِقلال في اليَومِ الرابِعِ من شَهْرِ تَمّوز.

عيدُ العُمّال

تَحتَفِلُ أمريكا بِعيدِ العُمّالِ في أوّلِ يَومِ إثنين مِن شَهرِ أيلول.

عيدُ مارتنِ لوثَر كِنغ

تَحتَفِلُ مُعظَمُ الولاياتِ الأمريكيّة بِهذا العيدِ في ثالثِ يَومِ إثنين مِن شَهرِ كانونَ الثاني.

سُعاد ريماوي

سُعاد ريماوي فَتاةٌ عِراقيّةٌ مِن مَدينةِ بَغداد. تَدرُسُ التِجارةَ في جامِعةِ بَغداد وتَسكُنُ مَعَ أبيها وأُمِّها وثَلاثةِ إخْوةٍ في بَيتٍ كَبيرٍ في شارعِ دِجلة.

وُلِدَتْ سُعاد في مَدينةِ بَغداد وعيدُ ميلادِها في ٢٠ آذار. هي أكبَرُ إخوَتِها. دَرَسَتْ في مَدارِسِ بَغدادَ مِن الصَفِّ الأوّلِ الابْتِدائيّ إلى الصفِّ الثامنِ المُتَوَسِّط. حينَ كانتْ في سِنِّ الرابِعةَ عَشْرةَ انتَقَلَتْ مَعَ أبيها وأُمِّها مِن بَغدادَ إلى مَدينةِ المَوصِلِ لأنَّ أباها صارَ مُديرَ التَربيةِ والتَعليمِ فيها. درَسَت هُناكَ في مَدارِسِ المَوصِلِ ثَلاثَ سَنَوات. بَعْدَ ذلكَ رَجَعوا إلى بَغدادَ. حينَ تَخَرَّجَتْ مِن المدرسةِ الثانَويّة ذَهَبَتْ إلى جامِعَةِ بَغداد.

سُعاد في سِنِّ العِشرين الآن. تَقولُ سُعاد إنَّها حينَ تَتَخَرَّجُ مِنَ الجامِعةِ بَعدَ سَنَتَين سَوفَ تَرجِعُ إلى المَوصِلِ وتَعمَلُ هُناكَ لأنَّها تُحِبُّ تِلكَ المدينة.

تمرين ١

A. Select the best alternative according to the reading passages.

١- عيدُ الثَورةِ في مِصر في ......

❑ ٤ تَمّوز ❑ ١٧ تَمّوز ❑ ٢٤ تَمّوز

٢- عيدُ ...... عيدٌ إسلاميّ.

❑ الفِصْح ❑ الفِطر ❑ الثَورة

٣- عيد استِقلالِ سورية في ......

❑ ١٧ نيسان ❑ ٨ آذار ❑ ٢٢ أيّار

٤- يُحتَفَلُ بعيدِ ...... في شهرِ كانَون الأوّل.

❑ الفِصح ❑ الأضحى ❑ الميلاد

٥- سَكَنَتْ سُعاد ريماوي في المَوصِل ......

❑ سَنةً واحدة ❑ ثَلاثَ سَنَوات ❑ خَمسَ سَنَوات

٦- رجَعَت سُعاد إلى بَغداد حينَ كانَت في سِنٍّ ......

❑ الثالثةَ عَشْرة ❑ السابِعةَ عَشْرة ❑ الثامِنةَ عَشْرة

٧- تَدرُسُ سُعاد ...... في جامِعةِ بَغداد.

❑ التِجارةَ ❑ الطِبَّ ❑ اللُغَةَ الإنكليزيّةَ

٨- تَسكُنُ سُعاد ......

❑ في شَقَّةٍ ❑ مَعَ عائِلَتِها ❑ في سَكَنِ الطالِبات

B. Mark the following sentences صح or خطأ and correct the false ones.

٩- تَحتَفِلُ الجزائِرُ بالأعيادِ الإسلاميَّةِ والمَسيحية.

١٠- يُحْتَفَلُ بِعيدِ الفِصحِ في ٢٢ آذار.

١١- يَأكلُ الأمريكيونَ ديكَ حَبَش في عيدِ الفِصح.

١٢- تَحتَفِلُ كُلُّ الولاياتِ الأمريكيةِ بِعيدِ مارتِن لوثَر كِنغ.

١٣- سُعادُ أكبرُ مِن إخوتِها الثَلاثة.

١٤- سَوفَ تَتَخرَّجُ سُعادُ مِنَ الجامِعَةِ بَعدَ سَنَةٍ واحِدة.

تمرين ٢

Complete the following sentences with appropriate words from the list.

(الاستِقلال، وُلِدَ، ذو الحِجّة، تَعليم، إسلاميّ، رَمَضان، طَعام، لأنَّ، نَوْع)

١- إيرانُ بَلَدٌ ...... لكِنَّهُ لَيسَ بلداً عَرَبياً.

٢- انتَقَلَتْ أُختي إلى قَطَر ...... عَمَلَ زَوجِها صارَ هُناكَ.

٣- ...... جورج واشنطُن في ولايةِ ڤرجينيا في سَنَةِ ١٧٣٢.

٤- تَحتَفِلُ سورية بعيدِ ...... في ١٧ نيسان.

٥- ما ...... سيّارتِك يا أستاذ؟

٦- يَصومُ المُسلِمونَ في شَهرِ ......

تمرين ٣

Select the word that does not belong in each set and explain your choice.

١-	تَربية	تعليم	فَجْر	مدرسة
٢-	الأضحى	الفِطر	الفِصح	الجَزيرة
٣-	إسلاميّ	ابتِدائيّ	مُتَوَسِّط	ثانَويّ
٤-	فَجْر	حَلوى	ظُهْر	مَغرِب

تمرين ٤

Write down matching words from the left-hand column in the blank spaces next to their matches in the right-hand column.

١- إسلاميّ	....	المَسيح
٢- عيدُ الشكر	....	رَمَضان
٣- عيدُ الأضحى	....	ثانويّة
٤- عيدُ الميلاد	....	٤ تَمّوز
٥- عيدُ الفِطر	....	مَسيحيّ
٦- عيدُ استِقلال أمريكا	....	الحَجّ
		ديك حَبَش

تمرين ٥

Rearrange the words in each set to make meaningful sentences.

١- يَحتَفِلُ - ميلادِه - بِعيدِ - أخوكَ - مَتى؟

٢- شَهر - أختي - آب - وُلِدَتْ - في

٣- جِدّاً - أستراليا - كَبيرة - جَزيرة

٤- في - إلى - الخَريف - هذِهِ - انتَقَلتُ - فَصلِ - الشقّة

تمرين ٦

Rearrange the following sentences to form a meaningful paragraph, leaving the first one intact.

١- وُلِد مازن المُدَرِّس في مَدينةِ حَلَب،

ثُمَّ رَجَعَ إلى حَلَب وَدَرَسَ في جامِعَةِ حَلَب في السَنَةِ الأولى.

بَعدَ ذلِكَ دَرَسَ في مَدرَسَةٍ ثانَويّة في مَدينةِ دِمَشق.

يَقولُ مازن إنّه سَوفَ يَرجِعُ إلى حَلَبَ حينَ يَتَخَرَّج.

دَرَسَ في مَدارِسِ حَلَبَ الابتِدائية والـمُتوَسِّطة.
ثُمَّ انتقلَ إلى جامِعةِ عَمّان في السنةِ الثانية.
لأنَّ أسرَتَه انتقَلَتْ إلى هُناك.

تمرين ٧

Select any occasion for festivities which has not been covered in this lesson and describe it in the manner the other occasions are described above, providing information about when, how, and by whom it is celebrated.

1. Structural Notes

a. **The Five Nouns Revisited**: The third of the five nouns is (ذو) "of, with, owner of." It is the first part of the name of the lunar month ذو الحجّة (the month of pilgrimage). It has the form ذي in the phrase شَهر ذي الحجة. This is the genitive form (مَجرور), because it is the second part of an *iḍāfa* structure (شَهرُ ذي الحجّة). Case is indicated by long rather than short vowels on the end of the five nouns.

In addition to أب, أخ, and ذو, there are two more. For your information, they are حَمو "*father in law*" and فو (=فَم) "*mouth.*" Here are the forms of the five nouns in the three cases: the nominative, accusative, and genitive.

مَرفوع:	أبو	أخو	ذو	فو	حَمو
مَنصوب:	أبا	أخا	ذا	فا	حَما
مَجرور:	أبي	أخي	ذي	في	حَمي

Remember that the nominative case (مَرفوع) is the case of subjects and predicates, the genitive (مَجرور) is the case of objects of prepositions and the second part of *iḍāfa* structures, and the accusative (مَنصوب) is that of objects of verbs and several other grammatical categories. Note that ذو has a feminine form (ذات) and that both forms have dual and plural forms which vary with case. However, accusative (مَنصوب) and genitive (مَجرور) forms are identical, as you can see in the table below:

Forms of ذو

	مَجرور	مَنصوب	مَرفوع
Singular masculine	ذي	ذا	ذو
Singular feminine	ذاتِ	ذاتَ	ذاتُ
Dual masculine	ذَوَيْ	ذَوَيْ	ذَوا
Dual feminine	ذَواتَيْ	ذَواتَيْ	ذَواتا
Plural masculine	ذَوي	ذَوي	ذَوو
Plural feminine	ذَواتِ	ذواتِ	ذَواتُ

تمرين ٨

Use the appropriate form of the noun in parentheses.

١ـ ما اسمُ (أب + ك)؟

٢ـ اشتريتُ بَيْتاً (ذو) أربعِ غُرَف.

٣ـ (أخ + ها) طالبٌ في هذه الجامعة.

٤ـ (أب) أحْمَد رجلٌ مِن مدينةِ دُبَي.

٥ـ هَل هذهِ السَيارة لِـ (أخ + ك)؟

٦ـ (ذو) الحِجّة اسْمُ شهرٍ من الأشْهرِ العَرَبيّة.

٧ـ أتَتْ سامية إلى هذه الجامِعةِ لأنَّ (أخ + ها) يَدرُسُ فيها.

٨ـ أين (أب + كِ) يا مَها؟

b. **Not Fully Inflected Nouns** (المَمْنوعُ مِن الصَرف) (diptotes): The name مكّةَ in the passage above has a *fatḥa* on its end although it is supposed to have a *kasra* because it is the second part of an *iḍāfa* structure. This is because some proper nouns (names) and plurals do not inflect fully (are indeclinable) in the indefinite state. They differ from regular nouns in two respects:

(1) They never take تَنوين when they are indefinite.

(2) They take a *fatḥa* for both the accusative (منصوب) and the genitive (مجرور) cases:

١ هذهِ دِمَشقُ الفَيحاءُ.

٢ وَصَلتُ دِمَشقَ الفَيحاءَ.

٣ في دِمَشقَ الفَيحاءِ.

٤ هذه شَوارِعُ نظيفةٌ.

٥ أعرفُ شَوارِعَ نظيفةً.

٦ في شَوارِعَ نظيفةٍ.

Note that adjectives of such nouns agree with what the ending on the noun is supposed to be, not with what it actually is. In examples 3-6, the adjectives take a *tanwīn* although the modified noun does not have a *tanwīn*. The adjective in 3 takes a *kasra* while the noun displays a *fatḥa*. In 6, the adjective takes a double *kasra* although the noun displays a *fatḥa*. This is because the name دِمَشق and the plural noun شَوارِع are indeclinable. They invariably take *fatḥa* in the accusative *and* genitive, whereas the modifying adjectives take *fatḥa* and *kasra*, respectively. In other words, an adjective modifying a noninflecting noun acquires the case of this noun as though it were fully inflected.

However, in the definite state, such nouns inflect just like other nouns and their adjectives agree with them completely:

٧ هذهِ الشَوارِعُ النَظيفةُ.

٨ أعرفُ الشَوارِعَ النَظيفةَ.

٩ في الشَوارِعِ النَظيفةِ.

The following are some of the noninflecting, or indeclinable, proper nouns that occurred in this lesson: دِمَشق، بَغداد، مَكّة، سورية، لُبنان، فلَسطين، مصر. And these are two plurals that do not inflect: شَوارِع، مَدارِس.

SUMMARY

- Some names and indefinite plurals do not inflect fully, that is, they are marked by a *fatḥa* in both the accusative and genitive cases.

- Noninflecting nouns do not take a *tanwīn* in the indefinite state.
- Adjective-modifying noninflecting nouns may be fully inflected.

❖المَمنوعُ مِنَ الصرف لا يُنوَّن ويُنصَبُ ويُجَرُّ بالفتحة ❖

تمرين ٩

Provide the appropriate inflections (short vowels) on the ends of nouns and adjectives:

١ـ دَرَسَتْ سامَيَةُ في مَدارِسَ مِصريّة.

٢ـ في مَدينةِ الرياضِ شَوارِعُ حَديثة.

٣ـ يَحُجّ المُسلِمونَ إلى مَكّةَ والمدينة.

٤ـ ذَهَبنا في شَهرِ نيسانَ الماضي إلى لُبنانَ والأردنِ بالحافِلة.

c. **The Passive Voice**: A verb in the passive voice is generally formed from a verb that takes an object (transitive). On the other hand, intransitive verbs, such as كـانَ and ذَهَبَ, cannot be made passive because they do not take an object. Unlike the English passive, which is made with a form of the verb *to be* and the past participle of the verb (e.g. has been bought), the Arabic passive is formed through internal changes in the form of the verb.

i. In the past tense, these changes are represented by a *ḍamma* on the first consonant of the verb and a *kasra* on the second:

	Passive		Active
١٠	was born وُلِدَ	⇦	to give birth وَلَدَ

Apart from changes in these two short vowels, no other changes in the different conjugations take place.

In hollow verbs that contain a long vowel in the middle, such as قـالَ, the long vowel changes into a *yā'* (ي) in the passive, as in example 11:

١١	قالَ	⇦	قيلَ

Defective verbs that end with an *alif* are made passive just like regular verbs (i.e. by placing a *ḍamma* on the first consonant and a *kasra* on the second) in addition to changing the final *alif* into a *yā'*:

١٢ سَمّى ⇦ سُمِّيَ

ii. The present tense verb is made passive also by internal changes, with a *ḍamma* on the present tense prefixes (أ، نـ، يـ، تـ) and a *fatḥa* on the middle consonant of the verb:

١٣ يَكتُبُ ⇦ يُكتَبُ

In active verbs that begin with a consonantal و, such as وَلَدَ "to give birth," the passive in the present is made with the long vowel و following the present tense prefix and a *fatḥa* on the middle consonant, as in example 14:

١٤ يَلِدُ ⇦ يولَدُ

Hollow present tense verbs with a long vowel (*alif* or *yā'*) as the middle character are made passive with a *ḍamma* on the present tense prefix and a regular *alif* replacing the long vowel:

١٥ يَقولُ ⇦ يُقالُ

Present tense verbs ending in a long vowel (*alif* or *yā'*) are made passive with an *alif maqṣūra* (ى) replacing the long vowel:

١٦ يُسَمّي ⇦ يُسَمّى

iii. **Agent** (فاعل) and **deputy agent** (نائب فاعل): The noun that follows the passive verb is actually the object of the active sentence, but it occupies the subject (or agent) position in the passive sentence and, therefore, it assumes its case: مَرفوع (nominative). It is called نائب فاعل in Arabic (literally, deputy agent). The verb should agree in gender with it:

١٧ تُسَمّى مَدينةُ نيويورك "التُفّاحةَ الكبيرة."

where the verb تُسَمّى is third person feminine that agrees with مَدينةُ.

SUMMARY

- **The passive of the past tense verb** is formed with a *ḍamma* on the first consonant and a *kasra* on the second. If the last letter is a long vowel, it changes into a *yā'* in addition to the short vowel changes. And if the middle letter is a long vowel, it changes into a *yā'*, which is the only change.
- **The passive in the present** is formed with a *ḍamma* on the present tense prefix and a *fatḥa* on the middle consonant. If the first letter is a consonantal *w*, the vowel و follows the prefix. If the middle letter is a long و or ي, it changes into an *alif*. If the final letter is a long vowel, it changes into an *alif maqṣūra*.

- The noun that follows the passive verb (نائِب فاعل) is the object of the active sentence. It acquires the nominative case (رَفع) because it assumes the subject position in the passive sentence.

تمرين ١٠

Provide the correct form of the passive. The agent specified in the parentheses should be dropped. Provide full voweling for the verb and the deputy agent, as in the example:

(كَتَب سامي) رسالةً مِن باريس. ⇦ كُتِبَتْ رسالةٌ مِن باريس.

١- (يَقولُ أصدقائي) إنَّ باريس مَدينة جَميلة.

٢- (وَلَدَتْ أمّي) هالة في بَيروت سَنَةَ ١٩٧٥.

٣- (يُسَمّي الأمريكيّون) وِلايةَ نيويورك "إمپاير ستيت."

٤- (يشرب الناس) القهوةَ بَعدَ الطعامِ عادةً.

٥- (سَمّى العرب) بَغداد "مَدينة السلام."

d. **The Verb** صارَ: Although the verb صارَ "*to become*" has a meaning different from the verb كانَ "*was, were,*" it shares with it the same grammatical function. Both of them belong to the same category of verbs (sisters of كانَ) that makes the predicate of a nominal sentence مَنصوب (accusative):

٢. صارَ الطَقسُ جيِّداً.

The subject الطَقسُ is مَرفوع and the predicate جيِّداً is مَنصوب marked by *tanwīn*.

تمرين ١١

A. Complete these sentences with information from the listening passage.

١- اسْمُ زَوْجَةِ مَحْمود ......

٢- مَحمود لَهُ صديقٌ أمريكي اسمُهُ ......

٣- يَعمَلُ صَديقُ مَحْمود في مَدينةِ ......

٤- تَخَرَّجَ مَحمود وَصَديقُهُ مِنَ الجامِعة في ......

B. Answer these questions according to the listening passage.

٥- كَم مَدينةً أمريكيةً زارَها مَحمود وَزَوْجَتُه؟ ما هِيَ؟

٦- ماذا يَعمَلُ صَديقُ مَحمود؟

٧- في أيِّ يَومٍ وشهر احْتَفَلَ الأصدِقاءُ الأربَعَة بِعيدِ الشُكْر؟

٨- ماذا أكلوا في عيدِ الشكر؟

C. Label the following statements صَــواب or خَطَأ and correct or comment on the false statements or parts thereof.

٩- يَسكُنُ محمود وزَوجَتُهُ في الولاياتِ المُتَّحِدَةِ الأمريكية.

١٠- كانَ مَحمود وصَديقُهُ طالبَين في جامِعةٍ واحدة.

١١- يَسكنُ صَديقُ مَحمود في بَيتٍ مَعَ زَوجَتِهِ كارلا.

١٢- أحَبَّت زَوجةُ مَحمود الطَعامَ كثيراً في بَيتِ صَديقِ مَحمود.

المُفرَدات

to celebrate .... احْتَفَلَ (يَحْتَفِلُ) احتِفال (v.)
independence .... اِسْتِقلال (n., m.)
Islam .... إسلام (n., m.)
to move, to relocate .... انتَقَلَ (يَنتَقِلُ) انتِقال (v.)
country .... بَلَد ج بِلاد (n., m.)
to graduate .... تَخَرَّجَ (يتخرَّجُ) تَخَرُّج (v.)
education, upbringing .... تَرْبِية (n., f.)
instruction, education .... تَعليم (n., m.)
revolution .... ثَوْرة ج ثَورات (n., f.)
pilgrimage .... حَجّ (n., m.)
dessert, sweets .... حَلْوى ج حَلوَيات (n., f.)
cock, rooster .... ديك ج دِيَكَة (n., m.)
turkey .... ديك حَبَش (n., m.)
with, of, owner of .... ذو ج ذَوو (n., m.)
Ramadan, the month of fasting .... رَمَضان (n., m.)
to save, to protect .... سَلَّمَ (يُسَلِّمُ) تَسْليم (v.)
age of a person .... سِنّ (n., m.)
to become .... صارَ (يَصيرُ) صَيْر، صَيْرورة، مَصير (v.)
to fast .... صامَ (يَصومُ) صَوْم (v.)
to pray, to bless .... صَلّى (يُصَلّي) (v.)
food .... طَعام ج أطْعِمة (n., m.)
Feast of Immolation/sacrifice (after Haj), Greater Bairam .... عيدُ الأضْحى (n., m.)
Thanksgiving .... عيدُ الشُكْرِ (n., m.)
Easter .... عيدُ الفِصْحِ (n., m.)
feast of breaking the Ramadan fast .... عيدُ الفِطْرِ (n., m.)

dawn, daybreak .... (n., m.) فَجْر

pie .... (n., f.) فَطيرة ج فَطائِر

pumpkin .... (n., m.) قَرْع

intermediate .... (adj., m.) مُتَوَسِّط

director, manager .... (n., m.) مُدير ج مُدَراء

Muslim, one of the Islamic faith .... (n., m.) مُسْلِم ج مُسْلِمون

Christ .... (n., m.) المَسيح

sunset .... (n., m.) مَغْرِب

birthday, birthplace .... (n., m.) مَوْلِد

birth, birthday .... (n., m.) ميلاد ج مَواليد

to be born (passive) .... (v.) وُلِدَ (يولَدُ)

Calligraphy of the words Allah and Muḥammad. Notice the phrase عَلَيْهِ السَلام following Muḥammad, where the *alif* after the *lām* is not spelled out.

Lesson Twenty-Two الدَرْسُ الثاني والعِشرون

Objectives

- Describing people, activities, and past events.
- Forms of the Arabic verb: Patterns and verb forms.
- Ordinal numbers revisited.
- Listen to recorded material for this lesson.
- Do relevant computer drills and exercises, Stage 7.

شَخصِيّاتٌ أمريكيّة وعَرَبيّة

إبراهام لنكَن
١٨٠٩-١٨٦٥

هُوَ رَئيسُ الجُمهوريّةِ الأمريكيُّ السادِسُ عَشَر. وُلِدَ في وِلايَةِ كِنتَكي سَنَةَ ١٨٠٩. انتَقَلَ إلى ولايةِ إلينوي في سَنَةِ ١٨٣١. دَرَسَ لِنكَن القانونَ، وفي سَنَةِ ١٨٣٦ صارَ مُحامِياً ثُمَّ صارَ رَئيسَ الجُمهورية في سَنَةِ ١٨٦٠. بَعدَ ذلِكَ قامَت الحَربُ الأهليّةُ الأمريكية. انْتُخِبَ مَرّةً ثانيةً في سَنَةِ ١٨٦٤. اغتيلَ إبراهام لِنكَن في واشِنطَن العاصِمة في شَهرِ نيسانَ سَنَةَ ١٨٦٥.

جورج واشنطَن
١٧٣٢-١٧٩٩

هو أوّلُ رَئيسٍ لِلولاياتِ المُتّحِدة الأمريكية. وُلِدَ في ولايةِ ڤرجينيا وتُوُفيَ فيها. كانَ قائدَ الجَيشِ في الثَورةِ الأمريكية وحارَب البريطانيين بَينَ سَنَتَيْ ١٧٧٦ و١٧٨١. صارَ رَئيسَ الجُمهوريةِ في سَنَةِ ١٧٨٩ وانتُخِبَ رَئيساً مَرّةً ثانيةً في ١٧٩٣، لكِنّهُ رَفَضَ في المرّةِ الثالِثة ورَجَعَ إلى دارِه في «ماونت ڤرنَن» في ڤرجينيا في سَنَةِ ١٧٩٧ حَيْثُ تُوُفِيَ بَعدَ سَنَتَيْن.

مارتن لوثَر كنغ
١٩٢٩-١٩٦٨

زَعيمٌ أمريكيٌّ أسْوَد. وُلِدَ في مَدينةِ أتلانتا في وِلايةِ جورجة. كانَ قِسّاً وخَطيباً وحارَبَ التَميِيزَ العُنْصُريّ. حَصَلَ على جائزَةِ نوبِل لِلسلام سَنَةَ ١٩٦٤. اغتيلَ في مَدينةِ مِمْفِس في ولايةِ تِنيسي سَنَةَ ١٩٦٨. تَحتَفِلُ مُعظَمُ الولاياتِ الأمريكية بعيدِ مارتِن لوثَر كِنغ في ثالِثِ يومِ إثنين مِن شَهرِ كانونَ الثاني.

عبدُ القادرِ الجَزائِري
١٨٠٧-١٨٨٣

أميرٌ وزعيمٌ جَزائِريّ. وُلِدَ في قريةٍ قُرْبَ وَهْران في الجَزائِر. حينَ دَخَلَتْ فَرَنسا الجزائِرَ في سَنَةِ ١٨٤٣ حارَبَ الأميرُ عبدُ القادِرِ الفَرَنسيينَ خَمسَ عَشْرَةَ سَنةً ثُمَّ نُفِيَ إلى طولون. وفي سَنَةِ ١٨٦٨ انتَقَلَ إلى دِمَشْقَ حَيْثُ سَكَنَ وتُوُفِّيَ فيها في سنةِ ١٨٨٣. كانَ الأميرُ عبدُ القادِرِ كاتِباً وشاعِراً أيضاً.

يوسُف العَظْمة
١٨٨٤-١٩٢٠

قائدٌ سوريٌّ وُلِدَ في مَدينةِ دِمَشْقَ في سَنَةِ ١٨٨٤. كانَ ضابِطاً في الجَيْشِ العُثْمانيّ ثُمَّ صارَ ضابِطاً في الجَيْشِ السوريّ. حينَ دَخَلَ الفَرَنسيّون سوريةَ في سَنَةِ ١٩٢٠ كان وَزيرَ الدفاع وخَرَجَ على رأسِ جَيشٍ صَغيرٍ وحارَبَهُم في مَيْسَلون قُرْبَ دِمَشقَ واستُشْهِدَ هُناك.

جَمال عَبْدُ الناصِر
١٩١٦-١٩٧٠

زَعيمٌ عَرَبيٌّ مِن مِصر وُلِدَ في قَريةِ بَني مُرٍّ قُربَ مَدينةِ أسْيوط في مِصر. انتَقَلَ إلى القاهِرة وهُوَ في سِنِّ الثامِنةِ وسَكَنَ مَعَ عَمِّهِ خَليل ودَرَسَ بِها ثُمَّ بِالإسْكَندَريّة. دَرَسَ بِالكلّيّةِ الحَربيّة وتَخَرَّجَ مِنها وصارَ ضابِطاً بِالجَيْشِ المِصريّ. حارَبَ في فِلَسطين سَنَةَ ١٩٤٨ حَيْثُ جُرِحَ في الحَرب. في سَنَةِ ١٩٥٢ قامَ بِثَورةٍ عَلى المَلِكِ وصارَتْ مِصرُ جُمْهوريّة. صارَ رَئيسَ الجُمهوريةِ المِصريةِ في ١٩٥٦ ثُمَّ رئيسَ الجُمهوريةِ العربيةِ المُتَّحِدةِ (مِصرَ وسورية) في سَنَةِ ١٩٥٨. تُوُفِيَ بِالقاهِرة في سنةِ ١٩٧٠.

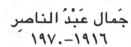

عبدُ الرحمن ابن خلدون
١٣٣٢-١٤٠٦

مُؤَرِّخٌ وفَيْلَسوفٌ وعالِمُ اجتِماعٍ عَرَبيّ. وُلِدَ في تونِس وتُوُفِيَ بِالقاهِرة. كَتَبَ كُتُباً في التاريخِ والاجتِماعِ والفَلْسَفَةِ والأدَب. أسَّسَ عِلْمَ الاجتِماع في مُقَدِّمَتِهِ المَشْهورة لِكتابِهِ "العِبَر." عَمِلَ وسَكَنَ في مدينةِ غِرناطَةَ في الأندَلُسِ وفي فاسَ في المَغرِبِ وفي تِلمسانَ في الجَزائِر وفي القاهِرةِ في مِصرَ حَيْثُ دَرَّسَ في الجامِعِ الأزْهَر.

تمرين ١

A. Check your reading comprehension by selecting the alternative in each item that agrees with the information in the reading passages above.

١- تُوُفِّيَ الأميرُ عَبدُ القادرِ الجَزائِريّ في سَنَةِ .....

❑ ١٨٤٣ ❑ ١٨٦٨ ❑ ١٨٨٣

٢- كانَ يوسُفُ العَظْمة ضابِطاً في الجَيْشِ ......

❑ العُثمانيّ ❑ الفَرَنسيّ ❑ الجَزائِريّ

٣- دَرَسَ جَمال عَبدُ الناصِر ....

❑ بِجامعةِ القاهِرة ❑ بِالجَيْشِ المِصريّ ❑ بِالكُليّةِ الحَرْبيّة

٤- أسَّسَ ابنُ خَلدون عِلمَ ......

❑ الاجتِماع ❑ الفَلْسَفة ❑ التاريخ

٥- صارَ جورج واشِنطُن رَئيساً ......

❑ مَرّةً واحِدةً ❑ مَرَّتَيْن ❑ ثلاثَ مَرّات

٦- انْتُخِبَ إبراهام لِنكَن رَئيساً لِلولاياتِ المُتَّحِدة أوّلَ مَرّةٍ في سَنَةِ ...

❑ ١٨٣٦ ❑ ١٨٦٠ ❑ ١٨٦٤

٧- حَصَلَ مارتِن لوثَر كِنغ على جائِزَةِ نوبِل لِلسلام في سَنَةِ ......

❑ ١٩٦٠ ❑ ١٩٦٤ ❑ ١٩٦٨

B. Complete the following sentences with information from the passages.

٨- نُفِيَ الأميرُ عَبدُ القادرِ الجَزائِريّ إلى ......

٩- حارَبَ يوسُفُ العَظْمة الفَرَنسيّينَ في ......

١٠- كانَ ...... رَئيسَ الجُمهوريّةِ العَرَبيّةِ المُتَّحِدة.

١١- دَرَّسَ ...... في الجامِعِ الأزهَر.

١٢- وُلِدَ ...... في سَنَةِ ١٧٣٢.

١٣- صارَ ...... مُحامِياً في سَنَةِ ١٨٣٦.

١٤- حارَبَ مارتِن لوثَر كِنغ ......

C. Mark the following sentences صَح or خَطَأ according to the passages above and correct the false ones.

١٥- سكَنَ الأميرُ عبدُ القادرِ الجَزائِري مَدينةَ دِمَشقَ بَعدَ سَنةِ ١٨٦٨.

١٦- كانَ يوسُفُ العَظْمة رَئيسَ سورية حينَ دَخَلَها الفَرَنسيّون.

١٧- وُلِدَ يوسُفُ العَظْمة في دِمَشقَ سَنةَ ١٨٨٤.

١٨- حارَبَ جَمال عَبد الناصِرِ البريطانيينَ في مِصْرَ.

١٩- كانَ ابنُ خَلْدون شاعِراً.

٢٠- تُوُفِيَ جورج واشِنطن في مَدينةِ واشِنطن.

٢١- قامَت الحَربُ الأهليّةُ الأمريكيّةُ قَبْلَ سَنَةِ ١٨٦٠.

٢٢- وُلِدَ مارتِن لوثَر كِنغ في مَدينةِ مِمفِس.

تمرين ٢

A. Check your understanding of the vocabulary by selecting the word in each item that best completes the sentence.

١- والت ويتمان ...... أمريكيٌّ مَشهور.

❑ شاعِرٌ ❑ زَعيمٌ ❑ رَئيسٌ

٢- ...... رونالد ريغن رئيساً مَرَّتَين.

❑ تُوُفِيَ ❑ وُلِدَ ❑ انْتُخِبَ

٣- أفلاطون* أشْهَرُ ...... في العالَم.

❑ مَلِك ❑ فَيْلَسوفٍ ❑ مُحامٍ

* Plato

٤- مَتى صارَتْ إليزابث الثانية ...... بريطانيا؟

❑ قَرية ❑ جائزَة ❑ مَلِكَة

٥- ڤرساي بَلْدَةٌ صَغيرةٌ ...... باريس.

❑ قُرْبَ ❑ حَرْبَ ❑ جَيْشَ

٦- كانَ هوميروس* أوّلَ ...... كَتَبَ التاريخ.

❑ مُؤَرِّخٍ ❑ قِسٍّ ❑ قائِدٍ

* Homer

B. Do the following:

٧- اكتُبْ أسْماءَ ثلاثةِ حُروبٍ مَشهورة.

٨- اكتُبْ اسْمَ كاتِبٍ أو كاتِبةٍ أمريكيّة واسْمَ كِتابٍ أو كُتُبٍ كَتَبَها.

تمرين ٣

Select the word that does not belong in each set and explain your choice.

١- وُلِدَ نُفِيَ تُوُفِّيَ اغتيلَ

٢- شاعِر جَيْش ضابِط قائِد

٣- أمير زَعيم رَئيس مُحامٍ

٤- كاتِب حَصَلَ قِسّ خَطيب

٥- مَدينة قَرْية بَلْدة فَلْسَفة

تمرين ٤

Copy the matching word from the left-hand column and write it down in the blank space provided next to its match.

١- حَرْب	....	خَرَجَ
٢- كِتاب	....	الأندَلُس
٣- تُوُفِّيَ	....	مَلِك
٤- قانون	....	اجتِماع
٥- غِرناطة	....	سَلام
٦- دَخَلَ	....	مُقَدِّمة
٧- رَئيس	....	وُلِدَ
		مُحامٍ

تمرين ٥

Rearrange the words in each set to make meaningful sentences.

١- شاعِرةً - كانَتْ - إميلي دِكَنسَن - مَشْهورةً - أمريكيةً

٢- مَكْتَبِ - أختي - مُحامٍ - تَخَرَّجَتْ - عَمِلَتْ - مِنَ - في - ثُمَّ - الجامِعةِ

٣- الأمريكيةِ - مَرَّتَيْن - بِل كلنتَن - المُتَّحِدةِ - رَئيساً - انتُخِبَ - لِلوِلايات

٤- سَنَةِ - كِنيدي - في - دالاس - اغتيلَ - بِمَدينةِ - ١٩٦٣ - الرَئيسُ

تمرين ٦

Rearrange the following sentences to form a meaningful paragraph, leaving the first sentence intact.

١- مُحَمَّد بن موسى الخُوارِزمي عالِمُ رِياضِيّاتٍ مُسْلِمٌ مَشْهور.

وكَتَبَ كتاباً في حِسابِ الجَبْرِ وتُرْجِمَ* إلى اللاتينية.		*was translated

عَرَفَتْ أوروبا عِلْمَ الجَبْرِ مِن هذا الكِتاب.

تُوُفِيَ الخُوارِزمي سَنَةَ ٨٤٠ ميلادية.

كَلِمةُ *algorithm* مأخوذة* مِن اسْمِه.		* taken, derived

وكَتَبَ أيْضاً عَن الصِفْر في الرياضيّات.

وُلِدَ الخُوارِزمي في مَدينةِ خُوارِزم.

أسَّسَ الخُوارِزمي عِلْمَ الجَبْرِ.

تمرين ٧

Compose a biographical sketch of a personality of your choice (contemporary or historical; American or otherwise), following the models in the reading passages.

1. Forms of the Arabic Verb

You have encountered so far a number of verbs and you may have noticed that they differ in form with respect to the number of consonants and type of short vowels that constitute each one. For example, the following verbs refer to the third person, masculine, singular in the past tense, yet they vary in the number of letters.

١ سَكَنَ دَرَّسَ أَسَّسَ انتَقَلَ حارَبَ استَحَمَّ

This kind of variation in the verb form pertains to a characteristic of Arabic morphology (i.e., structure of the word) whereby a given base verb acquires additional consonants and/or vowels to express shades of meaning or completely different meanings. A description of the so-called morphological patterns (الميزان الصَرْفي) might be useful, because an understanding of the system of patterns can serve as a road map for the student of Arabic. It allows one to determine the type and function of a given word and facilitate the process of looking up words in a dictionary significantly, because words are listed according to their **roots** (the base form) in most dictionaries, although there are today good Arabic dictionaries which classify entries according to the **stem** of a word, or how they appear in speaking and writing (an excellent example is *al-Mawrid* by R. Baalbaki).

a. **Patterns الأوزان and the Root System**: The basic word pattern is a combination of three letters that represent the three *original* letters of the basic Arabic verb (the triliteral verb). These are the letters ف, ع, and ل. Together they make the word فَعَلَ "*to do.*" The ف always stands for the first letter of a word, the ع represents the second, or middle, letter, and the ل denotes the third, or last, letter. So, the pattern for the verb سَكَنَ is فَعَلَ, where the three letters of the pattern correspond to those that make up the word in question. Note also that all the short vowels of the word are represented exactly in the pattern except for the final short vowel, which is not important for this purpose. If a word has *added* letters, these are also represented in the pattern intact. Take, for example, the word انْتَقَلَ "to move, to relocate" and let's construct its **pattern**:

٢ انْتَقَلَ ⇦ افْتَعَلَ

When you read the word and its pattern aloud, they should rhyme. An examination of the **pattern** should yield some useful information:

1. **It determines type of word**: This word is a verb because افْتَعَلَ is a verb pattern (as you will see below).

2. **It determines verb form**: This verb is not of the basic type, since it contains added letters (an *alif* ا and a *tā'* ت) in addition to the basic ones (ف+ع+ل).

3. **It identifies the root**: After stripping the item of added letters, its basic form (i.e., **root**) can be identified, which is نَقَل. It is useful for looking words up in a dictionary because, as noted above, words in most Arabic dictionaries are classified according to their roots. You arrive at this result by identifying the added letters and eliminating them. Then you can match the letters of the basic pattern (ف، ع، ل) with their counterparts in the word in question.

There are as many word **patterns** as there are word types. Patterns are representations of words which can be either nouns, adjectives, or verbs; thus they may be singular, dual, plural, masculine, or feminine and can display the prefixes and suffixes of verbs. Take the word مُسْلِمون "Muslims," for example, and try to create its pattern:

٣ مُسْلِمون ⇦ مُفْعِلون

As you can see, the **pattern** reflects the word faithfully. And if you want to identify the **root** of this word, you can do that easily by isolating the letters in the word that correspond to those in فَعَل, which represent the root. You will find that the **root** is سلم, that the first letter م is only a prefix, and the letters ون are a suffix. In summary, the **root** is a combination of the original letters of a word, excluding all added letters.

Verbs with doubled letters: If a verb has a doubled consonant as in دَرَّس "*to teach*" the **pattern** should also have a corresponding doubled consonant (فَعَّل). Words that seem to have only two letters, such as مَرَّ "*to pass through*" are in fact triliteral as indicated by the final doubled consonant. This word is represented by فَعَل, where the ع in the pattern stands for the first instance of ر in the verb and ل stands for the second ر.

Verbs with a long vowel: If a verb contains an original long vowel, it is represented in the pattern as a consonant. For example, the verb زار "*to visit*" is represented by the **pattern** فَعَل where the letter ع in the pattern stands for the long vowel ا in the verb.

Quadriliteral verbs: Verbs that have *four* original letters are represented with a pattern that has the final ل repeated, e.g.

٤ بَرْمَج *to program* ⇦ فَعْلَل

There are several other considerations to be taken into account when forming patterns, but they are not central to this discussion.

تمرين ٨

Construct patterns for the following words which occurred in this and previous lessons and identify the root of each one, as in the example:

Root	Pattern		Word
(وَزَر)	فَعيل	⇦	وَزير
		⇦	١ـ نِهايَة
		⇦	٢ـ مَشْهور
		⇦	٣ـ أخْبار
		⇦	٤ـ مُتَأخِّر
		⇦	٥ـ يَسْبَحون
		⇦	٦ـ جَديد

b. **Verb Forms** أوزان الفعل: A verb may be composed of three original letters (triliteral); for example, كَتَبَ "*to write*." This is the basic verb form, which will not be included in the table of increased forms below. This type of verb is known in Arabic as الفِعْل المُجَرَّد "*stripped verb*" because it has no added letters. A triliteral verb may have one or more added letters. This type of verb is known as الفِعْل المَزيد "*increased, or augmented, verb*," which may have one, two, or three added letters (e.g. تَكاتَبَ "*to correspond with*" where the first ت and the ا are added letters).

Each increased form has an inherent meaning or meanings of its own irrespective of the semantic meaning of the verb. For example, the form فَعَّلَ (Form II) has several meanings, including intensifying and transitive meanings. The intensifying meaning may be exemplified by the verb كَسَّرَ "*to smash or to break to pieces*" (Form II of كَسَرَ "*to break*"). The transitive meaning is exemplified by عَلَّمَ "*to teach, or cause others to know*" (Form II of عَلِمَ "to know").

The nine most common verb forms (II-X) are listed in the order in which they usually occur in Western grammars of Arabic, where they are also identified by Roman numerals. Examples from previous reading passages are listed below each form.

Forms of the Increased Triliteral Verb with Verbal Nouns

أوزان الفعل المَزيد مع المصدر

Form	Past Tense	Present Tense	Verbal Noun[6]	Inherent Meaning
II	فَعَّل	يُفَعِّل	تَفْعيل	intensive; transitive; causative
	حَضَّر	يُحَضِّر	تَحْضير	*to prepare, to make ready*
III	فاعَل	يُفاعِل	مُفاعَلة	reciprocal
	حارَب	يُحارِب	مُحارَبة	*to fight; to go to war*
IV	أفْعَل	يُفْعِل	إفْعال	transitive; causative
	أعْطى	يُعْطي	إعْطاء	*to give* (something to someone)
V	تَفَعَّل	يَتَفَعَّل	تَفَعُّل	reflexive; acquire quality in verb
	تَكَلَّم	يَتَكَلَّم	تَكَلُّم	*to speak*
VI	تَفاعَل	يَتَفاعَل	تَفاعُل	reflexive of III; mutual action
	تَكاتَب	يَتَكاتَب	تَكاتُب	*to correspond with*
VII	انْفَعَل	يَنْفَعِل	انْفِعال	passive meaning
	انْكَسَر	يَنْكَسِر	انْكِسار	*to break* (by itself, no external agent)
VIII	افْتَعَل	يَفْتَعِل	افْتِعال	reflexive
	انتَخَب	يَنتَخِب	انتِخاب	*to make one's choice, to elect*
IX	افْعَلَّ	يَفْعَلُّ	افْعِلال	acquisition of an attribute (e.g. color)
	اخْضَرَّ	يَخْضَرُّ	اخْضِرار	*to become green*
X	اسْتَفْعَل	يَسْتَفْعِل	اسْتِفْعال	seek to have the quality in the verb
	اسْتَحَمّ	يَسْتَحِمّ	اسْتِحْمام	*to take a bath*

---

[6] There may be more than one verbal noun for a given form.

تمرين ٩

Identify each of the following verbs (most of which you have encountered in this and previous lessons) by pattern and Roman numeral. Then strip each one of its added letters in order to identify the root, as in the example.

Root	Number	Pattern	Meaning	Verb
حَبَّ	III	أفْعَل	to like, to love	أحَبّ

١- احْتَفَل	٥- تَكَلَّم	٩- حارَب
٢- اسْتُشْهِد	٦- اشْتَرى	١٠- احْمَرّ
٣- دَرَس	٧- أعطى	١١- تَراسَل
٤- انْهَزَم	٨- تَخَرَّج	١٢- أخَّر

2. Ordinal Numbers Revisited

You may already know that lesson numbers in this textbook are listed in ordinal numbers (i.e., first, second, etc.). As you may recall, the ordinal number أوَّل differs in form from the cardinal number واحد. All the rest are, in fact, formed from cardinal numbers based on the pattern فاعل. So, ثَلاث, for example, becomes ثالِث, rhyming with فاعِل. Ordinal numbers 1-10 vary in case:

٥ هذا هُوَ الدَرسُ الثالثُ.

٦ قرأتُ الدَرْسَ الثالثَ.

٧ في الدَرْسِ الثالثِ.

However, ordinals over the number 10 have two important characteristics listed below.

1. Ordinal numbers *11-19* are invariable. They do not inflect for case:

٨ هذا هُوَ الدَرسُ الثالثَ عَشرَ.

٩ قرأتُ الدَرْسَ الثالثَ عشرَ.

١٠ في الدَرْسِ الثالثَ عشرَ.

Although the noun الدَرس occurs in the above examples in three different cases, the modifying phrase الثالثَ عَشَرَ has one form only with a *fatḥa* on the end of both constituents of the number.

2. Unlike cardinal numbers, both words of ordinal numbers *11-19* agree in gender with the modified noun:

١١ الدَرسُ الثالثَ عَشرَ

١٢ الصورةُ الثالثةَ عَشْرَةَ

Forming ordinal numbers for numbers *20*, *30*, etc. is easy. Simply prefix the definite article ال and you get an ordinal number:

١٣ عِشْرونَ دَرْساً *20 lessons* ⇦ الدَرسُ العِشْرون *the 20th lesson*

Ordinal numbers *20-29*, *30-39*, etc. are declinable, i.e., they change in form according to case, as you can see in these sentences:

١٤ هذا هُوَ الدَرسُ الثالثُ والعِشْرون.

١٥ قرأتُ الدَرْسَ الثالثَ والعِشْرينَ.

١٦ في الدَرْسِ الثالثِ والعِشْرين.

The first part of the number (الثالث) inflects to agree with the noun الدَرس; so does the second part العشرون, which has only two forms, العشرون for the nominative and العشرين for both the accusative and genitive.

Ordinal numbers over *100* are written with the hundred(s) separated from the tens by the preposition بَعْدَ "*after*", as in the example:

١٧ الدَرسُ الخامِسَ عَشَرَ بعدَ المِئة (the fifteenth lesson after the hundredth)

تمرين ١٠

A. Complete these sentences with the suitable alternative:

١- الصورةُ ...... في هذا الدَرسِ هي صورةُ إبراهام لِنكَن.

❑ الأوَّلُ ❑ الأولى ❑ الواحِدةُ

٢- قرأنا عَن هالة بُستاني في الدرسِ ......

❑ عَشْرة ❑ عاشِر ❑ العاشِر

٣- دَرسُ الكيمياءِ في الساعةِ ...... والنِصف.

❑ الثانيةُ عَشْرَةُ ❑ الثانيةَ عَشْرَةَ ❑ الثانيةِ عَشْرَةِ

٤- سَيكونُ الدرسُ ...... عَن الدِراسةِ والمَواعيد.

❑ الثالِثِ والعِشرين ❑ الثالِثَ والعِشرين ❑ الثالِثُ والعِشرون

٥- كان لِنكَن في السَنَةِ ...... حينَ اغتيلَ في واشنطن العاصِمة.

❑ الرابِعةِ والخَمسين ❑ الرابِعةَ والخَمسين ❑ الرابِعةُ والخَمسون

B. Form ordinal numbers and provide the short vowels on the ends of words, e.g.

الرَجُلُ ١٥ = الرَجُلُ الخامِسَ عَشَر

٦- البِنتُ ٩

٧- الكِتابُ ١٨

٨- في السَنَةِ ٢٥

٩ في عيدِ الثورةِ ١٠٥

١٠- على الصَفحةِ ١٢٢

١١- الطالِبُ ١

تمرين ١١

Complete these sentences with information from the listening passage.

١- كانَتْ هذه الشَخصيّةُ زَوْجَةَ رَئيسِ ......

٢- اغتيلَ زَوْجُها في ......

٣- اسمُ الزَوْجِ الثاني هُوَ ......

Select the best alternative according to the listening passage.

٤- صارَتْ هذهِ الشخصيّةُ زَوْجةً ......

❑ مَرّةً واحِدةً ❑ مَرَّتَيْن ❑ ثَلاثَ مَرّات

٥- اسْمُ هذهِ الشَخصيّة ......

❑ أمريكيّ ❑ فَرَنسيّ ❑ عَرَبيّ

٦- بعْدَ وَفاةِ زَوْجِها الثاني سكَنَتْ في ......

❑ مَدينةِ نيويورك ❑ مَدينةِ واشِنطُن ❑ وِلايةِ تكساس

Label the following statements صَـــواب or خَطَأ and correct or comment on the false statements or parts thereof.

٧- هذهِ الشَخصيّةُ فَرَنسيّةٌ.

٨- صارَتْ زَوْجةً مَرّةً ثانيةً في سَنَةِ ١٩٦٨.

٩- الزَوْجُ الثاني أمريكي.

10. Write down in English the name of the personality describing itself in the listening passage.

المُفْرَدات

social gathering .... (n., m.) اجتماع ج اجتماعات

to become a martyr .... (passive v.) اسْتُشْهِدَ (يُستَشْهَدُ) اسْتِشهاد

to establish, to found .... (v.) أسَّسَ (يُؤَسِّسُ) تأسيس

black .... (n., m.) أسْوَد ج سود

to be assassinated .... (passive v.) اغتيل (يُغتالُ) اغتِيال

prince .... (n., m.) أمير ج أُمَراء

to elect .... (v.) انتَخَبَ (يَنتَخِبُ) انتِخاب

Andalusia, Muslim Spain .... (n., f.) الأنْدَلُس

history .... (n., m.) تاريخ ج تَواريخ

discrimination .... (verbal n., m.) تَمييز

to pass away .... (passive v.) تُوُفِّيَ (يُتَوَفّى) وَفاة

mosque .... (n. ,m.) جامِع ج جَوامِع

prize, award .... (n., f.) جائِزة ج جَوائِز

algebra .... (n., m.) جَبْر

to be wounded, to be hurt .... (passive v.) جُرِحَ (يُجرَحُ) جَرح

republic .... (n., f.) جُمهوريّة ج جُمهوريّات

army .... (n., m.) جَيْش ج جُيوش

to fight .... (v.) حارَبَ (يُحارِبُ) حَرب/مُحارَبة

war .... (n., f.) حَرْب ج حُروب

to obtain, to get, to acquire .... (v.) حَصَلَ (يَحصُلُ) حُصول

to go out, to exit .... (v.) خَرَجَ (يَخرُجُ) خُروج

orator, preacher, speaker .... (n., m.) خَطيب ج خُطَباء

to enter .... (v.) دَخَلَ (يَدخُلُ) دُخول

defense .... (n., m.) دِفاع ج دِفاعات

head .... (n., m.) رأس ج رُؤوس

to reject.. (v.) رَفَضَ (يَرفُضُ) رَفْض
leader, president .... (n., m.) رَئيس ج رُؤَساء
leader (popular)... (n., m.) زَعيم ج زُعَماء
poet... (n., m.) شاعِر ج شُعَراء
personality, character .... (n., m.) شَخصيّة ج شَخصِيّات
ranking officer.. (n., m.) ضابِط ج ضُبّاط
Toulon (a town in southern France)... (n., f.) طولون
scholar, scientist.. (n., m.) عالِم ج عُلَماء
race, element.. (n., m.) عُنصُر ج عَناصِر
racial.. (adj.) عُنصُريّ
philosophy... (n., f.) فَلْسَفة ج فَلسَفات
philosopher.. (n., m.) فَيْلَسوف ج فَلاسِفة
to do, to perform... (v.) قامَ (يَقومُ) قِيام
law.. (n., m.) قانون ج قَوانين
leader (military).. (n., m.) قائد ج قُوّاد/قادة
nearby, close.. (adv.) قُرْب
village... (n., f.) قَرية ج قُرى
priest... (n., m.) قِسّ ج قَساوِسة
writer, scribe.. (n., m.) كاتِب ج كُتّاب/كَتَبة
lawyer, attorney at law, counsel.. (n., m.) مُحامٍ ج مُحامون
introduction.. (n., f.) مُقَدِّمة ج مُقَدِّمات
king.. (n., m.) مَلِك ج مُلوك
historian.. (n., m.) مُؤَرِّخ ج مُؤَرِّخون
to be sent into exile, to be expelled... (passive v.) نُفِيَ (يُنْفى) نَفْيٌ
minister.. (n., m.) وَزير ج وُزَراء

Lesson Twenty-Three الدَرْسُ الثالِثُ والعِشرون

Objectives

- Describing events and activities (e.g. appointments, festivities, schedules).
- Dual and plural nouns in *iḍāfa* structures.
- Expressing frequency (كُلّ – مَرّة – مَرَّتان).
- Expressing exception (ما عَدا).
- Explaining reason, using لِـ and المضارع المنصوب (subjunctive).
- Derived forms: اسم الفاعِل واسم المفعول (active and passive participles).
- Weak verbs (الفعل المعتل).
- Negating past tense verbs with لَم (المضارع المَجزوم).
- Listen to recorded material for this lesson.
- Do relevant computer drills and exercises, Stage 8.

عيدُ الفِطر

مايكل براون، كَما تَعلَمون، مَوْجودٌ الآنَ في القاهِرة لِدِراسةِ العربيّة. يَذهَبُ كُلَّ يَومٍ إلى دُروسِهِ في الجامِعةِ ماعَدا يَومَ الجُمْعةِ لأنَّ هذا اليَومَ عُطلَةُ نِهايَةِ الأسبوعِ في مِصرَ وفي مُعْظَمِ البِلادِ العربيةِ. كَتَبَ مايكل في يَوميّاتِهِ هذِهِ الكَلِمات:

الثُلاثاء ٢٠ فِبْرايِر (شُباط)

اليومُ عطلةٌ بسبَبِ عيدِ الفِطر، وهو عيدٌ يأتي بعدَ شَهْرِ رَمَضان. صامَ مُعظَمُ زُمَلائي المصريين في رَمَضان. فَفي هذا الشَهرِ يَصومُ الناسُ عَن الطَعامِ والشَرابِ مِنَ الصَباحِ حَتّى غُروبِ الشَمس. أمّا في العيدِ فَيَزورُ الناسُ بَعْضُهُم بَعْضاً عادةً ويأكُلونَ كثيراً مِنَ الطَعامِ والحَلوى ويَشرَبونَ الشايَ والقَهوة.

بِطاقَةُ مُعايَدة

أرسَلتُ أمسِ بِطاقاتِ مُعايَدة لِبَعضِ أصْدِقائي المِصريّين. وَجَدْتُ في المكتبة بِطاقاتٍ مَكْتوبٌ عَلَيها «كُلُّ عامٍ وأنتُم بِخَير» وبطاقات مكتوبٌ عَليها «عيدٌ مُبارَك.» اشترَيتُ من النَوع الأول، أمّا الناسُ فَيَقولونَ بَعْضُهُم لِبَعْضٍ «كُلّ سَنة وأنتَ طَيِّب.» وقالَ لي سَمير إنّ الناس في بلادِ الشام يقولون «كُلّ سَنة وأنتَ سالِم.»

الجُمْعة ١ مارس (آذار) ١٩٩٦

أمْسِ كان عِندي مَوعِدٌ عِندَ طَبيبِ الأسْنان في الساعةِ الثانيةِ والنِصْف. آلَمَني ضِرسي كَثيراً في الليلةِ الماضِية وأخَذتُ حَبَّتَي أسبِرين دونَ فائدةٍ كَبيرة. لَمْ

أنَمْ تلكَ اللَيلة مِن ألَمي. وَصَلتُ إلى عِيادةِ الطَبيبِ قَبل مَوعِدي بِخَمسِ دَقائق فَقَط، لكِنَّ الطبيب لَمْ يَرَني حتّى الساعةِ الثالثةِ وعَشْرِ دَقائق. قالَ لي إنَّ هناكَ الْتِهاباً في الضِرس. أعطاني حُبوباً ضِدَّ الالتِهاب. سأرجِعُ إلى الطَبيب بَعدَ ثَلاثةِ أيّام.

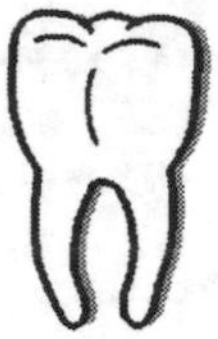

ضِرْس

عامٌ دراسيٌّ جديد

كَتَبَ عَدنان مارتيني هذِهِ اليَوْمِيّات حينَ كانَ طالِباً في جامِعةِ وِلاية أوهايو يَدرُسُ عِلمَ الحاسوب، وكانت هذِهِ هِيَ بِدايَةُ السَنَةِ الثانِيةِ لَهُ في كلمبس.

السبت ٢١ أيلول ١٩٩٦

بعد ثلاثةِ أيام يَبدأُ العامُ الدِراسيُّ الجَديد. في فَصلِ الصَيفِ الماضي لَمْ أرْجِع إلى سورِيَة بَل درَستُ ثَلاثَ مَواد وهي عِلمُ الحاسوب والرياضِيّاتُ والكيمياء. انتَهَت الدراسةُ في الشهرِ الماضي وذهبتُ إلى نيويورك وفلوريدا وزُرتُ كَنَدا أيضاً. رجَعتُ إلى كَلَمبَس في الأسبوعِ الماضي.

اليَومَ وغداً سأذهبُ بِسيارتي إلى مَطارِ كلمبس الدَوْليِّ ثلاثَ مَرّاتٍ لأستَقبِلَ بَعضَ الطلابِ العَرَب الجُدُد. أنا لا أعرِفُهم لكنّي عَلِمتُ أسماءَهم مِن مَكتَبِ الطُلابِ الأجانِبِ في الجامِعة. اليَوم سأستَقبِل هِشام تَميمي وخَديجة عَبد السلام. ولا أعرفُ عنهُما شَيْئاً الآن. سَتصِلُ طائِرةُ هِشام في الساعةِ الحاديةَ عَشْرة والربعِ صَباحاً، أمّا مَوعِدُ طائِرةِ خَديجة فَهُوَ في الساعةِ الرابِعة والنِصف بَعدَ الظُهر.

الإثنين ٢٣ أيلول ١٩٩٦

ذهبتُ أمسِ وأمسِ الأوّلِ إلى المطار. اسْتَقْبَلْتُ هِشام تَميمي وخديجة عبد السلام أمسِ الأول. وصَلَت طائرةُ هِشام مُتأخِّرةً عِشرينَ دَقيقة. كانَ مَعَهُ حَقيبَتان. حَمَلنا الحَقيبَتَينِ إلى السيارةِ ثُمَّ أخَذْتُهُ إلى سَكَنِ الطُلاب حَيثُ سَيَسكُنُ هذهِ السنة. رَجَعتُ مَرّةً ثانيةً إلى المَطار بَعدَ الظُهرِ لأَسْتَقبِلَ خَديجة. وَصَلَت طائرتُها في مَوعِدِها. وَجَدْتُ خَديجة جالِسةً بِجانِبِ البَوّابَة رَقْم تِسعة . كانَ مَعَها حَقيبتانِ أيْضاً. أخذتُها بِالسيّارةِ بَعدَ ذلِكَ إلى سَكَنِ الطالِباتِ حَيثُ سَتَسكُنُ هذهِ السنة.

عَرَفتُ من هِشام أنّه من مَدينةِ الخَليل في فِلَسطين. أتى إلى الولايات المُتَّحِدةِ لِيدرسَ الهَندسةَ الكَهرَبائيّة. هو من أُسْرة مُتَوَسِّطة. أبوهُ مُديرُ مَدْرسةٍ ثانَويةٍ وأمُّه مُدَرِّسَةُ عُلوم في مَدرَسةٍ مُتَوَسِّطة لِلبَنات.

هِشام تَميمي

عِندَهُ أربَعةُ إخْوة: اِثْنان في المدرسةِ الابتِدائية، واحدٌ في الصَفِّ الرابِع والثاني في السادِس، والأخ الثالث في الصفِّ الثامِن في المدرسة المُتوَسِّطة، والأخُ الرابِع في الصفِّ الحادي عَشَر في المدرسة الثانَويّة. لَهُ أختان، واحدةٌ تَسكُنُ في مَدينةِ القُدْسِ والثانيةُ طالِبةٌ في جامِعةِ «بير زَيْت».

خديجة عبد السلام

عَرَفْتُ مِن خَديجة أنّها تونَسيّةٌ مِن مَدينةِ تونِس. أتَت إلى جامِعةِ ولايةِ أوهايو لِتَدرسَ الأدَبَ الأمريكي. عِندَ خَديجة أخَوان وأختٌ واحدة. أخوها الكبير مُنير يَسكُنُ ويَعمَلُ في باريس. وأخوها الصَغير في المدرسةِ الثانوية في تونِس. أمّا أختُها فَهِي مُتَزَوِّجة وتَسكُنُ مَعَ زَوْجِها في تونِس. قالَت خَديجةُ إنّها فَقيرة، لكِنَّ أخاها الكبيرَ يُساعِدُها.

استَقبلتُ طالبَين أمْسِ وهُما فُؤاد عَبدُ الرَحيم وسامِر العاني. فُؤاد مِن مِصرَ وأتى مِنَ القاهِرة لِيدرُسَ علمَ الحاسوب. يقول إنَّه مِن أسرةٍ لَيسَت غَنيّة، فأبوهُ ساعي بَريد وأمُّه رَبّةُ بَيت، لكنَّه حَصَلَ على مِنحةٍ دِراسيّةٍ مِن حُكومَتِه.

فُؤاد عبد الرحيم

سامِر العاني

أمّا سامِر فهُوَ عِراقيٌّ، لكنّه لَمْ يأتِ مِن العِراق بَل مِن دُبَيْ حيثُ يعملُ أبوه وتسكن أسرتُه. يريد سامِر دِراسةَ الطِبِّ لأنَّ أباهُ طَبيبٌ، لكِنَّهُ لَيسَ في كُليّةِ الطبِّ الآن. سَيسكُنُ سامِر وفُؤاد في سَكَنِ الطلاّب في فَصلِ الخَريف، لكِنَّهُما يُريدانِ السَكَنَ في شَقّةٍ بَعدَ ذلِك.

تمرين ١

اختَر التكمِلة المُناسبة حَسَبَ النَص.

Select the most suitable alternative according to the reading passage.

١- يأتي عيدُ الفِطرِ ...... شهرِ رَمَضان.

❑ قَبلَ ❑ بَعدَ ❑ مَعَ

٢- عُطلَةُ نِهايةِ الأسبوعِ في مُعظَمِ البِلادِ العربية هِيَ يَومُ ......

❑ الجُمْعة ❑ السَبت ❑ الأحَد

٣- ...... المُسلِمون في شَهرِ رَمَضان.

❑ يَأكُلُ ❑ يَصومُ ❑ يَشرَبُ

٤- ...... الناسُ بعضُهُم بَعْضاً في العيدِ.

❑ يأكُل ❑ يَصوم ❑ يَزور

٥- وَجَد مايكل براون بِطاقات ...... في المكتبة.

❑ حلْوى ❑ مُعايَدة ❑ قَهْوة

٦- وَصَل مايكل إلى عِيادَةِ طَبيبِ الأسنانِ ......

❑ مُتأخِّراً ❑ في مَوعِدِه ❑ قَبلَ مَوعِدِه

٧- عَدنان مارتيني طالِبٌ في السنةِ ......

❑ الأولى　　❑ الثانية　　❑ الثالِثة

٨- دَرَس عَدنان ...... في فَصلِ الصَيف.

❑ مادّةً　　❑ مادّتَين　　❑ ثلاثَ مَواد

٩- انتهَت الدِراسة في جامِعةِ عَدنان في شَهرِ ......

❑ تَمّوز　　❑ آب　　❑ أيلول

١٠- استَقبَل عَدنان ...... طُلّابٍ عَرَب في المَطار.

❑ ثلاثةَ　　❑ أربَعَةَ　　❑ خَمسةَ

١١- وَصلَت طائرةُ خَديجة إلى المَطار ......

❑ في مَوعِدِها　　❑ مُتَأخِّرةً　　❑ قَبلَ مَوعِدِها

١٢- أبو هِشام تَميمي ......

❑ مُدَرِّس عُلوم　　❑ ساعي بَريد　　❑ مُديرُ مَدرَسة

١٣- كانت خَديجة جالِسةً بِجانِبَ ...... في المَطار.

❑ البَوّابةِ　　❑ الكُرسيِّ　　❑ الطائرةِ

١٤- تُريدُ خَديجة دِراسة ......

❑ الأدَبِ الأمريكي　　❑ عِلمِ الحاسوب　　❑ الطِبِّ

١٥- فُؤاد عَبد الرَحيم طالِبٌ ......

❑ عِراقيّ　　❑ سوريّ　　❑ مِصريّ

تمرين ٢

أجِبْ عَن هذِهِ الأسئلةِ حَسَبَ النَصّ.

Answer these questions according to the reading passage.

١- لِماذا لا يذهَبُ مايكل إلى الجامِعةِ في القاهرة يَومَ الجُمْعة؟

٢- لِماذا ذهَبَ مايكل إلى طَبيبِ الأسْنانِ؟

٣- أيّةَ بِلادٍ زار عَدنان مارتيني في الصَيف؟

٤- مِن أينَ حَصَل عَدنان على أسْماءِ الطلاّبِ العَرَب الجُدُد؟

٥- لِماذا يريدُ سامِر دِراسَةَ الطِبّ؟

تمرين ٣

اكتُبْ «خَطأ» أو «صَواب» جانِبَ كلّ جُملةٍ وصَحّح الجُمَلَ الخَطأ.

Mark these sentences خَطأ or صَواب and correct the false ones.

١- سَيَرى مايكل طَبيبَ الأسْنانِ مَرّتَين.

٢- رَجَع عَدنان إلى سورية في عُطلةِ الصَيف.

٣- مَدينةُ الخَليل في تونِس.

٤- تَدرُس أختُ خَديجة في جامِعةِ «بير زَيت».

٥- وَصَلَ سامِر إلى كَلَمبَس مِن بَغداد.

تمرين ٤

اختَر الكلِمة التي لا تُناسِب باقي الكلمات في كُلّ مَجموعة وبَيِّن السَبَب.

Select the word that does not belong in each set and explain your choice.

١- لأنَّ	بِسَبَب	ما عَدا	لِماذا
٢- عَرَب	رَمَضان	صامَ	غُروب
٣- عيد	الشام	مُعايَدة	حَلوى
٤- التِهاب	طائرة	مَطار	بَوّابة
٥- عِيادة	حَبّة	صَديق	التِهاب
٦- رَأى	جالِس	زارَ	استَقبَلَ
٧- طَبيب	مُدَرِّس	مُدير	طالِب

تمرين ٥

وافِق بَين كَلِمةٍ مِنَ العَمود الأوَّل وكَلَمةٍ مِنَ العَمودِ الثاني واكتبْهُما في الفَراغ.

١ـ أخَذ	....	نَسِيَ
٢ـ آلَمَ	....	فَقير
٣ـ بَدَأ	....	طَبيب
٤ـ عَلِمَ	....	انتَهى
٥ـ غَنيّ	....	أعْطى
		أسْبِرين

تمرين ٦

عَرِّفْ هؤلاءِ الأشْخاص كَما في المِثال حَسَبَ النص.

Identify the following people with reference to the information in the reading passage as in the example:

رَبّةُ بَيت ⇦ هِي أمُّ الطالِب المِصري فُؤاد عَبد الرَحيم.

١ـ طَبيب الأسنان

٢ـ مُدَرِّسةُ عُلوم

٣ـ ساعي بَريد

٤ـ أختُها مُتَزَوِّجة

٥ـ طَبيب

تمرين ٧

أعِدْ تَرتيبَ الكلِماتِ في كُلِّ مَجموعةٍ لِتَشكِّلَ جُمَلاً مُفيدة.

Rearrange the words in each set to form meaningful sentences.

١ـ المُسلِمونَ - رَمَضان - في - شَهْرِ - يَصومُ.

٢ـ عاصِمةِ - ما - تَعلَم - هَلْ - اسمُ - الأردُنّ؟

٣ـ الخَميس - المكتَبةِ - في - كُلَّ - ما عَدا - أدرُسُ - يَومٍ - يَومَ.

٤ـ شَهرِ - الدِراسةُ - حَزيران - تَنتَهي - الجامِعةِ - في - في.

٥ـ بَعْدَ - السينَما - وَصَلْتُ - الفيلم - دارِ - إلى - بِدايَة.

تمرين ٨

وافِق بَيْنَ هؤلاءِ الأشخاصِ وبِلادِهِم واكتُب اسْمَ بَلَدِ كُلٍّ مِنهُم عَلى الخَريطة.

Match these people with their countries and write down the name of their respective countries on the map.

سامِر

خديجة

هِشام

فُؤاد

عَدنان

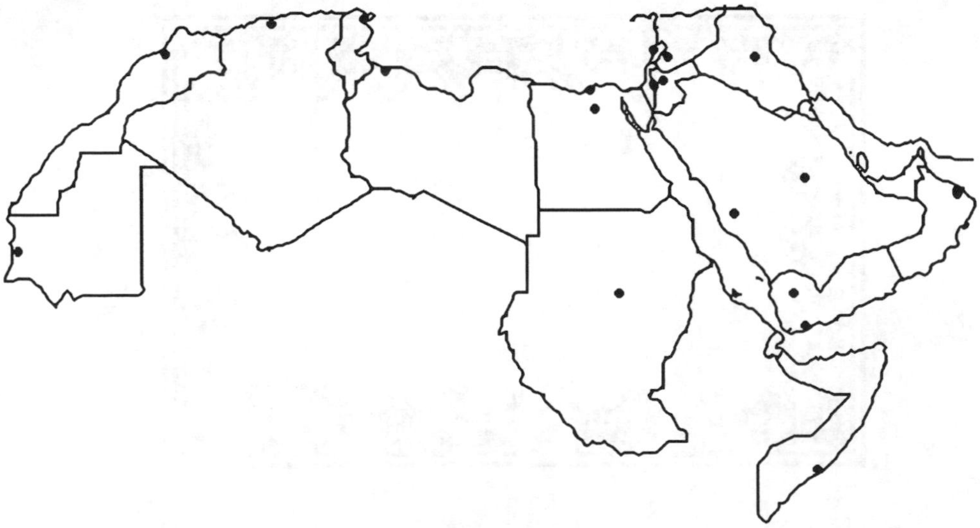

تمرين ٩

أعِدْ ترتيبَ الجُمَلِ لِتَشكِّلَ فِقرةً مُفيدة.

١- لَم أذْهَب اليَوْمَ إلى المدرسةِ بِسَبَبِ عيدِ الاستقلال.

سَبَحنا في البحرِ ساعَتين.

ثُمَّ أخذنا القِطارَ في الساعةِ الرابعةِ والنِصف ورَجَعنا إلى بُيوتِنا.

لِهذا السَبَبِ ذهبتُ أنا وأصدِقائي إلى شاطِئِ البَحْر.

بَعدَ الظُهرِ سَبَحنا قَليلاً مَرّةً ثانية.

ذَهبْنا إلى الشاطِئِ بِالقِطار.

بعد ذلِكَ أكَلْنا الغَداءَ في مَطعمٍ صَغيرٍ على الشاطِئ.

وَصَلنا إلى الشاطِئِ في الساعةِ العاشِرة والنِصفِ صَباحاً.

تمرين ١٠

املأ بِطاقةَ المُعايَدةِ هذِهِ بعِبارةٍ مُناسِبة ووَقِّعْ اسْمَكَ عليها.

Fill out this blank greeting card with an appropriate phrase and sign it in Arabic.

1. Dual and Plural Nouns in *Iḍāfa* Structures (المضاف (مُثَنّى وجَمع

As you may remember, dual nouns are formed by suffixing to them ان if they are nominative and ـَيْـن if they are accusative or genitive. However, if a dual noun happens to be مُـضـاف, or the first word of an *iḍāfa* structure, the final ن in the suffix is dropped, as in the example:

١ حَبَّتان *two pills* + أسبِرين ⇦ حَبَّتا أسبِرين *two pills of aspirin*

Similarly, some sound masculine plural nouns are formed by the suffixes ون and ـين. If such plurals serve as مُضاف in an *iḍāfa* structure, the ن in the suffix is also dropped:

مُدَرِّسون *teachers* + العُلوم ⇦ مُدَرِّسو العُلوم *teachers of science*

2. Expressing Frequency كُلّ، مَرّة

The two words كلّ and مـرّة are among several words used to express frequency. The word كُلّ "*every, each*" is considered a noun. Therefore, when it modifies another noun, as in كُلَّ يومِ خميس "*every Thursday*" the following word or words form with it an *iḍāfa* structure. Remember that كُلّ being مُضاف can be in any case, whereas the words following it (being مُـضـاف إلَيـه, or second or third word in an *iḍāfa* structure) must be in the genitive case (مَجرور).

The word مَـرّة, on the other hand, when used to express frequency, is in the **accusative** case (مَنصوب):

٢ زُرتُ دِمَشقَ مَرّةً.

٣ زُرتُ دِمَشقَ مَرَّتَين.

٤ زُرتُ دِمَشقَ ثَلاثَ مَرّات.

This form of the noun is called مَفعول مُطلَق, or absolute object.

3. Expressing Exception ما عَدا

The combination of ما and عَدا are used to express exception (though عَدا by itself may also be used). The following noun is always accusative مَنصوب:

٥ استقبَلَ عَدنان في المَطار كُلَّ الطلابِ الجُدُد ما عَدا طالبَين.

٦ كتَبتُ إلى كُلِّ أصدِقائي ما عَدا ثَلاثةً مِنهُم.

4. Explaining Reason, Using لِـ and المضارع المنصوب (Subjunctive)

A. **Reminder**: You have already learned to explain reason, using لأنَّ "because." If you recall, لأنَّ must be followed by a subject and a predicate, forming a nominal sentence. The subject (or topic) of لأنَّ is accusative (مَنصوب) and its predicate (or comment) is nominative (مَرفوع):

٨ لا نَسبَحُ في البُحَيرةِ لأنَّ الماءَ بارِدٌ..

We don't swim in the lake because the water is cold.

In sum, لأنَّ must be followed by a sentence.

B. In this lesson, another word is used to explain reason - بِسَبَب *"because of."* This word is a combination of a preposition (بِـ) and a noun (سَبَب), meaning *"reason, cause."* Together they mean *"by reason of."* It must be followed by a noun which is genitive because it forms with it an *iḍāfa* structure:

٩ اليَومُ عُطلةٌ بِسَبَبِ العيدِ.

C. Another way of explaining reason involves the use of the particle لِـ with a form of the present tense verb called المُضارِع المَنصوب (subjunctive). Note that this particle occurs as a prefix only. The table in Section 7 illustrates the three forms of المُضارِع (see Appendix C for conjugations of selected verbs).

Remember that with the particle لِـ (among other particles that share this function), the verb must be مُضارِع مَنصوب marked by either a *fatḥa* on the end of singular verb forms (as in 10) or the deletion of ن in the second person, feminine singular and in dual and plural masculine forms (as in 11, 12):

١٠ ذهبَتْ أختي إلى المطارِ لتَأخُذَ أولَ طائرةٍ إلى تونِس.

١١ أتى سامِر وفؤاد إلى الولاياتِ المتحدّة ليَدرُسا في الجامِعة.

١٢ ذَهَبوا إلى المطعمِ ليَحتَفِلوا بعيدِ ميلادِ صَديقِهِم.

5. **Derived Forms: Active and Passive Participles** اسمُ الفاعِل واسمُ المَفعول

As the Arabic terms indicate, these are nouns and are formed according to the patterns فاعل and مَفعول from الفعل المُجَرَّد (Form I). The passive participle, however, is formed only from transitive verbs (those that take objects).

The active participle (فاعل) may refer either to the agent (doer of the action):

١٣ هو طالبٌ في هذه الجامعة. He is a <u>student</u> at this university.

or to the action:

١٤ هو ذاهِبٌ إلى المكتبة. He <u>is going</u> to the library.

Like regular nouns, an active participle has dual and plural forms (e.g. طالبان، طُلاّب، ذاهبون، ذاهبان) which may be sound (requiring a plural suffix with no change in the order of letters) or broken (internal changes).

The passive participle refers to the *recipient* or *experiencer* of the action and has sound (as in 15) or broken (as in 16) plural forms:

١٥ مَشْهور ج مَشهورون/مَشاهير. *well known, famous*

١٦ مَعْجون ج مَعاجين. *paste*

All other active and passive participles for verb forms II-X begin with a مُـ prefix. In the active participle, the ع, or middle letter, takes a *kasra* (e.g. مُدَرِّس "*teacher*") and in the passive participle, it takes a *fatḥa* (e.g. مُدَرَّس "*taught*"). The table below lists the nine verb forms and corresponding active and passive participles with examples.

	وَزن الفعل *Verb Form*	اسم الفاعل *Active Participle*	مثال *Example*	اسم المفعول *Passive Participle*	مثال *Example*
II	فَعَّل (دَرَّس)	مُفَعِّل	مُدَرِّس *teacher*	مُفَعَّل	مُدَرَّس *taught*
III	فاعَل (حارَب)	مُفاعِل	مُحارِب *warrior*	مُفاعَل	مُحارَب *fought, resisted*
IV	أفْعَل (أعْطى)	مُفْعِل	مُعْطي *giver*	مُفْعَل	مُعْطى *given*
V	تَفَعَّل (تعلَّم)	مُتَفَعِّل	مُتَعلِّم *educated*	مُتَفَعَّل	مُتَعلَّم *learnable*
VI	تَفاعَلَ (تَقاسَمَ)	مُتَفاعِل	مُتَقاسِم *sharing*	مُتَفاعَل	مُتَقاسَم *shared*
VII	اِنْفَعَل (اِنْكَسَرَ)	مُنْفَعِل	مُنْكَسِر *broken, defeated*	مُنْفَعَل	-----
VIII	اِفتَعَل (احْتَفَل)	مُفْتَعِل	مُحْتَفِل *celebrator*	مُفْتَعَل	مُحتَفَل *celebrated*
IX	اِفْعَلّ (اخضرّ)	-----	-----	مُفْعَلّ	مُخْضَرّ *having the color green*
X	اِسْتَفْعَل (استقبَل)	مُسْتَفْعِل	مُسْتَقْبِل *receiver*	مُسْتَفْعَل	مُسْتَقْبَل *received*

6. Negating Past Tense Verbs with لَمْ (المُضارِع المَجزوم)

So far, you have used the particle ما to negate the past tense verb. As you may recall, ما does not cause any changes either in the form of the verb or in word order:

١٧ زُرنا بَيروت. *We visited Beirut* ⇦ ما زُرنا بَيروت. *We did not visit...*

The past tense verb (perfect), though, can be negated with another particle: لَمْ. This particle provides a more emphatic negation and it is more formal. However, لَمْ has an effect on the following verb. It changes a past tense verb into a form of the present tense المُضارِع (imperfect) called المضارع المَجزوم, or the **jussive**. This mood is marked by a *sukūn* on the end of singular verb forms and the deletion of ن in the second person, feminine singular and in dual and plural masculine forms. Although the verb form is called مُضارِع, the sentence still retains a sense of the past tense by virtue of لَم:

١٨ زُرنا بَيروت. *We visited Beirut* ⇦ لَم نَزُرْ بَيروت. *...We did not visit...*

تَصريف الفِعل المَضارِع (المَرفوع، المَنصوب، المَجزوم)

Conjugations of the Present Tense Verb (indicative, subjunctive, jussive)

الضَمير	المَرفوع	المَنصوب	المَجزوم	
أنا	أكتُبُ	أكتُبَ	أكتُبْ	
نَحنُ	نَكتُبُ	نَكتُبَ	نَكتُبْ	
أنتَ	تَكتُبُ	تَكتُبَ	تَكتُبْ	
أنتِ	تَكتُبينَ	تَكتُبي	تَكتُبي	
أنتُما	تَكتُبانِ	تَكتُبا	تَكتُبا	
أنتُم	تَكتُبونَ	تَكتُبوا	تَكتُبوا	silent *alif*
أنتُنَّ	تَكتُبْنَ	تَكتُبْنَ	تَكتُبْنَ	no change
هُوَ	يَكتُبُ	يَكتُبَ	يَكتُبْ	
هِيَ	تَكتُبُ	تَكتُبَ	تَكتُبْ	
هُما	يَكتُبانِ	يَكتُبا	يَكتُبا	
هُما	تَكتُبانِ	تَكتُبا	تَكتُبا	
هُمْ	يَكتُبونَ	يَكتُبوا	يَكتُبوا	silent *alif*
هُنَّ	يَكتُبْنَ	يَكتُبْنَ	يَكتُبْنَ	no change

7. **Weak**[7] **Verbs الفعل المُعتَلّ**: There are verbs that contain either و or ي as one of their original letters. Such verbs conjugate in a special manner in المضارع المجزوم as compared to the other two moods. Let's use two verbs as examples, one that contains a long vowel in the middle (زارَ) *"to visit,"* which is called hollow (أجوَف), and one with a long vowel as the third letter (مَشى) *"to walk,"* which is called defective (ناقص). The two tables below list the three forms of المضارع of the verbs زارَ and مَشى. Notice how in some conjugations the long vowel (و in this example) changes into its short counterpart *ḍamma* (ـُ) (see Appendix C for conjugations of selected verbs):

١٩ يَزورُ ⇦ يَزُرْ

تصريف الفعل (زار) بالمضارع المرفوع والمنصوب والمجزوم

	المَجزوم	المَنصوب	المَرفوع	الضَمير
	أزُرْ	أزورَ	أزورُ	أنا
	نَزُرْ	نَزورَ	نَزورُ	نَحنُ
	تَزُرْ	تَزورَ	تَزورُ	أنتَ
	تَزوري	تَزوري	تَزورينَ	أنتِ
	تَزورا	تَزورا	تَزورانِ	أنتُما
silent *alif*	تَزوروا	تَزوروا	تَزورونَ	أنتُم
no change	تَزُرْنَ	تَزُرْنَ	تَزُرْنَ	أنتُنَّ
	يَزُرْ	يَزورَ	يَزورُ	هُوَ
	تَزُرْ	تَزورَ	تَزورُ	هِيَ

[7] In Western grammars, Arabic verbs with long original vowels are known as "weak or sick." This is a literal translation of the term مُعتَلّ, where one of the meanings of علّة is "sickness." However, such verbs are thus called because they contain a حَرف علّة, i.e. a long vowel (و or ي), hence the term مُعتَلّ, which means "with or containing a long vowel."

هُما	يَزورانِ	يَزورا	يَزورا	
هُما	تَزورانِ	تَزورا	تَزورا	
هُمْ	يَزورونَ	يَزوروا	يَزوروا	silent *alif*
هُنَّ	يَزُرْنَ	يَزُرْنَ	يَزُرْنَ	no change

A similar process can be observed with verbs ending with a long vowel, such as مَشى:

تصريف الفعل (مَشى) بالمضارع المرفوع والمنصوب والمجزوم

الضَمير	المَرفوع	المَنصوب	المَجزوم .	
أنا	أمشي	أمشِيَ	أمشِ	
نَحنُ	نَمشي	نَمشِيَ	نَمشِ	
أنتَ	تَمشي	تَمشِيَ	تَمشِ	
أنتِ	تَمشينَ	تَمشي	تَمشي	
أنتُما	تَمشِيانِ	تَمشِيا	تَمشِيا	
أنتُم	تَمشونَ	تَمشوا	تَمشوا	silent *alif*
أنتُنَّ	تَمشينَ	تَمشينَ	تَمشينَ	no change
هُوَ	يَمشي	يَمشِيَ	يَمشِ	
هِيَ	تَمشي	تَمشِيَ	تَمشِ	
هُما	يَمشِيانِ	يَمشِيا	يَمشِيا	
هُما	تَمشِيانِ	تَمشِيا	تَمشِيا	
هُمْ	يَمشونَ	يَمشوا	يَمشوا	silent *alif*
هُنَّ	يَمشينَ	يَمشينَ	يَمشينَ	no change

تمرين ١١

Complete these sentences, taking into account the grammatical explanations above.

١- عِندي ...... كَبيرتان.

❏ دَرّاجَتان ❏ دَرّاجَتا ❏ دَرّاجَتَيْن

٢- يَعملُ في الشركةِ ...... سَيّاراتٍ مِن بِلادٍ عَديدة.

❏ سائِقون ❏ سائِقو ❏ سائِقين

٣- يأكُلُ مازِنُ العَشاءَ مَعَ زَوجَتِهِ في المطعَمِ ...... يَومِ جُمْعة.

❏ كُلّ ❏ مَرّةً ❏ ما عَدا

٤- زُرتُ مَدينةَ باريس ......

❏ مَرّتان ❏ مَرّتَيْن ❏ مَرّتا

٥- تَدرُسُ هالَة في المكتبةِ كُلَّ يَومٍ ...... يَومَ الجُمْعة.

❏ ما عَدا ❏ كُلّ ❏ مَرّة

٦- يَسكُنُ مايكل براون القاهِرَةَ الآنَ بِسَبَبِ ......

❏ يُريدُ العَمَلَ في البِلادِ العربية ❏ دِراسةِ العَرَبيّة

٧- عِندَ سالي سيارةُ تويوتا لأنَّ ......

❏ السياراتِ اليابانيةَ جَيِّدةٌ ❏ تحبّ اليابان

تمرين ١٢

1 Locate one instance of اسم فاعل in the paragraph on خديجة, and another one in Adnān's Monday journal.
2. Locate اسم مفعول in the third paragraph.
3. Locate مضارع مجزوم and مضارع منصوب in the fourth paragraph and in Adnān's Saturday journal.
4. Locate a simple and a compound ordinal number in the paragraph on هشام.
5. Find in the third paragraph verbs of these forms: افتَعَل، أفعَل ، فَعَل.
6. Find in the reading passage three instances of فعل مُعتل and list them in the third person singular masculine in the past and present.
7. Find in Michael's Friday journal an *iḍāfa* structure where the مُضاف is dual.

تمرين ١٣

اختَرِ التَصريفَ (conjugation) المُناسِبَ لِلفِعلِ لِتُكمِلَ الجُمَلَ التاليـة:

١ـ أتى سامِر إلى أمريكا لِـ ...... الطِبِّ.

❑ يَدرُسُ ❑ يَدرُسَ ❑ يدرُسْ

٢ـ لَمْ ...... الطَبيبُ هذا الشَيء.

❑ يَقولُ ❑ يَقولَ ❑ يَقُلْ

٣ـ ما ...... هاوائي حتّى الآن.

❑ زُرنا ❑ نَزورَ ❑ نَزُرْ

٤ـ لَمْ ...... بِعيدِ ميلادِ ابنَتِهِم هذا العام.

❑ يَحتَفِلونَ ❑ احتَفَلوا ❑ يَحتَفِلوا

٥ـ ذَهَب عَدنان إلى كاليفورنيا لِـ ...... ديزني لاند.

❑ يَرى ❑ يَرَ ❑ رأى

٦ـ لَمْ ...... الفَتاةُ في اللَيلِ بِسَبَبِ الألَم.

❑ تَنامُ ❑ تَنامَ ❑ تَنَمِ

تمرين ١٤

أـ أكمِلِ الجُمَلَ بالخِيارِ المناسب:

١ـ الشَخصُ في هذا التَمرينِ هُوَ ......

❑ أُم ❑ أب ❑ طَبيب

٢ـ «اللاذِقِيـةُ» هُوَ اسمُ ......

❑ بَحْرٍ ❑ عِيادَةٍ ❑ مَدينة

٣ـ لَمْ تَنَمِ البِنتُ بِالليلِ بِسَبَبِ ......

❑ البَطْنِ ❑ الألَمِ ❑ الأسْبِرين

٤- سَوفَ تَنامُ البِنتُ في النَهارِ بِسَبَبِ ......

❑ الإبْرَةِ ❑ الألَمِ ❑ حَبّاتِ الأسبِرين

ب - أكمِل الجُمَلَ التاليةَ بِعِباراتٍ مِنَ النص:

٥- اسمُ أبي البِنت ......

٦- يعملُ أبو البِنتِ ......

٧- أعطى الطَبيبُ لِلبِنتِ ...... في العِيادة.

٨- اسْمُ البِنتِ ......

ت - اكتبْ «خَطأ» أو «صَواب» جانِبَ كُلِّ جملةٍ وصَحِّحِ الجُمَلَ الخَطأ.

٩- الأمُّ لا تعمَل.

١٠- لَم تَنَمِ الأمُّ كثيراً بِسَبَبِ ألَمٍ في بَطنِها.

١١- أخَذَت البِنتُ الإبرةَ في عِيادَةِ الطَبيب.

١٢- سَتَأخُذُ البِنتُ حَبّةَ أسبِرين بعدَ كُلِّ طَعام.

ث - أجِبْ عن هذه الأسئِلةِ حَسَبَ النَصّ:

١٣- كَم وَلَداً في هذِهِ العائِلة؟

١٤- ماذا فَعَلَت الأمُّ في الليلِ لِتُساعِدَ ابنَتَها؟

١٥- إلى أين أخَذَت الأمُّ ابنَتَها في الصَباح؟

١٦- ما هو سَبَبُ ألَمِ البِنت؟

17. In the listening passage, there are three vocabulary items that you have not encountered before. You might be able to guess their meanings from the context. List these words with the meanings that you think they have in this passage.

18. The name of a certain body of water occurs in the passage. Write it down in Arabic and list its English equivalent.

المُفْرَدات

foreign .... أَجْنَبيّ ج أجانب (n., m.)
to take .... أَخَذَ (يَأخُذُ) أَخْذ (v.)
to send .... أَرْسَلَ (يُرسِلُ) إرْسال (v.)
to receive (someone) .... اسْتَقبَلَ (يَسْتَقبِلُ) اسْتِقبال (v.)
inflammation, infection .... الْتِهاب ج الْتِهابات (n., m.)
pain .... أَلَم ج آلام (n., m.)
to hurt .... آلَمَ (يُؤلِمُ) (v.)
as for, but, yet, however .... أمّا (particle)
to finish, to come to an end .... انْتَهى (يَنْتَهي) انتِهاء (v.)
to begin .... بَدَأَ (يَبدَأُ) بَدْء (v.)
beginning .... بِداية ج بِدايات (n., f.)
sitting .... جالِس ج جالِسون (n., m.)
pill .... حَبَّة ج حَبّات (n., f.)
government .... حُكومة ج حُكومات (n., f.)
to carry .... حَمَلَ (يَحْمِلُ) حَمْل (v.)
to see .... رأى (يَرى) رُؤية (v.)
housewife .... رَبَّةُ بَيْت ج رَبّات بُيوت (n., f.)
colleague, coworker .... زَميل ج زُمَلاء (n., m.)
mail carrier .... ساعٍ ج سُعاة (ساعي بَريد) (n., m.)
to help, to assist .... ساعَدَ (يُساعِدُ) مُساعَدة (v.)
safe, secure, healthy .... سالِم ج سالِمون (n., m.)
reason, cause .... سَبَب ج أسْباب (n., m.)
Syria, Damascus, Greater Syria .... الشام (n., f.)
drink, beverage, sherbet .... شَراب ج أشْرِبة، شَرابات (n., m.)
opposite, anti-, adversary, opponent .... ضِدٌّ ج أضْداد (n., m.)

molar tooth.......... (n., m.) ضِرْس ج أضْراس، ضُروس

physician, doctor.......... (n., m.) طَبيب ج أطِبّاء

good.......... (n., m.) طَيِّب ج طَيِّبون

year.......... (n., m.) عام ج أعْوام

to know.......... (v.) عَلِمَ (يَعْلَمُ) عِلْم

sunset.......... (n., m.) غُروب

rich, wealthy.......... (n., m.) غَنيّ ج أغنياء

and, then, so.......... (coordinating particle) فَـ

benefit, use, advantage.......... (n., f.) فائِدة ج فَوائِد

poor.......... (n., m.) فَقير ج فُقَراء

as.......... (particle) كَما

electricity.......... (n., f.) كَهْرَباء

not (particle used to negate past-tense verbs).......... (particle) لَمْ

(a) night.......... (n., f.) لَيْلة ج لَيالٍ

except.......... (particle) ما عَدا

previous, last, past.......... (adj.) ماضٍ (الماضي)

blessed.......... (n., m.) مُبارَك

school.......... (n., f.) مَدْرَسة ج مَدارِس

greetings.......... (n., f.) مُعايَدة ج مُعايَدات

written.......... (n., m.) مَكْتوب

scholarship, grant, gift.......... (n., f.) مِنْحة ج مِنَح

existing, present.......... (n., m.) مَوْجود ج مَوْجودون

kind, sort.......... (n., m.) نَوْع ج أنْواع

to find.......... (v.) وَجَدَ (يَجِدُ) وُجود

Lesson Twenty-Four الدَرْسُ الرابِعُ والعِشرون

Objectives

- Expressing opinion and supporting it.
- Describing activities past and present.
- Reading newspaper advertisements.
- Describing floor plans, house fixtures, and furniture.
- Describing neighborhood businesses and locations.
- Expressing intention (أراد أنْ (المضارع المنصوب.
- Noun of instrument اسم الآلة.
- Prepositions (حروف الجر): relational concepts.
- Listen to recorded material for this lesson.
- Do relevant computer drills and exercises, Stages 8 and 9 (Text 3).

شَقّةُ مايكل الجَديدة

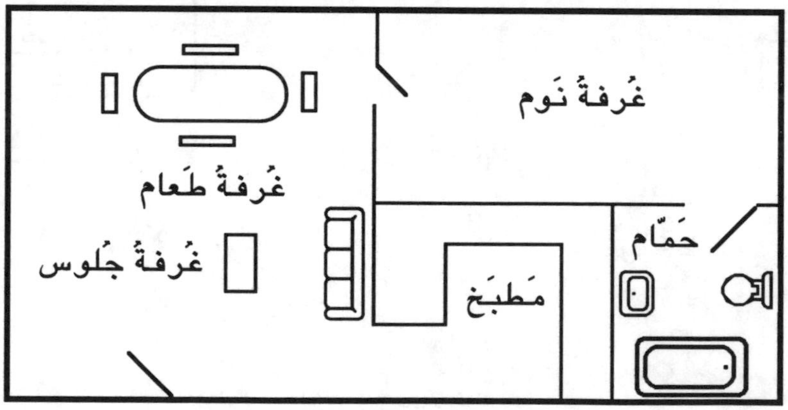

مُخَطَّطُ شَقّةِ مايكل

يَسكُنُ مايكل براون، كَما تَعلَم، في القاهِرةِ الآنَ لأنّهُ يَدرُسُ اللُغَةَ العَرَبيّةَ في الجامِعَةِ الأمريكيّةِ بِالقاهِرة. أرادَ مايكل أنْ يَنتَقِلَ مِن شَقّتِه القَديمَةِ إلى شَقّةٍ أُخرى أقرَبَ إلى الجامِعَةِ فيها هاتِفٌ وبَرّاد. قَرَأ في الجَريدةِ هذا الإعلانَ عَن شَقّةٍ لِلإيجار:

للإيجار
شقة ٦٠ م، ش الأندلس، غرفة نوم وجلوس بالتليفون، الطابق الثالث. قرب مطعم العمدة.

رَأى مايكل تِلكَ الشَقّةَ، وهِيَ تَقَعُ في «بابِ اللَوق» وأعْجَبَتْهُ، فاستَأجَرَها مِن سَيِّدةٍ عَلِم أنّها عَمِلَتْ في الكُويتِ عِدّةَ سَنَوات. أُجْرةُ الشَقّةِ الشَهريّةِ ٧٠٠ جُنَيهٍ مِصريٍّ بِالإضافةِ إلى الماءِ والكَهرَباء. توجَدُ غُرفَةُ جُلوسٍ واحِدةٌ في الشَقّةِ لكِنَّ هذهِ الغُرفةَ واسِعةٌ. هُناكَ طاوِلَةٌ وأربعُ كَراسٍ في جُزْءٍ مِنَ الغُرفةِ يَسْتَعْمِلُها مايكل لِلطَعامِ ولِلدراسَةِ أيضاً، وفي الجُزءِ الآخَرِ أريكةٌ كَبيرَةٌ لِلجُلوسِ يوجَدُ مُقابِلَها تِلفازٌ وخِزانَةُ كُتُبٍ صَغيرَةٌ وَضَعَ مايكل فيها كُتُبَهُ وعَلّقَ عَلى الجِدارِ صورَةَ أسرتِه. إلى جانِبِ الأريكَةِ هُناكَ مِصباحٌ وهاتِف.

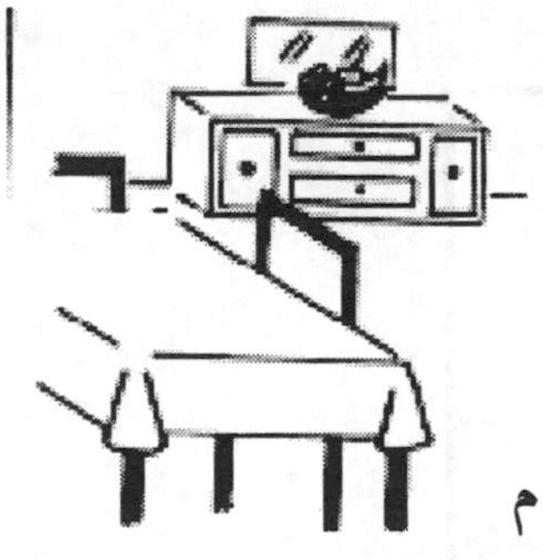

غُرفَةُ طَعام

غُرفَةُ جُلوس

أمّا في غُرفَةِ النَومِ فَهُناكَ سَريرٌ وطاوِلَةٌ صَغيرَةٌ عَلَيْها مِصْباحٌ كَهْرَبائِيٌّ وخِزانَةُ مَلابِس. إلى جانِبِ غُرفَةِ النَوْمِ يوجَدُ الحَمّامُ وفيهِ حَوضُ الاستِحْمامِ ومِرْحاضٌ أوروبيٌّ ومَغْسَلَة. فَوْقَ المَغسَلَةِ هُناكَ مِرآة.

غُرفَةُ نَوم

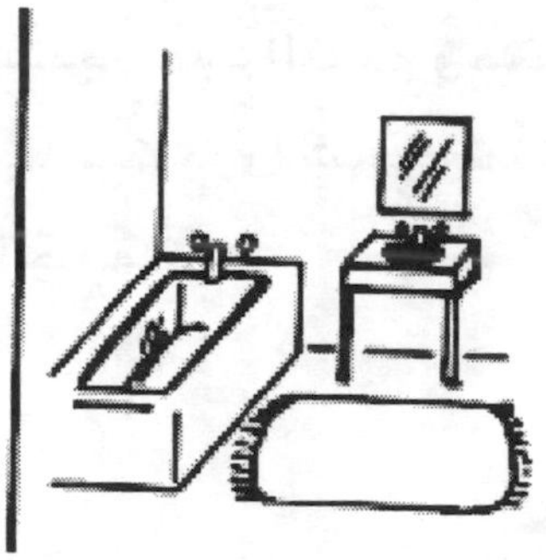

حمّام

المَطبَخُ لَيْسَ واسِعاً. فيهِ ثَلاّجةٌ ومَوْقِدٌ يَعمَلُ بِالغازِ ومَجْلى، لكِنْ لَيسَ فيهِ غَسّالةٌ ولا جَلاّيَةٌ كَهْرَبائِيَّة. مَطبَخُهُ هذا أكبَرُ من مَطبَخِهِ القَديم. يَستعمِلُ مايكل المَطبَخَ كلَّ يَومٍ لأنَّهُ يأكلُ فَطورَه في البَيتِ وأحْياناً يأكلُ الغَداءَ والعَشاءَ أيضاً.

مَطبَخ

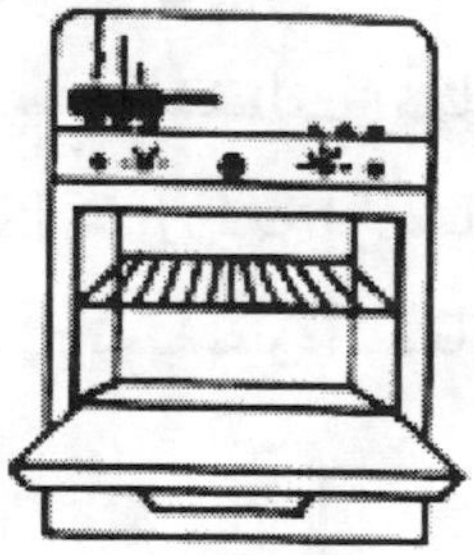

مَوقد

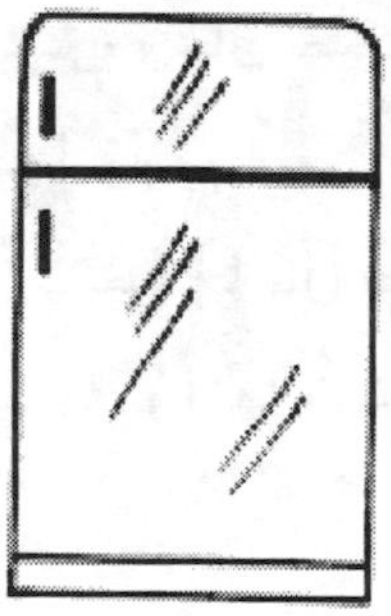

بَرّاد/ثَلاّجَة

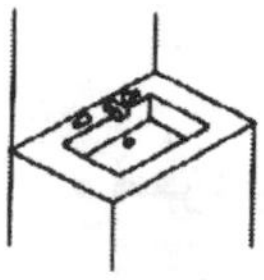

مَغسَلَة

مصْباح

حَوْض

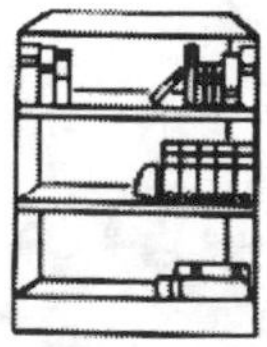

خزانَةُ كُتُب

مرحاض

حينَ انتَقَل مايكل من شَقَّتِه القَديمَة إلى شَقَّتِه الجَديدَة أتى صَديقاهُ المِصريّان سَمير عَبدُ الفتّاح وحُسَيْن أحْمَد ليُساعِداهُ في الانتِقال. حَمَلوا كُتُبَ مايكل وحَقائِبَهُ ثمَّ اسْتأجَروا شاحِنةً صَغيرَةً وذَهَبوا إلى الشَقَّةِ الجَديدة. لَم يذهبوا في ذلِكَ اليومِ إلى الجامِعة.

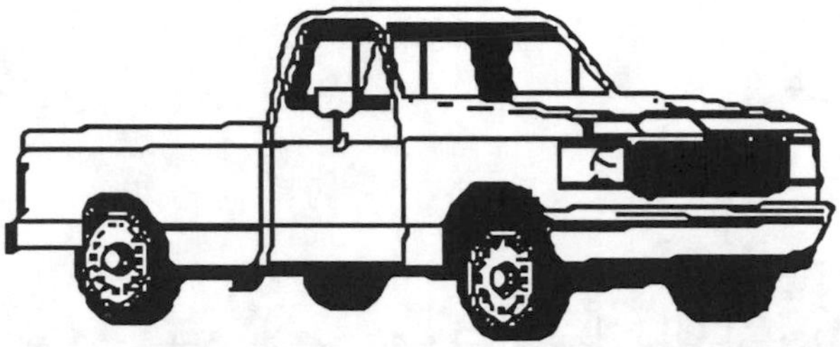

شاحنة

في مَساءِ يَومِ الخَميسِ مِنَ الأسبوعِ التالي زارَهُ في شَقَّتِه الجَديدَة أصدِقاؤُهُ سَمير وحُسَين وجِنِفَر وهِبَة. قالت هِبَة إنَّ الشَقَّةَ أعْجَبَتْها لأنَّها مُطِلّةٌ على شارِعٍ كَبيرٍ، وقال حُسَين إنَّها تُعجِبُهُ لأنَّها في بِنايَةٍ نَظيفَة، وقال سَمير إنَّ الشقة تُعجِبُهُ لأنَّها قَريبَةٌ مِنَ السوق. أمّا جِنِفَر فقالت إنّها لاتُريدُ أنْ تَسكُنَ في شَقّةٍ لأنّها لا تُحبُّ أنْ تُنَظِّفَها كلَّ يَوم. لكِنَّ مايكل قالَ لَها إنَّ خادِمةً تَأتي مَرَّتَينِ في الأسبوعِ لِتُنَظِّفَ الشَقّة، وإنَّها تُساعِدُه أحْياناً في تَحضيرِ الطَعام.

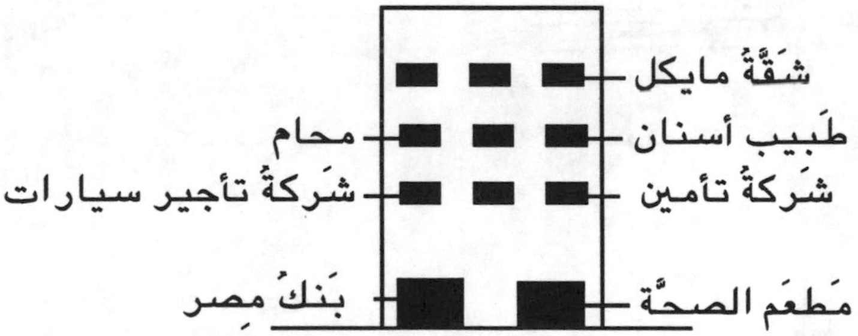

تَقَعُ شَقّةُ مايكل في بِنايةٍ في بابِ اللَوقِ قَريبَةٌ من وَسَطِ المَدينة. هُناكَ مَصرِفٌ في الطابَقِ الأرضِيِّ هو «بَنْكُ مِصرَ» ومَطعَمٌ صَغيرٌ يُسَمّى «مَطعَمُ الصِحّة». وفي الطابَقِ الأوّل توجد شَرِكَةُ تَأجيرِ سَيّاراتٍ وشَرِكةُ تأمين. أمّا في الطابَقِ الثاني فَهُناك عِيادَةُ طَبيبِ أسْنانٍ ومَكتَبُ مَحامٍ.

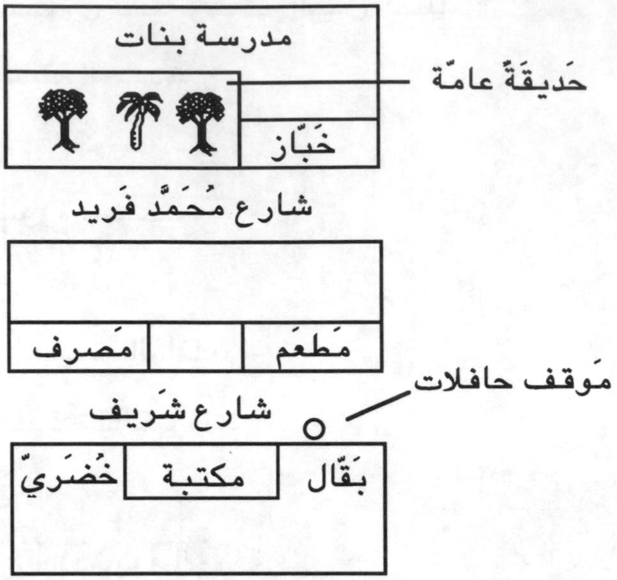

أمامَ البِنايةِ هُناك مَوقِفُ حافِلات، ويوجد مُقابِلَها مَكتَبة. إلى يَمينِ المكتَبة هُناكَ دُكّانُ بَقّال وإلى يَسارِها دُكّانُ الخُضَريّ. مَحَطّةُ المِترو «سَعْد زَغلول» لَيْسَتْ بَعيدةً جِدّاً عَنِ البِنايَة. في الشارعِ التالي بَعدَ شارعِ شَريف، ويُسَمّى شارعَ مُحَمّد فَريد، يوجدُ مَخبَزٌ يَبيعُ أنْواعاً مِن الخُبْزِ العَرَبيّ. اشترى مايكل مِنَ الخَبّازِ الخُبزَ الشاميَّ والعَيْشَ البَلَديَّ وأعجَبَهُ النوعانِ جِدّاً. هُناكَ أيْضاً حَديقَةٌ عامَّةٌ في ذلِكَ الشارعِ تَقَعُ خَلفَها مَدرَسةُ بَناتٍ ابتِدائيّة.

تمرين ١

أجِبْ عَن هذهِ الأسئِلةِ حَسَبَ نَصِّ القِراءَة:

١- لِماذا انتقل مايكل مِن شَقَّتِه القَديمة؟

٢- في أيِّ طابَقٍ توجَدُ شَقَّةُ مايكل الجَديدة؟

٣- ما مَعْنى الحَرفَين (م) و (ش) في الإعْلان؟

٤- مَن ساعَدَهُ في الانتِقالِ من الشَقَّةِ القَديمةِ إلى الجَديدة؟

٥- في أيِّ مَكانٍ مِن القاهِرةِ توجَدُ الشَقّةُ الجَديدَة؟

٦- هل تُعجِبُ الشَقّةُ الجَديدةُ حُسَين؟ لماذا؟

اكتُبْ «خَطَأ» أو «صَواب» بِجانب كلِّ جُملَةٍ وصَحِّحِ الجُمَلَ الخَطَأ.

٧- هُناكَ هاتِفٌ وبَرّادٌ في الشَقَّةِ الجَديدة.

٨- عَمِلَتْ هِبَةُ عِدّةَ سَنَواتٍ في الكُوَيت.

٩- علَّقَ مايكل على الجِدارِ صورةَ صَديقَتِه.

١٠- لا يَسْتَعمِلُ مايكل المَطبَخَ كَثيراً.

١١- انتقلَ مايكل إلى الشَقَّةِ الجَديدَة بِالحافِلة.

١٢- يَعْمَلُ المَوقِدُ في الشَقَّةِ الجَديدَةِ بِالكهرَباء.

١٣- المخبَزُ في شارِع الأندلُس.

١٤- انتَقَلَ مايكل إلى الشَقَّةِ الجَديدَةِ يَومَ الجُمْعة.

اكتُبْ أسئِلَةً لِهذِهِ الإجاباتِ كَما في المِثال.

Provide questions for these answers, as in the example.

لأنَّهُ يَدْرُسُ اللُغةَ العَرَبيّةَ بِالقاهِرة. ⇦ لماذا يَسكُنُ مايكل بِالقاهِرة؟

١٥- بِشاحِنَةٍ صَغيرة.

١٦- لأنَّها قَريبَةٌ مِنَ السوق.

١٧- في الطابَقِ الثاني.

١٨- تَقَعُ خَلْفَ الحَديقَةِ العامَّة.

أكمِلِ الجُمَلَ التاليةَ بِالكلِمَةِ المُناسِبَةِ حَسَبَ النَصّ:

١٩- شَقّةُ مايكل الجَديدةُ في الطابَقِ ......

❑ الأوَّل ❑ الثاني ❑ الثالِث

٢٠- عَلِمَ مايكل عَنِ الشَقّة مِن ......

❑ حُسَين ❑ الجَريدة ❑ المَجَلّة

٢١- أجرَةُ الشَقَّةِ السَنَويّةُ ...... جُنَيهٍ مِصريٍّ.
❑ ٧٠٠ ❑ ٤٨٠٠ ❑ ٨٤٠٠

٢٢- الهاتِفُ في غُرفَةِ ......
❑ الجُلوسِ ❑ النَومِ ❑ الطَعامِ

٢٣- المِرآةُ فوقَ ......
❑ المَجلى ❑ المَغسَلَة ❑ الأريكة

٢٤- يأكلُ مايكل طَعامَ ...... دائِماً في البَيت.
❑ الفَطورِ ❑ الغداءِ ❑ العشاءِ

٢٥- أصدِقاءُ مايكل زاروه ......
❑ صَباحاً ❑ ظُهراً ❑ مَساءً

٢٦- شَرِكةُ التَأمينِ في الطابَقِ ......
❑ الأوَّلِ ❑ الثاني ❑ الثالِثِ

٢٧- يوجد ...... مُقابِلُ بِنايةِ مايكل.
❑ مكتَبَةٌ ❑ مَدرسَةٌ ❑ مَحطّةُ مِترو

٢٨- اشترى مايكل العَيشَ البَلَديّ مِن ......
❑ الخُضَريّ ❑ البَقّال ❑ الخَبّاز

تمرين ٢

أكمِلِ الجُمَلَ التالِيَةَ بِالكَلِمَةِ المُناسِبَة:

١- ...... مايكل إلى شقّةٍ جديدة.
❑ اسْتَأجَرَ ❑ انتَقَلَ ❑ أعْجَبَ ❑ أحَبَّ

٢- أتكلَّمُ مَعَ أصدقائي بِـ ......
❑ البَرّاد ❑ المِصباح ❑ المِرآة ❑ الهاتِف

٣- أجلِسُ ...... التِلفاز.
❑ أمامَ ❑ خَلفَ ❑ تَحتَ ❑ فَوقَ

٤- تَضَعُ هالة ملابِسَها في ......

❑ الثلاّجةِ ❑ الخِزانةِ ❑ المِرحاضِ ❑ السَريرِ

٥- يَعْمَلُ أبو هِشام في ......

❑ مَصرِف ❑ مَوقِف ❑ مَجلى ❑ مِرحاض

٦- يَجلِسُ صَديقي أحمَد إلى ......

❑ نَوْمي ❑ يَميني ❑ مَلابِسي ❑ خِزانَتي

٧- ...... مايكل سَيّارَةً لِيَومَين حينَ كانَ في الإسكَندَرِيَّة.

❑ اشتَرى ❑ باعَ ❑ استَأجَر ❑ انْتَقَلَ

تمرين ٣

أعطِ عَكْسَ (opposite) هذهِ الكَلِمات:

١- يَمين ٢- فَوق

٣- أمامَ ٤- واسِع

تمرين ٤

وافِق بين الكلِماتِ في العَمودَين. .Match words in the two columns

١- بَرّاد	....	مِترو
٢- خُبز	....	تَليفون
٣- مَحَطّة	....	ثَلاّجة
٤- عِيادة	....	خَلْفَ
٥- بِناية	....	عَيش
٦- بَنْك	....	دُكّان
٧- هاتِف	....	طَبيب
٨- بَقّال	....	شقّة
		مَصْرِف

تمرين ٥

اخْتَرِ الكلِمَةَ غَيْرَ المُناسِبَةِ في كلِّ مَجموعةٍ وبَيِّن السَبَب.

١-	خَبّاز	بَقّال	نَوْع	خُضَريّ
٢-	مِرحاض	غَسّالة	بَرّاد	جَلاّية
٣-	مَغسَلة	حَوْض	هاتِف	مَجلى
٤-	فَوقَ	شارِع	تَحْتَ	أمامَ
٥-	غُرفة	شَقَّة	مَوْقِف	بِناية

تمرين ٦

إقرأ هذَين الإعلانَين ثم أجِب عَنِ الأسئِلة التالية:

> دار في شارع الجلاء مع هاتف وبراد وغسالة وجلاية وتلفزيون. ثلاث غرف نوم وحمامان. غرفة جلوس واسعة وغرفة طعام مع طاولة طعام وستة كراس. مطلة على حديقة المدفع. الإيجار السنوي ٦٤٠ ألف ليرة سورية.

> شقة فاخِرة في شارع الخليج مطلة على البحر. غرفتا نوم وغرفة جلوس وطعام وغرفة للخادمة، دون أثاث. مع هاتف. الإيجار الشهري ٥٨٠ دينار كويتي.

١- في أيِّ بَلَدٍ توجَدُ كُلٌّ مِنَ الدارِ والشَقَّة؟

٢- كَمْ غُرفَةً في الشَقّة؟

٣- ما عُمْلاتُ (currencies) كُلٌّ مِن مِصرَ وسورية والكُوَيْت؟

٤- اِقرأ الإعلانين في هذا التَمرين والإعلانَ في أوّلِ الدرس والإعلانَ في الدرسِ ١٧ تمرين ٧ مَرّةً ثانية ثمَّ اكتب إعلاناً مِثلَ هذه الإعلانات في جَريدةٍ عَرَبِيّة عَن غُرفتِك أو شَقّتِك أو بيتِك.

تمرين ٧

اكتب إلى جانب كُلِّ صورةٍ اسمَها.

١-  ....

٢-  ....

٣-  ....

٤-  ....

٥- 

....

٦- 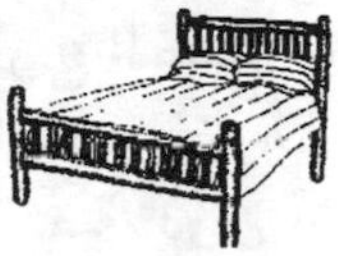 ....

٧-  ....

٨- 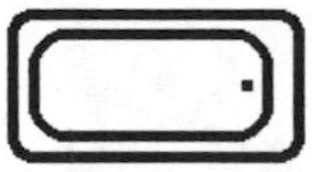 ....

٩-  ....

١٠-  ....

١١-  ....

١٢-  ....

١٣-  ....

١٤-  ....

تمرين ٨

أعِدْ تَرتيبَ الكلماتِ لِتُشكِّلَ جُمَلاً مُفيدة.

١- بَيتي - ابتدائية - هُناكَ - خَلفَ - مَدرَسة

٢- التِلفاز - الكبيرة - وَضَعْتُ - مُقابِلَ - الأريكة

٣- أصدقائي - سَيّارَتي - مِن - في - ساعَدَني - غَسْلِ - اثنان

٤- للإيجار - اليوم - قَرَأتُ - شَقَّة - إعلاناً - في - عَن - جَريدة

تمرين ٩

Rearrange the sentences to form a meaningful paragraph, leaving the first sentence intact.

١- مرحباً. أنا مُنى الأسوَد وأعملُ مَدَرِّسةً في وَسَطِ المدينة.

لأنَّ فيها غرفةَ مكتبٍ لَهُ وغرفةَ طعام ومَطبَخاً واسِعاً.

قالوا إنَّ الشقّةَ أعجبَتْهم لأنَّها مُطِلّة على حَديقَةٍ جَميلة.

انتَقَلْتُ وعائِلَتي في الشهْرِ الماضي إلى شَقّةٍ كبيرة.

لِذلِكَ أركبُ الحافِلةَ كلَّ يومٍ إلى المدرسة.

تقعُ شَقّتي الجَديدة في شارعٍ بَعيدٍ عَن وَسَطِ المدينة.

زارَنا أمسِ بَعضُ أصدقائِنا لِيشاهِدوا الشَقّةَ الجديدة.

تُعْجِبُني شَقّتي كثيراً وتُعجِبُ زَوْجي كذلِك.

1. **Expressing Intention**: أرادَ أنْ + المضارع المنصوب

One way of expressing intention, want, or need is by using the verb أراد, or other verbs of volition, followed by the particle أنْ. This particle is immediately followed by a form of the present tense: المضارع المنصوب, as in this example:

Michael wanted to move. ١ أرادَ مايكل أنْ ينتقِلَ.

Do not confuse this particle أنْ with إنَّ and أنَّ, which are used with nouns. The particle أنْ in this usage is similar to the particle *to* in English used with the infinitive (e.g. to eat).

Other verbs which are used to express preference may also be followed by أنْ and المُضارع المَنصوب. These include أحَبَّ and أعجَبَ. Examine these examples:

٢ أُحِبُّ أنْ آكلَ عَشائي في المَطعم.

I like to eat my dinner in the restaurant.

٣ يُعْجِبُه أنْ يدرُسَ اللُغَةَ العَرَبِيّةَ.

He likes to study Arabic (literally: [It] pleases him to study Arabic).

The أنْ-phrase may be replaced with a verbal noun. Thus, أنْ يدرسَ in sentence 3, for example, may be replaced with دِراسة. This change, however, entails a structural change. The verbal noun forms with the following noun an *iḍāfa* structure. In addition, the verb must agree in gender with the verbal noun, which is feminine. The modified sentence reads:

٤ تُعجِبُه دِراسةُ اللُغَةِ العَرَبِيَّةِ.

a. **The Verb أعْجَبَ:** Note that this verb translates "*to like,*" but it literally means "*to please.*" This might be a little confusing because in a sentence with أعجب, the agent, or doer of the action, seems to occupy the position of the direct object. Compare these two sentences which have a similar meaning:

٥ أحِبُّ الطعامَ العربيّ.

٦ يُعْجِبُني الطعامُ العربيّ.

In 5, الطعامَ is the direct object of the verb أحبُّ, while الطعامُ is the agent in 6. This sentence may be rephrased as follows to show its structure:

٧ يُعجِبُ الطَعامُ العَرَبيُّ (أنا).

Sentence 7 clearly shows that الطعامُ is the agent, or doer of the action, of the sentence and that the pronoun أنا is the direct object. If we substitute the object أنا with a noun, the case can be indicated, as in 8:

٨ الطَعامُ العَرَبيُّ يُعْجِبُ الطالبَ.

SUMMARY

Certain verbs, such as أرادَ and أحَبَّ, may be followed by a phrase starting with the particle أنْ, which is, in turn, followed by المضارع المنصوب.

تمرين ١٠

A. Express the following meanings, using أنْ and المضارع المنصوب.

1. You want to write to all your friends.
2. Your classmates like to sit in the sun.
3. You want to help your younger brother with his studies.
4. Your sister likes to sleep late.

5. Identify in the reading passages and list at least <u>four</u> *nisba* nouns, <u>two</u> verbal nouns (مَصْدَر), <u>two</u> instances of مُضارع منصوب, <u>one</u> instance of مُضارع مجزوم, and <u>two</u> comparative nouns (اسم تَفضيل).

2. **Noun of Instrument** اسْمُ الآلة

There are patterns in Arabic which are used to derive names for instruments. The most common of these are the following three listed with examples, two of which you already know:

مِفْعال	مِفْتاح *key*
مِفْعَلة	مِسْطَرة *ruler*

مِفْعَل *scissors* مِقَصّ

However, with the need in the modern world to coin words for new devices, other patterns are also used. Seven of these patterns are listed with examples from material covered so far in this textbook:

Pattern	Example
فاعِل	*telephone* هاتِف
فاعِلة	*calculator* حاسِبة
مُفَعِّل	*engine, motor* مُحَرِّك
مُفَعِّلة	*tape recorder* مُسَجِّلة
فاعول	*computer* حاسوب
فَعّال	*refrigerator* بَرّاد
فَعّالة	*washing machine* غَسّالة

تمرين ١١

List below each of the following patterns the appropriate names for devices which fit these patterns:

١ـ مِفْعَلة ٢ـ فَعّالة ٣ـ مِفْعال ٤ـ فَعّال ٥ـ فاعِلة ٦ـ فاعِل

مِرحاض، حاسِب (computer)، مِبراة، حافِلة، دَرّاجة، بَرّاد، جَلّاية،

مِرْآة، شاحِنة، خَلّاط (mixer)، مِمْحاة، مِصْباح، ثَلّاجة

3. Prepositions حُروفُ الجَرّ: Relational Concepts

The meaning of a preposition is largely determined by the context in which it occurs. The preposition في, for example, may have several meanings based on the context and purpose of the sentence, as in the following examples (there are several other meanings that have not been used in this text so far):

٩ يَدرُسُ الطِبَّ في جامِعَةِ بْرِنْسْتَن. *at* (signifying place)

١٠ سَأستَقبِلُهُ في الساعَةِ الثانِيَةِ. *at* (signifying time)

١١ نَحنُ في الصَفِّ. *in (place)*

١٢ زُرتُهُ في يَومِ العيدِ. *on (time)*

Prepositions covered thus far fall into two categories: those prefixed to the noun they modify and those that stand independent of it. They include the following, starting with attached prepositions, each listed with an example. Remember that a noun modified by a preposition is in the genitive case (مَجرور):

١٣ بِـ أكتبُ بِالقلمِ *write with*

أسكنُ بِبَيروت. *live in (place)*

اشتريتُ الكتابَ بِخَمسينَ دولاراً. *for $50*

وَصَلنا بِالطائِرة. *by plane*

تكلَّمتُ بِاللُّغَةِ العَرَبيَّة. *in Arabic*

قَرأتُ الكِتابَ بِيَومَين. *in two days (time)*

١٤ كَـ الأستاذُ، كَما تَعلَم، لُبنانيّ. *as you know*

١٥ لِـ لِسامِيَةِ أربَعَةُ أولاد. *Samia has four children*

كَتَبتُ لِجَميعِ أصدِقائي. *to all my friends*

١٦ مِن هِيَ مِن مَدينةِ بَغداد. *from the city of Baghdad*

١٧ إلى ذَهَبَتْ إلى المَكتَبة. *to the library*

١٨ عَن تَكلَّمَ عَن أُسرَتِه. *about his family*

١٩ عَلى الكِتابُ عَلى الطاولةِ. *on the table.*

٢٠ في هُوَ في غُرفَتِه. *in his room (see examples 9-12)*

٢١ حتّى دَرَستُ حَتّى الساعةِ الثانِية. *till two*

٢٢ وَ وَاللّه *by God, I swear*

٢٣ عَدا نَعمَلُ كلَّ يَومٍ عَدا يَومِ الجمعة. *except Friday*

The last example (23) has عَدا as a preposition. It can, however, have a verbal meaning when used with ما, whereby the following noun is منصوب:

٢٤ زارَني أصدِقائي ما عَدا واحداً.

a. **Adverbs and Prepositions of Place**: Some grammarians consider a number of adverbs and nouns as prepositions. These nouns and adverbs describe the relationship between entities in terms of location. The graph below illustrates some of the meanings of some of the items.

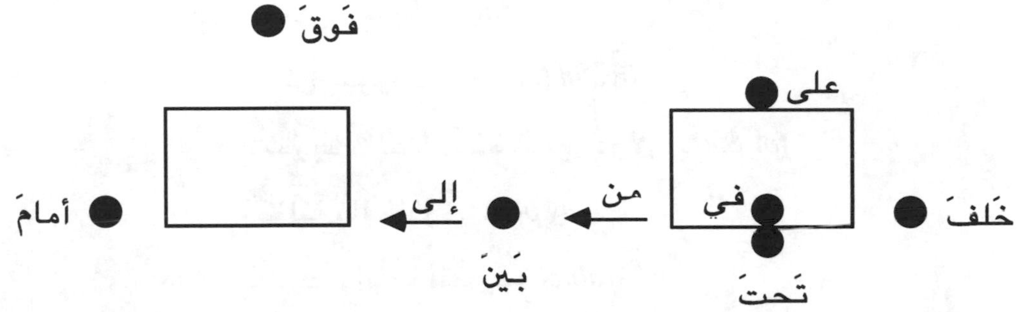

Preposition-like items (also considered adverbs of time and place) covered so far include the following. Note that they are nouns in the accusative case (منصوب) and that the modified noun is مجرور (genitive). They form with the modified noun an *iḍāfa* structure.

٢٤	عِندَ	سَأراكَ عِندَ بابِ المكتبةِ.	*at the door of*
٢٥	أمامَ	هُناكَ شَجَرةٌ أمامَ بابِ داري.	*in front of*
٢٦	قَبْلَ	المَخبَزُ قَبلَ الحَديقةِ.	*before the park (place)*
		سَأراكَ قَبلَ المَغرِبِ.	*before sunset (time)*
٢٧	بَعْدَ	دُكّانُ البَقّالِ بَعدَ المَحَطّةِ.	*after the station*
		سَتَزورُنا بَعدَ العُطلةِ.	*after the break*
٢٨	بَيْنَ	الحَديقةُ بَينَ داري ودارِك.	*between*
٢٩	خَلْفَ	هُناكَ مَصرِفٌ خَلفَ بَيتي.	*behind*
٣٠	جانِبَ	أحِبُّ أنْ أجلِسَ جانِبَ الشبّاكِ.	*by, next to*
٣١	بِجانِبِ	أحِبُّ أنْ أجلِسَ بِجانِبِ الشبّاكِ.	*by, next to*

٣٢	تَحْتَ	هُناكَ مَطعَمٌ تَحتَ شَقَّتي. *under*
٣٣	فَوْقَ	المِصباحُ فَوقَ الطاولة. *over*
٣٤	مُقابِلَ	مَحطّةُ القِطارِ مُقابِلَ المخبَز. *across from*
٣٥	دونَ	أشربُ الشايَ دونَ سُكّرٍ. *without*
٣٦	مَعَ	وَصلَتِ الطائرَةُ مَعَ اللَيلِ. *at night*
		سَكَنْتُ مَعَ طالِبَةٍ لُبنانِيّة. *with*

تمرين ١٢

أكمِلِ الجُملَ التالِيَةَ بِحَرفِ الجَرِّ المُنفصِلِ (separate) أو الظَرفِ (adverb) المُناسِب.

(في - إلى - حَتّى - مِن - عَلى - مَعَ - عَن)

١ـ وَصلَتِ الطائِرةُ ...... مَوعدِها.

٢ـ ذَهَبنا ...... الجَزائِرِ بِالطائِرة.

٣ـ وَجَدتُ كِتابي ...... طاولَةِ الأستاذ.

٤ـ سَأدرُسُ في المكتبةِ ...... الساعةِ الرابعة.

٥ـ تَسكُنُ أمّي ...... القُدسِ.

٦ـ قَرَأنا ...... الأميرِ عَبدِ القادِرِ الجَزائِريِّ في هذا الكِتابِ.

٧ـ هذِهِ الأزهارُ ...... صَديقي.

٨ـ ذَهَبتُ إلى السينَما ...... ثَلاثةٍ مِن أصدِقائي.

أكمِلِ الجُمَلَ التالِيةَ بأحَدِ حُروفِ الجَرِّ المُتَّصِلةِ (attached prepositions) (لَـ - بِـ - كَـ).

٩ـ اشْتَرَتْ هالَة هذا الكِتابَ ......خمسينَ دولاراً.

١٠ـ هي، .....ما تَعلَم، مَغرِبيَّة.

١١- هَل تَسكُنينَ ......هذهِ الشَقّةِ؟

١٢- هَل ......كِ إخوة؟

اختَرِ الكَلِمةَ المُناسِبةَ لِتكملَ الجُمَلَ التالية.

١٣- هل شَقَّتُك ...... عِيادةِ الطَبيب؟

❑ إلى ❑ فَوقَ ❑ بَينَ ❑ عِندَ

١٤- جَلَسْتُ في سَيارةِ الأُجرةِ (*taxicab*) ...... السائِق.

❑ خَلفَ ❑ بَينَ ❑ مَقابِلَ ❑ أمامَ

١٥- هل تَشرَبينَ القَهوةَ ...... سُكَّر؟

❑ بَعدَ ❑ قَبلَ ❑ دونَ ❑ جانِبَ

١٦- لَم يرجعْ أحمَد إلى المدرسةِ ...... الغَداء.

❑ أمامَ ❑ خَلفَ ❑ تَحتَ ❑ بَعدَ

١٧- تَقَعُ بَلدَتي ...... مَدينَتَينِ كَبيرَتَين.

❑ مُقابِلَ ❑ دونَ ❑ بَينَ ❑ خَلفَ

١٨- عَلّقتُ صورَةَ أمّي ...... صورةِ أبي.

❑ جانِبَ ❑ عِندَ ❑ دونَ ❑ أمامَ

١٩- هَل هُناكَ مَوقِفُ حافِلةٍ...... بابِ الشركة؟

❑ خَلفَ ❑ أمامَ ❑ فَوقَ ❑ تحتَ

٢٠- هُناكَ مَخبَزٌ ...... دُكّانِ البَقّالِ.

❑ بَينَ ❑ مُقابِلَ ❑ فَوقَ تحتَ

تمرين ١٣

استَمع (listen) إلى النَصِّ الأوَّلِ ثُمَّ أجِبْ عَنِ الأسئِلة التالية:

١- لماذا انْتَقَلَتْ العائِلةُ إلى شَقّةٍ جَديدة؟

٢- لماذا تُعجِبُ الشَقّةُ الجَديدةُ الزَوجة؟

٣- أينَ تَقَعُ الشَقّةُ الجَديدة؟

اكتُبْ «خَطأ» أو «صَواب» بِجانبِ كلِّ جُملَةٍ وصَحِّح الجُمَلَ الخطأ.

٤- الشَقّةُ القَديمةُ أكبرُ مِنَ الجديدة.

٥- تَعمَلُ الزَوجةُ في شَرِكة.

٦- اشتَرَت الزَوجةُ تِلفازاً.

أكمِلِ الجُمَلَ بِالكلِماتِ المُناسِبةِ حَسَبَ نَصِّ الاستِماع.

٧- الزَوجةُ والزَوجُ لَهُما ......

❑ وَلَدٌ واحِد		❑ وَلَدان		❑ ثَلاثَةُ أولاد		❑ أربَعَةُ أولاد

٨- في الشَقّةِ الجَديدةِ ...... نَوم.

❑ غُرفةُ		❑ غُرفتا		❑ ثلاثُ غُرَف		❑ أربَعُ غُرَف

٩- الشَقّةُ الجديدةُ قَريبَةٌ مِن ......

❑ عَمَلِ الزَوج		❑ بَيتِ أسرةِ الزَوجة

❑ بَيتِ أسرةِ الزَوج		❑ الجامِعة

١٠- سَوفَ تَشتَري هذِهِ العائِلةُ ......

❑ غَسّالةً		❑ بَرّاداً		❑ جَلّايةً		❑ أريكةً

١١- الشَقّةُ الجديدة مَوجودة في الطابَقِ ......

❑ الأوَّل		❑ الثاني		❑ الثالث		❑ الرابع

تمرين ١٤

اسـتَـمِعْ إلى الـنَـصِّ الـثـاني ثُمَّ اكتُبْ أسـمـاءَ الشـوارِعِ والأمـاكِنِ على المُـخَـطَّـطِ حَـسـبَ نَـصِّ الاستِماعِ الثاني (second listening passage) .

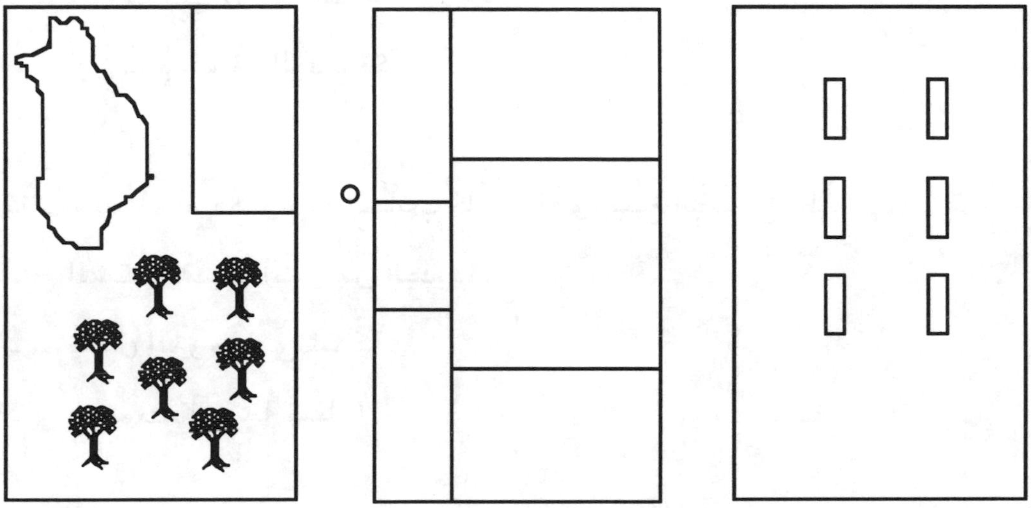

المُفْرَدات

furniture.. (n., m.) أثاث

to lease, to let.. أجَّرَ (يُؤَجِّرُ) تَأجير

rent, wage, fare.. (n., f.) أُجْرة ج أُجور

other.. (n., m.) آخَر ج آخَرون

ground, land.. أرض ج أراضٍ

couch.. (n., f.) أريكة ج أرائِك

to rent, to hire.. (v.) استأجَرَ (يَستأجِرُ) استِئجار

to please.. (v.) أعْجَبَ يُعْجِبُ

advertisement.. (n., m.) إعْلان ج إعْلانات

in front of.. (preposition) أمامَ

to (infinitive).. (particle) أنْ

Europe.. (n., f.) أوروبا

rent.. (n. m.) إيجار ج إيجارات

to sell.. (v.) باعَ (يَبيعُ) بَيْع

refrigerator (Syria).. (n., m.) بَرّاد ج بَرّادات

far.. (adv.) بَعيد

grocer.. (n., m.) بَقّال ج بَقّالون

local, popular.. (adj.) بَلَديّ

bank (colloquial).. بَنْك ج بُنوك

insurance.. (n., m.) تأمين ج تأمينات

telephone (colloquial).. (n., m.) تَليفون ج تَليفونات

refrigerator (Egypt).. (n., f.) ثَلاّجة ج ثَلاّجات

part.. (n., m.) جُزْء ج أجْزاء

dishwasher.. (n., f.) جَلاّية ج جَلاّيات

[Egyptian] pound.. (n., m.) جُنَيه ج جُنَيْهات

park, garden .... حَديقة ج حَدائِق (n., f.)
[bath] tub .... حَوْض ج أحْواض (n., m.)
servant .... خادِم ج خَدَم (n., m.)
baker .... خَبّاز ج خَبّازون (n., m.)
closet, cupboard .... خِزانة ج خَزائِن/خِزانات (n., f.)
greengrocer .... خُضَريّ ج خُضَريّون (n. m.)
behind .... خَلْفَ (preposition)
shop, store .... دُكّان ج دَكاكين (n., f.)
dinar (Kuwaiti currency) .... دينار ج دَنانير (n., m.)
truck .... شاحِنة ج شاحِنات (n. f.)
company .... شَرِكة ج شَرِكات (n., f.)
health .... صِحّة (n.)
floor, storey, flat .... طابَق ج طَوابِق
to hang .... عَلَّقَ (يُعَلِّقُ) تَعْليق (v.)
doctor's practice, clinic .... عِيادة ج عِيادات
bread (Egypt) .... عَيْش (n., m.)
[butane] gas .... غاز ج غازات (n., m.)
washing machine .... غَسّالة ج غَسّالات (n., f.)
deluxe, fancy, excellent, luxurious .... فاخِر (adj.)
[Syrian] pound; lira .... لَيْرة ج لَيْرات (n., f.)
meter .... م (مِتْر) ج أمْتار (n., m.)
metro .... مترو (n., m.)
kitchen sink .... مَجْلى ج مَجالٍ (n., m.)
bakery .... مَخْبَز ج مَخابِز (n., m.)
[floor] plan, map .... مُخَطَّط ج مُخَطَّطات (n., m.)
mirror .... مِرْآة ج مَرايا (n., f.)
toilet .... مِرْحاض ج مَراحيض (n., m.)
lamp .... مِصْباح ج مَصابيح (n., m.)
bank .... مَصْرِف ج مَصارِف (n., m.)

مُطلٌّ (verbal noun) .... overlooking
مَغْسَلة ج مَغاسِل (n., f.) .... washbasin, bathroom sink
مُقابِل (adv.) .... opposite, across from
مَلبَس ج مَلابِس (n., m.) .... clothes
مَوْقِد ج مَواقِد (n., m.) .... [cooking] range
مَوْقِف ج مَواقِف (n., m.) .... [bus] stop, parking lot
واسِع (adj.) .... spacious, large
وُجِدَ (يوجَدُ) (passive of وَجَد) .... there is/are, to exist
وَضَعَ (يَضَعُ) وَضْع (v.) .... to put
وَقَعَ (يَقَعُ) وُقوع/وَقْع (v.) .... to be located, fall down
يَسار (n., m.) .... left
يَمين (n., m.) .... right

دَيْر صيدنايا في سورية
Monastery of Seydnaya, Syria

Lesson Twenty-Five — الدَرْسُ الخامِسُ والعِشرون

Objectives:

- Describing activities in past, present, and future.
- Postcards and letters.
- Terms of address in written communication.
- Adverbs of time and place.
- Negating future time (لَنْ).
- Relative clauses (الّذي – الّتي) .
- Prepositions revisited.
- Possessive *iḍāfa.*
- Listen to recorded material for this lesson.
- Do relevant computer drills and exercises, Stages 8 and 9.

مايكِل بْراون في القاهِرَةِ والإسكَندَريَّة

القاهِرَة، الجُمْعَة ١٣ سِبتَمبر ١٩٩٦

أكتبُ هذهِ اليَوميّاتِ كَجُزءٍ مِن درسِ اللُغَةِ العَرَبيَّةِ، وأنا أستَمْتِعُ بِكِتابَتِها كثيراً. وَصَلتُ إلى القاهرة مُنذُ أسابيعَ وأعجَبَتْني هذهِ المدينةُ مَعَ أنَّها مَدينةٌ كبيرةٌ جِداً فيها أكثَرُ مِن ١٤ مِليون نَسَمة. بَعدَ وُصولي إلى

القاهِرة بِمُدّةٍ قَصيرةٍ ذَهَبْتُ مَعَ أصدقائي إلى «الجيزة» قُرْبَ القاهَرة لِمُشاهدةِ الأهراماتِ، والأهراماتُ مَبانٍ عَظيمةٌ بَناها الفَراعِنةُ مُنذُ آلافِ السِنين. التَقَطتُ صُوَراً كَثيرةً بِآلةِ تَصويري الجَديدَة، ورَكِبتُ هُناكَ عَلى الجَمَل. لَم أرَ جِمالاً إلاّ عِندَ الأهراماتِ وفي حَديقةِ الحَيَواناتِ الّتي زُرتُها في عُطلةِ عيدِ الأضْحى. شاهدتُ هُناكَ عَدَداً كبيراً من الحِيَواناتِ مِن كلِّ بِلادِ العالَم.

جَمَل

آلةُ تَصوير

القاهِرَة، السبت ١٩٩٦/٩/٢١

سافَرْتُ أوّلَ أمسِ الخَميسِ إلى الإسْكَنْدَرِيّةِ بالقِطارِ مَعَ بَعضِ الأصْدِقاء. الإسْكَنْدَرِيّةُ ميناءٌ هامٌّ على البَحرِ الأبيَضِ المُتَوَسِّطِ وهِيَ أقدَمُ مِن القاهِرةِ بِمِئاتِ السِنين. أخَذنا القِطارَ مِن مَحطّةِ رَمْسيسَ في مَيْدانِ رَمسيس في الساعةِ الثامنةِ والنِصْفِ صَباحاً. اشْتَرَيتُ تَذكرَةً ذَهاباً وإياباً بِعِشرينَ جُنَيهاً. مَرَرْنا في الطَريقِ إلى الإسكندَريّةِ بِمدينَةِ طَنطا ثالِثِ أكبَرِ مُدُنِ مصر. وَصَلنا إلى الإسْكَنْدَرِيّةِ بَعدَ الظُهرِ. ذَهَبنا أولاً إلى مَطعمٍ قَريبٍ مِنَ الشاطِئِ حَيثُ تَناوَلْنا طَعاماً مِصرِيّاً وشَرِبنا القَهوة.

مَشَينا قليلاً في شارعٍ طَويلٍ وجَميلٍ بِجانِبِ الشاطِئِ يُسَمّى «الكورنيش»، ثُمَّ نزَلنا إلى الشاطِئِ وسَبَحْنا ساعَتَين أو ثَلاث. كانَ الطقسُ دافِئاً وجَميلاً والشَمسُ

ساطِعةً. نَزَلنا تِلكَ اللَيلةَ في فُندُقٍ صَغيرٍ لكنَّهُ نَظيف. وفي اليومِ التالي ذَهَبنا إلى الشاطِئِ مَرَّةً ثانِيَةً، ثُمَّ ركِبنا القِطارَ ورَجَعنا إلى القاهِرةِ مَساءً. لَم أنسَ أنْ أكتُبَ بِطاقةً بَريدِيّةً لأستاذَتي. أعْجبَتْني الإسكندريَّةُ كَثيراً واستَمتَعتُ بِهذهِ الزيارة بِسبَبِ المناظِرِ الجَميلةِ ولأنَّ الإسكَندَرانيينَ طَيِّبونَ ويُحِبّونَ أنْ يُساعِدوا الناسَ الآخَرين.

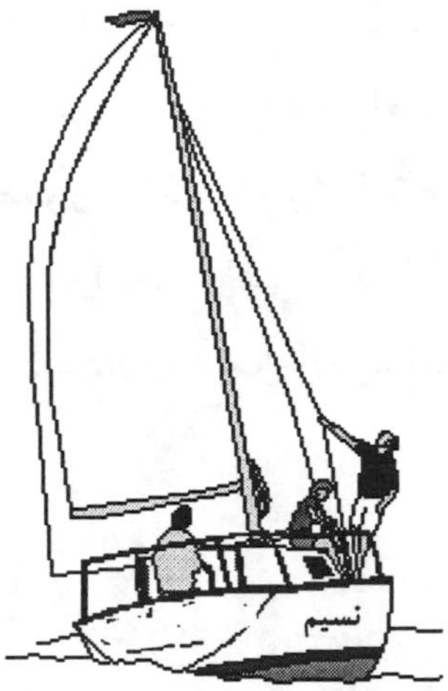

قارب في البحر المتوسط

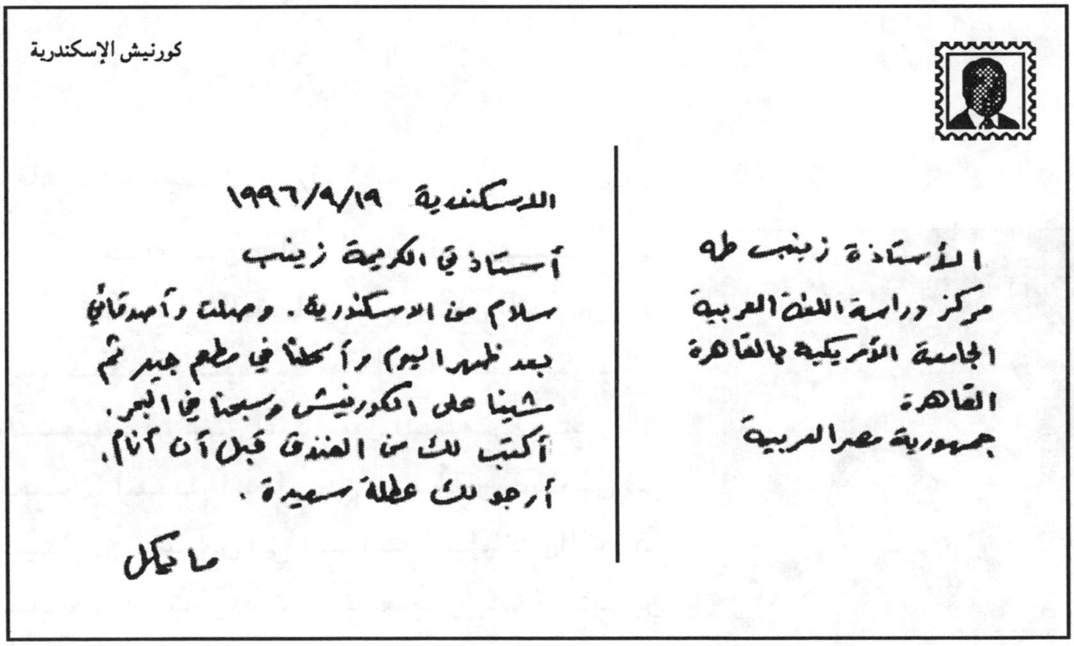

كورنيش الإسكندرية

الإسكندرية ١٩٩٦/٩/١٩
أستاذتي الكريمة زينب
سلام من الإسكندرية. وصلت وأصدقائي
بعد ظهر اليوم وأكلنا في مطعم جيد ثم
مشينا على الكورنيش وسبحنا في البحر.
أكتب لك من الفندق قبل أن أنام.
أرجو لك عطلة سعيدة.

مايكل

الأستاذة زينب طه
مركز دراسة اللغة العربية
الجامعة الأمريكية بالقاهرة
القاهرة
جمهورية مصر العربية

See a typed version of the above postcard in Appendix E 1.

القاهِرَة، الجُمْعة ٢٢ نوفمبر ١٩٩٦

إنَّ الشَيءَ الَّذي أعْجَبَني في القاهِرَةِ كَثيراً هو السَماءُ الزَرقاءُ ونَهرُ النيلِ العَظيمِ الَّذي يَبْدَأُ مِن وَسَطِ إفريقيا في «بُروندي». يَسيرُ النيلُ شَمالاً إلى الخَرطومِ عاصِمةِ السودانِ حَيثُ يَلتَقي نَهرا النيلِ الأبيَضِ والنيلِ الأزرَق، ومِن هُناكَ يَسيرُ النيلُ شَمالاً إلى القاهِرةِ ثُمَّ إلى البَحرِ الأبيَضِ المُتَوَسِّط. نَهرُ النيلِ أطولُ نَهرٍ في العالَم، وطولُهُ ٦٦٩٥ كيلومِتراً، لِذلِكَ فَهُو أطوَل مِن نَهرِ أوهايو ونَهرِ الميسيسيبي.

القاهِرَة، السَبت ٢١ ديسمبر ١٩٩٦

في كلِّ عُطلةِ نِهايةِ أسْبوع أزورُ مكاناً جَديداً. ذَهَبتُ صَباحَ أمسِ إلى المُتْحَفِ المِصريِّ ووَجَدتُ فيهِ عَدَداً كَبيراً مِنَ الآثارِ الفِرعَونيَّةِ القَديمَةِ وكذلِكَ آثاراً إسلاميَّةً وعَرَبيّة. إنّه مُتْحَفٌ جَيِّدٌ جِدّاً وسَأزورُهُ مَرّةً ثانيَةً إنْ شاءَ الله. اشتَرَيتُ مِنَ المُتحَفِ بَعضَ الصُوَرِ وكِتاباً عَن آثارِ مِصر. ومِن هُناكَ ذَهَبتُ إلى مَسجِدِ مُحَمَّد عَلي والتَقَطتُ بَعضَ الصُوَر. في الأسبوعِ المُقبِلِ سَوفَ أزورُ بَعضَ المَساجِدِ القديمةِ في القاهِرة، لكِنّي لَنْ أسافِرَ إلى مُدُنٍ أخْرى في ذلِكَ الأسبوع.

عَدنان مارتيني

في نيويورك وكندا وفلوريدا

كَلَمبَس، الأربعاء ٢٨ آب ١٩٩٦

أخَذتُ أمسِ آخِرَ امتِحانٍ في هذا الفصلِ الدراسيِّ وكانَ في مادّةِ الرياضِيّات. أظُنُّ أنّي أجَبْتُ عَنِ الأسئِلَةِ جَيِّداً، وأنا سَعيدٌ أنَّ الدراسةَ انتَهَت. أستطيعُ الآنَ أنْ أسافِرَ لِزيارةِ الأماكِنِ الجَميلةِ في الولاياتِ المُتَّحِدةِ وكَندا الَّتي أريدُ زِيارتَها.

اشْتَرَيتُ في الشهرِ الماضي تَذْكِرةَ طائِرةٍ إلى نيويورك ذَهاباً وإياباً بِمِئَةٍ وثَمانين دولاراً. أرَدْتُ زيارةَ نيويورك مُنذُ أشهُرٍ فأنا لا أعرِفُها، مَعَ أنَّ لي صَديقاً يَسكُنُ هُناكَ ويَدرُسُ الهَندَسةَ الصِناعيَّةَ في جامِعَةِ نيويورك. سَوفَ يستَقبِلُني غَسّان في المَطار. لَن أنزِلَ في فُندُق، بَل في شَقّةِ غَسّان.

نيويورك، السَبت ٣١ آب ١٩٩٦

وَصَلَتْ طائرَتي إلى مَطارِ «لاغوارديا» في مَوعِدِها وكانَ غَسّانُ أمامَ البوّابةِ وأخَذَني إلى شَقَّتِه حَيثُ وَضَعتُ حَقيبَتي وأشيائي. مَشَينا في الشوارعِ حَتّى وصَلْنا إلى ساحَةٍ مَشهورَةٍ تُسمّى «تايم سكوير». ثمَّ زُرْنا بَعدَ ذلِكَ مَحلاّتٍ تِجاريَّةً مِثلَ «ساكْس فيفث أفِنيو» و«ماسيز»، لكِنَّنا لَم نَشتَرِ أيَّ شيءٍ.

مَشَينا في الشارعِ الخامِسِ لِزيارةِ مَبْنى «إمپايَر ستيت» الَّذي يَقَعُ بَين الشارِعِ الثالِثِ والثَلاثين والشارِعِ الرابعِ والثَلاثين والَّذي بُنِيَ مُنذُ أكثَرَ مِن خَمسةٍ وستِّينَ عاماً. أخَذنا المِصْعَدَ إلى الطابَق ١٠٢ وشاهَدْنا مَدينةَ نيويورك مِن فَوق. كان هذا المَبْنى أطولَ مَبنىً في العالَمِ إلى أنْ بُنِيَ مَبنى «سيَرز» في شيكاغو.

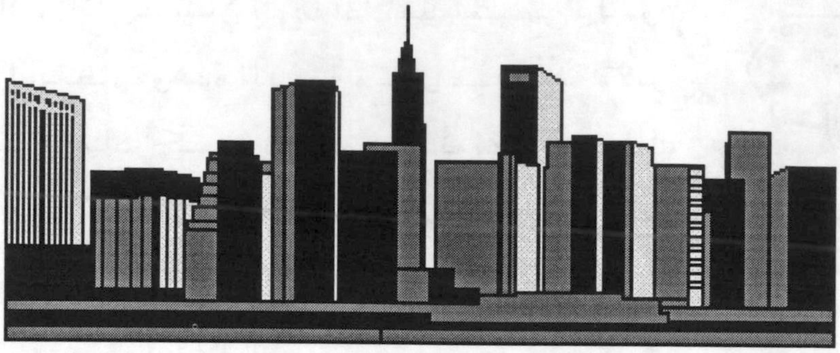

بعدَ ذلِك تَناوَلنا طَعامَ العَشاءِ في مَطعَمٍ فرَنسيٍّ جَيِّدٍ قَريبٍ مِن مَسْرَحِ «راديو سيتي». كانَ الطَعامُ جيِّداً لكِنَّهُ كانَ غالِياً جِدّاً. شاهَدْنا فيلماً في راديو سيتي. لَن أستطيعَ أن أزورَ جامِعَةَ نيويورك غَداً لأنّنا سَنُسافِرُ بِالقِطارِ صَباحاً إلى شَلاّلاتِ نَياغَرا.

شَلاّلاتُ نَياغَرا، الإثنين ٢ أيلول ١٩٩٦

وَصَلْنا أمسِ ظُهراً إلى الشَلاّلاتِ الّتي يَقَعُ جُزءٌ مِنها في الولاياتِ المُتَّحِدَةِ والجُزءُ الآخَرُ في كَنَدا. ذَهَبنا أوّلاً إلى الجانِبِ الكَنَديّ، وقال غَسّانُ إنَّ الشلالات على الجانِبِ الكَنَديِّ أجمَل. لَم أرَ أعْظَمَ مِن هذِهِ الشَلاّلاتِ مِن قَبل. أعْجَبَتْني الحَدائِقُ والأزهارُ الجَميلةُ في الجانِبِ الكَنَديّ.

في اليَومِ التالي ذَهَبنا إلى الجانِبِ الأمريكيِّ ورَكِبنا قارِباً مَعَ ناسٍ آخَرين سارَ بِنا تَحتَ الشلالات. كانَ مَنظَرُ الشلاّلاتِ مِن تَحتُ عَظيماً جِدّاً، والتَقطتُ صُوَراً كَثيرةً مِنَ القارِب.

سَنَرجِع غَداً إلى نيويورك حَيثُ سأزورُ تِمثالَ الحُرِّيَّةِ و«ستاتن آيلاند». شاهَدتُ صُوَرَ التِمثالِ في المَجلاّتِ والأفلامِ وقرأتُ عَنهُ كَثيراً مُنذُ كنتُ صَغيراً، لكنّي لَمْ أرَهُ إلى الآن.

سَنُسافِر أنا وغَسّان إلى «أتلانتِك سيتي» لِيَومٍ واحِدٍ فَقَط بِالقِطار، وهذه المَدينَةُ مِثلُ مَدينَةِ «لاس ڤيغاس» فيها أماكِنُ كَثيرَةٌ لِلقِمارِ بِأنواعِه. بَعدَ ذلِكَ سَأسافِرُ وَحدي إلى فلوريدا بالطائرة لِزيارةِ «ديزني وُرلد» في «أورلاندو».

أورلاندو، السَبت ٧ أيلول ١٩٩٦

وَصَلتُ إلى هُنا أوّلَ أمسِ بَعدَ الظُهر. نَزَلتُ في فُندُق «رامادا» وهُوَ قَريبٌ مِن «ديزني وُرلْد». في ذلِكَ المَساءِ ذَهَبتُ إلى العَشاءِ في مَطعَمٍ يُقدِّمُ أطعِمَةً من الغَربِ الأمريكي. لَم يُعجِبْني الطَعامُ أبَداً.

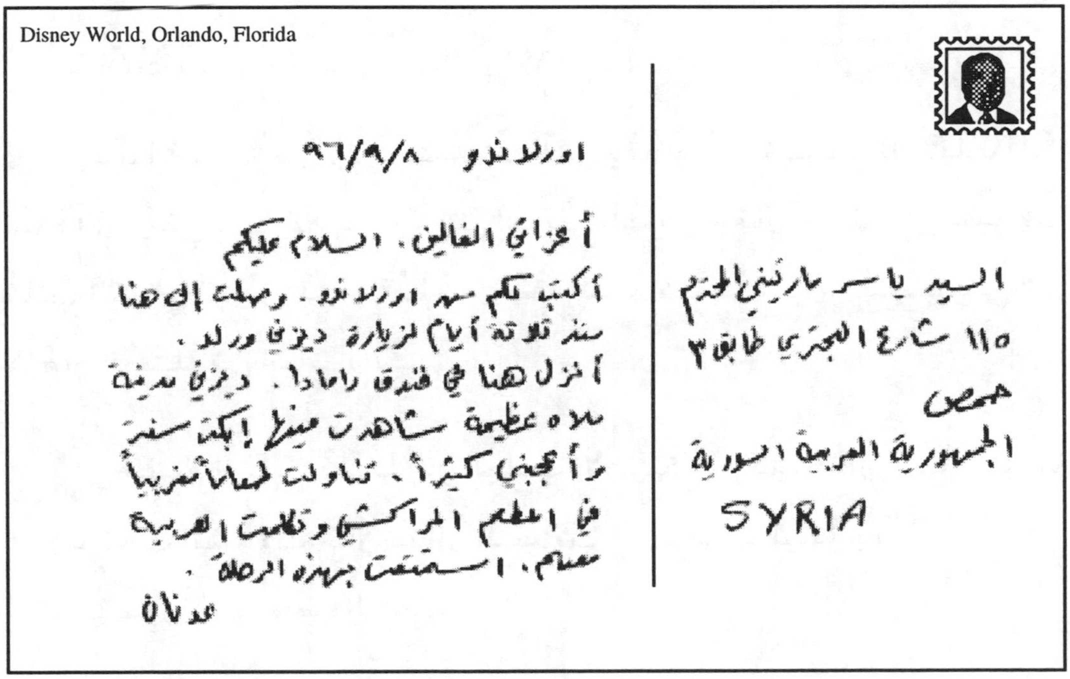
Disney World, Orlando, Florida

اورلاندو ٨/٩/٩٦

أعزائي الغالين، السلام عليكم
أكتب لكم من اورلاندو. وصلت إلى هنا
منذ ثلاثة أيام لزيارة ديزني ورلد.
أنزل هنا في فندق رامادا. ديزني مدينة
ملاه عظيمة شاهدت فيها [illegible]
وأعجبني كثيراً. تناولت طعاماً مغربياً
في المطعم المراكشي وكانت العربية
ممتاز. استمتعت بهذه الرحلة.
عدنان

السيد ياسر مارتيني المحترم
١١٥ شارع البحتري طابق ٣
حمص
الجمهورية العربية السورية
SYRIA

See a typed version of this postcard in Appendix E 2.

في صَباحِ اليَومِ التالي ذَهَبْتُ مِنَ الفُندُقِ مَعَ بَعضِ الناسِ الآخَرينَ في حافِلَةٍ صَغيرةٍ إلى ديزني وُرلد، وهي مَدينةُ مَلاهٍ واسِعةٌ جِداً فيها عَدَدٌ كبيرٌ مِن العُروضِ

والألعابِ والمَطاعمِ والمَحلاّتِ التِجاريةِ مِن كُلِّ بَلَدٍ في العالَم. أعْجَبَني «إبكَت سِنتَر» كَثيراً وكَذلِكَ «ماجِك كِنغدَم». لَم أرَ كلَّ شَيءٍ في اليَومِ الأوّل، لِذلِكَ رَجَعتُ في اليَومِ التالي وشاهَدْتُ الأشياءَ الّتي لَم أشاهِدْها وزُرتُ «إبكَتْ» مَرَّةً ثانيَة. تَناولتُ العَشاءَ مَساءً في ديزني وُرلد في المَطعَمِ المَرّاكِشيِّ الّذي يُقدِّم أطعِمَةً مَغربيَّةً. أعجَبَني المَطعَمُ والموسيقا العربية الّتي قَدَّمَتْها فِرقةٌ مَغربية. لم يَكُنْ الطعامُ غالياً.

رِسالةُ عَدنانَ إلى صَديقِهِ مازِن

كلمبس في ٢١ أيلول ١٩٩٦

أخي العزيز مازن، سلام حار لك من كلمبس.

كيف حالك يا أخي؟ لم تصلني منك أية رسالة منذ مدة طويلة. كتبت لك رسالة في شهر آذار الماضي ولم يصلني منك أي شيء، لذلك ظننت أنك انتقلت من عنوانك القديم في حلب. علمت من مروان بعد ذلك أنك انتقلت إلى جامعة عمان وهو الذي أعطاني عنوانك الجديد. هل يعجبك السكن والدراسة في عمان؟

أنا كما تعلم أدرس علم الحاسوب في جامعة ولاية أوهايو. بعد أيام سيبدأ العام الدراسي الجديد، وهذه هي سنتي الثانية هنا. أنا سعيد في كلمبس وأستمتع بالسكن هنا وبالدراسة كذلك.

في الأسابيع الثلاثة الماضية زرت مدينة نيويورك وأتلانتك سيتي وشلالات نياغرا في كندا وكذلك "ديزني ورلد" وهي مدينة ملاهٍ كبيرة جداً في مدينة أورلاندو في فلوريدا. استمتعت بهذه الزيارات كثيراً. أرجو أن أزور ولاية كاليفورنيا في السنة المقبلة إن شاء الله، و"لاس فيغاس" أيضاً.

أرجو أن تكتب لي عنك وعن دراستك. لك مني أطيب السلام وإلى لقاء قريب في حلب.

أخوك المخلص
عدنان

See a typed version of this letter in Appendix E 3.

تمرين ١

أجِب عَن هذهِ الأسئِلَةِ حَسَبَ النَصِّ:

١- مَتى زارَ مايكل الأهرامات وفي أيِّ مَكانٍ تَقَعُ؟
٢- ماذا يُعجِبُ مايكل في القاهِرَةِ؟
٣- مِن أينَ اشترى مايكل كُتُباً عَن آثارِ مِصرَ؟
٤- ما اسمُ المَحَطَّةِ الَّتي سافَرَ مِنها مايكل إلى الإسكندَريَّةِ؟
٥- لماذا أعْجَبَتْ الإسكندريَّةُ مايكل؟
٦- مَتى كَتَبَ مايكل البِطاقَةَ البَريدِيَّةَ لأستاذَتِهِ؟
٧- في أيِّ يَومٍ أخَذَ عَدنانُ امتِحانَ الرياضِيّاتِ؟
٨- أينَ تَناوَلَ عَدنانُ طَعامَ العَشاءِ في نيويورك ومَعَ مَن؟
٩- في أيِّ يَومٍ زارَ عَدنانُ تِمثالَ الحُرِيَّةِ؟
١٠- مَعَ مَن سافَرَ عَدنانُ إلى أورلاندو؟
١١- أينَ تَكَلَّمَ عَدنانُ العَرَبيةَ في أورلاندو؟
١٢- أينَ يَدرُسُ مازِنُ الآنَ؟

تمرين ٢

أكمِلِ الجُمَلَ حَسَبَ النَصِّ:

١- يَومِيّاتُ مايكل جُزءٌ مِن ......

❑ رَسائلِهِ ❑ دِراستِهِ ❑ زيارتِهِ

٢- رَأى مايكل الجمالَ في ......

❑ حَديقَةِ الحَيَوانات ❑ كلِّ مَكانٍ ❑ شوارِعِ القاهِرَةِ

٣- الإسكندَرِيةُ ......

❑ مَدينةٌ حَديثَةٌ ❑ أقدَمُ مَدينةٍ ❑ ميناءٌ هامٌّ

٤- الناسُ في الإسكندريةِ ......

❑ جَميلون ❑ يُحِبّون ❑ طَيِّبون

٥- يَلتَقي النيلانُ الأبيَضُ والأزرَقُ في ......

❑ الخَرطوم ❑ القاهِرَةِ ❑ الإسكندَريَّةِ

٦- عَدنانُ سَعيدٌ لأنّ ......

❑ الفَصلَ الدِراسيَّ الجديدَ ابتَدأ ❑ الدراسةَ انتَهَتْ

❑ تَذكَرَةَ الطائِرَةِ بِمِئةٍ وخَمسةٍ وثَمانين دولاراً

٧- نَزَلَ عَدنانُ في نيويورك في ......

❑ فُندُقِ رَمادا ❑ إمپايَر ستيت ❑ شَقَّةِ صديقِهِ

٨- بُنِيَت «إمپاير ستيت» مُنذُ أكثَرِ مِن ...... عاماً.

❑ ٥٥ ❑ ٦٥ ❑ ٩٥

٩- كانَ الطَعامُ في المَطعَمِ الفَرَنسيِّ ......

❑ غالياً ❑ طَويلاً ❑ جَميلاً

١٠- لم يَزُرْ عَدنانُ جامِعةَ نيويورك بِسَبَبِ ......

❑ العُطلَةِ السَنَويةِ ❑ زِيارَتِهِ لِلشَلاّلاتِ ❑ الطَقسِ

١١- التَقَطَ عَدنانُ صُوَراً لِلشَلاّلاتِ مِن ......

❑ الجانِبِ الكَنَديّ ❑ القارِبِ ❑ الحَدائِقِ

١٢- سافَرَ عَدنانُ إلى أتلانتيك سيتي ......

❑ بِالقِطارِ ❑ بِالسَيّارةِ ❑ بِالطائِرَةِ

١٣- لَم يُعجِبْ مايكل الطَعامُ ......

❑ الفَرَنسي ❑ المُرّاكِشيّ ❑ الأمريكي الغَربيّ

١٤- تَسكُنُ أسرةُ عَدنانَ في ......

❑ دِمَشقَ ❑ حَلَبَ ❑ عَمّانَ

١٥- يُريدُ عَدنانُ زِيارَةَ ...... في السنةِ المُقبِلة.

❑ فلوريدا ❑ كَنَدا ❑ كاليفورنيا

تمرين ٣

اكتب إلى جانبِ كُلِّ جُمْلَةٍ «صَواب» أو «خَطأ» وصَحِّح الجُمَلَ الخطأ.

١- اشترى مايكل صُوَراً عِندَ الأهرامات.

٢- يَسيرُ النيلُ شَمالاً مِنَ القاهِرةِ إلى الخَرطوم.

٣- الإسكندَريَّةُ أقدَمُ مِنَ القاهِرةِ بِمِئاتِ السِنين.

٤- نامَ مايكل وأصدِقاؤهُ عَلى الشاطِئِ في الإسكندرية.

٥- لَم يَرَ عَدنانُ تِمثالَ الحُريَّةِ مِن قَبل.

٦- ذَهَبَ عَدنانُ إلى مَبنى إمپاير سْتيت بِالسيّارَة.

٧- يَظُنُّ غَسّانُ أنَّ الشلّالاتِ عَلى الجانِبِ الأمريكيِّ أجمَل.

٨- زارَ عَدنانُ «ديزني ورلد» لِيَومٍ واحِدٍ فقط.

٩- انتَقَلَ مازِن صَديقُ عَدنانَ مِن جامِعَةِ عَمّانَ إلى حَلَب.

تمرين ٤

أكمِلِ الجُمَلَ التالِيَةَ بِأفضَلِ كَلِمةٍ مُناسِبة (most suitable):

١- ...... أخي سَيّارةً حينَ زارَ سان فرانسيسكو.

❑ اسْتأجَرَ ❑ اسْتقبَلَ ❑ اسْتَمتَعَ

٢- أريدُ أنْ أزورَ مَدينةَ المَلاهي ..... تَبدأ الدراسة.

❑ مَعَ أنَّ ❑ إلى أنْ ❑ قَبلَ أنْ

٣- تَقَعُ شَقَّتي ..... مَحطّةِ القِطار.

❑ قُرْبَ ❑ شَمالاً ❑ أطوَلَ

٤- ..... عَشَراتِ الصُوَرِ في حَديقةِ الحَيَوانات.

❑ انتَقَلتُ ❑ التَقَطتُ ❑ احتَفَلتُ

٥- هل ..... الغَداءَ؟
❑ شاهَدتُم ❑ زُرتُم ❑ تَناوَلتُم

٦- ..... نَهرَ النيلِ أطوَلُ نهرٍ في العالَم.
❑ لَنْ ❑ إنَّ ❑ أنْ

٧- ..... تشاهِدْ أختي فيلمَ «عيدِ الاستِقلال» حتّى الآن.
❑ لَم ❑ لَن ❑ أنْ

٨- تَناوَلْتُ ..... عَرَبِيّاً في مَطعمٍ مَرّاكِشيّ.
❑ طَعاماً ❑ موسيقا ❑ فِرقةً

٩- ..... الفيلمُ التلفزيوني في الساعةِ الحاديةَ عَشْرَةَ.
❑ أعجَبَ ❑ التَقَطَ ❑ انتَهى

١٠- ..... أدرُسَ الرياضيّاتِ في الفَصلِ المُقبِل.
❑ لَم ❑ لَنْ ❑ لا

تمرين ٥

وافِقْ بَينَ الكلماتِ في العمودين:

١- شاهَدَ	....	أحَبَّ
٢- مَشى	....	شَلاّل
٣- بِنايَة	....	رأى
٤- طَريق	....	مَيْدان
٥- ساحَة	....	دُكّان
٦- دافِئ	....	سارَ
٧- طَيِّب	....	حَتّى
٨- أعْجَبَ	....	شارِع
٩- مَحَلٌّ تِجاريّ	....	مَبنى
١٠- إلى أنْ	....	جَيِّد
		حارّ

تمرين ٦

ضَعْ خَطّاً تحتَ الكلِمَةِ الّتي لا تُناسِبُ باقي الكلِماتِ وبَيِّنِ السَبَب.

١ـ قِطار ـ سَيّارة ـ حَديقَة ـ قارِب ـ طائِرة

٢ـ شَلاّل ـ نَهر ـ بُحَيرة ـ مَبنى ـ ماء

٣ـ طَيِّب ـ دافِئ ـ حارّ ـ بارِد ـ مُعتَدِل

٤ـ أعجَبَ ـ أحبَّ ـ استَمتَعَ ـ استَحَمَّ

٥ـ دِراسة ـ امتِحان ـ مَحَطّة ـ سُؤال ـ مَدرَسة

تمرين ٧

Certain words go together forming phrases which have reference to places, objects, people, etc. Match words that form such phrases and list their meanings.

١ـ شَلاّلات	....	حَيَوانات
٢ـ تِمثالُ	....	المَلاهي
٣ـ آلَةُ	....	طائِرة
٤ـ حَديقَةُ	....	نَياغَرا
٥ـ عيدُ	....	الحُرِيّة
٦ـ بِطاقَةُ	....	تِجاريّ
٧ـ تَذْكَرةُ	....	تَصوير
٨ـ مَحَلٌّ	....	تَأمين
٩ـ مَدينَةُ	....	بَريديّة
		الأضحى

تمرين ٨

أعِدْ تَرتيبَ الكلِماتِ في كلِّ جُملَةٍ لِتَشكِّلَ جُملةً مُفيدَةً.

١- لُغاتٍ - جيِّداً - أختي - أنْ - ثَلاث - تتكَلَّمَ - تَستَطيعُ

٢- العِشرين - المِصعَدَ - الطابَقِ - يَأخُذُ - إلى - الناسُ

٣- فيلماً - بِهِ - واستَمتَعتُ - في - السينَما - شاهَدْتُ - دارِ

٤- آلافِ - بُنِيَتْ - السِنين - الأهراماتُ - مُنْذُ

٥- الإسكَندريّةِ - رَمسيس - إلى - رَكِبْنا - مِن - القِطارَ - مَحَطّةِ

٦- تَسْتَمتِعوا - لمَدينَتِنا - بزيارَتِكُم - أنْ - أرجو

٧- تَصويري - صورةً - بآلَةِ - لأصدقائي - الجَديدة - التَقَطتُ

تمرين ٩

أعِدْ تَرتيبَ الجُمَلِ لِتُشكِّلَ فِقرةً. لا تُغَيِّرْ مكانَ الجُملةِ الأولى.

Rearrange the items below to construct a paragraph, leaving the first sentence intact.

١- أردتُ أنا وعائلَتي زيارةَ مَدينةِ اللاذقيّةِ في عطلةِ الرَبيع.

في الطريقِ إلى اللاذِقِيَّةِ مَرَرْنا بِمدينَتَيْ حِمصَ وطَرطوس.

في اليومِ التالي ذهَبْنا إلى الشاطئِ وسَبَحْنا.

سارَتِ الحافِلةُ في الثامِنةِ صَباحاً.

ذَهَبنا أولاً إلى الفُندُقِ حَيثُ وَضَعنا حَقائِبَنا.

واللاذقيّةُ ميناءُ سوريةَ الأوّلِ عَلى البَحرِ الأبيَضِ المتوَسِّط.

بَعدَ الغَداءِ ركِبنا قارِباً صَغيراً لِساعةٍ أو أكثَر.

عِندي عائِلةٌ كَبيرةٌ مِن أربعَةِ أبناءٍ وثلاثِ بَنات.

ثمَّ ذَهَبنا إلى شاطِئِ البَحرِ حَيثُ تَناوَلنا الغَداء.

اسْتَمْتَعنا كثيراً بهذه الزيارة.

وجَلَسْتُ أنا وزَوجَتي خَلفَ السائِق.
وَصَلنا إلى اللاذِقِيَّةِ في الثانِيَةِ بَعدَ الظُهر.
جَلَسَ ابني الكَبير إلى جانِبِ السائِق.
لِذلِكَ اسْتأجَرنا حافِلةً صَغيرة مَعَ سائِقِها.

تمرين ١٠

اكتُبْ بطاقةً بَريديَّةً إلى صَديقٍ عَرَبيٍّ مِن مدينةٍ زُرتَها إمّا في الوِلايات المُتَّحِدَةِ أو في مَكانٍ آخَر.

Write a postcard to an imaginary Arab pen pal from a real or fictitious town you have visited or are visiting in or outside the United States. Address the person properly, provide the date, and write a plausible address. Describe the town briefly, say where you are staying, what you have seen, what you plan to do in the near future, when you are returning home, and whether or not you enjoyed this visit and why. Use the form provided below so that you do not exceed the normal length of a postcard.

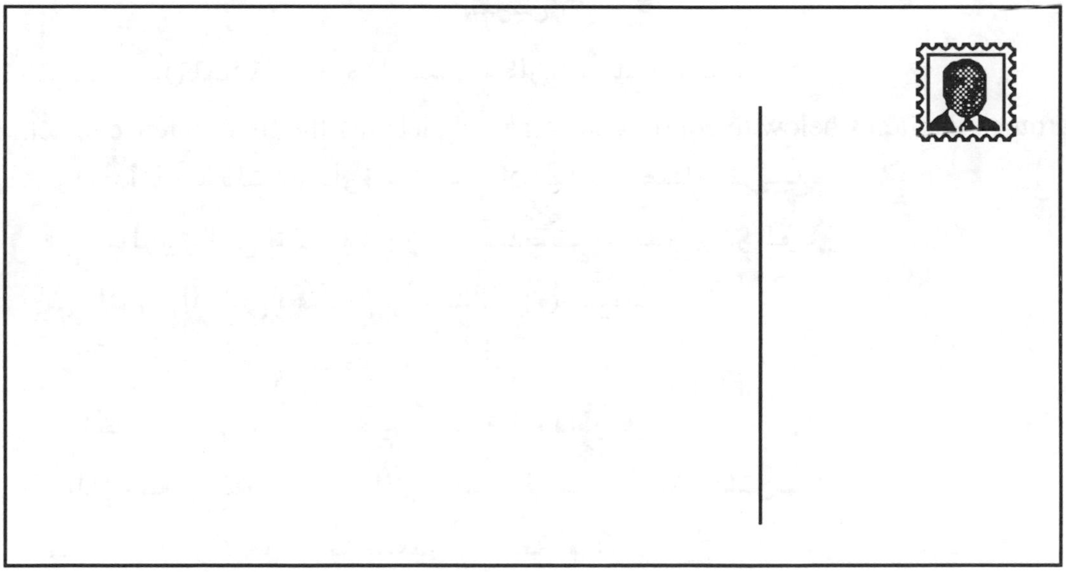

1. Terms of Address in Written Communication

When writing postcards, letters, and the like, one needs to address the person to whom he/she is writing appropriately. For this purpose certain terms of address, or salutations, are used, such as عَـزيز "dear", حَـبـيـب "loved one, darling", and variations thereof. In addition, to add formality to a letter, for example, one might use the noun والد instead of أب and والدة for أم. Therefore, a letter to a father, for instance, may be started as follows:

والِدي الحَبيب or والِدي العَزيز

A friend may be addressed in this manner:

أخي العَزيز فُلان*

أختي العَزيزة فُلانة

* A generic term that stands for a person's name (e.g., so and so).

However, a man addressing a woman may not use الحَبيبة or حَبيبَتي unless she is his wife, fiancée, sister, daughter, etc.

Generally, the writer signs off, by using one of these terms:

المُخلِص / المُخلِصة *sincerely*

المُشتاق / المشتاقة *the one missing you*

المُحِبّ / المُحِبّة *lovingly*

2. Adverbs of Time and Place ظَرفُ الزَمانِ والمَكان

Adverbs are nouns in the accusative case (منصوب) which indicate the time or place of an action. In Arabic, as the Arabic term signifies, adverbs are considered vessels or containers in which an action occurs. Adverbs of time denote the time when an action occurs, e.g.

١ وَصَلَتِ الطائِرةُ مَساءً. *The plane arrived in the evening.*

Some frequent adverbs of time include the following:

دَقيقَة، ساعَة، يَوم، لَيلَة، أُسبوع، شَهر، سَنَة، عام، زَمان، حينَ، مُنذُ.

٢ وُلِدْتُ عامَ ١٩٥٢. *I was born in 1952*

Similarly, adverbs of place denote the place where an action takes place:

٣ مَشَيْتُ شَمالاً. *I walked in a northerly direction.*

٤ شَقَّتي تَحتَ عِيادةِ الطَبيب. *My apartment is below the doctor's office*

Some frequently used adverbs of place include directions (words in parentheses have not been covered yet):

أمامَ، خَلفَ، تحتَ، فَوقَ، شَمالَ، غَربَ (جَنوبَ، شَرقَ، يَمينَ، يَسارَ)

٥ تَقَعُ الإسكَندَريَّةُ شَمالَ القاهِرَةِ. *Alexandria is north of Cairo*

٦ الأهراماتُ في الجيزةِ قُرْبَ القاهِرَةِ. *The pyramids are in Giza near Cairo*

Note, however, that these adverbs of time and place also function as regular nouns, acquiring the case of their particular syntactic contexts:

٧ وُلِدْتُ في عامِ ١٩٥٢. *I was born in 1952*

٨ مَشَيْتُ إلى الشَمالِ. *I walked north.*

where عامِ and الشَمالِ are objects of prepositions and display the marker of the genitive case.

3. **Negating Future Time** (لَنْ)

You already know that future time is expressed by using the particles سَـ (which is a prefix) and سَوْفَ (which is an independent word) immediately before a present tense verb:

٩ سَأسافِرُ إلى مُدُنٍ أخرى.

١٠ سَوفَ أزورُ جامِعَةَ نيويورك.

As you have seen in Michael Brown's and Adnan Martini's journals, future time may be negated by using the particle لَنْ:

١١ لَنْ أسافرَ إلى مُدُنٍ أُخرى.

١٢ لَنْ أزورَ جامِعَةَ نيويورك.

However, the use of لَنْ entails two changes in the verb form:

1. The future markers سَ or سَوفَ are dropped.

2. The مُضارِع مَرفوع (indicative) is changed into مُضارِع مَنصوب (subjunctive).

By examining examples 9-12, you'll find that أسافرُ and أزورُ, which are مُضارِع مرفوع, change into أسافرَ and أزورَ, respectively. These are مُضارِع مَنصوب marked by a *fatḥa.*

SUMMARY

Verbs indicating future time are negated by using لَنْ immediately before such verbs. Two changes must be made:
1. Drop the future markers سَ or سَوفَ.
2. Change the mood of the verb to مُضارِع مَنصوب.

تمرين ١١

اِنْفِ (negate) الجُمَلَ التالِيَةَ:

١- سَوفَ أدرسُ اللُغةَ العَرَبيَّةَ في جامِعَةِ عمّان.

٢- سَتَزورُني أمّي في الشَهرِ المُقبِل.

٣- سَوفَ أشاهِدُ فيلمَينِ في عُطلةِ الأسبوعِ هذهِ.

٤- سَأستَمتِعُ بالسِباحةِ في هذا الطَقس.

4. **Relative Clauses** (الَّذي، الَّتي) الأسْماءُ المَوصولة

In English sentence structure, a relative clause has a modifying function which is similar to that of an adjective. A relative clause is, in fact, a sentence modifying a noun phrase. Examine the following example:

13 The student who speaks Arabic lived in Damascus for two years.

The sentence *[he] speaks Arabic* modifies the noun phrase, or the head noun (*the student*), but unlike an adjective, a relative clause *follows* the modified noun phrase in exactly the same order as in Arabic. An Arabic sentence parallel to *13* may be:

١٤ الطالِبُ الّذي يَتَكلّمُ العَرَبيّةَ سكَنَ في دِمَشقَ سَنَتَين.

The sentence يَتَكَلَّمُ العَرَبيةَ modifies (refers back to) the head noun الطالب, which is called the antecedent. If the antecedent is definite, the relative sentence is introduced by a relative *noun*, as it is considered in Arabic. In the example above, the relative noun is الذي (pronounced: *al-ladī*). Its role is to link the antecedent to the relative clause.

A. **Restrictive Relative Nouns** الأسماءُ المَوصولةُ الخاصّة: There are Arabic relative nouns which are restricted to a specific noun, that is, they modify a noun and agree with this modified noun (antecedent) in number and gender. Moreover, dual relative nouns vary also according to case. Thus, the relative noun assumes different forms, depending on the form of the antecedent. Notice how the relative noun (in a box) varies as the antecedent (the first word in the sentences below) changes:

١٥ الطالِبَةُ الّتي تَتَكلّمُ العَرَبيّةَ ...

١٦ الطالِبانِ اللّذانِ يَتَكلّمانِ العَرَبيّةَ ...

١٧ الطالِبَتانِ اللّتانِ تَتَكلّمانِ العَرَبيّةَ ...

١٨ الطُلاّبُ الّذينَ يَتَكلّمونَ العَرَبيّةَ ...

١٩ الطالِباتُ اللاتي يَتَكلّمْنَ العَرَبيّةَ ...

Agreement in case requires that the middle *alif* in the two dual forms of the relative noun change into ي if the antecedent is مَنصوب (accusative) or مَجرور (genitive). Compare sentences *20* and *21* below with *16* and *17* above.

٢٠ أعرفُ الطالبَينِ اللّذَين يَتَكلّمانِ العَرَبيّةَ ...

٢١ أعرفُ الطالبَتَينِ اللّتَين يَتَكلّمانِ العَرَبيّةَ ...

الأسماءُ المَوصولةُ الخاصّة

	Plural	Dual (nom./acc.-gen.)	Singular
Masculine	الّذينَ	اللّذانِ/اللّذَيْنِ	الّذي
Feminine	اللاتي/اللّواتي	اللّتانِ/اللّتَيْنِ	الّتي

B. **Agreement with Nonrational Plurals**: Just like adjectives modifying nouns, nonrational plural antecedents agree with third person feminine singular relative nouns regardless of their gender (see Noun-Adjective Agreement in Lesson 16):

٢٢ هذه هي الكتُبُ الّتي اشتريتُها. *These are the books which I've bought*

٢٣ أعْطِني المَجلاّتِ الّتي قَرَأتَها. *Give me the magazines which you have read*

In 22, the noun الكُتُبُ is plural masculine and in 23, the noun المَجلاّت is plural feminine, yet both are modified by الّتي, a third person feminine singular relative noun.

تمرين ١٢

اسْتخدِم الاسمَ الموصولَ المُناسِبَ في الجُمَلِ التاليةِ (use the appropriate relative):

١ـ هَل قَرأتِ المَجلّةَ ...... اشتريتُها أمس؟

٢ـ هؤلاءِ هُنَّ الطالباتُ ...... يَسْكُنَّ في سكَنِ الطالبات.

٣ـ أحمَدُ وأيْمَنُ هُما الطالِبانِ ...... يَدرُسانِ الرياضِيّاتِ.

٤ـ مَن هُوَ الأستاذُ ...... كَتَبَ هذا الكِتاب؟

٥ـ أعرفُ الرَجُلَينِ ...... يَعمَلانِ في هذِهِ الشَركة.

٦ـ مَن هُم أصدِقاؤكَ ...... زاروا مِصر؟

٧ـ كَتَبْتُ إلى السَيِّدَتَيْنِ ...... تَسكُنانِ في تِلكَ البِناية.

٨ـ سَلمى وهَنا هُما ...... تَعمَلانِ في هذه الدُكّان.

C. **Nonrestrictive Relative Nouns** مَن and ما: There are a number of relative nouns which are common to antecedents that vary in number and gender. That is to say, one such noun is used with masculine, feminine, singular, dual, and plural antecedents. You are already familiar with one of them (مَنْ), which we have used thus far for asking questions about the identity of a person or persons:

٢٤ مَنْ زارَ الإسكَندَريّة ؟ *Who visited Alexandria?*

By such a question, we may be asking about a man, a woman, two people, or more. It can also be used as a common, or nonrestrictive, relative noun, as in this example:

٢٥ أعْجَبَتEالإسكَندَريّةَ مَنْ زارَها.

The nonrestrictive nature of مَن can be demonstrated by varying the number and gender of the sentence modified by it (*he visited it, she visited it,* etc.):

٢٦ أعْجَبَتِ الإسكندريّةُ مَنْ زارها/زارَتها/زاراها/زارَتاها/زاروها/زُرنَها.

(lit.) Alexandria pleased [that/those] who visited it.

Bear in mind that مَنْ is generally used with rational nouns (humans). Its nonrestrictive counterpart, which generally refers to nonrational nouns, is ما:

٢٧ إقرأي مِن تِلكَ الكُتُبِ/ المَجَلاّتِ ما تُريدينَ.

Read which[ever] of those books/magazines you like.

Obviously, ما does not change with the gender of the antecedent. Both كُتُب, which is masculine, and مَجَلاّت, which is feminine, are modified by ما.

D. **Combining with Prepositions**: The relative nouns مَن and ما, when preceded by certain prepositions, combine with them, forming single words:

٢٨ كَتَبَ عدنانُ عَمّا (عَن + ما) فَعَلَ في العُطلةِ الصَيفيّة.

Adnan wrote about what he did during the summer break.

٢٩ تَكَلَّمَ عدنانُ عَمَّن استقبَلَ مِن الطُلاّبِ الجُدُد. (عَن + مَن)

Adnan talked about whom he met [at the airport] of the new students.

٣٠. هل تُريدُ أنْ تَشربَ مِمّا أشرَبُ؟ (مِن + ما)

Would you like to drink some of what I'm drinking?

٣١ وَصَلَتْني رَسائِلُ مِمَّن كَتَبتُ لَهُم. (مِن + مَن)

I have received letters from those to whom I wrote.

٣٢ قَرَأتُ فيما قَرأتُ يَومِيّاتِ طالِبٍ في القاهِرة. (في + ما)

Part of what I have read are the journals of a student in Cairo.

٣٣- عَرَفتُ فيمَن عَرَفتُ في الجامِعَةِ طالِبَةً تونِسيَّةً. (في + مَن)

Among those whom I knew at the university is a female Tunisian student.

E. **Indefinite Antecedents**. In the examples cited so far, the antecedent, or the noun modified by the relative noun, has been definite either by prefixing the definite article ال, suffixing a possessive pronoun, or using a proper name:

٣٤ الطالب، الكتُب، المجلات، أصدقاؤك، سلمى وهَنا، الإسكندرية

However, antecedents can be indefinite, in which case *no* relative noun may be used. In Michael's journal we read:

٣٥ الأهراماتُ مَبانٍ عظيمةٌ بَناها الفراعِنةُ.

The pyramids are great buildings *[which] the pharaohs built.*

Although there is no relative noun in the Arabic sentence, the English translation requires one because the sentence بناها الفراعنة is still a relative clause. The relative pronoun is not used because the head noun مبانٍ is indefinite.

F. **The Referent as Object in the Relative Clause**: Another feature which you may have noticed in 35 is the suffix ها attached to the verb بَنى. This suffix, which refers back to the antecedent مَبانٍ, is the object of the verb بنى. Thus, according to the rules of Arabic sentence structure, if the referent in the relative clause is an object of a verb or a preposition, or if it forms an *iḍāfa* with a noun, it must be used. It is, however, deleted in a similar English structure. Compare the Arabic and English examples:

٣٦ خَديجةُ هِيَ الطالِبةُ الّتي استَقبَلَها عَدنانُ في المَطار.

37 Khadīja is the student whom Adnan met (not met *her*) at the airport.

Literally, the verb in the Arabic relative sentence translates *he met her*, whereas in the English translation no such pronoun is permissible. Consider these examples where the referent is the object of a verb or a preposition:

٣٨ هذِهِ هِيَ السَيّارَةُ الّتي اشْتَرَيتُها.

This is the car which I bought (it).

٣٩ هذِهِ هِيَ السَيّارَةُ الّتي رَكِبتُ فيها.

This is the car which I rode in (it).

٤٠ هذِهِ هِيَ السَيّارَةُ الّتي أعرفُ سائقَها.

This is the car whose driver I know. (lit.) *This is the car which I know its driver.*

In sentences *38-40*, the object pronoun (ها) refers to السيارة in the main sentence and it functions as the object of the verb in *38*, the object of the preposition in *39*, and it forms an *iḍāfa* with the noun سائق in *40*.

With the relative nouns مَن and ما, however, the object pronoun is *not* used:

٤١ اشتَريتُ مِن الكُتُبِ ما أريدُ. *I bought books I want.*

٤٢ زرتُ مِن الأصدقاءِ مَن أحِبُّ. *I visited friends I like.*

تمرين ١٣

Fill in the blanks with the appropriate relative noun, restrictive or nonrestrictive, in the sentences that require one. Use relatives from the table above in addition to ما and مَن.

١- أعرفُ طالباً ...... يدرسُ اللغتَينِ العَرَبيَّةَ والصينيَّةَ.

٢- أعطِني الكِتابَ ...... كُنتُ أقرأ فيه.

٣- هل تُريدينَ أنْ تَقرأي ...... كَتَبتُ؟

٤- أين الرجالُ ...... وصَلوا بِالطائرة المِصْريَّة؟

٥- أعرف ...... يُحِبُّ هذا النوعَ مِن الطَعام.

٦- استقبلتُ في المطار طالبَتَين ...... ستَدرسانِ عِلمَ الحاسوب.

٧- هل شاهدتَ الحيوانات ...... وَصَلتْ إلى الحَديقةِ مِن كينيا؟

٨- هؤلاءِ هُنَّ الأمَّهاتُ ...... أتَينَ لِمُشاهَدَةِ أبنائِهِنَّ على المَسْرَحِ؟

5. Prepositions Revisited

In the reading passages above, we have encountered prepositions in combination with other prepositions, particles, adverbs, and demonstrative nouns. While the resulting meanings are straightforward and predictable in most cases, some combinations have special new meanings:

مِن فَوق / مِن تَحت (preposition+adverb of place) *from above/from below*

إلى الآن (prep.+adverb of time) *until now*

إلى أنْ (prep.+particle) *till, until* — Must be followed by a verbal sentence.

مع أنَّ (prep.+particle) *although*

This combination can be followed by either a noun or an attached pronoun (e.g. مَعَ أنَّها *= although she;* مَعَ أنَّ البنتَ *= although the girl).*

كَذلِكَ (preposition+demonstrative noun) *also, too, in addition, as well*

لِذلِكَ (preposition+demonstrative noun) *therefore, for this reason*

تمرين ١٤

أ- أكمِلِ الجُمَلَ التالية بكلمات مُناسبة من الفقرة ٥.

Complete the following sentences with prepositional combinations from section 5 above.

١- اشترى سالِم بَيتاً جديداً و...... سيارةً جَديدة.

٢- عِصام رَجلٌ فَقير، ...... لا يَستَطيعُ أنْ يَشتريَ بَيتاً.

٣- لَم تَزُرْ سامية بَيروت ...... صَديقتَها تَسكُنُ هُناك.

٤- جَلَسنا على شاطِئِ البَحْرِ ...... غابَت (set) الشَمسُ.

B. Express these meanings in Arabic.

1. So far, I haven't been able to visit the Grand Canyon.
2. The view of the city is beautiful from above.
3. He is not happy although he is rich.
4. We studied at the library until my friends wanted to go to the movies.

6. Possessive *Iḍāfa*

You already know one way of rendering nouns possessive: by suffixing attached pronouns to them (e.g. كتابي، سيارتُهُم). But when you want to make an *iḍāfa* phrase possessive, you may not know to which item the pronoun should be attached. In the majority of cases, the possessive pronoun must be suffixed to the second (or last) item of the *iḍāfa* structure. Examine the following examples:

٤٣ آلةُ تصويري *my camera*

٤٤ عُنوانُ شَقَّتِه *his apartment address*

٤٥ مِفتاحُ بابِ سَيّارتِها *the key to the door of her car*

تمرين ١٥

Express these meanings in Arabic, using *iḍāfa* structures with possessive suffixes.

1. My bedroom.
2. Her (male) friend's car.
3. His wife's mother.
4. Their house floor plan.
5. Our grocer's store.

تمرين ١٦

استَمِعْ إلى الشَريط ثُمَّ أجِبْ عن الأسئلة:

١- كم وَلَداً في هذه العائلة؟

٢- أينَ هذه العائلةُ الآنَ؟

٣- أيُّ فَصلٍ مِن السنةِ في هذا النصّ.

أكمِل الجُمَلَ التالية حَسَبَ النص:

٤- للأردنّ ......

☐ ميناءٌ واحد ☐ ميناءان ☐ ثلاثةُ مَوانِئ

٥- سافَرَتْ العائلةُ إلى العَقَبةِ ......

☐ بالسيارةِ ☐ بالطائرةِ ☐ بالقِطار

٦- زارَتْ عائِلةُ مَيساء العَقَبَةَ لِمُدَّةِ ...... أيّام.

❑ ثلاثة ❑ أربعة ❑ خَمسة

٧- سَبَحوا في البَحرِ ...... في اليوم.

❑ مَرَّتَين ❑ ساعتَين ❑ يَومين

٨- كان الطقسُ في العَقَبةِ ......

❑ حارّاً ❑ مُعتَدلاً ❑ بارِداً

٩- اسْتأجَرَت العائلةُ ...... في الفُندُق.

❑ غُرفةً ❑ غرفتَين ❑ ثلاثَ غُرَف

اكتبْ «صَواب» أو «خَطأ» إلى جانِبِ كلِّ جملة وصَحِّحْ الجُمَلَ الخطأ.

١٠- الامرأةُ في النصِ مُتَزَوِّجةٌ واسمُ زَوجِها هِشام.

١١- تَناوَلَت مَيساء وعائلَتُها العَشاءَ في مَطعَم «نَخيل».

١٢- العَقَبةُ ميناءٌ على البحرِ الأبيَضِ المتوسِّط.

١٣- الفُندُقُ في شارِعٍ قَريبٍ مِن الشاطِئ.

١٤- سَتركب العائلةُ قارِباً بَعد الظُهر.

١٥- اكتبْ على الخريطة اسمَ البَلَدِ الموجود في النص واسمَ المدينتَين واسمَ البحر.

المُفْرَدات

to return .... آبَ (يَؤوبُ) إياب (v.)
white .... أبيَض ج بيْض (n., m.)
ruin, antiquity, artifact, relic .... أثَر ج آثار (n., m.)
to respond, to answer .... أجابَ (يُجيبُ) إجابة (v.)
to be able, can .... استَطاعَ (يَستَطيعُ) استِطاعة (v.)
to enjoy .... استَمتَعَ (يَستَمتِعُ) استِمتاع (v.)
until .... إلى أنْ
device, gadget, machine, apparatus .... آلة ج آلات (n., f.)
to meet, converge, encounter .... التَقى (يَلتَقي) التِقاء (v.)
to take, make (a picture) .... التَقَطَ (يَلتَقِطُ) التِقاط (v.)
who, that .... الَّتي (n., f.)
who, that .... الَّذي (n., m.)
to examine, to test .... امتَحَنَ (يَمتَحِنُ) امتِحان (v.)
mail, post .... بَريد (n., m.)
to build, to construct .... بَنى (يَبني) بِناء (v.)
ticket .... تَذكِرة ج تَذاكِر (n., f.)
statue .... تمثال ج تَماثيل (n., m.)
to eat, to take, to reach for something .... تَناوَلَ (يَتَناوَلُ) تَناوُل (v.)
camel .... جَمَل ج جِمال (n., m.)
liberty, freedom .... حُرِّيّة ج حُرِّيّات (n., f.)
animal .... حَيَوان ج حَيَوانات (n., m.)
to hope .... رَجا (يَرجو) رَجاء (v.)
to ride, to mount .... رَكِبَ (يَركَبُ) رُكوب (v.)
square, courtyard .... ساحة ج ساحات (n., f.)
to move, to walk, to travel, to march, to flow .... سارَ (يَسيرُ) سَيْر (v.)

happy, pleased, joyful........ (n., m.) سَعيد ج سُعَداء
question, query........ (n., m.) سُؤال ج أسئلة
to see, to watch, to witness........ (v.) شاهَدَ (يُشاهِدُ) مُشاهَدة
waterfall........ (n., m.) شَلاّل ج شَلاّلات
north........ (n., m.) شَمال
thing, object........ (n., m.) شَيْء ج أشياء
industry........ (n., f.) صناعة ج صناعات
to make a picture, to portray, to illustrate........ (v) صَوَّرَ (يُصَوِّرُ) تَصوير
way, road........ (n., f.) طَريق ج طُرُق، طُرُقات
number (quantity)........ (n., m.) عَدَد ج أعْداد
show, demonstration, performance........ (n., m.) عَرْض ج عُروض
dear, esteemed, beloved........ (n., m.) عَزيز ج أعِزّاء
great, important, imposing........ (adj./n., m.) عَظيم ج عُظَماء
expensive, dear........ (n., m.) غالٍ
often, mostly, generally........ (adv.) غالباً
west........ (n., m.) غَرْب
pharaoh........ (n., m.) فِرعَون ج فَراعِنة
band, company, troupe........ (n., f.) فِرقة ج أفْرِقة
boat........ (n., m.) قارِب ج قَوارِب
to gamble........ (v.) قامَرَ (يُقامِرُ) مُقامَرة، قِمار
to serve, to provide........ (v.) قَدَّمَ (يُقَدِّمُ) تَقديم
also, as well........ كَذلِكَ
kilometer........ (n., m.) كيلومِتر ج كيلومِترات
game, play, ride........ (n., f.) لُعبة ج لُعبات، ألعاب
building, construction........ (n. m.) مَبنى ج مَبانٍ
something similar, like, such as........ (n., m.) مِثْلُ ج أمْثال
museum........ (n., m.) مُتحَف ج مَتاحِف
loving........ (n.) مُحِبّ ج مُحِبّون
sincere, faithful, (sincerely yours)........ (n., m.) مُخلِص ج مُخلِصون

period, duration .... (n., f.) مُدّة ج مُدَد
to pass, to go by .... (v.) مَرَّ (يَمُرُّ) مُرور
mosque .... (n., m.) مَسجِد ج مَساجِد
theater, stage .... (n., m.) مَسرَح ج مَسارِح
one who is longing, yearning .... (n.) مُشْتاق ج مُشْتاقون
elevator, lift .... (n., m.) مصعَد ج مَصاعِد
though, although .... مَعَ أنَّ
coming, next, following .... (n., m.) مُقبِل ج مُقبِلون
place, location .... (n., m.) مَكان ج أمْكِنة
million .... (n., m.) مليون
since, for .... (preposition) مُنْذُ
square, field, arena .... (n., m.) مَيدان ج مَيادين
port .... (n., m.) ميناء ج مَوانِئ
person (used in population counts) .... (n., f.) نَسَمة ج نَسَمات
important, significant .... (n./adj.) هامٌّ ج هامّون
pyramid .... (n., m.) هَرَم ج أهرام / أهرامات
father, parent .... (n., m.) والِد ج والِدون

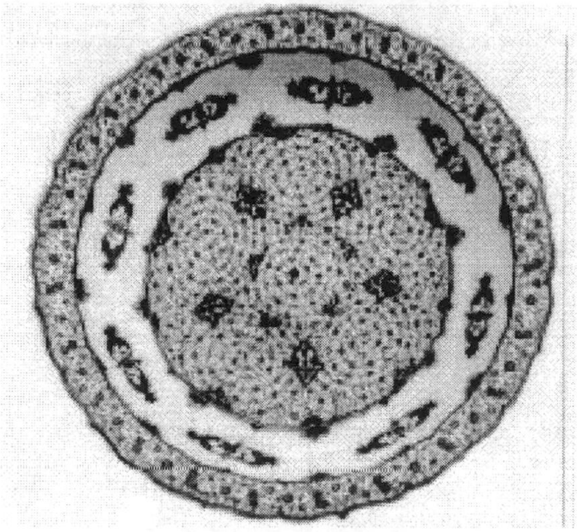

China plate صَحْنٌ خَزَفيٌّ

Lesson Twenty-Six الدَرْسُ السادِسُ والعِشرون

Objectives

- Expressing preferences.
- Expressing frequency (مرة ـ أحياناً ـ دائماً ـ غالِباً ـ يَوميّاً – أبداً).
- Expressing degree (قليلاً ـ كثيراً ـ جيّدا ـ جِداً).
- Expressing uncertainty (رُبّما).
- Habitual and progressive past.
- Colors.
- Comparative nouns with doubled consonants.
- Weak verbs revisited الفعل المعتل.
- Listen to recorded material for this lesson.
- Do relevant computer drills and exercises, Stages 10 and 11.

رِياضاتٌ وأطعِمةٌ مُفَضَّلة

مِن يَوميّات عَدنان مارتيني

كرة السلّة

حينَ كنتُ في المدرسةِ الثانوية في حَلَب لَعِبتُ كُرةَ السلّةِ مع فَريقِ المدرسةِ مِنَ الصفِّ العاشِر حَتّى الثاني عَشَر. كانت كُرةُ السلّةِ في ذلِكَ الوَقتِ رياضَتي المُفَضَّلة. كُنتُ ألعَبُها كلَّ يومٍ تَقريباً. كُنتُ أذهبُ مع أصدِقائي إلى مُبارَياتِ كُرةِ السلّةِ دائِماً وأشاهِدُها على التِلفاز.

أمّا هُنا في أمريكا فَلا ألعَبُ كرةَ السلّةِ كثيراً، مرّتين أو ثلاثَ مرّاتٍ فَقَط في الشهرِ بِسبَبِ الدراسة. صِرتُ ألعبُ الآنَ كُرةَ الطاولة. هُناكَ مَكانٌ واسِعٌ للألعابِ في الطابَقِ الأرضيِّ حَيثُ توجدُ شَقّتي. أنزِلُ إلى هذا المكان مَساءً وفي صَباحِ يومِ السَبت وألعَبُ مَعَ أصدِقائي أو مَعَ بَعضِ السُكّانِ الآخَرين. تُعجِبني كرةُ الطاولةِ كثيراً.

بيسبول

مُنذُ ثلاثةِ شُهور أخَذَني صَديقي تِم نِكلز إلى مُباراةٍ في لُعبَةٍ تُسمّى هُنا «بيسبول». لا أعرف لَها اسماً بالعربية رُبَّما لأنّنا لا نَلعَبُها في البِلادِ العَرَبية. يُحِبُّ الأمريكيون هذه اللُعبَةَ جِداً، وهي تُلعَبُ بِعَصا طَويلةٍ وكُرةٍ صَغيرةٍ بَيضاءِ اللَون. شَرَحَ لي تِم كيفَ تُلعَب البيسبول، لكنّي لَم أفهَمْ قَواعِدَ اللُعبةِ مِن أوّلِ مَرّة. لكِنَّني الآن أفهَمُها أكثَر وبدَأَتْ تُعجِبُني.

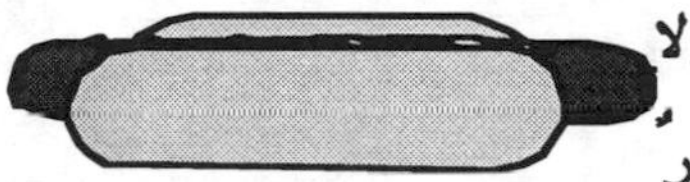

بَقينا في الملعبِ أربعَ ساعاتٍ تقريباً. شَرِبنا كولا وأكلنا شَطائِر «هَط ضَغ»، وهذا النَوعُ مِن الطعامِ مَشهور جداً في أمريكا ويأكلُه الناسُ في كلِّ وَقتٍ تَقريباً. الـ«هَط ضَغ» مِثلُ النَقانِقِ في بِلاد الشام، لكنّها أكبر ومَصنوعة من لَحمِ البَقَر. صِرتُ أحِبُّ أنْ آكلَ شطائِرَ الهط ضَغ الآن وكذلك شَطائِرَ الـ«هامبرغر»، لكنّ النَقانِقَ ألَذُّ من الهَط ضغ لأنَّ فيها تَوابِل كَثيرة.

السباحة

السِباحةُ مِنَ الرياضاتِ الّتي أُفَضِّلُها كثيراً بالإضافةِ إلى كرةِ السَلّةِ وكرةِ الطاولة. هُناكَ مَسبَحٌ في الجامِعةِ أذهَبُ إليه دائِماً قبلَ دروسي في الصَباح ثَلاثَ مَرّاتٍ أو أكثَر في الأسبوع.

أفَضِّل السِباحةَ في البَحْرِ في فَصلِ الصيف وكلمبس لَيسَتْ على شاطئ البَحر، لكِنّها قَريبة من عددٍ من البُحَيرات الكبيرة الّتي يوجد على شواطِئها حَدائقُ عامّة واسِعة. سَبَحتُ في بَعضِها في الصَيف حينَ ذَهَبتُ إلى هُناكَ مَعَ

بَعضِ الأصدِقاء. كان في تِلكَ الحَدائق عائلاتٌ كثيرة، وكان الكِبارُ والصِغارُ يَلعَبون الكُرةَ الطائِرة وكرةَ القَدَم الأوروبيـةَ وغَيرَهُما مِن الألعاب. لَم أرَ أحداً يَلعَبُ كرةَ القَدَم الأمريكية.

كرة القدم الأمريكية

يوجدُ أيْضاً في هذِه الحدائق مَشاوٍ عامّة يَستَخدِمُها الناسُ لِشَيِّ اللَحمِ و«الهَط ضَغ»، واللحمُ المشويّ هو الطعامُ المُفضَّل للناسِ في الحدائق. هذه الحدائق نَظيفةٌ غالباً وفيها الكثيرُ مِن الأشجارِ وأماكِنُ واسعة لِلَّعِب. وَصَلنا إلى الحَديقة عِندَ الظهرِ تَقريباً وبَقيْنا فيها حَتّى الساعةِ التاسِعة مَساءً. استَمتَعتُ كثيراً في ذلك اليوم.

من يوميّات مايكل براون

الرياضة المفضّلة عند المصريين هي كُرَةُ القَدَم، لكِنّها لَيسَت كرةَ القدمِ الّتي نَعرفُها في أمريكا، بَل كرةَ القَدَم الأوروبية. هُناك فِرَقٌ كثيرة لِكرةِ القَدَمِ في مِصر، لكنَّ الفَريقَين المشهورَين في القاهرة هُما «الأهلي» و«الزَمالِك». ذَهَبتُ إلى إحدى المباريات بَينَهُما مَعَ سَمير في مَلعَب القاهِرة الدَوْلي الّذي يتَّسِع لِمِئةٍ وعِشرين ألفَ مُتَفَرِّج. وكان هناكَ عَشرات الآلاف مِن المُتَفَرِّجين، رِجالاً ونِساءً وأولاداً وبَناتا. يأكلُ الناسُ في الملعبِ عادةً «السَميط»

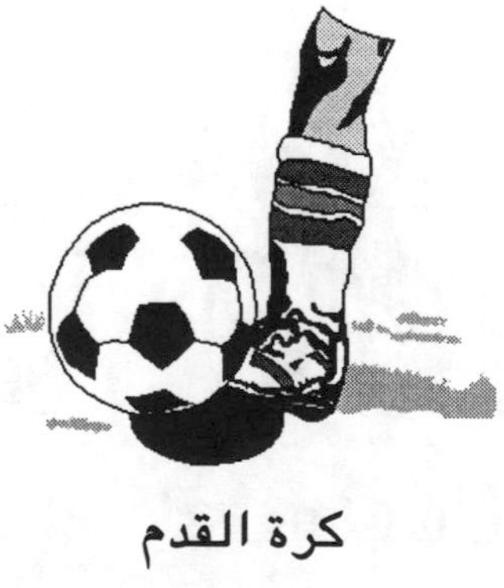

كرة القدم

ويَشرَبونَ الشايَ والقهوةَ والمِياهَ الغازيّة. يأكلُ كَثيرٌ مِن الناسِ اللُبَّ (أو اللِبّ كما يَقولون) وهو بُذور البَطّيخ المُحَمَّصة، وكذلِك الفولَ السوداني.

قال لي سَمير إنّه يَلبَسُ قَميصاً أحمرَ لأنّ اللونَ الأحمَر هو لونُ «الأهلي»، أمّا لونُ «الزمالك» فَهو الأبْيَض. وقال إنّ لِكلِّ فَريقٍ بالقاهِرة مَلعَبَه، لكنّ الفِرَق الكبيرة تَلعَبُ في مَلعَبِ القاهرة الدَولي عادةً. شَرَح لي سَمير قَواعِدَ اللُعبة وفهِمتُها واستَمتَعتُ بالمباراة جداً. وكانَ سَمير سَعيداً جِداً لأنّ فَريقَهُ (الأهلي) فازَ بالمباراة. صِرتُ أشاهِدُ مُباريات كرةِ القدم على التلفاز وأذهبُ أحياناً إلى الملعب حينَ يكونُ عِندي وقت.

الجري

صار عِندي في القاهرة رِياضة مُفضّلة أخرى وهي المَشي. هُنا في القاهرة أمشي إلى كلِّ مَكان. أكثر الناس يَمشون ولا يَركبون السيارات أو الحافِلات دائماً. أفضّل أنْ أمشيَ مَساءً خُصوصاً في الصَيف. أمّا في الفُصولِ الأخرى فَأيُّ وَقتٍ مِن اليَومِ مُناسِبٌ لِلمَشي. وبِسَبَبِ المشي يومياً صِرتُ أعرف شوارعَ القاهرة جيّداً ومكانَ مُعْظَم المحلات التِجارية القَريبة والشَركات وغَيْرِها. لا تجِدُ ناساً يَجرون في شوارع القاهرة كَما في أمريكا. الجَري هُنا رِياضةٌ يَلعَبُها بَعضُ الناسِ في المَلعبِ فقط وليس في الشارِع. جَميعُ الألعابِ التي نَعرفُها مَوجودة في مِصر وكذلك في البِلادِ العَرَبية الأخرى كَكُرةِ المَضرِب وكرةِ الماء ورُكوبِ الخَيل ورُكوبِ الدَرّاجاتِ وغَيرِ ذلك.

كُرة المَضرِب

رُكوب الخَيل

رُكوب الدَرّاجات

الخُضَرُ والفواكِه في مصر لَذيذة جداً. صِرتُ آكل الآن الكثيرَ من الخُضَرِ كَالفاصوليةِ والبازِلّاء والخَسِّ والبامية والباذِنجانِ والكوسا والفُلَيفُلة الخَضراء وغَيرِها. أفضِّل الباذِنجانَ من الخُضَر.

جَزَر

ثوم

خيار

باذِنجان

ذُرة

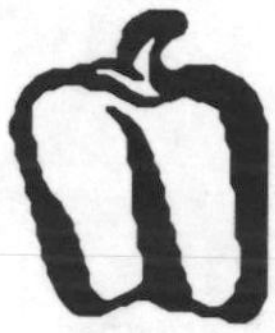
فُلَيفُلة خَضراء

خَسّ

بازِلّاء

زَيتون

بَنَدورة

قَرْع

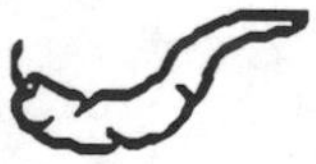
فُلَيفُلة حارّة

لايوجدُ تُفّاح كَثير في مِصر، لكِن هُناكَ فَواكِهُ كثيرةٌ أخرى كَالبُرتُقالِ والعِنَبِ والمَوزِ والتوتِ والبِطّيخِ والمَنجةِ والإجّاص. فاكِهَتي المُفَضّلة في مِصر هي المنجة المصرية لأنَّها لَذيذةٌ وأكبرُ من أيِّ نوعٍ آخَر أعرفه.

توت

عِنَب

بِطّيخ

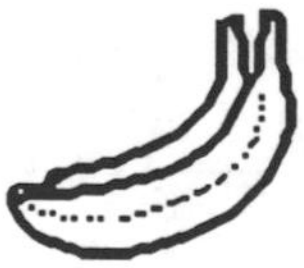
مَوز

إجّاص

ومِنَ الأطعِمةِ المصريةِ أُفَضِّلُ الطَعميّة والكُشَري. أجِدُ هذه الأطعِمةَ لَذيذةً بِسَبَبِ التَوابِلِ الموجودةِ فيها. لَم أكُنْ آكلُ طَعاماً فيه تَوابِل كثيرة، لكِن بعدَ أن تناوَلتُه في مصر صارَ يعجِبُني.

تمرين ١

أجِب عن هذه الأسئلة حسَب النص.

١- ما الرياضةُ المفضّلةُ الّتي كانَ يلعَبُها عَدنان حينَ كانَ في المدرسة الثانوية؟

٢- ماذا يوجد تَحتَ شَقّة عَدنان؟

٣- ماذا يأكلُ الأمريكيونَ في مباراةِ البيسبول؟

٤- أينَ يَسبحُ عَدنان في الصيف أحياناً؟

٥- ماذا يأكلُ الناسُ ويَشرَبون في مَلاعِبِ كُرَةِ القَدَمِ في القاهِرة؟

٦- ما الرياضاتُ الأخرى في البلادِ العربية؟

٧- لماذا صارَ مايكل يَعرفُ شَوارِعَ القاهرةِ جيّداً؟

٨- ما فاكهةُ مايكل المُفَضَّلة في مصر؟ لماذا يُفَضِّلُها؟

تمرين ٢

اكتُبْ «خَطَأ» أو «صَواب» جانِبَ كلِّ جُملةٍ وصَحِّح الجُمَلَ الخَطَأ.

١- يَلعَبُ عَدنان كرةَ الطاولةِ في الجامعة.

٢- لَيسَ لِرياضةِ البيسبول كلِمةٌ عَرَبية لأنّ العَرَبَ لا يَلعَبونَها.

٣- النَقانِقُ مَصنوعةٌ مِنَ اللَحم.

٤- يوجد في كلمبس بُحَيراتٌ كبيرة.

٥- شاهَدَ مايكل مُباراةَ كرة قَدَم في مَلعَبِ فَريق «الأهلي».

٦- كان مايكل يَلعَبُ رِياضَةَ الجَري في شَوارِعِ القاهرة.

٧- لا يوجدُ تُفّاح وبِطيخ كثير في مِصر.

٨- الكُشَري من أطعِمَة مايكل المفَضَّلة لأنّ مايكل صارَ يأكلُ كثيراً مِن الخُضَر.

تمرين ٣

اختَر التكملة المناسبة حَسَب النَص.

١- لَعِبَ عَدنان كرةَ السلّة في أمريكا ......

❑ يَومياً ❑ مَرّة في الأسبوع ❑ مَرّة في الشهر

٢- لُعبةُ عَدنان المفضّلة في أمريكا هي ......

❑ كرةُ السلّة ❑ كرةُ الطاولة ❑ البيسبول

٣- لَم ...... عَدنان رياضةَ البيسبول مِن أوّلِ مرة.

❑ يَفهمْ ❑ يُشاهدْ ❑ يُعجبْ

٤- أكل عَدنان في الملعَب ......

❑ هامبرغر ❑ هَط ضَغ ❑ نَقانق

٥- يَظُنُّ عَدنان أنَّ النَقانقَ ...... مِن الهط ضَغ.

❑ ألَذّ ❑ أصغَر ❑ أكبَر

٦- يَسبَحُ عَدنان في أيّام الدِراسة في ......

❑ البُحيرة ❑ المسبَح ❑ البَحر

٧- طَعامُ الناس المُفضَّل في الحدائق العامّة هو اللَحم ......

❑ المَشويّ ❑ المُحَمَّص ❑ الحارّ

٨- بَقِيَ عَدنان في الحَديقة العامّة حتّى ......

❑ الظُهر ❑ المَساء ❑ اللَيل

٩- يتَّسِع مَلعَب القاهِرة الدولي لِـ ...... ألف مُتَفَرِّج.

❑ ٢٠ ❑ ٦٠ ❑ ١٢٠

١٠- يأكلُ المصريون في الملعَب ......

❑ اللحمَ المَشوي ❑ النَقانق ❑ السَميط

١١- الوقت المناسب للمَشي بالقاهرة في الصَيف هو ......

❑ الظهر ❑ المساء ❑ أيّ وقت

١٢- يُفضِّل مايكل مِن الخُضَر ......

❑ الباذنجان ❑ المنجة ❑ الفاصولية

١٣- تُعجب المنجةُ مايكل لأنّها ......

❑ صَغيرة ❑ مصرية ❑ لَذيذة

١٤- صار مايكل يُحِبُّ أن يَتَناولَ طعاماً فيه ......

❑ كُشَري ❑ تَوابل ❑ طعمية

تمرين ٤

اختر الكلمة المناسبة لِتُكمِلَ الجمل التالية:

١- ...... كرةَ الطاولة في المدرسة.

❑ أعجِبُ ❑ ألعبُ ❑ أشتري ❑ أنزلُ

٢- في المَبنى حَيثُ أسكنُ، هُناك ...... من عَدَدٍ مِن بِلادِ العالَم.

❑ سُكّان ❑ شَطائِر ❑ مَلاعِب ❑ نَقانِق

٣- شَرَح لي صَديقي كَيفَ ...... كرة القدم الأمريكية.

❑ تُشاهَدُ ❑ تُؤكَلُ ❑ تُفهَمُ ❑ تُلعَبُ

٤- أحبُّ الفلافِل لأنّ فيها ......

❑ خُضَر ❑ تَوابِل ❑ شَطائِر ❑ فَواكه

٥- الغُيوم في السماء ...... اللَون.

❑ خَضْراء ❑ بَيْضاء ❑ زَرْقاء ❑ حَمْراء

٦- ألعبُ ...... السلّةِ في المدرسة.

❑ عَصا ❑ كرةَ ❑ ملعَبَ ❑ طابَقَ

٧- ...... ناديا اللغةَ الفَرَنسية وتَتكلّمُها جَيِّداً.

❑ تَلعَبُ ❑ تَضَعُ ❑ تَنزِلُ ❑ تَفهَمُ

٨- تُعجِبُ أخي السياراتُ اليابانيةُ ...... تويوتا.

❑ أحياناً ❑ دائِماً ❑ خُصوصاً ❑ جِدّاً

٩- أكلتُ ...... جُبن مَعَ فِنجان شاي صَباحاً.

❑ شَطيرة ❑ لَذيذة ❑ فُليفُلة ❑ أطعِمة

١٠- ما طعامُك ......؟

❑ اللَذيذ ❑ المشوي ❑ النَظيف ❑ المُفَضَّل

١١- ما اسمُ ...... كرةِ السلّةِ المشهور في لوس أنجِلس؟

❑ جَري ❑ رياضة ❑ فَريق ❑ لُعبة

١٢- هل تفهمين .... لعبةِ كرةِ القَدَم الأمريكية؟

❑ فِرق ❑ قَواعِد ❑ رياضات ❑ مُباريات

١٣- حَضَّرنا طَعامَ الغَداءِ على ...... في حَديقةِ داري.

❑ مِشواة ❑ عَصا ❑ كُرة ❑ بَقَرة

تمرين ٥

اختَر الكلِمة التي لا تُناسِب باقي الكلمات وبَيِّن السَبَب.

١-	بِسَبَبِ	لأنَّ	أوّلاً	لِذلِكَ	
٢-	مَصنوع	بَقِيَ	سَكَنَ	جَلَسَ	
٣-	مَلعَب	مُتَفَرِّج	شاطئ	مُباراة	فَريق
٤-	سَميط	لُبّ	مِياه غازية	عَصا	شاي
٥-	دائِماً	أحياناً	عادةً	غالِباً	تَقريباً
٦-	قَرنبيط	توت	باذِنجان	بامية	خَس
٧-	لَذيذ	جَيِّد	شَرَح	مُفَضَّل	مَشْويّ

تمرين ٦

وافق بين كلٍّ كلمتين تناسبان بعضهما بَعضاً.

مثال: إمرأة / نِساء

١ـ إجّاص	....	عَرَبية
٢ـ حِصان	....	سودانيّ
٣ـ مَوعِد	....	وَقت
٤ـ طابَق	....	مُفَضَّل
٥ـ فُلَيفُلة	....	بَقَر
٦ـ لحم	....	تِجاري
٧ـ فول	....	فاكِهة
٨ـ مَحَلّ	....	أرضيّ
٩ـ بِلاد	....	خَضْراء
		خَيل

تمرين ٧

أعِدْ تَرتيب الكلمات في كُلِّ مَجموعة لِتَشكِّلَ جُمَلاً مُفيدة.

١ـ بِسَبَبِ ـ تَوابِلِها ـ العَرَبيةِ ـ أحِبُّ ـ الأطعِمةِ ـ بَعْضَ

٢ـ الوطنِ ـ هي ـ العربيِّ ـ القدمِ ـ اللُعبةُ ـ في ـ كرةُ ـ المفضّلةُ

٣ـ لَذيذةٌ ـ أنَّ ـ عَدنان ـ النَقانقَ ـ يَظُنُّ

٤ـ في ـ المَشاوي ـ العامّةِ ـ تُستَخدَم ـ الحدائقِ ـ اللحمِ ـ لِشَيِّ

٣ صِرتُ أعرف شَوارِعَ القاهرةِ جيّداً.

This sentence might be translated as:

I now know (have come to know) the streets of Cairo well.

Verbs which refer to the senses can also convey a progressive meaning:

٤ رَأى سامي هالة تَمشي على شاطئِ البَحر.

Sami saw Hala walking/walk on the beach.

تمرين ١٢

Express these meanings in Arabic, using sequences of past and present verbs.

1. Hala used to play tennis twice a week.
2. I saw Adnan riding a bicycle.
3. I now know the names of all my classmates.
4. We watched the two teams play basketball.

2. Colors

Names for the six basic colors may be used as nouns and adjectives. In either case, they change in number and gender, just like other nouns. However, when forming the dual (by adding ان) the *hamza* changes into و. The same process applies when forming the plural of feminine nouns (by adding ات):

٥ بَيْضاء ⇦ بَيْضاوان ⇦ بَيْضاوات

The table below lists the six basic colors, as adjectives, in the singular, dual, and plural in the masculine and feminine. Note that feminine and masculine plurals are identical (e.g. بنات/أولاد بيض).

	m. sing.	m. dual	m. plural	f. sing.	f. dual	f. plural
white	أبْيَض	أبْيَضان	بيض	بَيْضاء	بَيْضاوان	بيض
black	أسْوَد	أسْوَدان	سود	سَوداء	سَوداوان	سود

green	أخْضَر	أخْضَران	خُضْر	خَضْراء	خَضْراوان	خُضْر
blue	أزرَق	أزرَقان	زُرْق	زَرْقاء	زَرْقاوان	زُرْق
red	أحْمَر	أحْمَران	حُمْر	حَمراء	حَمراوان	حُمْر
yellow	أصْفَر	أصْفَران	صُفْر	صَفْراء	صَفْراوان	صُفْر

3. **Comparative Nouns with Doubled Consonants**

As you may recall, a comparative (and superlative) noun is formed on the pattern أفْـعَل, such as أكْـبَـر. This noun in the example is derived from the adjective كَـبـيـر, which contains four different letters. If, however, an adjective contains two similar letters, as in جـديـد, قـلـيـل, and لذيـذ where the د, ل, and ذ are repeated in each word, respectively, the two similar consonants are collapsed in the derived comparative noun into one doubled consonant:

٦ سيارتي أجَدُّ من سيارتك. *newer than* (not أجْدَدُ)

٧ عددُ سُكّانِ الإسكندرية أقلُّ من عدد سكان القاهرة. (not أقلَل) *less than*

٨ النَقانِقُ ألَذُّ من الهط ضغ. *more delicious than* (not ألذَذُ)

(See Lesson 17, Section 5 for information on forming comparative and superlative nouns).

تمرين ١٣

اشتقّ (derive) اسمَ تَفضيل مِن الصِفة بينَ القَوسين.

١- مَبنى «سِيَرز» (طويل) مِن مَبنى «إمپايَر ستيت».

٢- ما (صَغير) وِلاية في الولايات المتحدة الأمريكية؟

٣- هذه (لَذيذ) حَلوى أكلتُها حتّى الآن.

٤- تَظُنُّ رانية أنَّ زَوجَةَ سامي (جَميل) فَتاةٍ في البَلدة.

٥- عَدَدُ دَفاتِري (قليل) مِن عَدَدِ دَفاتِرك.

٦- يَسكُنُ أحمَد في (جديد) شَقّةٍ في البِناية.

4. **Weak Verbs Revisited (الفعل المعتلّ)**

In Lessons 19 and 23, there is reference to two types of verbs that contain a long vowel, or rather a semivowel: defective and hollow. In fact, there are as many types as there are positions in the verb form for those vowels (five altogether). Of these different types, we have encountered the following so far:

a. الناقص: This type is called *defective* and is characterized by a vowel (و or ي) at the end of the word:

٩ مشى، جرى، بقِيَ، نَسِيَ

b. الأجوَف: This type is called *hollow* because it contains a vowel in the medial position:

١٠ قالَ، فازَ

c. المثال: This type has the vowel in the initial position:

١١ وَضَعَ، وَجَدَ، وَسِعَ، وَصَلَ

In English, المثال is called *assimilated* for good reason. When verbs of this type are on the pattern افـتَـعَل (Form VIII), the initial vowel (و) changes to ت because the ت of the pattern assimilates it (i.e. it changes it into ت). Examine the process as illustrated by وَسِع (to hold, to contain) and وَصَل (to arrive, to connect, to establish contact).

١٢ فَعَلَ ⇦ افتَعَلَ

وَسِعَ ⇦ اوتَسَعَ ⇦ اتَّسَعَ (to hold)

وَصَلَ ⇦ اوتَصَلَ ⇦ اتَّصَلَ (to call on the phone, to contact)

Note that the ت of the pattern and the assimilated ت are spelled as one تّ with a *shadda* to indicate a double consonant.

All weak verbs, including the three types listed above, share some common characteristics. One of these is that in the present tense conjugation, the long vowel is replaced with its short counterpart when the mood changes from مرفوع to مجزوم (from indicative to jussive):

١٣ يَقول ⇦ يَقُلْ

يَجري ⇦ يَجرِ

يَبقى ⇦ يَبقَ

Second, the vowel may be lost completely in the present and the imperative:

١٤ وَصَلَ ⇦ يَصِلُ ⇦ صِلْ

Third, when the vowel is in the final position, it is dropped in اسم الفاعل (active participle) if it is indefinite, but it is restored when definite:

	Active Participle Definite		Indefinite		Verb	
to remain	الباقي	⇦	باقٍ	⇦	بَقِيَ	١٥
to run	الجاري	⇦	جارٍ	⇦	جَرى	١٦
to walk	الماشي	⇦	ماشٍ	⇦	مَشى	١٧
to forget	الناسي	⇦	ناسٍ	⇦	نَسِيَ	١٨

تمرين ١٤

انفِ الجُملَ التالية باستعمال (لَم).

Negate these sentences with لَم, taking into account the changes that take place in weak verbs:

١- بَقيتُ في المكتبة أكثرَ مِن ساعتين.

٢- مَشى رياض إلى المدرسة.

٣- فَهِمَتْ سَلمى الدرسَ كلَّه.

٤- نَسيتُ أن أكتبَ رسالةً لِصديقي.

٥- سكنوا في الدارِ البَيضاء.

تمرين ١٥

أجِبْ عن هذه الأسئلة حسب نصِّ الاستِماع.

١- أين شاهَدَ رِياض مُباراةَ كُرةِ القدَم؟

٢- لماذا لَم يكُنْ سُهَيل سَعيداً في نِهايةِ المُباراة؟

٣- مَن حَضَّر الحلوى؟

اكتُبْ «خَطَأ» أو «صَواب» جانِبَ كلِّ جُملةٍ وصَحِّح الجُمَلَ الخَطَأ.

٤- حَضَّر سُهَيل الشايَ والحِمَّص.

٥- استَمتَعَ رِياض وأصدقاؤه بالمباراة.

٦- لَم يكُنْ والِدا سُهَيل في البَيتِ في وَقتِ المباراة.

أكمل الجمل التالية بكلمات مناسبة حسب النص.

٧- في وَقتِ المباراة كانَ هُناكَ ...... أشْخاصٌ في بَيتِ سُهَيل.

❑ أربعةُ ❑ خَمسةُ ❑ سِتّةُ ❑ سَبعةُ

٨- أكَلَ الأصدِقاءُ الحِمَّص مَعَ ......

❑ الشاي ❑ الحلوى ❑ أم سهيل ❑ الفليفلة

٩- لَم يكُنْ الأصدقاءُ سُعَداء في نهايةِ المباراة لأنَّ ...... لم يفُزْ.

❑ صَديقَهُم سهيل ❑ فَريقَهُم

❑ والِدَ سُهيل ❑ رِياض

١٠- شاهد الأصدِقاء ...... المباراة على التِلفاز.

❑ كلَّ ❑ بعضَ ❑ جزءاً مِن ❑ معظمَ

١١- شاهَدَ رِياض المُباراةَ في ......

❑ دارِه ❑ بَيتِ صَديقِهِ ❑ الملعَبِ ❑ المدرسةِ

١٢- شَرِبَ الأصدِقاءُ الشايَ ...... أنْ أكَلوا الحِمَّص.

❑ قَبلَ ❑ بَعدَ ❑ مَعَ ❑ عِندَ

المُفْرَدات

never, not at all ... (adv.) أبَداً
to hold, to contain ... (v.) اتَّسَعَ (يَتَّسِعُ) اتِّساع
pear ... (n., m.) إجّاص
red ... (adj.) أحمَر ج حُمْر
blue ... (adj.) أزرَق ج زُرْق
to use, to utilize, to employ ... (v.) استَخدَمَ (يَستَخدِمُ) استِخدام
yellow ... (adj.) أصْفَر ج صُفْر
eggplant ... (n., m.) باذِنجان
green peas ... (n., f.) بازِلاء
ochra ... (n., f.) بامْيَة
seed, kernel ... (n., f.) بِذرة ج بُذور
watermelon ... (n., m.) بِطّيخ
cow, cattle ... (n., f.) بَقَرة ج أبْقار / بَقَر
to remain, to stay ... (v.) بَقِيَ (يَبْقى) بَقاء
tomato ... (n., f.) بَنَدورة (طَماطِم في مصر)
white ... (n./adj., f.) بَيضاء ج بيض/ بَيضاوات
spice, condiment, seasoning ... (n., m.) تابِل ج تَوابِل
approximately, about, nearly, roughly ... (adv.) تَقريباً
berry ... (n., m.) توت
garlic ... (n., m.) ثوم
to run, to flow, to hurry, to rush, to happen, to occur ... (v.) جَرى (يَجري) جَري
horse ... (n., m.) حصان ج أحْصِنة
lettuce ... (n., m.) خَسّ
especially, particularly ... (adv.) خُصوصاً
corn ... (n., f.) ذُرة

perhaps, probably .... رُبَّما (adv.)
basket .... سَلّة ج سِلال (n., f.)
a kind of toasted thin bread .... سَميط (n., m.)
to explain, to expound, to illustrate .... شَرَحَ (يَشرَحُ) شَرْح (v.)
sandwich .... شَطيرة ج شَطائِر (n., f.)
to grill, to broil .... شَوى (يَشوي) شَيّ (v.)
public .... عامّ (adj.)
stick, rod, cane .... عَصا ج عُصِيّ (n., f.)
grape .... عِنَب (n., m.)
non-, un-, other than, different from .... غَيْر (n., m.)
to win .... فازَ (يفوزُ) فَوز (v.)
green beans .... فاصولية (n., f.)
team, company, band, troupe .... فَريق ج أفرِقة (n., f.)
green (bell) pepper .... فُلَيفُلة (n., f.)
to understand, to comprehend, to realize .... فَهِمَ (يَفْهَمُ) فَهْم (v.)
peanuts .... فول (سوداني) (n., m.)
rule, principle, basis, foundation, base .... قاعدة ج قَواعِد (n., f.)
cauliflower .... قَرنَبيط (n., m.)
like, as .... كَـ (prep.)
ball, sphere .... كُرة ج كُرات (n., f.)
basketball .... كُرةُ السلة
table tennis .... كرة الطاولة
volleyball .... الكرة الطائرة
football/soccer .... كرة القدم
water polo .... كُرةُ الماء
tennis .... كُرةُ المَضرِب
zucchini .... كوسا (n., m.)
kernel, seed .... لُبّ ج لُبوب (n., m.)
delicious, delightful, tasty .... لَذيذ (adj., m.)

لَعِبَ (يَلعَبُ) لَعْب (v.) .... to play
ماء غازيّ ج مِياه غازيّة (n., f.) .... soda
مُباراة ج مُباريَات (n., f.) .... match, game
مُتَفَرِّج ج ـون (n., m.) .... spectator
مُحَمَّص (n./adj.) .... roasted, toasted
مِشواة ج مَشاوٍ (n., f.) .... grill, gridiron
مَشويّ (adj.) .... grilled
مُفَضَّل (n./adj., m.) .... preferred, favorite
مَوْز (n., m.) .... banana
نَقانِق (أو مَقانِق) (n., pl.) .... small, spicy mutton sausage
وَقْت ج أوْقات (n., m.) .... time

بائِعُ العِرقسوس
باب شرقي، دمشق

Lesson Twenty-Seven — الدَرْسُ السابِعُ والعِشرون

Objectives

- Describing geographical directions and features.
- Describing countries, populations, and products.
- The noun كِلا.
- Expressing exception with إلاّ and غَير.
- Listen to recorded material for this lesson.
- Do relevant computer drills and exercises, Stage 9.

جُغرافِيَّةٌ

الوَطَنِ العَرَبيّ والولاياتِ المُتَّحِدةِ الأمريكية

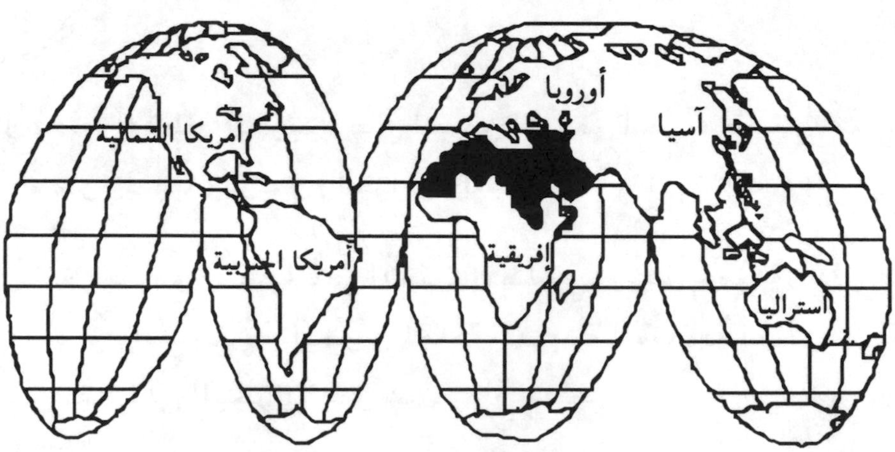

خريطة الوطن العربي والعالم

يَقَعُ الوَطَنُ العَرَبِيّ في قارّتَين هُما آسيا وإفريقية. تَقَعُ تِسعةُ أقطارٍ عربية في إفريقية واثنا عَشَرَ قُطراً في آسيا. يَتألَّفُ الوَطَنُ العربيّ مِن خَمسةِ أقاليمَ

جُغرافيَّةٍ هي بِلادُ الشامِ وما بَينَ النَهرَين (العِراق) وشِبْهُ الجَزيرةِ العَربيةِ ووادي النيل وشمالُ إفريقية.

بلاد الشام

العراق

شِبْهُ الجزيرة العربية

شمال إفريقيا

مصر والسودان

تُطِلُّ بَعضُ الأقطارِ العربيةِ على البَحرِ الأبْيَضِ المُتوَسِّط مِثلُ سورية ولُبنان وفِلَسطين ومِصرَ وليبيا وتونس والجزائِر والمغرِب.

يُطِلُّ المغربُ وموريتانيا على المُحيطِ الأطلَسيّ، وتُطِلُّ خَمسةُ بُلْدانٍ على البَحرِ الأحمَر هِي مِصرُ والسودانُ واليَمَنُ والمَملكةُ العربيةُ السُعوديّةُ والأردُنّ. لكنَّ الأردنَّ لَهُ مَنفَذٌ ضَيِّق فَقَط على البحرِ الأحمر هُو ميناءُ العَقَبة.

يُطِلُّ على الخَليجِ العربيِّ الكويتُ والمَملَكةُ العربيّةُ السعودية وقَطَرُ والإماراتُ العربية، ولِلعراقِ مَنفَذٌ ضَيِّق عَلى الخَليج. أمّا البَحرين فَهُوَ جَزيرةٌ صَغيرة تَقَعُ في الجزءِ الغَربي مِنَ الخليجِ العَربيّ وهُوَ أصْغَرُ بَلَدٍ عَربيّ. ويُطِلُّ اليَمَنُ وعُمانُ على بَحرِ العَرَب. أمّا الصومالُ وجيبوتي فيُطِلاّنِ على بَحرِ العَرَبِ والمحيطِ الهِنْديّ.

يَحُدُّ الوَطَنَ العَربيَّ مِنَ الشَمالِ تُركيا والبَحرُ الأبْيَضُ المُتَوَسِّط، ومِن الشَرقِ إيرانُ وبَحرُ العَرَب، ومِنَ الجَنوبِ المُحيطُ الهِنديُّ والصَحراءُ الكُبرى، ومِنَ الغَربِ المُحيطُ الأطلَسيّ.

خريطة الوطن العربي

الوِلاياتُ المُتَّحِدةُ الأمريكية

تَقَعُ الوِلاياتُ المُتَّحِدةُ الأمريكيّةُ في أمريكا الشَماليّة إلاّ ولايةَ هَوائي. يَحُدُّها مِنَ الشَرقِ المُحيطُ الأطْلَسيّ، ومِنَ الغَربِ المُحيطُ الهادي، ومِنَ الشَمالِ كَندا، ومِنَ الجَنوبِ المِكسيك وخَليجُ المِكسيك.

أمّا وِلايةُ ألاسكا فَتَقَعُ شَمالَ غَربِ كَندا، ووِلايةُ هَوائي في وَسَطِ المُحيطِ الهادي. أصغر ولاية أمريكية من حيثُ المَساحةُ هِيَ « رود آيلاند » في شَرقِ الوِلاياتِ المُتَّحِدةِ على المُحيطِ الأطلَسي، وأكبرُها ألاسكا، لكِنَّها أقَلُّ الوِلاياتِ بِعَدَدِ السُكّان.

خَريطةُ الولاياتِ المتحدةِ الأمريكية

سوريَة

تَقَعُ سورية في شَمالِ الوَطَنِ العَربيّ. يَحُدُّها مِنَ الشَمالِ تُركيا ومِنَ الشَرقِ العِراقُ ومِنَ الجَنوبِ الأرْدُنُّ ومِنَ الجَنوبِ الغَربيّ لُبنانُ وفِلَسطينُ ومِنَ الغَربِ البَحرُ الأبْيَضُ المُتَوَسِّط.

عاصِمةُ سورية هي دِمَشقُ وتَقَعُ في جَنوبِها الغَربيّ وهي أكبرُ مُدُنِها وأقدمُ مَدينةٍ في العالَمِ سُكِنَت دونَ انقِطاع.

ثاني أكبرِ مَدينةٍ هي حَلَب وتَقَعُ في الشَمال. هُناكَ صِناعاتٌ عَديدةٌ في كِلتا المدينتينِ وبالقُربِ مِنهُما. تَقَعُ مَدينتا حِمصَ وحَماةَ بَينَ حَلَبَ ودِمَشق. اللاذِقيّةُ ميناءُ

سوريةَ الأوَّل، وطَرطوسُ ميناءٌ آخَرُ على الساحِلِ السوريّ. أمّا بانياسُ فهي ميناءٌ نِفطيّ. تَقَعُ السُوَيداء في جَنوبِ سورية والقامِشلي في شَمالِها الشَرقي. أمّا مَدينةُ دَيرِ الزَوْرِ فَتَقَعُ على نَهْرِ الفُراتِ الَّذي يَنْبُعُ مِن تُركيا ويمُرُّ بِسورية ثُمَّ بِالعِراق.

خريطة الجُمهورية العربية السورية

عَلَم الجمهورية العربية السورية
(آحمر وأبيض وأسود ونَجمتان خضراوان)

مِساحَةُ سورية ١٨٥١٠٠ كيلومِتراً مُرَبَّعاً (٧١٤٦٧ ميلاً مُرَبَّعاً) وعَدَدُ سُكّانِها ١٦ مِليون نَسَمة تَقْريباً. توجَدُ في سورية زِراعَةُ الحُبوبِ والفَواكِهِ والخُضَرِ والقُطنِ والتَبْغ. هُناكَ أيْضاً صِناعاتُ النَسيجِ والأجهِزَةِ الكَهرُبائيَّةِ والنِفْطُ ومُنتَجاتُ الحَليبِ وغيرُ ذلِك.

مِساحاتٌ كَبيرةٌ مِن أراضي سورية صَحْراءُ أو شِبهُ صَحْراءَ كَبادِيةِ الشام، لكِنْ هُناكَ أيْضاً سُهولٌ خَصيبةٌ جِداً مِثلُ حَوْرانَ جَنوبيّ دِمَشق، وسَهْلُ الغابِ قُربَ الساحِلِ السوريّ، وسُهولُ الجَزيرةِ في شَمالِ شَرقيٍّ سورية.

بِالإضافةِ إلى نَهرِ الفُراتِ هُناكَ نَهرُ العاصي الَّذي يَنْبُعُ مِن لُبنانَ ويَجري شَمالاً إلى حِمصَ وحَماةَ ثُمَّ يَصُبُّ في البَحرِ المُتَوَسِّط. وهُناكَ نَهرُ الخابورِ الَّذي يَنبُعُ مِن تُركِيّا ويَسيرُ جَنوباً لِيَصُبَّ في نَهرِ الفُرات. أمّا نَهرُ بَرَدى فَهو نَهرٌ صَغيرٌ يَروي السُّهولَ قُربَ دِمَشق.

شِعار سورية القديم

شِعارُ سورية الجَديد مِثلُ الشِعارِ القَديمِ لكِنَّ فيهِ نَجمَتَينِ ولَيْسَ ثلاث، والكلِماتُ المكتوبَةُ على الشِعارِ الجَديد هي «الجُمهوريةُ العَربيةُ السوريةُ».

يوجَدُ جِبالٌ عاليةٌ في سورية كَجَبَلِ الشَيخِ في جَنوبِ غَربِ دِمَشق الَّذي يَصِلُ إلى ٢٨١٤ متراً (٩٢٣٢ قَدَماً) وهو جزءٌ من سِلسِلةِ جِبالِ لُبنانَ الشَرقيةِ ويُعْتَبَرُ أعلى جَبَلٍ فيها. وهُناكَ جِبالُ العَلَويين على طولِ الساحِلِ السوريّ، وجَبَلُ العَرَبِ في الجَنوب.

وِلايةُ أوهايو

تَقَعُ وِلايةُ أوهايو في الجُزءِ الشَرقيِّ مِنَ الولاياتِ المُتَّحِدة، وتُعْتَبَرُ أيْضاً واحدةً مِن ولاياتِ الغَربِ الأوسَط. يَحُدُّها مِنَ الشَمالِ بُحَيرةُ إيري، ومِنَ الشَمالِ الغَربيّ وِلاية ميشِغَن، ومِنَ الغَربِ وِلايةُ إنديانا، ومِنَ الجَنوبِ وِلايةُ كِنتَكي، ومِنَ الجَنوبِ الشَرقيِّ وِلايةُ ڤِرجينيا الغَربيّة (وِسْت ڤِرجينيا)، ومِنَ الشَرق وِلايةُ پِنْسِلڤانيا.

عاصِمةُ أوهايو هي مَدينة كَلَمبَس وتَقَعُ في وَسَطِ أوهايو. أكبَرُ مُدُنِ أوهايو هي كليڤلَند وتَقَعُ في شَمالِ شَرقِ الوِلايةِ وتُطِلُّ على بُحَيْرةِ إيري. تُعتَبَرُ سِنسِناتي مِن أجمَلِ مُدُنِ أوهايو وهِيَ تَقَعُ في الجَنوبِ الغَربيِّ مِنَ الوِلاية. أمّا توليدو فَتَقَعُ في شَمالِ غَربِ أوهايو عَلى الحُدودِ بَينَ وِلايَتَي أوهايو وميشِغَن، وهي مَدينةٌ صِناعيّة. وهُناكَ آكرَن وكانتَن في شَمالِ شَرقِ أوهايو وكِلتاهُما مَدينتانِ صِناعيَّتانِ كذلِك.

مساحةُ أوهايو ١٠٦٧٦٥ كيلومتراً مُرَبَّعاً (٤١٢٢٢ ميلاً مُرَبَّعاً) وعَدَدُ سُكّانها ١١ مِليونَ نَسَمة تَقريباً. أوهايو وِلايةٌ صِناعيّةٌ تأتي في إنتاجِها الصِناعيِّ بَعدَ ولايَتَي نيويورك وكاليفورنيا، وهي زِراعِيَّةٌ كذلِك وتُنتِجُ الذُرَةَ والقَمحَ ومُنتَجاتِ الحَليبِ والأبقار.

لأوهايو ميناءانِ هامّانِ على بُحَيْرَةِ إيري هُما كليڤلَند وتوليدو. وتُعتَبَرُ سنسِناتي ميناءً هامّاً أيْضاً على نَهرِ أوهايو الّذي يُشَكِّل الحُدودَ الجَنوبِيَّةَ ونِصفَ الحُدودِ الشَرقيّةِ لِلوِلاية.

مُعظَمُ أوهايو سُهولٌ خَضْراءُ ولا يوجَدُ فيها جِبال إلاّ في الجَنوبِ الشَرقيِّ عَلى الحُدودِ مَعَ ڤِرجينيا الغربِية. هُناكَ بُحَيْراتٌ عَديدةٌ وعِدّةُ أنهار صَغيرة. أمّا نَهرُ أوهايو فَلا يَنْبَعُ مِن أوهايو بَل يَبْدَأُ عِندَ مَدينة بِتسبرغ في وِلاية بِنسلڤانيا ويَصُبُّ في نَهرِ الميسيسيپي عِندَ بَلدة كايرو في ولايةِ إلينوي. طوله ١٥٧٩ كيلو مِتراً وتَسيرُ فيهِ سُفُنُ الرُكّابِ والبَضائِع.

تمرين ١

أجِب عَن هذه الأسئِلةِ حَسَبَ النَصّ.

١- ما القُطر العَرَبيُّ الّذي تَحُدُّهُ مِصرُ مِنَ الشرقِ والجَزائِرُ مِنَ الغَرب؟

٢- أيُّ قُطرٍ يَقَعُ في شَمالِ الوَطَنِ العَرَبِيّ؟

٣- ما البَحْرُ الّذي يُطِلُّ الأردُنُّ عَليه؟

٤- ماذا يَحُدُّ الولاياتِ المُتَّحِدةَ مِنَ الغَرب؟

٥- أيُّ بَلَدٍ غَيرِ عَرَبيّ لَهُ حُدودٌ مَعَ سورية؟

٦- ما بَعضُ مُنتَجاتِ سورية؟

٧- كَم وِلايةً تَحُدُّ وِلايةَ أوهايو؟

٨- هَلِ الإنتاجُ الصِناعِيُّ في أهايو كَبير؟ اشْرَحْ ذلِك.

تمرين ٢

اكتُبْ «خَطَأ» أو «صَواب» جانِبَ كلِّ جُملةٍ وصَحِّح الجُمَلَ الخَطَأ.

١- يُطِلُّ البَحْرَين على الخَليجِ العَرَبي.

٢- أكبَرُ الولاياتِ الأمريكيةِ بالمِساحَةِ هي تِكساس.

٣- يَنبُعُ نَهرُ العاصي مِن تُركِيّا ويَصُبُّ في الخَليجِ العَرَبي.

٤- كانتَن ميناءٌ هامّ عَلى بُحَيْرَةِ إيري.

تمرين ٣

اكتبْ أسئلةً مُناسِبَةً لِهذه الإجابات. Write questions for the following answers.

١- ثَلاثةُ أقطارٍ عَرَبِيَّةٍ تُطِلُّ على هذا البَحْر.

٢- هُما تُركيّا وإيران.

٣- خَليجُ المكسيك والمِكسيك.

٤- هو مَدينةُ بانياس.

٥- أحَدَ عَشَرَ مليون نسمة.

تمرين ٤

اختَر التكملةَ المُناسبةَ حسَبَ النَص.

١- تَقَعُ ...... أقطارٍ عَرَبِيَّةٍ في إفريقية.
❑ ٩ ❑ ١٢ ❑ ٢٠ ❑ ٢٢

٢- يُطِلُّ الأردنُّ على ......
❑ البَحرِ المُتوَسِّط ❑ البَحرِ الأحْمَر
❑ الخَليجِ العَربي ❑ بَحرِ العَرَب

٣- ...... أصغرُ قُطرٍ عَرَبيّ.
❑ عُمانُ ❑ قَطَرُ ❑ البَحرَينُ ❑ لُبنانُ

٤- تَقَعُ وِلايَةُ ألاسكا في ......
❑ المُحيطِ الهادي ❑ المُحيطِ الأطلَسيّ
❑ أمرِيكا الشَمالية ❑ كَنَدا

٥- تُعتَبَرُ ...... أصْغَرَ ولايةٍ أمرِيكية مِن حَيثُ عَدَدِ السُكّان.
❑ رود آيلاند ❑ ديلاوير ❑ ألاسكا ❑ هوائي

٦- أقدمُ مَدينةٍ في العالَم هي ......
❑ دِمَشق ❑ حَلَب ❑ القاهِرة ❑ بَغداد

٧- ...... من المُنتَجات السورية.
❑ النِفط ❑ التَبْغ ❑ القُطْن ❑ كلّ ما سَبَق

٨- تَقَعُ جِبالُ العَلَوِيّين ...... سورية.
❑ في جَنوبَ ❑ على ساحِلِ ❑ في شَرقِ ❑ في وَسَطِ

٩- يَحُدُّ أوهايو مِنَ الشَمال ......
❑ كَنَدا ❑ ميشِغن ❑ بُحَيرةُ إيري ❑ بِنسلڤانيا

١٠- يُشَكِّلُ نَهرُ أوهايو ......
❑ أكبرُ أنهارِ الولاية ❑ الحُدودَ الجَنوبيةَ الشرقيةَ والجنوبية
❑ حُدودَ الوِلاية ❑ ميناءً هاماً

١١- ...... مِن أجملِ مُدن أوهايو.

❑ سِنسِناتي ❑ كَلَمبَس ❑ كليڤلَند ❑ توليدو

١٢- لا يوجدُ ...... في وَسَطِ وشَمالِ أوهايو.

❑ صِناعاتٌ ❑ جِبالٌ ❑ سُهولٌ ❑ مَوانِئُ

تمرين ٥

اختَر الكلِمة الّتي لا تُناسِب باقي الكلمات في كُلِّ مَجموعة وبَيِّن السَبَب.

١- مَحيط بَحر وَطَن بُحَيرة نَهر

٢- صِناعة ساحِل جَبَل صَحراء سَهْل

٣- قُطن تَبغ قَمح خُضار نَسَمة

٤- ذُرة شَمال شَرق غَرب جَنوب

٥- خَليج سُكّان ميناء بَحر سَفينة

تمرين ٦

وافِق بَين كُلِّ كَلِمةٍ وضِدِّها.
Match antonyms

١- واسِع.........فَقير
٢- كبير ....صَبٌّ
٣- طَويل.........تَحْتَ
٤- غَنيّ..........ضَيِّق
٥- بَعيد ....جَميل
٦- كَثير ....قَصير
٧- نَبَعَ..........صَغير
٨- فَوق..........قَريب
قَليل

وافِق بَين كُلِّ كَلِمة ومثيلَتِها.
Match related words

٩- عَلَم ....بَحر
١٠- بَلَد .... ميناء
١١- جَزيرة..........شِعار
١٢- سَفينة ....زِراعة
١٣- صناعة ....رِياضة
١٤- نِفْط..........قُطْر
غاز

تمرين ٧

أكمل الجُمَلَ بالاختيار المناسب.

١- كوبا ...... تَقَعُ في البَحرِ الكاريبي.

❑ مَنفَذٌ ❑ جَزيرةٌ ❑ مُحيطٌ ❑ ميناءٌ

٢- ...... الولاياتُ المتّحِدة الأمريكية مِن ٥٠ ولاية.

❑ تُطِلُّ ❑ تَقَعُ ❑ تُشَكِّلُ ❑ تَتَألَّفُ

٣- زُرْتُ بِلادَ شَمالِ إفريقية ...... تونِس.

❑ إلاّ ❑ إلى ❑ بِـ ❑ لِذلكَ

٤- يوجدُ مَصارِفُ ...... في مدينة نيويورك.

❑ ضَيِّقةٌ ❑ خَصيبةٌ ❑ عَديدةٌ ❑ شَرقيّةٌ

٥- كَم ...... في العَلَمِ الأمريكي؟

❑ نَجمةً ❑ جَزيرةً ❑ وادياً ❑ قُطراً

٦- ماذا ...... كَنَدا من الشمال؟

❑ يوجدُ ❑ يَقَعُ ❑ يَتَألَّفُ ❑ يَحُدُّ

٧- الجُبنُ مِن ...... الحَليب.

❑ صِناعاتِ ❑ مُنتَجاتِ ❑ أجهِزةِ ❑ مِساحاتِ

٨- هُناكَ ...... كثيرةٌ في الدُكّان.

❑ رُكّابٌ ❑ سُكّانٌ ❑ حُدودٌ ❑ بَضائعُ

تمرين ٨

أعِدْ ترتيب الكلمات في كُلِّ مَجموعة لِتَشكِّلَ جُمَلاً مُفيدة.

١- ساحِلِ - على - تَقَعُ - مِلبورن - الجَنوبيِّ - أستراليا

٢- العَرَبيِّ - ضَيِّقٌ - على - مَنفَذٌ - الخَليجِ - لِلعراقِ

٣- الوَطَنِ - مِنَ - واحِدَةٌ - الأقاليم - الشام - العَرَبِيِّ - في - بِلادُ - الجُغرافيةِ

٤- النِفطَ - الزراعيّةَ - تُنتِجُ - والمَنتوجاتِ - الجزائرُ

تمرين ٩

١ـ اقرأ النَصَّ التالي ثم اكتُب على الخَريطةِ المَوجودةِ تَحتَهُ اسمَ البَلَدِ الَّذي يَصِفُهُ النَصُّ وأسْماءَ مُدُنِهِ وأنهارِهِ وجِبالِهِ وصَحرائِهِ والأقطارَ الَّتي تَحُدُّه. بَيِّنْ بَعضَ الصِناعاتِ والزِراعاتِ حَسَبَ مَكانِها.

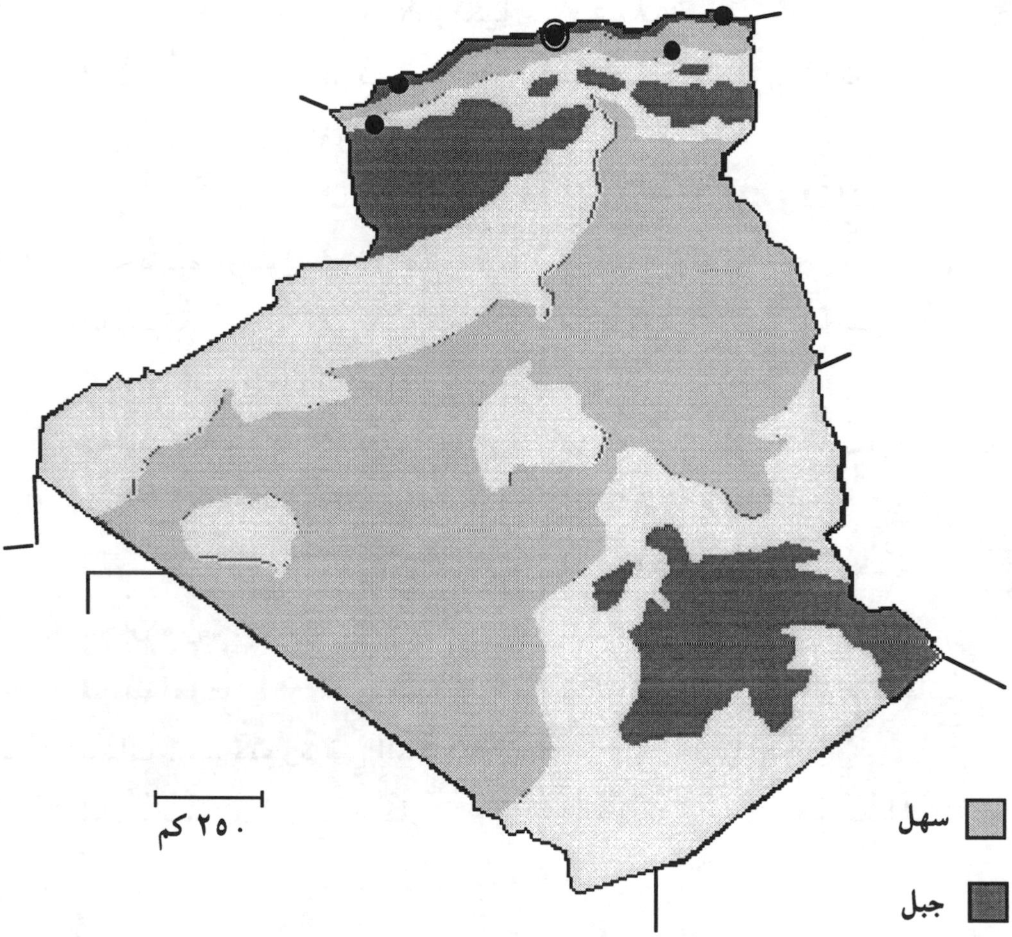

يَحُدُّ القُطرَ الجَزائريَّ مِنَ الشَمالِ البَحرُ الأبْيَضُ المُتَوَسِّط ومِنَ الغَربِ المَغرِبُ ومِنَ الجَنوبِ الغَربيِّ موريتانيا ومالي، ومِنَ الجَنوبِ الشَرقيِّ النيجَر، وتَحُدُّه مِنَ الشَرقِ ليبيا وتونِس. عاصِمةُ الجَزائِرِ هي مَدينةُ الجَزائِرِ وتَقَعُ في شَمالِ البِلادِ على ساحِلِ البَحرِ المُتَوَسِّط، وهي ميناءٌ هامٌّ وفيها صِناعةُ النِفطِ والسيارات. ومِن أهمِّ المُدُنِ الأخرى وَهرانُ وتَقَعُ على الساحِلِ في غَربِيِّ الجَزائِر، وتَقَع تِلِمسان في الشَمالِ

الغَربيِّ مِنَ البِلاد لكِنَّها لَيسَتْ على الساحِل. أمّا مَدينة عَنّابة فتَقَعُ في الشَمالِ الشرقيِّ على ساحِلِ البحر، وقَسَنطينة في الشَمالِ الشَرقي أيْضاً، لكِنَّها إلى الجَنوبِ الغَربي مِن عَنّابة.

تَقَعُ جِبالُ الأطْلَسِ على طولِ الساحِلِ إلى الجَنوبِ مِنه قَليلاً، ويَقَعُ بَينَ هذه الجِبالِ والبحرِ المُتَوَسِّطِ سُهولٌ خَصيبةٌ تُسْتَخدَمُ لِلزِراعة. مُعظَمُ الأراضي جَنوبَ جِبالِ الأطلَسِ صَحْراويّة.

عَدَدُ سُكّانِ الجَزائرِ ٢٨ مليون نَسَمَة تَقريباً. يَعمَلُ نِصْفُ السُكّانِ في الزِراعةِ ويُنتِجونَ العِنَبَ والبُرتُقالَ والحُبوبَ والفَواكِه. تُنتِجُ الجَزائرُ أيْضاً النِفطَ والغاز. ويوجَدُ إلى جانِبِ الزِراعةِ صِناعةُ السياراتِ بِالإضافةِ إلى صِناعاتٍ أخرى.

أجِب عَن هذه الأسئلة:

٢ـ كَم عَدَدُ سُكّانِ الجَزائر؟

٣ـ اكتُب اِسمَ صِناعَةٍ مِنَ الصناعاتِ الهامّة؟

٤ـ ماذا يوجدُ جَنوبَ جِبالِ الأطلَس؟

تمرين ١٠

اكتبْ وصفاً لمدينتك أو ولايتك أو بَلَدِك مِثلَ الوَصفِ في التَمرينِ السابِقِ (٩) وفي وَصْفِ سورية. بَيِّنْ اسمَ البَلَدِ ومَكانَه مِن حَيثُ البِلادِ الأخرى والمُدُنِ والأنهارِ والبُحَيراتِ والزِراعةِ والصِناعةِ والسُكّان.

تمرين ١١

صِف القُطرَ العِراقيَّ حَسَبَ المَعلوماتِ المَوجودة على الخَريطة. استَخدِمِ النَصَّ في التَمرينِ ٩ والنَصّينِ عَن سورية وأوهايو كأمثِلة.

خريطة العراق

1. **Geographical Directions**

The basic directions شَمال، جَنوب، شَرق ، غَرب may be used as adverbials with a *fatḥa*, denoting the accusative case (نَصب). For example, here is how to indicate the geographical relationship between two places:

١ تَقَعُ الإسكندريّةُ شَمالَ القاهِرةِ.

The sentence shows that Alexandria is *to the north of* Cairo. This usage may be represented graphically as follows:

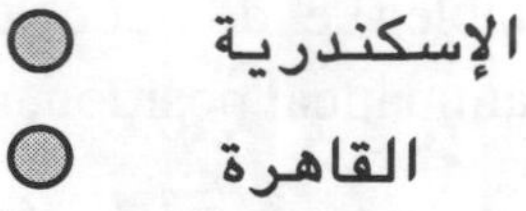

Remember that شَـمال is a noun, and in sentence 1 it forms an *iḍāfa* structure with the following noun.

However, if you use a prepositional phrase containing a geographical direction, the relationship is a little different, as in sentence 2:

٢ تَقَعُ الإسكندريةُ في شَمالِ مِصر. أو...
تَقَعُ الإسكندريةُ في شَماليِّ مِصر.

In sentence 2, the relationship is inclusive; that is, we are told that Alexandria is *in northern* Egypt, not to the north of something. Again, graphically, this relationship may represented as follows:

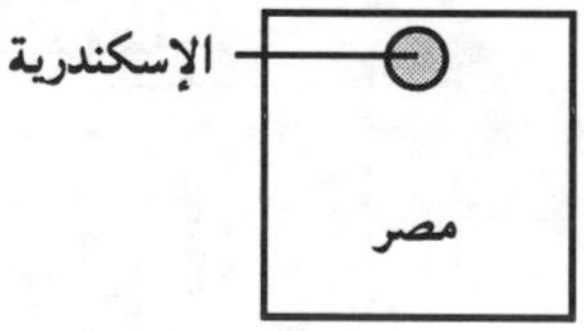

The word شَماليّ in the alternative sentence in 2 is a *nisba* noun.

2. The Noun كِلا

The word كِـلا is a singular masculine noun which has a dual meaning. It also has a feminine form (كِلتا). Both the masculine and feminine forms usually constitute an *iḍāfa* structure with another noun:

٣ كِلا الكتابين كُتِبَ بالعربية.

٤ كِلتا السيارتَينِ أتَتْ مِن ديترويت.

Note that the verbs that have reference to a noun phrase containing كِـلا have singular reference, because this noun is singular despite the fact that it has a dual meaning.

The nouns كلا and كلتا are invariable (i.e. do not change form) when they form an *iḍāfa* with a noun, regardless of their grammatical position, as in 3-8.

٥ قَرَأتُ كلا الكتابَين.

٦ زُرْنا كلتا المَدينتَين.

٧ كَتَبْتُ إلى كلا الطالبين.

٨ أعْرِفُ طُلّاباً مِن كلتا الجامِعَتَين.

However, the final *alif* in كلا and كلتا changes into ي (كِلَي، كِلتَي) when these nouns form an *iḍāfa* with an attached pronoun and refer at the same time to a noun that is the object of a verb (9) or a preposition (10):

٩ قَرَأتُ الكِتابَينِ كِلَيْهما.

١٠ اسْتَمتَعنا بِالزيارتَين كِلتَيْهما.

تمرين ١٢

Convey these meanings in Arabic, using appropriate forms of كلا.

1. Arabic and Hebrew are Semitic (ساميّ) languages, and both of them are written from right to left.
2. Both his sisters study medicine at this university.
3. I read both his letters.
4. There is a telephone in both houses.

3. Expressing Exception with إلاّ and غَيْر

Exception may be expressed with several words. So far, you are familiar with three of them. As you may recall, ما عَدا is used to express exception, where the following noun is مَنصوب, as it is considered the object of ما عَدا (see Lesson 23):

١١ أتى جَميعُ الطُلّابِ ما عَدا واحداً.

a. The word إلاّ is a particle used for exception, and it has no effect grammatically on the excepted noun (the noun immediately following it) if the sentence in which it is used is **negative** and the noun from which exception is made is not mentioned. The case of the excepted noun in such a sentence is determined according to its position in the sentence, as though إلاّ does not exist:

١٢ ما وَصَلَ إلاّ أحْمَدُ.

١٣ لا تُحِبُّ أختي إلاّ الحِمَّصَ.

١٤ لا يُطِلُّ الأردُنُّ إلاّ عَلى البَحرِ الأحْمَر.

In 12, the noun is مَرفوع because it is the doer of the action. In 13, it is the object of the verb and, therefore, مَنصوب. In 14, it is مَجرور because it is the object of a preposition.

b. In an **affirmative** sentence, the particle إلاّ causes the excepted noun, which follows it immediately, to be منصوب regardless of its position in the sentence.

١٥ وَصَلَ الطلاّبُ إلاّ خالداً.

١٦ نَظَّفَ الرَجُلُ كُلَّ السيّاراتِ إلاّ سيّارَتَك.

١٧ كَتَبْتُ إلى كُلِّ أصْدِقائي إلاّ واحِداً مِنهُم.

c. **The noun** غَيْر: This noun is used to express exception. However, since غَيْر is a noun, the excepted noun that follows it forms with it an *idāfa* and, therefore, must be مَجرور. Nonetheless, the case of غَير itself is determined just as the case of the excepted noun after إلاّ is determined; that is, غَير must be مَنصوب in affirmative sentences (18) and must acquire the case appropriate for its position in negative sentences (19-21):

١٨ وَصَلَ الطُلابُ غيرَ خالِدٍ (= إلاّ خالداً).

١٩ ما وَصَلَ طُلاّبٌ غَيْرُ خالدٍ.

٢٠ لا تَعْرِفُ أُمّي غَيْرَ العَرَبيّة.

٢١ ما كَتَبْتُ لِغيرِ خالِدٍ.

In 19, غَيْر is the doer of the action, in 20 it is the object of the verb, and in 21 it is the object of the preposition لِ.

تمرين ١٣

Express these meanings in Arabic, using إلاّ or غَيْر.

1. I haven't seen anything but books in his room.
2. He wrote to no one but his teacher.
3. No one came but your brother.

تمرين ١٤

١ـ اسْتَمِعْ إلى النَصِّ ثُمَّ اكتبْ على الخَريطَة اسمَ البَلَدِ الَّذي يَصِفُهُ النَصُّ واسمَ مُدُنِه وجِبالِه وسُهولِهِ والبِلادَ الَّتي تَحُدُّه مِن كُلِّ جانِب.

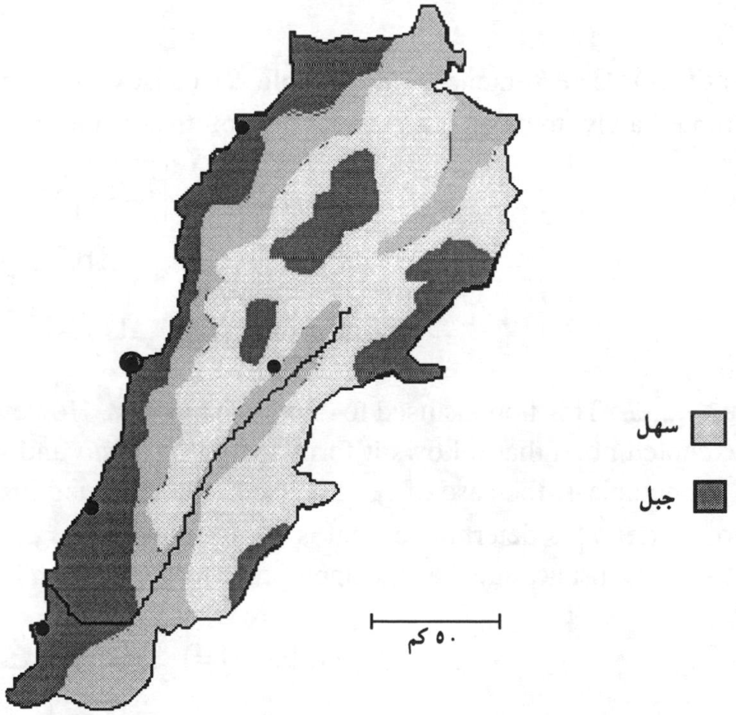

أجِبْ عَنِ الأسْئِلَةِ التالية.

٢ـ لماذا تُعتبَر عاصِمَةُ هذا البَلَدِ العاصِمةَ التِجاريّةَ لِلشَرق الأوسط؟

٣ـ ما المُنتَجاتُ الزِراعيّةُ في هذا البَلَد؟

٤ـ اَلسُهولُ أكْثَرُ في هذا القُطرِ أمِ الجِبالُ ؟ (أ+السُهولُ)

المُفْرَدات

Asia	آسيا (n., f.)
to overlook (s.t.)	أطلَّ (يطِلُّ) إطْلال (v.)
Atlantic	أطلَسيّ (adj.)
to consider	اعتَبَرَ (يَعتَبِرُ) اعتِبار (v.)
Africa	إفريقية (n., f.)
region	إقليم ج أقاليم (n., m.)
to produce	أنتَجَ (يُنتِجُ) إنتاج (v.)
to be interrupted, to be severed	انقَطَعَ (يَنقَطِعُ) انقِطاع (v.)
Iran	إيران
semiarid desert	بادِية ج بَوادٍ (n., f.)
merchandise, goods	بِضاعة ج بَضائِع (n., f.)
to consist of, to comprise	تَألَّفَ (يتَألَّفُ) تَألُّف (v.)
dates	تَمْر ج تُمور (n., m.)
mountain	جَبَل ج جِبال (n., m.)
island	جَزيرة ج جُزُر (n., f.)
geography	جغرافية (n., m.)
south	جَنوب (n., m.)
device, apparatus, appliance	جِهاز ج أجهِزة (n., m.)
to border, to demarcate, to limit	حَدَّ (يَحُدُّ) حَدّ (v.)
border, edge, boundary, borderline	حَدّ ج حُدود (n., m.)
map	خَريطة ج خَرائِط (n., f.)
fertile	خَصيب (adj.)
gulf, bay	خَليج ج خُلجان (n., m.)
passenger, rider	راكِب ج رُكّاب (n., m.)
to irrigate, to water	رَوى (يَروي) رَيّ (v.)
to plant, to cultivate	زَرَعَ (يَزرَعُ) زَرْع، زِراعة (v.)
coast, shore	ساحِل ج سَواحِل (n., m.)
range, series, chain	سِلسِلة ج سَلاسِل (n., f.)

plain	سَهل ج سُهول (n., m.)
semi-, quasi, similarity	شِبْه ج أشباه (n., m.)
emblem, sign, slogan	شعار ج شعارات، أشعِرة (n., m.)
to form, to constitute	شَكَّلَ (يُشَكِّلُ) تَشكيل (v.)
to flow into	صَبَّ (يصُبُّ) صَبّ (v.)
desert	صَحْراء ج صَحاري (n., f.)
to manufacture, to make	صَنَعَ (يَصنَعُ) صِناعة (v.)
narrow, tight	ضَيِّق (adj.)
capital city	عاصِمة ج عَواصِم (n., f.)
high, elevated	عالٍ (العالي) (adj.)
several, multiple	عَديد (adj.)
flag, banner	عَلَم ج أعْلام (n., m.)
continent	قارّة ج قارّات (n., f.)
country (almost exclusively used for Arab countries)	قُطْر ج أقْطار (n., m.)
cotton	قُطْن (n., m.)
wheat	قَمْح (n., m.)
both	كِلا (n.)
what	ما (adverbial particle)
ocean	مُحيط ج مُحيطات (n., m.)
square	مُرَبَّع (adj.)
area	مِساحة ج مِساحات (n., f.)
Mexico	المَكسيك
product	مُنْتَج ج مُنتَجات (n., m.)
outlet	مَنْفَذ ج مَنافذ (n., m.)
to spring, to originate, to flow	نَبَعَ (يَنبُعُ) نَبْع (v.)
textile, tissue, fabric	نَسيج (n., m.)
petroleum, crude oil	نِفْط (n., m.)
Pacific	الهادي (adj.)
middle, central	وَسَط ج أوساط (n., m.)

Lesson Twenty-Eight الدَرْسُ الثامِنُ والعِشرون

Objectives

- Describing events (television and radio programs).
- Expressing obligation with على ... أن.
- Expressing possibility with يُمكِنُ.
- The particle لَمْ.
- The structure لم يَعُدْ.
- The relative noun ما.
- The particle أنْ after adverbs of time.
- The noun بِضْعُ.
- Listen to recorded material for this lesson and sample Arabic songs.
- Do relevant computer drills and exercises, Stages 10 and 11.

الإذاعَةُ والتلفاز

في الولاياتِ المتحدة والوَطنِ العربي

مِن يَومِيّاتِ عَدنان مارتيني

مُنذُ أنْ أتَيتُ إلى الولاياتِ المُتَّحِدةِ لَمْ أعُدْ أشاهِدُ التلفازَ كَما كُنْتُ أشاهِدُهُ في حَلَب، رُبَّما لأنَّني الآنَ مَشغولٌ بِدِراسَتي ولَيْسَ عِندي الوَقتُ لِمُشاهدةِ البَرامِجِ والمُسَلسَلاتِ الكثيرة. لكِنَّني أشاهِدُ الأخبارَ كلَّ يَومٍ صَباحاً قَبلَ أنْ أذْهَبَ إلى الجامِعةِ ومَساءً بَعدَ عَودَتي مِنها، وأشاهِدُ كَذلِكَ بَعضَ المُسَلسَلاتِ أحْياناً.

أشاهد غالباً برنامجَ «صَباحُ الخَيْرِ يا أمريكا» عَلى القَناةِ ستة في الساعةِ السابِعةِ صَباحاً مِن مَحطّةِ «إي بي سي». نَشْرَةُ الأخبارِ في هذهِ المحطّةِ مُدّتُها نِصفُ ساعةٍ لكِنَّها سَريعة. يَقرأُ المُذيعُ أو المُذيعةُ الخَبَرَ في بِضعِ دَقائِقَ ثُمَّ تَظهَرُ الإعلاناتُ التِجاريّة. وهذهِ الإعلاناتُ تَظهرُ في أيِّ وَقتٍ خِلالَ المُسلسَلاتِ والأفلامِ والبَرامِجِ، وهذا شَيءٌ لا يُعجِبُني.

في المَساءِ أشاهِدُ الأخبارَ أوّلاً على القناةِ ٣٤ مِن مَحطّةِ «پي بي إس»، ونَشرةُ الأخبارِ في هذهِ المحطّةِ طويلةٌ وفيها أخبارٌ مِن أمريكا والعالَمِ وكَذلِكَ مُقابَلاتٌ مَعَ أشخاصٍ عَديدين. تَبُثُّ هذهِ المَحطّةُ بَرامِجَ عِلميّةً مُمتازة عنِ الحَيَواناتِ والطَبيعة، وهي مَحَطّةٌ عامّة ولَيْسَتْ تِجاريّة. حينَ يكونُ عِندي وَقتٌ أفَضِّلُ أنْ أشاهِدَ هذهِ البَرامِج.

في الساعةِ السادسةِ والنِصفِ أشاهِدُ الأخبارَ على إحْدى القَنَواتِ الّتي تَبُثُّ عَليها المحطّاتُ التِجاريّةُ «إن بي سي» و«سي بي إس». أشاهِدُ أحياناً بَعضَ المُسَلسَلاتِ مِثلَ «ساينفلد» و«فريجر» و«فريندز»، أيْ «الأصدِقاء». يُعجِبُني أيْضاً بَرنامَجَي «عِشرين على عِشرين» و«سِتّونَ دقيقة».

يوجَدُ في أمريكا نِظامان لِلبَثِّ التِلفزيوني واحِدٌ لاسِلكيّ وهو مَجّانيّ والآخَرُ سِلكيّ (ويُسَمّى كيبل هُنا) ويُمْكِنُ أنْ تَحصُلَ عليهِ مُقابِلَ اشتِراكٍ شَهريّ. يَحْصُلُ الناسُ مِنَ النِظامِ اللاسِلكيّ عَلى المحطّاتِ الكبيرةِ الثلاث (سي بي إس، أي بي سي، إن بي سي) بِالإضافةِ إلى «پي بي إس» (المَحَطّةِ العامّة) وكذلِكَ مَحَطةِ «فوكس».

أمّا النِظامُ السِلكيُّ فَفيهِ عَشَراتُ القَنَواتِ لِلأفلامِ السينَمائيةِ والأطفالِ والتاريخِ والعُلومِ والموسيقا وبَيعِ البَضائعِ التِجاريّةِ وغَيْرِ ذلكَ كثير. شاهدتُ مَرّةً قَناةَ «ديسكڤري» وأعْجَبَتْني جِداً بِسَبَبِ البَرامِجِ العِلميّةِ الّتي تَبُثُّها يَومِيّاً.

حينَ أقرأُ دُروسي مَساءً في الشَقّةِ أحِبُّ أنْ أسْتَمِعَ إلى الإذاعةِ وهُناكَ عَدَدٌ كَبيرٌ مِنَ المحطات. أستَمِعُ عادةً إلى ما يُعجِبُني مِنَ الأغاني والموسيقا مِن مَحطّاتٍ

عَلى المَوجةِ «إف إم» لكِنَّ هُناكَ أَيْضاً مَحطّاتٌ كثيرةٌ على المَوجَةِ المُتَوَسِّطة. إذاعَتي المُفَضَّلةُ هي الإذاعةُ العامّة «إن پي آر» لأنَّ فيها أخباراً وبرامجَ مُمتازة. في الشُهورِ الأولى حينَ أتَيْتُ إلى الوِلاياتِ المُتَّحِدةِ كُنْتُ أستَمِعُ إلَيها عِدّةَ ساعاتٍ كُلَّ يوم وساعَدَتني كَثيراً في تَحسينِ لُغَتي الإنكليزيّة.

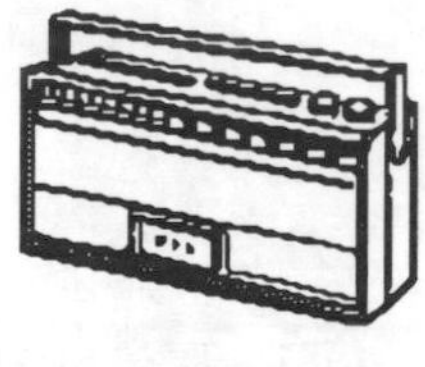
جهاز راديو

غلوريا إستِفان

مادونا

ستيڤي وَندَر

أمّا مِن أجلِ الأغاني والموسيقا فأستَمِعُ إلى عِدّةِ مَحطّات. تُعجِبُني الموسيقا الحَديثة وأغاني «ستيڤي وَندَر» و«مادونا» و«غلوريا إستِفان» وغيرِهِم. لكِنَّ عِندي أيضاً أشْرِطةٌ لِمُغَنّينَ عَرَبٍ مِثلِ فَيروز وصَباح فَخري ووَديع الصافي وراغِب عَلامة ومُحَمَّد عَبدُه. وَصَلَتني هذهِ الأشرِطة مِن أخي رامي.

وَديع الصافي

راغِب عَلامة

فَريد الأطرَش

مِن يَومِيّات مايكل براون

مايكل براون

صِرتُ الآنَ أفهَمُ كَثيراً مِمّا أسمَعُ في الإذاعةِ والتِلفاز. أشاهِدُ التِلفاز ساعةً أو ساعتَين كلَّ يَومٍ مَساءً ويُساعِدُني هذا كثيراً في تَحسينِ لُغَتي العربية، الفَصيحةِ والعامِيّة. هُناكَ بَرامجُ بِالعَرَبيةِ الفَصيحةِ كَالأخبارِ والمقابلاتِ والبَرامجِ العِلميّة وغَيرِها. أمّا المُسَلسَلاتُ الإذاعيةُ والتِلفزيونيةُ فَمُعظَمُها بِالعامِيَّة، وأنا أريدُ تَحسينَهما كِلتَيهِما.

في شَهرِ رَمَضان بَثَّ التلفزيون المِصري بَرنامَجاً غِنائياً أحَبَّه مُعظَمُ المِصريين اسمُهُ «فَوازير رَمَضان»، وعَلِمتُ أنَّهُ يُبَثُّ أيْضاً في أقطارٍ عَرَبيةٍ أُخرى. قَدَّمَتْ هذا البَرنامَجَ اليَومِيَّ مُمَثِّلةٌ ومُغَنِيَّةٌ اسمُها «نيللي»، كانَت تَرقُصُ وتُغَنّي أغنيةً تَصِفُ فيها شَيئاً وكان عَلى مُشاهِدي البَرنامَج أن يَحزِروا هذا الشَيء. لكِنّي لَم أحْزِرْ أيَّ شَيءٍ وَصَفَتْه.

مُعظَمُ المِصريينَ يُحِبّونَ أمَّ كُلثوم ويَسمَعونَها كُلَّ يَوم. كانَت أمُّ كُلثوم مُغَنِيّةً مَشهورةً جِداً في مِصرَ وفي كُلِّ الوَطَنِ العَرَبيّ. بَدَأت الغِناءَ في العِشرينات وغَنَّتْ دونَ انقِطاع في مِصرَ وفي عَدَدٍ مِنَ الأقطارِ العَرَبيّةِ حَتّى تُوُفيَت في عامِ ١٩٧٥.

عبد الحليم حافظ

أم كُلثوم

ومِنَ المُغنّين المَشهورين الّذين ماتوا ولا يَزالُ الناسُ يَسمَعونَ أغانيَهُم ويُحِبّونَها مُحَمَّد عبدُ الوَهّاب وفَريدُ الأطْرَش وعَبدُ الحَليم حافِظ وفايزة أحمَد وغيرُهم.

طَبْعاً هُناكَ عَدَدٌ كبيرٌ مِنَ المُغَنّين الأحياء، ومِن أشهرِهِم اليَوم وَردَة الجَزائرية ومَيّادة حِنّاوي وعَمْرو[8] دياب. الأولى أتَتْ إلى القاهِرة مِنَ الجزائر في الستينات، والثانية مِن سورية، أما الأخير فَهُوَ مِصري.

وردة الجزائرية

ميّادة حِنّاوي

هُناكَ طَبعاً مُغنّون ومُغنّيات في الأقطارِ العَرَبيةِ الأخرى. مُغَنيَتي المُفَضَّلَة مِن غَيْرِ المِصريّات هي فَيروز. لا تُسمَعُ أغانيها في مِصر كثيراً لكنَّها مُسَجَّلةٌ على أشرِطة و مَوجودةٌ في السوق. بَدَأَتْ فَيروزُ الغِناءَ في لُبنانَ وسورية في الخَمسيناتِ وهي لاتَزالُ تُغَنّي إلى الآن. صَوتُ فَيروز جَميلٌ جِداً ويُحِبُّهُ اللبنانيونَ والسوريونَ خُصوصاً. كانَت مُتَزَوِّجةً مِن عاصي الرَحَباني الّذي كانَ موسيقِياً مُمْتازاً، ولَها ابنٌ مِنه اسمُه زِياد الرَحَباني وهو موسيقيٌ ومُغَنٍّ أيضاً. غَنَّتْ فَيروزُ في مُعظَمِ الأقطارِ العربيةِ وفي أوروبا وأوستراليا والولاياتِ المتحدةِ حَيثُ كانَت أولَ مُغَنيةٍ عَرَبيّةٍ تُغَنّي في قاعَةِ «كارنِغي» في نيويورك وكانَ ذلِكَ في ٢٩ أيلول ١٩٧٢.

فَيروز

[8] This name is pronounced عَمْر. The final و is silent.

بَرامِجُ إذاعة وتلفزيون

من الجرائدِ العربية

هُناكَ مَحَطّةُ إذاعةٍ أو أكثَر مَحَطّةُ تِلفزيونٍ أو أكثر في كُلِّ قُطرٍ عَربي. يوجدُ اليومَ أيْضاً مَحطاتٌ فَضائيةٌ، أيْ بَرامجُ تِلفزيونيةٌ مِن عِدّةِ أقطارٍ عَربيةٍ تُبَثُّ مِن خِلالِ القَمَرِ الصِناعيِّ العربيِّ «عَرَبسات».

الفضائية المغربية

١٢,١٥	نور الإيمان، صلاة الجمعة، الأخبار
١,٣٠	السلسلة العربية التاريخية «ميراث السنين»
٢,٣٠	النشرة الجوية
٣,٠٠	«مرايا» برنامج عن المرأة
٣,٣٠	الفلم العربي «القانون واللعبة»
٥,٣٠	الأخبار الدولية
٥,٥٥	ألعاب القوى من مدينة كولونيا
٨,٣٠	الجريدة المتلفزة الرئيسية
٩,١٠	ركن المفتي
٩,٣٥	السهرة السينمائية العربية «لعبة الانتقام»
١١,٠٠	منوعات غنائية
١١,١٥	الأخبار الأخيرة
١١,٣٠	حفلات أقيمت بالمغرب
١,٢٠	ما تيسر من الذكر الحكيم
١,٣٠	ختام البرامج

تلفزيون

١,٠٠	صور وموسيقا
٣,٣٠	برنامج أجنبي
٤,٠٠	لبنان هذا النهار
٤,٣٠	رسوم متحركة
٥,٠٠	ستاديوم
٥,٣٠	رياضة من حول العالم
٦,٠٠	الأرض الطيبة
٦,٣٠	برنامج عربي
٧,٣٠	أخبار لبنان والعالم هذا المساء
٨,٠٠	برنامج أجنبي
٨,٣٠	فيلم أجنبي
١٠,٠٠	أوتوغراف
١١,٠٠	خليك بالبيت
١٢,٠٠	أخبار آخر السهرة

يُمكنُكَ أنْ تَقرأَ بَرامِجَ الإذاعةِ والتِلفزيون في مُعظَمِ الجَرائدِ العربيةِ، بِما في ذلِكَ بَرامِجُ المحطاتِ الفَضائيةِ. في ما يَلي بَعضُ هذهِ البَرامِجِ مِن جرائدَ عَربيةٍ. اقرأها

وحاوِلْ أنْ تَعرِفَ مِن أيِّ قُطرٍ عربي كلٌّ مِن هذِهِ البَرامج، وهَل هي بَرامِجُ إذاعيةٌ أو تِلفزيونية.

القناة الأولى

٧,٠٠ صباح الخير يا مصر والقرآن الكريم ومن أقوال الصحف
١٠,١٣ سينما الأطفال
١١,٠٧ نشرة الأخبار
١١,٢٧ مجلة المرأة
١٢,٢٠ إذاعة خارجية
١,٣٠ مسلسل سر الأرض
١,٤٩ اللقاء الأسبوعي للشيخ الشعراوي
٢,٣٥ مع النجوم
٢,٤٦ فلم الزهور الفاتنة
٤,٥٨ لقاء الأجيال
٥,٢٨ صندوق الدنيا
٦,٠٠ الأخبار وحدث في مثل هذا اليوم
٦,٣٠ رسالة مهرجان القراءة للجميع
٧,٣٠ مسلسل من الذي لا ينساك
٨,٣٠ حديث الروح
٩,٠٠ الأخبار
٩,٥٣ فكّر ثواني واكسب دقائق
١١,٣٦ حلقتان من مسلسل الفرسان
١٢,٠٠ آخر الأنباء
١,١٠ مسلسل ألف ليلة وليلة
١,٤٢ فوازير أم العريف
٢,٠٨ ابتسامة آخر الليل
٢,٣٣ القرآن الكريم

برامج الإذاعة

٥,٢٧ الافتتاح
٦,١٥ الأخبار الأولى
٦,٤٥ معكم على الهواء
١١,٣٠ مسابقة الأغاني المحلية
١,٠٠ قصص من العالم
١,٣٠ الشرطة في خدمة الشعب
٢,١٥ الأخبار الثالثة
٣,٠٠ برنامج قصة في تمثيلية
٤,١٥ المجلة الاقتصادية
٥,٠٠ المسلسل اليومي
٥,٣٠ صوت القوات المسلحة
٦,٠٠ في رحاب اللغة
٨,٠٠ حكاية شاعر
١٠,٠٠ سورية اليوم
١٢,٠٠ الشعر والليل موعدنا
١٢,٣٠ معالم من الوطن العربي الكبير
١,١٥ الأخبار السابعة
١,٣٠ شخصيات روائية
٢,١٥ آخر المشوار

تمرين ١

أجِب عن هذه الأسئِلة حسَب النص.

١- ما الّذي ساعدَ عَدنان على تَحسينِ لُغَتِهِ الإنكليزية؟

٢- أين شاهد عَدنان بَرامِجَ عَن الحَيَوانات؟

٣- اكتُبْ اسمَ أحدِ البَرامِجِ التلفزيونيةِ في رَمَضان بِمِصر؟

٤- مَن المُغنّي المشهور مِنَ المُغنّينَ الأحياء في مِصر؟

٥- كَم نَشرةَ أخبارٍ يَبُثُّ التلفزيون المِصري؟

٦- في أيِّ وَقتٍ تَبدأ بَرامِجُ الإذاعةِ السوريةِ ومَتى تَنتَهي؟

٧- ما اسمُ بَرنامَجِ المرأةِ في التلفزيون المَغربي؟

٨- ما الكلمةُ المُستَعمَلَةُ في المغربِ بَدَلاً مِن «مَسلسَل»؟

٩- مَتى يُمكِنُ أنْ تَسمَعَ الموسيقا والأغاني في تلفزيون لُبنان؟

١٠- ما البَرنامَجُ الّذي يُبَثُّ مِن مِصرَ في الساعةِ السادِسَةِ مَساءً. اشرحْهُ كَما تَفهَمُهُ بِالعَربيّةِ أو الإنكليزيّة.

اكتب اسمَ الشخصِ أو الشيءِ الّذي تَصِفُهُ الجُمَلَ التالية:

١١- هِيَ مِنَ الجَزائر.

١٢- يُشاهِدُهُ عَدنان مِن مَحطّةِ «إن بي سي».

١٣- هي بِالعاميّةِ المِصرية.

١٤- يُحِبُّها اللُبنانيونَ والسوريون.

اكتُبْ «خَطَأ» أو «صَواب» جانِبَ كلِّ جُملةٍ وصَحِّح الجُمَلَ الخَطَأ.

١٥- كانَ عَدنان يُشاهِدُ التِلفزيون في حَلَبَ أكثَرَ مِن أمريكا.

١٦- لا تُعجِبُ عَدنان الإعلاناتُ التِجارية.

١٧- عَلى مُشاهِدي بَرنامَج «فَوازير رَمَضان» أنْ يُغَنّوا مَعَ المُغَنية.

١٨- تُوُفِيَتْ فايزة أحمَد عامَ ١٩٧٥.

١٩- يُبَثُّ مُسَلسَلُ «ألف لَيلة ولَيلة» مِنَ التِلفزيون المَغربي.

٢٠- «ابتسامةُ آخِرِ اللَيل» هي آخِرُ فِقرةٍ في التلفزيون المِصري.

عَرِّف العبارات التالية حَسَبَ النصّ(define these phrases according to the text):

٢١- التِلفاز السِلكي

٢٢- اللُغَة العَربية الفَصيحة

٢٣- فَوازير رَمَضان

٢٤- زياد الرَحباني

٢٥- مَعالِم من الوَطَنِ العربي الكبير

٢٦- رِياضة مِن حَولِ العالَم

اختَر التكمِلة المناسبة حَسَب النَص.

٢٧- يُشاهِدُ عَدنان الأخبارَ ......

❑ صَباحاً ❑ مَساءً

❑ صَباحاً وظُهراً ❑ صَباحاً ومَساءً

٢٨- نَشرةُ الأخبارِ في المحطّاتِ التِجارية الأمِريكية ......

❑ طَويلة ❑ سَريعة ❑ جَميلة ❑ قَصيرة

٢٩- تَظهَرُ الإعلاناتُ التِجاريةُ ...... الأخبارِ في أمريكا.

❑ دونَ ❑ قَبلَ ❑ بَعدَ ❑ خِلالَ

٣٠- مَحطّةُ «بي بي إس» ......

❑ طَويلة ❑ تِجارية ❑ عامّة ❑ عِلميّة

٣١- نِظامُ البَثِّ التلفزيوني اللاسلكي ......

❑ مَجّاني	❑ عِلمي	❑ عَديد	❑ عاميّ

٣٢ـ المغنية المُفضّلة في مِصر هي ......

❑ فَيروز	❑ أمّ كُلثوم	❑ مادونا	❑ فَريد الأطرَش

٣٣ـ غنّتْ فَيروز في ......

❑ لُبنان	❑ الوَطَنِ العَرَبيّ

❑ أوروبا وأمريكا	❑ كُلِّ ما سَبَق

٣٤ـ هُناكَ ...... نَشَراتِ أخبارٍ في الإذاعة السورية.

❑ أربعُ	❑ خَمسُ	❑ سِتُّ	❑ سَبعُ

٣٥ـ يُمكِنُ أنْ يُشاهَدَ التلفزيون المغربي في لُبنان مِن خِلالِ ......

❑ القَمَرِ الصِناعي العَرَبيّ	❑ مَحَطّةٍ تلفزيونيةٍ مَغربية

❑ البَثِّ التلفزيوني المِصري	❑ الإذاعةِ المَغربيّة

تمرين ٢

وافِق بَين الكلمات التالية.

١ـ إذاعة	....	مُمتاز

٢ـ قناة	....	سوق

٣ـ إعلانات	....	أكثر

٤- توفيَ	....	بَثّ

٥ـ مُغَنٍّ	....	مَوجة

٦ـ جَيِّد	....	عامية

٧ـ فَصيحة	....	أغنية

٨ـ مُعظَم	....	تجارة

مات

تمرين ٣

اكتبْ بَرنامَجَ إحدى مَحطّاتِ الإذاعةِ أو التلفزيون الّتي تَسمَعُها أو تُشاهِدُها أو جُزْءاً مِنه.

تمرين ٤

اختَر الكلِمة التي لا تُناسِب باقي الكلمات في كُلٍّ مَجموعة وبَيِّن السَبَب.

١ـ	بَرنامَج	مُسَلسَل	أخبار	لُغة
٢ـ	بَثّ	مَجّاني	قَناة	مَوجة
٣ـ	عَودة	موسيقا	أغنية	مُغَنِية
٤ـ	حَيَوان	طَبيعة	تِجارة	أشجار
٥ـ	مَوْجة	إذاعة	مَحَطّة	مَجّانيّ

تمرين ٥

صَنِّف كلِماتٍ مِن هذا الدَرس تَحتَ الفِئات التالية.

List words that occurred in this lesson under the following categories.

١ـ محطات تلفزيون	٢ـ مسلسلات	٣ـ برامج	٤ـ إذاعة	٥ـ مغنون ومغنيات	٦ـ لغة

تمرين ٦

أكمِل الجُمَلَ بالكلمة المناسبة.

١ـ أشاهِدُ مُسَلسَلي المُفَضَّل على ...... سِتّة.

❑ المَحَطّة ❑ القَناة ❑ اللاسِلكي ❑ المَوجَة

٢ـ تُريدُ أختي أنْ تَعملَ ...... بَعدَ تَخَرُّجِها.

❑ فَصيحة ❑ عاميّة ❑ أُغنِية ❑ مُذيعة

٣ـ شاهَدْتُ ...... على التِلفاز مَعَ المُغنِية مَيّادة حنّاوي.

❑ مُقابَلة ❑ موسيقا ❑ مُمتازة ❑ مُسَلسَلاً

٤ـ ...... إلى الأغاني مِن مُسَجِّلتي.

❑ أستمِعُ ❑ أشاهِدُ ❑ أفهَمُ ❑ أحَسِّنُ

٥ـ أختي الكبيرة ...... مِن رجل جَزائري.

❑ مُغَنية ❑ مُمَثِّلة ❑ مُتَزَوِّجة ❑ موسيقيّة

تمرين ٧

أعِدْ تَرتيبَ الكلمات في كُلِّ مَجموعة لِتَشكِّلَ جُمَلاً مُفيدة.

١ـ مِن ـ إلى ـ المفضّلة ـ المُسجِّلة ـ أغانيَّ ـ أستَمِعُ

٢ـ دِمَشقَ ـ صَباحاً ـ إذاعةُ ـ الخامسة ـ بَثُّها ـ تَبدأ ـ الساعةِ ـ في

٣ـ مُذيعةً ـ إذاعةِ ـ أختُ ـ محطةِ ـ في ـ حَلَب ـ تَعمَلُ ـ صَديقي

تمرين ٨

أعِدْ تَرتيبَ الجُمَلِ لِتَشكِّلَ فِقرةً مُفيدةً دونَ تغييرِ مَكانِ الجُملةِ الأولى.

١ـ أوّلُ شَيءٍ أفعَلُهُ صَباحاً هو الذهابُ إلى الحَمّام.

بَعدَ مُشاهدةِ مُسَلسَلي المفضّل أنامُ نِصفَ ساعةٍ فَقَط.

في الساعةِ الثامِنة صَباحاً أذهَبُ إلى عَمَلي.

في المَساءِ أشاهِدُ أنا وزَوجي فيلماً مِنَ التِلفاز أو من شَريط مُسَجَّل.

بَعدَ ذلكَ أجلِسُ أمامَ التِلفاز وأشاهِدُ الأخبارَ خِلالَ تَناوُلِ الفَطور.

حينَ أعودُ إلى البَيتِ بَعدَ الظُهرِ أشاهِدُ مُسَلسَلي المُفَضَّل.

خِلالَ العَمَلِ أستَمِعُ إلى الإذاعة.

1. Expressing Obligation with على ... أنْ

In English, obligation may be expressed with *must, ought to, have to*, among other words. Similarly, in Arabic, there are multiple ways for doing that. In this lesson, the structure

على ... أن is introduced. This structure starts with a preposition, but a deleted verb that precedes it is implied (يجب *"must"*). The preposition على is immediately followed by a noun or a noun phrase, as in this sentence which occurred in this lesson.

١ على مُشاهِدي البَرنامَج أنْ يَحزِروا هذا الشَيء.

The viewers of the show should guess what this thing is.

In this example, على is followed by a noun phrase which is an *iḍāfa* (مشاهدي البرنامج) (refer to Lesson 17 for a discussion of the form of dual and plural *iḍāfa* structures). This noun phrase acts as the agent, or the entity supposed to do the action. It is in the genitive case (مجرور). The action is expressed in the form of a verb preceded by the particle أنْ. This particle must be followed by (مضارع منصوب), a mood of the present tense (refer to Lesson 24 for a discussion of المضارع المنصوب).

The preposition على in this structure may also be followed by a pronoun. Remember, however, that the final *alif* in على changes into a *yā'* when a suffix (a pronoun) is attached to it. Thus, if you want to replace the noun with a corresponding pronoun in example 1, it would look as follows:

٢ عليهم أنْ يَحزِروا هذا الشَيء. *They should guess what this thing is.*

Moreover, instead of the verbal phrase أنْ يحزروا, you may use the verbal noun:

٣ عليهِم حَزْرُ هذا الشَيء. *They should guess what this thing is.*

If you want to use the past tense with such structures, insert the verb كان at the beginning of the sentence:

٤ كان عَلَينا أنْ نَحزِرَ هذا الشَيء. *We had to guess what this thing was.*

تمرين ٩

Express these meanings in Arabic, using على... أنْ.

1. The students must come to class at seven o'clock.
2. You have to write a letter to your teacher.
3. Her father had to carry her from the car to the house.
4. I must wash my mother's car tomorrow.

2. **Expressing Possibility with the Verb أمكَنَ**

One way of expressing possibility is with the verb أمكَنَ (to be possible). This is a regular verb that varies according to tense, number, and gender. It normally has a subject (doer of the action, or فاعل). However, its direct object may be either a verbal noun:

٥ هَلْ يُمكِنُكَ مُساعَدَتي؟ *Can you help me?*

or a verbal phrase starting with the particle أن:

٦ هَلْ يُمكِنُكَ أنْ تُساعِدَني؟

The doer of the action (فاعل) (i.e. agent) in examples 5 and 6 is in the form of a pronoun (ك). The فاعل can be, however, a noun:

٧ هَلْ يُمكِنُ أحمَدُ أنْ يُساعِدَني؟ *Can Ahmed help me?*

Remember that certain verbs can take a direct object either as a noun or as an attached pronoun (e.g. ساعَدَ "help"). Attached pronouns serving as direct objects are the same as those attached to nouns except for the first person singular. In 5 above, مُساعَدَتي is a noun with the suffix ي (*my*). In 6, تُساعِدَني is a verb with the attached pronoun ي as well. However, the verb and the pronoun are separated by an intervening letter ن that has no grammatical function.

In sum, the first person singular pronoun attached to nouns is ي, e.g. بَيتي. The first person singular pronoun attached to verbs is ني, e.g. شاهَدَني.

3. **The Structure لَمْ يَعُدْ**

This structure uses the verb عادَ (يَعود) "to return." Its meaning, however, is equivalent to the English phrase "no longer," as in:

Ahmed no longer lives here. ٨ لَمْ يَعُدْ أحمَدُ يَسكُنُ هُنا.

Note that the verb in the phrase لَمْ يَعُدْ is مُضارِع مَجزوم (jussive) followed by a present tense verb, which provides present tense reference. Both verbs have the same agreement with the doer of the action. That is, both are, in the jussive case, third person masculine singular. If the doer of the action were سلمى, for example, both verbs must be feminine:

٩ لَمْ تَعُدْ سَلمى تَسكُنُ هُنا.

تمرين ١٠

تَرجِمْ إلى العَربيةِ ما يلي (translate the following into Arabic):

1. Mrs. Boustani no longer eats in the cafeteria.
2. Khalid is no longer a student in this school.
3. I no longer want to study chemistry.
4. Nizar and Hisham no longer play basketball.

4. The Relative Noun ما

The relative noun ما generally refers to inanimate, or nonrational, objects. In this sense, it is similar to "*what*," as in:

10 *I eat what I want.* آكُلُ ما أريد.

In the above example, ما stands for الشَيء الَّذي (refer to Lesson 25 for a discussion of relative nouns).

Prepositions may be prefixed to ما:

١١ لَمْ يُعجِبْني شَيءٌ مِمّا سَمِعتُ. *I didn't like what I heard.*

In the example above, مما is a combination of مِن and ما. Similar examples include:

١٢ لا أعرفُ عَمّا يَتَكلْمون. *I don't know what they are talking about.*

The word عَـمّا in 12 is made up of عَن and ما.

١٣ يُمكِنُكَ أنْ تَأتيَ إلى هُنا بِما علَيْكَ مِن مَلابِس.

You can come in whatever you are wearing.

تمرين ١١

تَرجِم إلى العربية ما يلي بِاسْتِعمالِ «ما»:

Translate into Arabic, using ما.

1. You may purchase these Arabic books with whatever US dollars you have on you.
2. Write down in Arabic what you have heard on the news bulletin.
3. I like what I see (what I see pleases me).
4. She is happy with what she has.

5. The Particle أنْ after Adverbs of Time

In English, you may use a sentence immediately after an adverb of time or place:

14 We had dinner after we had gone to the movies.

In Arabic, an adverb of time, such as بَعد and قَبل, must be followed by أنْ. Remember that أنْ must be followed by المُضارِع المَنصوب, as in 15:

١٥ تَناوَلنا العَشاءَ بَعدَ أنْ ذَهَبْنا إلى السينَما.

6. The Noun بِضْع

This noun is a quantifier and it refers to a number of things from three to about ten. Like numbers from 3 to 10, it has **reverse gender agreement** with the modified noun. That is, masculine nouns are modified by بِضْعة and feminine nouns by بِضْع. The noun بِضْع assumes a case consistent with its position in the sentence. The modified noun is always indefinite:

١٦ عِندي بِضْعُ صَديقات في الدارِ البَيضاء.

١٧ قَرَأتُ بِضْعَةَ كُتُبٍ عَن تاريخ أوروبا.

تمرين ١٢

Express the following meanings in Arabic with reference to Sections 5 and 6 above.

1. I read a few newspapers on the plane.
2. I'll eat an apple before I go to bed.
3. My friend bought a few books on the Arab world when she was in Tunis.
4. They went to the library after they had seen their favorite television series, *Friends.*

تمرين ١٣

اكتُبْ «خَطَأ» أو «صَواب» جانِبَ كلّ جُملة وصَحِّح الجُمَلَ الخَطَأ.

١- السيِّدة الّتي تَتَكَلَّمُ على الشَريطِ المُسجَّل مُتَزَوِّجة.

٢- مُسَلسَل «الجَوارِح» مِن دَولةِ الإمارات.

أجِب عن هذه الأسئلة حسب النص المسجَّل.

٣- لماذا يُعجِبُ هذه السيِّدة مُسَلسَلُ الجَوارِح؟

٤- أينَ تُشاهِدُ السَيِّدةُ البَرامِجَ التونِسية والمَغربية؟

اختر التكملة المناسبة حسب النص المسجَّل.

٥- صُوِّرَ مُسَلسَلُ «الجَوارِح» في ......

❑ الصَحراء ❑ سورية ❑ المغرِب

٦- مَوعِدُ مُسَلسَلِ «الجَوارِح» ......

❑ التاسعةَ صَباحاً ❑ التاسعةَ مَساءً ❑ الحاديةَ عَشرةَ

٧- لُغةُ مُسَلسَلِ «الجَوارِح» ......

❑ العاميّةُ السورية ❑ العاميّةُ المصرية ❑ العَربية الفَصيحة

٨- تُشاهِدُ السيِّدة المُسلسلاتِ العاميَّةَ مِن تلفزيون ......

❑ تونِس ❑ المَغرِب ❑ دِمَشقَ وعَمّان

أكمل الجمل التالية من النصّ المسجَّل.

٩- يَبُثُّ التلفزيون هذه الأيّام مُسَلسَلاً ......

١٠- هُناكَ طَبعاً مُسَلسَلاتٌ أُخرى لكِنَّها لَيْسَتْ تاريخيّة ......

المُفْرَدات

أجْل (مِن أجْلِ)	for the sake of, because of
إذاعَة ج –ات (n. f.)	broadcasting station
اسْتَمَعَ (يَسْتَمِعُ) اسْتِماع (v.)	to listen
اشْتَرَكَ (يَشْتَرِكُ) اشْتِراك (v.)	to enroll in, to subscribe to
أُغنِيَة ج أغانٍ (n., f.)	song
أمْكَنَ (يُمكِنُ) إمْكان (v.)	to be possible
بَثَّ (يَبُثُّ) بَثّ (v.)	to broadcast
بِضْع (n.)	a few
حَزَرَ (يحْزِرُ) حَزْر (v.)	to guess
حَسَّنَ (يحَسِّنُ) تَحْسين (v.)	to improve, to make better
حَيّ ج أحْياء (n., m.)	a living person
رَقَصَ (يرقُصُ) رَقْص (v.)	to dance
سِلْك ج أسْلاك (n., m.)	wire
شَريط ج أشْرِطَة (n., m.)	tape
شَخْص ج أشْخاص (n., m.)	person
طَبْعاً (adv.)	of course
طَبيعة (n., f.)	nature
طِفْل ج أطْفال (n., m.)	child
ظَهَرَ (يَظهَرُ) ظُهور (v.)	to appear, to become visible
عادَ (يعودُ) عَوْد (v.)	to go back, to return
عاميّ (adj.)	colloquial, common, dialectal
غَنّى (يُغَنّي) غِناء (v.)	to sing
فَزّورة ج فَوازير (n., f.)	riddle
فَصيح (adj.)	pure, good, clear, standard, or literary, Arabic
فَضاء (n., m.)	space

moon, satellite .... (n. m.) قَمَر ج أقْمار
channel .... (n., f.) قَناة ج قَنَوات
cable .... (n., m.) كيبِل
what .... (relative noun) ما
to die .... (v.) ماتَ (يموت) مَوْت
married man .... (n., m.) مُتَزَوِّج ج –ون
free of charge .... (adj.) مَجّانيّ
announcer .... (n., m.) مُذيع ج –ون
series, serial .... (n., m.) مُسَلسَل ج مَسَلسَلات
singer .... (n., m.) مُغَنٍّ ج –ون
interview .... (n. f.) مُقابَلة ج –ات
excellent .... (adj.) مُمْتاز ج –ون
actor, representative .... (n., m.) مُمَثِّل ج –ون
wave .... (n., f.) مَوْجة ج –ات
bulletin, report .... (n., f.) نَشْرة ج نَشَرات
system .... (n., m.) نِظام ج أنْظِمة

Lesson Twenty-Nine الدَرْسُ التاسِعُ والعِشرون

Objectives

- Professions.
- Describing activities in present, past, and future.
- Travel-related activities.
- The use of the particle فَـ.
- Functions of the particle قَدْ.
- البَدَل (substitution, the permutative).
- The particle إنْ.
- Listen to recorded material for this lesson.
- Do relevant computer drills and exercises, Stage 12.

عَدنان في مَدينةِ دِنْقَر

في عُطلةِ فَصلِ الربيعِ سافَرَ عَدنان مارتيني بِالطائرةِ مِن مَدينةِ كلمبس في أوهايو حَيثُ يَدرُسُ عِلمَ الحاسوبِ في جامِعةِ ولايةِ أوهايو إلى مَدينةِ دِنقَر عاصِمةِ ولايةِ كولورادو. نَزَلَ في دِنقَر في مَنزِلِ عائلةٍ أمريكيةٍ هي عائلةُ السَيِّدِ والسَيِّدةِ آلَن. تَستَضيفُ عائلةُ آلَن الطُلّابَ الأجانِبَ خِلالَ العُطلاتِ لِمُدّةِ أسبوعٍ أو أسبوعَين.

أوهايو وكولورادو على خريطة الولايات المتحدة

منزل عائلة آلن

يَعملُ السَيِّدُ تشارلز آلن صَحَفِيّاً ويَكتُبُ لِمَجلّةٍ في دنفر ولِصُحُفٍ ومَجلّاتٍ أُخرى في الولاياتِ المتحدة، وتَعملُ زَوجَتُهُ آليس مُحاسِبةً في مَصْرِفٍ. تشارلز وآليس لَهُما ابنٌ وابنة. الابنُ، واسمُهُ پول، طالبٌ في جامعة كولورادو في بولدَر حَيثُ يَدرُسُ العُلومَ السِياسيّةَ وهُو لاعِبُ كُرةِ قَدَمٍ أيْضاً. أمّا ابنَتُهُما هِذَر فَهيَ تَدرُسُ التِجارةَ في جامِعةِ كاليفورنيا في سانتا كروز وتَعملُ أيْضاً نادِلةً في مَطعَمٍ هُناكَ ثَلاثَ ساعاتٍ كلَّ يَوم.

هِذَر آلن نادِلة

السيد تشارلز آلن صَحَفيّ

پول آلن لاعِبُ كُرةِ قَدَم

زارَ عَدنان وَسَطَ المَدينةِ وعَدَداً مِنَ البُيوتِ القَديمة هُناك. وفي يَومِ السَبتِ حَضَرَ مَعَ عائِلةِ آلن مُباراةَ كُرةِ قَدَمٍ في مَلعَبِ المدينةِ الّذي يُسمّيهِ أهْلُها «المَلعَبَ العالي» لأنَّهُ يَرتَفِعُ ميلاً عَن سَطْحِ البَحر.

في اليَومِ التالي ذَهَبوا بِالسيارَةِ إلى جِبالِ «الروكي» وتَناوَلوا طَعامَ الغَداءِ في مَطعَمٍ قَديمٍ في الجِبالِ وقَد أعجَبَهُ ذلكَ جِدّاً. في طَريقِ العَودَةِ مَرّوا بِمَصنَعِ بيرَةِ «كورز» وهو مَصنَعٌ كَبيرٌ يَعمَلُ فيهِ مِئاتُ العُمّال.

لَقَد استَمتَعَ عَدنان بِهذِهِ الزِيارةِ استِمتاعاً كَبيراً، وفي نِهايَتِها شَكَرَ السَيِّدَ والسَيِّدةَ آلن على كَرَمِهِما واستِضافتِهِما لَهُ. قَدَّمَ لَهُما هَديّةً وهي شَريطٌ مُسَجَّلٌ عَلَيهِ موسيقا وأغانٍ عَرَبية. وقَدّمَ كذلِكَ مِفْرَشاً جَميلاً لِطاولةِ الطَعامِ مَصنوعاً في دِمَشق. عادَ عَدنان إلى كَلَمبَس كَما أتى مِنها بِالطائرة.

تمرين ١

أكمل الجُملَ التالية مِن نصِّ القراءة.

١- سافَرَ عَدنان إلى دِنڤَر بـ ......

٢- تَعمَلُ هِذَر ......

٣- تَستَضيفُ عائِلةُ السَيِّدِ آلَن الطُلابَ ...

٤- شاهَدَ عَدنان في جِبال الروكي مَصنَعَ ......

٥- يُسَمّي الناسُ في دِنڤر مَلعَبَ المدينةِ «الملعبَ العالي» لأنَّهُ ......

اكتُبْ «خَطَأ» أو «صَواب» جانِبَ كلِّ جُملةٍ وصَحِّح الجُمَلَ الخَطَأ.

٦- مَدينةُ دِنڤَر عالية.

٧- يوجَدُ خَمسةُ أشخاصٍ في عائِلةِ آلَن.

٨- يَدرُسُ پول آلَن التِجارةَ في جامِعة كولورادو.

٩- قَدَّم عَدنان هَديّةً لِلسَيِّدِ والسَيِّدَةِ آلَن.

أجِب عَن هذه الأسئلة حسب النص.

١٠- مَن يَعمَلُ مُحاسِباً؟

١١- ماذا يَعمَلُ السَيِّدُ آلَن؟

١٢- ماذا فَعَلَ عَدنان يَومَ السَبت؟

١٣- أينَ صُنِعَ مَفرَشُ الطاولة؟

وافِق بين كلمات من السَطرِ الأوّل وكلمات مِنَ السَطرِ الثاني.

Match a word from the first line with another word from the second line.

١٤- جريدة ١٥- شَريط ١٦- نادِل ١٧- عائلة ١٨- مَصرِف ١٩- لاعِب ٢٠- مَنزِل

رياضة، أسرة، استَضاف، صَحيفة، دار، مطعم، نُقود، مَسَجِّلة

لالينيا تَزورُ المِنيا

لالينيا غولدزبري طالِبةٌ أمريكيةٌ تَدرُسُ اللُغَةَ العَرَبيةَ في جامِعةِ وِلايةِ أوهايو، وقَد ذَهَبَتْ إلى الجامِعَةِ الأمريكيةِ في القاهِرة لمدةِ سَنَةٍ دراسيةٍ لِدِراسةِ العربيةِ هُناك. في العُطلاتِ زارَتْ لالينيا أماكِنَ عَديدَةً في مِصرَ وخارِجِها. هذا ما كَتَبَتْهُ إلى أستاذِها عَن رِحلَتِها إلى المِنيا:

في اليَومِ الأوَّل مِن عيد الفطر ركبتُ سَيارةَ أجرةٍ مِن حَيِّ العَجوزة إلى مَحَطَّةِ الجيزة للقطارات ودَفَعْتُ للسائقِ ثَلاثةَ جُنَيهاتٍ أجْرَةَ السيارة. كانَتِ المَحطةُ مُزدَحِمَةً بالناس، رُبَّما بِسَبَبِ العيد. أعتَقِد أنّ مَحَطَّةَ رَمسيس كانَت مُزدَحِمَةً أيضاً، لكنَّني لَمْ أذهَبْ إليها في ذلِكَ اليَوم. اشتَريتُ تَذكرةً بالدرَجَةِ الثانية بأربَعَةَ عَشَرَ جُنَيهاً، وتَدافَعْتُ مَعَ مِئاتِ الرُكّاب للحُصولِ عَلى مَقعَد مَعَ أنَّ لي مَقعَداً مَحجوزاً. أظُنُّ أنَّ النّاسَ تَعَوَّدوا عَلى التَدافُعِ في المُواصَلاتِ العامّة.

قطار

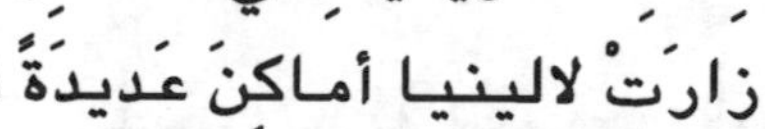

مَرَّ القطارُ بِقُرى عَديدَةٍ ووَصَلتُ المِنيا بعد ثلاث ساعات ونصف حيثُ كانَ أخو صَديقي في استِقبالي في المَحطة. ركِبتُ مَعَهُ سيارَتَهُ الّتي

ساقَها في شَوارِعِ البَلدَةِ لأتعرَّفَ عَلَيها. المنيا بَلدَةٌ لَيْسَت كَبيرة ولا أعرفُ عَدَدَ سُكّانها تَماماً. كانَ فيها الكثيرُ مِنَ الأشجارِ الخَضراءِ وكان الهَواءُ نَقيّاً غَيْرَ مُلَوَّثٍ والشوارِعُ هادِئةٌ بِعَكْسِ القاهِرة، حَتّى أنّي شاهَدْتُ عَدَداً كَبيراً مِنَ النُجومِ في السماءِ في اللّيل.

مَرَرْنا بِشارِعٍ يُسَمّى الكورنيش تَقَعُ على أحَد جانِبَيه حَديقةٌ عامّة واسعة كانَ فيها عَدَدٌ كَبيرٌ مِنَ الناسِ بَعضُهم يَمشي وبَعْضُهم يَلعَبُ ويَتَنَزَّه. قال لي أخو صَديقي إنَّ الحَديقةَ لا يوجَدُ فيها هذا العَدَدُ مِنَ الناسِ عادةً، لكنّها كانَت مُزدَحمةً في ذلكَ اليَوم بِسَبَبِ العيد. عَبَرنا إلى الجانِبِ الآخَرِ من نَهرِ النيلِ حَيثُ توجَدُ مَزارِعُ المَوز، وشاهَدْنا أنواعاً مُختَلِفةً مِنَ الناسِ مُعظَمُهم مِنَ الفلاّحين.

بَقيْتُ مَعَ أسرةِ صَديقي ثلاثةَ أيّامٍ وهي أيّامُ العيد. كُلُّ شَيءٍ في المَنزِل كانَ يَدُلُّ عَلى العيد، الحَلوى الّتي تُسَمّى «كَعكَ العيدِ» وبَرامِجُ الإذاعةِ والتلفاز الخاصة والزِياراتُ إلى بيوتِ الأصدِقاءِ والأقرِباء.

في نِهايَةِ عُطلة العيد رَجَعتُ إلى القاهِرة. كانَ مَوعِدُ القطار في الساعة السادِسَة صَباحاً وأخَذَني الأبُ إلى المَحطّةِ بِسيّارَتِه وانتَظَرني هُناكَ حَتّى غادَرَ القِطارُ المَحطّة.

جَلَستُ في القِطارِ إلى جانِبِ شاب، وقَد قَدَّمَ لي حَلوى وهي كَعكُ العيد فَرَفَضْتُ، لكنَّهُ أصَرَّ فأخذتُ واحدة. ثُمَّ مَرَّ بائِعُ الشاي فَسألَني إنْ كُنتُ أريدُ كأسَ شايٍ فَقُلتُ لا. بَعدَ قَليل سألَني إنْ كُنتُ مِنَ القاهِرة أم مِنَ المنيا، فَضَحِكتُ بَيني وبَينَ نَفسي من هذا السؤالِ السَخيف لأنّه لا شَكلي ولا كَلامي يَدُلاّن عَلى أنّي مصريّة، لكنّني كُنتُ سَعيدةً أنّهُ ظَنَّ أنّي مِصريَّة. قالَ لي هذا الشابُ إنَّهُ مِن أسْوان وتَكَلَّمنا عَنِ الدِراسة،

وسرّهُ كثيراً أنّي كنت أدْرُسُ العَربية. كانَ يَقرَأ كِتاباً خلالَ الرحلَة وأصرّ أنْ يُقَدِّمَهُ لي كَهَديّة. كانَ الكتابُ عَن الخَليفَة الرابِع. لَقَد استَمتَعتُ بِهذهِ الرِحْلَةِ أيَّما استِمتاع وقَد أزورُ المِنيا ثانيةً.

تمرين ٢

أكمِلِ الجمل التالية مِن نصِّ القراءةِ الثاني.

١ـ كتبَتْ لالينيا إلى أستاذِها عَن ......

٢ـ تَسكُنُ لالينيا في حَيّ ......

٣ـ كانت المحطّةُ ...... بِسَبَبِ العيد،

٤ـ تَقعُ مَزارِعُ المَوزِ ......

٥ـ تَستَغرِقُ الطَريقُ مِنَ القاهِرةِ إلى المِنيا ......

٦ـ كانَ الشابُّ في القِطارِ يَقرأ كِتاباً عَن ......

اكتُبْ «خَطأ» أو «صَواب» جانِبَ كلِّ جُملةٍ وصَحِّح الجُمَلَ الخَطأ.

٧ـ تَدافَعَ الناسُ لِلحُصولِ عَلى مَقعَدٍ في القِطارِ لأنَّ المقاعِدَ قَليلَة.

٨ـ لالينيا طالِبةٌ مِصرية.

٩ـ استَقبَلَ لالينيا في المحطةِ أخو صَديقِها.

١٠ـ جَلَسَتْ لالينيا في طَريق العَودَةِ إلى جانِبِ سَيِّدةٍ مِصرية.

١١ـ حَصَلَتْ لالينيا عَلى هَدِيَّةٍ مِن عائِلةِ صَديقِها.

١٢ـ هَواءُ القاهِرةِ مُلَوَّث.

وافِق بين الكلِمات ذاتِ الأرقامِ وكلِمات مِن المُستَطيلين.

Match the numbered words with those in the two boxes.

١٣ـ جُنَيه ١٤ـ مَقعَد، ١٥ـ قَرية ١٦ـ اعتَقَدَ

أُسْرة – انتَظَرَ – لَيرة – كُرسيّ –

١٧ـ مِثل ١٨ـ قَريب ١٩ـ مُلَوَّث ٢٠ـ غادَرَ

عَكْس – ظَنَّ – وَصَلَ – بَلدة – نَقِيّ –

List words from the above passage under each of the following categories:

21. Agriculture	22. Transportation	23. Environment	24. Festivity

تمرين ٣

اختَر الكلِمة التي لا تُناسِب باقي الكلمات في كُلِّ مَجموعة وبَيِّن السَبَب.

١- صَحَفِيّ مَجلّة عاصِمة جَريدة

٢- مَصرِف عائِلة أسرة أقرِباء

٣- مُواصَلات قِطار طائِرة حَلوى

٤- نامَ تجوَّلَ سافَرَ مَشى

تمرين ٤

أعِدْ ترتيب الكلمات في كُلِّ مَجموعة لِتَشكِّلَ جُمَلاً مُفيدة.

١- الأجانِبَ - آلَن - الطلاّبَ - عائِلةُ - تَستَضيفُ

٢- جُنَيهاً - القِطار - عَشَرَ - تَذكِرةَ - بأربعةَ - اشتَرَيتُ

٣- مُزدَحِمةٌ - القاهرةِ - مُلَوَّث - شوارعُ - وهَواؤُها - بالناسِ

٤- العيد - لالينيا - في - المِنيا - مَدينة - زارَتْ

تمرين ٥

أعِدْ ترتيبَ الجُمَلِ لِتَشكِّلَ فِقرةً مُفيدة.

١- أراد بْرِتْ آدَمز أن يَزورَ المغرب.

كانَت الرِحلةُ طويلةً واستَغرقَت ١٥ ساعةً تَقريباً.

ركِبَ بْرِتْ سَيارةَ أجرةٍ مِنَ المَطارِ إلى الفُندُق.

اتَّصَلَ بِأمِّهِ بِالهاتِفِ مِنَ الفُندُقِ وأخبَرَها بِوُصولِه إلى المَغرب.

ثانياً اشترى تَذكِرةَ طائِرة على الخطوطِ المَلكيةِ المغربية.

في يَومِ السَفَرِ أخذتْهُ أمُّهُ إلى المطارِ بِسيّارتِها.

وحَصلَ في الفُندُقِ على غُرفَةٍ بِسَريرٍ واحِدٍ مَعَ حَمّام بِداخِلِها.

أوّلاً كانَ عليه أن يَحصُلَ على تأشيرة دُخول.

فَقد وَصَلَ إلى مَطارِ الدارِ البيضاء في اليَومِ التالي.

لِذلِكَ أرسَلَ جَوازَ سَفَرِهِ إلى السفارةِ المغربيةِ بِواشِنطَن.

1. **The Use of the Particle فَـ**

This particle is a conjunction. It means different things in different contexts. It may be prefixed to nouns and verbs alike. With nouns, it may signify a gradual process:

١ يَوماً فَيَوماً *day by day* ، شَيئاً فَشَيْئاً *gradually*

Or it may purport a sequence (then):

٢ مَرَرنا بِحَلَبَ فَحماةَ فَحِمصَ فَدمشق.

We passed through Aleppo, Hama, Hims, and then Damascus.

With verbs, it may mean *then, thus, and so*, among other meanings. In this lesson, there are four occurrences of فَـ in two consecutive sentences, which are stylistically acceptable:

٣ قدَّم لي حَلوى وهي كعك العيدِ فَرَفَضتُ، لكِنَّهُ أصَرَّ فَأخذتُ واحِدة.

ثُمَّ مَرَّ بائِعُ الشاي فَسَألَني إنْ كُنتُ أريدُ كأسَ شاي فَقُلتُ لا.

2. **Functions of the Particle قَدْ**

There are two main functions for قَدْ, depending on whether the verb following it is past or present.

a. With Past Tense Verbs (Perfect): It denotes completed action similar to the use of the perfective in English (present and past perfect):

٤ أرجو أنْ يَكونَ الكِتابُ قَدْ أعجَبَكَ. *I hope the book has pleased you.*

More idiomatically*: I hope you like the book.*

Note that it does not translate into English. If the sentence contains two verbs in the past, then the verb following قَـد may be the one that occurred before the other one, which makes its use similar to that of the English past perfect when used with كان:

٥ وصلتُ إلى الصَفِّ في التاسِعةِ والرُبعِ وكانَ الدَرسُ قَد بَدَأ.

I arrived in the classroom at 9:15 and the lesson had already started.

However, ordering of actions in the past is not the only attribute of this particle. The verb with قد may not represent the action in the past that preceded the other past action in the sentence. It simply emphasizes the verb:

٦ تَناوَلتُ الغَداءَ في مَطعَمٍ قَديمٍ وقَد أعجَبَني.

I had lunch in an old retaurant and I liked it.

In this usage, the act of *liking* follows the act of *eating* lunch, not the other way around. In this context, the particle قد simply provides emphasis.

Certain particles may be prefixed to قـد, a process which might entail some changes in meaning:

٧ لَقَد دَرَسَ العربيّةَ في المَغرِب. *He has studied Arabic in Morocco*

٨ شاهدْتُ فيلماً مُمتازاً وقَد نَسَيتُ اسمَهُ الآن.

I saw an excellent movie, and/but I have forgotten its title now.

٩ لَمْ أشتَرِ كِتابَ غَسّان كَنَفاني فَقَد قَرَأتُهُ مِن قَبل.

I didn't buy Kanafani's book because I had read it before.

b. With Present Tense Verbs: If the following verb is in the present tense (imperfect), the use of قد denotes possibility. No change in the verb form takes place:

١٠ قَد أسافِرُ إلى عَمّانَ غداً. *I may travel to Amman tomorrow*

SUMMARY

- The particle قد, when followed by a past tense verb, denotes either completed action or emphasis. It also denotes a past action preceding another action when preceded by كانَ.
- When it is followed by a present tense verb, it denotes possibility (e.g. may, might).

تمرين ٦

Express these meanings in Arabic, using قد with reference to the section above.

1. They (m., p.) may travel to Damascus by plane.
2. I saw her house and I did like it.
3. When we got to our friends' house, they had already had dinner.

3. البَدَل (Substitution or the Permutative)

Sometimes a noun stands for another noun that immediately precedes it. In a sense, it substitutes the preceding noun completely, as the Arabic term indicates. Several instances of البَدَل have occurred so far:

١١ سافَرَ عَدنان إلى مَدينةِ دِنفَر عاصِمةِ ولايةِ كولورادو.

Adnan traveled to the city of Denver, capital of the state of Colorado.

In example 11, the phrase عاصمة ولاية كولورادو stands for the noun phrase مَدينة دِنفَر. In fact, you can delete the first phrase without losing much of the meaning because the second phrase explains what the first phrase is and can substitute for it entirely. It even has the same case as the substituted noun (compare مَدينةِ and عاصِمةِ).

Remember that noninflecting المَمنوع من الصَرف (or rather partially inflecting) nouns display a *fatḥa* in both الجَرّ (genitive) and النصب (accusative) (see Lesson 21 for further information):

١٢ سافَرَ رامي إلى عَمّانَ عاصِمةِ الأردُن.

The noun عاصمة is بَدَل substituting for the noun عَمّانَ, which has a *fatḥa* on its end because it is a noninflecting noun. The inflectional marker which this noun is supposed to have on its end is *kasra*, hence the *kasra* on the end of عاصِمةِ.

تمرين ٧

Identify البَدَل in the following sentences and provide the appropriate inflectional ending.

١- دفعتُ لِلسائقِ ثَلاثةَ جُنَيهاتٍ أجرة السيارة.

٢- زُرنا القاهِرةَ أكبر مُدُنِ إفريقيا.

٣- وصلنا صباحاً إلى الرِباطِ عاصمة المغرب.

٤- سكَنَت لَيلى في «بيز ووتر» حيٍّ العَرَبِ في لَندَن.

A Reminder about *Iḍāfa*

The first word of an *iḍāfa* structure (i.e. المضاف) can never have the definite article ال, nor a *tanwīn*, nor the final *nūn* (ن) of the dual and plural suffixes. In the last passage of this lesson, the following sentence occurs:

١٣ أرَدتُ أنا وصَديقتايَ آن ورينا أن نَزورَ سورية. *my two friends*

The noun صَديقتايَ is a combination of the dual noun صديقتان plus the possessive suffix ي which forms an *iḍāfa* with the noun. And since the noun is the first word of the structure, or the مُضاف, it loses the final *nūn* of the dual suffix.

4. The Particle إنْ

The particle إنْ has a conditional meaning "if." The most common usage is in a conditional sentence containing two verbs; the first one expresses the condition and the second is the "answer" to the condition. The two verbs can be in either the present tense, past tense, or a combination of the two tenses:

١٤ إنْ تَزُرْ حَلَبَ تُعجِبْكَ. *If you visit Aleppo, you'll like it.*

١٥ إنْ زُرتَ حَلَبَ أعجَبَتْكَ.

١٦ إنْ تَزُرْ حَلَبَ أعْجَبَتْكَ.

١٧ إنْ زُرتَ حَلَبَ تُعجِبْكَ (أو تُعجِبُكَ).

There are four different alternative structures. If the verb following إنْ directly is in the present, it must be مُضارع مَجزوم (jussive), as in 14 and 16. If the verb in the "answer" is present tense (example 17), then it can be either a regular present (indicative مَرفوع) or jussive (مَجزوم).

You already know the familiar phrase إنْ شاءَ الله (God willing). This and the token of إنْ occurring in this lesson follow example 17 in its structure. The conditional clause contains the past tense verb كنتُ أريدُ with the answer omitted:

١٨ سألَني إنْ كُنتُ أريدُ كأسَ شاي.

تمرين ٨

أجب عن الأسئلة حسب نص الاستماع.

١- إلى أيِّ بَلَدٍ سَتَكونُ الرِحلة؟

٢- كَم يَوماً ستَبقى الصَديقات في القاهَرة؟

٣- هل سَتُسافِرُ المُتكلِّمَةُ (speaker) مَعَ صَديقاتِها؟ لماذا؟

اكتُبْ «خَطَأ» أو «صَواب» جانِبَ كلِّ جُملةٍ وصَحِّح الجُمَلَ الخَطَأ.

٤- مَسجِدُ مُحَمَّد عَلي في الإسكَندَريّة.

٥- مُدَّةُ الرِحلة إلى الإسكندرية ثَلاثَةُ أيّام.

٦- سَيكونُ السَفَرُ إلى الأقصُر بالحافِلة.

٧- لَن تَسافِرَ الفَتاةُ مَعَ صَديقاتِها لأنَّها تَعرِف مِصر.

أكمل الجمل بالاختيار المناسب حسب نص الاستماع.

٨- سَتَزورُ الصَديقاتُ في القاهِرة ...

❏ المكتباتِ الكُبرى ❏ المُتحَفَ المِصريّ ❏ البَحرَ المُتَوَسِّط

٩- الأهرامات مَوجودةٌ ...

❏ قُربَ القاهِرة ❏ في الأقصُر ❏ في جَنوبِ مِصر

١٠- ستأخُذُ الصَديقاتُ رِحلةً ...

❏ خاصّة ❏ عامّة ❏ جامِعِيّة

١١- لَيْسَ عِندَ الفَتاةِ ...

❏ وَقتٌ ❏ هَويّةٌ ❏ صَديقاتٌ

١٢- الآثارُ الفِرعَونيّةُ مَوجودَةٌ ...

❏ على الطَريقِ إلى الأقصُر ❏ في الإسكندرية

❏ في مَسجِدِ مُحَمَّد عَلي

المُفْرَدات

to rise, to be higher .... ارتَفَعَ (يرتَفِعُ) ارتِفاع (v.)
to host .... استَضافَ (يستَضيفُ) استِضافة (v.)
to insist .... أصرَّ (يُصِرُّ) إصْرار (v.)
to believe .... اعتَقَدَ (يعتَقِدُ) اعتِقاد (v.)
if .... إنْ (particle)
to wait .... انتَظَرَ (يَنْتَظِرُ) انتِظار (v.)
immensely, greatly (intensifies the following noun) .... أيَّما (n.)
to push, shove one another .... تَدافَعَ (يتَدافَعُ) تَدافُع (v.)
to be acquainted with .... تَعَرَّفَ (يتَعَرَّفُ) تَعَرُّف (على) (v.)
to be accustomed to .... تَعَوَّدَ (يتَعَوَّدُ) تَعَوُّد (v.)
to stroll, to have a good time, to go on a picnic .... تَنَزَّهَ (يتَنَزَّهُ) تَنَزُّه (v.)
to attend, to be present .... حَضَرَ (يحْضُرُ) حُضور (v.)
outside .... خارِج (n.)
caliph, successor .... خَليفة ج خُلَفاء (n., m.)
class, step, level, degree .... دَرَجة ج دَرَجات (n., f.)
to pay .... دَفَعَ (يَدْفَعُ) دَفْع (v.)
trip, journey, flight .... رِحْلة ج رِحلات (n., f.)
to drive .... ساقَ (يَسوقُ) سِياقة (v.)
silly, absurd, foolish .... سَخيف ج سُخَفاء (n./adj.)
to please, to be glad .... سَرَّ (يَسُرُّ) سُرور (v.)
surface, level .... سَطْح ج سُطوح (n., m.)
political .... سِياسيّ (adj.)
journalist .... صَحَفِيّ ج ـون (n., m.)
newspaper .... صَحيفة ج صُحُف (n., f.)
to laugh .... ضَحِكَ (يَضْحَكُ) ضِحْك (v.)

to cross.. عَبَرَ (يَعبُرُ) عُبور (v.)
opposite, reverse, contrary.. عَكْس (n.)
to leave.. غادَرَ (يُغادِرُ) مُغادَرة (v.)
peasant, farmworker.. فَلاّح ج ـون (n., m.)
no meaning, denotes completed action, emphasis, or possibility.. قَد (particle)
a relative.. قَريب ج أقارِب (n., m.)
heart.. قَلْب ج قُلوب (n., m.)
as, like.. كَـ (prep.)
hospitality, generosity.. كَرَم (n., m.)
speech, speaking.. كَلام (n., m.)
player.. لاعِب ج ـون (n., m.)
a variation of *qad*.. لَقَد (particle)
accountant.. مُحاسِب ج ـون (n., m.)
crowded.. مُزدَحِم (adj.)
farm.. مَزْرَعة ج مَزارِع (n., f.)
recorded.. مُسَجَّل (adj./n.)
factory, plant.. مَصْنَع ج مَصانِع (n., m.)
tablecloth.. مَفْرَش ج مَفارِش (n., m.)
seat, bench, armchair.. مَقْعَد ج مَقاعِد (n., m.)
polluted.. مُلَوَّث (adj.)
house, residence.. مَنزِل ج مَنازِل (n., m.)
means of transportation.. مُواصَلة ج مُواصَلات (n., f.)
waiter.. نادِل ج نُدُل (n., m.)
pure.. نَقيّ (adj.)
quiet, serene.. هادِئ (adj.)
present, gift.. هَدِيّة ج هَدايا (n., f.)

Lesson Thirty الدَّرْسُ الثَّلاثون

Objectives

- Family members and relations.
- Describing professions.
- Relational concepts.
- Terms of address (أبو and أم).
- Comparative and superlative degrees revisited.
- Expressing reason with كَي and لِـ.
- Verbal nouns (المَصدَر) revisited.
- Writing the *hamza.*
- Listen to recorded material for this lesson.
- Do relevant computer drills and exercises, Stages 14 and 15.

أُسرَةُ عَدنان مارتيني

هذِهِ صورةُ أسرةِ عَدنان مارتيني. لقد أرسَلَ أبو عدنان صورةَ العائلةِ مع رسالةٍ إلى ابنِهِ عَدنان الَّذي يَدرُسُ عِلمَ الحاسوبِ في جامِعةِ ولاية أوهايو في الولاياتِ المُتحدةِ الأمريكية. يَظهَرُ في الصورةِ أبو عدنان في أعلى الصورةِ إلى اليَمينِ وتَظهَرُ أمُّ عَدنان إلى جانِبِهِ إلى يَسارِ الصورة. تَظهَرُ في أسفلِ الصورةِ إلى اليَمين أختُ

عَدنان الصُغرى أماني، وعُمرُها إحدى عَشْرةَ سَنةً وهي في الصفِّ السادسِ الابتدائي. إلى جانبِ أماني تَبدو أختُها أمينة، وعُمرُها خَمسَ عَشْرَةَ سَنة. أمينة في الصَفِّ العاشرِ وهي تَذهَبُ إلى المدرسةِ الثانَويّةِ الجَديدةِ لِلإناثِ في مَدينةِ حَلَبَ في سورية. يَجلِسُ مَروان إلى جانبِ أمينة، وهو طالِبٌ في الصَفِّ الثاني عَشَرَ العِلمِيّ في المدرسةِ الثانويةِ لِلبَنين وعُمرُهُ سَبعةَ عَشَرَ عاماً. لا يَظهَرُ أخوهُم رامي في الصورةِ وكذلِكَ أيمَن لأنَّهُما ما كانا في حَلَب حينَ التُقِطَتْ الصورة.

ياسر مارتيني
أبو عدنان

أبو عَدنان، واسمُهُ ياسِر مارتيني، تاجِرٌ في الخامسةِ والخَمسين من عُمره. لَهُ مَحَلٌّ تِجاري في حَلَب فَتَحَهُ مُنذُ خَمسةٍ وعِشرين عاماً يَبيعُ فيهِ قِطَعَ غِيارٍ لِبعْضِ السياراتِ الألمانيّة كَفولكسڤاكن وأوپل. مَحَلُّ أبي عَدنان واسِعٌ وهو مُؤَلَّفٌ مِن دُكّانٍ لِبَيعِ قِطعِ الغِيارِ ومكتَبٍ لَهُ وآخَرَ لِلمُحاسِب، وهُناكَ مَخزَنٌ كَبيرٌ لِتَخزينِ البِضاعة. يَعملُ عِندَهُ في المحلِّ مُحاسِبٌ واحدٌ وبائِعانِ وثَلاثةُ عُمّالٍ لِنَقلِ البِضاعةِ من المحلِّ وإليه. يَستَورِدُ السَيِّدُ ياسِر مارتيني بِضاعتَه مِن ألمانيا وتَصِلُه إلى حَلَبَ بالشاحِناتِ غالِباً و أحياناً بالبَحرِ عَن طريقِ ميناءِ اللاذِقيّة، لكنّها تَتَأخَّرُ عادةً بِهذه الطَريق. لِذلكَ فَهو يُسافِرُ إلى ميونيخ وكولون وفرانكفورت ليَشتريَ البِضاعةَ بِنَفسِهِ مِن ألمانيا.

سامية كحّال

أمُّ عَدنان، واسمُها سامية كَحّال، عُمرُها خَمسونَ عاماً. هي رَبَّةُ بَيتٍ الآنَ ولا تَعمَل، لكِنَّها كانَت مَدَرِّسةَ لُغةٍ فَرَنسيّة في إحدى مَدارسِ الإناثِ الثانويةِ في حَلَب. تَقاعَدَتْ السَيِّدةُ سامية كَحّال عَنِ العَمَلِ مُنذُ ثَماني سَنَوات كَي تَعتَنيَ بِوالِدَتِها المريضة وبِمَنزِلِها وزَوجِها وأولادِها. فَكانت تَعمَلُ في المنزِلِ في النهارِ وتَزورُ صَديقاتِها مَساءً، وفي اللَيلِ تَبقى مَعَ عائِلَتِها.

الجمهورية العربية السورية
REPUBLIQUE ARABE SYRIENNE
وزارة الداخلية
MINISTERE DE L'INTERIEUR
إدارة الهجرة والجوازات
DEPARTEMENT DE L'IMIGRATION & DES PASSPORTS

صدر بمدينة: حلب Fait a: Alep
في اليوم: السادس من شهر نيسان ١٩٩١
le 6 avril 1991
وينتهي مفعوله بتاريخ ٥ نيسان ١٩٩٧
et expire le 5 avril 1997
رقم التسجيل ٩١/٢٥٤٣

الاسم والشهرة: ياسرِ مارتيني
اسم الأب: عَبد الغَني
اسم الأم: رُقَيّة
مكان الإقامة الحالي: حلب
تاريخ ومكان الولادة: حلب ١٥ آب ١٩٤١
المهنة: تاجِر
الشعر: أسوَد
الطول: ١٧١ سنتيمتر
اللون: أسمَر
العينان: بُنيتان
التوقيع

صفحتان من جواز سفر السيد ياسر مارتيني

سافَرَتْ أمُّ عَدنان خارجَ سورية مَرَّةً واحِدةً مَعَ زَوجِها إلى ألمانيا مُنذُ سَنَتَين ومَرّةً أخرى إلى الولاياتِ المتحِّدة لِزيارةِ ابنِها عدنان، لكنّها سافَرَتْ وَحدَها ومَعَ زَوجِها عِدّةَ مرّاتٍ إلى دِمشق واللاذقية وكذلك إلى لُبنانَ والأردُن.

كَتَبَ أبو عَدنان الرسالةَ التاليةَ إلى ابنِهِ عَدنان في أمريكا وأرسَلَ لَهُ مَعَها صورةَ العائِلة. يُخبِرُ أبو عَدنان ابنَهُ في الرِسالةِ أنَّ والِدتَهُ سَتَزورُهُ في الولايات المتحدةِ في الصيفِ المُقبِلِ وأنَّهُ لَن يَستَطيعَ أنْ يَكونَ مَعَها في هذهِ الزِيارة.

مُلاحَظة حَولَ الدِراسة .. حينَ يَصِلُ الطالِبُ إلى الصفِّ الحادي عَشَر يَختارُ الفَرْعَ العِلمِيَّ أو الفَرعَ الأدبيَّ ويَبقى فيهِ سَنَتَين. في الفَرعِ العِلميِّ يَدْرُسُ الرياضياّت والكيمياء والفيزياء وعِلمَ الأحْياء والجيولوجيا. أمّا في الفَرعِ الأدَبيِّ فَيَدرُسُ لُغَتَينِ أجنَبِيَّتَينِ والأدَبَ والشِعْرَ العَرَبيَّ والفَلسَفَةَ والتاريخَ والجُغرافيا وعِلمَ الاجتِماع.

رسالةُ ياسرِ مارتيني إلى ابنِه عَدنان

بسم الله الرحمن الرحيم

حمص في ٢٢ أيار ١٩٩٧

ابني الحبيب عدنان، السلام عليك ورحمة الله.

أرجو أن تصلك رسالتي هذه وأنت في أحسن حال. كلنا بخير والحمد لله. كتبت لك رسالة في الشهر الماضي وما وصلني منك رد عليها. أما وصلتك رسالتي؟ آخر رسالة منك كان تاريخها ٧ كانون الثاني. أرجو أن تكتب لنا دون تأخير.

أكتب لك هذه الرسالة لأخبرك أن والدتك تريد أن تسافر إليك في شهر آب. لن أستطيع أن أسافر معها هذه المرة لأنني مشغول جداً. يجب أن أسافر إلى ألمانيا في آب المقبل من أجل استيراد بضاعة للمحل.

اشتريت تذكرة طائرة لوالدتك على الخطوط الجوية الهولندية. تغادر طائرتها مطار دمشق في يوم الخميس ١٤ آب وتصل إلى شيكاغو في اليوم نفسه. أرجو أن تستقبلها في المطار لأنها كما تعلم لا تتكلم الإنكليزية ولا تعرف أحداً على الطائرة.

والآن إليك أخبار الأسرة. أخوك أمين كلمنا بالهاتف من دمشق وهو بخير ويرسل لك سلامه. أخوك رامي لا يزال يدرس في الجامعة ويعمل سائقاً في شركة البرادات، وهو سعيد بذلك. خالك أحمد انتقل في الشهر الماضي وعائلته إلى دمشق حيث سيعمل مدرساً للفيزياء في إحدى المدارس الثانوية. تقاعد عمك زهير من عمله في وزارة التربية وهو يقول إن حياة المتقاعد تعجبه كثيراً.

جدتك أم ياسر ترسل لك سلامها وتشكرك على الهدية التي أرسلتها لها. اكتب لنا عن أخبارك وإلى اللقاء.

والدك

The typed version of the above letter is in Appendix E 4.

تمرين ١

أجِب عَن الأسئلةِ التالية مِن النص:

١- في أيِّ صَفٍ أمينة؟
٢- ما اسم أختِ عَدنان الصُغرى؟
٣- أينَ يَجلِسُ مَروان في الصورة؟
٤- مِن أينَ يَستَوْرِدُ ياسِر ما رتيني بِضاعَتَهُ؟
٥- كَمْ مُوَظَّفاً يَشتَغِلُ في مَحلِّ أبي عَدنان؟
٦- لماذا يُسافِرُ أبو عَدنان إلى ألمانيا؟
٧- ماذا كانَت تَعمَلُ أمُّ عَدنان؟
٨- مَتى تَقاعَدَت عن العمل ولماذا؟
٩- مَتى كَتَبَ عَدنان آخِرَ رِسالةٍ إلى أسرَتِه؟
١٠- مَن أم ياسر؟

اكتُبْ «خَطَأ» أو «صَواب» إلى جانِبَ كلِّ جُملةٍ وصَحِّح الجُمَلَ الخَطَأ.

١١- تَذهَبُ أمينة إلى مَدرَسةٍ ثانويَّةٍ لِلبَنين.
١٢- يَدرُسُ رامي عِلمَ الحاسوبِ في أمِريكا.
١٣- مَروان أصْغَر إخوَةِ عَدنان وهو في السابِعةِ عَشْرَةَ مِن عُمرِه.
١٤- تَصِلُ بِضاعَةُ السَيِّد مارتيني إلى ميناءِ اللاذِقيَّةِ دائماً.
١٥- لَمْ تَزُرْ أمُّ عَدنان أمِريكا.
١٦- خالُ عَدنان مُتَقاعِدٌ الآن.

اختَر التكمِلة المناسبة حَسَب النَص.

١٧- ياسِر مارتيني لَهُ ...

❑ مَحَلٌّ تِجاري ❑ سَيّارة ألمانية

❑ سَيارة فولكسڤاكن ❑ مَحَلٌّ في ألمانيا

١٨- يَستَوْرِدُ ياسِر مارتيني بِضاعَتَهُ مِن ...

❑ حَلَب ❑ الشاحِنات

❑ البَحَر ❑ ألمانيا

١٩- مَحَلٌّ أبي عَدنان مَوجودٌ في ...

❑ دِمَشق ❑ حَلَب

❑ اللاذِقية ❑ ألمانيا

٢٠- أوپل اسمُ ...

❑ سَيّارةٍ ألمانية ❑ مَحَلٍّ ياسِر مارتيني

❑ قِطَعِ غِيارِ السيّاراتِ ❑ مَخْزَنِ سَيّارات

٢١- يَستَورِدُ أبو عَدنان بَضاعَتَهُ غالباً عَن طَريقِ ...

❑ البَحرِ ❑ الشاحِناتِ

❑ الجَوِّ ❑ القِطاراتِ

٢٢- أمُّ عَدنان ... الآنَ.

❑ مُدرِّسةُ لُغَةٍ فَرنسيّة ❑ رَبَّةُ بَيت

❑ جَدّة ❑ مُوَظَّفة

٢٣- أحمَد هو ... عَدنان.

❑ خالُ ❑ عَمُّ

❑ جَدُّ ❑ أخو

٢٤ سَتُسافِرُ أمُّ عَدنان إلى أمرِيكا عَلى الخُطوطِ الجَويّة ...

❑ السوريّة ❑ الألمانيّة

❑ الهولنديّة ❑ الأردُنيّة

تمرين ٢

اختَر الكلِمة الّتي لا تُناسِب باقي الكلمات في كُلٍّ مَجموعة وبَيِّن السَبَب.

١ـ	استيراد	صورة	التَقَطَ	ظَهَرَ
٢ـ	عام	سَنة	عَمّ	عُمْر
٣ـ	رِسالة	طِبّ	تِجارة	عِلمُ الحاسوب
٤ـ	بِضاعة	دُكّان	مُدَرِّس	مَحَلّ تِجاري
٥ـ	كَيْ	أيُّ	لِذلِكَ	لِـ
٦ـ	جَواز سَفَر	عامِل	مُحاسِب	مُوَظَّف

تمرين ٣

اكتب في كلّ عمود (column) كلمات من النص تناسب الكلمة في أعلاه.

١ـ جواز سفر	٢ـ عائلة	٣ـ تجارة	٤ـ مدارس	٥ـ مِهَن	٦ـ بلاد

تمرين ٤

وافِق بين كلماتٍ مِنَ العَمودِ الأيْمَن وكلماتٍ مِنَ العَمودِ الأيْسَر واكتُب الكَلِمَتَين في الوسط.

١ـ كُبرى	....	نَهار
٢ـ لَوْن	....	بَحر
٣ـ يَمين	....	بَنات
٤ـ سَفينة	....	صُغرى
٥ـ مَحَلٌّ تِجاري	....	يَسار
٦ـ بَنون	....	واسِع
٧ـ لَيْل	....	أسْمَر
		دُكّان

تمرين ٥

أعِدْ تَرتيبَ الكَلِماتِ في كُلِّ مَجموعة لِتَشكِّلَ جُمَلاً مُفيدة.

١ـ لِلبَنين، في، مَروانُ، بحلب، ثانَوِيَّةٍ، يَدرُسُ، مَدرَسَةٍ

٢ـ لِبَيعِ، السَيّاراتِ، أبو، غِيارِ، عِندَ، واسِعٌ، عَدنان، قِطَعِ، مَحَلٌّ

٣ـ كَيْ، عَدنان، بِعائِلَتِها، عَمَلِها، تَقاعَدَتْ، تعتنيَ، أمُّ، مِن

٤ـ مارتيني، ومُحاسِبٌ، في، ياسِرِ، عُمّالٍ، ثَلاثَةُ، وبائِعان، يَعمَلُ، مَحَلٍّ

تمرين ٦

أعِدْ ترتيبَ الجُمَلِ لِتَشكِّلَ فِقرةً مُفيدة. لا تغيِّر مكان الجملة الأولى.

١- دَرَسَتْ هالة الصيدَلة في جامِعَةِ دِمشق. — pharmacy, pharmacology

اشتَريا داراً كَبيرةً في دِمشق مُؤلَّفةً مِن ثلاثةِ طوابِق.

تَعَرَّفَتْ في المُستَشفى على زَوجِها مازِن الَّذي كانَ يَعمَلُ طَبيباً. — hospital

أمّا الطابَقُ الثاني فَسَكنوا فيه.

وتَخَرَّجَتْ مِنَ الجامِعةِ في العامِ ١٩٧٥.

حينَ صارَ أولادُهُما في سِنِّ المَدرَسة انتَقَلا إلى دِمَشق.

بَعدَ تَخرُّجِها عَمِلَت صَيدَلانِيَّةً في مُستَشفى في مَدينةِ الكُوَيت. — pharmacist

والطابَقُ الأوَّل صارَ عِيادَةً لمازن.

صارَ لِهالة ومازِن بِنتان ووَلَدان.

في الطابَقِ الأرضِيِّ مَحَلٌّ تِجارِيٌّ واسِعٌ فَتَحَتْهُ هالة صيدلية. — pharmacy

تمرين ٧

تَصوَّر أنَّ هذه الصورةَ تُمَثِّل اجتماعَ أساتِذةٍ وطُلابٍ مِن قِسْمِ اللُغةِ العَربية. أعطِ لكلِّ شَخصٍ في الصورةِ اسماً ثمَّ اكتب وَصفاً مِثلَ الوَصفِ المَوجودِ في الفقرةِ الأولى من الدَرسِ مُستَخدِماً أفعالاً وكلماتٍ مِثلَ (يَظهَرُ، يَجلِسُ، يَقِفُ، يَبدو، إلى جانِبِ، إلى يَمينِ، إلى يَسارِ، أعلى، أسفَل، أمامَ، خَلفَ).

Imagine that the picture on page 495 depicts a meeting attended by faculty and students in the Arabic Department. Provide fictitious names for the five individuals in the picture and then describe the role of each and their places in the picture in relation to one another in a manner similar to that found in the first paragraph of this lesson, using similar verbs and words expressing relational concepts.

1. **Terms of Address: أبو and أم**

As is the case in many languages, there are several ways in which people address one another. You have already learned that men may be addressed by أخ، سَيِّد، أستاذ، دكتور and women by أخت، آنسة، سَيِّدة، ست، أستاذة، and دكتورة. However, in many parts of the Arab world, the use of أبو and أم followed by the name of the eldest son is a common practice. Addressing a man by أبو سَليم rather than by his first name, for example, may be interpreted as a sign of respect, an indication of solidarity, or a manifestation of a formal situation. It is not uncommon for someone to be known only by their nickname (e.g. أبو سامِر، أم هِشام). Not all communities, though, assign positive interpretations to the use of these two terms. In urban centers in Egypt, for instance, the use of أبو and أم as terms of address is almost restricted to the lower working class.

2. **Comparative and Superlative Degrees Revisited**

As you may recall, the comparative form (e.g. longer than) is formed after the pattern أفعل and followed by the preposition مِن (e.g. أنا أطوَلُ مِن عَدنان). The superlative form (e.g. the longest) is formed after the same pattern as the comparative, but it is followed, not by مِن, but rather by another noun which possesses the superlative attribute. It forms with it an *iḍāfa* structure (e.g. أطولُ رجلٍ). The superlative may also have the

definite article ال prefixed to it (e.g. أخي الأكبَر). Both nouns are اسم تَفضيل.

اسم التفضيل

Feminine Plural	Feminine Superlative	Masculine Plural	Masculine Superlative	Adjective
كُبرَيات	كُبرى	أكابِر	أكبَر	كَبير
صُغرَيات	صُغرى	أصاغِر	أصْغَر	صَغير
- - - -	عُليا	أعالي	أعلى	عالٍ
سُفلَيات	سُفلى	أسافِل	أسفَل	سافِل
- - - -	يُمنى	- - - -	أيمَن	يَمين
- - - -	يُسرى	- - - -	أيْسَر	يَسار

Table 1

The Arabic comparative and superlative forms are nouns. And while most of them are masculine only, some have feminine counterparts as well. In this lesson, you have seen the following phrase:

١ أختُ عَدنان الصُغرى — *Adnan's youngest sister*

The pattern after which the feminine superlative is formed is فُعْلى. Other adjectives from which feminine superlative nouns are derived include those listed in Table 1. Note also that some of these superlatives have plurals.

3. The Particles كَيْ and لِـ

The particles كَيْ and لِـ (*in order to*) are two of a group of particles used to express reason, which can be used separately or in combination (لِكَي):

٢ حَضَرَتْ أمُّ عَدنان إلى أمريكا كَيْ تزورَ ابنَها.

Umm Adnān came to America in order to visit her son.

٣ ذَهَبَ الطُلابُ إلى دِمشق لِيَدرُسوا العَرَبيةَ.

The students went to Damascus to study Arabic.

Remember that other particles with which you are already familiar include لَنْ (used to negate verbs denoting future time) and أنْ (*to,* which follows certain verbs, such as أراد). All these particles must be followed by the form of the present called المُضارع المَنصوب, which is marked by a *fatḥa* on its end (e.g. لَنْ يَكتُبَ) or by the deletion of the final ن in the suffix (e.g. لَنْ يَكتُبا).

تمرين ٨

Provide in the box the appropriate form of المضارع المنصوب of the verb in parentheses which is listed in the past tense. Indicate the correct ending. Example:

أظُنُّ أنَّني لَنْ (زار) أزورَ فلوريدا هذا الشِتاء.

١- يُريدُ هِشام وأماني أنْ (سكَن) .... في مَدينةٍ كبيرة.

٢- أظُنُّ أنَّ أصدقائي لَنْ (أتى) .... إلى الصَفِّ اليَوم.

٣- هَل تُحِبُّ أنْ (شَرِب) .... الشايَ مَعَ السُكَّر؟

٤- حَضَرتُ إلى هذهِ الجامِعة كَيْ (دَرَس) .... العَرَبية.

٥- مَنْ يُريدُ أنْ (اعتَنى) .... بِقِطَّتي حينَ أسافِر؟

٦- ذَهَبْنا إلى مَطعَمٍ عَرَبيّ لِـ (أكَل) .... الفَلافِل.

4. **Verbal Nouns Revisited** المَصدَر

In Lesson 16 different patterns of المَصْدَر are introduced. You have seen verbal nouns of Verb Forms I-X. Each verb form, I-X, has a different verbal noun pattern.

Notice that only the Verb Form فَعَل (I) has multiple verbal noun patterns. All the rest have either one or two patterns of المَصْدَر (see table in Lesson 22). In this lesson, several instances of المَصْدَر occur. Some of them are used with the preposition لِـ to indicate purpose, and therefore, they are objects of this preposition:

٤ لِبَيْعِ قِطَعِ الغيار *for selling spare parts*

لِتَخزينِ البِضاعة *for storing the merchandise*

The two instances of the verbal noun in 4 function as objects of the preposition لـ. Being nouns, they can function as subjects of sentences (as in 5) and as objects of verbs (6):

٥ تُعجِبُني دِراسةُ الأدَب.

٦ أريدُ بَيعَ سَيّارَتي القَديمة.

تمرين ٩

Underline verbal nouns (المصدر) in these sentences, indicate their grammatical function (i.e. subject, agent, object), and then write down the root of each one in the box next to the sentence, as in the example. There may be more than one مَصْدَر in each sentence.

مِثال: ذَهَبَت الزَوجَةُ إلى عَمَلِها بَعدَ تَحضيرِ الفَطور. [عمل، حضر]

١- يُريدُ أحمَد بَيْعَ سَيارتِه القَديمة لِيَشتَرِيَ سَيّارةً جَديدة. [ ]

٢- لَم أرَ أختي مُنذُ كِتابةِ هذِه الكلِمات. [ ]

٣- أعرِفُ اللُغةَ الألمانية لكِنْ لا يُمكِنُني التَكلُّمُ بِها. [ ]

٤- سَوفَ أعمَلُ في شَرِكةٍ تِجاريّة بَعدَ تَخَرُّجي. [ ]

٥- اسْتِضافَتُكُم في بَيتي تَسُرُّني جِداً . [ ]

٦- يُعجِبُني التَنَزُّهُ على شاطِئِ البَحر. [ ]

5. Writing the *Hamza*

Two types of *hamza*: Rules for writing the letter *hamza* are somewhat numerous and characterized by exceptions. It occurs in particles, nouns, and verbs. There are two types of the *hamza*, همزة الوصل *hamzatu-l-waṣl* (literally, *hamza* of connection, or conjunctive *hamza*) and همزة القطع *hamzatu-l-qaṭ'* (disjunctive *hamza*).

A. ***Hamzatu-l-waṣl*** همزة الوَصل (**conjunctive *hamza***). This type of *hamza*

serves a phonetic need. Because Arabic phonological rules do not allow a consonant cluster, especially in the initial word position, this conjunctive *hamza* helps to break the cluster. For example, Arabic does not allow two consonants in a row as in (جْلس). In order to break it, an initial *hamza* with a following short vowel are used (اِجْلس). It is spelled on an *alif* without the diacritic (ء) and occupies the initial position only of certain words which include the following:

1. The definite article ال, which is pronounced (*al*) if the word modified by it is in the initial position, i.e., no other words or particles precede it. Thus, the word for *house* البَيت is pronounced *al-bayt* when it occurs independently. But with a preceding noun with which it forms an *iḍāfa* or with any prefix, the *hamza* is lost:

   ٧ وَالبَيت *wa-l-bayt*

   بِالبَيت *bi-l-bayt*

   بابُ البَيت *bābu-l-bayt*

   In all three examples, the *a-* of ال is not pronounced, though the *alif* is retained.

2. A **restricted class of nouns** starts with *hamzatu-l-waṣl*. The most common of those nine nouns are the following: اِبن، اِبنة، اسم، اثنان، اثنتان، امرأة، امرُؤ. You have already encountered them except for اِمرؤ (*man, one, person*). Example:

   ٨ اِسْمُهُ (*ismuhu*) ⇦ واسْمُهُ. The *i* is dropped. (*wa-smuhu*)

3. Some augmented verbs (الفعل المزيد) and their derivatives:

   i. The imperative of Form I, e.g. أُكْتُبْ (*uktub*), (*ijlis*) اِجْلِسْ . The initial sound of *hamza* (i.e. *a-*, *u-*, *i-*) will be lost, but note that the *alif* is retained in writing (e.g. واجلِسْ *wa-jlis,* واكتُبْ *wa-ktub*).

   ii. The past tense, imperative, and verbal noun of Form VIII: اِنتَظَرَ اِنتَظِرْ اِنتِظار.

   iii. The past tense, imperative, and verbal noun of Form X: اِسْتَخْدَمَ اِسْتَخدِمْ اِسْتِخدام.

   اِسْتَخدَمَ (*istakhdama*) ⇦ واسْتَخدَمَ (*wa-stakhdama*)

B. ***Hamzatu-l-qaṭʻ*** همزة القطع (**disjunctive *hamza***). This is the type of *hamza* that is pronounced (and spelled) in all word positions. It occurs in particles, nouns, and verbs. Examples of particles include:

٩ أ (interrogative particle used with yes/no questions) أتدرسين في المكتبة؟
أ (used as a vocative to call the attention of someone) أمروانُ!
أ (the first person singular indicative prefix-- *I*) أكتبُ
إلى (preposition) ، أينَ (question particle)

The spelling of *hamza* in the initial position is not affected by prefixes:

١٠ لأنّ، سأكتبُ، لأسكُنَ

However, there are three exceptions: (1) when the preposition لـ is prefixed to ألاّ (*not to*), the combination is spelled لئلاّ (*in order not to*), (2) when the letter هـ is prefixed to the demonstrative أولاء (*these, those*), it is spelled هؤلاء, and (3) when the particle لَـ is prefixed to the particle إنْ (*if*), the word is spelled لَئِنْ.

Examples of nouns with *hamza* include: أحمد, فؤاد, and مساء.

Examples with verbs (first person singular prefix *I*): أساعِدُ، أعْمَلُ.

You have already covered the rules associated with the initial position. These can be summarized as follows:

1. **In the initial position**: The *hamza* is spelled over a silent *alif* which serves as a seat only. If the *hamza* is followed by a *kasra*, it may be written either over the *alif* with a *kasra* indicated below it or, more frequently, below the *alif* with no *kasra*:

أَ أُ إِ

2. **In the medial position**: Spelling the *hamza* correctly involves its seat and the immediately preceding and following vowels. As for the seat, there are four possibilities: the three long vowels as seats and placing it flush on the line. The seat is determined on the basis of the more powerful vowel adjacent to it. Each short vowel has a corresponding long vowel to serve as a seat: a *fatḥa* and an *alif* correspond to an *alif*, a *ḍamma* and a *wāw* to a *wāw*, and a *kasra* and a *yā'* to a *yā'*. It is placed on the line medially when it is preceded by a long *alif* and followed by a *fatḥa* (e.g. تساءَلَ). Remember that a suffix renders a final *hamza* a medial one.

The weighting system is easy. The *sukūn*, or absence of a vowel, is the weakest. The *fatḥa* and the *alif* are more powerful than the *sukūn*, but weaker than the *ḍamma* and the *wāw*. The most powerful vowels are the *kasra* and the *yā'*. Examine the following illustration:

Most Powerful							Least Powerful
Seat	Vowel	Seat	Vowel	Seat	Vowel	Seat	Vowel
ي	ـِ/ي	و	ـُ/و	ا	ـَ/ا	——	ـْ

Thus, if the preceding vowel is a *fatḥa* and the following vowel is a *kasra*, for example, the *hamza* should be seated on a dummy *yā'* (with no dots) because the *kasra* prevails. Now let's look at instances of the *hamza* in the medial position classified according to the vowel preceding it.

i. A *sukūn* Preceding: In the absence of a preceding vowel (marked with a *sukūn*), the seat corresponds to the vowel that follows:

١١ مَسْأَلَة It is placed above an *alif* because the *fatḥa* is more powerful than the *sukūn.*

١٢ مَسْؤول The *wāw* is more powerful and, therefore, the *hamza* is placed on a *wāw.*

١٣ مَرْئِيّ The *kasra* prevails and the *hamza* is placed on a *yā'*.

However, a preceding *yā'*, be it a long vowel or a semivowel, causes the *hamza* to be seated on a *yā'*:

١٤ بيئة شَيْئُك شَيْئِك شَيْئان هَيْئَة بَذيئون

ii. A *fatḥa* Preceding: When the *hamza* is preceded by a *fatḥa* and followed by a *sukūn*, a *fatḥa* or an *alif*, the seat is an *alif*; when the following vowel is a *ḍamma* or a *wāw*, the seat is a *wāw*; and when the next vowel is a *yā'* or a *kasra*, the seat is a *yā'*:

١٥ رَأس سَأَل بَؤُس سَئِم رَئيس رَؤوف

iii. A *ḍamma* Preceding: The *hamza* followed by vowels that are weaker than a *ḍamma* is seated on a *wāw*. But a following *kasra* or a *yā'* require a *yā'* for the *hamza* as a seat:

١٦ لُؤْلُؤ بُؤَر سُؤال سُئِل

iv. A *kasra* Preceding: Since the *kasra* is the most powerful vowel, all instances of a medial *hamza* following *a kasra* are seated on a *yā'*:

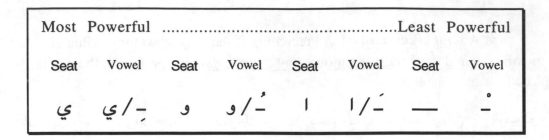

١٧ بِئْر مِئَة مِئات مِئَين

v. An *alif* (ا) or a *wāw* (و) Preceding: If the long vowel preceding is either *alif* (ا) or *wāw* (و) and the *hamza* is followed by a *fatḥa, ḍamma,* or an *alif*, the medial *hamza* is placed flush on the line:

١٨ ساءَل قِراءَة ضَوْءُك يَسوءُك مَملوءان مَملوءاً

vi. *A yā'* (ي) Preceding. If the preceding long vowel is *yā'* (ي) (as either a vowel or a semivowel) and the *hamza* is followed by a *fatḥa, ḍamma,* or an *alif*, a medial *hamza* is spelled on the letter *yā;* (without the dots):

١٩ شَيْئاً شَيْئان شَيْئُك شَيْئَك بَذيئان بيئات

vii. *An alif* (ا) Preceding: A *hamza* after an *alif* is spelled according to the rule of the more powerful vowel if it has a *ḍamma*, *kasra*, *wāw*, or *yā'* following it:

٢٠. تَساؤُل عائِلة مُراؤون مُرائين

viii. A *wāw* (و) Preceding: A *hamza* after a *wāw* is spelled according to the rule of the more powerful vowel if it has a *ḍamma*, *kasra*, *wāw*, or *yā'* following it:

٢١ يَنوؤون تَسوئين يَسوؤُكُم سوئِل

ix. A *yā'* (ي) Preceding: Since the *yā'* is the most powerful vowel, all instances of a medial *hamza* following a *yā'* are seated above a *yā'* regardless of the following vowel.

٢٢ بيئَة بيئات يَجيئان يَجيئون شيْئَين

3. In the final position: A *hamza* in the final position is placed on a letter that corresponds to the *short* vowel preceding it:

٢٣ يَقرَأ لُؤلُؤ سَيِّئ

If no short vowel (a *sukūn*) or a long vowel precedes the final *hamza*, then it is placed on the line:

٢٤ شَيْء جُزْء ماء سوء بَريء

i. Placement of Double *Fatḥa* and Other Suffixes on a Final *Hamza*: You may remember that a double *fatḥa* requires a seat, which is an *alif*. However, not all final *hamzas* need an *alif* for the *tanwīn*. There are two cases where you don't need an *alif*:

(1) If the final *hamza* follows a long *alif* (e.g. مَساءً).

(2) If the final *hamza* is placed above an *alif* (e.g. مَرْفَأً).

On the other hand, you will need an *alif* as a seat for a double *fatḥa* in all other cases. This *alif* may either be connected to the *hamza* or not:

(1) If the letter preceding the final *hamza* is a nonconnector, the *alif* should be independent and unconnected (e.g. جُزْءاً).

(2) If the letter preceding the final *hamza* is a connector, the *alif* should be connected (e.g. عِبْئاً).

SUMMARY

- There are two types of *hamza*: *waṣl* and *qaṭ'*. The former is initial only and is spelled on an *alif* without the diacritic (ء) that distinguishes the *hamza*. It serves a phonetic purpose. The latter occurs in all word positions and is spelled with the diacritic (ء).
- In the initial position the *hamza* is placed above or below an *alif* (أب، إلى).
- In the medial position, it is placed on a silent long vowel corresponding to the stronger of two vowels preceding and following it, or it may be placed on the line.
- In the final position, it is placed on a silent long vowel, corresponding to the preceding vowel, or it may be placed on the line.

التمرين ١٠

Check the correct spelling of each item below and explain your choice in English if necessary.

١ـ	❑ المَرْأة	❑ المَرْءَة	❑ المَرْئَة
٢ـ	❑ لُأيّ	❑ لُئَيّ	❑ لُؤَيّ
٣ـ	❑ تَوْأم	❑ تَوْءَم	❑ تَوْئَم

٤- ❑ مَوْءِل ❑ مَوْإِل ❑ مَوْئِل

٥- ❑ آباء ❑ ءَاباء ❑ أاباء

٦- ❑ رَجاءُها ❑ رَجاؤُها ❑ رَجاأُها

٧- ❑ يَجيْئونَ ❑ يَجيْؤونَ ❑ يَجيْءونَ

التمرين ١١

Provide the correct spelling of the following combinations, where the *hamza* in the items is spelled with an independent *hamza*.

١- مَ + رْ + ءَ + و + س = ...

٢- مُ + ءَ + ا + مَ + ر + ة = ...

٣- ج + ا + ءَ = ...

٤- ح + ا + ءِ + ل = ...

٥- فَ + ءْ + س = ...

٦- رِ + ءَ + ة = ...

٧- ءَ + ثَ + ر = ...

٨- بَ + ذ + ي + ء = ...

٩- مَ + س + ا + ء + ً = ...

١٠- ذِ + ءْ + ب = ...

١١- وَ + طْ + ء + ً = ...

١٢- ن + ا + ء + ي = ...

١٣- س + ا + ءِ + ل = ...

١٤- دَ + و + ا + ءِ + يّ = ...

١٥- يَ + ب + و + ء + و + نَ = ...

١٦- دَ + ء + و + ب = ...

تمرين ١٢

أجِب عن السؤالَين حَسَبَ نَصِّ الاستماع.

١- أينَ تَسكُنُ الفَتاة ووالِدُاها؟

٢- مَنْ يَعمَلُ ويسكُنُ في الدارِ البَيْضاء؟

اكتُبْ «خَطَأ» أو «صَواب» جانِبَ كلِّ جُملةٍ وصَحِّح الجُمَلَ الخَطَأ.

٣- تَدرُسُ الفَتاةُ الهَندسةَ الكَهرُبائية.

٤- للفَتاةِ أخٌ يَدرُسُ في أمرِيكا.

أكمل الجُمَلَ بالاختيار المناسب حَسَبَ نَصِّ الاستماع.

٥- سَتَصِلُ أسرةُ نِزار إلى فيلادلفيا على طائرةٍ ...

❑ سورية ❑ مَغربية ❑ أمرِيكية

٦- اشترى الوالِدُ ...... سَفَر.

❑ تَذكِرةَ ❑ تَذكِرَتَي ❑ ثلاثَ تذاكِرَ

أكمل الجملَ التالية حَسَبَ نَصِّ الاستماع.

٧- تُريدُ الفَتاةُ أنْ تَرى ......

٨- سَتَبقى الفَتاةُ ووالِداها في الدارِ البَيضاء مُدّةَ ......

المُفْرَدات

to select .... اختار (يَختارُ) اختِيار (v.)

last, latest .... آخِر (adjective)

department .... إدارة ج إدارات (n., f.)

to import .... استَوْرَدَ (يَسْتَوْرِد) اسْتيراد

bottom, lowest point, lower .... أسفَل ج أسافِل (n., m., superlative form)

to take care of, to tend .... اعتَنى (يَعْتَني) اعتِناء

top, highest point, upper .... أعْلى ج أعالٍ (n., m., superlative form)

to reside in .... أقام (يُقيم) إقامة

to take (a picture), to pick up .... التَقَطَ (يلتَقِط) التِقاط

female .... أنثى ج إناث (n., f.)

salesman .... بائِع ج بائِعون (n., m.)

to appear, to seem .... بَدا (يَبْدو) بُدُوّ/بَداء

brown .... بُنّيّ (adjective)

merchant, businessman .... تاجِر ج تُجّار (n., m.)

to be late .... تَأخَّر (يَتَأخَّر) تَأخُّر

to retire (from work) .... تَقاعَدَ (يَتَقاعَد) تَقاعُد

signature .... تَوْقيع (n., m.)

grandfather .... جَدّ ج جُدود (n., m.)

geology .... جِيولوجيا (n., f.)

maternal uncle .... خال ج أخْوال (n., m.)

to store .... خَزَّن (يخَزِّن) تَخْزين

to refer to, to review .... راجَعَ (يراجِع) مُراجَعة (v.)

to respond, to answer .... رَدَّ (يَرُدّ) رَدّ

to register .... سَجَّل (يُسَجِّل) تَسجيل

hair .... شَعْر ج شُعور/أشْعار (n., m.)

poetry, poem, knowledge.. (n., m.) شِعْر ج أشعار
last name, surname.. (n., f.) شُهْرة
to issue.. صَدَر (يَصْدُر) صُدور
youngest, smallest.. صُغرى superlative of صَغيرة
height.. (n., m.) طول
paternal uncle.. (n., m.) عَمّ ج أعْمام
age.. (n., m.) عُمْر ج أعْمار
eye.. (n., f.) عَيْن ج عُيون
spare [part], change.. (n., m.) غِيار ج غِيارات
branch, subdivision.. (n., m.) فَرْع ج فُروع
to talk to, to speak.. كَلَّم (يُكَلِّم)
expresses completed action with a verb.. (particle) لَقَدْ
retired person.. (n., m.) مُتَقاعِد ج مُتَقاعِدون
store, shop, place, location.. (n., m.) مَحَلّ ج مَحَلاّت
store, warehouse.. (n., m.) مَخْزَن ج مَخازِن
teacher.. (n., m.) مُدَرِّس ج مُدَرِّسون
sick, ill, patient.. (n., m.) مَريض ج مَرْضى
effectiveness.. (passive participle) مَفعول
note, observation.. (n., f.) مُلاحَظة ج مُلاحَظات
occupation, profession.. (n., f.) مِهْنة ج مِهَن
consisting of, comprising.. (passive participle) مُؤَلَّف
same.. (n., f.) نَفْس ج أنْفُس
ministry, department in an administration.. (n., f.) وِزارة ج وِزارات

Dictionary

Vocabulary items are listed in alphabetical order. Nouns are followed by their plurals after the letter ج for جَمع "plural," and verbs are listed in the past tense third person masculine singular form, followed by the present tense form in parentheses and the verbal noun after the parentheses. Nouns starting with the definite article are listed according to the first letter of the word. The number of the lesson in which an item first occurs is listed in brackets next to the English meaning.

father [11] .... (n., m.) أب ج آباء

to return (round trip) [25] .... (v.) آبَ (يَؤوبُ) إياب (ذَهاباً وإياباً)

August [17] .... (n., m.) آب

elementary [11] .... (adj., m.) ابتدائِيّ

never, at all [26] .... (adv.) أَبَداً

son [11] .... (n., m.) ابن ج أبْناء

14th-century Arab historian and sociologist [9] .... (proper noun) ابْنُ خَلْدون

daughter [11] .... (n., f.) ابنَة ج بَنات

Abu Dhabi (*abū ẓabī*) [4] .... (n., f.) أبو ظَبي

white [25] .... (n., m.) أبيَض ج بيض

to come [17] .... (v.) أتى (يَأتي) اتيان، أتيّ

to hold, to contain [26] .... (v.) اتَّسَعَ (يَتَّسِعُ) اتِّساع

furniture [24] .... (n., m.) أَثاث

ruin, antiquity, artifact, relic [25] .... (n., m.) أثَر ج آثار

two [9] .... (n., m.) اثنان

Monday [17] .... (n., m.) اَلإثْنَين

to respond, to answer [25] .... (v.) أجابَ (يُجيبُ) إجابة

pear [26] .... (n., m.) إجّاص

social gathering [22] .... (n., m.) اجتماع ج اجتماعات

to lease, to let [24] .... أَجَّرَ (يؤجِّر) تأجير

rent, wagc, farc [24] .... (n., f.) أجْرة ج أُجور

for the sake of, because of [28]	أجْل (مِن أجْلِ)
foreign [23]	أجْنَبِيّ ج أجانِب (n., m.)
to like [14]	أحَبَّ (يُحِبُّ) حُبّ، مَحَبّة (v.)
to celebrate [21]	احْتَفَلَ (يَحْتَفِلُ) احْتِفال (v.)
one, someone [15]	أحَد ج آحاد (n., m.)
Sunday [17]	الأحَد (n., m.)
statistics [15]	إحْصاء (n., m.)
to bring [29]	أحْضَرَ (يُحْضِرُ) إحْضار (v.)
red [26]	أحمَر (adj.)
biology [10]	أحْياء (n., f.)
sometimes [13]	أحياناً (adv.)
brother [11]	أخ ج إخوة (n., m.)
sister [11]	أُخت ج أخَوات (n., f.)
to select [30]	اختار (يختار) اختِيار (v.)
to take [23]	أَخَذَ (يَأخُذُ) أخْذ (v.)
other [24]	آخَر ج آخَرون (n., m.)
last, latest [30]	آخِر (adjective)
green [18]	أخْضَر ج خُضْر (adj., m.)
department [30]	إدارة ج إدارات (n., f.)
literature [8]	أدَب ج آداب (n., m.)
proper noun (man's name) [2]	أديب (n., m.)
March [17]	آذار (n., m.)
broadcasting station [28]	إذاعة ج –ات (n., f.)
to want [14]	أرادَ (يُريدَ) إرادة (v.)
Wednesday [17]	الأرْبِعاء (n., m.)
four [9]	أرْبَعة (n., f.)
ground, land [8, 24]	أرض ج أراضٍ
to rise, to be higher [29]	ارتَفَعَ (يَرتَفِعُ) ارتِفاع (v.)
Jordan (*al-urdun*) [4]	الأرْدُن (n., m.)
rice [20]	أرُزّ (n., m.)
to send [23]	أرْسَلَ (يُرسِلُ) إرْسال (v.)
Arizona [4]	أريزونا (n., f.)

أريكة ج أرائك (n., f.) .... couch [24]
أزرق ج زُرْق (adj.) .... blue [26]
أُسْبوع ج أسابيع (n., m.) .... week [17]
استأجَرَ (يَستأجِر) استئجار (v.) .... to rent, to hire [24]
أستاذ ج أساتذة (n., m.) .... professor, teacher [7]
اسْتَحَمَّ (يَستحِمُّ) استِحْمام (v.) .... to bathe, to take a bath or shower [19]
اسْتُشْهِدَ (يُستَشْهَدُ) اسْتِشهاد (passive v.) .... to become a martyr [22]
استَضافَ (يستَضيفُ) استِضافة (v.) .... to host [29]
استَطاعَ (يَستَطيعُ) استِطاعة (v.) .... to be able, can [25]
استَغرَقَ (يَستَغرِقُ) استِغراق (v.) .... to take (time) [29]
اسْتَقبَلَ (يَسْتَقبِلُ) اسْتِقبال (v.) .... to receive (someone) [23]
اسْتِقلال (n., m.) .... independence [21]
استَخدَمَ (يَستَخدِمُ) استِخدام (v.) .... use, utilize, employ [26]
استَمتَعَ (يَستَمتِعُ) استِمتاع (v.) .... to enjoy [25]
استَمَعَ (يَسْتَمِعُ) استِماع (v.) .... to listen [28]
استَوْرَدَ (يَسْتَورِد) اسْتِيراد .... to import [30]
أُسْرة ج أُسَر (n. f.) .... extended family [20]
أسَّسَ (يُؤَسِّسُ) تأسيس (v.) .... to establish, to found [22]
آسِف (n., m.)/ آسِفة (n., f.) .... sorry [12]
أسفَل ج أسافِل (n., m., superlative form) .... bottom, lowest point, lower [30]
إسلام (n., m.) .... Islam [21]
اِسْم ج أسْماء (n., m.) .... name [1]
أسْوَد ج سود (n., m.) .... black [22]
آسيا (n., f.) .... Asia [27]
اشتَرى (يَشتَري) اشتِراء (v.) .... to buy, to purchase [17]
اشْتَرَكَ (يَشْتَرِكُ) اشْتِراك (v.) .... to enroll in, to subscribe to [28]
أصَرَّ (يُصِرُّ) إصْرار (v.) .... to insist [29]

yellow [26] .... (adj.) أصْفَر ج صُفْر

to overlook (s.t.) [27] .... (v.) أطلّ (يطِلُّ) إطلال

Atlantic [27] .... (adj.) أطلَسيّ

to consider [27] .... (v.) اِعتَبَرَ (يَعتَبِرُ) اعتِبار

to believe [29] .... (v.) اعتَقَدَ (يَعتَقِدُ) اعتِقاد

to take care of, to tend [30] .... اِعتَنى (يَعْتَني) اعتِناء

to please [24] .... (v.) أعْجَبَ (يُعْجِبُ) إعْجاب

to give [13] .... (verbal noun) إعْطاء (imperative) (v.) أعْطِ أعطى (يُعطي)

top, highest point, upper [30] .... (m. n., superlative form) أعْلى ج أعالٍ

advertisement, notice, announcement [24] .... (n., m.) إعْلان ج إعْلانات

most knowledgeable [12] .... (n. superlative) أعلَمُ

to be assassinated [22] .... (passive v.) اغتيل (يُغتالُ) اغتِيال

song [28] .... (n., f.) أُغنية ج أغانٍ

Africa [27] .... (n., f.) إفريقية

to reside in [30] .... أقام (يُقيم) إقامة

region [27] .... (n., m.) إقليم ج أقاليم

to eat [14] .... (v.) أكَلَ (يأكُلُ) أكْل

good-bye [1] .... إلى اللِقاء

except, minus [15] .... (particle) إلاّ

until .... إلى أنْ

now [9] .... (n., m.) الآن

device, gadget, machine, apparatus [25] .... (n., f.) آلة ج آلات

to meet, converge, encounter [25] .... (v.) اِلتَقى (يَلتَقي) التِقاء

to take, make (a picture) [25] .... (v.) اِلتَقَطَ (يَلتَقِطُ) التِقاط

inflammation, infection [23] .... (n., m.) اِلْتِهاب ج التِهابات

who, that [25] .... (n., f.) الّتي

who, that [25] .... (n., m.) الَّذي

God [9] .... (n., m.) الله

thousand [15] .... (n., m.) أَلْف ج آلاف

name of the letter *alif* [1] .... (n., f.) أَلِف

pain [23] .... (n., m.) أَلَم ج آلام

to hurt [23] .... (v.) آلَمَ (يُؤلِمُ) ألَم

Germany [16] .... (n., f.) ألمانيا

German [16] .... (adj.) ألمانيّ

mother [11] .... (n., f.) أُمّ ج أُمَّهات

or (particle used in questions) [9] .... (conjunction) أَمْ

as for, but, yet, however [23] .... (particle) أمّا

United Arab Emirates (*al-imārāt*) [4] .... (n., f.) الإمارات

in front of [25] .... (preposition) أمامَ

to examine, to test [25] .... (v.) اِمتَحَنَ (يَمتَحِنُ) امتِحان

woman [9] .... (n., f.) إمرأة ج نِساء

yesterday [17] .... (adv.) أمْسِ

to be possible [28] .... (v.) أمكَنَ (يُمكِنُ) إمْكان

prince [22] .... (n., m.) أمير ج أُمَراء

librarian [12] .... (n., m./f.) أمين/ أمينةُ مكتَبةٍ

to (infinitive) [24] .... (particle) أنْ

that (after verbs similar to "think") [17] .... (particle) أنَّ

if [29] .... (particle) إنْ

hopefully (lit. God willing) [17] .... (set phrase) إنْ شاءَ الله

that (after the verb for "say") [17] .... (particle) إنَّ

I [1] .... (pronoun) أنا

you (singular, masculine) [2] .... (pronoun) أنتَ

you (singular, feminine) [2] .... (pronoun) أنتِ

to produce [27] .... أنتَجَ (يُنتِجُ) إنتاج (v.)
to elect [22] .... انتَخَبَ (يَنتَخِبُ) انتخاب (v.)
to wait [29] .... اِنتَظَرَ (يَنْتَظِرُ) انتظار (v.)
to move, to relocate [21] .... اِنتَقَلَ (يَنتَقِلُ) انتِقال (v.)
you [5] .... أَنتُمْ (pro., m., pl.)
you [5] .... أنْتُما (pro., f./m. dual)
you [5] .... أنتُنَّ (pro., f., pl)
to finish, come to an end [23] .... انْتَهى (يَنْتَهي) انتِهاء (v.)
female [30] .... أنثى ج إناث (n., f.)
Andalusia, Muslim Spain [22] .... الأنْدَلُس (n., f.)
Indiana [4] .... إنديانا (n., f.)
to be interrupted, to be severed [27] .... انقَطَعَ (يَنقَطِعُ) انقِطاع (v.)
English [11] .... إنْكليزيّ (adj.)
English (language) [9] .... الإنكليزيّة (adj.)
hello, welcome (response to a greeting) [1] .... أهلاً (n., m.)
or (particle used with statements) [9] .... أو (conjunction)
Europe [27] .... أوروبا (n., f.)
first [11] .... أوّل ج أوائِل (n., m.)
those [8] .... أولائكَ (pl., demonstrative)
which [13] .... أيُّ (n., m.)/أيّةُ (n., f.)
May [17] .... أيّار (n.)
rent [24] .... إيجار ج إيجارات (n. m.)
Iran [27] .... إيران
too, also [7] .... أيْضاً (adv.)
September [17] .... أيْلول (n., m.)
immensely, greatly (intensifies the following noun) [29] .... أيّما (n.)
where (question particle) [4] .... أيْنَ
on, in, by, with, for [7] .... بِـ (preposition)
name of the letter *bā'* [2] .... باء (n., f.)
door [6] .... باب ج أبواب (n., m.)
Baton Rouge [4] .... باتِن روج (n., f.)

semiarid desert [27] ...... بادِية ج بَوادٍ (n., f.)
eggplant [26] ...... باذِنجان (n., m.)
cold [18] ...... بارِد (adj., m.)
green peas [26] ...... بازَلاّء (n., f.)
Pakistan [16] ...... الباكِسْتان (n., f.)
to sell [24] ...... باعَ (يَبيعُ) بَيْع (v.)
ocra [26] ...... بامْية (n., f.)
salesman ...... بائِع ج بائِعون (n., m.)
to broadcast [28] ...... بَثَّ (يبُثُّ) بَثّ (v.)
sea [18] ...... بَحْر ج بِحار (n., m.)
Bahrain (*al-baḥrayn*) [4] ...... البَحرَين (n., f.)
lake [18] ...... بُحَيْرة ج بُحَيْرات (n., f.)
fine, well [3] ...... بِخَير
to appear, to seem [30] ...... بَدا (يَبْدو) بُدُوّ، بَداء (v.)
to begin [23] ...... بَدَأَ (يَبدَأُ) بَدْء (v.)
beginning [23] ...... بِداية ج بِدايات (n., f.)
seed, kernel [26] ...... بِذرة ج بُذور (n., f.)
refrigerator (Syria) [24] ...... بَرّاد ج بَرّادات (n., m.)
orange [14] ...... بُرتُقال (n., m.)
program [19] ...... بَرنامَج ج بَرامِج (n., m.)
mail, post [25] ...... بَريد (n., m.)
onion [20] ...... بَصَل (n., m.)
merchandise, goods [27] ...... بِضاعة ج بَضائِع (n., f.)
a few [28] ...... بِضْع (n.)
card (n.) [9] ...... بِطاقة ج بِطاقات (n., f.)
watermelon [26] ...... بِطّيخ (n., m.)
after [15] ...... بَعْدَ (prep.)
some [18] ...... بَعْض (n., m.)
far [24] ...... بَعيد (adv.)

Baghdad (*baġdād*) (capital of Iraq) [4] .... (n., f.) بَغداد
grocer [24] .... (n., m.) بَقّال ج بَقّالون
cow, cattle [26] .... (n., f.) بَقَرة ج أبْقار / بَقَر
to remain, to stay [26] .... (v.) بَقِيَ (يَبْقى) بَقاء
rather, but [10] .... (particle) بَلْ
country [21] .... (n., m.) بَلَد ج بِلاد
small town [9] .... (n., f.) بَلْدة ج بَلْدات
local, popular [24] .... (adj.) بَلَديّ
to build, to construct [25] .... (v.) بَنى (يَبني) بِناء
building [10] .... (n., f.) بِناية ج بِنايات
girl [11] .... (n., f.) بِنْت ج بَنات
tomato [26] .... (n., f.) بَنَدورة (طَماطِم في مصر)
bank [24] .... بَنْك ج بُنوك
brown [30] .... (adjective) بُنّيّ
Porsche (German car) .... (n.) پورشَة
Boise [4] .... (n., f.) بويزي
home, house [8] .... (n., m.) بَيْت ج بُيوت
Beirut (capital of Lebanon) [4] .... (n., f.) بَيروت
egg [14] .... (n., m.) بَيْض
white [26] .... (n./adj., f.) بَيضاء ج بيض/ بَيضاوات
name of the letter *tā'* [2] .... (n., f.) تاء
spice, condiment, seasoning [26] .... (n., m.) تابِل ج تَوابِل
merchant, businessman [30] .... (n., m.) تاجِر ج تُجّار
to be late [30] .... تَأخَّر (يَتَأخَّر) تَأخُّر
history [22] .... (n., m.) تاريخ ج تَواريخ
ninth [11] .... (adj.) تاسِع
(entry) visa [29] .... (n., f.) تأشيرة (دُخول) تأشيرات
to consist of, to comprise [27] .... (v.) تَألَّفَ (يَتَألَّف) تَألُّف
insurance [24] .... (n., m.) تأمين ج تأمينات

those [8].. (dual, nom.) تانِكَ

salad made with finely chopped parsley, cracked wheat, tomatoes, lemon juice, and olive oil [19].. (n., f.) تَبّولة

trade, business, commerce [8].. (n., f.) تِجارة

to wander about, to tour [29].. (v.) تَجَوَّلَ (يَتَجَوَّلُ) تَجَوُّل

to graduate [21].. (v.) تَخَرَّجَ (يتخرَّجُ) تَخَرُّج

push, shove one another [29].. (v.) تَدافَعَ (يَتَدافَعُ) تَدافُع

ticket [25].. (n., f.) تَذكِرة ج تَذاكِر

education, upbringing [21].. (n., f.) تَرْبِية

nine [9].. (n., f.) تِسْعة

nice to meet you [1]... تَشَرَّفنا

to be acquainted with [29].. (v.) تَعَرَّفَ (يَتَعَرَّفُ) تَعَرُّف (على)

instruction, education [21]... (n., m.) تَعليم

to be accustomed to [29].. (v.) تَعَوَّدَ (يَتَعَوَّدُ) تَعَوُّد

apple [14].. (n., m.) تُفّاح

differential equations [11]... (n., m.) تَفاضُل

if you please [13].. (imperative verb) تَفَضَّلْ/تَفَضَّلي

to retire (from work) [30].. تَقاعَدَ (يَتَقاعَدُ) تَقاعُد

approximately, about, nearly, roughly [26]... (adv.) تَقريباً

calendar [17].. (n., m.) تَقويم ج تَقاويم

to speak [12].. (v.) تَكَلَّمَ (يَتَكَلَّمُ) تَكَلُّم

television [5].. (n., m.) تلفاز ج تلفازات

that [8].. (demonstrative, f. s.) تِلْكَ

telephone (colloquial) [24].. (n., m.) تَليفون ج تَليفونات

exactly [29].. (adv.) تَماماً

statue [25].. (n., m.) تمثال ج تَماثيل

dates [27].. (n., m.) تَمْر ج تُمور

July [17].. (n., m.) تَمّوز

discrimination [22].. (verbal n., m.) تَمييز

to eat, to take, to reach for something [25].. (v.) تَناوَلَ (يَتَناوَلُ) تَناوُل

to stroll, to have a good time, to go on a picnic [29]........................ (v.) تَنَزَّهَ (يَتَنَزَّهُ) تَنَزُّه

tanwīn (diacritical mark) [6].. (n., m.) تَنوين

berry [26]… (n., m.) توت
to pass away [22]… (passive v.) تُوُفِّيَ (يُتَوَفّى) وَفاة
signature [30]… (n., m.) تَوْقيع
Tunis, Tunisia [4]… (n., f.) تونس
those [8]… (dual, acc., g.) تَيْنِكَ
name of the letter *ṯā'* [2]… (n., f.) ثاء
third [11]… (adj.) ثالث
eighth [11]… (n., m.) ثامِن
second [11]… (n., m.) ثانٍ (الثاني)
secondary [16]… (adj.) ثانَوِيّ
Tuesday [17]… (n., m.) الثُلاثاء
three [9]… (n., f.) ثَلاثة
refrigerator (Egypt) [24]… (n., f.) ثَلاّجة ج ثَلاّجات
a third [15]… (n., m.) ثُلْث ج أثْلاث
snow [18]… (n., m.) ثَلْج ج ثُلوج
then, and again [19]… (conjunction) ثُمَّ
eight [9]… (n., f.) ثَمانِيَة
revolution [21]… (n., f.) ثَوْرة ج ثَورات
garlic [26]… (n., m.) ثوم
sitting [23]… (n., m.) جالِس ج – ون
mosque [22]… (n., m.) جامِع ج جَوامِع
university [7]… (n., f.) جامِعة ج جامِعات
side [7]… (n., m.) جانِب
prize, award [22]… (n., f.) جائِزة ج جَوائِز
algebra [22]… (n., m.) جَبْر
mountain [27]… (n., m.) جَبَل ج جِبال
name of a town in Syria [9]… (n., f.) جَبْلة
cheese [14]… (n., m.) جُبْن ج أجْبان
grandfather [30]… (n., m.) جَدّ ج جُدود
wall [7]… (n., m.) جِدار ج جُدران
new [16]… (adj., m.) جَديد ج جُدُد
to run, to flow, to hurry, to rush, to happen, to occur [26]… (v.) جرى (يَجري) جَرْي

to be wounded, to be hurt [22] .... (passive v.) جُرِحَ (يُجرَحُ) جَرح
newspaper [5] .... (n., f.) جَريدة ج جَرائِد
Algiers (*al-jazā'ir*), Algeria (*al-jazā'ir*) [4] .... (n., f.) الجَزائِر
part [24] .... (n., m.) جُزْء ج أجْزاء
island [27] .... (n., f.) جَزيرة ج جُزُر
geography [27] .... (n., m.) جغرافية
dishwasher [24] .... (n., f.) جَلاّية ج جَلاّيات
to sit down [14] .... (v.) (imperative) جَلَسَ (يَجلِسُ) جُلوس (اجلِسْ)
sitting [17] .... (verbal n.) جُلوس
Islamic month (*Jumādā al-ākira*) [17] .... (n., f.) جُمادى الآخِرة
Islamic month (*Jumādā al-'ūlā*) [17] .... (n., f.) جُمادى الأولَى
Friday [17] .... (n., m.) الجُمْعَة
camel [25] .... (n., m.) جَمَل ج جِمال
republic [22] .... (n., f.) جُمهوريّة ج جُمهوريّات
beautiful, goodlooking [16] .... (adj.) جَميل
south [27] .... (n., m.) جَنوب
[Egyptian] pound [24] .... (n., m.) جُنَيه ج جُنَيْهات
device, apparatus, appliance [27] .... (n., m.) جِهاز ج أجهِزة
passport [29] .... (n., m.) جَواز (سَفَر) ج جَوازات
Djibouti (*jībūti*) [4] .... (n., f.) جيبوتي
good [12] .... (adj.) جَيِّد
well [12] .... (adv.) جَيِّداً
army [22] .... (n., m.) جَيْش ج جُيوش
name of the letter *jīm* [3] .... (n., f.) جيم
geology [30] .... (n., f.) جيولوجيا
hot [18] .... (adj., m.) حارّ
to fight [22] .... (v.) حارَبَ (يُحارِبُ) حِراباً/مُحارَبة
calculator [6] .... (n., f.) حاسِبة ج حاسِبات
computer .... حاسوب ج حَواسيب
ready, present (polite expression) [14] .... (n., m.) حاضِر
bus, tram [19] .... (n., f.) حافِلة ج حافِلات
condition, circumstance [3] .... (n., f.) حالَ (أحوال)

name of the letter *ḥā'* [3] .... (n., f.) حاء
grain, cereal [14] .... (n., m.) حَبّ ج حُبوب
pill [23] .... (n., f.) حَبّة ج حَبّات
till, until [17] .... (particle) حَتّى
pilgrimage [21] .... (n., m.) حَجّ
to border, to demarcate, to limit [27] .... (v.) حَدَّ (يَحُدُّ) حَدّ
border, edge, boundary, borderline [27] .... (n., m.) حَدّ ج حُدود
conversation [15] .... (n., m.) حَديث ج أحاديث
modern [16] .... (adj.) حَديث
park, garden [24] .... (n., f.) حَديقة ج حَدائِق
shoe [29] .... (n., m.) حذاء ج أحْذِية
heat [18] .... (n., f.) حَرارة
war [22] .... (n., f.) حَرْب ج حُروب
campus, sacred possession [29] .... (n., m.) حَرَم ج أحْرام
liberty, freedom [25] .... (n., f.) حُرِّيّة ج ‑ات
silk [29] .... (n., m.) حَرير
to guess [28] .... (v.) حَزَرَ (يحْزِر) حَزْر
June [17] .... (n., m.) حَزيران
to improve, to make better [28] .... (v.) حَسَّنَ (يحَسِّنُ) تَحْسين
good [29] .... (adj.) حَسَن
horse [26] .... (n., m.) حصان ج أحْصِنة
to obtain, to get, to acquire [22] .... (v.) حَصَلَ (يَحصُلُ) حُصول
to attend, to be present [29] .... (v.) حَضَرَ (يحْضُرُ) حُضور
to prepare, to make [19] .... (v.) حَضَّرَ (يُحَضِّرُ) تَحْضير
right, law [8] .... (n., m.) حَقّ ج حُقوق
bag, briefcase [6] .... (n., f.) حَقيبة ج حَقائِب
government [23] .... (n., f.) حُكومة ج حُكومات
Aleppo [7] .... (n., f.) حَلَب
to shave [19] .... (v.) حَلَقَ (يَحْلِقُ) حَلْق
dessert, sweets [21] .... (n., f.) حَلْوى ج حَلْوِيات

ornament, jewelry [29] .... (n., m.) حَلي ج حُليّ
milk [14] .... (n., m.) حَليب
bathroom [19] .... (n., m) حَمّام ج حمّامات
Thank God, praise be to God [3] .... الحَمدُ لِلّه
dip prepared from chickpeas, sesame seed paste, lemon juice [15] .... (n., m.) حمّص
to carry [23] .... (v.) حَمَلَ (يَحْمِلُ) حَمْل
[bath] tub [24] .... (n., m.) حَوْض ج أحْواض
around [29] .... (adv.) حَوْلَ
neighborhood, borough [20], a living person[28] .... (n., m.) حَيّ ج أحْياء
where [12] .... (adv.) حَيْثُ
when [17] .... (adv.) حينَ
animal [25] .... (n., m.) حَيَوان ج –ات
name of the letter *ḳā'* [3] .... (n., f.) خاء
servant [24] .... (n.,m.) خادِم ج خَدَم
outside [29] .... (n.) خارِج
maternal uncle [30] .... (n., m.) خال ج أخْوال
fifth [11] .... (adj.) خامِس
news story [19] .... (n., m.) خَبَر ج أخْبار
baker [24] .... (n., m.) خَبّاز ج خَبّازون
bread [14] .... (n., m.) خُبْز
to stamp, to seal [29] .... (v.) خَتَمَ (يَخْتِمُ) خَتْم
to go out, exit [22] .... (v.) خَرَجَ (يَخرُجُ) خُروج
Khartoum (*al-ḳurṭūm*) (capital of the Sudan) [4] .... (f.) الخُرطوم
map [27] .... (n., f.) خَريطة ج خَرائِط
autumn [18] .... (n., m.) خَريف
closet, cupboard [24] .... (n., f.) خزانة ج خَزائِن/خِزانات
to store [30] .... خَزَّن (يخَزِّن) تَخْزين
lettuce [26] .... (n., m.) خَسّ
horse [26] .... (n., m.) حصان ج خَيل

especially, particularly [26]............ (adv.) خُصوصاً
fertile [27]............ (adj.) خَصيب
green [18]............ (n., f.) خَضْراء ج خَضْراوات
vegetables [19]............ (n., f.) خُضْرة ج خُضَر
greengrocer [24]............ (n., m.) خُضَريّ ج خُضَريّون
orator, preacher, speaker [22]............ (n., m.) خَطيب ج خُطَباء
to take off, to undress [29]............ (v.) خَلَعَ (يَخلَعُ) خَلْع
behind [24]............ (preposition) خَلْفَ
gulf, bay [27]............ (n., m.) خَليج ج خُلجان
caliph, successor [29]............ (n., m.) خَليفة ج خُلَفاء
five [9]............ (n., f.) خَمْسة
Thursday [17]............ (n., m.) الخَميس
pig, swine [14]............ (v.) خِنزير ج خَنازير
house [16]............ (n., f.) دار ج دور
warm [18]............ (adj., m.) دافِئ
name of the letter *dāl* [1]............ (n., f.) دال
to enter [22]............ (v.) دَخَلَ (يَدخُلُ) دُخول
bicycle [5]............ (n., f.) دَرّاجة ج دَرّاجات
study, studying [16]............ (n., f.) دِراسة ج دِراسات
of school, academic [11])............ (adj.) دِراسيّ
degree (temperature), step, class [18/29]............ (درجة حرارة) (n., f.) دَرَجة ج دَرَجات
to study [10]............ (v.) دَرَسَ (يَدرُسُ) دِراسة/دَرْس
lesson [17]............ (n., m.) دَرْس ج دُروس
defense [22]............ (n., m.) دِفاع ج دِفاعات
notebook [5]............ (n., m.) دَفتَر ج دَفاتر
to pay [29]............ (v.) دَفَعَ (يَدْفَعُ) دَفْع
minute [15]............ (n., f.) دَقيقة ج دَقائِق
shop, store [24]............ (n., f.) دُكّان ج دَكاكين
to show, to indicate, to point out [29]............ (v.) دَلَّ (يَدُلُّ) دَلالة

Damascus (*dimašq*) (capital of Syria) [4] .... (n., f.) دمشق
Doha (*ad-dawḥa*) (capital of Qatar) [4] .... (n., f.) الدَوحة
international [15] .... (n., m.) دَوْلِيّ
without [14] .... (prep.) دونَ
cock, rooster [21] .... (n., m.) ديك ج ديَكة
turkey [21] .... (n., m.) ديك حَبَش
dinar (Kuwaiti currency) [24] .... (n., m.) دينار ج دَنانير
name of the letter *ḏāl* [1] .... (n., f.) ذال
corn [26] .... (n., f.) ذُرة
chin (when used with 'shave' it signifies facial hair) [19] .... (n., f.) ذَقْن ج ذُقون
that (demonstrative) [8] .... (n., m. s.) ذلكَ
to go [16] .... (v.) ذَهَبَ (يذْهَبُ) ذَهاب (إلى)
with, of, owner of [17] .... (n., m.) ذو ج ذَوو
Islamic month (*ḏū al-ḥijja*) [17] .... (n., m.) ذو الحجّة
Islamic month (*ḏū al-Qi'da*) [17] .... (n., m.) ذو القِعدة
name of the letter *rā'* [1] .... (n., f.) راء
to see [23] .... (v.) رَأى (يَرى) رُؤية
fourth [11] .... (adj.) رابِع
to refer to, to review [30] .... (v.) راجَعَ (يراجِع) مُراجَعة
head [22] .... (n., m.) رأس ج رُؤوس
passenger, rider [27] .... (n., m.) راكِب ج رُكّاب
Rabat (*ar-rabāṭ*) (capital of Morocco) [4] .... (n., f.) الرَباط
housewife [23] .... (n., f.) رَبّةُ بَيْت ج رَبّات بُيوت
quarter [15] .... (n., m.) رُبْع ج أرْباع
perhaps, probably [26] .... (adv.) رُبَّما
spring [18] .... (n., m.) رَبيع
Islamic month (*Rabī' al-'āḵir*) [17] .... (n., m.) رَبيع الآخر
Islamic month (*Rabī' al-'awwal*) [17] .... (n., m.) رَبيع الأوّل
to hope [25] .... (v.) رَجا (يَرجو) رَجاء
Islamic month (*Rajab*) [17] .... (n., m.) رَجَب
to return, to go back [19] .... (v.) رَجَعَ (يَرْجِعُ) رُجوع

man [9] .... (n., m.) رَجُل ج رِجال
trip, journey, flight [29] .... (n., f.) رِحْلة ج رِحلات
cheap, inexpensive [29] .... (adj.) رَخيص
to respond, to answer [30] .... رَدَّ (يَرُدّ) رَدّ
letter, message [19] .... (n., f.) رِسالة ج رَسائِل
to reject [22] .... (v.) رَفَضَ (يَرفُضُ) رَفْض
number [9] .... (n., m.) رَقْم ج أرْقام
to ride, to mount [25] .... (v.) رَكِبَ (يَركَبُ) رُكوب
to dance [28] .... (v.) رَقَصَ (يرقُصُ) رَقْص
Ramadan, the month of fasting [21] .... (n., m.) رَمَضان
to irrigate, to water [27] .... (v.) رَوى (يَروي) رَيّ
Roman [29] .... (adj.) رومانيّ
Riyadh (*ar-riyāḍ*) (capital of Saudi Arabia) [4] .... (n., f.) الرياض
sport [8] .... (n., f.) رِياضة ج رِياضات
of sports [8] .... (adj.) رِياضيّ
mathematics, calculus [7] .... (n., f.) رِياضِيّات
leader, president [22] .... (n., m.) رَئيس ج رُؤَساء
wind [18] .... (n., f.) ريح ج رِياح
to visit [20] .... (v.) زارَ (يَزورُ) زِيارة
name of the letter *zāy* [1] .... (n., f.) زاي
plus [9] .... (n., m.) زائد
butter [14] .... (n., f.) زُبْدَة
to plant, to cultivate [27] .... (v.) زَرَعَ (يَزرَعُ) زِراعة
leader (popular) [22] .... (n., m.) زَعيم ج زُعَماء
alley, narrow street [29] .... (n., m.) زُقاق ج أزِقّة
colleague, coworker [23] .... (n., m.) زَميل ج زُمَلاء
flower [18] .... (n., f.) زَهْرة ج زَهْرات، أزْهار
husband [11] .... (n., m.) زَوْج ج أزْواج
wife [11] .... (n., f.) زَوْجة ج زَوْجات
olive [14] .... (n., m.) زَيْتون
shall, will [17] .... (future particle) سَـ
seventh [11] .... (adj.) سابِع

square, courtyard [25] .... (n., f.) ساحة ج ساحات
coast, shore [27] .... (n., m.) ساحِل ج سَواحِل
sixth [11] .... (adj.) سادِس
to move, to walk, to travel, to march, to flow [25] .... (v.) سارَ (يَسير) سَيْر
brilliant, shining [18] .... (adj., m.) ساطِع
mail carrier [23] .... (n., m.) ساعٍ ج سُعاة (ساعي بَريد)
watch, clock, o'clock, hour [5] .... (n., f.) ساعة ج ساعات
to help, to assist [23] .... (v.) ساعَدَ (يُساعِدُ) مُساعَدة
watch, clock [15] .... (n., f.) ساعة ج ساعات
to drive [29] .... (v.) ساقَ (يَسوقُ) سِياقة
safe, secure, healthy [23] .... (n., m.) سالِم ج سالِمون
equals [9] .... (v.) ساوَى (يُساوي) مُساواة
driver, chauffeur [16] .... (n., m.) سائِق ج سائِقون
reason, cause [23] .... (n., m.) سَبَب ج أسْباب
Saturday [17] .... السَبْت
to swim [18] .... (v.) سَبَحَ (يَسْبَحُ)
seven [9] .... (n., f.) سَبْعة
six [9] .... (n., f.) سِتّة
to register [30] .... سَجَّلَ (يُسَجِّلُ) تَسجيل
prisoner [29] .... (n., m.) سَجين ج سُجَناء
silly, absurd, foolish [29] .... (n./adj.) سَخيف ج سُخَفاء
to please, to be glad [29] .... (v.) سَرَّ (يَسُرُّ) سُرور
bed [10] .... (n., m.) سَرير ج أسِرّة
surface, level [29] .... (n., m.) سَطْح ج سُطوح
Saudi Arabia (*as-suçūdiyya*) [4] .... (n., f.) السُعودية
happy, pleased, joyful [25] .... (n., m.) سَعيد ج سُعَداء
embassy [29] .... (n., f.) سِفارة ج سَفارات
to fall [18] .... (v.) سَقَطَ (يَسْقُطُ) سُقوط
sugar [14] .... (v.) سُكَّر
to live [9] .... (v.) سَكَنَ (يَسْكُنُ) سَكَن
(student) living, residence, dormitory [9] .... (verbal noun, m.) سَكَن (الطلاب)
sukūn (absence of a vowel) [6] .... (n., m.) سُكون

peace be upon you (greeting) [1] … السلامُ عَلَيْكُمْ
basket [26] … (n., f.) سَلّة ج سِلال
range, series, chain [27] … (n., f.) سلسلة ج سَلاسِل
salad [14] … (n.) سَلَطة ج سَلَطات
wire [28] … (n., m.) سِلْك ج أسْلاك
to save, to protect, to greet, to hand, to deliver [21] … (v.) سَلَّمَ (يُسَلِّمُ) تَسْليم
sky [18] … (n., f.) سَماء ج سَماوات
a kind of toasted thin bread [26] … (n., m.) سَميط
tooth [19] … (n., m.) سِنّ ج أسْنان
age of a person [21] … (n., m.) سِنّ
year [17] … (n., f.) سَنَة ج سَنَوات، سُنون
plain [27] … (n., m.) سَهل ج سُهول
question, query [25] … (n., m.) سُؤال ج أسئِلة
the Sudan (*as-sūdān*) [4] … (n., m.) السودان
Syria (*sūrya*) [4] … (n., f.) سورية
shall, will [17] … (future particle) سَوْفَ
market [16] … (n., f.) سوق ج أسْواق
car [5] … (n., f.) سَيّارة ج سَيّارات
political [29] … (adj.) سِياسيّ
name of the letter *sīn* [3] … (n., f.) سين
to want, to will [9] … (v.) شاءَ (يَشاءُ)
truck [24] … (n. f.) شاحِنة ج شاحِنات
street [9] … (n., m.) شارِع ج شَوارِع
beach [18] … (n., m.) شاطِئ ج شَواطِئ
poet [22] … (n., m.) شاعِر ج شُعَراء
vacant, empty, unoccupied, free [29] … (adj.) شاغِر
Syria, Damascus, Greater Syria [23] … (n., f.) الشام
to see, to watch, to witness [25] … (v.) شاهَدَ (يُشاهِدُ) مُشاهَدة
tea [14] … (n., m.) شاي
February [17] … (n., m.) شُباط
semi-, quasi, similarity [27] … (n., m.) شِبْه ج أشباه
winter [18] … (n., m.) شِتاء

tree [18] .... شَجَرة ج شَجَرات (n., f.)
personality, character [22] .... شَخصيّة ج شَخصيّات (n., m.)
šadda (diacritical mark that signifies a doubled consonant) [6] .... شَدّة (n., f.)
drink, beverage, sherbet [23] .... شَراب ج أشْرِبة، شَرابات (n., m.)
to drink [14] .... شَرِبَ (يَشْرَبُ) شُرْب (v.)
to explain, to expound, to illustrate [26] .... شَرَحَ (يَشرَحُ) شَرْح (v.)
bedsheet [17] .... شَرْشَف ج شَراشِف (n., m.)
company [24] .... شَرِكة ج شَرِكات (n., f.)
tape [28] .... شَريط ج أشْرِطة (n., m.)
person [28] .... شَخْص ج أشْخاص (n., m.)
sandwich [26] .... شَطيرة ج شَطائِر (n., f.)
emblem, sign, slogan [27] .... شِعار ج شِعارات، أشعِرة (n., m.)
Islamic month (*ša'bān*) [17] .... شَعبان (n., m.)
hair [30] .... شَعْر ج شُعور، أشْعار (n. m.)
poetry, poem, knowledge [30] .... شِعْر ج أشعار (n., m.)
apartment [9] .... شَقّة ج شُقَق (n., f.)
thank you [9] .... شُكْراً (adv.)
to form, to constitute [27] .... شَكَّلَ (يُشَكِّلُ) تَشكيل (v.)
waterfall [25] .... شَلاّل ج شَلاّلات (n., m.)
north [25] .... شَمال (n., m.)
sun [18] .... شَمْس ج شُموس (n., f.)
of the sun [7] .... شَمسيّ (adj.)
month [17] .... شَهْر ج أشْهُر، شُهور (n., m.)
last name, surname [30] .... شُهْرة (n., f.)
Islamic month (*šawwāl*) [17] .... شَوّال (n., m.)
to grill, to broil [26] .... شَوى (يَشوي) شَيّ (v.)
thing, object [25] .... شَيْء ج أشياء (n., m.)
name of the letter *šīn* [3] .... شين (n., f.)
soap [19] .... صابون (n., m.)
to become [21] .... صارَ (يَصيرُ) صَيْر، صَيْرورة، مَصير (v.)
pure, clear, not cloudy [18] .... صافٍ (adj., m.) صافية (adj., f.)
to fast [21] .... صامَ (يَصومُ) صَوْم (v.)

to flow into [27].. صَبَّ (يصُبُّ) صَبّ (.v)
morning [14].. صَباح (.n., m)
good morning [3].. صَباحُ الخَير
good morning (response) [3].. صَباحُ النور
journalism [24].. صحافة (.n., f)
health [24].. صِحّة (.n)
journalist [29].. صَحَفيّ ج ـون (.n., m)
desert [27].. صَحْراء ج صَحاري (.n., f)
clear, fine (of weather) [18].. صَحْوٌ (.adj., m)
newspaper [29].. صَحيفة ج صُحُف (.n., f)
to issue [30].. صَدَر (يَصْدُر) صُدور
friend [16].. صَديق ج أصْدِقاء (.n., m)
youngest, smallest [30].. صُغرى superlative of صَغيرة
small, child, young child [16].. صَغير ج صِغار (.n., m)
class, classroom [7].. صَفّ ج صُفوف (.n., m)
Islamic month (*ṣafar*) [17].. صَفَر (.n., m)
zero [9].. صِفر ج أصْفار (.n., m)
to pray, to bless [21].. صَلّى (يُصَلّي) صَلاة (.v)
industry [25].. صِناعة ج صِناعات (.n., f)
to manufacture, to make [27].. صَنَعَ (يَصنَعُ) صِناعة (.v)
San'a (*ṣançā'*) (capital of Yemen) [4].. صَنعاء (.n., f)
to make a picture, to portray, to illustrate [25].. صَوَّرَ (يُصَوِّرُ) تَصوير (v)
picture [6].. صورة ج صُوَر (.n., f)
Somalia (*aṣ-ṣōmāl*) [4].. الصومال (.n., m)
pharmacology [12].. صَيْدَلَة (.n., f)
ranking officer [22].. ضابِط ج ضُبّاط (.n., m)
to laugh [29].. ضَحِكَ (يَضْحَكُ) ضِحْك، ضَحِك (.v)
opposite, anti-, adversary, opponent [23].. ضِدّ ج أضْداد (.n., m)
molar tooth [23].. ضِرْس ج أضْراس، ضُروس (.n., m)
narrow, tight [27].. ضَيِّق (.adj)
floor, storey, flat [24].. طابَق ج طَوابِق
male student [7].. طالِب ج طُلاّب (.n., m)

female student [7] .... (n., f.) طالِبة ج طالِبات
table [6] .... (n., f.) طاوِلة ج طاوِلات
airplane [17] .... (n., f.) طائِرة ج طائِرات
medicine [8] .... (n., m.) طِبّ
physician, doctor [23] .... (n., m.) طَبيب ج أطِبّاء
of course [28] .... (adv.) طَبْعاً
nature [28] .... (n., f,) طَبيعة
Tripoli (*ṭarāblus al-ġarb*) (capital of Libya) [4] .... (n., f.) طَرابلُس الغَرب
way, road [25] .... (n., f.) طَريق ج طُرُق، طُرُقات
food [21] .... (n., m.) طَعام ج أطْعِمة
taste, flavor [29] .... (n., m.) طَعْم ج طُعوم
patty made from ground beans and spices fried in oil (Egypt) [14] .... (n., f.) طَعْمِيّة
child [28] .... (n., m.) طِفْل ج أطْفال
weather [18] .... (n., m.) طَقْس ج طُقوس
good [23] .... (n., m.) طَيِّب ج طَيِّبون
bird [29] .... (n., m.) طَيْر ج طُيور
to think, to believe [17] .... (v.) ظَنَّ (يَظُنُّ) ظَنّ
to appear, to become visible [28] .... (v.) ظَهَرَ (يَظهَر) ظُهور
noon [14] .... (n., m.) ظُهْر
height [30] .... (n., m.) طول
Toulon (a town in southern France) [22] .... (n., f.) طولون
tall [16] .... (n., m.) طَويل ج طِوال
to go back, to return [28] .... (v.) عادَ (يعودُ) عَوْد
usually [13] .... (adv.) عادَةً
tenth [11] .... (adj.) عاشِر
capital city [27] .... (n., f.) عاصِمة ج عَواصِم
high, elevated [27] .... (adj.) عالٍ (العالي)
world [19] .... (n., m.) عالَم ج عَوالِم
scholar, scientist [22] .... (n., m.) عالِم ج عُلَماء
year [23] .... (n., m.) عام ج أعْوام
public [26] .... (adj.) عامّ
colloquial, vulgar, dialectal [28] .... (adj.) عامّيّ

worker, laborer (Labor Day) [20]................................ عامِل ج عُمّال (n., m.) (عيد العُمّال)
family [11].. عائِلَة ج عائِلات (n., f.)
cloak, woolen wrap [29].. عَباءَة ج عَباءات (n., f.)
to cross [29].. عَبَرَ (يَعبُرُ) عُبور (v.)
a number of, several [8]... عِدّةُ (adj.)
number (quantity) [25].. عَدَد ج أعْداد (n., m.)
lentils [20].. عَدَس (n., m.)
several, multiple [27]... عَديد (adj.)
Iraq (*al-çirāq*) [4].. العِراق (n., m.)
Arabic (language) [9].. العَرَبِيّة (n., f.)
Arab [4].. عَرَبِيّ ج عَرَب (n., m.)
show, demonstration, performance [25]............................ عَرْض ج عُروض (n., m.)
to know [9].. عَرَفَ (يَعرِفُ) مَعْرِفة، عِرْفان (v.)
dear, esteemed, beloved [25].. عَزيز ج أعِزّاء (n., m.)
honey [14].. عَسَل (n., m.)
dinner [18].. عَشاء ج أعْشِية (n., m.)
ten [9].. عَشَرة (n., f.)
stick, rod, cane [26].. عَصا ج عُصِيّ (n., f.)
juice [14].. عَصير (n., m.)
break, vacation [20].. عُطْلة ج عُطلات (n., f.)
weekend [20].. عُطْلَةُ نِهايَةِ الأُسْبَوعِ (n., f.)
great, important, imposing [25]................................ عَظيم ج عُظَماء (adj./n., m.)
you're welcome (response to "thank you") [9].. عَفْواً (adv.)
cord used to hold *fūfiyya* in place [16]................................ عِقال ج عُقُل (n., m.)
group of ten [12].. عَقْد ج عُقود (n., m.)
opposite, reverse, contrary [29].. عَكْس (n.)
on [7].. عَلى (prep.)
relation [15].. عَلاقة ج عَلاقات (n., f.)
to hang [24].. عَلَّقَ (يُعَلِّقُ) تَعْليق (v.)
flag, banner [27].. عَلَم ج أعْلام (n., m.)
to know [23].. عَلِمَ (يَعْلَمُ) عِلْم (v.)
science, discipline [8].. عِلْم ج عُلوم (n., m.)

of science, scientific [8] .... (adj.) عِلميّ
response to السلامُ عَلَيْكُمْ [1] .... وَعَلَيْكُمُ السلام
knowledgeable [12] .... (adj.) عَليم
Amman (*çammān*) (capital of Jordan) [4] .... (n., f.) عَمّان
Oman (*çumān*) [4] .... (n., f.) عُمان
mayor [20] .... (n., m.) عُمْدة ج عُمَد
paternal uncle [30] .... (n., m.) عَمّ ج أعْمام
age [30] .... (n. m.) عُمْر ج أعْمار
to work [16] .... (v.) عَمِلَ (يَعْمَلُ) عَمَل
to mean [15] .... (v.) عَنَى (يَعْني) عَني، عِناية
grape [26] .... (n., m.) عِنَب
at (expresses possession with possessive pronouns) [5] .... (prep.) عِنْدَ
race, element [22] .... (n., m.) عُنْصُر ج عَناصِر
racial [22] .... (adj.) عُنْصُريّ
address [9] .... (n., m.) عُنوان ج عَناوين
doctor's practice, clinic [24] .... عِيادة ج عِيادات
celebration, festivity, holiday, feast day [20] .... (n., m.) عيد ج أعْياد
Feast of Immolation (after Haj), Greater Bairam [21] .... (n., m.) عيدُ الأضْحى
Thanksgiving [21] .... (n., m.) عيدُ الشُكْر
Easter [21] .... (n., m.) عيدُ الفِصْح
feast of breaking the Ramadan fast [21] .... (n., m.) عيدُ الفِطْر
bread (Egypt) [24] .... (n., m.) عَيش
eye [30] .... (n., f.) عَيْن ج عُيون
to leave [29] .... (v.) غادَرَ (يُغادِرُ) مُغادَرة
[butane] gas [24] .... (n., m.) غاز ج غازات
expensive, dear [25] .... (n., m.) غالٍ
often, mostly, generally [25] .... (adv.) غالِباً
cloudy [18] .... (adj., m.) غائِم
a male's headdress [16] .... (n., f.) غُتْرة ج غُتَر، غُتْرات
tomorrow [17] .... (adv.) غَداً
lunch [18] .... (n., m.) غَداء ج أغْدية
west [25] .... (n., m.) غَرْب

room [7] .... (n., f.) غُرفة ج غُرَف
sunset [23] .... (n., m.) غُروب
washing machine [24] .... (n., f.) غَسّالة ج غَسّالات
to wash [19] .... (v.) غَسَلَ (يَغْسِلُ) غَسْل
to sing [28] .... (v.) غَنّى (يُغَنّي) غِناء
rich, wealthy [23] .... (n., m.) غَنيّ ج أغنياء
spare [part], change [30] .... (n., m.) غِيار ج غِيارات
non-, un-, other than, different from [27] .... (n., m.) غَيْر
cloud [18] .... (n., f.) غَيْمة ج غُيوم
and, then, so [23] .... (coordinating particle) فَـ
name of the letter *fā'* [3] .... (n., f.) فاء
to win [26] .... (v.) فازَ (يفوزُ) فَوز
Fez (*fās*) (town in Morocco) [4] .... (n., f.) فاس
green beans [26] .... (n., f.) فاصوليَة
benefit, use, advantage [23] .... (n., f.) فائدة ج فَوائد
girl, young woman [16] .... (n., f.) فَتاة ج فَتَيات
dawn, daybreak [21] .... (n., m.) فَجْر
brush .... (n., f.) فُرْشاة ج فَراشٍ
pharaoh [25] .... (n., m.) فِرعَون ج فَراعِنة
band, company, troupe [25] .... (n., f.) فِرقة ج فِرَق
French (language) [9] .... (adj.) الفَرنسيَة
branch, subdivision [30] .... (n., m.) فَرْع ج فُروع
team, company, band, troupe [26] .... (n., f.) فَريق ج أفرِقة
riddle [28] .... (n., f.) فَزّورة ج فَوازير
(academic) term, season [11] .... (n., m.) فَصْل ج فُصول
pure, good, clear, standard, or literary, Arabic [28] .... (adj.) فَصيح
space [28] .... (n., m.) فَضاء
silver [29] .... (n., f.) فِضّة
breakfast [19] .... (n., m.) فَطور
pie [21] .... (n., f.) فَطيرة ج فَطائر
to do [13] .... (v.) فَعَلَ (يَفعَلُ)
only, no more [11] .... فَقَطْ

poor [23] .... (n., m.) فَقير ج فُقَراء
peasant, farmworker [30] .... (n., m.) فَلاّح ج فَلاّحون
philosophy [22] .... (n., f.) فَلْسَفة ج فَلسَفات
patty made from ground beans and spices fried in oil [14] .... (n., m.) فُلفُل ج فَلافِل
Palestine (*filasṭīn*) [4] .... (n., f.) فِلَسطين
green (bell) pepper [26] .... (n., f.) فُلَيفُلة
cup [14] .... (n., m.) فِنْجان ج فَناجين
hotel [17] .... (n., m.) فُنْدُق ج فَنادِق
to understand, to comprehend, to realize [26] .... (v.) فَهِمَ (يَفْهَمُ) فَهْم
fava bean [14] .... (n., m.) فول
peanuts [26] .... (n., m.) فول (سوداني)
in [4] .... (prep.) في
physics [11] .... (n., f.) فيزياء
philosopher [22] .... (n., m.) فَيْلَسوف ج فَلاسِفة
to drive [29] .... (v.) قادَ (يَقودُ) قِيادة
boat [25] .... (n., m.) قارِب ج قَوارِب
continent [27] .... (n., f.) قارّة ج قارّات
rule, principle, basis, foundation, base [26] .... (n., f.) قاعِدة ج قَواعِد
name of the letter *qāf* [3] .... (n., f.) قاف
to say [17] .... (v.) قالَ (يَقولُ) قَوْل
to do, to perform [22] .... (v.) قامَ (يَقومُ) قِيام
to gamble [25] .... (v.) قامَرَ (يُقامِرُ) مُقامَرة، قِمار
law [22] .... (n., m.) قانون ج قَوانين
Cairo (*al-qāhira*) (capital of Egypt) [4] .... (n., f.) القاهِرة
leader (military) [22] .... (n., m.) قائِد ج قُوّاد، قادة
before [17] .... (adv.) قَبْلَ
no meaning, denotes completed action, emphasis, or possibility [29] .... (particle) قَد
Jerusalem (*al-quds*) (capital of Palestine) [4] .... (n., f.) القُدس
foot [29] .... (n., f.) قَدَم ج أقدام
to serve, to provide, give [25] .... (v.) قَدَّمَ (يُقَدِّمُ) تَقديم
old, ancient [16] .... (adj.) قَديم ج قُدَماء
to read [13] .... (v.) قَرَأَ (يَقرَأُ) قِراءة

nearby, close [22]........ (adv.) قُرْب
pumpkin [21]........ (n., m.) قَرْع
cauliflower [26]........ (n., m.) قَرَنبيط
close, near [17]........ (adj.) قَريب
a relative [29]........ (n., m.) قَريب ج أقارِب
village [22]........ (n., f.) قَرية ج قُرى
priest [22]........ (n., m.) قَسّ ج قَساوِسة
story [29]........ (n., f.) قِصّة ج قِصَص
short [16]........ (n./adj., m.) قَصير ج قِصار
train [20]........ (n., m.) قِطار ج قِطارات
Qatar (*qaṭar*) [4]........ (n., f.) قَطَر
country (almost exclusively used for Arab countries) [27]........ (n., m.) قُطْر ج أقْطار
piece [14]........ (n., f.) قِطْعة ج قِطَع
cotton [29]........ (n., m.) قُطْن ج أقْطان
pen, pencil [5]........ (n., m.) قَلَم ج أقلام
little [12]........ (n,. m.) قَليل
a little [12]........ (adv.) قَليلاً
wheat [27]........ (n., m.) قَمْح
moon, satellite [28]........ (n. m.) قَمَر ج أقْمار
of the moon [7]........ (adj.) قَمَريّ
shirt [17]........ (n., m.) قَميص ج قُمْصان
channel [28]........ (n., f.) قَناة ج قَنَوات
coffee [14]........ (n., f.) قَهْوة
powerful, strong [16]........ (n., m.) قَويّ ج أقوِياء
like, as [26]........ (prep.) كَـ
writer, scribe [22]........ (n., m.) كاتِب ج كُتّاب، كَتَبة
glass [14]........ (n., m.) كَأس ج كُؤوس
to be (was, were) [17]........ (v.) كانَ (يَكونُ) كَون
December [17]........ (n., m.) كانون الأوّل
January [17]........ (n., m.) كانون الثاني
kebob, minced meat on a skewer with parsley and onion [15]........ (n., m.) كَباب
big, large, old (in age) [16]........ (n., m.) كَبير ج كِبار

to write [13, 19]	كَتَبَ (يَكْتُبُ) كِتابة
book [5]	(n., m.) كتاب ج كُتُب
much, a great deal [19]	(n., m.) كَثير ج كَثيرون، كِثار
a great deal [14]	(adverbial) كَثيراً
also, as well [25]	كَذلك
ball, sphere [26]	(n., f.) كُرَة ج كُرات
basketball [26]	كُرَةُ السلة
table tennis [26]	كرة الطاولة
volleyball [26]	الكرة الطائرة
football, succor [26]	كرة القدم
water polo [26]	كُرَةُ الماء
tennis [26]	كُرَةُ المَضرب
chair [6]	(n., m.) كُرسي ج كَراسٍ
hospitality, generosity [29]	(n., m.) كَرَم
every, all, the whole [18]	(n., m.) كُلّ
both [27]	(n.) كلا
speech, speaking [29]	(n., m.) كَلام
to cost [29]	(v.) كَلَّفَ (يُكَلِّفُ) تَكليف، تَكلِفة
to talk to, to speak [30]	كَلَّم (يُكَلِّم) تَكليم، كَلام
word [9]	(n., f.) كَلِمة ج كَلِمات
college [8]	(n., f.) كُلِّيَة ج كُلِّيات
how many/much (question particle) [9]	(interrogative particle) كَم
as [23]	(particle) كَما
electricity [23]	(n., f.) كَهْرَباء
zucchini [26]	(n., m.) كوسا
headdress [16]	(n., f.) كوفيّة ج (ات)
Kuwait (*al-kuwayt*) [4]	(n., f.) الكُوَيت
cable [28]	(n., m.) كيبل
how [3]	(particle) كَيفَ
How are you? [3]	كَيفَ الحال؟
kilometer [25]	(n., m.) كيلومتر ج كيلومِترات
chemistry [11]	(n., f.) كيمياء

to, for, by [12] .... (prep.) لـِ
no (negative particle) [2] .... لا
player [29] .... (n., m.) لاعِب ج لاعِبون
because [19] .... (particle) لأنَّ
kernel, seed [26] .... (n., m.) لُبّ ج لُبوب
to wear [16] .... (v.) لَبِسَ (يَلبَس) لُبْس
yogurt [19] .... (n., m.) لَبَن
Lebanon (*lubnān*) [4] .... (n., m.) لُبنان
meat [14] .... (n., m.) لَحْم ج لُحوم
for this reason, therefore [20] .... (demonstrative) لذلكَ
delicious, delightful, tasty [26] .... (adj., m.) لَذيذ
to play [26] .... (v.) لَعِبَ (يَلعَبُ) لَعْب
game, play, ride [25] .... (n., f.) لُعبة ج لُعبات، ألعاب
language [8] .... (n., f.) لُغة ج لُغات
of language, linguistic [8] .... (adj.) لُغَويّ
expresses completed action with a verb [29] .... (particle) لَقَدْ
but (weak version) [7] .... لكنْ
but (strong version) [7] .... لكنَّ
not (particle used to negate past-tense verbs) [23] .... (particle) لَمْ
why [19] .... (particle) لماذا
blackboard [6] .... (n., m.) لَوح ج ألواح
color [18] .... (n., m.) لَوْن ج ألْوان
Libya (*lībyā*) [4] .... (n., f.) ليبيا
not (negative particle) [7] .... لَيْسَ
[Syrian] pound; lira [24] .... (n., f.) لَيْرة ج لَيْرات
night [18] .... (n., m.) لَيْل
(a) night [23] .... (n., f.) لَيْلة ج لَيال
meter [24] .... (n., m.) م (مِتْر) ج أمْتار
what (question particle used in front of nouns) [9] .... ما
particle used to negate past tense verbs [16] .... (particle) ما
except [23] .... (particle) ما عَدا
what [27] .... (adverbial particle) ما

what [28] .... (relative noun) ما
to die [28] .... (v.) ماتَ (يموتُ) مَوْت
water [14] .... (n., m.) ماء ج مِياه
soda [26] .... (n., f.) ماء غازيّ ج مِياه غازيّة
school subject, course [10] .... (n., f.) مادّة ج مَوادّ
what (question particle used with verbs) [9] .... ماذا
previous, last, past [23] .... (adj.) ماضٍ (الماضي)
rainy [18] .... (adj., m.) ماطِر
match, game [26] .... (n., f.) مُباراة ج مُبارَيات
blessed [23] .... (n., m.) مُبارَك
pencil sharpener [6] .... (n., f.) مبراة ج مبرايات
one coming early [19] .... (n., m.) مُبَكِّر ج مُبَكِّرون
building, construction [25] .... (n. m.) مَبنى ج مَبانٍ
when (question particle) [14] .... مَتى
one coming late [19] .... (n., m.) مُتَأخِّر ج مُتَأخِّرون
united [15] .... (adj., m.) مُتَّحِد
museum [25] .... (n., m.) مُتحَف ج مَتاحِف
metro [24] .... (n., m.) مترو
married man [28] .... (n., m.) مُتَزَوِّج ج مُتَزَوِّجون
spectator [26] .... (n., m.) مُتَفَرِّج ج مُتَفَرِّجون
retired person [30] .... (n., m.) مُتَقاعِد ج مُتَقاعِدون
intermediate [21] .... (adj., m.) مُتَوَسِّط
something similar, like, such as [25] .... (n., m.) مِثْلُ ج أمْثال
free of charge [28] .... (adj.) مَجّانيّ
kitchen sink [24] .... (n., m.) مَجْلى ج مَجالٍ
magazine [13] .... (n., f.) مَجَلّة ج مَجَلّات
accountant [29] .... (n., m.) مُحاسِب ج مُحاسِبون
accounting [15] .... (n., f.) مُحاسَبة
lawyer, attorney at law, counsel [22] .... (n., m.) مُحامٍ ج مُحامون

loving [25]	مُحبّ ج مُحبّون (n.)
engine, motor [16]	مُحَرِّك ج مُحَرِّكات (n., f.)
Islamic month (*muḥarram*) [17]	مُحَرَّم (n., m.)
station [20]	مَحَطّة ج مَحَطّات (n., f.)
store, shop, place, location [30]	مَحَلّ ج مَحَلاّت (n., m.)
roasted, toasted [26]	مُحَمَّص (n./adj.)
ocean [27]	مُحيط ج مُحيطات (n., m.)
laboratory [8]	مَخْبَر ج مَخابِر (n., m.)
bakery [24]	مَخْبَز ج مَخابِز (n., m.)
store, warehouse [30]	مَخْزَن ج مَخازِن (n., m.)
[floor] plan, map [24]	مُخَطَّط ج مُخَطَّطات (n., m.)
sincere, faithful, (sincerely yours) [25]	مُخلِص ج مُخلِصون (n., m.)
madda (a diacritical mark that signifies a *hamza* followed by *alif*) [6]	مَدّة ج مَدّات (n., f.)
teacher [30]	مُدَرِّس ج مُدَرِّسون (n., m.)
school [23]	مَدْرَسة ج مَدارِس (n., f.)
stewed [19]	مُدَمَّس (adj.)
director, manager [21]	مُدير ج مُدَراء (n., m.)
period, duration [25]	مُدّة ج مُدَد (n., f.)
town, city [5]	مَدينة ج مُدُن (n., f.)
announcer [28]	مُذيع ج مُذيعون (n., m.)
to pass, to go by [25]	مَرَّ (يَمُرُّ) مُرور (v.)
mirror [24]	مِرْآة ج مَرايا (n., f.)
jam, preserve [14]	مُرَبّى ج مُرَبَّيات (n., m.)
square [27]	مُرَبَّع (adj.)
once, one occurrence [19]	مَرّة ج مَرّات (n., f.)
toilet [24]	مِرْحاض ج مَراحيض (n., m.)
hello (greeting) [1]	مَرحَباً (sdv.)
center [29]	مَركَز ج مَراكِز (n., m.)
sick, ill, patient [30]	مَريض ج مَرْضى (n., m.)

crowded [29] .... (adj.) مُزدَحِم
farm [29].................... (n., f.) مَزْرَعة ج مَزارِع
area [27].................... (n., f.) مِساحة ج مِساحات
evening [14].................... (n., m.) مَساء
swimming pool [8].................... (n., m.) مَسْبَح ج مَسابِح
mosque [25].................... (n., m.) مَسجِد ج مَساجِد
recorded [29] .... (adj./n.) مُسَجَّل
tape recorder [5] .... (n., f.) مُسَجِّلة ج مُسَجِّلات
theater, stage [25].................... (n., m.) مَسرَح ج مَسارِح
ruler [6].................... (n., f.) مِسطَرة ج مَساطِر
Muscat (*masqaṭ*) (capital of Oman) [4].................... (n., f.) مَسْقَط
television series, serial [19].................... (n., m.) مُسَلسَل ج مُسَلسَلات
Muslim, one of the Islamic faith [21].................... (n., m.) مُسْلِم ج مُسْلِمون
Christ [21] .... (n., m.) المَسيح
watching [19].................... (verbal noun) مُشاهَدة
to walk [17] .... (v.) مَشى (يَمْشي) مَشي
one who is longing, yearning [25].................... (n.) مُشْتاق ج مُشْتاقون
busy [19].................... (n., m.) مَشْغول ج مَشْغولون
famous, well known [20].................... (participle) مَشْهور ج مَشْهورون، مَشاهير
grill, gridiron [26].................... (n., f.) مِشواة ج مَشاوٍ
grilled [26].................... (adj.) مَشويّ
lamp [24].................... (n., m.) مِصْباح ج مَصابيح
Egypt (*miṣr*) [4].................... (n., f.) مِصر
bank [24] .... (n., m.) مَصْرِف ج مَصارِف
elevator, lift [25].................... (n., m.) مِصعَد ج مَصاعِد
factory, plant [29].................... (n., m.) مَصْنَع ج مَصانِع
airport [17].................... (n., m.) مَطار ج مَطارات
kitchen [14] .... (n., m.) مَطْبَخ ج مَطابِخ
rain [18].................... (n., m.) مَطَر ج أمْطار

overlooking [24]............ (verbal noun) مُطلٌّ
restaurant [14]............ (n., m.) مَطْعَم ج مَطاعِم
with [10]............ (prep.) مَعَ
though, although [25]............ مَعَ أنَّ
good-bye [1]............ مَعَ السلامَة
together [19]............ (adv.) مَعاً
greetings [23]............ (n., f.) مُعايَدة ج مُعايَدات
moderate [18]............ (adj.) مُعْتَدِل
meaning [9]............ (n., m.) مَعْنى ج مَعانٍ (المعاني)
paste [19]............ (n., m.) مَعْجون ج مَعاجين
most [18]............ (n.,. m.) مُعْظَم
pasta, macaroni [20]............ (n., f.) مَعْكَرونة
sunset [21]............ (n., m.) مَغْرِب
Morocco (*al-maġrib*) [4]............ (n., m.) المَغْرِب
washbasin, bathroom sink [24]............ (n., f.) مَغْسَلة ج مَغاسِل
singer [28]............ (n., m.) مُغَنٍّ ج مُغَنّون
key [5]............ (n., m.) مِفتاح ج مَفاتيح
tablecloth [29]............ (n., m.) مِفْرَش ج مَفارِش
preferred, favorite [26]............ (n./adj., m.) مُفَضَّل
effectiveness [30]............ (passive participle) مَفعول
opposite, across from [24]............ (adv.) مُقابِل
interview [28]............ (n. f.) مُقابَلة ج مُقابَلات
coming, next, following [25]............ (n., m.) مُقبِل ج مُقبِلون
introduction [22]............ (n., f.) مُقَدِّمة ج مُقَدِّمات
cafeteria [14]............ (n., m.) مَقْصَف ج مَقاصِف
seat, bench, armchair [29]............ (n., m.) مَقْعَد ج مَقاعِد
fried [19]............ (adj.) مَقليّ
place, location [25]............ (n., m.) مَكان ج أمْكِنة
office [8]............ (n., m.) مَكْتَب ج مَكاتِب

library, bookstore, bookcase [8] .... (n., f.) مَكْتَبة ج مَكْتَبات
written [23] .... (n., m.) مَكْتوب
Mexico [27] .... المكسيك
note, observation [30] .... (n., f.) مُلاحَظة ج مُلاحَظات
clothes [24] .... (n., m.) مَلبَس ج مَلابِس
playground, sports field [8] .... (m.) مَلْعَب ج مَلاعِب
king [22] .... (n., m.) مَلِك ج مُلوك
queen [29] .... (n., f.) مَلِكة ج مَلِكات
place of entertainment [20] .... (n., m.) مَلْهًى ج مَلاهٍ
polluted [29] .... (adj.) مُلَوَّث
million [25] .... (n., m.) مليون
excellent [28] .... (adj.) مُمْتاز ج مُمْتازون
actor, representative [28] .... (n., m.) مُمَثِّل ج مُمَثِّلون
eraser [6] .... (n., f.) ممحاة ج ممحايات
kingdom [29] .... (n., f.) مَمْلَكة ج مَمالِك
who (question particle and relative noun) [11] .... مَنْ
from, of [4] .... (prep.) مِن
please [13] .... مِنْ فَضْلِك
Manama (*al-manāma*) (capital of Bahrain) [4] .... (n., f.) المَنامة
product [27] .... (n., m.) مُنتَج ج مُنتَجات
scholarship, grant, gift [23] .... (n., f.) مِنْحة ج مِنَح
house, residence [29] .... (n., m.) مَنزِل ج مَنازِل
since, for [25] .... (preposition) مُنْذُ
outlet [27] .... (n., m.) مَنْفَذ ج مَنافِذ
occupation, profession [30] .... (n., f.) مِهْنة ج مِهَن
engineer [20] .... (n., m.) مُهَنْدِس ج مُهَندِسون
means of transportation [29] .... (n., f.) مُواصَلة ج مُواصَلات
wave [28] .... (n., f.) مَوْجة ج مَوْجات
existing, present [23] .... (n., m.) مَوْجود ج مَوْجود ون

historian [22] ... (n., m.) مُؤَرِّخ ج مُؤَرِّخون

Mauritania (*mōritānyā*) [4] ... (n., f.) موريتانيا

banana [26] ... (n., m.) مَوْز

time, appointment [15] ... (n., m.) مَوْعِد ج مَواعيد

Mogadishu (*muqadīšō*) (capital of Somalia) [4] ... (n., f.) موقاديشو

[cooking] range [24] ... (n., m.) مَوْقِد ج مَواقِد

[bus] stop, parking lot [24] ... (n., m.) مَوْقِف ج مَواقِف

birthday, birthplace [21] ... (n., m.) مَوْلِد ج مَواليد

consisting of, comprising [30] ... (passive participle) مُؤَلَّف

hundred [12] ... (n., f.) مِئة ج مِئات

square, field, arena [25] ... (n., m.) مَيدان ج مَيادين

birth, birthday [21] ... (n., m.) ميلاد ج مَواليد

port [25] ... (n., m.) ميناء ج مَوانِئ

waiter [29] ... (n., m.) نادل ج نُدُل

window [6] ... (n., f.) نافِذة ج نَوافِذ

minus [9] ... (n., m.) ناقِص

to sleep [17] ... (v.) نامَ (يَنامُ) نَوم

plant [29] ... (n., m.) نَبات ج نَباتات

to spring, to originate, to flow [27] ... (v.) نَبَعَ (يَنبُعُ) نَبْع

we [5] ... (pronoun) نَحْنُ

proper noun (man's name) [2] ... نزار

to stay (in a place), to go down [17] ... (v.) نَزَلَ (يَنْزِلُ) نُزول

relative adjective [5] ... (n., f.) نسبة

person (used in population counts) [25] ... (n., f.) نَسَمة ج نَسَمات

to forget [19] ... (v.) نَسِيَ (يَنسى) نِسْيان

textile, tissue, fabric [27] ... (n., m.) نَسيج

bulletin, report [28] ... (n., f.) نَشْرة ج نَشَرات

half [15] ... (n., m.) نِصْف ج أَنْصاف

eye glasses [5] ... (n., f.) نَظّارة ج نَظّارات

system [28] ... (n., m.) نظام ج أَنْظِمة

to clean [19] ... (v.) نَظَّفَ (يُنَظِّفُ) تَنظيف

clean [20] ... (adj., m.) نَظيف ج نَظيفون

yes [2] .... نَعَم

same [30] .... (n., f.) نَفْس ج أَنْفُس

petroleum, crude oil [27] .... (n., m.) نفْط

to be sent into exile, to be expelled [22] .... (passive v.) نُفِيَ (يُنْفى) نَفْيٌ

small, spicy mutton sausage [26] .... (n., pl.) نَقانِق (أو مَقانق)

to move, to transport [29] .... (v.) نَقَلَ (يَنقُلُ) نَقْل

pure [29] .... (adj.) نَقِيّ

day, daytime [18] .... (n., m.) نَهار ج

end [20] .... (n., f.) نهاية ج نهايات

to get up [19] .... (v.) نَهَضَ (يَنهَضُ) نُهوض

Nwakshot (*nwakšot*) (capital of Mauritania) [4] .... (n., f.) نواكشوط

kind, sort [23] .... (n., m.) نَوْع ج أَنْواع

sleeping [17] .... (verbal n.) نَوْم

name of the letter *nūn* [2] .... (n., f.) نون

April [17] .... (n., m.) نيسان

these [8] .... (dual, f., nominative) هاتانِ

telephone [5] .... (n., m.) هاتف ج هَواتِف

these [8] .... (dual, f., acc., g.) هاتَيْنِ

quiet, serene [29] .... (adj.) هادِئ ج هادِئون

important, significant [25] .... (n./adj.) هامٌّ ج هامّون

present, gift [29] .... (n., f.) هَدِيّة ج هَدايا

this [6] .... (n., m.) هذا

these [8] .... (dual, m., nom.) هذانِ

this [6] .... (n., f.) هذه

these [8] .... (dual, m., accusative, genitive) هذَيْنِ

pyramid [25] .... (n., m.) هَرَم ج أهرام، أهرامات

question particle for yes-no questions [9] .... (particle) هَلْ

they [5] .... (pro., m., pl.) هُمْ

they [5] .... (pro., m., pl.) هُما

they [5] .... (pro., f., pl.) هُنَّ

here [15] .... (demonstrative) هُنا
there, there is/are [7] .... (demonstrative) هُناك
Pacific [27] .... (adj.) الهادي
India [16] .... (n., f.) الهِنْد
engineering [8] .... (n., f.) هَنْدَسة
he [2] .... (pronoun) هُوَ
air [29] .... (n., m.) هَواء
these [8] .... (pl., m.) هؤُلاء
identity [9] .... (n., f.) هَوِيّة ج هَوِيّات
she [2] .... (pronoun) هِيَ
one [9] .... (n., m.) واحِد
spacious, large [24] .... (adj.) واسِع
by God, I swear, really (used to add emphasis) [19] .... وَاللّهِ
father, parent [25] .... (n., m.) والِد ج والِدون
and [7] .... (conjunction) وَ
name of the letter *wāw* [1] .... (n., f.) واو
to find [23] .... (v.) وَجَدَ (يَجِدُ) وُجود
there is/are, exist [24] .... (passive of وَجَدَ) وُجِدَ (يوجَدُ)
face [19] .... (n., m.) وَجْه ج وُجوه
alone, by himself [15] .... وَحْدَهُ
sole, only [11] .... (n., m.) وَحيد ج وَحيدون
sheet of paper [6] .... (n., f.) وَرَقة ج وَرَقات
ministry, department in an administration [30] .... (n., f.) وِزارة ج وِزارات
minister [22] .... (n., m.) وَزير ج وُزَراء
pillow [17] .... (n., f.) وِسادة ج وَسائد
middle, central [27] .... (n., m.) وَسَط ج أوساط
handsome [16] .... (adj., m.) وَسيم ج وَسيمون
scarf, sash [29] .... (n., m.) وِشاح ج أوشِحة، وَشائح
to arrive, to reach a destination [17] .... (v.) وَصَلَ (يَصِلُ) وُصول

to put [24] .... (v.) وَضَعَ (يَضَعُ) وَضْع

homeland [4] .... (n., m.) وَطَن ج أوطان

time [26] .... (n., m.) وَقْت ج أوْقات

to be located, to fall down [24] .... (v.) وَقَعَ (يَقَعُ) وُقوع، وَقْع

the United States of America [15] .... (n., f.) الولايات المُتَّحِدة الأمريكيّة

state [6] .... (n., f.) ولاية ج ولايات

to be born (passive) [21] .... (v.) وُلِدَ (يولَدُ) ولادة

boy [11] .... (n., m.) وَلَد ج أوْلاد

Wichita [4] .... (n., f.) ويتشيتا

vocative particle used to call the attention of the addressee [9] .... (particle) يا

name of the letter *yā'* [2] .... (n., f.) ياء

Japan [16] .... (n., f.) اليابان

Japanese (language) [9] .... (n.) اليابانية

hand [19] .... (n., f.) يَد ج أيْدٍ

left [24] .... (n., m.) يَسار

Yemen (*al-yaman*) [4] .... (n., m.) اليَمَن

right [24] .... (n., m.) يَمين

Utah [4] .... (n., f.) يوتا

day [17] .... (n., m.) يَوْم ج أيّام

today [17] .... (n,. m.) اليَوْم

diary, daily journal [17] .... (n., f.) يَوْمِيّة ج يومِيّات

Appendix A

Arabic Alphabet and Diacritical Marks

حروف الهجاء العربية

وعلامات التشكيل

الرمز		أشكال الحرف في مواضع الكلمة		اسم الحرف	الحرف
Symbol	Final	Medial	Initial	Name	Letter
ā	ـا	ـا	ا	ألف	ا
b	ـب	ـبـ	بـ	باَء	ب
t	ـت	ـتـ	تـ	تاء	ت
ṯ	ـث	ـثـ	ثـ	ثاء	ث
j	ـج	ـجـ	جـ	جيم	ج
ḥ	ـح	ـحـ	حـ	حاء	ح
ḳ	ـخ	ـخـ	خـ	خاء	خ
d	ـد	ـد	د	دال	د
ḏ	ـذ	ـذ	ذ	ذال	ذ
r	ـر	ـر	ر	راء	ر
z	ـز	ـز	ز	زاي	ز
s	ـس	ـسـ	سـ	سين	س
š	ـش	ـشـ	شـ	شين	ش
ṣ	ـص	ـصـ	صـ	صاد	ص
ḍ	ـض	ـضـ	ضـ	ضاد	ض
ṭ	ـط	ـطـ	طـ	طاء	ط
ẓ	ـظ	ـظـ	ظـ	ظاء	ظ
‘/ *ç*	ـع	ـعـ	عـ	عَيْن	ع
ġ	ـغ	ـغـ	غـ	غين	غ
f	ـف	ـفـ	فـ	فاء	ف
q	ـق	ـقـ	قـ	قاف	ق
k	ـك	ـكـ	كـ	كاف	ك
l	ـل	ـلـ	لـ	لام	ل
m	ـم	ـمـ	مـ	ميم	م
n	ـن	ـنـ	نـ	نون	ن
h	ـه	ـهـ	هـ	هاء	ه

w/ū	ـو	ـو	و	واو	و
y/ī	ـي	ـيـ	يـ	ياء	ي
ā	ـى	–	–	ألف مَقصورة	ى
t	ـة	–	–	تاء مَربوطة	ة
ʾ	ـأ ـؤ ـئ	ـأ ـؤ ـئـ	أإ	هَمزة	ء
a		(*fatḥa*)		فَتحة	ـَ
u		(*ḍamma*)		ضَمّة	ـُ
i		(*kasra*)		كَسْرة	ـِ
-an		(*tanwīn*)		تَنوين بالفَتح	ـً
-un		(*tanwīn*)		تَنوين بالضَم	ـٌ
-in		(*tanwīn*)		تَنوين بالكَسْر	ـٍ
	(*sukūn*) signifies absence of a short vowel			سُكون	ـْ
	(*shadda*) indicates a doubled consonant			شَدّة	ـّ
	(*madda*) denotes a *hamza* and a long *alif*			مَدّة	آ
	(short *alif*) represents a long *alif*			ألِف قَصيرة	

Appendix B

A Key to the Arabic Sound System and the Transliteration System Used in This Textbook

Arabic Letter	Roman Symbol	Example/Description
ا	ā	*a* as in *far* and *bad*
ب	b	*b* as in *bet*
ت	t	*t* as in *tip*
ث	ṯ	*th* as in *thin*
ج	j	*j* as in *judge*
ح	ḥ	*h*-like sound produced with constriction
خ	ḳ	*ch* as in Scottish *loch* or German *Bach*
د	d	*d* as in *dip*
ذ	ḏ	*th* as in *then*
ر	r	*r* as in Spanish *pero* (trilled *r*)
ز	z	*z* as in *zip*
س	s	*s* as in *sad*
ش	š	*sh* as in *show*
ص	ṣ	*s* as in *sod*
ض	ḍ	*d* as in *dark*
ط	ṭ	*t* as in *tar*
ظ	ẕ	*th* as in *thyne*
ع	ç/ʻ	a fricative sound produced in the throat
غ	ġ	roughly similar to German *r*; a gargling sound
ف	f	*f* as in *fit*
ق	q	roughly similar to the *c* in *cot*, but further back
ك	k	*k* as in *kit*

ل	l	*l* as in *leak*
م	m	*m* as in *mint*
ن	n	*n* as in *nill*
هـ / ه	h	*h* as in *hat*
و	ū	*oo* as in *pool*
و	w	*w* as in *wet*
ي	ī	*ee* as in *feel*
ي	y	*y* as in *yet*
ى	ā	*a* as in *dad* (a form of *alif* in the final position)
ـة / ة	t	See the discussion on *tā' marbūṭa* in Lesson 3.
ء	'	glottal stop; the stop before *a* in *above*
َ	a	roughly similar to *u* as in *but*
ُ	u	*u* as in *pull*
ِ	i	*i* as in *bill*

Appendix C

Verb Conjugations

This appendix contains a representative sample of verb conjugation paradigms. At the top of each table, الماضي (past) with المضارع (present) are listed next to each other followed by the pattern of the verb and its Roman number, then المصدر (verbal noun), اسم الفاعل (active participle) and اسم المفعول (passive participle). Each table has separate pronouns in the right-hand column followed by the conjugations of المضارع: المرفوع والمنصوب والمجزوم (indicative, subjunctive, jussive) in this order, and الأمر (imperative). All are in the active voice. The conjugations are classified according to person: first, second, third. Only one conjugation for the second person dual masculine and feminine (أنتما) is provided. Feminine pronouns follow masculine pronouns.

to think, to presume ظَنَّ (يَظُنُّ) (فَعَلَ I) (ظَنٌّ – ظانّ – مَظنون)

Imperative	Jussive	Subjunctive	Indicative	Past	Pronoun
الأمر	المضارع المجزوم	المضارع المنصوب	المضارع المرفوع	الماضي	الضمير
	أظُنَّ	أظُنَّ	أظُنُّ	ظَنَنْتُ	أنا
	نَظُنَّ	نَظُنَّ	نَظُنُّ	ظَنَنّا	نَحنُ
ظُنَّ	تَظُنَّ	تَظُنَّ	تَظُنُّ	ظَنَنْتَ	أنتَ
ظُنّي	تَظُنّي	تَظُنّي	تَظُنّينَ	ظَنَنْتِ	أنتِ
ظُنّا	تَظُنّا	تَظُنّا	تَظُنّانِ	ظَنَنْتُما	أنتُما
ظُنّوا	تَظُنّوا	تَظُنّوا	تَظُنّونَ	ظَنَنْتُم	أنتُم
أُظْنُنَّ	تَظْنُنَّ	تَظْنُنَّ	تَظْنُنَّ	ظَنَنْتُنَّ	أنتُنَّ
	يَظُنَّ	يَظُنَّ	يَظُنُّ	ظَنَّ	هُوَ
	تَظُنَّ	تَظُنَّ	تَظُنُّ	ظَنَّتْ	هِيَ
	يَظُنّا	يَظُنّا	يَظُنّانِ	ظَنّا	هُما
	تَظُنّا	تَظُنّا	تَظُنّانِ	ظَنَّتا	هُما
	يَظُنّوا	يَظُنّوا	يَظُنّونَ	ظَنّوا	هُم
	يَظْنُنَّ	يَظْنُنَّ	يَظْنُنَّ	ظَنَنَّ	هُنَّ

تَكَلَّمَ (يَتَكَلَّمُ) (تَفَعَّل V) (تَكَلُّمٌ – مُتَكَلِّم – مُتَكَلَّم) *to talk, to speak*

Imperative الأمر	Jussive المضارع المجزوم	Subjunctive المضارع المنصوب	Indicative المضارع المرفوع	Past الماضي	Pronoun الضمير
	أتَكَلَّمْ	أتَكَلَّمَ	أتَكَلَّمُ	تَكَلَّمتُ	أنا
	نَتَكَلَّمْ	نَتَكَلَّمَ	نَتَكَلَّمُ	تَكَلَّمْنا	نَحنُ
تَكَلَّمْ	تَتَكَلَّمْ	تَتَكَلَّمَ	تَتَكَلَّمُ	تَكَلَّمْتَ	أنتَ
تَكَلَّمي	تَتَكَلَّمي	تَتَكَلَّمي	تَتَكَلَّمينَ	تَكَلَّمْتِ	أنتِ
تَكَلَّما	تَتَكَلَّما	تَتَكَلَّما	تَتَكَلَّمانِ	تَكَلَّمتُما	أنتُما
تَكَلَّموا	تَتَكَلَّموا	تَتَكَلَّموا	تَتَكَلَّمونَ	تَكَلَّمتُم	أنتُم
تَكَلَّمْنَ	تَتَكَلَّمْنَ	تَتَكَلَّمْنَ	تَتَكَلَّمْنَ	تَكَلَّمتُنَّ	أنتُنَّ
	يَتَكَلَّمْ	يَتَكَلَّمَ	يَتَكَلَّمُ	تَكَلَّمَ	هُوَ
	تَتَكَلَّمْ	تَتَكَلَّمَ	تَتَكَلَّمُ	تَكَلَّمَتْ	هِيَ
	يَتَكَلَّما	يَتَكَلَّما	يَتَكَلَّمانِ	تَكَلَّما	هُما
	تَتَكَلَّما	تَتَكَلَّما	تَتَكَلَّمانِ	تَكَلَّمَتا	هُما
	يَتَكَلَّموا	يَتَكَلَّموا	يَتَكَلَّمونَ	تَكَلَّموا	هُم
	يَتَكَلَّمْنَ	يَتَكَلَّمْنَ	يَتَكَلَّمْنَ	تَكَلَّمْنَ	هُنَّ

كانَ (يَكونُ) (فَعَل I) (كَونٌ – كائِن – مَكون) *to be*

Imperative الأمر	Jussive المضارع المجزوم	Subjunctive المضارع المنصوب	Indicative المضارع المرفوع	Past الماضي	Pronoun الضمير
	أكُنْ	أكونَ	أكونُ	كُنتُ	أنا
	نَكُنْ	نَكونَ	نَكونُ	كُنّا	نَحنُ
كُنْ	تَكُنْ	تَكونَ	تَكونُ	كُنتَ	أنتَ
كوني	تَكوني	تَكوني	تَكونينَ	كُنتِ	أنتِ
كونا	تَكونا	تَكونا	تَكونانِ	كُنتُما	أنتُما
كونوا	تَكونوا	تَكونوا	تَكونونَ	كُنتُم	أنتُم
كُنَّ	تَكُنَّ	تَكُنَّ	تَكُنَّ	كُنتُنَّ	أنتُنَّ
	يَكُنْ	يَكونَ	يَكونُ	كانَ	هُوَ
	تَكُنْ	تَكونَ	تَكونُ	كانَتْ	هِيَ
	يَكونا	يكونا	يَكونانِ	كانا	هُما
	تَكونا	تَكونا	تَكونانِ	كانَتا	هُما
	يَكونوا	يكونوا	يكونونَ	كانوا	هُم
	يَكُنَّ	يَكُنَّ	يَكُنَّ	كُنَّ	هُنَّ

أعطى (يُعْطي) (أَفْعَلَ IV) (إعْطاء – مُعْطٍ – مُعْطىً) *to give*

Imperative الأمر	Jussive المضارع المجزوم	Subjunctive المضارع المنصوب	Indicative المضارع المرفوع	Past الماضي	Pronoun الضمير
	أُعْطِ	أُعْطِيَ	أُعْطي	أعْطَيْتُ	أنا
	نُعْطِ	نُعْطِيَ	نُعْطي	أعْطَيْنا	نَحنُ
أعْطِ	تُعْطِ	تُعْطِيَ	تُعْطي	أعْطَيْتَ	أنتَ
أعْطي	تُعْطي	تُعْطي	تُعْطينَ	أعْطَيْتِ	أنتِ
أعْطِيا	تُعْطِيا	تُعْطِيا	تُعْطِيانِ	أعطَيْتُما	أنتُما
أعْطوا	تُعْطوا	تُعْطوا	تُعْطونَ	أعطَيْتُم	أنتُم
أعْطينَ	تُعْطينَ	تُعْطينَ	تُعْطينَ	أعطَيْتُنَّ	أنتُنَّ
	يُعطِ	يُعطِيَ	يُعطي	أعطى	هُوَ
	تُعطِ	تُعطِيَ	تُعطي	أعطَتْ	هِيَ
	يُعطِيا	يُعطِيا	يُعطِيانِ	أعطَيا	هُما
	تُعْطِيا	تُعْطِيا	تُعطِيانِ	أعطَيَتا	هُما
	يُعطوا	يُعطوا	يُعطونَ	أعطَوا	هُم
	يُعطينَ	يُعطينَ	يُعطينَ	أعطَيْنَ	هُنَّ

أحبَّ (يُحِبُّ) (أَفْعَلَ IV) (حُبٌّ – مُحِبّ – مُحَبٌّ) *to like, to love*

Imperative الأمر	Jussive المضارع المجزوم	Subjunctive المضارع المنصوب	Indicative المضارع المرفوع	Past الماضي	Pronoun الضمير
	أُحِبَّ	أُحِبَّ	أُحِبُّ	أحبَبْتُ	أنا
	نُحِبَّ	نُحِبَّ	نُحِبُّ	أحبَبْنا	نَحنُ
أحْبِبْ	تُحِبَّ	تُحِبَّ	تُحِبُّ	أحبَبْتَ	أنتَ
أحِبّي	تُحِبّي	تُحِبّي	تُحِبّينَ	أحبَبْتِ	أنتِ
أحِبّا	تُحِبّا	تُحِبّا	تُحِبّانِ	أحبَبْتُما	أنتُما
أحِبّوا	تُحِبّوا	تُحِبّوا	تُحِبّونَ	أحبَبْتُم	أنتُم
أحْبِبْنَ	تُحبِبْنَ	تُحبِبْنَ	تُحبِبْنَ	أحبَبْتُنَّ	أنتُنَّ
	يُحِبَّ	يُحِبَّ	يُحِبُّ	أحبَّ	هُوَ
	تُحِبَّ	تُحِبَّ	تُحِبُّ	أحبَّتْ	هِيَ
	يُحِبّا	يُحِبّا	يُحِبّانِ	أحبّا	هُما
	تُحِبّا	تُحِبّا	تُحِبّانِ	أحبّتا	هُما
	يُحِبّوا	يُحِبّوا	يُحِبّونَ	أحبّوا	هُم
	يُحْبِبْنَ	يُحْبِبْنَ	يُحْبِبْنَ	أحْبَبْنَ	هُنَّ

أرادَ (يُريدُ) (أفْعَلَ IV) (إرادة– مُريد – مُراد) *to want*

Imperative الأمر	Jussive المضارع المجزوم	Subjunctive المضارع المنصوب	Indicative المضارع المرفوع	Past الماضي	Pronoun الضمير
	أُرِدْ	أُريدَ	أُريدُ	أرَدْتُ	أنا
	نُرِدْ	نُريدَ	نُريدُ	أرَدْنا	نَحنُ
أرِدْ	تُرِدْ	تُريدَ	تُريدُ	أرَدْتَ	أنتَ
أريدي	تُريدي	تُريدي	تُريدينَ	أرَدْتِ	أنتِ
أريدا	تُريدا	تُريدا	تُريدانِ	أرَدْتُما	أنتُما
أريدوا	تُريدوا	تُريدوا	تُريدونَ	أرَدْتُم	أنتُم
أرِدْنَ	تُرِدْنَ	تُرِدْنَ	تُرِدْنَ	أرَدْتُنَّ	أنتُنَّ
	يُرِدْ	يُريدَ	يُريدُ	أرادَ	هُوَ
	تُرِدْ	تُريدَ	تُريدُ	أرادَتْ	هِيَ
	يُريدا	يُريدا	يُريدانِ	أرادا	هُما
	تُريدا	تُريدا	تُريدانِ	أرادَتا	هُما
	يُريدوا	يُريدوا	يُريدونَ	أرادوا	هُم
	يُرِدْنَ	يُرِدْنَ	يُرِدْنَ	أرَدْنَ	هُنَّ

عنى (يَعْني) (فَعَلَ I) (عَني – عانٍ – مَعْني) *to mean*

Imperative الأمر	Jussive المضارع المجزوم	Subjunctive المضارع المنصوب	Indicative المضارع المرفوع	Past الماضي	Pronoun الضمير
	أعْنِ	أعْنيَ	أعْني	عَنَيْتُ	أنا
	نَعْنِ	نَعْنيَ	نَعْني	عَنَيْنا	نَحنُ
اِعْنِ	تَعْنِ	تَعْنيَ	تَعْني	عَنَيْتَ	أنتَ
اِعْني	تَعْني	تَعْني	تَعْنينَ	عَنَيْتِ	أنتِ
اِعْنيا	تَعْنيا	تَعْنيا	تَعْنيانِ	عَنَيْتُما	أنتُما
اِعْنوا	تَعْنوا	تَعْنوا	تَعْنونَ	عَنَيْتُم	أنتُم
اِعْنينَ	تَعْنينَ	تَعْنينَ	تَعْنينَ	عَنَيْتُنَّ	أنتُنَّ
	يَعْنِ	يَعْنيَ	يَعْني	عَنى	هُوَ
	تَعْنِ	تَعْنيَ	تَعْني	عَنَتْ	هِيَ
	يَعْنيا	يَعْنيا	يَعْنيانِ	عَنَيا	هُما
	تَعْنيا	تَعْنيا	تَعْنيانِ	عَنَتا	هُما
	يَعْنوا	يَعْنوا	يَعْنونَ	عَنَوا	هُم
	يَعْنينَ	يَعْنينَ	يَعْنينَ	عَنَيْنَ	هُنَّ

اشتَرى (يَشْتَري) (اِفْتَعَل VIII) (اشتِراء – مُشْتَرٍ – مُشْتَرى) *to buy*

Imperative الأمر	Jussive المضارع المجزوم	Subjunctive المضارع المنصوب	Indicative المضارع المرفوع	Past الماضي	Pronoun الضمير
	أشْتَرِ	أشْتَرِيَ	أشْتَري	اشْتَرَيْتُ	أنا
	نَشْتَرِ	نَشْتَرِيَ	نَشْتَري	اشْتَرَيْنا	نَحنُ
اشْتَرِ	تَشْتَرِ	تَشْتَرِيَ	تَشْتَري	اشْتَرَيْتَ	أنتَ
اشْتَري	تَشْتَري	تَشْتَري	تَشْتَرينَ	اشْتَرَيْتِ	أنتِ
اشْتَرِيا	تَشْتَرِيا	تَشْتَرِيا	تَشْتَرِيانِ	اشْتَرَيْتُما	أنتُما
اشْتَرَوا	تَشْتَرَوا	تَشْتَرَوا	تَشْتَرَونَ	اشْتَرَيْتُم	أنتُم
اشْتَرينَ	تَشْتَرينَ	تَشْتَرينَ	تَشْتَرينَ	اشْتَرَيْتُنَّ	أنتُنَّ
	يَشْتَرِ	يَشْتَرِيَ	يَشْتَري	اشْتَرى	هُوَ
	تَشْتَرِ	تَشْتَرِيَ	تَشْتَري	اشْتَرَتْ	هِيَ
	يَشْتَرِيا	يَشْتَرِيا	يَشْتَرِيانِ	اشْتَرَيا	هُما
	تَشْتَرِيا	تَشْتَرِيا	تَشْتَرِيانِ	اشْتَرَتا	هُما
	يَشْتَرَوا	يَشْتَرَوا	يَشْتَرَونَ	اشْتَرَوا	هُم
	يَشْتَرينَ	يَشْتَرينَ	يَشْتَرينَ	اشْتَرَيْنَ	هُنَّ

وَصَلَ (يَصِلُ) (فَعَلَ I) (وُصول – واصِل – مَوْصول) *to arrive*

Imperative الأمر	Jussive المضارع المجزوم	Subjunctive المضارع المنصوب	Indicative المضارع المرفوع	Past الماضي	Pronoun الضمير
	أصِلْ	أصِلَ	أصِلُ	وَصَلْتُ	أنا
	نَصِلْ	نَصِلَ	نَصِلُ	وَصَلْنا	نَحنُ
صِلْ	تَصِلْ	تَصِلَ	تَصِلُ	وَصَلْتَ	أنتَ
صِلي	تَصِلي	تَصِلي	تَصِلينَ	وَصَلْتِ	أنتِ
صِلا	تَصِلا	تَصِلا	تَصِلانِ	وَصَلْتُما	أنتُما
صِلوا	تَصِلوا	تَصِلوا	تَصِلونَ	وَصَلْتُم	أنتُم
صِلْنَ	تَصِلْنَ	تَصِلْنَ	تَصِلْنَ	وَصَلْتُنَّ	أنتُنَّ
	يَصِلْ	يَصِلَ	يَصِلُ	وَصَلَ	هُوَ
	تَصِلْ	تَصِلَ	تَصِلُ	وَصَلَتْ	هِيَ
	يَصِلا	يَصِلا	يَصِلانِ	وَصَلا	هُما
	تَصِلا	تَصِلا	تَصِلانِ	وَصَلَتا	هُما
	يَصِلوا	يَصِلوا	يَصِلونَ	وَصَلوا	هُم
	يَصِلْنَ	يَصِلْنَ	يَصِلْنَ	وَصَلْنَ	هُنَّ

اتَّصَلَ (يَتَّصِلُ) (اِفْتَعَلَ VIII) (اِتِّصال – مَتَّصِل – مُتَّصَل) *to contact, to connect*

Imperative الأمر	Jussive المضارع المجزوم	Subjunctive المضارع المنصوب	Indicative المضارع المرفوع	Past الماضي	Pronoun الضمير
	أتَّصِلْ	أتَّصِلَ	أتَّصِلُ	اتَّصَلْتُ	أنا
	نَتَّصِلْ	نَتَّصِلَ	نَتَّصِلُ	اتَّصَلْنا	نَحنُ
اتَّصِلْ	تَتَّصِلْ	تَتَّصِلَ	تَتَّصِلُ	اتَّصَلْتَ	أنتَ
اتَّصِلي	تَتَّصِلي	تَتَّصِلي	تَتَّصِلينَ	اتَّصَلْتِ	أنتِ
اتَّصِلا	تَتَّصِلا	تَتَّصِلا	تَتَّصِلانِ	اتَّصَلْتُمَا	أنتُمَا
اتَّصِلوا	تَتَّصِلوا	تَتَّصِلوا	تَتَّصِلونَ	اتَّصَلْتُم	أنتُم
اِتَّصِلْنَ	تَتَّصِلْنَ	تَتَّصِلْنَ	تَتَّصِلْنَ	اتَّصَلْتُنَّ	أنتُنَّ
	يَتَّصِلْ	يَتَّصِلَ	يَتَّصِلُ	اتَّصَلَ	هُوَ
	تَتَّصِلْ	تَتَّصِلَ	تَتَّصِلُ	اتَّصَلَتْ	هِيَ
	يَتَّصِلا	يَتَّصِلا	يَتَّصِلانِ	اتَّصَلا	هُما
	تَتَّصِلا	تَتَّصِلا	تَتَّصِلانِ	اتَّصَلَتا	هُما
	يَتَّصِلوا	يَتَّصِلوا	يَتَّصِلونَ	اتَّصَلوا	هُم
	يَتَّصِلْنَ	يَتَّصِلْنَ	يَتَّصِلْنَ	اِتَّصَلْنَ	هُنَّ

عَلَّقَ (يُعَلِّقُ) (فَعَّلَ II) (تَعْليق – مُعَلِّق – مُعَلَّق) *to hang*

Imperative الأمر	Jussive المضارع المجزوم	Subjunctive المضارع المنصوب	Indicative المضارع المرفوع	Past الماضي	Pronoun الضمير
	أُعَلِّقْ	أُعَلِّقَ	أُعَلِّقُ	عَلَّقْتُ	أنا
	نُعَلِّقْ	نُعَلِّقَ	نُعَلِّقُ	عَلَّقْنا	نَحنُ
عَلِّقْ	تُعَلِّقْ	تُعَلِّقَ	تُعَلِّقُ	عَلَّقْتَ	أنتَ
عَلِّقي	تُعَلِّقي	تُعَلِّقي	تُعَلِّقينَ	عَلَّقْتِ	أنتِ
عَلِّقا	تُعَلِّقا	تُعَلِّقا	تُعَلِّقانِ	عَلَّقْتُما	أنتُما
عَلِّقوا	تُعَلِّقوا	تُعَلِّقوا	تُعَلِّقونَ	عَلَّقْتُم	أنتُم
عَلِّقْنَ	تُعَلِّقْنَ	تُعَلِّقْنَ	تُعَلِّقْنَ	عَلَّقْتُنَّ	أنتُنَّ
	يُعَلِّقْ	يُعَلِّقَ	يُعَلِّقُ	عَلَّقَ	هُوَ
	تُعَلِّقْ	تُعَلِّقَ	تُعَلِّقُ	عَلَّقَتْ	هِيَ
	يُعَلِّقا	يُعَلِّقا	يُعَلِّقانِ	عَلَّقا	هُما
	تُعَلِّقا	تُعَلِّقا	تُعَلِّقانِ	عَلَّقَتا	هُما
	يُعَلِّقوا	يُعَلِّقوا	يُعَلِّقونَ	عَلَّقوا	هُم
	يُعَلِّقْنَ	يُعَلِّقْنَ	يُعَلِّقْنَ	عَلَّقْنَ	هُنَّ

انْتَقَلَ (يَنْتَقِلُ) (اِفتَعَلَ VIII) (انتِقال – مُنْتَقِل – مُنْتَقَل) *to move, to relocate*

Imperative الأمر	Jussive المضارع المجزوم	Subjunctive المضارع المنصوب	Indicative المضارع المرفوع	Past الماضي	Pronoun الضمير
	أنْتَقِلْ	أنْتَقِلَ	أنْتَقِلُ	انْتَقَلْتُ	أنا
	نَنْتَقِلْ	نَنْتَقِلَ	نَنْتَقِلُ	انْتَقَلْنا	نَحنُ
انْتَقِلْ	تَنْتَقِلْ	تَنْتَقِلَ	تَنْتَقِلُ	انْتَقَلْتَ	أنتَ
انْتَقِلي	تَنْتَقِلي	تَنْتَقِلي	تَنْتَقِلينَ	انْتَقَلْتِ	أنتِ
انْتَقِلا	تَنْتَقِلا	تَنْتَقِلا	تَنْتَقِلانِ	انْتَقَلْتُما	أنتُما
انْتَقِلوا	تَنْتَقِلوا	تَنْتَقِلوا	تَنْتَقِلونَ	انْتَقَلْتُم	أنتُم
انْتَقِلْنَ	تَنْتَقِلْنَ	تَنْتَقِلْنَ	تَنْتَقِلْنَ	انْتَقَلْتُنَّ	أنتُنَّ
	يَنْتَقِلْ	يَنْتَقِلَ	يَنْتَقِلُ	انْتَقَلَ	هُوَ
	تَنْتَقِلْ	تَنْتَقِلَ	تَنْتَقِلُ	انْتَقَلَتْ	هِيَ
	يَنْتَقِلا	يَنْتَقِلا	يَنْتَقِلانِ	انْتَقَلا	هُما
	تَنْتَقِلا	تَنْتَقِلا	تَنْتَقِلانِ	انْتَقَلَتا	هُما
	يَنْتَقِلوا	يَنْتَقِلوا	يَنْتَقِلونَ	انْتَقَلوا	هُم
	يَنْتَقِلْنَ	يَنْتَقِلْنَ	يَنْتَقِلْنَ	انْتَقَلْنَ	هُنَّ

اسْتَخْدَمَ (يَسْتَخدِمُ) (اِسْتَفْعَلَ X) (استِخْدام – مَسْتَخْدِم – مُسْتَخْدَم) *to use*

Imperative الأمر	Jussive المضارع المجزوم	Subjunctive المضارع المنصوب	Indicative المضارع المرفوع	Past الماضي	Pronoun الضمير
	أسْتَخْدِمْ	أسْتَخْدِمَ	أسْتَخْدِمُ	اسْتَخْدَمْتُ	أنا
	نَسْتَخْدِمْ	نَسْتَخْدِمَ	نَسْتَخْدِمُ	اسْتَخْدَمْنا	نَحنُ
اسْتَخْدِمْ	تَسْتَخْدِمْ	تَسْتَخْدِمَ	تَسْتَخْدِمُ	اسْتَخْدَمْتَ	أنتَ
اسْتَخْدِمي	تَسْتَخْدِمي	تَسْتَخْدِمي	تَسْتَخْدِمينَ	اسْتَخْدَمْتِ	أنتِ
اسْتَخْدِما	تَسْتَخْدِما	تَسْتَخْدِما	تَسْتَخْدِمانِ	اسْتَخْدَمْتُما	أنتُما
اسْتَخْدِموا	تَسْتَخْدِموا	تَسْتَخْدِموا	تَسْتَخْدِمونَ	اسْتَخْدَمْتُم	أنتُم
اسْتَخْدِمْنَ	تَسْتَخْدِمْنَ	تَسْتَخْدِمْنَ	تَسْتَخْدِمْنَ	اسْتَخْدَمْتُنَّ	أنتُنَّ
	يَسْتَخْدِمْ	يَسْتَخْدِمَ	يَسْتَخْدِمُ	اسْتَخْدَمَ	هُوَ
	تَسْتَخْدِمْ	تَسْتَخْدِمَ	تَسْتَخْدِمُ	اسْتَخْدَمَتْ	هِيَ
	يَسْتَخْدِما	يَسْتَخْدِما	يَسْتَخْدِمانِ	اسْتَخْدَما	هُما
	تَسْتَخْدِما	تَسْتَخْدِما	تَسْتَخْدِمانِ	اسْتَخْدَمَتا	هُما
	يَسْتَخْدِموا	يَسْتَخْدِموا	يَسْتَخْدِمونَ	اسْتَخْدَموا	هُم
	يَسْتَخْدِمْنَ	يَسْتَخْدِمْنَ	يَسْتَخْدِمْنَ	اسْتَخْدَمْنَ	هُنَّ

Appendix D

Answer Key

The answer key provides answers to all the exercises in the textbook, including listening comprehension exercises.

Lesson 1

Exercise 4 ١ـ دارو ٢ـ زار ٣ـ راوا ٤ـ ذاد ٥ـ زود ٦ـ زارو ٧ـ واد ٨ـ داذو

Exercise 5

١ـ زارو	Vowel	☑	☐	Consonant
٢ـ دوذا	Vowel	☑	☐	Consonant
٣ـ راواد	Vowel	☐	☑	Consonant
٤ـ واداد	Vowel	☐	☑	Consonant
٥ـ زادور	Vowel	☑	☐	Consonant

Exercise 6 ١ـ دور ٢ـ واد ٣ـ زودا ٤ـ وادود ٥ـ ذاد ٦ـ دار

Exercise 7 (g-greeting; r=response)

١– أهلاً g/r ٢– إلى اللقاء r ٣– مع السلامة r ٤– وعليكم السلام r ٥– الحمد لله بخير r ٦– كيف الحال؟ g

Lesson 2

تمرين ٢ تين، نبيذ (vowel) - بيان، ثياب (semivowel)

تمرين ٣ ١– دَب short ٢– زور long ٣– ديب long ٤– بُن short ٥– يار long ٦– ثوب short
٧– دار long ٨– بَرد short

تمرين ٥ ١– داني ٢– بارود ٣– روبي ٤– داري ٥– ثُبور ٦– نادِر ٧– بَريد ٨– رَباب

تمرين ٦ ١– رَبيب ٢– ثابِت ٣– نوري ٤– باري ٥– نابي ٦– بوران

تمرين ٧ ١ـ نُريد ٢ـ زُبَيدي ٣ـ رَتيب ٤ـ يابان ٥ـ بُدور

Ex. 8	Self	Addressee (f.)	Addressee (m.)	Third person (f.)	Third person (m.)
Example:	☐	☑	☐	☐	☐
1.	☑	☐	☐	☐	☐
2.	☐	☐	☐	☐	☑
3.	☐	☐	☑	☐	☐
4.	☐	☐	☐	☑	☐
5.	☐	☑	☐	☐	☐
6.	☐	☐	☑	☐	☐

Lesson 3 الدرس الثالث

تمرين ٢ ١ـ تَسْديد ٢ـ شَراب ٣ـ روسي ٤ـ داش ٥ـ شَنَبْ ٦ـ ناشِزْ ٧ـ يَسار ٨ـ سودان

تمرين ٣ ١ـ تشرين ٢ـ شَريد ٣ـ سَيارين ٤ـ شَراشيب ٥ـ تَشويش ٦ـ يابوس

تمرين ٤ ١ـ داسو ٢ـ سَردين ٣ـ شين ٤ـ ديدان ٥ـ شادور ٦ـ رَشاش

تمرين ٦ ١ـ خَراب ٢ـ حَرير ٣ـ حَديث ٤ـ جَرَش ٥ـ خَرير ٦ـ تَحذير

تمرين ٧   ١ـ رِحاب ٢ـ سِنجاب ٣ـ شَخير ٤ـ خَسيس ٥ـ رَبيح ٦ـ جوري ٧ـ ساخِرون ٨ـ سَحاب

تمرين ٨   ١ـ حَراج ٢ـ جَبان ٣ـ خَروف ٤ـ حَبيبي ٥ـ حَشيش ٦ـ خاسِر

تمرين ١٠   ١ـ خُسوف ٢ـ ثُقب ٣ـ فَنادِق ٤ـ خَفيف ٥ـ رِفاق ٦ـ فُستُق ٧ـ فِردَوس

تمرين ١١   ١ـ رَقيب ٢ـ تَقارير ٣ـ فُنون ٤ـ ثاقِب ٥ـ فُرات ٦ـ نُقود

تمرين ١٢   ١ـ خشية ٢ـ جَريدة ٣ـ دَفينة ٤ـ شَريفة ٥ـ حارِسة ٦ـ قارورَتي

تمرين ١٤   ١ـ ضَروح ٢ـ خَيش ٣ـ رَديفة ٤ـ قَريبة ٥ـ خوري ٦ـ شَيخ

Lesson Four

الدرس الرابع

تمرين ٢   ١ـ فَضيحة ٢ـ رَصين ٣ـ صَفيح ٤ـ صوص ٥ـ فُرصة ٦ـ صاد ٧ـ رَصيف ٨ـ داري
٩ـ صاري ١٠ـ يُسرِف

تمرين ٣   ١ـ ضَرير ٢ـ صُدور ٣ـ فُرَص ٤ـ ضَفيرة ٥ـ يَصفِر ٦ـ قَوارِض ٧ـ رَصين ٨ـ قَوانِص

تمرين ٤   ١ـ صَرصور ٢ـ صَفيح ٣ـ ضَروري ٤ـ وَصفة ٥ـ صَرير ٦ـ حَصير

تمرين ٦   ١ـ رَتيب ٢ـ ظَريف ٣ـ ظافِر ٤ـ بِطريق ٥ـ بِساط ٦ـ فَيص

تمرين ٧   ١ـ طَربوش ٢ـ قِطار ٣ـ فَظاظة ٤ـ رُطَب ٥ـ بوظ ٦ـ ظَبي

تمرين ٨   ١ـ طَيش ٢ـ قَرار ٣ـ ظَبية ٤ـ طَريف ٥ـ قارِس ٦ـ شَوط

تمرين ١٠   ١ـ عَديد ٢ـ يَعرِف ٣ـ يُزيغ ٤ـ طِباع ٥ـ عَريف ٦ـ يَغار

تمرين ١١   ١ـ عِفريت ٢ـ فَراغ ٣ـ شُغور ٤ـ دَعد ٥ـ بَديع ٦ـ تُبوغ

تمرين ١٢

1. Beirut	2. Utah	3. Arizona	4. Baton Rouge	5. Indiana
6. Syria	7. Boise	8. Tunis/Tunisia	9. Damascus	10. Wichita

تمرين ١٤   ١ـ سَليل ٢ـ ظَربان ٣ـ غَدير ٤ـ ذَرف ٥ـ رُتَب ٦ـ داري ٧ـ ثَعلَب ٨ـ لُعَب

Lesson Five

الدرس الخامس

تمرين ٢   ١ـ نَبيل ٢ـ والي ٣ـ بِلال ٤ـ لادِن ٥ـ لَباب ٦ـ بِلادي ٧ـ والِدي ٨ـ روبي

تمرين ٣   ١ـ لَيل ٢ـ بُلبُل ٣ـ عَسَل ٤ـ جَلال ٥ـ صَليب ٦ـ نَوال

تمرين ٤   ١ـ لَسنا ٢ـ خَليل ٣ـ رِسالة ٤ـ دال ٥ـ بَلَل ٦ـ لَذيذ

تمرين ٦   ١ـ كُوَيت ٢ـ شاكِر ٣ـ كُفوف ٤ـ قاسي ٥ـ كَسَب ٦ـ تَدليك

تمرين ٧   ١ـ كَشكول ٢ـ كُسوف ٣ـ شُكوك ٤ـ بُركان

تمرين ٨   ١ـ كَليلة ٢ـ كان ٣ـ صُكوك ٤ـ كُفوف ٥ـ كاري ٦ـ شاك

تمرين ١٠   ١ـ ميسان ٢ـ ديماس ٣ـ صَمَم ٤ـ مارِد ٥ـ لَميس ٦ـ سَلام

تمرين ١١   ١ـ بَلسَم ٢ـ مُسلِمون ٣ـ كِرام ٤ـ مُقيم

تمرين ١٢   ١ـ مَلايين ٢ـ سُموم ٣ـ شاي ٤ـ مِرحاض ٥ـ صَميم ٦ـ تَمرين

تمرين ١٤   ١ـ حُسام ٢ـ نَبيه ٣ـ مَحروم ٤ـ دَواليه ٥ـ زَهرة ٦ـ حافِلة

تمرين ١٥   ١ـ بَهلول ٢ـ مُهاتَرات ٣ـ المَلاهي ٤ـ سَفيه ٥ـ فِداهُ

تمرين ١٦   ١ـ هارون ٢ـ مَهزوم ٣ـ تيه ٤ـ هامِش ٥ـ تاه ٦ـ هِمَم

تمرين ١٧   ١ـ هندي/هندية ٢ـ قَطَري/قَطَرية ٣ـ سُعودي/سُعودية ٤ـ أخَوي/أخَوية ٥ـ لُغَوي/لُغَوية
٦ـ فَرَنسي/فَرَنسية ٧ـ عِراقي/عِراقية ٨ـ دِمَشقي/دِمَشقية

تمرين ١٨   ١ـ كَيفَ الحال؟/الحمدُ لله ٢ـ اِسمي خالِد/تَشَرَّفنا ٣ـ مَرحَباً/أهلاً ٤ـ أنتَ/هِيَ ٥ـ لا/نَعَم
٦ـ مصر/المَغرِب ٧ـ مَعَ السلامة/إلى اللقاء

تمرين ١٩   ١ـ مُسَجِّلة ٢ـ نَظّارة ٣ـ مِفتاح ٤ـ دَرّاجة

Lesson Six

الدرس السادس

تمرين ٢ ١ـ علَى ٢ـ لاما ٣ـ سودي ٤ـ رَمى ٥ـ لُبنى ٦ـ دَوي

تمرين ٣ ١ـ رَمى ٢ـ يُشتَرى ٣ـ وَفى ٤ـ فَدوى

تمرين ٤ ١ـ هَمى ٢ـ ذُرى ٣ـ سُدى ٤ـ هُدى

تمرين ٦ ١ـ أديب ٢ـ نَقاء ٣ـ نَشاء ٤ـ أُذُن ٥ـ أبي ٦ـ إناء

تمرين ٧ ١ـ أُستاذ ٢ـ إزاء ٣ـ أبوك ٤ـ رِياء

تمرين ٩ ١ـ شُبّاك ٢ـ ثَمان ٣ـ سَحّار ٤ـ ساحِر ٥ـ هَجّان ٦ـ مَرّ

تمرين ١٠ ١ـ بَشّار ٢ـ حَدّاد ٣ـ خَبّاز ٤ـ رَسّام

تمرين ١٢ ١ـ أَثَر ٢ـ مأرِب ٣ـ مرِآب ٤ـ آثار ٥ـ أدَب

تمرين ١٣ ١ـ آراء ٢ـ مرِآة ٣ـ آلاف ٤ـ آفة ٥ـ قُرآن

تمرين ١٥ ١ـ عَفواً ٢ـ بَيت ٣ـ أهلٌ ٤ـ مَساءً ٥ـ دينٌ ٦ـ جيمٍ

تمرين ١٦ ١ـ صَباحاً ٢ـ شُكراً ٣ـ سيّارةٌ ٤ـ قَلَمٍ ٥ـ صَفٌّ ٦ـ عَلَماً

تمرين ١٧ Variable responses.

تمرين ١٨ مِمحاة/مِبراة باب/نافِذة كُرسي/طاوِلة حاسوب/حاسِبة عَرَبي/أمريكي

Lesson Seven

الدرس السابع

تمرين ١ ١ـ دِمَشق ٢ـ جامعة ٣ـ ساعة... صورة ٤ـ كرسي ٥ـ صورة ٦ـ رِياضِيّات

تمرين ٢ عندي سيارة وَدرّاجَة وَحاسوب وكِتاب. في غُرفتي طاوِلة وكرسي ونافذة.

تمرين ٣ في غرفتي صورة. هُناكَ حَقيبة على الأرض.

تمرين ٤ ١ـ هذا هاتف ٢ـ هذه ورَقة ٣ـ هذا قلَم ٤ـ هذا تلفاز ٥ـ هذا لَوح ٦ـ هذه طالبة

تمرين ٥ ١ـ أستاذُنا لَيسَ مصرِياً. ٢ـ سوزان لَيْسَتْ أسترالِيّة. ٣ـ نَحنُ لَسْنا سورِيِّين. ٤ـ هؤلاءِ الطُلّابُ لَيسوا مِن جامِعَتِنا. ٥ـ هُما لَيْسَتا طالِبَتَينِ أمريكيّتَين.

تمرين ٦ ١ـ صَورةُ هالة علَى الجِدار لكِنَّ صورتَك على الباب. ٢ـ دمَشْقُ في سورية لكِنَّ عمّانَ في الأردُنّ. ٣ـ أنتِ مِصريّةٌ لكنّني سودانيّ. ٤ـ حاسوبُ الأستاذ أمريكيٌّ لكِنَّ حاسوبَ الطالِب يابانيّ.

تمرين ٧ ١ـ جامعَتُكَ في دمَشق، لكِنَّ جامعتَه في القاهِرة. ٢ـ لَيسَ عندَها درّاجة ، لكِنْ سيّارة. ٣ـ لَيسَ هُناكَ جَريدة في حَقيبَتي، لكِنْ كتاب. ٤ـ هذه مَسَجِّلة، لكِنَّ هذا تلفاز. ٥ـ لكِنْ ليس هُناكَ حاسِبة على الطاوِلة، لكِنْ مِمحاةٌ وَمسطَرة . ٦ـ سيّارَتُهُ أمريكيّةٌ، لَكِنَّ حاسوبَهُ يابانيّ.

تمرين ٧ ١ـ لَوْح/صَفّ ٢ـ غُرفة/باب ٣ـ أستاذ/ طالِب ٤ـ جدار/صورة ٥ـ هُنا/هُناك ٦ـ علَى/في

تمرين ٨ ١ـ الطاولة ٢ـ الجَريدة ٣ـ المفتاح ٤ـ الساعة ٥ـ القَلَم ٦ـ الباب ٧ـ النافذة ٨ـ الكُرسي

تمرين ٩ ١ـ سيّارَتُك ٢ـ هاتِفٌ ٣ـ كِتابي ٤ـ الجامِعةُ ٥ـ درّاجتُها ٦ـ مسجِّلةٌ ٧ـ جريدتُه ٨ـ لَوحٌ ٩ـ المِفتاحُ ١٠ـ غُرفةٌ

Lesson Eight

الدرس الثامن

تمرين ١ (١) هَيثَم نَجّار كُليّة العُلوم جامِعة دمشق (٢) راغِب طَبّاع كُليّة العُلوم الجامعة الأردنية

١ـ عِدّةُ ٢ـ ملعَب رياضي ومسبَح ٣ـ مَخبَر لُغَويّ ٤ـ أستاذ رِياضِيّات ٥ـ رِياضِيّات ٦ـ كليّة العُلوم ٧ـ هاتِف ٨ـ الأرض

تمرين ٤ ١ـ جانِب ٢ـ هندسة ٣ـ عِدّة ٤ـ رِياضيّ

تمرين ٥ ١ـ رِياضة/ملَعَب ٢ـ مَخبَر/لُغَويّ ٣ـ ذلكَ/تلكَ ٤ـ كليّة/طِبّ ٥ـ كتاب/مَكتَبة

تمرين ٦ ١ـ رياضيّة ٢ـ طِبّيّ ٣ـ تِجاريّة ٤ـ صَباحيّ ٥ـ جامعيّة ٦ـ يابانيّة

تمرين ٧ ١ـ كُلِّيَّة العلومِ ٢ـ جامعة دمَشق ٣ـ عدّة كُليّات ٤ـ كُلِّيَّةُ الهَندَسة ٥ـ كُلِّيَّةُ العلومِ ٦ـ كليّة الآداب ٧ـ كُلِّيَّةُ الطِبِّ ٨ـ كُلِّيَّةُ التِجارةِ ٩ـ كُلِّيَّةُ الحُقوق ١٠ـ كُلِّيَّةُ الآدابِ ١١ـ جانِبَ كُلِّيَّةِ الحُقوق ١٢ـ غُرفَةُ

مكتبي   ١٣ـ أستاذُ رياضيّات ١٤ـ غُرفَة مكتبي   ١٥ـ جانبَ الطاولة ١٦ـ كُلّيّة العُلومِ

تمرين ٨   ١ـ كُلّيّة الطبّ   ٢ـ نافذةُ غُرفَتي   ٣ـ مفتاحُ السيّارة   ٤ـ نَظّارةُ طالبةٍ   ٥ـ أستاذُ ساندي   ٦ـ دَرّاجةُ طالبةٍ

تمرين ٩   ١ـ ذلكَ لِنكَن   ٢ـ تلكَ سيّارة   ٣ـ ذلكَ بَيت   ٤ـ تلكَ سيّارة

تمرين ١٠   ١ـ سَمهوري   ٢ـ بير زيت   ٣ـ الآداب   ٤ـ القُدس   ٥ ـ خَطأ: عِندهُ حاسوب   ٦ـ صَح   ٧ـ صَح

الدرس التاسع

تمرين ١   ١ـ نِزار   ٢ـ شقّة   ٣ـ سيّارة   ٤ـ ٦٠١٥٧٩٤   ٥ـ جَبلة بَلْدةٌ في سورية.   ٦ـ لا نعرف اسمَها.   ٧ـ ٥ شارع ابن خلدون.

تمرين ٢   Variable responses.

تمرين ٣   ١ـ أينَ المكتبة؟   ٢ـ عِندك سيّارة؟   ٣ـ كَم غرفةً في بيتِك؟   ٤ـ ما رَقمُ هاتِفِك؟   ٥ـ مِن أينَ أستاذُ اللغةِ الغربية؟

تمرين ٤   Variable responses.

تمرين ٥   ١ـ أينَ تَسكُنين؟   ٢ـ لا أسكُنُ في شارع لِنكَن.   ٣ـ هل تَسكُنينَ في شقّة؟   ٤ـ يسكُن أستاذي في مدينة ....

تمرين ٦   ما مَعنى كَلمةُ dear بالعَرَبيّة؟

تمرين ٧   ١ـ درّاجةً   ٢ـ مفتاحاً   ٣ـ قَلَماً   ٤ـ مُسَجِّلَةً   ٥ـ هاتِفاً   ٦ـ جامعةً   ٧ـ كَلِمةً   ٨ـ أستاذاً

تمرين ٩   ١ـ ٨   ٢ـ ٨   ٣ـ ٥   ٤ـ ٧   ٥ـ ١٠   ٦ـ ١٠   ٧ـ ٧   ٨ـ ٤

تمرين ١٠   Variable responses.

تمرين ١١   ١ـ تسعة not a residence   ٢ـ لَيسَ a negative particle   ٣ـ عِلميّ not a nationality   ٤ـ طاولة not an address

تمرين ١٢   Variable responses.

تمرين ١٣   ١ـ بَلدة الباب   ٢ـ التِجارة   ٣ـ هاتف   ٤ـ خطأ. في سكَن الطالبات.   ٥ـ صَح   ٦ـ خطأ. لغتين.

تمرين ١٤   ١ـ بلدة/مدينة   ٢ـ عنوان/شارع   ٣ـ العربية/لغة   ٤ـ رقم/ثلاثة   ٥ـ بطاقة/هَويّة   ٦ـ شُكراً/عَفواً

الدرس العاشر

تمرين ١   ١ـ كليّة الطبّ   ٢ـ شقّة   ٣ـ مَعَ   ٤ـ مِن   ٥ـ تسعة   ٦ـ التِجارة

تمرين ٢   ١ـ خطأ. ليسَت أختَها. هي تسكن معها.   ٢ـ خطأ. لا نعرف من النص.   ٣ـ صَح   ٤ـ خطأ. في جامعة حَلَب   ٥ـ سَرير واحد

تمرين ٣   ١ـ مادّة/أحياء   ٢ـ لُغة/الإنكليزيّة   ٣ـ كُرسي/سَرير   ٤ـ بناية/شَقّة   ٥ـ تَعرِف/تَسكُن   ٦ـ في/مَعَ

تمرين ٤   ١ـ الفرنسية the only language in the set   ٢ـ كُلّيّة not a residence   ٣ـ درّاجة not a piece of furniture

تمرين ٥   ١ـ ثَلاث طاوِلات   ٢ـ سيّارة واحِدة   ٣ـ سبعةُ دَفاترِ   ٤ـ هاتِفان   ٥ـ حَقيبَتان   ٦ـ حاسوب واحِد   ٧ـ ثَماني مَساطِر   ٨ـ ستّةُ أقلام

تمرين ٦   Variable responses

تمرين ٧   ١ـ كَم لُغةً تَعرِفين؟   ٢ـ كَم بَيتاً في شارِعك؟   ٣ـ كم مدينةً عَرَبيّةً تعرف؟   ٤ـ كم طالباً في درسِ اللغةِ العربية؟   ٥ـ كم طالباً تعرفينَ في هذا الصفّ؟   ٦ـ كَم طالباً عَرَبيّاً تعرف؟

تمرين ٨   ١ـ هذهِ حَقيبة   ٢ـ هذه كَراسٍ   ٣ـ تلكَ ساعة   ٤ـ هذه بُيوت   ٥ـ هؤلاءِ طُلّاب   ٦ـ هذا تِلفاز   ٧ـ تِلكَ مَفاتيح   ٨ـ هذه طالبة   ٩ـ تلك نظّارة   ١٠ـ هذه سيّارات

تمرين ٩   ١ـ عَبدُ الرحمن   ٢ـ الطِبّ   ٣ـ وُجدة   ٤ـ سَريران   ٥ـ صَح   ٦ـ صح   ٧ـ خطأ. أردنيّ   ٨ـ صح

الدرس الحادي عَشَر

تمرين ١   ١ـ ابن واحد   ٢ـ الرابع   ٣ـ لبناني   ٤ـ علم الحاسوب   ٥ـ ثلاث مَواد   ٦ـ شقّة   ٧ـ أوهايو   ٨ـ مازِن   ٩ـ زِياد نابُلسي   ١٠ـ يسكن مع وَليد صايِغ وزياد نابُلسي   ١١ـ يدرس مادّتَين   ١٢ـ الهندسة

تمرين ٢ ١ـ صح ٢ـ خطأ. هو زوج ناديا. ٣ـ صح ٤ـ خطأ. هي أخت أحمَد. ٥ـ صح ٦ـ خطأ. هو ابن مازن.
٧ـ خطأ. هو ابن ناديا.

تمرين ٣ Variable responses.

تمرين ٤ ١ـ أخت not a school subject ٢ـ وحـــيـــد does not pertain to school ٣ـ أوَّل not a family relation ٤ـ ابنة not a preposition

تمرين ٥ ١ـ فلَسطين/لُبنان ٢ـ فَصل/دِراسيّ ٣ـ بِنت/وَلَد ٤ـ سِتّة/سادِس

تمرين ٦ ١ـ تدرس ٢ـ مادّةً ٣ـ الثاني ٤ـ الإبتِدائيّ

تمرين ٧ Variable responses.

تمرين ٨ Variable responses.

تمرين ٩ ٦ـ حافِظ last (grandfather's) name ب ـ الشيباني، هويدي

تمرين ١٠ ١ـ يسكنُ أحمد شقّةً في شارع الاستقلال. ٢ـ أدرسُ مادّتَين في هذا الفصل. ٣ـ لا تعرفُ سامية عُنوانَ أمين. ٤ـ تدرس هالة مادّةَ الأحياء في جامعة حلَب.

تمرين ١١ ١ـ أدرسُ مادّتين في هذا الفصلِ. ٢ـ أسكنُ في شقّةٍ معَ طالبَين. ٣ـ أدرسُ عِلمَ الحاسوب. ٤ـ أعرفُ ثلاثةَ طلاّبٍ فَرَنسيين. ٥ـ أسكنُ في مدينة ....

تمرين ١٢ ١ـ هذه هي المِبراة. ٢ـ هذا هو الأستاذ راغِب طَبّاع. ٣ـ أخي هو نِزار. ٤ـ هذا هو دفتر العائلة.

تمرين ١٣ Variable responses.

تمرين ١٤ Variable responses.

تمرين ١٥ ١ـ الفَرَنسية ٢ـ ابنان ٣ـ سميح ٤ـ السابع ٥ـ خطأ. تسكن مع نَدى وسَميح. ٦ـ صح ٧ـ خطأ. زَوجتُهُ أستاذة في مدرسةِ بَنات. ٨ـ صح

الدرس ١٢

تمرين ١ ١ـ الغرفة رقم ٣٧ ٢ـ شقة رقم ٩ ٣ـ نِداء خَيّاط ٤ـ ليس معَهُ كتاب ٥ـ لا تعرِفُ ٦ـ طالب

تمرين ٢ ١ـ الأستاذ وليد طَرَزي ٢ـ يا سَيِّد مَحمود! ٣ـ يا آنِسة ريم! ٤ـ السيِّدة رَباب كَحّال ٥ـ السيِّد عبد الرحمن حُسَين ٦ـ دكتور قَدّورة ٧ـ الآنِسة زَينَب حَمدي

تمرين ٣

The young woman apologizes for not knowing where the school of Law is located, hence the form آسِفة.

تمرين ٤ ١ـ آسِف ٢ـ آسِفة ٣ـ آسِفان ٤ـ آسِفَتان ٥ـ آسِفات ٦ـ آسِفون

تمرين ٥ ١ـ جَيِّداً/قَليلاً ٢ـ آنِسة/سَيِّدة ٣ـ يَتَكَلَّم/لُغة ٤ـ أمينَة/مَكتبة ٥ـ الله/أعلَم

تمرين ٦ ١ـ الآنِسة ٢ـ آسِف ٣ـ سَيِّداتي ٤ـ اللهُ أعلَم ٥ـ قَليلاً

تمرين ٧ ١ـ لا. آسِفة. ٢ـ ٤٥ شارع الكَواكِبي، شقّة رَقم ٩، حلَب، سورية. ٣ـ سَيِّداتي وَسادَتي .... ٤ـ أتكلَّم العربية قَليلاً. ٥ـ اللهُ أعلَم. ٦ـ آسِفة. آسِف

تمرين ٨ ١ـ حَيثُ ٢ـ جَيِّد ٣ـ أمينةُ ٤ـ آسَف ٥ـ تتكلّم

تمرين ٩ ١ـ أتَكَلَّمُ الإنكليزية جيِّداً. ٢ـ أتكلّم العربية قليلاً. ٣ـ أتكلّم الإسبانية قليلاً. ٤ـ لا أتكلّم الفَرَنسية. ٥ـ لا أتكلّم اللاتينية.

تمرين ١٠ ١ـ ثَماني نَظّارات ٢ـ أربَعةُ مَخابِر ٣ـ أحَدَ عَشَرَ دَفتَراً ٤ـ أربَعَ عَشْرَةَ دَرّاجةً ٥ـ خَمسونَ طالباً ٦ـ ثَمانون بِنتاً ٧ـ مِئَةُ قَلَمٍ ٨ـ مِئَتا جامعة ٩ـ سَبعُمِئَة رَجُل

تمرين ١١ ١ـ الإسكندريّة ٢ـ أخو ٣ـ الإسكندريّة ٤ـ ثلاث أخَوات ٥ـ سكَن الطالبات ٦ـ لَها أختان ٧ـ زَينَب أختُ سامية وهي في المدرسة الثانوية ٨ـ تَهاني تسكن مع سامية وهي من مدينة المنصورة وتدرس الصيدلة. ٩ـ في الغُرفةِ مكتَبَةٌ وَتِلفاز وَطاوِلة وكُرسيّان وسَريران. هُناكَ أربَعُ صُوَرٍ علَى الجِدار. ١٠ـ Variable responses

الدرس ١٣

تمرين ١ ١ـ جَريدة ٢ـ مجلاّت وجَرائِد ٣ـ مجلة ٤ـ يعرفون العربيّة ٥ـ جريدة لبنانيّة ٦ـ الدُستور ٧ـ المعرِفة ٨ـ الأهرام ٩ـ الثَّورة

تمرين ٢ ١ـ أيّةَ ٢ـ عادةً ٣ـ من فَضلك ٤ـ آسِفة

تمرين ٣ ١ـ جريدة/مجلّة ٢ـ عادةً/أحياناً ٣ـ اعطني/تفضَّل ٤ـ يقرأ/يكتب

تمرين ٤ ١ـ اعطِني قلَماً من فضلِك. / معك قلَم من فَضلِك؟ ٢ـ تَفَضَّلي مجلّةَ «تايم». ٣ـ عندك جريدةُ لرأي؟ ٤ـ آسِف / آسِفة ليس معي ممحاة.

تمرين ٥ ١ـ الصَفِّ: مجرور، مضاف إليه/مدينة: مجرور بحرف الجر ٢ـ السيارةُ: مرفوع، مبتدأ ٣ـ طالباً: منصوب، تمييز ٤ـ أحمدُ: مرفوع، فاعل ٥ـ عنوانَ: منصوب، مفعول به

تمرين ٦ ١ـ عند ريما درّاجتان. ٢ـ لِبَيتِنا ثلاثةُ أبواب. ٣ـ مع أحمد سيارة الآن. ٤ـ عندي أخٌ وأخت. ٥ـ هل نظّارتُك معك؟ ٦ـ السيّدة بستاني لها ابنٌ وابنة.

تمرين ٧ ١ـ (أنا) أعرفها. ٢ـ أعطانا جريدةً. ٣ـ يعرفون العربيةَ ويتكلّمونها في البيت. ٤ـ اِعطني تلك المجلةَ من فضلك. ٥ـ هنَّ يعرفنَني. ٦ـ هل تعرفينَهم؟ ٧ـ اعطِه رقمَ هاتفك.

تمرين ٨ ١ـ جون كلارك غيبل John Clark Gable – كلايَد وير Clyde Wier – جيم Jim – جيمس برولين James Brolin – ريتشارد راوندتري Richard Roundtree ٢ـ غراهام غرين Graham Greene – جون لو كاريه John le Carré – برلين Berlin

تمرين ٩ ١ـ فاطمة ٢ـ الأهرام ٣ـ ابن ٤ـ رانية وسميرة ٥ـ الشرق الأوسط ٦ـ الدستور ٧ـ خطأ. لا يقرأ أحمد مجلات. ٨ـ صح ٩ـ خطأ. يسكنون في مدينة عمّان.

الدرس ١٤

تمرين ١ Variable responses. Please note the first person singular conjugation of أكل in the present tense is آكُلُ.

تمرين ٢ ١ـ المطعم ٢ـ عصير برتقال ٣ـ البَيض ٤ـ القهوة العربية ٥ـ دون سكر ٦ـ العَسَل ٧ـ مطعم نِعمة ٨ـ اللَحم ٩ـ جريدة ١٠ـ البيت

تمرين ٣ ١ـ شاي/قهوة ٢ـ مُربّى/عَسَل ٣ـ لَحم/خنزير ٤ـ صباحاً/مساءً ٥ـ مع/دون ٦ـ مطعم/ مَقصَف ٧ـ يشرب/يأكل ٨ـ عصير/برتقال

تمرين ٤ ١ـ مُـربّى only sweet food ٢ـ دون does not pertain to time ٣ـ برتقـال not a drink ٤ـ خبز not a drink

تمرين ٥ ١ـ عصير برتقال ٢ـ مطعم ٣ـ العسَل ٤ـ الماء ٥ـ الحُبوب

تمرين ٦ ١ـ أريدُ كأسَ ماءٍ من فضلك. ٢ـ يأكل سمير الخبزَ والجبنَ ويشرب الشايَ صباحاً. ٣ـ يحبُّ مايكل الفلافِلَ لكنّه لا يحبُّ اللحمَ (the third and last words may be interchangeable).

تمرين ٧ ١ـ اجلِسي مِن فضلِك. ٢ـ اجلِسوا من فضلكم. ٣ـ اجلس من فضلك. ٤ـ اجلسنَ من فضلكنّ. ٥ـ اجلسوا من فضلكم.

تمرين ٨ Variable responses.

تمرين ٩ ١ـ السيّاراتُ اليابانيّة سيّاراتٌ جَيِّدة. ٢ـ هؤلاءِ طلاّبٌ ماليزيّون. ٣ـ هُناكَ بَناتٌ و أبناءٌ كثيرون في عائلاتِ المصريّين. ٤ـ في كُلِيّتي حَواسيبُ كَثيرة. ٥ـ يأكُلُ السوريّونَ الجُبنَ والزَيتونَ صَباحاً. ٦ـ مَن مَعَهُ أقلامٌ في حَقيبَتِه؟

تمرين ١٠ ١ـ عندنا ثلاث طالبات فرنسيات في صفِّنا. ٢ـ معي ثلاثة أقلام. ٣ـ هناك خمسة هواتف في هذه الغرفة. ٤ـ هل تعرف أيَّ طلابٍ كوريين؟ ٥ـ يوجد ثلاث طاولات وستة كراسٍ في غرفة الأساتذة.

تمرين ١١ Variable responses.

تمرين ١٢ ١ـ عصير برتقال ٢ـ فنجان قهوة ٣ـ كأس ماء ٤ـ فنجان شاي ٥ـ جامعة آركانسو ٦ـ قطعة خبز

تمرين ١٣ ١ـ قهوة ٢ـ الخبز والجبن ٣ـ الدجاج أو اللحم ٤ـ خطأ. هي تأكل اللحم أوالدجاج. ٥ـ خطأ. هي تأكل السلطة ظهراً. ٦ـ صح ٧ـ هي تأكل البرتقال ظهراً. ٨ـ هي تأكل الخبز والجبن والزيتون مساءً.

الدرس ١٥

تمرين ١ ١ـ دمشق ٢ـ مع طالبة ٣ـ اللغة الإنكليزية ٤ـ مقصف ٥ـ الواحدة بعد الظهر ٦ـ لين ٧ـ القاهرة ٨ـ سمير عبد الفتّاح ٩ـ الهندسة ١٠ـ خطأ. تدرس أربع مواد. ١١ـ خطأ. قبل درس المحاسبة. ١٢ـ صح ١٣ـ صح ١٤ـ صح

تمرين ٢ الساعة الثامنة: ليس عندها دروس. الساعة التاسعة: موعد درس الرياضيات. الساعة العاشرة: موعد اللغة الإنكليزية. الساعة الحادية عشرةَ: تقرأ مجلات وجرائد في المكتبة. الساعة الثانيةَ عَشْرة: تأكل في مقصف الجامعة. الساعة الواحدة: موعد درس المحاسبة. الساعة الثانية: ليس عندها دروس. الساعة الثالثة: موعد درس الإحصاء. الساعة الرابعة والساعة الخامسة: تدرس في المكتبة مع طلاب وطالبات من صفها.

تمرين ٣ جاك ـ مارثا، مايكل ـ لين ـ ريتشارد، B and C: variable responses.

تمرين ٤ ١ـ أول/واحد ٢ـ الولايات المتحدة/أمريكا ٣ـ ساعة/دقيقة ٤ـ مادة/العلاقات الدولية

تمرين ٥ ١ـ كثير not a fraction ٢ـ موعد not food ٣ـ دقيقة not a school subject ٤ـ حاضر not a number

تمرين ٦ ١ـ أريدُ كأسَ شاي مِن فضلِك. ٢ـ يأكل سمير الخبزَ والجبنَ صباحاً ويشرب الشاي. ٣ـ موعد درس المحاسبة في الساعة الواحدة بعد الظهر.

تمرين ٧ ١ـ الساعةُ الثانيةَ عَشْرةَ والربع ٢ـ الساعةُ الثامنةَ إلاّ عشرَ دقائق ٣ـ الساعةُ السادسة والنصف ٤ـ الرابعة ٥ـ الساعةُ الحادية عَشْرةَ وخمسٌ وثلاثونَ دَقيقة ٦ـ الساعةُ الثالثة إلاّ ثُلثاً ٧ـ الساعةُ الحاديةَ عَشْرةَ والنصف إلاّ خمسَ دقائق ٨ـ الساعةُ العاشرة والثُلث

تمرين ٨ ١ـ برتقالة ٢ـ خبزة ٣ـ زَيتونة ٤ـ بَيضة ٥ـ فولة ٦ـ سُكَّرة

تمرين ٩ ١ـ تسعُمئة وسَبعة ٢ـ أربعةُ آلاف وسبعُمئة وثَلاثٌ وثَمانون ٣ـ ثلاثةَ عَشرَ ألفاً وستُّمئة وخمسٌ وثمانون

تمرين ١٠ ١ـ متى تأكل سَحَر في المقصَف؟ تأكل فيَ المقصَف ظهراً. ٢ـ في أيّةِ ساعة مَوعِد درسِ سَحَر في الإحصاء؟ موعد درس الإحصاء في الساعة الثالثة. ٣ـ ما اسمُ أستاذة مايكل في مادّة اللغة العربيّة؟ اسمُها الأستاذة زَينب طه. ٤ـ أين يسكن والدا مايكل (أو: أبو مايكل وأمه)؟ يسكنان في مدينة سنسناتي.

تمرين ١١ ١ـ عادل ٢ـ الإنكليزي ٣ـ جزائري ٤ـ بريطانيا ٥ـ خطأ. في الجامعة الأردنية. ٦ـ صح ٧ـ خطأ. هو عربي مِن عمّان. ٨ـ صح ٩ـ الساعة التاسعة: مادة اللغة الإنكليزية. الساعة الواحدة: مادة الأدب الإنكليزي ١٠ـ الدكتور

الدرس ١٦

تمرين ١ ١ـ الدَوحة عاصمةُ قَطَر. ٢ـ سيارةُ حسين بورش ألمانية. ٣ـ شارع حَمَد المُبارَك في الكويت .

تمرين ٢ ١ـ قَطَر ٢ـ اللغة الإنكليزية ٣ـ المكتبة ٤ـ دار أسرتها ٥ـ ثلاث سيارات ٦ـ لندن ٧ـ الكويت ٨ـ ألمانية ٩ـ خطأ. سبع غُرَف ١٠ـ صح ١١ـ خطأ. في المكتبة ١٢ـ خطأ. مُحَرِّك قوي ١٣ـ خطأ. حسين ليس له زَوجة ويسكن وحدهُ. C. Variable responses

تمرين ٣ ١ـ مُحَرِّك ٢ـ غرفة ٣ـ دار ٤ـ صديق ٥ـ سائقاً

تمرين ٤ ١ـ سيارة/سائق ٢ـ مكتبة/مجلات ٣ـ دار/بيت ٤ـ طويل/قصير ٥ـ وسيم/جميلة ٦ـ قديم/حديث

تمرين ٥ ١ـ حليب nothing to do with books or reading ٢ـ نصف not related to cars or driving ٣ـ محاسبة not a county ٤ـ أرض not a family member

The Gulf: ١ـ إيران وتركيا

٢ـ الإمارات العربية المتحدة، البحرين، فلسطين، لبنان، الأردن

تمرين ٦ ١ـ أحبُّ القراءةَ في الصباح. ٢ـ يريد صديقي عُمَر دراسةَ الرياضيات. ٣ـ أسكن في سكَنِ الطلاب. ٤ـ أنا وأصدقائي نحبُّ شُربَ القهوةِ دون سكَّر. ٥ـ تحبّ أختي الصغيرة الأكلَ العربيّ. ٦ـ يحب حَسَين العملَ في الكويت. ٧ـ يحِبّ أخوها لِبسَ الكوفية

تمرين ٧ ١ـ يابانيّان ✗ يابانيّ ٢ـ صغير ✓ ٣ـ قديمات ✗ قديمة ٤ـ طِوال ✓ ٥ـ الصغير ✗ الصغار ٦ـ قديم ✗ قديمة

تمرين ٨ ١ـ فَرَنسيّ ✗ فرنسية ٢ـ سوريّ ✓ ٣ـ أمريكيّة ✓ ٤ـ كبير ✗ كبيرة ٥ـ صغير ✓ ٦ـ قَطَريّة ✗ قَطَريّ

تمرين ٩ ١ـ جديدَين ✗ جديدان ٢ـ جديدةٌ ✗ جديدةٌ ٣ـ الأمريكية ✓ ٤ـ وَسيمون ✗ وسيمين ٥ـ السوريّةُ ✗ السوريّة

تمرين ١٠ ١ـ phrase ✓ ٢ـ phrase ✓ ٣ـ sentence ✓ ٤ـ phrase ✗ حديثةٌ ٥ـ phrase ✗ جميلةٌ ٦ـ sentence ٧ـ phrase ✓ ٨ـ phrase ✗ وَسيمٌ ٩ـ phrase ✓ ١٠ـ sentence ✗ جديدةٌ ١١ـ sentence ✓ ١٢ـ phrase ✓

تمرين ١١ ١ـ الجديدةُ ٢ـ القديمةُ ٣ـ القديمةَ ٤ـ فَرَنسيّتان ٥ـ الجديدِ ٦ـ الجديداتُ

تمرين ١٢ ١ـ صغيرةٌ ٢ـ الصغيرة ٣ـ الصغارَ ٤ـ صغيرتان ٥ـ صغيرةٌ ٦ـ صغيرتَانِ ٧ـ صغيرةٌ ٨ـ الصغيرِ

تمرين ١٣ ١ـ تونسي ٢ـ عِلم الحاسوب ٣ـ سكَن الطلاب ٤ـ أختان ٥ـ صح ٦ـ خطأ. يريد دراسةَ الطبّ ٧ـ خطأ. فرَح أخت سَعيد ٨ـ خطأ. هي لا تدرس. هي في البيت. ٩ـ صح ١٠ـ خطأ. عنده درّاجة ١١ـ variable

الدرس ١٧

تمرين ١ ١ في الساعة السادسة ٢ـ العاشرة والنصف ٣ـ صديق رامي ٤ـ المطار ٥ـ غرفتا نوم ٦ـ هاني ٧ـ قميصاً ٨ـ ٢٧٦ ٩ـ خطأ. سيسكن في غرفة صغيرة ١٠ـ صح ١١ـ خطأ. في يوم الأربعاء ١٢ـ خطأ. يظنُّ أنّها أكبر جامعة في الولايات المتحدة.

تمرين ٢ ١ـ شهر the only noun ٢ـ غرفة not an establishment ٣ـ أيلول a month, not a day
٤ـ حينَ does not pertain to place ٥ـ ساعة not related to sleeping

تمرين ٣ ١ـ آب/أغسطس ٢ـ مساءً/ظهراً ٣ـ نام/فندق ٤ـ شباط/فبراير ٥ـ وِسادة/سَرير ٦ـ فاهيتا/المكسيك
٧ـ شهر/أسبوع ٨ـ الأحَد/السبت ٩ـ كانون الثاني/يَناير ١٠ـ مَطار/طائرة

تمرين ٤ ١ـ حَزيران ٢ـ نيسان ٣ـ حَزيران ٤ـ كانون الأوّل ٥ـ آب ٦ـ سبعة ٧ـ الجُمُعة ٨ـ الأحَد ٩ـ الجُمُعة ١٠ـ السبْت والأحَد

تمرين ٥ ١ـ سَوفَ أقرأ مجلّةً في المكتبة. ٢ـ سوف ينزِلُ صديقي العربيّ في شقّتي في هذا الشهر. ٣ـ سأذهبُ إلى واشنطن يومَ الإثنَين. ٤ـ سوف أنامُ في الساعة العاشرةِ يومَ الأحَد.
٥ـ سأدرسُ الكيمياءَ يومَي الإثنَين والأربعاء. ٦ـ ستَصِلُ طائرةُ صديقي في الساعة السابِعةِ والنِصف مساءً.
٧ـ سآكُلُ دَجاجاً في المطعم غداً. ٨ـ سأشتري مجلّةً وجريدتَين وثلاثةَ كُتُبٍ من السوق.

تمرين ٦ ١ـ أنَّ الجامعةَ ٢ـ إنَّ سيّارَتَها ٣ـ أنَّ الكتابَين ٤ـ أنَّ مدينةً ٥ـ إنَّ الطلابَ ٦ـ إنَّ السيّارَتَين جديدَتان.

تمرين ٧ ١ـ أجمل من ٢ـ أكبَر ٣ـ أطوَل ٤ـ أقدَم ٥ـ أكبَر من ٦ـ أحدَث ٧ـ أجمَل ٨ـ أطوَل منّي

تمرين ٨ ١ـ سائقو شاحنات ٢ـ شركة المطاحن ٣ـ مئَتي دينار ٤ـ ثلاثمئة دينار ٥ـ شارع الجَلاء ٦ـ ثلاث غُرَف نوم ٧ـ غُرفَتا جُلوس ٨ـ غرفة طَعام ٩ـ ٦٠٠ ألف لَيرة

تمرين ٩ ١ـ سَيَكون ٢ـ كانا ٣ـ كانَ ٤ـ كُنّا ٥ـ كانوا ٦ـ كانا ٧ـ كُنْتِ ٨ـ تكونُ

تمرين ١٠ ١ـ لأخيها ٢ـ اللُغةَ ٣ـ أبو ٤ـ الكتابُ ٥ـ جامعةِ ٦ـ أبا

تمرين ١١ ١ـ دمشق ٢ـ ابن وبنت ٣ـ دار أبيه ٤ـ أربع غُرَف نَوم ٥ـ خطأ. ذهب إلى دمشق بالطائرة مَعَ عائلَتِه. ٦ـ صح ٧ـ خطأ. حَسّان أستاذ في مدرسة ثانَوية في الرياض ٨ـ صح

الدرس ١٨

تمرين ١ ١ـ فصول ٢ـ الخريف ٣ـ معتدل ٤ـ البحر ٥ـ أريزونا ٦ـ الخريف ٧ـ في فصلَي الربيع والصيف ٨ـ في فصل الصيف ٩ـ variable ١٠ـ يكون الطقسُ حاراً في فصل الصيف عادةً. ١١ـ خطأ. يسقط الثلج في الشتاء. ١٢ـ صح ١٣ـ خطأ. تكون الشمس ساطعةً في الصيف. ١٤ـ variable

تمرين ٢ ١ـ ربيع/خريف ٢ـ حار/بارد ٣ـ غائم/صحو ٤ـ شاطئ/بحر ٥ـ ليل/نهار ٦ـ ثلج/مَطَر ٧ـ درجة/مئوية

تمرين ٣ ١ـ ثلج not a plant or color of one ٢ـ بحيرة not weather related ٣ـ مَطَر not body of water ٤ـ فصل does not pertain to temperature ٥ـ أسبوع not a weather condition

تمرين ٤ Variable responses.

تمرين ٥ ١ـ سيارتُها هذه ليست أمريكية. ٢ـ هذا مفتاحُ بابِ شقةِ أختي. ٣ـ يأتي شهرُ حَزيران بعد شهرِ أيّار. ٤ـ سيكون الطقسُ صحواً بعد غد. ٥ـ يذهب الناسُ إلى شاطئِ البحر في الصيف. ٦ـ قالت زينَبُ لصديقاتها إنَّها ستسافرُ إلى المغربِ غداً. ٧ـ قال لي أستاذي إنَّ لغتي العربيةَ جيِّدةٌ. ٨ـ ذهبتُ من حلب إلى دمشق بالقطار في يوم السبت.

تمرين ٦ ١ـ وصلَتْ طائرةُ هاني في الساعة التاسعة والنصف. ٢ـ وَصَلْتُ إلى هذه المدينة في سنةِ ١٩٩٠. ٣ـ تصلُ درجةُ الحرارةِ في الصيفِ إلى ٤٠ دَرَجة مِئويّة في بَلَدَتي. ٤ـ وَصَلْنا إلى الدرس ١٨. ٥ـ ستصِل درجة الحرارة إلى ناقص خمسة في الليل.

تمرين ٧ ١ـ ٣٨ مئوية = ١٠٠,٤ فارنهايت ٢ـ 20C=78.8F ٣ـ ٨٤ فرنهايت=٢٨,٨ مئوية ٤ـ 32F=0C

تمرين ٨ ١ـ كُلّ الكُتُب ٢ـ كلّ شهرٍ ٣ـ بعض أصدقائي ٤ـ معظم النهارِ ٥ـ كلّ الأسبوعِ ٦ـ بعض السنة

تمرين ٩ ١ـ معتدلاً ٢ـ الربيع ٣ـ الخميس ٤ـ حلب ٥ـ خطأ. بالسيارة. ٦ـ صح ٧ـ خطأ. تريد السَكَنَ في صافيتا. ٨ـ صح. بارد قليلاً.

الدرس ١٩

تمرين ١ ١ـ حَلَب ٢ـ السابعة ٣ـ بالحافلة ٤ـ غادة ٥ـ الثالثة ٦ـ الجبن ٧ـ في موعده ٨ـ مشغولة ٩ـ خمس عشرة ساعة ١٠ـ برنامج ٦٠ دقيقة ١١ـ سَحَر ١٢ـ الخامسة ١٣ـ العاشرة والنصف ١٤ـ في وقت مُبَكِّرٍ جداً ١٥ـ العَشاء ١٦ـ المكتبة ١٧ـ خطأ. تاكل الفول يومَ الجُمُعة ١٨ـ خطأ. في العاشرة والنصف ١٩ـ خطأ. تنظِّف وجهها بالماء والصابون ٢٠ـ صح ٢١ـ خطأ تحبّ مشاهدة المسلسلات العربية والأمريكية وبرامج الأخبار ٢٢ـ خطأ. بعد النوم ٢٣ـ خطأ. نسي موعد العشاء ٢٤ـ خطأ. ليسا تكلّمتْ بالهاتف وقالت إنّها مشغولة ٢٥ـ صح ٢٦ـ خطأ. يوم الخميس

تمرين ٢ ١ـ الشاي ٢ـ الصابون ٣ـ الحلوى ٤ـ تنهضين ٥ـ المعجون ٦ـ تَبّولة

تمرين ٣ ١ـ استحمّ/غسَلَ ٢ـ فرشاة/معجون أسنان ٣ـ نسي/موعد ٤ـ سَرير/نوم ٥ـ كباب/فَلافِل ٦ـ حلَق/ذَقَن ٧ـ مَقصَف/مطعم

تمرين ٤ ١ـ فرشاة not a drink ٢ـ طِبّ not a meal ٣ـ حاسبة not a means of transportation ٤ـ صابون not food ٥ـ لَبَن not a body part ٦ـ مادّة not a TV program ٧ـ مَرّة not a verb ٨ـ مشاهَدة has nothing to do with writing

تمرين ٥ ١ـ اسمي رَوضة قَطّان. ٢ـ أعملُ أمينةَ مكتبة في الجامعة الأردنيّة في عَمّان. ٣ـ أذهب إلى عملي في الساعة السابعة كُلَّ يوم. ٤ـ لكنّني أنهَضُ مُتَأخِّرةً في يوم الجُمُعَة (في التاسعة أو العاشرة). ٥ـ أُحضِّرُ عادةً فُطوراً كبيراً لي ولِزَوجي وأولادي. ٦ـ أُحَضِّرُ أحياناً الفولَ المُدَمَّسَ والبَيضَ المَقليّ. ٧ـ وأحياناً نأكُلُ الحمّص إلى جانبِ الزيتون والجُبن. ٨ـ بعدَ الفُطور أُنظِّفُ الدارَ وأغسلُ القُمصان. ٩ـ في الساعة الرابعة بعد الظُهر أذهب وأولادي إلى دارِ أبي وأمّي. ١٠ـ حَيثُ أتكلَّمُ مَعَهُما ومَعَ أُختي وأخي. ١١ـ نرجعُ إلى البيتِ في الساعة الثامنة

مساءً.

تمرين٦ ١ـ تأكل كاثي الفول المدَّمس على الغداء ٢ـ أحبُّ مشاهدة برامج الأخبار صباحاً ٣ـ يغسل زوجي السيارة يوم السبت

تمرين ٧ Variable responses

تمرين ٨ Variable responses

تمرين ٩ ١ـ كأس عصيرِ برتقال ٢ـ فنجان قهوة ٣ـ قطعة جبن

تمرين ١٠ ١ـ لا تكتب/تكتبوا على الجدران. ٢ـ لا تنسَ موعدَ طائرتِك . ٣ـ لا تعطِهِ رقم هاتفك. ٤ـ لا تجلِسْ على ذلك الكرسي. ٥ـ لا تذهبوا إلى الدرس اليوم.

تمرين ١١ ١ـ ليس عند سامي سيارة لأنّه طالب. ٢ـ لا يعرف ماذا تقول لأنّه لا يتكلّم الإنكليزية. ٣ـ سأزور بعضَ البلادِ العربية في فصلِ الربيعِ المقبلِ لأنّني أتعلّم العربية.

تمرين ١٢ ١ـ يدرسون ٢ـ وصلَتْ ٣ـ عَمِلَ ٤ـ يسكنان ٥ـ انتقلوا ٦ـ يلبس ٧ـ تدرس

تمرين ١٣ ١ـ الجُمُعة ٢ـ دار صديقه ٣ـ جامعة دمشق ٤ـ بريطانيا ٥ـ الصحّة ٦ـ خطأ. عند أبيه سيارة ٧ـ خطأ. يدرس الأدب الإنكليزي ٨ـ خطأ. سيذهبون إلى المطعم بعد السينما. ٩ـ صح ١٠ـ سيغسل سيارة أبيه وسينظّف غرفتَه ويغسل قمصانَه. ١١ـ غسّان طالب في جامعة دمشق يدرس الأدب الإنكليزي وسوف يذهب في السنة المقبلة إلى بريطانيا ليدرسَ الأدبَ الإنكليزي.

الدرس ٢٠

تمرين ١ ١ـ مطعم ٢ـ مصرية ٣ـ نَظيفاً ٤ـ محطة الجيزة ٥ـ المكتبة ٦ـ مَلاه ٧ـ الإثنين ٨ـ تم ٩ـ خطأ. ثلاث ساعات ونصف. ١٠ـ خطأ. السابعة صباحاً. ١١ـ خطأ. كانت الشمس ساطعة. ١٢ـ صح ١٣ـ variable

تمرين ٢ ١ـ مَشهور ٢ـ عُطلة ٣ـ حَيّ ٤ـ المُقبِل ٥ـ بَصَل not weather related ٦ـ سَرير not related to transportation ٧ـ طقس not a kind of food ٨ـ عيد not related to bodies of water

تمرين ٣ ١ـ «المسخَّن» أكلةٌ فلسطينية مشهورة. ٢ـ زار مايكل براون مدينةَ الإسكندرية. ٣ـ كان هناك ناسٌ كثيرون على شاطئِ البحر. ٤ـ وصلَتْ سامية إلى محطة القطار مساءً.

تمرين ٤ ١ـ أحْمَد حجازي رجلٌ من مدينةِ حلَب. ٢ـ أرادَ أحْمَد زيارةَ مَدينة طَرطوس مَعَ عائلَته. ٣ـ وطَرطوس مَدينةٌ صَغيرة على الشاطئِ السوريّ. ٤ـ لكنَّ طَرطوس لَيْسَت قَريبة ولَيْسَ عندَ أحمد سيّارة. ٥ـ لذلكَ ذَهَبوا إلى هُناكَ بِالقطار. ٦ـ كانوا في محطّة القطارِ في حلَب في الساعة السابِعة صَباحاً. ٧ـ بَعدَ أربعِ ساعاتٍ ونصْف وَصَلوا إلى طَرْطوس. ٨ـ نَزَلوا في طَرطوس في فُندُقٍ قَريبٍ مِن شاطئِ البَحْر. ٩ـ بَعْدَ خَمسةِ أيّام رَجَعوا إلى حلَب بِالقطارِ أيْضاً.

تمرين ٥ ١ـ نهرُ النيل طويل، أمّا نهرُ بَرَدى فَقصير. ٢ـ يَسكنُ نادر في شقّة، أمّا ناديا فَتسكنُ في سَكَنِ الطالبات. ٣ـ أخي مُهَندس، أمّا أختي فَأستاذة. ٤ـ اشتَرَيتُ محفظةً، أمّا زَوجَتي فَاشتَرَتْ نَظّارة. ٥ـ مدينةُ طَرابلُس الشام في لبنان، أمّا مدينةُ طَرابلُس الغَرب فَفي ليبيا. ٦ـ أحبُّ عصيرَ البُرتُقال، أمّا أنت فَتحبّين الحَليب.

تمرين ٦ ١ـ المكتبة قريبة، لذلكَ مَشَيْتُ إليها. ٢ـ يحبّ مَحْمود البيتزا كثيراً، لذلكَ هو يأكلُها كُلَّ يوم. ٣ـ سَحَر من دمشق وتدرسُ في جامعة حلَب، لذلكَ هي تسكن في شقّة هناك. ٤ـ ليس عندي سيارة، لذلك ذهبتُ بالقطار. ٥ـ جلَسنا في غرفة الصفِّ لمدّة نصف ساعة، لكنَّ الأستاذَ لم يأتِ، لذلكَ ذهبنا إلى المكتبة. ٦ـ تحبّ سِهام السِباحة، لذلك تسكن على شاطئِ بحيرة.

تمرين ٧ ١ـ قال لي أستاذي إنّه سيكون في مكتبه في الساعة التاسعة. ٢ـ قال محمود لزوجته إنّه نزل في فندق شيراتون في دمشق. ٣ـ وقال لَها أيضاً إنّه أكل في مَطعم الشرق كلَّ يوم. ٤ـ يقول مروان إنَّ أخاهُ سيصل إلى محطة القطار في الساعة الرابعة بعد الظهر.

تمرين ٨ ١ـ هذا هوَ أستاذنا. ٢ـ عطلتك هذه. ٣ـ أصدقائي هؤلاء. ٤ـ هذه سيّارتي. ٥ـ نظارة أمي هذه.

تمرين ٩ ١ـ أوروبيّ ٢ـ سَنَويّ ٣ـ سَماويّ ٤ـ شَتَويّ ٥ـ ميلاديّ ٦ـ مِئَويّ ٧ـ خَريفيّ ٨ـ أسْرَويّ

تمرين ١٠ Variable responses

تمرين ١١ ١ـ حمص ٢ـ سيأكلان غداءً كبيراً. ٣ـ الحاديةَ عَشْرة ٤ـ أطعمة لبنانية ٥ـ مُهَندساً ٦ـ حمص ٧ـ الربيع ٨ـ لبنان الأخضَر ٩ـ صح ١٠ـ صح ١١ـ خطأ. كان الطقسُ جَميلاً والشمسُ ساطِعَةً. ١٢ـ خطأ. بالسيارة.

الدرس ٢١

تمرين ١ ١ـ ٢٤ تموز ٢ـ الفطر ٣ـ ١٧ نيسان ٤ـ الميلاد ٥ـ ثلاث ٦ـ السابعة عشرة ٧ـ التجارة ٨ـ مع عائلتها ٩ـ خطأ. تحتفل بالأَعياد الإسلامية. ١٠ـ خطأ. في يوم أحد بين ٢٢ آذار و٢٥ نيسان ١١ـ خطأ. في عيد الشكر. ١٢ـ خطأ. بعض الولايات لا تحتفل به. ١٣ـ صح ١٤ـ خطأ بعد سنتين

تمرين ٢ إسلاميّ ٢ـ لأنّ ٣ـ وُلِدَ ٤ـ الاستقلال ٥ـ نوع ٦ـ رَمَضان

تمرين ٣ ١ـ فجر has nothing to do with education ٢ـ الجزيرة not a festivity ٣ـ إسلاميّ not a school level ٤ـ حلوى not a time of day

تمرين ٤ ١ـ إسلاميّ/مَسيحيّ ٢ـ عيد الشكر/ديك حَبَش ٣ـ عيد الأضحى/الحج ٤ـ عيد الميلاد/المسيح ٥ـ عيد الفطر/رمضان ٦ـ عيد استقلال أمريكا/٤ تموز

تمرين ٥ ١ـ متى يحتفل أخوك بعيد ميلاده؟ ٢ـ وُلِدَتْ أختي في شهر آب. ٣ـ أستراليا جزيرة كبيرة جداً. ٤ـ انتَقَلتُ إلى هذه الشقّة في فصل الخريف.

تمرين٦ ١ـوُلِد مازِن المُدَرِّس في مدينةِ حلَب، ٢ـ درس في مدارِسِ حلَب الإبتِدائية والمتوَسِّطة. ٣ـ بعد ذلكَ درسَ في مدرسة ثانوية في مدينةِ دمشق. ٤ـ ثم رجع إلى حلَب ودرسَ في جامعةِ حلَب في السنةِ الأولى. ٥ـ ثمَّ انتقلَ إلى جامعةِ عَمّان في السَنةِ الثانية. ٦ـ لأنَّ أسرَتَه انتقلَتْ إلى هُناك. ٧ـ يقول مازِن إنّه سوفَ يرجِعُ إلى حلَب حين يتخرَّج.

تمرين ٧ Variable responses

تمرين ٨ ١ـ أبيك ٢ـ ذا ٣ـ أخوها ٤ـ أبو ٥ـ لأخيك ٦ـ ذو ٧ـ أخاها ٨ـ أبوك

تمرين ٩ ١ـ مدارسَ مصريّةٍ ٢ـ شوارعُ حديثةٌ ٣ـ مكّةَ والمدينة ٤ـ نيسانَ... لبنانَ والأردنِّ

تمرين ١٠ ١ـ يُقالُ إنَّ باريسَ مدينةٌ جميلة. ٢ـ وُلِدَتْ هالة ... ٣ـ تُسَمّى ولايةُ نيويورك ... ٤ـ تُشرَبُ القهوةُ... ٥ـ تُسَمّى بغدادُ ...

تمرين ١١ ١ـ أماني ٢ـ أندرو هارت ٣ـ أوستن ٤ـ مدينة أوستن ٥ـ زارا ست مدن هي نيويورك وشيكاغو وسياتل وسان فرانسيسكو ولوس أنجيلس وأوستن ٦ـ يعمل مهندساً ٧ـ يوم الخميس ٢٣ تشرين الثاني ٨ـ ديك حبش وفطيرة القرع ٩ـ خطأ. زارا الولايات المتحدة. ١٠ـ صح ١١ـ صح ١٢ـ خطأ. ما أحبّتْ ديك الحبَش.

الدرس ٢٢

تمرين ١ ١ـ ١٨٨٣ ٢ـ العُثماني ٣ـ بالكليّة الحربية ٤ـ الاجتماع ٥ـ مرّتين ٦ـ ١٨٦٠ ٧ـ ١٩٦٤ ٨ـ طولون ثمّ إلى دمشق ٩ـ مَيْسَلون ١٠ـ جمال عبد الناصر ١١ـ ابن خَلدون ١٢ـ جورج واشنطن ١٣ـ لنكَن ١٤ـ التمييز العُنصُري ١٥ـ صح ١٦ـ خطأ. كان وزير الدفاع ١٧ـ صح ١٨ـ خطأ. حارب في فلسطينَ ١٩ـ خطأ. كان مؤرِّخاً وفيلسوفاً ٢٠ـ خطأ. في «ماونت ڤرنَن» ٢١ـ خطأ. بعد سنة ١٨٦٠ ٢٢ـ خطأ. اغتيل في مدينة ممفيس.

تمرين ٢ ١ـ شاعِر ٢ـ انتُخب ٣ـ فَيلَسوف ٤ـ مَلَكة ٥ـ قُرب

تمرين ٣ ١ـ نُفيَ not related to birth and death ٢ـ شاعِر nothing to do with the army ٣ـ محامٍ not a leader ٤ـ حصل the only verb ٥ـ فلسفةَ not a town

تمرين ٤ ١ـ حرب/سَلام ٢ـ كتاب/مُقدِّمة ٣ـ تُوفي/وُلِد ٤ـ قانون/مُحام ٥ـ غِرناطة/الأندلُس ٦ـ دخل/خَرَج ٧ـ رئيس/مَلك

تمرين ٥ ١ـ كانت إملَي ديكنسَن شاعرة أمريكية مشهورة. ٢ـ تخرّجتْ أختي من الجامعة ثم عمِلتْ في مكتب محام.

٣ـ انتُخب بِل كلينتَن رئيساً للولايات المتحدة مرّتين. ٤ـ اغتيل الرئيس كنيدي بمدينة دالاس في سنة ١٩٦٣.

تمرين ٦ ١ـ مُحَمَّد بن موسى الخُوارزمي عالمُ رياضيّات مُسْلمٌ مَشْهور. ٢ـ وُلِدَ الخُوارزمي في مَدينة خُوارزم. ٣ـ أسَّسَ الخُوارزمي عِلْمَ الجَبْر. ٣ـ وكتَبَ كتاباً في حسَاب الجَبْرِ وتُرْجم إلى اللاتينية. ٥ـ عَرَفَتْ أوروبا عِلْمَ الجَبْرِ مِن هذا الكِتاب. ٦ـ وكَتَبَ أيْضاً عَن الصِفْرِ في الرياضيّات. ٧ـ تُوُفِّيَ الخُوارِزمي سنةَ ٨٤٠ ميلادية.

تمرين ٧ Variable

تمرين ٨ ١ـ فعالة، نَهو/نَهي ٢ـ مَفعول، شَهَر ٣ـ أفْعال، خَبَر ٤ـ مُتَفَعِّل، أخَر ٥ـ يفعَلون، سَبَح ٦ـ فَعيل، جَدّ

تمرين ٩ ١ـ to celebrate افتعَل، VIII، حفَل ٢ـ to die as a martyr، استُفعل، X، شَهد ٣ـ to study، فَعَل، I، دَرَس ٤ـ to be defeated، انفَعَل، VII، هزَم ٥ـ to talk، تَفَعَّل، V، كَلم ٦ـ to buy، افتعَل، VIII، شَرى ٧ـ to give، أفعَل، IV، عَطو ٨ـ to graduate، تفَعَّل، V، خَرَج ٩ـ to fight، فاعَل، III، حَرَب ١٠ـ to turn red افْعَلّ، IX، حمَر ١١ـ to correspond تفاعَل، III، رَسَل ١٢ـ to delay، فعَّل، II، أخَر.

تمرين ١٠ ١ـ الأولى ٢ـ العاشر ٣ـ الثانيةَ عَشْرَةَ ٤ـ الثالثُ والعشرون ٥ـ الرابعة والخمسين ٦ـ التاسعة ٧ـ الكتاب الثامنَ عَشَرَ ٨ـ في السنة الخامسة والعشرين ٩ـ في عيدِ الثورةِ الخامسِ بعدَ المئة ١٠ـ على الصفحةِ الثانيةِ والعشرين بعد المئة ١١ـ الطالبُ الأوّلُ

تمرين ١١ ١ـ الولايات المتحدة الأمريكية ٢ـ سنة ١٩٦٣ في تكساس ٣ـ أريسطو أوناسيس ٤ـ مرّتين ٥ـ فرنسي ٦ـ مدينة نيويورك ٧ـ خطأ. هي أمريكية ٨ـ صح ٩ـ خطأ. يونانيّ ١٠ـ Jacqueline Lee Bouvier Kennedy Onassis

الدرس ٢٣

تمرين ١ ١ـ بعد ٢ـ الجُمُعة ٣ـ يصوم ٤ـ يزور ٥ـ مُعايَدة ٦ـ قبل موعده ٧ـ الثانية ٨ـ ثلاث مَواد ٩ـ آب ١٠ـ ثلاثة ١١ـ في موعدها ١٢ـ مدير مدرسة ١٣ـ البوابة ١٤ـ الأدَب الأمريكي ١٥ـ مصري

تمرين ٢ ١ـ لأنّ يومَ الجمعة عطلة ٢ـ لأنّ ضرسه آلمه ٣ـ زار نيويورك وفلوريدا وكندا ٤ـ من مكتب الطلاب الأجانب ٥ـ لأنّ أباه طبيبٌ.

تمرين ٣ ١ـ خطأ. سيرى الطبيب مرّة واحدة ٢ـ خطأ. لم يرجِعْ إلى سورية بل درس ثلاث مواد ٣ـ خطأ. في فلسطين ٤ـ خطأ. أختها متزوِّجة ولا تدرس ٥ـ خطأ. من دُبَيّ

تمرين ٤ ١ـ ما عدا nothing to do with explaining reason ٢ـ عرب not related to fasting ٣ـ الشام not related to festivities ٤ـ التهاب not related to airport ٥ـ صديق nothing to do with illness ٦ـ جالس not a verb ٧ـ طالب not a paid profession

تمرين ٥ ١ـ أخذ/أعطى ٢ـ ألم/أسبرين ٣ـ بدأ/انتهى ٤ـ عَلِمَ/نَسي ٥ـ غني/فقير

تمرين ٦ ١ـ ذهب مايكل إلى عيادة الطبيب بسبب ألَمٍ في ضرسه. ٢ـ هي أم الطالب الفلسطيني هشام ٣ـ أبو الطالب المصري فؤاد ٤ـ الطالبة التونسية خديجة ٥ـ أبو الطالب العراقي سامر

تمرين ٧ ١ـ يصوم المسلمون في شهرِ رَمَضان. ٢ـ هل تعلم ما اسمَ عاصمةِ الأردنّ؟ ٣ـ أدرسُ في المكتبة كلَّ يوم ماعدا يوم الخميس. ٤ـ تنتهي الدراسة في الجامعة في شهرِ حَزيران. ٥ـ وصلتُ إلى دارِ السينما بعد بداية الفلم.

تمرين ٨ سامر/العراق خديجة/تونس هشام/فلسطين فؤاد/مصر عدنان/سورية

تمرين ٩ ١ـ لَم أذهب اليوم إلى المدرسة بسَبَب عيد الاستقلال. ٢ـ لهذا السَبَب ذهبتُ أنا وأصدقائي إلى شاطئِ البحر. ٣ـ ذهبنا إلى الشاطئِ بالقطار. ٤ـ وَصَلنا إلى الشاطئِ في الساعة العاشرة والنصف صَباحاً. ٥ـ سبحنا في البحرِ ساعتين. ٦ـ بعدَ ذلكَ أكلنا الغداءَ في مطعمٍ صغيرٍ على الشاطئ. ٧ـ بعد الظهرِ سَبَحنا قَليلاً مرةً ثانية. ٨ـ ثُمَّ أخذنا القطارَ في الساعةِ الرابعةِ والنِصف ورجَعنا إلى بُيوتِنا.

تمرين ١٠ كلُّ عامٍ وأنتم بخير، أوَ: عيدٌ مُبارك

تمرين ١١ ١ـ دراّجتان ٢ـ سائقو ٣ـ كلّ ٤ـ مرّتين ٥ـ ماعَدا ٦ـ دراسته الجامعيّة ٧ـ السيارات اليابانية جيّدة

تمرين ١٢ — ١. مُـتـأخِّـرة، مُـتَـزوِّجة ٢. مَكتـوب ٣. أنمْ، يَرَني، أرجِعْ، لأستـقـبلَ ٤. الثـاني، الحـادي عَـشَـر ٥. وجدتُ، اشترَيتُ، أرسلتُ ٦. وجَدَ (يَجِدُ)، صامَ (يَصومُ)، اشترَى (يَشتَري) ٧. حبّتَي أسبرين

تمرين ١٣ — ١. يدرسَ ٢. يَقُلْ ٣. زرنا ٤. يحتَفَلوا ٥. يَرى ٦. تَنَمْ

تمرين ١٤ — ١. أم ٢. مـدينة ٣. الألَم ٤. الإبْرة ٥. عـصـام ٦. مُـدَرِّس رياضـيّـات ٧. إبْرةً ٨. نادية ٩. خطأ. هي تعمل ١٠. خطأ. بسبب ألَمٍ في بَطنِ ابنَتِها ١١. صح ١٢. خطأ. ستأخذ حبّتين كلّ ست ساعات بعد الطعام ١٣. ثلاثة ١٤. أعطتها أربع حبّات أسبرين للأطفال ١٥. إلى عيادة الطبيب ١٦. لا نعرف من النص ١٧. صَبي *boy* ، بَطن *abdomen* ، إبْرة *shot* ١٨. البَحر الأبيَض المُتَوسِّط *Mediterranean*

الدرس ٢٤

تمرين ١ — ١. يريد مايكل شقة قريبة من الجامعة فيها هاتف ٢. الطابق الثالث ٣. م=متر، ش=شارع ٤. صديقاه سمير وحسين ٥. في باب اللوق ٦. نعم لأنّها في بناية نظيفة ٧. صح ٨. خطأ. استأجر مايكل الشقة من سيّدة كانت تعمل في الكويت ٩. خطأ. علّق صورة أسرته ١٠. خطأ. يستـعـمله كلّ يوم ١١. خطأ. بشاحنة استأجرها هو وصديقاه ١٢. خطأ. يعمل بالغاز ١٣. خطأ. في شارع محمد فريد ١٤. خطأ. انتقل في يوم فيه دروس في الجامعة ١٥. كيف انتقل مايكل إلى شقته الجديدة؟ ١٦. لماذا تعجبه الشقة؟ ١٧. أين توجد عيادة طبيب الأسنان ١٨. أين تقع مدرسة البنات؟ ١٩. الثالث ٢٠. الجريدة ٢١. ٨٤٠٠ ٢٢. الجلوس ٢٣. المغسلة ٢٤. الفطور ٢٥. مساءً ٢٦. الأول ٢٧. مكتبة ٢٨. الخبّاز

تمرين ٢ — ١. انتقل ٢. الهاتف ٣. أمام ٤. الخزانة ٥. مصرف ٦. يميني ٧. استأجر

تمرين ٣ — ١. يَسار ٢. تحت ٣. خلف ٤. صغير

تمرين ٤ — ١. برّاد/ثلاّجة ٢. خبز/عيش ٣. مترو/محطة ٤. عيادة/طبيب ٥. بناية/شقة ٦. بنك/مصرف ٧. هاتف/تليفون ٨. بقّال/دكّان

تمرين ٥ — ١. نوع not a store ٢. مرحاض not an appliance ٣. هاتف not a house fixture ٤. شارع not a location or direction ٥. موقف not a residence

تمرين ٦ — ١. سورية، الكويت ٢. خمس غرف ٣. الجنيه، الليرة، الدينار ٤. variable

تمرين ٧ — ١. قطار ٢. بناية ٣. تلفاز ٤. موقف حافلة ٥. محطة وقود ٦. سرير ٧. أريكة ٨. حوض ٩. مصباح ١٠. مرحاض ١١. مَغسلة ١٢. حقيبة ١٣. حديقة ١٤. شاحنة

تمرين ٨ — ١. هناك مدرسة ابتدائية خلف بيتي ٢. وضعتُ التلفاز مقابل الأريكة الكبيرة ٣. ساعدني اثنان من أصدقائي في غسل سيارتي ٤. قرأتُ في الجريدة إعلاناً عن شقة للإيجار.

تمرين ٩ — ١. مرحباً. أنا مُنى الأسوَد وأعملُ مُدَرِّسةً في وَسَط المدينة. ٢. انتقلتُ وعـائلتي في الشهر الماضي إلى شقةٍ كبيرة. ٣. تقعُ شقتي الجديدة في شارعٍ بعيد عَن وَسَطَ المدينة. ٤. لذلكَ أركبُ الحافلةَ كلَّ يومٍ إلى المدرسة. ٥. تعجبُني شقتي كثيراً وتعجبُ زوجي كذلك. ٦. لأنّ فيها غرفةُ مكتَبٍ لهُ وغرفةُ طَعامٍ ومَطبَخٌ واسِع. ٧. زارنا أمس بعضُ أصدقائنا ليشاهدوا الشقة الجديدَة. ٨. قالوا إنَّ الشقّةَ أعجبَتْهُم لأنّها مُطلّة على حديقة جميلة.

تمرين ١٠ — ١. أريد أن أكتبَ لكلّ أصدقـائي. ٢. يحبُّ طلابُ صفّي أن يجلسوا في الشـمـسِ. ٣. أريد أن أسـاعـدَ أخي الصغير بالدراسة. ٤. تحبُّ أختي أن تنامَ مُبكّرةً. ٥. (أن ينتقلَ، ليساعداه)، (مصري، أوروبي، كهربائي، عربي)، (الانتقال، دراسة)، (أقرب، أكبر)، (لم يذهبوا)

تمرين ١١ — ١. مِبراة، مرآة، ممحاة ٢. درّاجة، جلاّية، ثلاّجة ٣. مرحاض، مصباح ٤. برّاد، خلاّط ٥. حافلة، شاحنة ٦. حاسب

تمرين ١٢ — ١. في ٢. إلى ٣. على ٤. حتّى ٥. في ٦. عن ٧. من/إلى ٨. مع ٩. لِـ ١٠. كَـ ١١. بِـ ١٢. لَـ ١٣. فوق ١٤. خلف ١٥. دون ١٦. بعد ١٧. بين ١٨. جانب ١٩. أمام ٢٠. مقابل

تمرين ١٣ — ١. لأنّهما عندهما ثلاثة أطفال ويريدان شقةً أكبر. ٢. لأنّها مطلّة على الحديقة العامّة. ٣. تقع بين بيت أسرتها وبيت أسرة زوجها. ٤. خطأ. الجديدة أكبر. ٥. خطأ. هي ربّة بيت. ٦. خطأ. سوف تشتري تلفازاً. ٧. ثلاثة أولاد ٨. ثلاث غرف ٩. عمل الزوج ١٠. برّاداً ١١. الرابع

تمرين ١٤

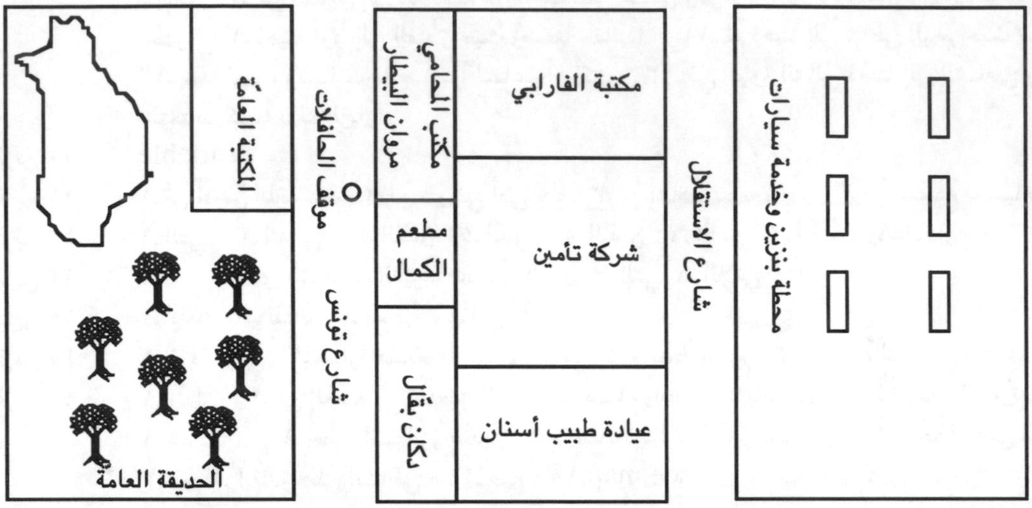

الدرس ٢٥

تمرين ١ ١ـ زار الأهرامات بعد وصوله إلى القاهرة بمدة قصيرة وتقع الأهرامات في الجيزة. ٢ـ السماء الزرقاء ونهر النيل. ٣ـ من المتحف المصري ٤ـ محطة رمسيس ٥ـ بسبب المناظر الجميلة ولأنّ الإسكندرانيين طيّبون ٦ـ كتب البطاقة قبل أنْ ينام ٧ـ يوم الأربعاء ٢٨ آب (أغسطس) ٨ـ في مطعم فرنسي مع صديقه غسان ٩ـ يوم الثلاثاء ٣ أيلول (ستيمبر) ١٠ـ سافر لوحده ١١ في المطعم المراكشي ١٢ـ يدرس في الجامعة الأردنية.

تمرين ٢ ١ـ دراسته ٢ـ حديقة الحيوانات ٣ـ ميناء هام ٤ـ طيّبون ٥ـ الخرطوم ٦ـ الدراسة انتَهتْ ٧ـ شقة صديقه ٨ـ ٦٥ ٩ـ غالياً ١٠ـ زيارته للشلالات ١١ـ القرب ١٢ـ بالقطار ١٣ـ الأمريكي الغربي ١٤ـ حلَب ١٥ـ كاليفورنيا

تمرين ٣ ١ـ خطأ. من المتحف المصري ٢ـ خطأ. من الخرطوم إلى القاهرة ٣ـ صح ٤ـ خطأ. في فندق صغير ٥ـ صح ٦ـ خطأ. مشى إلى مبنى إمپاير ستيت ٧ـ خطأ. يظنُّ أنّها أجمل على الجانب الكَنَديّ ٨ـ خطأ. زار أتلانتيك سيتي ليوم واحد ٩ـ خطأ. انتقل من حلب إلى عمّان

تمرين ٤ استأجر ٢ـ قبل أنْ ٣ـ قُرب ٤ـ التَقَطتُ ٥ـ تناولتُم ٦ـ إنّ ٧ـ لم ٨ـ طَعاماً ٩ـ انتهى ١٠ـ لَنْ

تمرين ٥ ١ـ شاهَد/رأى ٢ـ مَشى/سارَ ٣ـ بناية/مَبنى ٤ـ طريق/شارِع ٥ـ ساحة/مَيْدان ٦ـ دافِئ/حارّ ٧ـ طَيِّب/جَيِّد ٨ـ أعجب/أحبَّ ٩ـ مَحَلّ تجاري/دُكّان ١٠ـ إلى أنْ/حَتّى

تمرين ٦ ١ـ صديقة not a means of transportation ٢ـ مبنى not a body of water ٣ـ طَيِّب has nothing to do with temperature ٤ـ استحمّ does not pertain to enjoyment ٥ـ محطّة has nothing to do with school and study

تمرين ٧ ١ـ شلالات نَياغَرا ٢ـ تمثالُ الحُرِيّة ٣ـ آلةُ تَصوير ٤ـ حديقةُ حَيَوانات ٥ـ عيدُ الأضحى ٦ـ بِطاقةٌ بَريديّة ٧ـ تَذكَرةُ طائرة ٨ـ مَحَلٌّ تجاريّ ٩ـ مَدينةُ المَلاهي

تمرين ٨ ١ـ تَستَطيعُ أختي أنْ تَتَكَلَّمَ ثلاثَ لُغات جَيِّداً. ٢ـ يأخُذُ الناسُ المِصعَدَ إلى الطابَقِ العشرين. ٣ـ شاهَدتُ فيلماً في دارِ السينَما واستَمتَعتُ به. ٤ـ بُنِيَتْ الأهراماتُ مُنذُ آلافِ السنين. ٥ـ ركِبنا القِطارَ من مَحطّةِ رَمسيس إلى الإسكندريّة. ٦ـ أرجو أنْ تَستَمتِعوا بزيارَتِكم لِمَدينَتِنا. ٧ـ التَقَطتُ صورةً لأصدِقائي بآلةِ تَصويري الجديدة.

تمرين ٩ ١ـ أردتُ أنا وعائلَتي زيارةَ مدينةِ اللاذقيّة في عطلة الرَبيع. ٢ـ واللاذقيّةُ ميناءُ سورية الأوّل على البحر الأبيَض المتوسِّط. ٣ـ عندي عائلةٌ كبيرةٌ من أربعة أبناء وثَلاث بَنات. ٤ـ لذلكَ استأجَرنا حافلةً صغيرة مع سائقها. ٥ـ جَلَسَ ابني الكبير إلى جانبِ السائق. ٦ـ وجَلَستُ أنا وزوجَتي خَلفَ السائق. ٧ـ سارَت الحافلةُ في الثامنة

صَباحاً. ٨ـ في الطريق إلى اللاذقية مَرَرنا بمدينتَي حمصَ وطَرطوس. ٩ـ وصَلنا إلى اللاذقية في الثانية بعدَ الظهر. ١٠ـ ذهبنا أولاً إلى الفُندُقِ حَيثُ وَضَعنا حَقائبَنا. ١١ـ ثمَّ ذهبنا إلى شاطئِ البحرِ حيثُ تناوَلنا الغداء. ١٢ـ بعدَ الغداء ركبنا قارباً صغيراً لِساعةٍ أو أكثر. ١٣ـ في اليومِ التالي ذهَبنا إلى الشاطئِ وسَبحنا. ١٤ـ استمتَعنا كثيراً بهذه الزيارة.

تمرين ١٠ Variable

تمرين ١١ ١ـ لَنْ أدرسَ اللغةَ ... ٢ـ لَنْ تزورَني أمي ... ٣ـ لنْ أشاهدَ فيلمَين ... ٤ـ لَنْ أستَمتِعَ بالسباحةِ ...

تمرين ١٢ ١ـ الّتي ٢ـ اللاتي ٣ـ اللّذانِ ٤ـ الّذي ٥ـ اللّذَيْنِ ٦ـ الّذينَ ٧ـ اللّتَيْنِ ٨ـ اللّتانِ

تمرين ١٣ ١ـ __ ٢ـ الّذي ٣ـ ما ٤ـ الّذينَ ٥ـ مَنْ ٦ـ __ ٧ـ الّتي ٨ـ اللاتي

تمرين ١٤ ١ـ كَذلكَ ٢ـ لذلكَ ٣ـ مَعَ أنَّ ٤ـ إلى أنْ

تمرين ١٥ ١ـ غرفَةُ نَومي ٢ـ سيّارةُ صَديقها ٣ـ أمُّ زَوجته ٤ـ مُخَطَّطُ بَيْتهم ٥ـ دُكّانُ بَقّالنا

تمرين ١٦ ١ـ ولَدان ٢ـ في العَقَبة ٣ـ فَصل الرَبيع ٤ـ ميناء واحد ٥ـ بالسيّارة ٦ـ أربعة ٧ـ مرّتين ٨ـ مُعتَدلاً ٩ـ غرفتَين ١٠ـ خطأ. اسم الزوج نَديم ١١ـ خطأ. نَزَلوا في فندق «نَخيل» ١٢ـ خطأ. على البحر الأحمَر ١٣ـ خطأ. الفندق على الشاطئ ١٤ـ صح ١٥ـ see map

الدرس ٢٦

تمرين ١ ١ـ كرة السلّة ٢ـ مكان واسع للألعاب ٣ـ هَط ضَغ ٤ـ في البُحيرة ٥ـ يأكلون السَميط واللُبَّ ويشربون الشاي والقهوة والمياه الغازية ٦ـ كرة المَضرِب والكرة الطائرة وكرة الماء وركوب الدرّاجات وركوب الخَيل ٧ـ لأنّه كان يمشي كثيراً ٨ـ المنجة لأنّها لذيذة وكبيرة

تمرين ٢ ١ـ خطأ. في الطابَق الأرضي حيث توجد شقته ٢ـ صح ٣ـ صح ٤ـ خطأ. هي قريبة من بحيرات كبيرة ٥ـ خطأ. في ملعَب القاهرة الدولي ٦ـ خطأ. كان يمشي في شوارع القاهرة ٧ـ خطأ. البطيخ موجود في مصر ٨ـ خطأ. يفضّل الكُشَري بسبب التوابل الموجودة في ذلك الطعام

تمرين ٣ ١ـ مرّة في الشهر ٢ـ كرة الطاولة ٣ـ يفهَم ٤ـ هَط ضَغ ٥ـ ألَذّ ٦ـ المَسبَح ٧ـ المشوي ٨ـ المساء ٩ـ ١٢٠ ١٠ـ السميط ١١ـ أيّ وقت ١٢ـ الباذنجان ١٣ـ لذيذة ١٤ـ توابل

تمرين ٤ ١ـ ألعب ٢ـ سُكّان ٣ـ تُلعَب ٤ـ توابل ٥ـ بَيضاء ٦ـ كرة ٧ـ تَفهم ٨ـ خُصوصاً ٩ـ شَطيرة ١٠ـ المفضّل ١١ـ فريق ١٢ـ قَواعِد ١٣ـ مشواة

تمرين ٥ ١ـ أولاً not used to express reason ٢ـ مصنوع the only nonverb ٣ـ شاطئ not related to games ٤ـ عَصا not food or drink ٥ـ تقريباً not used to express frequency ٦ـ توت not a vegetable ٧ـ شَرَح the only verb in the set

تمرين ٦ ١ـ إجاص/فاكهة ٢ـ حصان/خَيل ٣ـ مَوعد/وَقت ٤ـ طابَق/أرضي ٥ـ فليفلة/خضراء ٦ـ لحم/بَقَر ٧ـ فول/سوداني ٨ـ مَحَلّ/تجاري ٩ـ بلاد/عَرَبية

تمرين ٧ ١ـ أحبُّ بعضَ الأطعمَة العربية بسَبَبِ تَوابلها. ٢ـ اللعبة المفضّلة في الوطن ا لعربي هي كرةُ القَدَم. ٣ـ يظنُّ عدنان أنَّ النَقانقَ لَذيذة. ٤ـ تُستَخدَمُ المشاوي لِشَيِّ اللَحمِ في الحدائق العامّة.

تمرين ٨ ١ـ أردتُ أنْ أشاهدَ مباراةَ كرة القدم مع أصدقائي في الملعب. ٢ـ لذلكَ اشتريتُ تذاكر المباراة قبل يومين. ٣ـ وصلنا أنا وأصدقائي إلى المَلعب في الساعة الثالثة إلا ربعاً. ٤ـ وكان في الملعب آلاف المتفرّجين. ٥ـ الذين كانوا يأكلون الفول السودانيّ ويشربون المياه الغازية. ٦ـ بدأتْ المباراة في الثالثة والنصف. ٧ـ بقَينا في الملعب ساعتين حتّى انتهتْ المباراة. ٨ـ رجعنا إلى بيوتِنا سعداء في الساعة السادسة مساءً. ٩ـ لأنَّ فريقنا فاز بالمَباراة.

تمرين ٩ Variable

تمرين ١٠ ١ـ أفهم اللغةَ العربيةَ وأتكلّمُها جيِّداً. ٢ـ مطعمُ «الأمير» غالٍ جداً. ٣ـ نِمتُ قليلاً في الليلةِ الماضية. ٤ـ أيّةَ فاكِهةٍ تحبّين كثيراً؟

تمرين ١١ ١ـ هل تلعب الكرةَ الطائرةَ أحياناً؟ ٢ـ أتّصلُ بأمّي بالهاتف ثلاثَ مرّاتٍ في الشهر. ٣ـ لا تلعبُ أختي الصغيرة «البيسبول» أبداً. أشاهد مُباريَات كَرة القَدَم على التلفاز غالباً. ٥ـ يلعبُ صديقي كُرةَ الطاولةِ كلَّ يومِ سَبت. ٦ـ هل تأكلُ الفُلَيفلة الحارّةَ مع الطَعامِ دائماً؟ ٧ـ variable ٨ـ variable

تمرين ١٢ ١ـ كانت هالة تلعب كرةَ المَضرِب مرّتين في الأسبوع. ٢ـ رأيتُ عدنان يركبُ دراّجة ٣ـ صرتُ أعرف الآنَ أسماءَ كلِّ طلاّبِ صَفّي. ٤ـ شاهدنا الفَريقَين يلعَبان مُباراةً بكُرة السلّة

تمرين ١٣ ١ـ أطول ٢ـ أصغَر ٣ـ ألذّ ٤ـ أجمَل ٥ـ أقلّ ٦ـ أجَدّ

تمرين ١٤ ١ـ لم أبْقَ... ٢ـ لم يَمشِ... ٣ـ لم تَفهَمْ... ٤ـ لم أنسَ... ٥ـ لم يسكُنوا...

تمرين ١٥ ١ـ في دارِ صديقِه سُهَيل. ٢ـ لأنّ فريقَه لم يَفُزْ. ٣ـ أمّ سُهَيل ٤ـ خطأ. حضَر سهيل الشاي، لكنّ أمّه حضّرت الحِمّص ٥ـ صح ٦ـ صح ٧ـ ٧ ٨ـ الفليفلة ٩ـ فريقهم ١٠ـ كُلّ ١١ـ بيت صديقه ١٢ـ بعد

الدرس ٢٧

تمرين ١ ١ـ ليبيا ٢ـ سورية ٣ـ البحر الأحمر ٤ـ المحيط الهادي ٥ـ تركيا ٦ـ القطن والحبوب والفواكه والخضار والنفط ٧ـ خمس ولايات ٨ـ نعم، إنتاج أوهايو الصناعي كبير فهي تأتي بعد ولايَتَي نيويورك وكاليفورنيا.

تمرين ٢ ١ـ خطأ. البحرين في الخليج العربي ٢ـ خطأ. الاسكا أكبر الولايات الأمريكية بالمساحة ٣ـ خطأ. ينبع نهر العاصي من لبنان ويسير في سورية ثم يصبّ في البحر المتوسِّط ٤ـ خطأ. كليفلند ميناء هام.

تمرين ٣ ١ـ كم قطراً عربياً يطلّ على بحر العرب؟ ما هما البلدان اللذان يحدّان الوطن العربي من الشمال والشرق؟ ٣ـ ماذا يحد الولايات المتحدة الأمريكية من الجنوب؟ ٤ـ ما هو ميناء سورية النفطي؟ ما عدد سكان أوهايو؟

تمرين ٤ ١ـ ١٢ ٢ـ البحر الأحمر ٣ـ البحرين ٤ـ أمريكا الشمالية ٥ـ ألاسكا ٦ـ دمشق ٧ـ كل ما سبق ٨ـ على ساحل ٩ـ بحيرة إيري ١٠ـ الحدود الجنوبية والجنوبية الشرقية ١١ـ سنسناتي ١٢ـ جبال

تمرين ٥ ١ـ وطن not a body of water ٢ـ صناعة not a geographical feature ٣ـ نسمة not a product ٤ـ ذرة not a geographical direction ٥ـ سكّان not related to the sea

تمرين ٦ ١ـ واسع/ضيِّق ٢ـ كبير/صغير ٣ـ طويل/قصير ٤ـ غني/فقير ٥ـ بعيد/قريب ٦ـ كثير/قليل ٧ـ نَبَع/صَبّ ٨ـ فوق/تحت ٩ـ عَلَم/شِعار ١٠ـ بلد/قُطر ١١ـ جزيرة/بحر ١٢ـ سفينة/ميناء ١٣ـ صناعة/زراعة ١٤ـ نفط/غاز

تمرين ٧ ١ـ جزيرة ٢ـ تتألّف ٣ـ إلاّ ٤ـ عديدة ٥ـ نجمة ٦ـ يحدّ ٧ـ مُنتَجات ٨ـ بَضائع

تمرين ٨ ١ـ تقع ملبورن على ساحِل أستراليا الجنوبي. ٢ـ للعراق منفذ ضَيِّق على الخليج العربي. ٣ـ بلاد الشام هي أحد الأقاليم الجغرافية في الوطن العربي. ٤ـ تنتج الجزائر النفط والمنتوجات الزراعية.

تمرين ٩ ١ـsee map of Algeria ٢ـ ٢٨ مليون نَسَمة ٣ـ صناَعة السيارات ٤ـ صحراء

تمرين ١٠ Variable responses

تمرين ١١ يحدُّ العراق من الشمال تركيا ومن الشرق إيران ومن الجنوب الشرقي الكويت ومن الجنوب المملكة العربية السعودية ومن الغرب سورية والأردن. عاصمة العراق بغداد وتقع في وسط البلاد. يدخل نهر دجلة العراق من الشمال ويسير جنوباً ويمرُّ ببغداد والبصرة ويصبّ في شَطِّ العرب. ينبع نهر الزاب من شمال شرق العراق ويسير نحو الجنوب ليصبَّ في دجلة جنوب بغداد. أمّا نهر الفرات فيدخل العراق من سورية من الغرب ويسير إلى الجنوب الشرقي ويصبّ في شطِّ العرب عند البصرة. تقع بحيرة الحَمّار غرب البصرة. الرمادي مدينة على الفرات في غرب العراق، والموصل على دجلة في شماله. أمّا كركوك فهي في الشمال الشرقي. يوجد النفط في شمال شرق العراق وفي جنوبه. هناك زراعة الحبوب في جنوب العراق بين نهري دجلة والفرات، ويوجد كذلك التمر قرب البصرة.

تمرين ١٢ ١ـ اللغتان العربية والعبرية ساميّتان وكلتاهما تُكتَبان من اليمين إلى اليَسار. ٢ـ كلتا أختيه تدرسان الطبّ في هذه الجامعة. ٣ـ قرأتُ كلتا رسالتيه. ٤ـ يوجد هاتف في كلا البيتين.

تمرين ١٣ ١ـ لم أرَ شيئاً في هذه الغرفة غيرَ الكتب. ٢ـ لم يكتب لغَيرِ أستاذه ٣ـ لم يأتِ غيرُ أخيك.

تمرين ١٤ ١ـ see the map of Lebanon ٢ـ بسبب المصارفَ والشَركات التجارية العَديدة الموجودة فيها ٣ـ الحبوب والزيتون والبرتقال والخضار ٤ـ الجبال أكثر

الدرس ٢٨

تمرين ١ ١ـ الاستماع إلى الإذاعة العامّة «إن پي آر» ٢ـ على محطّة «پي بي إس» ٣ـ فَوازير رَمَضان ٤ـ عَمرو دياب ٥ـ أربع نشرات أخبار ٦ـ تبدأ في الخامسة وسبع وعشرون دقيقة صباحاً وتنتهي في الثانية والربع صباحاً ٧ـ اسم برنامج المرأة «مَرايا» ٨ـ سلسلة ٩ـ في الساعة الواحدة ١٠ـ الأخبار وبرنامج يقدِّم أخباراً وقعت في يوم مثل ذلك اليوم في سَنَوات ماضية ١١ـ وردة الجزائرية ١٢ـ مسلسل «ساينفلد» ١٣ـ مسلسلات إذاعية وتلفزيونية مصرية ١٤ـ فيروز ١٥ـ صح ١٦ـ صح ١٧ـ خطأ. عليهم أن يحَزروا ١٨ـ خطأ. أم كلثوم تُوفيَتْ عام ١٩٧٥ ١٩ـ خطأ. من التلفزيون المصري، القناة الأولى ٢٠ـ صح ٢١ـ اسمه «كيبل» ويحصل عليه الناس مقابل اشتراك شهري ٢٢ـ تُستعمَل العربية الفصيحة في الأخبار والمقابلات والبرامج العلمية ٢٣ـ برنامج يُبَثّ في رمضان تصف فيه الممثّلة شيئاً بالرقص وعلى الناس أن يحزروا هذا الشيء ٢٤ـ ابن فيروز ٢٥ـ اسم برنامج من الإذاعة السورية يُبَثّ في الساعة الثانية عَشْرة والنصف صباحاً ٢٦ـ اسم برنامج يبثّه تلفزيون لبنان ٢٧ـ صباحاً ومساءً ٢٨ـ سريعة ٢٩ـ خِلال ٣٠ـ عامّة ٣١ـ مجّانيّ ٣٢ـ أم كلثوم ٣٣ـ كل ما سبق ٣٤ـ سبع ٣٥ـ القَمَر الصناعي العربي

تمرين ٢ ١ـ إذاعة/بَثّ ٢ـ قناة/موجة ٣ـ إعلانات/تجارة ٤ـ تُوفي/مات ٥ـ مُغنٍ/أغنية ٦ـ جيِّد/ممتاز ٧ـ فصيحة/عامية ٨ـ مُعظم/أكثر

تمرين ٣ Variable

تمرين ٤ ١ـ لغة: ليستْ برنامج ٢ـ مَجّاني has nothing to do with broadcasting ٣ـ عَودة has nothing to do with music ٤ـ تجارة has nothing to do with nature ٥ـ فزّورة has nothing to do with nature

تمرين ٥ ١ـ إن بي سي، سي بي إس، آي بي سي، فوكس، ديسكڤري ٢ـ ساينفلد، فريجر، فريندز ٣ـ صباح الخير يا أمريكا، أخبار، ٢٠ على ٢٠، ٦٠ دقيقة، فَوازير رَمَضان ٤ـ موجة، بَرامِج، مُسلسَلات، أخبار، أغانٍ، مُقابلات ٥ـ غلوريا إستفان، مادونا، ستيڤي وَنْدَر، فيروز، صَباح فَخري، وديع الصافي، راغب علامة، فَريد الأطرش، نيللي، أم كلثوم، عبد الحَليم حافظ، محمّد عبد الوَهّاب، فائزة أحمَد، وَردة الجَزائرية، مَيّادة حِنّاوي، عَمرو دياب، زياد رَحَباني ٦ـ عاميّة، فَصيحَة

تمرين ٦ ١ـ القناة ٢ـ مُذيعة ٣ـ مُقابلة ٤ـ أستَمِعُ ٥ـ مُتزوِّجة

تمرين ٧ ١ـ أستمع إلى أغانيَّ المُفضّلة من المسجلة. ٢ـ تبدأ إذاعة دمشق بَثّها في الساعة الخامسة صباحاً. ٣ـ تعمل أختُ صَديقي مُذيعةً في محطّة إذاعة حَلَب.

تمرين ٨ ١ـ أول شيء أفعلُه صباحاً هوَ الذهابَ إلى الحمّام. ٢ـ بعد ذلك أجلسُ أمام التلفاز وأشاهد الأخبار خلال تناول الفطور. ٣ـ في الساعة الثامنة صباحاً أذهب إلى عملي. ٤ـ خلال العملِ أستَمِعُ إلى الإذاعة. ٥ـ حين أعودُ إلى البيت بعد الظهر أشاهدُ مسلسلي المفضّل. ٦ـ بعد مشاهدة مسلسلي المفضل أنام نصف ساعة فقط. ٧ـ في المساء أشاهد أنا وزوجي فلماً من التلفاز أو من شَريط مسجَّل.

تمرين ٩ ١ـ على الطلاب أنْ يأتوا إلى الصف في الساعة السابعة. ٢ـ عليك أن تكتبَ رسالةً لأستاذِك. ٣ـ كان على أبيها أن يحملَها من السيارة إلى البيت. ٤ـ عليَّ أن أغسلَ سيارةَ أمي غداً.

تمرين ١٠ ١ـ لَم تعُدْ السيدة بستاني تأكلُ في المقصف. ٢ـ لم يعُدْ خليل طالباً في هذه المدرسة. ٣ـ لم أعُدْ أريدُ أنْ أدرسَ الكيمياء. ٤ـ لم يعُدْ نزار وهِشام يلعبان كرةَ السلّة.

تمرين ١١ ١ـ يمكنك أنْ تشتريَ هذه الكتب العربية بما معك مِن دولاراتٍ أمريكية. ٢ـ اكتب بالعربيةِ ما سمعتَ في نشرةِ الأخبار. ٣ـ يعجبني ما أرى. ٤ـ هي سعيدةٌ بِما عِندَها.

تمرين ١٢ ١ـ قرأتُ بِضعَ جَرائد على الطائرة. ٢ـ ساكلُ تفّاحةً قبلَ أنْ أذهبَ إلى النوم. ٣ـ اشترتْ صديقتي بضعةَ كُتُبٍ عربيةٍ عن الوطن العربي حين كانت في تونس. ٤ـ ذهبوا إلى المكتبةِ بعدَ أنْ شاهدوا مسلسلَهم المُفَضَّلَ «فريندز».

تمرين ١٣ ١ـ صح ٢ـ خطأ. هو سوري لكنّه صوَّرَ في دولة الإمارات. ٣ـ لأنّهُ بالعربيةِ الفَصيحة. ٤ـ على التلفاز من المحطّات الفضائية. ٥ـ الصحراء ٦ـ التاسعة مساءً ٧ـ العربية الفَصيحة ٨ـ دمشق وعمّان ٩ـ تاريخياً ١٠ـ وهي بالعامية السورية والمصرية

الدرس ٢٩

تمرين ١ ١ـ بالطائرة ٢ـ نادلة ٣ـ الأجانب ٤ـ بيرة «كورز» ٥ـ يرتفع ميلاً عن سطح البحر ٦ـ صح ٧ـ خطأ. أربعة أشخاص ٨ـ خطأ. يدرس العلوم السياسية ٩ـ صح ١٠ـ السيِّدة آلَن ١١ـ صحافياً ١٢ـ حضر مباراة كرة قدم ١٣ـ في دمشق ١٤ـ جريدة/صحيفة ١٥ـ شريط/مُسجِّلة ١٦ـ نادل/مطعم ١٧ـ عائلة/أسرة ١٨ـ مصرف/نُقود ١٩ـ لاعِب/رياضة ٢٠ـ منزل/دار

تمرين ٢ ١ـ رحلتها إلى المنيا ٢ـ العجوزة ٣ـ مُزدحمة ٤ـ على الجانب الآخَر من النيل ٥ـ ثلاث ساعات ونصف ٦ـ الخليفة الرابع ٧ـ خطأ. لأنَّ الناس ربَّما تعوَّدوا على التدافُع ٨ـ خطأ. أمريكية ٩ـ صح ١٠ـ خطأ. إلى جانب شاب مصري ١١ـ خطأ. من الشاب في القطار ١٢ـ صح ١٣ـ جنيه/لَيرة ١٤ـ مقعَد/كرسي ١٥ـ قرية/بلدة ١٦ـ اعتَقَد/ظنَّ ١٧ـ مِثل/عَكس ١٨ـ قريب/أسرة ١٩ـ مُلَوَّث/نَقي ٢٠ـ غادر/وصل ٢١ـ شجرة، مزرعة، فلاّح، مَوز ٢٢ـ طائرة، سيارة، سيارة أجرة، قطار ٢٣ـ نقيّ، ملوَّث، هادئ، مزدحِم ٢٤ـ عطلة الربيع، عيد الفطر، لَعِبَ، تَنَزَّهَ، حَلوى، كعك العيد، برامج تلفزيون خاصّة، زيارات للأقارب

تمرين ٣ ١ـ عاصمة not related to journalism ٢ـ مَصرِف not a family member ٣ـ حلوى not a means of transportation ٤ـ نامَ not related to travel

تمرين ٤ ١ـ تستضيف عائلة آلَن الطلاب الأجانب ٢ـ اشتريتُ تذكرةَ القطار بأربعةَ عَشَرَ جنيهاً ٣ـ شوارع القاهرة مزدحمة بالناس وهواؤها ملوَّث

تمرين ٥ ١ـ أراد بْرِتْ آدَمز أن يزورَ المغرِب. ٢ـ أولاً كان عليه أن يحصُلَ على تأشيرة دُخول. ٣ـ لذلك أرسل جوازَ سفره إلى السفارة المغربية بواشنطن. ٤ـ ثانياً اشترى تذكرة طائرة على الخطوط المَلَكية المغربية. ٥ـ في يوم السَفَر أخذتْه أمُّه إلى المطار بسيارتها. ٦ـ كانت الرحلة طويلة واستغرقَت ١٥ ساعة تقريباً. ٧ـ فقد وصل إلى مطار الدار البيضاء في اليوم التالي. ٨ـ ركِبَ برت سيارة أجرة من المطار إلى الفندق. ٩ـ وحصل في الفندق على غرفة بسرير واحد مع حمّام بداخلها. ١٠ـ اتَّصَل بأمِّه بالهاتف من الفندق وأخبرها بوصوله إلى المغرب.

تمرين ٦ ١ـ قَد يسافرون إلى دمشق بالطائرَة. ٢ـ رأيتُ بيتَها وقد أعجبني. ٣ـ حين وصلنا إلى بيتِ أصدقائنا كانوا قد تناولوا العشاء.

تمرين ٧ ١ـ أجرةَ ٢ـ أكبرَ ٣ـ عاصمةِ ٤ـ حَيٍّ

تمرين ٨ ١ـ إلى مصر ٢ـ ثلاثة أيام ٣ـ لا، لأنّها مشغولة وليس عندها وقت وموعد الرحلة قريب ٤ـ خطأ. في القاهرة ٥ـ خطأ يومان ٦ـ خطأ. بالقطار ٧ـ خطأ. لن تسافرَ لأنّها مشغولة ٨ـ المتحف المصري ٩ـ قرب القاهرة ١٠ـ جامعية ١١ـ وقت ١٢ـ على الطريق إلى الأقصر

الدرس ٣٠

تمرين ١ ١ـ في الصف العاشر ٢ـ أماني ٣ـ إلى جانب أمينة ٤ـ من ألمانيا ٥ـ ستة موظفين ٦ـ ليشتريَ بضاعتَه ٧ـ مُدَرِّسة لغة فرنسية ٨ـ تقاعدتْ منذ ثماني سنوات لتعتنيَ بوالدتها وبمنزلها وعائلتها ٩ـ في ٧ كانون الثاني ١٠ـ هي جدّة عدنان ١١ـ خطأ. تذهب إلى مدرسة ثانوية للإناث ١٢ـ خطأ. عدنان يدرس علم الحاسوب ١٣ـ صح ١٤ـ خطأ. أحياناً ١٥ـ خطأ. زارتها مرّة ١٦ـ خطأ. عمُّه تقاعد ١٧ـ محل تجاري ١٨ـ ألمانيا ١٩ـ حلب ٢٠ـ سيارة ألمانية ٢١ـ الشاحنات ٢٢ـ ربّة بيت ٢٣ـ خال ٢٤ـ الهولندية

تمرين ٢ ١ـ استيراد not related to taking photographs ٢ـ عَمّ not related to age ٣ـ رسالة not a

not used to express reason ٥- أيّ not related to business ٤- مُدَرِّس school subject
٦- جواز سَفَر not related to personnel

تمرين ٣ ١- وزارة الداخلية، هجرة، صدر، مفعول، تسجيل، شُهرة، إقامة، ولادة، مهنة، شَعر، توقيع، طول، لَون ٢- والِد، والِدة، أب، أم، أخ، أخت، عَمّ، خال، جَدّ، جَدّة ٣- استيراد، بيع، مُحاسِب، بائع، عامِل محلّ تجاري ٤- ثانوية، ابتدائية، صفّ، مُدَرِّس، طالب، إناث، بَنين ٥- مُدَرِّس، تاجِر، ربّة بَيت، سائق، مُتَقاعِد ٦- الجمهورية العربية السورية، الولايات المتحدة الأمريكية، ألمانيا، لبنان، الأردن

تمرين ٤ ١- كُبرى/صُغرى ٢- لَون/أسمَر ٣- يَمين/يَسار ٤- سفينة/بحر ٥- محل تجاري/دكان ٦- بَنون/بَنات ٧- لَيل/نَهار

تمرين ٥ ١- يدرس مروان في مدرسة ثانوية بحلب. ٢- عند أبو عدنان محلّ واسع لبيع قطع غيار السيارات. ٣- تقاعدتْ أمّ عدنان من عملها كي تعتنيَ بعائلتها. ٤- يعمل في محلّ ياسر مارديني ثلاثة عُمّال ومحاسب وبائعان.

تمرين ٦ ١- درست هالة الصيدلَة في جامعة دمشق. ٢- وتخرّجَت من الجامعة في العام ١٩٧٥. ٣- بعد تخرُّجِها عمِلَت صيدَلانيّةً في مستشفى في مدينة الكويت. ٤- تعرّفَتْ في المُستَشفى على زوجِها مازِن الذي كان يعمل طبيباً. ٥- صار لهالة ومازن بنتان وولدان. ٦- حين صار أولادُهما في سنِّ المدرسة انتقلا إلى دمشق. ٧- اشتريا داراً كبيرة في دمشق مؤلفةً من ثلاثة طوابق. ٨- في الطابَق الأرضي محلّ تجاري واسع فتحَتْه هالة صيدلية. ٩- والطابَقُ الأوّل صار عيادةً لمازن. ١٠- أمّا الطابَق الثاني فَسَكنوا فيه.

تمرين ٧ Variable responses

تمرين ٨ ١- يسكنا ٢- يأتوا ٣- تشربَ ٤- أدرسَ ٥- يعتنيَ ٦- ناكلَ

تمرين ٩ ١- بَيْع (بيع) ٢- كتابة (كتب) ٣- التكلّم (كلم) ٤- تخرّجي (خرج) ٥- استضافتكم (ضيف) ٦- التنزّه (نزه)

تمرين ١٠ ١- المرأة ٢- لُؤي ٣- تَوْأم ٤- مَوْئِل ٥- آباء ٦- رَجاؤُها ٧- يجيئون

تمرين ١١ ١- مَرؤوس ٢- مُؤامَرة ٣- جاءَ ٤- حائل ٥- فَأْس ٦- رِئة ٧- أثر ٨- بَذيء ٩- مساءً ١٠- ذِئْب ١١- وَطْئاً ١٢- نائي ١٣- ساءَل ١٤- دوائيّ ١٥- يبوؤون ١٦- ذؤوب

تمرين ١٢- ١- في دمشق ٢- عمّ الفتاة ٣- خطأ. أخوها يدرس الهندسة الكهربائية ٤- صح ٥- أمريكية ٦- ثلاث تذاكر ٧- تريد الفتاةُ أن ترى أخاها والولايات المتحدة الأمريكية كذلك ٨- أسبوعين

Appendix E

Texts of Postcards and Letters from Lessons 25 and 30

١ـ بِطاقةُ مايكِل بْراون إلى أُستاذَتِه:

الإسْكَندَريّة ١٩/٩/١٩٩٦

أُسْتاذَتي الكَريمة زَيْنَب.

سَلامٌ مِنَ الإسكَندَريّة. وَصَلتُ وأصدِقائي بَعْدَ ظُهرِ اليوم وأكَلْنا في مَطْعَمٍ جيِّدٍ ومَشَيْنا عَلى الكورنيشِ وسَبَحنا في البَحر. أكتُبُ لَكِ مِنَ الفُندُقِ قَبْلَ أنْ أنام. أرجو لَكِ عُطلَةً سَعيدة.

مايكل

الأُستاذة زَيْنَب طه
مَرْكَزُ دراسَةِ اللُغَة العَرَبيَّة
الجامِعَةُ الأمرِيكيَّةُ بِالقاهِرة
القاهِرة
جُمهورِيَّةُ مِصْرَ العَرَبيَّة

٢ـ بِطاقةُ عَدنان مارتيني إلى أسرَتِه:

أورلاندو ٨/٩/٩٦

أعِزّائي الغالين، السلامُ عَلَيكُم
أكتُبُ لَكُم من أورلاندو. وَصَلتُ إلى هُنا مُنذُ ثَلاثَةِ أيّام لِزيارَةِ ديزني وُرلد. أنزِلُ هُنا في فُندُقِ رامادا. ديزني مَدينَةُ مَلاهٍ عَظيمة شاهَدْتُ فيها إبكَتْ سِنتَر وأعجَبَني كَثيراً. تَناوَلْتُ طَعاماً مَغرِبيّاً في المَطعَمِ المَرّاكِشيِّ وتَكَلَّمتُ العَرَبِيَّةَ مَعهُم. استَمتَعْتُ بِهذِهِ الرِحْلة.

عَدنان

السيِّد ياسر مارتيني المُحْتَرَم
١١٥ شارِع البُحتُري، طابَق ٣
حمص، الجُمهوريّة العَرَبيّة السوريّة

٣ـ رِسالَةُ عَدنان إلى صَديقِهِ مازِن (الدرس ٢٥):

كَلَمبَس في ٢١ أيلول ١٩٩٦
أخي العَزيز مازِن، سَلامٌ حارٌ لَكَ مِن كَلَمبَس.

كَيفَ حالُكَ يا أخي؟ لم تَصِلْني منكَ أيّةُ رِسالةٍ مُنذُ مُدّةٍ طويلة. كَتَبتُ لَكَ رِسالةً في شَهرِ آذارَ الماضي ولَمْ يصِلْني منكَ أيُّ شَيْءٍ، لِذلكَ ظَنَنْتُ أنّكَ انتقلتَ مِن عُنوانكَ القَديمِ في حلَب. عَلِمتُ مِن مَروانَ بَعدَ ذلكَ أنّكَ انْتَقَلْتَ إلى جامِعَةِ عَمّان، وَهُوَ الّذي أعْطاني عُنْوانَكَ الجَديد. هَل يُعجِبُكَ السكَنُ والدِراسَةُ في عَمّان؟

أنا كَما تَعْلَم أدرُسُ عِلمَ الحاسوبِ في جامِعَةِ وِلايَةِ أوهايو. بَعْدَ أيّامٍ سَيَبدَأُ العامُ الدِراسِيُّ الجَديد، وهذِهِ هِيَ سَنَتي الثانِيَةُ هُنا. أنا سَعيدٌ في كَلَمبَس وأسْتَمْتِعُ بِالسَكَنِ فيها وبِالدِراسَةِ كَذلِك.

في الأسابيعِ الثلاثةِ الماضِيَةِ زُرتُ مَدينَةَ نيويورك وأتلانتك سيتي وشلّالاتِ نَياغَرا في كَنَدا وكَذلِكَ «ديزني ورلد» وهِيَ مَدينَةُ مَلاهٍ كَبيرةٌ جَدّاً في مَدينَةِ أورلاندو في فلوريدا. استَمتَعتُ بِهذِهِ الزِياراتِ كَثيراً. أرجو أنْ أزورَ وِلايَةَ كاليفورنيا في السَنَةِ المُقبِلَةِ إنْ شاءَ الله، و«لاس ڤيغاس» أيْضاً.

أرجو أنْ تَكتُبَ لي عَنكَ وعَن دِراسَتِك. لَكَ مِنّي أطيَبُ السَلامِ وإلى لِقاءٍ قَريبٍ في حلَب.

أخوكَ المُخلص
عَدنان

٤ـ رِسالةُ ياسِر مارتيني إلى ابنِهِ عَدنان (الدرس ٣٠).

حَلَب في ٢٢ أيّار ١٩٩٧

ابني الحَبيب عَدْنان، السلامُ علَيكَ ورَحمةُ الله.

أرْجو أنْ تَصِلَكَ رِسالَتي هذهِ وأنتَ في أحسَنِ حال. كُلُّنا بِخَير والحَمْدُ لِلّه. كَتَبتُ لَكَ رِسالةً في الشهرِ الماضي وما وَصَلَني مِنكَ رَدٌّ عَلَيْها. أما وَصَلَتْكَ رِسالَتي؟ آخِرُ رِسالةٍ مِنكَ كانَ تاريخُها ٧ كانونَ الثاني. أرجو أنْ تكتُبَ لَنا دونَ تأخير.

أكتُبُ لَكَ هذه الرسالةَ لأُخبِرَكَ أنّ والدَتَكَ تُريدُ أنْ تُسافِرَ إلَيكَ في شَهرِ آب. لَن أستَطيعَ أنْ أسافِرَ مَعَها هذهِ المرّة لأنّي مَشغولٌ جداً. يَجِبُ أنْ أسافِرَ إلى ألمانيا في آبَ المُقبِلِ مِن أجلِ استيرادِ بِضاعَةٍ لِمَحَلّي.

اشتَرَيتُ تَذكِرةَ طائِرةٍ لِوالدتك على الخُطوطِ الجَويّةِ الهولَنديّة. تُغادِرُ طائِرتُها مَطارَ دِمَشقَ في يومِ الخَميس ١٤ آب وتَصِلُ إلى شيكاغو في اليَومِ نَفسِه. أرجو أنْ تَستَقبِلَها في المطار لأنّها كَما تَعلَم لا تَتَكلّمُ الإنكليزيّة ولا تَعرِفُ أحَداً على الطائِرة.

والآنَ إليكَ أخبارَ الأُسْرَة. أخوكَ أيْمَن كَلَّمَنا بالهاتِفِ مِن دِمَشقَ وهُوَ بِخَيْرٍ ويُرسِلُ لَكَ سَلامَه. أخوكَ رامي لايَزالُ يَدْرُسُ في الجامِعةِ ويَعمَلُ سائِقاً في شَرِكةِ البَرّادات، وهُوَ سَعيدٌ بِذلِك. خالُكَ أحْمَد انتَقَلَ في الشَهرِ الماضي وعائِلَتَهُ إلى دِمَشق حَيْثُ سَيَعمَلُ مُدَرِّساً لِلفيزياءِ في إحدى المدارسِ الثانَويَّة. تَقاعَدَ عَمّكَ زُهَيْر مِن عَمَلِهِ في وزارةِ التَربِية، وهو يَقولُ إنّ حَياةَ المُتقاعِدِ تُعجِبُهُ كَثيراً. جَدَّتُكَ أُم ياسِر تُرسِلُ لَكَ سَلامَها وتَشكُرُكَ على الهَدِيَّةِ الّتي أرسَلتَها لَها. اكتُبْ لَنا عَن أخبارِكَ وإلى اللِقاء.

والِدُك

Index

Index

Index

Index

فِهرِس

فِهرِس